LITERARY
THEORIES
IN PRAXIS

LITERARY THEORIES IN PRAXIS

Edited by
Shirley F. Staton

upp

The University of Pennsylvania Press
Philadelphia

Grateful acknowledgment is made for permission to include the following: Excerpt from *Everything That Rises Must Converge* by Flannery O'Connor. Copyright © 1961, 1965 by the estate of Mary Flannery O'Connor. Reprinted by permission of Farrar, Straus and Giroux, Inc. Poems nos. 70, 271, 273, 315, 435, 488, 505, 508, 601, 754, 1677, and lines from poem no. 1737 by Emily Dickinson. Reprinted by permission of the publishers and the Trustees of Amherst College from *The Poems of Emily Dickinson*, edited by Thomas H. Johnson, Cambridge, Mass.: The Belknap Press of Harvard University Press. Copyright 1951, © 1955, 1979, 1983 by the President and Fellows of Harvard College. *The Complete Poems of Emily Dickinson*, edited by Thomas H. Johnson. Copyright © renewed 1957, 1963 by Mary L. Hampson. By permission of Little, Brown and Company. "Sailing to Byzantium" by W. B. Yeats. Reprinted with permission of Macmillan Publishing Company from *The Variorum Edition of the Poems of W. B. Yeats*, ed. Peter Allt and Russell K. Alspach. Copyright 1928 by Macmillan Publishing Company, renewed 1956 by Georgie Yeats.

Library of Congress Cataloging-in-Publication Data

Staton, Shirley F.
  Literary theories in praxis.

  Bibliography: p.
  Includes index.
  1. Criticism. 2. American literature—History and criticism. 3. English literature—History and criticism. I. Title.
PN94.S73 1987   801'.95   86-24898
ISBN 0-8122-8037-7 (alk. paper)
ISBN 0-8122-1234-7 (pbk.: alk. paper)

Printed in the United States of America

Second printing, 1988

CONTENTS

CONTENTS ARRANGED BY TOPIC

LITERARY
THEORIES
IN PRAXIS

Introduction: Pre-Text, Con-Text, and Sub-Text

PRE-TEXT

Literary Theories in Praxis introduces you to nine different types of contemporary criticism by showing how various cultural theories actually work in practice. Each of these forty-four essays anchors its theory to familiar topics—short stories, poems, films, or popular culture. Many of the essays focus on the same six, well-known, poems or stories: Dickinson's "My Life had stood—," Hawthorne's "The Birthmark," Poe's "The Purloined Letter," Yeats's "Sailing to Byzantium," Faulkner's "A Rose for Emily," or O'Connor's "Revelation." You are encouraged to read these critical selections in two different but complementary ways. You can choose to read several essays from the various critical modes clustered about one subject, such as New Critical, archetypal, structuralist, historical, Marxist, psychoanalytic, and humanist analyses of "Sailing to Byzantium." (Con-Text [below] explains what these terms mean. Use the Contents Arranged by Topic to select the essays grouped around one particular subject.) Or you can read several essays from one critical perspective but on various topics: New Critical interpretations of "My Life had stood—," "Sailing to Byzantium," "The Birthmark," "The Purloined Letter," "A Rose for Emily," and "Revelation." (For this perspective, consult the Contents.)

Both approaches have certain obvious advantages. Reading several essays from the same critical stance emphasizes similarities. We get the feel of a particular criticism more easily. On the other hand, reading selections from different critical positions enables us to compare the relative effectiveness of certain types of criticism with certain types of literature. Taken together, this double perspective sheds light on how literature interacts with "theory," by which I mean the self-conscious examination of ideas, values, and presuppositions involving literary culture.

Literary Theories in Praxis also helps readers map critical terrains by providing bare-bones ancillary materials. Along with the Con-Text, which outlines general theoretical principles, the text provides brief prefaces to each of the nine critical sections as well as headnotes to individual essays. These discuss methodologies, or how critics put theory into practice. The Provocateurs, or questions, concluding each of the critical sections, pinpoint current critical issues and so foment discussion. The extensive Bibliography guides those who want to read further.

All of these supporting materials, however, are but brief indexes of the mixed chorus that is literary, or cultural, criticism. Therefore, I strongly recommend that the reader also use a reliable literary handbook along with this text (see Bibliography for suggestions). Reading more extensively about critical theory clarifies how theory shapes practice, including our own critical responses.

Contemporary theory holds that there is no such thing as an innocent, value-free reading. Instead, each of us has a viewpoint invested with presuppositions about 'reality' and about ourselves, whether we are conscious of it or not. People who deny having a critical stance, who claim they are responding "naturally" or being "completely objective," do not know themselves. One of the aims of this text is to encourage readers to see around the corners of their own assumptions. The phrase "in praxis" means putting something into action, putting it to work. *Literary Theories in Praxis* aims not only at helping you see how theories work but also at making you a working theorist.

CON-TEXT

This section presents a bird's-eye view of the theoretical principles informing today's major critical modes. The subject is abstract and, at first acquaintance, formidable. Thus, the Con-Text may not make a lot of sense at first reading. You will find, however, that rereading this section again as you get into the essays will be helpful. So survey the next several pages much as you would scan a map of a country you are going to visit in the near future. Then put it in your mental pocket for later reference.

This is an exciting time to join the ongoing dialogue of literary criticism. But it is also an unsettling time because we in literary studies are asking ourselves tough questions.

For example, we are asking, What should literary critics aim at doing? Is our job to interpret the meaning of a literary work—to add another to the 1,001 extant interpretations of "A Rose for Emily"? Or should we interpret our interpretation—explain how a text comes to have meaning? We are asking, How does critical theory intersect with practical criticism? How does criticism relate to literature, especially contemporary literature? Is criticism a second-level discourse "about" literature? Or, following deconstructionist insights, are theory and criticism on a discursive par with literature? Moreover, just what and where is this "literature" we seem to take for granted? Does some essential literariness decree what shall be included in the literary canon—Virginia Woolf's novels but not her letters? her letters but not Louis L'Amour's westerns? L'Amour's westerns but not Jordache's TV advertisements? Or do cultural conventions determine what "literature" our institutions pass along? What interests and values are at stake here?

These unsettling questions, however, are but the shock waves from the larger shake-up in the humanities and social sciences that has been under way for several decades. We are slowly changing the way we think about ourselves and the world, and, as a result, about literary culture. Much of what is happening in literary studies now results from a radical revisioning of 'reality' already under way at the turn of the century in such disciplines as physics, linguistics, anthropology, psychology, and philosophy.

The older, nineteenth-century, commonsense view had depicted an objective world which people knew through direct experience of their senses. In that dualistic empirical model, the words people used to describe the world corresponded to objects "out there." Meaning itself was not called into question as it is today. Finding meaning depended upon determining the right correspondences between mind and matter. If a poet wrote the phrase "a red, red rose," we knew what was meant because the word "rose" evoked the essence, the rose-ness, of the rose out there. A rose by any other name was not a rose.

In some important ways the older, so-called New Critics, the first group you will read here, still share this earlier empirical world view. They see a literary work as an independent object with laws of its own which can be experienced and studied scientifically. Reacting against earlier "unprofessional" (by their definition) criticism which focused on the author's biography or on the critic's own impressions, the New Critics concentrate on "the poem itself." By this they mean the work's formal elements—its language, structures, tone—those things that distinguish literature from ordinary discourse. The critic's job is to interpret the way words are used, to show how a poem's special iconic language reveals 'reality.' They transpose content into form by analyzing not *what* the poem means but rather *how* the poem means. Form is meaning, they say. Theoretically at least, New Critics pay no heed to the author's intention, to the reader's role, or to the work's social and historical contexts. They aver that if we closely and sensitively read the poem, we will experience the work's meaning. These views, which have been expressed by New Critics such as John Crowe Ransom, Cleanth Brooks, W. K. Wimsatt, Robert Penn Warren, Allen Tate, R. P. Blackmur, and others, energized Ameri-

3

can (and to a lesser extent, English) literary studies through the 1940s, 1950s, and 1960s.

Since 1960, however, New Criticism as a theoretical approach has fallen out of general favor. Not only have its close readings and techniques become routine, but more important, its beliefs, especially the idea that the work exists as a self-sufficient object, have been strongly challenged. Structuralists, Marxists, feminists, and others argue that because the literary work is always bound up with language and social structures, it is never as independent and value-free as the New Critics would have us think.

If the New Critics fail to deal successfully with the problem of the subject/object dualism—of how we subjects know the literary work—phenomenological critics offer a different solution. Jettisoning the New Critical empiricist stance that sense experience provides the basis for knowledge, phenomenologists attend to those things we can know. They deliberately put aside the subject/object problem as a dead end. What we can know, what has meaning, they say, is phenomena, or everything that appears in human consciousness. For most phenomenological literary critics, this translates into knowing what the author intended, or had in mind, during the composing time. His intentionality inscribes the text, especially its temporal and spatial images. The critic, then, functions as a kind of transparent medium who describes the authorial mind by recording these deep modes of perception.

Since the 1960s, however, phenomenology, New Criticism, and literary studies in general have been rocked by something equivalent to an Einsteinian revolution—structuralism. Structuralist thinkers have recast the subject/object polarity into linguistic terms. The structuralists claim that language, not sense experience or modes of consciousness, shapes who we are, what we think, what we take reality to be. In a way, their view coincides with that of twentieth-century physicists who posit a world model of indeterminacy, relativity, and uncertainty. In lieu of the nineteenth-century correspondence model between words and things, structuralists depict a self-reflexive world of language which is attached only arbitrarily and conventionally to things out there.

The view that language encloses and so shapes us, instead of vice versa, took form around the turn of the century when linguist Ferdinand de Saussure showed that the supposed bond between word and thing is not natural but arbitrary. He argued that there is no inherent connection between *rose* and the flower it refers to. A rose by any other name would smell as sweet. As significantly, Saussure and other philosophers like semiotician Charles S. Peirce established that language was a system of signs (a sign being composed of a signifier, the individual utterance, and a signified, the concept), and that these signs, only arbitrarily linked to things, were both relational and differential. We recognize the word *rose*, or rather its signifier, because *rose* differs from *rise* or *ruse* or *peony* or all other signifiers ad infinitum. Words, or signs, mean something, then, in relation to other signs which mean something in relation to yet other words, and so on. Thus these theorists concluded that social and cultural meaning has to do not with stable essences—with rose-ness out there—but rather with differential relations among signifiers—with *rose* not *rise* not *ruse* not . . .

Much as the shift from Newtonian to Einsteinian physics decentered, or relativized, our ideas of time and space, so structuralist insights into language systems have "decentered" the text by challenging the belief that a literary text is unified by one meaning. No longer can we assume that textual ambiguities can be resolved by an authority—be it that of the work's formal coherence as the New Critics hold, or that of the author's intention as the phenomenologists believe. Instead, structuralist views on the relational and differential character of language see meaning as the product of various signifying systems; this opens the possibility to many, including contradictory ("polysemic") meanings. By using the term *text* for *work* and the term *discourse* for *language,* critics emphasize that texts, like words, have meaning(s) only as parts of a larger linguistic system.

Semiotics, or the structuralist science of signs (Saussure's term was "semiology," Peirce's "semiotics"), investigates this part-to-whole relationship by using structural linguistics as a model, not only to analyze literary texts, but to examine all forms of social behavior. In radical contrast to the nineteenth-century empirical world view, semiotics interprets behavior as signs whose meanings depend not on facts out there but on conventions and self-contained signifying systems. Thus semiotics tends to study the organization, or grammar, or codes of language systems instead of particular works: it is more interested in what Saussure called *langue,* the general language systems which are always already there, than in *parole,* the particular utterance.

Semioticians apply linguistic models in various ways to different areas of literary discourse. For example, structuralists employing the insights of anthropologist Claude Lévi-Strauss along with those of Saussure analyze texts into structural levels of binary oppositions: up/down, life/death, youth/age, and so on. This fondness for polarities indicates some structuralists' belief that such oppositional binaries shape the human mind itself. Another kind of structuralist poetics explores what makes poetry poetry. These theoreticians often use linguist Roman Jacobson's insights about the two basic processes of language—metaphor (which replaces one word with another that is equivalent: *my love* for *red, red rose*) and metonymy (which strings associated words together: *rose, thorn, Sleeping Beauty*). They then examine how poetry is "sparked"—much like an electric current—by the oppositions between the metaphoric and the metonymic functioning of words. Another branch of structuralist poetics, narratology, focuses on narrative theory, on what makes a story a story. Using structural linguistics, narratology accounts for the way the story is told—for those subjective elements of a narrative which formerly were assumed to be "outside" the story, existing in either the author's or the character's psychological reality.

Semioticians analyze other cultural discourses besides literature. Using language models, they map, or decode, the conventions and rules of various communicative systems, be they kinship patterns, dress styles, or cinema. But whatever the structuralists' area of examination, they all focus not on what something means but on how signifying systems produce meanings.

While some Marxist and feminist literary critics make use of structuralist insights into language, these critics are especially concerned with the ideology those discourses convey. (Although "ideology" has various meanings, it generally refers to the collective values and ideas which we take for granted and which frame 'reality' for us.) To study the interaction of literary discourse and the world, these critics situate literature within its historical and social contexts. They explore how the asymmetric power relations of class, sex, and race inform texts, and vice versa. In their analyses, Marxist critics use various strategies derived from the writings of Karl Marx and other Marxists; feminists and Third World critics, more recent participants in literary discourse, are more eclectic in their methodologies, drawing on a number of critical approaches. Unlike the literary historians who also view literature within a temporal and spatial frame, feminists and Marxists do so with the aim not only of studying but also of changing things. When reading a literary text, feminists, Marxists, and Third World critics often discern a sub-text, a disruptive covert narrative that undercuts the text's socially acceptable meaning and, by so doing, exposes what the critic sees as a contradiction between actual experience and ideology.

Within the last decade or so, yet another critical term—"post-structuralism"—has come into prominence. Post-structuralists are so called because they reject some aspects of structuralism while radically developing others. They fault earlier structuralist interpretations for being too static and centered. They argue that viewing a text as a copy of more general, rule-bound language models as classical structuralists do freezes discourse into something fixed and unchangeable. Instead, post-structuralists accentuate the fluidity and openness of discourses; they see texts as dynamic processes. For example, Roland Barthes's *S/Z* suggests we read texts as instances of *parole* without *langue*. From this perspective, texts are continually reconstituted by the reading process; they are fragmented and polysemic, or open to the voices of other texts. Such "intertextuality" establishes the text's ongoing plurality of meanings.

As important, post-structuralists criticize earlier interpretations not only of "structure" but also of "sign." They contend that although theoretically structuralism emphasizes the signifier, not the signified, our habit of taking the physical sign as a mere vehicle for the idea (a sign as a sign *of* something) keeps creeping back. In part, this results from Saussure's concept of sign as signifier *bonded* to signified. Post-structuralists contend this bonding encourages us to view the sign as a stable idea or entity, a habit of thought that supports what philosopher Jacques Derrida describes as "logocentrism" (*logos* = word, reason). Logocentrism, our dominant Western way of thinking, privileges certain metaphysical notions (e.g., truth, presence, self, nature, cause, origin, and such) above others by endowing them with a kind of self-presencing or Being.

The operations of "deconstruction"—Derrida's term for complex strategies of discourse analysis—calls such thinking into question by accounting for and simultaneously undoing its basic presuppositions. To do this, deconstruction emphasizes the arbitrariness of the link between signifier and signified as well as their structure of difference. Signs are to be seen as chainings of signifiers indicating the absence of signifieds, not their presence. For instance, if you ask me what *rose* means, I must reply with more signifiers: "a prickly shrub with multi-foliate, sweet smelling flowers or a perforated nozzle for spraying water from my garden hose; or a hemispheric gem cut; or a reddish color; or the past tense of rise. . . ." We see, then, that meaning is dispersed, deferred, or, to use Derrida's word, "disseminated" along an evanescent web of signifiers. Each signifier, moreover, is distinguished by its difference from others (*rose* not *ruse* not *mousse* not . . .) as well as from "itself." For example, Gertrude Stein's phrase, "a rose is a rose is a rose" evokes an endless chaining of different signs distinguished in time and space. As a result of this endless play of signifiers, texts are "decentered"—meaning is not focused but disseminated; the meaning cannot be verified by referring to an author or subject.

I have deliberately used *subject* in an ambiguous way to refer both to traditional literary content and to one's self, one's subjectivity. For along with decentering the text, post-structuralists have also drawn on linguistic insights to decenter the subject (our selves). They point out that our self-conscious *I*, like all signs, is inscribed within language and is a function of the differential system of language: I can say, "I like roses, do you?" becaue *I* (a form of consciousness) can reflect upon my self as an I. *I* (not-you) have posited myself as the subject of the sentence. You may answer, "Sure, I like roses, too." You, then, have now reflected upon your self as an I, or subject. But if language offers the possibility of meaning only within a system of differences, then the differentiated each of us refers to as representing a self-conscious identity, or entity, becomes problematic.

This post-structuralist insight into the primacy of language over subjectivity is explored by psychoanalysist Jacques Lacan's reading of Sigmund Freud. Yet even before structuralist and post-structuralist views disrupted our common-sense notions about knowable objects, unified texts, and subjective identity, Freud's psychoanalytic theories had jolted belief in the unified self. The comforting nineteenth-century image of ourselves as individuals controlling our destiny was, Freud had insisted, an illusion. The Horatio Alger "self-made man" myth which had valorized our drama, our romantic novels, our free-enterprise system, and our sense of ourselves, Freud exposed as a sham, a thread-bare security blanket. Instead, psychoanalysis depicted the human psyche as a fragmented, multi-layered, largely unconscious, and, hence, largely unknowable process.

Classical psychoanalysts metaphorically describe this fragmenting psychic activity as the dynamic interacting of ego and id. Governed by the reality principle, the over-worked ego must restrain yet satisfy the libidinal id. The id, in turn, is motivated by the pleasure principle with all its repressed, unconscious unmentionables—its incestual and erotic desires. Traditional psychoanalytic literary critics use these theories to analyze literature. Thus they examine how the author's psyche is revealed in the work—what *Hamlet* tells us about Shakespeare. Or they psychoanalyze the work's characters—Aylmer of "The Birthmark" has problems with female sexuality. Nontraditional critic Harold Bloom projects the Oedipal situation between father and son onto the ambivalent relation, the "anxiety of influence," the poet feels toward his precursors—Yeats toward Shelley, for example.

Another group of critics—reader-response and reception critics—examines not how the author creates but how the reader creates, as well as interprets, textual meaning in the process of reading. Although in the 1930s I. A. Richards had examined the reader's role, general critical attention to the reader's role has been fairly recent. The theoretical positions and methodologies of these critics span a wide theoretical range. Some who think that meaning is inscribed in the text see the reader's responses as constrained and controlled. Other "subjective" critics find that each reader creates his own meaning. Still other critics, the reception theorists, are concerned not so much with the individual reader as with how, throughout history, readers' "horizons of expectations" have actualized various readings of the open text.

In a special way, psychoanalyst Jacques Lacan is also involved with reader response—albeit with a deconstructionist version. His post-structuralist reading of "The Purloined Letter," for example, allows us to glimpse the unrecognizable processes by which our subjectivity is constituted. Lacan rereads Freud from a post-structuralist position which stresses the primacy of language and the fluidity of the signifier. Unlike the classical Freudians who understand the unconscious as prior to and independent of language, Lacan holds that the unconscious comes into being when the subject enters language. As a result, Lacan says, "the unconscious is structured like a language." Our unconscious desires operate like chainings of signifiers whose signifieds, like our never-fulfilled wants, are not present but always absent. Much as signifiers constantly link with other signifiers and so never possess one 'true' meaning, so our subjectivity ("imaginary self"/unconscious) is structured by the process of displacement and deferral.

Lacan's view of the unconscious as relational and differential "decenters" the subject in the same way that structuralism decenters the text. According to Lacan, we use the self-reflexive language system not to communicate with one another but to communicate with ourselves, that is, to constitute our subjectivity. The unconscious, as the discourse of the Other, shores up our "imaginary" ego. Like the neurotic's symptoms which express his unconscious desires yet keep him sane, words are the linguistic symptoms of the unconscious, the signs of our fragmented, differentiated selves. By inserting the subject into the objective structure of language, post-structuralists such as Lacan propose yet another solution to the subject/object dilemma.

Not everyone in literary studies is comfortable with decentering the subject and the text. Not everyone believes that free-floating signifiers and a plurality of contradictory meanings are useful ways to talk about literary discourse. Foremost among these disclaimers are the humanists—an umbrella term for a common-sense view that puts the individual person at the center of a knowable world. Fearing that too much theorizing will shrivel literary studies by restricting critical practice to an academic coterie, humanists emphasize instead the value of a coherent literary tradition. This means passing on to others the traditional literary canon as well as the reasons why these works should be taught and read. Humanists suggest critics explore the individuality of particular texts, not their general similarities. Above all, they urge critics to evaluate literary works on the basis of whether or not the piece reveals our existence to us, whether or not the poem or story says something to us in terms of our thoughts and emotions. By so relating criticism to actual life experience, they argue, we are historicizing literature, keeping open the life lines between criticism and culture out there. Humanists charge "de(con)struction," as they put it, with destroying literary studies. They accuse these post-structuralists of being so lost in a textual swirl of signifiers that they have not only decentered the text but, even worse, have severed literature from life.

Have they? What is the relation of literature and life? Those of us in literary studies must answer such questions for ourselves. *Literary Theories in Praxis* can help you do this. Those who bridle against theory, who assert they just study literature "naturally" without any critical fuss, are but grasped by older theoretical conventions so familiar as to be unrecognizable. These people are like the American traveling in Greece who kept nodding his head up and down for yes and could not figure out why he was misunderstood. (In Greece, a nod means no, a shake from side to side, yes.)

Over a century ago biologist Thomas Huxley suggested that the two

great leaps of humankind were, first, from unconsciousness to consciousness, and then from consciousness to self-consciousness. As this
Con-Text tries to make clear, the general paradigm for 'reality' is shifting
from an essentialist, static, unified, closed self and world to a relativistic,
in-process, decentered, open universe. As a result, we in literary studies
find ourselves betwixt and between, forced to consciously rethink what
we take for granted. This text provides directions for charting your way
in these critical zones.

SUB-TEXT

In contemporary literary parlance, "sub-text" refers to the hidden
agenda underlying and subverting the apparent, literal text. Sub-texts
occur when writers are either devious or not self-conscious enough
about their basic values and assumptions. This section attempts to clarify
the ulterior motives informing *Literary Theories in Praxis.*

Part of a sub-text of any work lies in the selection of its materials.
Many of the critical essays in this text focus on one of six literary works:
Dickinson's "My Life had stood—," Hawthorne's "The Birthmark," Poe's
"The Purloined Letter," Yeats's "Sailing to Byzantium," Faulkner's "A
Rose for Emily," and O'Connor's "Revelation." I chose these six because
they are short, easy to keep in mind, and familiar. Most of us have read
them several times over in high school or college. In addition, a few essays deal with yet other stories or poems but describe these fully in their
commentaries. The remaining selections analyze well-known aspects of
popular culture. Overall, the forty-four essays were chosen because they
illuminate a major critical position, focus on an accessible topic, and are
lucidly written, and because I like them.

I have to admit, too, that these choices involve other, less obvious,
values. By centering many critical essays on specific texts, *Literary Theories in Praxis* ranks "literature" over criticism: the literary work appears as
a kind of privileged body about which criticism hovers.

Further, the kinds of literary texts chosen here determine the kinds
of criticism represented. For example, New Critical, psychoanalytic, and
reader-response criticisms seem to deal more effectively with short fiction and lyric poems than do semiotic and Marxist approaches which
perform better on longer, sociocultural discourse—novels or essays or
cultural systems. In short, focusing on lyric poems or short stories encourages interpretive criticism but may discourage other, more speculative critical approaches.

In addition, the particular literary works chosen typify the "traditional" canon prescribed by the literary establishment, most of which is
white, middle-class, and male. Evidently these works do not speak to
Third World peoples; I could not locate any relevant black or Latino
criticism on these works. I think it important, therefore, that the femi-

nist, Marxist, and deconstructionist essays call attention to some of the value assumptions implicit in our traditional literary canon.

Choosing what critical essays to include seemed less value-laden than selecting the literary works. My criterion was that an essay clearly exemplify a specific literary mode. But because the more recent trend in literary criticism has been to combine two or more approaches, as, for example, semiotics and Marxism, feminism and phenomenology, or psychoanalysis and deconstruction, even this became problematic. Such crossovers may indicate future shifts in general critical categorizations; for now I merely point out such overlapping in the respective headnotes. Finally, while I did not necessarily seek out essays from "the foremost authorities in their fields," in many instances their essays did the job best.

Categorizing and naming involved still other kinds of value choices. As for the nine critical categories, I confess I used the generally accepted classifications, although some of these such as humanism and reader-response, for example, exist on different conceptual levels than the others. Terminology raised problems: for example, at times deconstructionism has been classified under the rubric of post-structuralism. Yet I am uneasy with that term because it suggests a more complete severence from structuralism than in fact it is. Another question I wrestled with was, How far should the nine categories be subdivided? Would it be helpful to subdivide phenomenological criticism, say, into Husserlian and Heideggerian groups? or structuralism-semiotics into structuralist linguistics, narratology, and semiotics? My solution here was to compromise: such subdivisions are omitted from the Contents but are indicated in the headnotes and Index.

My final ordering of the critical modes also suggests certain priorities and judgments I am not entirely comfortable with. For instance, *Literary Theories in Praxis* begins with New Criticism because historically these critics preceded the others, and so they established certain literary conventions and concerns which later critics take into account. Yet beginning with New Criticism seems to privilege that critical attitude. It implies that we should begin analysis with a close reading of the text. Likewise, since endings, as well as beginnings, are special places in discourse, concluding with a humanist essay appears to give them the last word.

As you read through *Literary Theories in Praxis,* you will raise issues and questions I have neither mentioned nor thought of. Perhaps one will be to challenge these traditional methods of boxing-in, of categorizing, literary criticism.

CHAPTER 1

New Criticism

THE NEW CRITICS DOMINATED American criticism from the 1940s through the 1960s. The group, which included John Crowe Ransom, Cleanth Brooks, W. K. Wimsatt, and others, aimed at raising the status of poetry (their cover term for all literature) by establishing it as an object. If a poem could be seen as an independent linguistic object, they reasoned, it could be studied scientifically. This would counter positivist views, prevalent since the nineteenth century, which had dismissed literature as scientifically unverifiable. However, by attending to "the poem itself," that is, to literature's special use of language, New Critics could distinguish literature from ordinary discourse and so affirm its particular value as a provider of insights into reality.

To these ends, the New Critics defined a poem as a unified linguistic object, ontologically independent (having its own Being), with laws of its own. These laws, usually in the forms of metaphor, paradox, and irony, structure the poem's language. Through the complex organization of these analogical structures, they claim, a poem works to resolve tensions and ambiguities.

As a result, form (structure) and content are inseparable; form is content, and hence, form is meaning. Thus the job of the critics is to interpret *how* a poem means, not *what* it means. Critics should describe how the literary work unifies its complex oppositional patterns into a coherent whole. They should concern themselves with the "iconicity" of poetic language, that is, the way its verbal signs embody, or share, the concrete properties of the "real" objects they denote. On the other hand, critics must avoid equating meaning with the "heresy of paraphrase" (Brooks's phrase). Nor should critics concern themselves with extrinsic issues such as the author's intention (what W. K. Wimsatt and Monroe Beardsley called "the intentional fallacy"), or the reader's response ("the affective fallacy"), or the social and historical conditions of the poem's production. The New Critics believe that such extrinsic considerations only distract us from properly experiencing the poem itself.

Instead, these interpreters choose "close reading" techniques. This means paying special attention to how the text's formal elements work to reconcile structural tensions and so make meaning. By being "open" to the work, New Critics say, readers will experience and hence understand the poem itself.

Most New Critics concern themselves with poetry, not prose, in part because poetic language differs markedly from everyday discourse. In addition, prose, especially realist fiction, seems to refer to the actual world in ways that complicate the independent, objective status of the literary work. Cleanth Brooks and Robert Penn Warren, however, were among those New Critics who first extended their field of study to prose—especially short fiction. These coauthors followed their extremely popular and pedagogically revolutionary textbook *Understanding Poetry* (1938), which provided models of New Critical poetry analyses, with *Understanding Fiction* (1943) which applied close-reading techniques to fiction. The selections here are from that text. You will note how Brooks and Warren attend not only to the story's language and imagery but also to its tone and style, that is, to *how* the story is told—its viewpoint, narrator, characterization, and genre. New Critics see these as formal aspects which inhere within the work itself.

Ecstasy: Dickinson's "My Life had stood— a Loaded Gun—"

CHARLES R. ANDERSON

As a New Critic, Anderson accords the poem status as a 'real' object, an ontological entity. Earlier in this essay he has argued that Dickinson's poems should be read not as the expression of the author's intention but as feelings reshaped in language and transformed into symbolic forms. To explore form as meaning, Anderson applies the New Critical techniques of "close reading": he examines the poem's language, including its imagery and style, to resolve the thematic tensions in the poem, especially in its problematic last stanza.

From *Emily Dickinson's Poetry: Stairway of Surprise*, by Charles R. Anderson (New York: Holt, Rinehart and Winston, 1960), 172–77. Copyright 1960 by Holt, Rinehart and Winston. Reprinted by permission.

LOVE IS DOING as well as being, however, and this opened up new possibilities. Once [Emily Dickinson] found an instrument adequate to render her need for fulfillment through absolute commitment to love's service:

My Life had stood—a Loaded Gun—
In Corners—till a Day
The Owner passed—identified—
And carried Me away—

And now We roam in Sovereign Woods—
And now We hunt the Doe—
And every time I speak for Him—
The Mountains straight reply—

And do I smile, such cordial light
Upon the Valley glow—
It is as a Vesuvian face
Had let its pleasure through—

And when at Night— Our good Day done—
I guard My Master's Head—
'Tis better than the Eider-Duck's
Deep Pillow—to have shared—

To foe of His—I'm deadly foe—
None stir the second time—
On whom I lay a Yellow Eye—
Or an emphatic Thumb—

Though I than He—may longer live
He longer must—than I—
For I have had the power to kill,
Without—the power to die—

The poem begins with a brilliant conceit. Fused from the ambiguous abstraction "Life" and the explicit concretion "Loaded Gun," it expresses the charged potential of the human being who remains dormant until "identified" into conscious vitality. "At last, to be identified!" another poem began. And when she heard of a friend's engagement to be married she wrote: "The most noble congratulation it ever befell me to offer—is that you are yourself. Till it has loved—no man or woman can become itself—Of our first Creation we are unconscious."

The paradox of finding oneself through losing oneself in love is rendered in her poem by one word: she achieves *identity* when the lover claims her as his own. The ecstasy of being swept up into the possession of another led her once to an extravagant succession of similes. She was borne along "With swiftness, as of Chariots," then lifted up into the ether by a balloon, while "This World did drop away." In the gun poem she puts far more in a single line, "And carried Me away," the double meaning encompassing both the portage of the gun and the transport of the beloved. The first stanza presents a tightly knit unit:

My Life had stood—a Loaded Gun—
In Corners—till a Day
The Owner passed—identified—
And carried Me away—

Its shock value inheres in the extreme disparity between the two things compared, incongruous in all ways except the startling points of likeness that can be ferreted out. The trap lies in the great precision needed to avoid confusing them, the vital but subjective "Life" and the objective but inanimate "Gun." If she had chosen to use the strict method of metaphysical poetry, the succeeding stanzas would have been devoted to complicating and reconciling these disparities until they coalesce violently in the end.

Instead, after a brief setting introducing her over-image, she proceeds to develop it by the ballad narrative, to which her chosen metrical pattern was so well suited. In another sense, her poem is a domestication on American soil of the tradition of courtly love. The knight has turned pioneer, his quest a hunting expedition in the wilderness, his bower a cabin with feather-pillow and trusty rifle at his head, his lady the frontier wife who shares his hardships and adventures. In such a folk version of the troubadour lyric, the ballad stanza properly replaces the intricate Provençal forms. In the special climate of frontier America, another turn is given to the convention. Since the male provider is unavoidably committed to the strenuous life, here it is the woman who celebrates the softer arts, pledging eternal fidelity and the rapture of love's service. So the courtly roles are reversed: he is only the adored "Master" while she is the joyous servant, which accounts for her assuming the active role in the love-game.

The hunting action of the second and third stanzas is given over to its devotional aspects. As steadfast companion, her words of love ring out in the gun's explosion, echoed by the mountains; her looks of love are the "cordial light" of its fire, like the glow of Vesuvius in eruption. The quarry they hunt, "the Doe," is appropriate to the romantic theme. But to counterbalance the danger of sentimentalism she makes a pervasive use of hyperbole, suggesting the tall-tale mode of western humor. The protective action of the next two stanzas portrays the service of love. To guard his sleep is better than to share his bed. This may only mean that she places a higher value on giving him peace than on enjoying connubial bliss, though there is a curious suggestion that the love is never fulfilled in physical union. To give him security also calls forth an unquestioning loyalty destructive of his enemies, the jealous anger of the flashing muzzle's "Yellow Eye" being a particularly happy extension of the image with which she began, the "Loaded Gun." Standing for the amorous potential of a newly vitalized life, this has been sustained through all the narrative center, successfully taking the risks inherent in this anatomical-mechanical fusion of part to part—"speak," "smile," "face," and "eye" applying to the gun as well as to love's servant. With "thumb" it seems to break down in a shift of agency. Only the "Owner" has a thumb to raise the hammer, and a finger to fire the gun, but here it fires itself. Her gun-life has so usurped the initiative as to reduce his function to hunting while she herself does the shooting. One of the hazards of the private poet is that the self tends to become the only reality. The lover here certainly plays a negative role.

The final stanza presents a more serious problem to be resolved. A metaphysical poet would have brought his series of shocks to rest in some unexpected figure evolved out of the initial conceit, but her gun only survives in the teasing antithesis of "kill" and "die." A balladist would have rung down the curtain with an ending in surprise comedy or stark tragedy. Instead, she makes a third switch in technique and concludes with an aphorism that seems to have little structural relation to the rest of the poem:

> Though I than He—may longer live
> He longer must—than I—
> For I have but the power to kill,
> Without—the power to die—

If this poem was a deliberate attempt to weld a new form from all these disparate ones—folk ballad, troubadour lyric, tall tale, metaphysical and aphoristic verse—it was a bold experiment even though it did not quite come off. But though the conclusion is a disturbing departure in mode, it may be ventured that its thematic relevance is such as to make it a resolution of all that has gone before. Perhaps this is a poem about the limitations of mortal love and a yearning for the superior glories of the immortal kind. If this is so, then the last stanza is not a moralistic commentary on the narrative but the very meaning which the elaborated image finally creates.

The clues for such an interpretation are not planted thick enough, but there are some. The joys of merely sheltering the beloved are preferred to sharing the marriage bed. And this is the kind of love that finds its expression not in an earthly paradise but in roaming woods that are described here as "Sovreign," one of a cluster of words running through her poems to evoke the celestial estate. Earthly love, in spite of the ecstasy of passion and the bliss of service, she was forced to conclude is mortal. Such is the inanimate but loaded gun, once it has been touched into life by being identified by the owner. The physical existence of the gun, her mortal love, may outlast the earthly life of her master, the

"Owner," but in immortality he will outlive it. So she too must have the "power to die" into heavenly love in order to become immortal. Limited by her gun-body she has only the "power to kill," including paradoxically the soul of the beloved, by making him too enamored of the Eden of this life. In the plaintive "I have but the power to kill" there may even be the backfire of a suicidal wish, to free him from the encumbrance of her mortal love. It may be reasonably objected that this meaning is too fragmentarily embodied in the poem; and the breakdown of the conclusion into prose brands it, when judged by the highest poetic standards, as a failure. But it is a brilliant one, repaying close study. Moreover, the theme here suggested, though conjectural, is in keeping with the whole trend of her love poetry and will help to illuminate it.

Worldly love, whether fully realized or not, has been the paradoxical image and counter-image of all human aspiration towards spiritual union with God. The lure of the flesh must be overcome, yet mystics have found no language except that of sexual love to express the ineffable they were seeking. The painful transition from one to the other is the direct theme of a key poem:

> You constituted Time—
> I deemed Eternity
> A Revelation of Yourself—
> 'Twas therefore Deity
>
> The Absolute—removed
> The Relative away—
> That I unto Himself adjust
> My slow idolatry—

Once again, entrapment in time rather than in the body symbolizes the mortal conditioning. The earthly lover, in the first stanza, comprises the whole realm of temporal reality in which she has been a willing subject. So imprisoned, she could not even conceive of Eternity except as a projected image of the face of Now.

Yeats's "Sailing to Byzantium"

CLEANTH BROOKS

Brooks contends that Yeats's poems reenact and so unify the complex paradoxes involved in human existence. In this selection from *The Well-Wrought Urn*, Brooks, having just discussed

From *The Well-Wrought Urn: Studies in the Structure of Poetry.* Copyright 1947; renewed 1975 by Cleanth Brooks. Reprinted by permission of Harcourt Brace Jovanovich, Inc.

the metaphorical logic of "Among School Children," demonstrates how the golden bird image of "Sailing to Byzantium" ironically dramatizes the human dilemma of body/soul, of natural/supernatural. He asserts that the poem's meaning cannot be logically paraphrased because the image works analogically. However, the complex of attitudes which is the poem itself presents "a controlled experience which must be experienced to be understood." Close reading, then, enables us to see how the poem 'means'.

"AMONG SCHOOL CHILDREN," as Kenneth Burke has suggested in his article on "Symbolic Action," balances "Sailing to Byzantium." (The two poems, by the way, according to Yeats's biographer, were written in the same year.) One seems to celebrate "natural" beauty, the world of becoming; the other, intellectual beauty, the world of pure being. To which world is Yeats committed? Which does he choose?

The question is idle—as idle as the question which the earnest school-marm puts to the little girl reading for the first time "L'Allegro–Il Penseroso": which does Milton *really* prefer, mirth or melancholy? Does Yeats choose idealism or materialism—the flowering chestnut or the golden bird whose metal plumage will not molt?

Yeats chooses both and neither. One cannot know the world of being save through the world of becoming (though one must remember that the world of becoming is a meaningless flux apart from the world of being which it implies).

If the last sentence seems to make Yeats more of a metaphysician than we feel he really was, one can only appeal to the poems themselves. Both of them are shot through and through with a recognition of the problem which the reflective human being can never escape—the dilemma which is the ground of the philosophic problem; and the "solution" which is reached in neither case *solves* the problem. The poet in both cases comes to terms with the situation—develops an attitude toward the situation which everywhere witnesses to the insolubility of the problem. As I. A. Richards has suggested of Wordsworth's "Ode," so here: "Among School Children" (or, for that matter, "Sailing to Byzantium") is finally a poem "about" the nature of the human imagination itself.

It is true that the reader is tempted to say that "Among School Children" makes a protest against the imposition of all disciplines from the outside—a protest against all that "bruises" the body "to pleasure soul." Yet since all idealisms are categorized as

. . . self-born mockers of man's enterprise

it is evident that the poet does not think that one could or should do away with them. If they break hearts, still they are the "Presences / That passion, piety or affection knows." The human world of passion, piety, and affection will necessarily be a world in which those Presences exist. They are not merely a concoction of the philosophers. If the philosophers and even the nuns constitute a special case, the mothers are not special. Their worship of images is taken for granted.

The last stanza does not refute Plato—is not intended to refute him. For if we try to read into the vision of the chestnut-tree an affirmation of the beautiful, careless play of nature, and thus a rebuke to Plato's holding nature a mere play "of spume" upon a "ghostly paradigm of things"; or a taunt at Aristotle's "playing" the taws on the behind of the youthful Alexander, we remember that Pythagoras' activity is play too—fingering "upon a fiddle-stick or strings." (Perhaps one weights the word *play* too heavily. Yet the word is used specifically with regard to Plato's thought and Aristotle's action, and Pythagoras is definitely represented as playing upon an instrument. The word *play* has senses which can encompass the activity of all three and that of the dancer of the last stanza as well.)

Or, one may approach the matter in this way: Is Yeats less respectful to the Greek sages of "Among School Children" than he is to the sages whom he invokes in "Sailing to Byzantium"? It is true that he visualizes these last as "standing in God's holy fire" and concerned with no activity so mundane as that of administering a spanking. Yet his last petition to them is to

> . . . gather me
> Into the artifice of eternity.

The word "artifice" fits the prayer at one level after another: the fact that he is to be taken *out of nature*; that his body is to be an artifice hammered out of gold; that it will not age but will have the finality of a work of art. But "artifice" unquestionably carries an ironic qualification too. The prayer, for all its passion, is a modest one. He does not ask that he be gathered into eternity—it will be enough if he is gathered into the "artifice of eternity." The qualification does not turn the prayer into mockery, but it is all-important: it limits as well as defines the power of the sages to whom the poet appeals.

The golden bird of "Sailing to Byzantium" and the flowering chestnut-tree of our poem are not, it should be apparent, on precisely the same level. Indeed, we need to add another term: the scarecrow. For the golden bird and the scarecrow are, as it were, limiting terms—or, if the scarecrow is not strictly a limiting term, it points to the other limit: the utter wreck and dissolution of the body in the grave. Between the limits of "unageing intellect" and the wreck of the body, are the blossoming chestnut-tree or the dancer moving through the mazes of the dance or golden-thighed Pythagoras fiddling away at his intuition of the music of the spheres. All of them represent something divine or supernatural, but as man can know it, always intermixed with the "natural." The divinely beautiful woman has not really subsisted on shadows and the wind, even if it seems that her flesh could not have been nourished on common food; the golden thighs of Pythagoras do turn to the spindly shanks of the scarecrow. Yet the tone of the poem indicates that the speaker is not mocking these intimations of the supernatural as mere easy illusions. The beloved is really worthy of the name "Ledaean"; the music of Pythagoras does give one an intimation of the song of the golden bird.

The irony of both poems is directed, it seems to me, not at our yearning to transcend the world of nature, but at the human situation itself in which supernatural and natural are intermixed—the human situation which is inevitably caught between the claims of both natural and supernatural. The golden bird whose bodily form the speaker will take in Byzantium will be withdrawn from the flux of the world of becoming. But so withdrawn, it will sing of the world of becoming—"Of what is past, or passing, or to come." Removed from that world, it will *know* as the chestnut-tree immersed in life, drenched in the world of becoming cannot know. Full life is instinctive like the life of Wordsworth's child. It is a harmony which is too blind to be aware of its own harmony. Here we have the dilemma of Wordsworth's "Intimations" ode all over again. The mature man can see the harmony, the unity of being, possessed by the tree or the lamb or the child; but the price of being able to see it is not to possess it in one's self, just as the price of possessing it in one's self is an unawareness that one does possess it. Or to state the matter in Yeats's own terms:

> For wisdom is the property of the dead,
> A something incompatible with life. . . .

Or, again, as Yeats liked to put it in the letters of his last years: "man can embody truth but he cannot know truth."

But, in attempting to reconcile the "meanings" of the two poems, one should not tempt the reader to substitute another abstract proposition for the "meaning." What is important is that, in the case of either poem, any statement which we attempt to abstract from the whole context as the "meaning" of the poem is seen to be qualified and modified by the context of the poem taken as a whole.

The poem is a dramatization, not a formula; a controlled experience which has to be *experienced,* not a logical process, the conclusion of which is reached by logical methods and the validity of which can be checked by logical tests. In each case, the unifying principle of the organization which *is* the poem is an attitude or complex of attitudes. We can discover, to be sure, propositions which seem to characterize, more or less accurately, the unifying attitude. But if we take such propositions to be the core of the poem we are contenting ourselves with reductions and substitutions. To do this, is to take the root or the blossoms of the tree for the tree itself.

The point is not a very abstruse one. It seems worth repeating here only because many of our professors and popular reviewers continue to act as if it were an esoteric principle. Our staple study of literature consists in investigations of the root system (the study of literary sources) or in sniffing the blossoms (impressionism), or—not to neglect Yeats's alternative symbol—in questioning the quondam dancer, no longer a dancer, about her life history (the study of the poet's biography).

I want to use the metaphor fairly: it is entirely legitimate to inquire into the dancer's history, and such an inquiry is certainly interesting for its own sake, and may be of value for our understanding of the dance. But we cannot question her as dancer without stopping the dance or waiting until the dance has been completed. And in so far as our interest is in poetry, the dance must be primary for us. We cannot afford to neglect it; no amount of notes on the personal history of the dancer will prove to be a substitute for it; and even our knowledge of the dancer qua dancer will depend in some measure upon it: How else can we know her? "How can we know the dancer from the dance?"

The Rhyme Structure of the Byzantium Poems

MARJORIE PERLOFF

As a branch of New Criticism, stylistics examines specific linguistic forms of various kinds of literature. Some stylistic studies focus on the general properties all literature shares; others, like Perloff's, on the particularized features of an author or a work. In this selection on "Sailing to Byzantium," Perloff shows how rhyme words establish thematic meanings. In a subsequent section on "Byzantium" not included here, Perloff argues that the difference in the two poems' rhyme schemes embodies the difference in their meaning: the rhymes in "Sailing" reflect sharp tensions while those in "Byzantium" emphasize unity. Thus stylistic studies draw our attention to aspects of literature we often take for granted and so alert us to how form makes meaning.

From *Rhyme and Meaning in the Poetry of Yeats,* by Marjorie Perloff (New York: Humanities Press; The Hague and Paris: Mouton, 1970), 122–31; 141–43. Copyright by The Humanities Press and Mouton, 1970. Reprinted by permission.

> Our words must seem to be inevitable
> —Yeats

THE TWO BYZANTIUM poems—"Sailing to Byzantium" (1926) and "Byzantium" (1930)—represent perhaps the most perfect expression of Yeats's mature rhyming technique. The poems are, of course, thematically related, but there is a basic contrast in meaning which is, interestingly, reflected in the rhymes themselves. A careful consideration of the rhyme structures of these two major poems will give us a clearer picture of the overall relationship between rhyme and meaning in Yeats's poetry which has been studied thus far.

1. Sailing to Byzantium

I

That is no country for old men. The *young*
In one another's arms, birds in the *trees*
—Those dying generations—at their *song,*
The salmon-falls, the mackerel-crowded *seas,*
Fish, flesh, or fowl, commend *all summer long*
Whatever is begotten, born, and dies.
Caught in that sensual music all neglect
Monuments of unageing intellect.

II

An aged man is but a *paltry thing,*
A tattered coat upon a stick, unless
Soul clap its hands and sing, and louder *sing*
For every tatter in its *mortal dress,*
Nor is there singing school but *studying*
Monuments of its own *magnificence;*
And therefore I have sailed the seas and come
To the holy city of Byzantium.

III

O sages standing in *God's holy fire*
As in the *gold mosaic of a wall,*
Come from the holy fire, perne in a *gyre,*
And be the singing-masters of my *soul.*
Consume my heart away; sick with *desire*
And fastened to a *dying animal*
It knows not what it is; and gather me
Into the artifice of eternity.

IV

Once out of nature I shall never take
My bodily form from any *natural thing,*
But such a form as Grecian goldsmiths make

Of hammered gold and *gold enamelling*
To keep a drowsy Emperor awake;
Or set upon a gold bough to sing
To lords and ladies of *Byzantium*
Of what is *past, or passing, or to come.*

The four ottava rima stanzas of "Sailing to Byzantium" contain twenty-eight rhymes which may be classified as follows:

EXACT RHYMES

song/long
trees/seas
thing/sing
unless/dress
fire/gyre
gyre/desire
take/make
take/awake
make/awake
thing/sing

APPROXIMATE RHYMES

1. *Phonemic Variation*
   A. *Consonance-Rhyme*
      young/song
      young/long
      trees/dies
      seas/dies
      wall/soul
2. *Stress Variation*
   A. *Tertiary-stress Rhyme*
      neglect/intellect
      thing/studying
      sing/studying
      come/Byzantium
      me/eternity
      thing/enamelling
      enamelling/sing
      Byzantium/come
3. *Combinations*
   A. *Tertiary-stress-and-Contrast*
      unless/magnificence
      dress/magnificence
   B. *Weak-and-Consonance*
      wall/animal
      soul/animal

Seventeen of the twenty-eight rhymes (60%) are approximate, and the approximations are marked by great variety: there are five rhymes that have phonemic variation, eight rhymes that have stress variation, and four that have combinations. The distribution of approximate rhymes is particularly interesting. One may note, first of all, that the closing couplet of each stanza has tertiary-stress rhyme ("neglect"/"intellect," "come"/"Byzantium," "gather me"/"eternity" and "Byzantium"/"come"); the last couplet differs slightly from the other three in that the rhyming unit that has tertiary stress precedes the one that has primary stress; the

23

variation that is thus produced is, as will be explained below, relevant to the meaning of the poem.

In Stanza I, the first two *a* rhymes are consonance-rhymes ("young"/ "song," "young"/"long"), while the third is an exact rhyme ("song"/ "long"); the *b* rhymes have precisely the same pattern but in reverse order—the first *b* rhyme is an exact rhyme ("trees"/"seas"), while the second two *b* rhymes are consonance-rhymes ("trees"/"dies," "seas"/"dies"). In Stanza II, the first *a* rhyme is exact ("thing"/"sing"); the second and third *a* rhymes are tertiary-stress rhymes ("thing"/"studying," "sing"/ "studying"). The first *b* rhyme is similarly exact ("unless"/"magnificence," "dress"/"magnificence"). In Stanza III Yeats introduces a new variation. All three *a* rhymes are now exact ("fire"/"gyre"/"desire"), while all three *b* rhymes are approximate: "wall"/"soul" is consonance-rhyme; "wall"/ "animal" and "soul"/"animal" are weak-and-consonance rhymes. Finally, in stanza IV the three *a* rhymes are exact ("take"/"make"/"awake"), while only the second *b* rhyme is exact ("thing"/"sing"), the other two being tertiary-stress rhymes ("thing"/"enamelling," "sing"/"enamelling").

Yeats thus combines exact rhyme and approximate rhyme in a great variety of ways; no two stanzas have the same distribution of approximate rhyme, and in no stanza are all the rhymes exact or all approximate. The balance thus achieved is very delicate: on the one hand, Yeats avoids the monotony that *ababab* might have if all the rhymes were exact; on the other, he avoids the chaos that would result from an exclusive use of approximate rhyme—there is just enough exact rhyme to fix the ottava rima rhyme scheme firmly in the mind.

The meaning of "Sailing to Byzantium" must now be considered. While controversies continue to rage over specific details of this poem,[1] it is generally agreed that the speaker of "Sailing to Byzantium" feels he must turn away from one complex of values (life, sex, the body, the natural—the world of becoming) and commit himself to another (art, intellect, the soul, the supernatural—the world of pure being). Yeats described his purpose in a manuscript book:

> Now I am trying to write about the state of my soul, for it is right for an old man to make his soul, and some of my thoughts upon that subject I have put into a poem called "Sailing to Byzantium." When Irishmen were illuminating the Book of Kells and making the jewelled croziers in the National Museum, Byzantium was the center of European civilization and the source of its spiritual philosophy, so I symbolize the search for the spiritual life by a journey to that city.[2]

The early drafts of "Sailing to Byzantium" shed light on the relationship of rhyme to meaning in the poem. In the discussion that follows all references are to Curtis Bradford's arrangement of the notebook drafts.[3]

Yeats was evidently dissatisfied with his early version of the beginning of "Sailing"; in the first draft, designated as *A* by Bradford, the opening Stanza has no resemblance whatsoever to the opening stanza of the finished poem, beyond the fact that it is written in ottava rima (the rhyme words are "Byzantium," "mariners," "come," "stairs," "foam," "oars," "lies," "Paradise"). The germ of the first stanza as we know it is found in the third draft. C1 is reproduced below, except that, in the interest of conciseness, lines that were completely cancelled are omitted. Bradford explains that "internal cancellations are lined out; then, following a slanting rule, the revised version is given" (p. 112).

C1

~~This~~/ ~~Here~~/ That is no country for old men—the young
~~Pass by me~~/ That travel singing of their loves, the trees
~~Break~~/ Clad in such foliage that it seems a song
The shadow of the birds upon the seas
The leaping fish, the fields all summer long
~~The leaping fish~~/ The crowding fish commend all summer long
Deceiving [?] ~~abundance~~/ Plenty, but no monument
Commends the never aging intellect
The salmon rivers, the ~~fish~~/ mackerel crowded seas
~~Flesh~~/ ~~All~~/ Fish flesh and fowl, all spring all summer long
~~What~~/ Commemorate what is begot and dies.

In the final version of Stanza I, Yeats alters every word in lines 2, 3 and 4, except for the rhyme word; he seems, in other words, to begin with the rhyme words "trees," "song," and "seas," and then goes back to fill in the rest of each line. Thus line 8 reshapes line 4, bringing it closer to its final version. At the end of C1, the rhyme words of the first six lines are all intact; only the couplet rhymes are missing.[4]

The first draft of the second stanza is found in C3 and C4:

C3

~~The~~/ An aged man is but a paltry thing
~~A Paltry business to be old~~, unless
~~My~~/ Soul clap ~~hands~~/ its hands and sing, and then
~~sing more~~/ louder sing

                                                              dress
                                                              oar
For every tatter in its mortal dress

C4

An aged man is but a paltry thing
Nature has cast him like a shoe unless
Soul clap its hands and sing, and louder sing
For every tatter in its mortal dress
And there's no singing school like studying

The monuments of ~~its old~~/ our magnificence
And therefore have I sailed the seas and come
To the holy city of Byzantium.

In C3, Yeats seems to be searching for the right rhyme words: in line 2 he crosses out every word except the rhyme word "unless," which he retains in the final version of the stanza. The words "dress" and "oar" are jotted down in the margin as possible rhyme words; Yeats retains the former but not the latter. In C3, the first four rhyme words are in place; in C4, all the rhyme words are in place, although the lines themselves still receive a great deal of revision (e.g., line 2, "Nature has cast him like a shoe unless . . ." becomes "A tattered coat upon a stick unless . . .").

The first version of Stanza III appears in the A draft:

A6

Procession on procession, tier on tier
Saints and apostles in the gold of a wall
As in God's love will refuse my prayer
When prostrate on the marble step I fall
And cry aloud—"I sicken with desire
~~Though~~/ And fastened to a dying animal
Cannot endure my life—O gather me
Into the artifice of eternity."

This draft is only the germ of the final version, yet five of the eight rhyme words are in place: "wall," "desire," "animal," "me," "eternity." It is interesting that the *a* rhyme words are revised in the direction of exact rhyme rather than vice-versa: they become "fire," "gyre," "desire." The substitution of "soul" for "fall" in line 4 creates two interesting relationships between rhyme and meaning which will be discussed below.

A7 is the first draft of Stanza IV:

And if it be the dolphin's back   take
                                          spring
                                          sake
Of hammered gold and gold enamelling
That the Greek goldsmiths make
And set in gold leaves to sing
Of present past and future to come
For the instruction of Byzantium

Only five of the projected eight lines of the fourth stanza appear here, and these five lines are almost totally changed in the final version; nevertheless, six of the eight final rhyme words are in place: "take," "enamelling," "make," "sing," "come," "Byzantium." One concludes that in this stanza, as in the other three, Yeats generally works from right to left; he gets his rhyme words in place first and then works out the details of each line: the "golden leaves" of line 30, for example, are transmuted into the "golden bough," an image with more specific mythological reference. The rhyme structure of the finished poem follows:

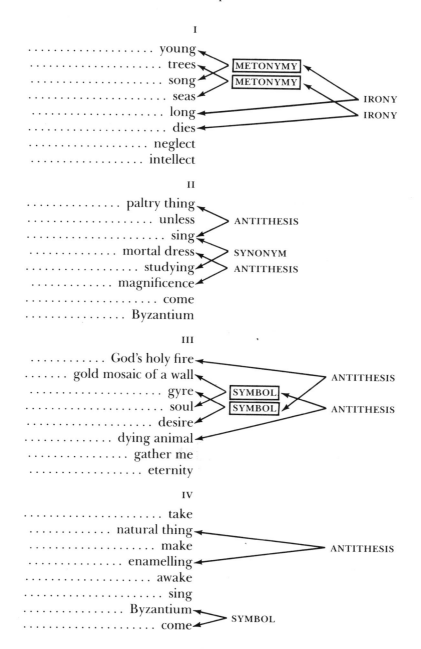

I

.... young
.... trees ⟩ METONYMY
.... song ⟩ METONYMY
.... seas   IRONY
.... long   IRONY
.... dies
.... neglect
.... intellect

II

.... paltry thing
.... unless ⟩ ANTITHESIS
.... sing
.... mortal dress ⟩ SYNONYM
.... studying   ANTITHESIS
.... magnificence
.... come
.... Byzantium

III

.... God's holy fire
.... gold mosaic of a wall ⟩ ANTITHESIS
.... gyre ⟩ SYMBOL
.... soul ⟩ SYMBOL   ANTITHESIS
.... desire
.... dying animal
.... gather me
.... eternity

IV

.... take
.... natural thing
.... make ⟩ ANTITHESIS
.... enamelling
.... awake
.... sing
.... Byzantium ⟩ SYMBOL
.... come

This diagram indicates that seventeen of the twenty-eight rhymes involve semantic relationships. In the first stanza, the *a* rhymes and *b*

27

rhymes exhibit similar semantic patterns: in both cases, the first two rhyme words are metonymically associated, while the third rhyme word ironically qualifies the meaning of the first two. Those who are "young" are traditionally associated with the joy and gaiety of "song," but here both "young" and "song" are ironically modified by the phrase "all summer long." "All summer" may seem like a "long" time to the young lovers, but obviously the summer cannot last, the implication being that the "song" of the "young" is merely transient, unlike the "song" of the golden bird in Stanza IV. Similarly, the words "trees" and "seas," both images of natural life, of fruition, of vitality, are qualified by the third *b* rhyme word "dies." All living things, the speaker reminds himself, must "die"; he therefore turns his back on "those dying generations" and sails to the "holy city of Byzantium."

In Stanza I, the rhyme words revolve about the life-death antinomy; in Stanza II, the rhyme words involve the related antinomy between body and soul. In terms of his material existence, an "aged man" is "but a paltry thing," but in the immortal world of Byzantium, the soul can "sing." The song of the soul is an intellectual activity; it is the process of "studying" the "monuments" of a permanently valuable civilization such as Byzantium. "Sing"/"studying" is, then, synonym-rhyme. The rhyme "mortal dress"/"magnificence" again contains the central tension between body and soul, life and art. The tattered "mortal dress" is the very opposite of the "magnificence" of the Byzantine artifacts.

In Stanza III, the rhymes constitute a distinct improvement, not only over the first version, but also over the B draft, in which lines 19 and 20 are:

> Consume this heart and make it what you were
> Unwavering, indifferent, fanatical. . . .

The word "were" has no particular semantic relationship to "fire" or to "desire"; the new rhyme word "gyre," on the other hand, is a Yeatsian symbol for flux or conflict; as he writes in *A Vision,* the gyres or cones "mirror reality but are in themselves pursuit and illusion."[5] The "gyre" thus aptly symbolizes the painful "desire" for rebirth of the speaker, who prays to the sages to "gather" him "into the artifice of eternity."[6] Both "gyre" and "desire" are, furthermore, antithetical to the phrase "God's holy fire" in line 17; the supernatural is opposed to the natural, the immortal to the mortal. The internal rhyme "holy fire"/"gyre" in line 19 intensifies this crucial antithesis.[7] The revision of line 20 has an equally effective rhyme change. The word "fanatical" has no specific relationship to the "gold mosaic of a wall" or to the "dying animal" while "soul" relates to both. In its stylized splendor, the "gold mosaic of a wall" symbolizes the perfection of the "soul" in the afterlife; the symbol-rhyme "gold mosaic of a wall"/"soul" is further antithetical to the "dying animal" or body of line 22. In Stanza IV, the rhyme "natural thing"/"gold enamelling" is a variation on the antithesis-rhyme "gold mosaic of a wall"/ "dying animal." Again Yeats opposes the natural to the artificial, the mutable to the permanent.

Nothing has been said so far about the four closing couplets. Taken together, they exhibit a very interesting pattern. In the first three couplets, the rhymes all involve the syntactic relationship: VERB/COMPLEMENTARY NOUN; each one can be read as an independent imperative sentence:

I neglect/intellect
II come/to Byzantium
III gather me/into the artifice of eternity

The fourth and final couplet does not have this structure, for noun and verb are reversed in position: "Byzantium"/"come." Rather, this rhyme is symbol-rhyme: "Byzantium" has become the symbol of the eternal, of that which is "past, or passing, or to come." The four couplet rhymes are related to the narrative movement of the whole poem. The first three define the state of becoming, as the speaker moves toward Byzantium. In the fourth stanza, however, the speaker has arrived at his destination; Byzantium is now revealed as the symbol of timelessness, encompassing past, present and future. Interestingly, the phonetic nature of the four rhymes supports this shift in narrative movement; as was pointed out above, all four are tertiary-stress rhymes, but whereas in the first three rhymes the rhyming unit with primary stress precedes the one with tertiary-stress, the process is reversed in the fourth rhyme: "Byzantium"/"come."

In summary, the following seventeen relationships between rhyme and meaning (R-M's) are found in "Sailing to Byzantium":

SEMANTIC CONGRUITY		SEMANTIC DISPARITY	
Symbol	3	Antithesis	7
Synonym	1	Irony	4
Metonymy	2		
Total	6		11

Grand Total: 17

Commenting on the symbolic value of the golden bird of Stanza IV, Yeats wrote, "I use it as a symbol of the intellectual joy of eternity, as contrasted with the instinctive joy of human life" (cited by Bradford, 111). These two poles—"the intellectual joy of eternity" and "the instinctive joy of human life"—remain in sharp opposition or contrast throughout the poem. It is therefore appropriate that antithesis-rhyme is the predominant R-M; the antithesis-rhymes convey the central tension between body and soul, change and permanence, life and art. Surely it is no coincidence that "dying animal" rhymes with "soul," "natural thing" with "gold enamelling," or "gyre" with "God's holy fire."

"Sailing to Byzantium" depicts a sharp tension in the speaker's mind between the claims of the natural and the supernatural. The central antithesis is reflected in its rhymes: there are eleven rhymes that involve semantic disparity as compared to six that involve semantic congruity, and antithesis-rhyme, the predominant class of meaning relationships, constitutes 41% of the total. In "Byzantium," on the other hand, the point of view has shifted. The speaker has arrived in the holy city and proceeds to define its character. Despite the return of the sea of life in the last stanza, the overall emphasis in "Byzantium" is on Unity of Being itself; therefore rhymes that have semantic congruity appropriately outnumber those that have semantic disparity, the count being as follows:

SEMANTIC CONGRUITY		SEMANTIC DISPARITY	
Symbol	1	Antithesis	1
Synonym	1	Irony	1
Metonymy	2	Pun	1
Symbolic Association	5		—
	9		3

Grand Total: 12

Rhyme involving semantic congruity is a suitable device for Yeats's description of his Eternal City, and, because this City is essentially mysterious and indescribable, he renders it in terms of symbol: symbol-rhyme and symbolic association–rhyme, taken together, constitute 67% of the rhymes that have semantic congruity and 50% of all the R-M's.

We are now in a better position to understand the function of epiphora in lines 9–11 and lines 17–18. "Byzantium" is a poem of harmonies rather than of contrasts; epiphora, like rhyme that involves semantic congruity, helps to intensify and to coordinate the images in the poem. Both devices are supported by the frequent use of word repetition within the lines: "images" occurs five times; "complexities" and "flames" four times each; "shade," "blood," "mire," "golden" and "fury" three times each. There is also anaphora in lines 6–7, 15–16, and 31–32. Furthermore, the rhymes involving a semantic relationship in "Byzantium" have a lower percentage of approximate rhyme than do those in "Sailing to Byzantium." In "Sailing," of the seventeen rhymes that involve a semantic relationship, eleven or 65% are approximate. In "Byzantium," of the twelve rhymes that involve a semantic relationship, only six or 50% are approximate. Exact rhymes, such as "song"/"gong," "dance"/"trance," and "metal"/"petal" contribute to the incantatory effect of "Byzantium"; the Yeatsian antinomies are momentarily resolved as the speaker has a mystical vision of Unity of Being.

In his article on Rhyme in *Encyclopedia of Poetry and Poetics*, A. M. Clark argues that "rhyme is wasted unless its sound cooperates in some way with the sense. That being so, the poet who has many insignificant words in rhyming places is losing some of his opportunities" (p. 707). The comparative study of the rhymes of the Byzantium poems has indicated Yeats's profound awareness of precisely such opportunities. Having studied Yeats's rhymes, one comes to demand similar effects from other poets; one assumes, as does Karl Shapiro, that "rhyming words need to be important words in the meaning of the line."[8]

But the examination of Yeats's rhyming practice also suggests an important corollary: rhyme has semantic value not only when it involves disparity (Clark places himself squarely in the Wimsatt tradition when he says that rhyme contributes to verse a "semantic factor . . . that underlines irony, litotes, and the unexpected collocation of dissimilars,"[9] but also when the meanings of the rhyming partners are congruous. Thus, although the rhymes of "Sailing to Byzantium" pinpoint such contraries as body-soul, mortal-immortal, or life-art, the rhymes of "Byzantium" underline and intensify the poet's vision of Unity of Being. One suspects, moreover, that a detailed study of the rhymes of other modern poets, such as Ezra Pound, Robert Frost, and Robert Lowell, would similarly reveal the importance of rhymes that involve semantic congruity.

In Yeats's major poems, rhyme functions as a kind of signal, reminding us of the larger poetic context in which it is embedded. Consider the last stanza of "A Dialogue of Self and Soul":

I am content to follow to its source
Every event in action or in thought;
Measure the lot; forgive myself the lot!
When such as I cast out remorse
So great a sweetness flows into the *breast*
We must laugh and we must sing,
We are blest by everything
Everything we look upon is *blest.*

The poem has dramatized the doctrine that blessedness is to be sought, not in the "pure" realm of the soul (the "breathless starlit air"), but in the "impure" one of the "self" or body ("the frog-spawn of a blind man's ditch"). The metonymy-rhyme "breast"/"blest" resolves the poem's central conflict between self and soul; it epitomizes the Yeatsian paradox that man is "blest" precisely when he comes to terms with the mortal limitations of his own "breast."

NOTES

1. For a detailed bibliography, see George Brandon Saul, *Prolegomena to the Study of Yeats's Plays* (Philadelphia: University of Pennsylvania Press, 1958), 122–23. The best general account of the Byzantium poems is that of T. R. Henn

in *The Lonely Tower: Studies in the Poetry of W. B. Yeats* (New York: Pellegrini and Cudahy, 1952), chapter 12.

2. Cited by Curtis Bradford in "Yeats's Byzantium Poems: A Study of Their Development" *PMLA* 75 (1960): 111.

3. I refer to Bradford's version of the drafts rather than to Jon Stallworthy's (*Between the Lines: Yeats's Poetry in the Making* [London: Oxford University Press, 1963], 87–136), which is slightly different, because the Bradford essay is readily available, having been reprinted in *Yeats: A Collection of Critical Essays*, ed. John Unterecker (Englewood Cliffs, N.J.: Prentice-Hall, 1963).

4. In the C draft, the closing couplet of stanza 1 is

And man has made no monument to extoll
The unborn, undying, unbegotten soul.

The closing couplet of stanza 1 in the final version first appears in the first printed version of "Sailing to Byzantium" in *October Blast* (Dublin: Cuala Press, 1927).

5. [Yeats, *A Vision* (New York: Macmillan Paperbacks, 1961), 73.]

6. Cleanth Brooks ("Yeats's Great-Rooted Blossomer," *The Well-Wrought Urn* [New York, 1947], 188–90) and Richard Ellmann (*The Man and the Masks* [London: 1961], 256) believe that Stanza III contains the speaker's ambivalent attitude toward Byzantium; he wants to be taken "out of nature," but even while he longs to be an artificial golden bird, he is "sick with desire" for the "sensual music" of the natural world. Ellmann writes, "the eternity into which the poet longs to be gathered is described with deliberate ambivalence as an artifice." But, as T. R. Henn notes (*Lonely Tower*, 214, n. 3), "artifice of eternity" is used in the time-honored sense of Sir Thomas Browne, who wrote, "In brief all things are artificial, for nature is the art of God." As for "sick with desire," the grammar of lines 21–22 suggests that it is the soul that is "sick with desire" for eternity. Even if we adopt the Brooks-Ellmann reading, however, "gyre"/"desire" is a symbol-rhyme and "fire"/"desire" an antithesis-rhyme.

7. Stallworthy suggests that "the close internal rhyme of 'fire' and 'gyre' brilliantly suggests a narrowing spiral and the approaching climax" (*Between the Lines*, 111).

8. Karl J. Shapiro, *A Prosody Handbook* (New York: Harper and Row, 1965), 101.

9. Clark, *Encyclopedia of Poetry and Poetics*, ed. Alex Preminger (Princeton: Princeton University Press, 1965), 708.

Interpretation: "The Birthmark"

CLEANTH BROOKS *and* ROBERT PENN WARREN

Brooks and Warren want us to see "The Birthmark" as something more than a parable, a story with a moral message (e.g.,

From *Understanding Fiction*, by Cleanth Brooks, Jr., and Robert Penn Warren (New York: Appleton-Century-Crofts, 1943), 103–6. Copyright 1943 by F. S. Crofts & Co., Inc. Reprinted by permission.

Perfection is something never achieved on earth). To this end, they explore Aylmer's character, especially his complex motivation for his ruinous experiment. Agreeing with what they interpret to be Hawthorne's own attitude, these New Critics conclude that Aylmer is both foolish and noble.

THIS STORY [HAWTHORNE's "The Birthmark"] amounts to a sort of parable. Indeed, Hawthorne frankly applies the term "parable" to one or two of his other stories of this kind. In the second paragraph of this story, Hawthorne says quite explicitly that the story of Aylmer and Georgiana has a "deeply impressive moral." But if we as readers are deeply impressed with the moral, we will be so because the presentation has been sufficiently concrete and sufficiently dramatic to impress us: the moral will hardly be "deeply impressive" in isolation. Even if we grant that Hawthorne is primarily interested here in the theme and does not hesitate to bring his theme to the fore, we are still compelled to ask the same questions with regard to this story which we have had to ask with regard to other stories. We may well begin with the problem which will probably present itself early to any reader: the problem of motivation.

Why is Aylmer anxious to remove the birthmark from his wife's cheek? She herself is frankly shocked when her husband first suggests removing it. She had not thought of it as a blemish; she had actually been complimented on it as something which was rather charming; and obviously, the birthmark had not prevented Aylmer from thinking her very beautiful, or from marrying her. Indeed, we are told, only a few women, jealous of her surpassing beauty, had ever regarded it as a disfigurement.

It is ironical that even Aylmer would not have come to regard the birthmark as a blemish if Georgiana had been less beautiful. As it is, the birthmark arrests his attention and gradually provokes his desire to remove it from the very fact that it remains the only possible blemish upon otherwise perfect beauty: ". . . his eyes wandered stealthily to her cheek, and beheld, flickering with the blaze of the wood fire, the spectral hand that wrote mortality where he would fain have worshiped."

Even so, had Aylmer not been a scientist, a daring experimenter, the birthmark on his wife's cheek would hardly have come to obsess him; for it was neither so large nor so prominent that it might not have been dismissed from mind, had not the thought that it lay within his power to remove it insinuated itself into Aylmer's imagination. That this is a very prominent part of his motivation is indicated in his remark to Georgiana: "I feel myself fully competent to render this cheek as faultless as its fellow; and then, most beloved, what will be my triumph when I shall have corrected what Nature left imperfect in her fairest work!"

We are not, of course, to conceive of Aylmer as a monster, a man who would experiment on his own wife for his own greater glory. Hawthorne does not mean to suggest that Aylmer is depraved and heartless. The triumph of which Aylmer speaks will not be for vulgar display and self-advertisement. It will be a triumph which his wife will share and a triumph to be won for her sake. And he *is* confident that he will be successful. The element of pride is there, but the kind of pride, it is suggested, is that which enters into and colors many of man's nobler purposes. What the story emphasizes is not Aylmer's self-conceit but rather his possession of the questing spirit which will not resign itself to the limitations and imperfections of nature. Nature itself is to be corrected, to be made perfect.

The decision to attempt to remove the birthmark is, of course, not arrived at in a moment, but by stages. Aylmer, before he allows the experiment to become a part of his conscious purpose, finds himself dreaming of it. His wife, who had paid no attention to her birthmark, soon begins to become self-conscious about it, and finally the mark becomes something hateful to her. Moreover, when she finds how much the thought of its removal has come to mean to her husband, she urges him on as a proof of her love for him. Others had counted the blemish charming, and other lovers would have risked life to kiss it; but just before the final experiment is to be made Georgiana can say that she fears only one thing—not death, but "that this horrible stigma shall be left upon my cheek!" As for Aylmer, the enterprise, which at the beginning was little more than a fantastic notion, has become a "rapture."

Aminadab, Aylmer's assistant, provides a sort of measuring stick for the folly and nobility of the husband and wife. He is, as Aylmer calls him, a "man of clay." He lacks the imagination for the noble enterprise of daring to surpass nature. The tiny blemish in a woman so beautiful as Georgiana would cause him no uneasiness at all, and he says, with a shrewd and solid common sense, "If she were my wife, I'd never part with that birthmark."

The birthmark is removed. Aylmer has his "peerless bride" in entire perfection for a moment, but the birthmark, symbol of the earthy, the mortal, can be eradicated only at the price of life itself. Aylmer has not realized that perfection is something never achieved on earth and in terms of mortality.

Here, of course, appears the theme of the story, the "impressive moral" which we have been told the story contains. But if the story is to be merely the vehicle for this moral, why has Hawthorne chosen to use the method of fiction at all? It is true that the story, as he has constructed it, is a rather transparent symbol for the basic idea, and that the characters have a rather obvious symbolic reference: Aminadab stands for the earthy, gross side of man's nature; Aylmer, for the aspiring and imaginative element in man. But, even so, why has Hawthorne written a story at all rather than an essay, say, or a sermon?

An obvious reason in favor of the story, of course, is our basic interest as human beings in a story, even a story which is closely tied to an idea. The story allows the author to develop suspense, to provide a dramatic form for the situation, to engage our interests more intensely. But there are other things which Hawthorne gains from his use of fiction here, matters usually overlooked but perhaps more important ultimately than the added interest and intensity. We shall see what these things are if we consider Hawthorne's attitude toward the situation which he has described. What, for example, is Hawthorne's attitude toward the various characters and toward the decisions which they make? Aminadab, for instance, would seem to support Hawthorne's moral, but does Hawthorne consider him to be a higher type than Aylmer? Hardly. Aminadab is for the author, too, a "man of clay," gross, animal-like, easily satisfied. Aylmer tries to achieve what is impossible and thus commits a folly; but it would be misreading the story to infer that Hawthorne dismisses him as merely a foolish man. The author is sympathetic to him, and obviously sees in his ruinous experiment a certain nobility.

What is the author's attitude toward the moral itself? Is man to give up all his attempts to conquer nature? Would Hawthorne have men settle down into a supine and passive acceptance of what nature gives? A careful reading of the story will suggest that Hawthorne himself does not take his own moral in these terms. There are many qualifications to be made, one would gather—matters of emphasis and matters of application to be taken into account. One cannot range the characters into two absolute categories, the good and the bad, the right and the wrong; and the moral itself is not a rule to be applied absolutely and without qualification.

Most important of all, it should be apparent that Hawthorne is *not interested in having us apply a rule*—he is not interested merely in trying to win our assent to a particular generalization, or in trying to make us adopt a certain course of action. His story, even with its heavy emphasis on a particular theme, is something more than a sermon or a lawyer's brief. His total intention, like that of any writer of fiction, is wider than this. . . .

Hawthorne's "The Birthmark": Science as Religion

ROBERT BECHTOLD HEILMAN

Heilman's essay illustrates the New Critical approach to thematic which traces how significant themes inform the language of a literary work. He claims "The Birthmark" approaches greatness

From *South Atlantic Quarterly* 48 (1949): 575–83. Copyright 1949 by Duke University Press. Reprinted by permission of Duke University Press.

because it has a great theme which it does not oversimplify. You will notice how careful he is to ground his discussion of theme in the story's formal aspects of words and imagery.

HAWTHORNE'S "THE BIRTHMARK" has been called, not inappropriately, a parable. The "truth" which it aims to set forth can be disengaged from the narrative: in a rational attempt to "perfect" nature man may destroy the organic life from which the imperfection is inseparable. But, as Messrs. Brooks and Warren have made clear, it is necessary to guard against an oversimplification of what the story says, to guard particularly against converting even a parabolic drama into melodrama. Aylmer, the overweening scientist, resembles less the villain than the tragic hero: in his catastrophic attempt to improve on human actuality there is not only pride and a deficient sense of reality but also disinterested aspiration. The story does not advocate total resignation or a flat acquiescence in the immediate state of affairs. Despite its firm expository conclusion, "The Birthmark" hardly advocates at all; it enters the neighborhood of greatness because it has a great theme, but is not tempted into pat answers. The theme which Hawthorne explores may be defined as the problem of mediating between irrational passivity and a hyperrational reorganization of life. Failure in this problem, as in others, may coincide with urgent good will; this is the formulation of the tragic actor which Hawthorne adopts, in contrast with the tragic structure in which an evil or perverted will is joined to saving qualities such as the capacity for repentance. But Hawthorne makes a more precise definition of the tragic error—one which is worth a brief examination.

This definition is made implicitly in the language of the story—language which may be either literal or figurative but in either case has influential overtones. What we find recurrently in "The Birthmark," and therefore insistently asking to be taken into account, is the terminology and imagery of religion. Specifically religious problems are not overtly introduced into the story, but the language of religion is there so unfailingly that, like iterative imagery in drama and poetry, it must be closely inspected if a final reading of the story is to be complete. What it does is create a story that transcends the parabolic: the foreground parable concerns man's relations with nature, but the immanent story is about man's conceptions of evil. The further we trace the implications of language, the less simple we discover Hawthorne's tale to be.

The scientific progress of Aylmer's day, we are told, "seemed to open paths into the region of *miracle*"; scientists are called *votaries;* Aylmer may have shared their "*faith* in man's ultimate control over Nature." The subjects of their study are called *secrets,* but also, repeatedly, *mysteries;* at the end, the "*mysterious* symbol had passed away," but it had been inseparable from the very "*mystery* of life." When Georgiana's and Aylmer's union has been virtually identified with the scientific effort to remove the birthmark, Georgiana thinks of Aylmer's devotion to her—to the perfected her—as "*holy* love." What is made clear by such terms, which function precisely like poetic images, is that science itself has become religion, able to provide an ultimate account of reality and therefore to exact complete human dedication. It has become religion not only for Aylmer but also for Georgiana—". . . she *prayed* that, for a single moment, she might satisfy his highest and deepest conception." Indeed, her taking of Aylmer's final potion, which is to effect her transformation, is recorded in terms which make it virtually a Christian act. The drink is "bright enough to be the draught of *immortality*"; to Georgiana it is "like water from a *heavenly* fountain," and it will allay "a feverish thirst that had parched me for many days." Since Biblical language makes frequent use of metaphors of thirst to express spiritual yearnings, it is difficult not to read in such a passage a reminiscence of John 4:14— ". . . whosoever drinketh of the waters that I shall give him shall never thirst; but the water that I shall give him shall be in him a well of water springing up into everlasting life."

The question, of course, is whether Georgiana's draught is really heavenly and has the power to allay the thirst that from the soul doth rise; whether, in other words, the auspices under which she drinks are spiritual principles. The irony of her illusion is subtly carried on by her blunt command, "Give me the goblet." At one level the analogy with communion is amplified; but *goblet* also has a metaphorical value, and we are inevitably reminded of the cup which is an ordeal: ". . . the cup which my Father hath given me, shall I not drink it?" Georgiana has overcome her dread and has come to conceive of herself, at least in part, as a sacrifice. The end is the secular salvation of mortal man.

The cup has been given by Aylmer. The language-pattern of the story indicates that in the religion of science Aylmer is less priest than God. The votaries believed, Hawthorne records, that the scientist would "lay his hands on the *secret of creative force* and perhaps *make new worlds* for himself." The word *wonders* is used repeatedly to describe what Aylmer and other scientists achieved. Aylmer, though he speaks jokingly, does apply the term *sorcerer* to himself; a laboratory exploit of his is *magical;* he is confident that he can "draw a *magic* circle around her within which no evil might intrude." He could make, he intimates, "an *immortal* nostrum"; he has created an "elixir of *immortality*"; the potion which he prepares for Georgiana may be the draught "of *immortal* happiness or misery." Aylmer has given to the problems offered by the birthmark such deep thought that he feels almost able "to *create* a being less perfect" than Georgiana. He is sure that he can make her cheek *faultless*. And then he makes an allusion which contributes importantly to this part of the meaning: "Even Pygmalion, when his sculptured woman assumed life, felt not greater ecstasy than mine will be." Formally, Aylmer rarely

37

fails to exhibit a consciousness of human limitations; but still he cannot discipline that part of himself which aspires to infinite power. At the conclusion of the experiment he exclaims spontaneously, "By *Heaven!* it is well nigh gone!" What is this Heaven? Has a superhuman power aided him? Or has his power itself seemed to go beyond the terrestrial? A minute later he lets "the light of *natural* day" enter the room, and Aminadab, "the *earthly* mass," chuckles grossly. It is as though Aylmer has descended for a moment into another kind of reality from that which is proper to him. Indeed, he distinguishes two kinds of force which he declares have been at work: "Matter and spirit—*earth and heaven*—have both done their part in this!" But the question is whether Aylmer really accepts the dualism to which his words give expression.

In fact, we have almost a parody of the Father who gives the bitter cup to drink. Aylmer, as we have seen, is virtually translated into the godhead: His "*sorcerer's* book," Georgiana insists to him, "has made me *worship* you more than ever." The confusion of values has spread to Georgiana. Aylmer's own confusion is shown further in his paradoxical inclination to adore as well as create: "the spectral hand wrote mortality where he would fain have *worshiped.*" Yet later, in a context which shows that his evaluation is moral, he assures her, "You are fit for heaven without tasting death!" Perhaps, then, she ought to be almost suitable for adoration, and the hand itself should seem a negligible flaw. Yet over it Aylmer is almost hysterical, while, as we shall see, he is blind to more serious flaws closer to home.

That Aylmer is a confused man has always been plain to readers of the story. But, when we examine it in detail, we discover that the language of the story defines his confusion very precisely—defines it as the mistaking of science for religion. The essential story, I have said, is about man's conception of evil: Aylmer does not, in the long run, regard evil as real. Without actually denying its reality, Aylmer in effect simplifies and attenuates it by treating it as manageable, subject to human control, indeed removable. Aylmer's religion reverses the Christian sense of the reality of evil—a reality which can ultimately be dealt with only by divine grace. Aylmer is a romantic perfectibilitarian, who suffers from a dangerous fastidiousness in the presence of complex actuality. "You are perfect!" he assures Georgiana—as she is dying. He believes in perfectibility without retaining the modifying concept of damnability. Man's confidence in his ability to deal with evil by some physical or psychological or social surgery makes him an earthly god: in his presumption he proposes to establish a heaven on earth. Thus, like Aylmer, man becomes committed to a hyperrational—that is, a shallowly grounded—reorganization of life. Hawthorne brilliantly summarizes the metaphysics of the scientific religion in Aylmer's explication of the series of steps in his rehabilitation of Georgiana. He tells her, "I have already administered agents powerful enough to change your entire physical system. Only one thing remains to be tried." ". . . to change your entire physical system" is, in this cosmology, the equivalent of regeneration or conversion. Aylmer's faith becomes, in effect: improve the body, and you save the soul.

Hawthorne repeatedly underlines the error of Aylmer's ways. His confusion of values shows in the fact that his husbandly love can have strength only "by intertwining itself with his love of science." The birthmark which he proposes to remove is "fairy," "mysterious," "magic"—terms which indicate how much more is at stake than Aylmer suspects at his most acute. He accepts uncritically Georgiana's assurance that from his hand she is willing "to take a dose of poison," an ironic anticipation of the way in which his elixir actually does work. He demands complete "trust" and is angry when, following him into the laboratory, she throws "the blight of that fatal birthmark over my labors"—his own word, *blight*, having a summary accuracy of which he is ironically innocent. Aylmer accepts entirely his wife's passionate exclamation that if the birthmark is not removed "we shall both go mad!" What the reader must see in this madness is a simple inability to accept the facts of life. It is precisely this inability of which Hawthorne, throughout the story, keeps reminding us, almost overwhelmingly.

Hawthorne could hardly have found a better symbol than the birthmark, which speaks of the imperfection born with man, with man as a race. Here is original sin in fine imaginative form. Aylmer does not altogether fail to see what is involved; he is not crudely stupid; but his sense of power leads him to undervalue the penalties of life. His tragedy is that he lacks the tragic sense; he is, we may say, a characteristic modern, the exponent of an age which has deified science and regards it as an irresistibly utopianizing force. His tragic flaw is to fail to see the tragic flaw in humanity. Hawthorne never lets the reader forget the deep significance of the "human hand" which scars Georgiana. He comments ironically on the lovers who hoped to see "one living specimen of ideal loveliness without the semblance of a flaw," a suggestion of a common attitude for which Aylmer speaks. The birthmark is a "symbol of imperfection," "the spectral hand that wrote mortality," the "sole token of human imperfection." This "fatal flaw of humanity"—the terms are virtually Christian—implies that all the productions of nature are "temporary and finite" and that "their perfection must be wrought by toil and pain." For spiritual discipline Aylmer wants to substitute magic—not quite pushbutton magic perhaps, but still a shortcut, a kind of prestidigitation. It is not that he is ignorant in a gross way; he sees much, but his premises stop him at the threshold of wisdom. He recognizes that the blemish on Georgiana's face is a "mark of earthly imperfection"; he even selects it "as the symbol of his wife's liability to sin, sorrow, decay, and death." The frequency of images of death in the story is a thematic reminder of the reality from which Aylmer doggedly turns away. Although here he actually puts his finger upon the realities which the mature man must come to terms with, his faith leads him to feel, as we have seen, "that he could draw a magic circle round her within which no evil might intrude." Evil is manageable: the symbol itself has become the reality.

What we finally come to is the problem of spirit, and the test of Aylmer's creed is the kind of spiritual values it embodies. We hear repeatedly about Aylmer's spirit and his interest in the spiritual. He had "attempted to fathom," we learn, "the very process by which Nature assimilates all her precious influences from earth and air, and from the *spiritual* world, to create and foster man, her masterpiece." Aminadab represents "man's physical nature"; in Aylmer we see "the *spiritual* element." Georgiana is almost convinced "that her husband possessed sway over the *spiritual* world." As she reads his record of experiments, the author, apparently speaking for her, comments: "He handled physical details as if there were nothing beyond them; yet *spiritualized* them all, and redeemed himself from materialism by his strong and eager aspiration towards the *infinite*. In his grasp the veriest clod of earth assumed a *soul*." His failures are those of "the *spirit* burdened with clay and working in matter"; "his *spirit* was ever on the march, ever ascending"—the spirit, one is tempted to say, of progress. But as a result of this spiritual yearning of his, another's "angelic spirit" leaves on its "heavenward flight."

At the end Hawthorne, distinguishing "mortal" and "celestial," reaffirms a dualism which he has insisted upon throughout the story and which, as various words of theirs make clear, is formally assented to also by Georgiana and Aylmer. But the first defect of Aylmer's religion, as the drama makes clear, is that in practice he does not accept dualism at all: for him, spirit is not distinct from matter but is the perfecting of matter. The material stigma that shocks him he is said, just once, to regard as symbol; but his efforts at amelioration are directed wholly at the symbol, not at its antecedent substance. Aylmer is actually symptom-doctoring and is unaware that the locus of the disease is elsewhere. His creed is secular and monistic. All the talk about spirit is an ironic commentary upon his essential lack of insight into real problems of spirit.

The story specifies what level of spiritual comprehension Aylmer does reach. He aspires, and his aspiration is presented with a good deal of sympathy, as is just; as between aspiration and passivity, the choice is, in the main, clear; but a judgment must be made between one kind of aspiration and another. So the question becomes: how, and toward what, does Aylmer actually aspire? Does he, for instance, aspire toward better insight? Toward charity? Toward wisdom? Or is it not rather that his aspiration is inextricably involved with the exercise of power? "There is no taint of imperfection on thy spirit," he tells Georgiana. Why? Because Georgiana has just indicated an unreserved willingness to accept his potion; her faith in him is total. He is not content with her perfection of "spirit." For him, immense knowledge is a means of doing things, of achieving physical, visible ends. We see in him no evidence of concern with the quality of his own life, or perception, or thought.

In this man of science divine discontent is with others; as Georgiana puts it, his love "would accept nothing less than perfection nor miserably make itself contented with an earthlier nature than he had dreamed of." It is of course Georgiana who shall be "all perfect." The romantic scientist has no thought of the problem of perfecting himself; indeed, his spiritual perception is very close to that of uplift and do-good-ism. He begs the real problem of spirit and is fanatical about the shortcomings of the world. Hawthorne is very acute in analyzing further the especial quality of Aylmer's outward-bound perfectionism and in discerning in it a core of intense fastidiousness. This hypersensitivity rushes in, indeed, at the very moment at which Aylmer fleetingly achieves a kind of wholeness of response to Georgiana, an acceptance of her which implies a spiritual modification of himself. "Yet once, by a strange and unaccountable impulse, he pressed it [the birthmark] with his lips." Here is virtually a redefinition of his love. But immediately his fastidiousness reasserts itself and gives the parting tone to the action: "His *spirit* recoiled, however, in the very act. . . ." That is his spirit: a primary awareness of the flaws of others and of the demand which they appear to make for remedy from without.

The heir of Prometheus kills his beneficiary, not by conferring a single blessing, but by endeavoring to eradicate the imperfections humanity is heir to. Upon this aspiration to divinity Hawthorne comments in his account of Aylmer's library, of the works of "these antique naturalists" who "perhaps imagined themselves to have acquired from the investigation of Nature a power above Nature, and from physics a sway over the spiritual world." Hawthorne has already remarked that the "great creative Mother . . . is yet severely careful to keep her own secrets." What Hawthorne has done, really, is to blueprint the course of science in modern imagination, to dramatize its persuasive faith in its omnipotence, and thus its taking on the colors of religion.

This very formulation commits Hawthorne to a critique—a critique which he makes by disclosing the false spirituality of Aylmer. It is the false spirituality of power conjoined with fastidiousness, of physical improvement, of external remedy, of ad hoc prescriptions, of reform: Aylmer's surgery is a fine symbol for a familiar code. Yet the code would have only an innocuous life in a museum-case if it did not gain converts. Thus we have Georgiana's very important role in the story: she is less the innocent victim than the fascinated sharer in magic who conspires in her own doom. Georgiana, the woman killed with kindness by the man who would be god, is really humanity—with its share of the heroic, its common sense, which enables it to question heroes, and yet its capacity for being beguiled, for combining good intention, devotion, and destructive delusion. In the marriage of science and humanity we see the inevitably catastrophic interaction of a mechanical perfectionism and the "birth-mark of mortality." Science has no way of coming to terms with human imperfection, and humanity, tutored by science, can no longer accept its liability to sin and death.

Ironically, it is Georgiana who cuts off, or at least helps cut off, a final path of spiritual rectification for Aylmer. "Do not *repent*," she says, "that . . . you have rejected the best earth could offer." Not only is Aylmer's definition of "the best" inadequate, but he is encouraged in a hardening of spirit which precludes his entering upon a reconsideration of values. His religion offers no way of dealing with his pride. And his pride—with its intense demand that the world submit itself to his limited criteria—gives us another definition of the spiritual defect of this man who is so convinced that spirit is his concern. When Georgiana confesses her de-sire to worship him more fully, he scarcely bothers to be deprecatory: "Ah, wait for this one success, . . . then *worship* me if you will. I shall deem myself hardly unworthy of it." These are the ultimate marks of his moral infatuation.

The critical problem in "The Birthmark" has to do with the kind of mistake Aylmer makes. Hawthorne's language tells us, subtly but insis-tently, that Aylmer has apotheosized science; and the images and drama together define the spiritual shortcoming of this new revelation—its be-lief in the eradicability of evil, its Faustian proneness to love power, its incapacity to bring about renunciation or self-examination, its pride. I once thought that Hawthorne had stopped short of the proper goal of the story by not including the next phase of Aylmer's experience—the phase in which, if the tragic view of Aylmer were to prevail, Aylmer would entertain the Furies. But the summation of Aylmer's defects is that he cannot see the Furies. The story stops where it must.

The Shadow's Shadow: The Motif of the Double in Edgar Allan Poe's "The Purloined Letter"

LIAHNA BABENER

Babener discovers meaning in the formal aspects of "The Pur-loined Letter" by analyzing its structural repetitions. Whereas the pervasive doubling motif (Dupin-Minister; the series of par-allel plot elements) unifies the work, the repetition calls attention

Reprinted from *Mystery and Detection Annual* 1 (1972): 21–32 by permission of the author.

to the structures as formal structures. By highlighting these formal aspects, Babener contends that the story calls into question the ethical norms of the detective tale which traditionally distinguish the sleuth from the criminal.

IN 1845, EDGAR ALLAN POE published "The Purloined Letter," his third contribution to the form he had himself invented. While critics of the work have generally recognized its superiority to Poe's other detective stories, particularly in light of its additions to the new genre, few have attributed its merit to factors other than skillful handling of the "ratiocinative" method, or effective rendering of structural unity.[1] But these qualities do not sufficiently account for the distinctive achievement of the work. The author himself admonished against overvaluing his detective tales merely "on account of their method or *air* of method,"[2] and encouraged the prudent reader to discover meaning beneath the surface as "an undercurrent of suggestion."

One aspect of the work, often noticed but as yet unexplained, is the pervasive doubling motif[3] which underlies the structure of the tale as a whole and characterizes particularly the relationship between M. Dupin and his rival, the Minister D——. Poe's insistent use of doublings in the story considerably exceeds that which is necessary for presenting Dupin's method of investigation, which in this case stresses detection through psychological identification with an adversary. Rather, the prominent pattern of doubles suggests that the protagonist and his foil are moral duplicates and may ultimately be two phases of the same mind.

The double principle informs the basic action of the story, the major event of which is Dupin's retrieval of the purloined letter and consequent triumph over the resourceful D——. The action revolves around Dupin's method of detection, which is based primarily on two logical premises from which he will eventually reason forth the solution to the mystery. One is that the cunning investigator must achieve an "identification of the reasoner's intellect with that of his opponent."[4] The other is the recognition that the truth "may escape observation by dint of being excessively obvious" (p. 47). Both axioms are exemplified by means of an analogy to game strategy. For the first, Dupin describes the familiar schoolboys' game of "even and odd." "One player holds in his hand a number of . . . [marbles], and demands of another whether that number is even or odd. If the guess is right, the guesser wins one; if wrong, he loses one" (p. 40). The shrewder player wins by anticipating the strategy of the other competitor. Dupin illustrates his second postulate with the old sport of locating place names printed on a map. While "a novice in the game generally seeks to embarrass his opponents by giving them the most minutely lettered names . . . the adept selects such words as stretch, in large characters, from one end of the chart to the other" (p. 47). The prudent player correctly presumes that the other will overlook the larger and more diffused letters in favor of the smaller, more compact words, and wins by subverting the expectations of his opponent. It is significant that both of these illustrations incorporate the use of parallel reasoning between contenders, and both epitomize in miniature the primary action of the tale as a whole. Dupin's casual game analogies thus serve as metaphors for the more consequential rivalry between him and D——.

Acting upon these paired axioms, the detective approaches the two-fold problem of the missing letter and the astute thief. Dupin knows that the Minister, who has purportedly stolen the document for purposes of political extortion, must fulfill two requirements if he is ever to utilize his spoils. He must be able to produce the letter at momentary notice, and he must protect it from frequent searches by the police. Given these circumstances, the sleuth reasons that the letter must be secreted on the premises of D——'s lodgings, despite the failure of the Prefect's men to find it. At this point, Dupin applies the first supposition of his method on the basis of a prior knowledge of the character of his adversary, and proceeds to recreate the Minister's reasoning in the current situation:

> Such a man, I considered, could not fail to be aware of the ordinary policial modes of action. He could not have failed to anticipate . . . the waylayings to which he was subjected. He must have foreseen, I reflected, the secret investigations of his premises. . . . I felt also, that the whole train of thought, which I was at some pains in detailing to you just now . . . would necessarily pass through the mind of the Minister. It would imperatively lead him to despise all the ordinary *nooks* of concealment. . . . I saw, in fine, that he would be driven, as a matter of course, to *simplicity*, if not deliberately induced to it as a matter of choice. (pp. 45–46)

In this extract, Dupin is actually reproducing the Minister's own method of reasoning: he "admeasures" the mind of his competitor (as D—— has appraised the intelligence of his police assailants) and predicts his tactics (as D—— has anticipated the tactics of his pursuers). In this way, the detective deduces D——'s plan for concealment of the letter—the paradoxical scheme of the conspicuous hiding place—which is the practical embodiment of Dupin's own axiom about the difficulty of perceiving the obvious. Like the game players' strategy in his analogies, Dupin's is to outguess his antagonist.

It remains for Dupin, having unriddled the mystery, to verify his solution and to retrieve the letter. He makes an unsolicited visit to the Minister's apartment, where, camouflaged behind a "pair of green spectacles," he scans the room for the letter which he locates, revamped and resealed, in a letter rack in plain view of the observer. A second visit, on a spurious excuse, furnishes the occasion for a surreptitious exchange of letters, where Dupin, repeating the method used initially by D—— to steal the letter, replaces the original document with a counterfeit one. Dupin describes his replica as "a *fac-simile,* (so far as regards externals) which I had carefully prepared at my lodgings; imitating the D—— cipher, very readily, by means of a seal formed of bread" (pp. 50–51). The vital letter itself is present in two guises. Dupin, studying the one in D——'s letter rack, recognizes that though "it was, to all appearance, radically different from the one of which the Prefect has read us so minute a description" (p. 49), nevertheless this document is the one sought. "It was torn nearly in two, across the middle" and it "had been turned, as a glove, inside out, re-directed and re-sealed." So the purloined letter becomes a double of itself. Thus, the entire process of crime solution incorporates a series of noticeable doublings and parallelings: the twin analytical axioms, the pair of game analogies, the two successive intellectual gambols between the police and D—— and between D—— and Dupin, the sequence of mimicked stratagems by which Dupin trips up his enemy, and the twofold nature of the chief clue.

While Poe unquestionably sets up the tale to enable Dupin to demonstrate his imitative method of detection against an antagonist of equal powers, this explanation does not sufficiently account for other insistent uses of the double pattern in the story.

This doubling technique appears especially in the portraits of the two major characters. Dupin's own reasoning processes are frequently depicted by means of coupled thoughts and parallel ideas. He is particularly fond of elaborate, point by point analogies. "The material world," he observes, "abounds with very strict analogies to the immaterial." He is fascinated by semblances and correspondences and often uses them as indirect means of communication. In one occurrence, Dupin induces the Prefect to acknowledge and reward his assistance in the present case by means of the "Abernethy" anecdote. The sleuth recounts the fable of a miser who uses hypothetical questions to maneuver advice from a doctor, and the Prefect, inferring Dupin's point, properly sees in the analogy an image of his own avarice. "'But,' said the Prefect, a little discomposed, 'I am *perfectly* willing to take advice, and to pay for it. I would *really* give fifty thousand francs to any one who would aid me in the matter'" (p. 38), and Dupin correspondingly interprets the Prefect's allusion as a reluctant offer of compensation. Dupin's anecdote illustrates again the gaming psychology and emphasizes his tendency to devise fictional doubles as means of expression. Moreover, Dupin himself is often described in terms of paired images. He is first pictured to us relaxing in his secluded quarters, "au troisième, No. 33. Rue Dunôt" (note the repetition of the numbers and the echo of the protagonist's name in that of his street), where he and the nameless narrator enjoy the "twofold luxury of meditation and a meerschaum" (p. 28). Correspondingly, the Minister D—— is frequently depicted by means of yoked images. The Prefect portrays him as a man who "dares all things, those unbecoming

as well as those becoming a man." He practices a thievery "not less ingenious than bold." Dupin knows him as poet and mathematician, courier
and intrigant. D——'s residence, the D—— Hotel, is also a reverberation
of his name.

These parallelisms and mated adjectives used to describe the major
characters are compounded by an almost compulsive duplication of
structural elements in the tale. Nearly every major movement of plot occurs twice. There are two consultations between the Prefect and Dupin.
On the occasion of the second call, we are told by the narrator that the
Prefect "found us occupied very nearly as before" (p. 37). Both visits are
at night and both times the caller is supplied with pipe and chair. There
are two interviews as well between Dupin and D——, and on each occasion they discuss the same subject. There are two major searches of the
Minister's apartment by the police. (When the Prefect expresses bewi-
lderment after the first fruitless inspection, Dupin's advice is "to make a
thorough re-search of the premises" [p. 37].) Similarly, we are informed
that D—— "has been twice waylaid" in the streets by the inspector's men;
both times the men are costumed as thugs, both times the search is exe-
cuted under the covert supervision of the Prefect himself, and both
times D—— is found without the stolen document. There are also two
instances of "blackmail": the Minister's against "a personage of most exalted station," and Dupin's of the prefect to obtain payment for his assistance. There are two rewards paid for the recovery of the letter—both
are "very liberal." (The Prefect notes that the prize offered "has been
lately doubled" [p. 38].) In addition, there are two instances of papers
being purloined, both involving the furtive substitution of the original
with a facsimile. Finally, there are two political power struggles, both involving the high deputies of state and both associated with possession of
the letter. In the first, D—— plots, and nearly accomplishes, the political
collapse of the royal lady; in the second, Dupin extricates the same lady
from the grip of her enemies and arranges the downfall of D——.

These numerous and striking instances of mirroring all underscore
the paramount doubling in the tale—that between Dupin and the Minister D——. From the perspective of the detective story genre, the two
function respectively as sleuth and criminal, protagonist and antagonist.
Dupin traps his quarry by adopting his rationale and duplicating his
method. But the resemblance between the two far exceeds that which
results from Dupin's conscious imitation of his foil, and renders inapplicable the conventional moral separation between detective and culprit.

The doubling which links Dupin and D—— is readily exhibited by
the astonishing similarity of their minds. Both possess the same intellectual capacities and interests. The Minister, author of a treatise on "the
differential Calculus," has gained some fame as a mathematician, a subject for which Dupin also demonstrates fondness by his frequent use of
mathematical models to illustrate abstract ideas and by his fascination

with probabilities. D—— has also "acquired renown as a poet," and Dupin admits to the same talent: "I have been guilty of certain doggerel myself." Dupin clearly recognizes D—— as a like mind: "I knew him . . . as both mathematician and poet" (p. 45), a man of equal mental make-up and a perfect peer.

If Dupin and D—— are intellectual counterparts, they are more significantly moral equivalents, whose motives and methods are equally dubious from an ethical standpoint. While D——'s villainy is never questioned by critics, few regard Dupin as other than an artist, who solves crimes for sheer aesthetic pleasure and hence is exempt from moral scrutiny, or else as a representative of the forces of morality. Neither appraisal is appropriate. Unquestionably, Dupin displays his characteristic preoccupation with sophisticated epistemological puzzles. In this sense, his interest in the case at hand is "artistic," though it does *not* distinguish him from D——, who shares an attraction to the artistic dimension of the problem.

Dupin cannot be regarded simplistically as a moral agent whose able solution of the crime represents a triumph for the cause of virtue. Dupin's mode of procedure, while successful, is nevertheless ethically suspicious; he does, after all, imitate D——'s own tactics which are clearly pernicious. Both men employ ingenious forms of trickery to execute their plans and to deceive their antagonists. The Minister's talent for duplicity is plain. The letter was first pirated by means of one clever deception, and secreted by another "to delude the beholder into an idea of the worthlessness of the document" (p. 49). Once the letter is "hidden," the Minister uses an elaborate ruse to safeguard it. He arranges to be regularly absent from his residence during the evenings in order to facilitate what he knows will be a futile search by the police, and thus to convince the Prefect that the letter is not secreted there. During Dupin's visit, the Minister enacts the role of the unsuspecting innocent in order to discourage speculation that he has anything to hide.

Dupin likewise employs deception to confound his opponent. His ostensibly "accidental" call upon D—— is really calculated to gain him entry into the man's lodgings, and once there, he resorts to a series of crafty pretenses to promote his search: he pretends a sight handicap to disguise his survey of the room; he diverts D—— with conversation in order to prolong his inspection; he purposefully leaves behind a snuff box to provide an excuse for a second visit; he stages a commotion outside the D—— Hotel to distract the Minister's attention and he substitutes a fraudulent letter for the real one in the precise manner that D—— had once used to purloin it himself. He practices a similar kind of deception against the prefect. Clearly, then, Dupin is not above using the same kind of duplicity practiced by his rival.

While Dupin's methods do not differ materially from those of his adversary, neither, in fact, do his motives. It may be argued that, like

D——, Dupin is moved to participate in the affair for reasons which are morally dubious. First, there is the submerged but abiding rivalry with the Prefect, a lesser instance of the more momentous competition with D——. While the Prefect assuredly admires Dupin, he regards the detective as an eccentric and scoffs at his attitudes. For example, he ridicules Dupin's preference for meditation in the dark as "another of your odd notions" (p. 29), and disdainfully equates poets with fools, though he knows Dupin to be a poet himself. His contempt for Dupin's idiosyncracies induces a subtle competitiveness in Dupin to vindicate himself and to deflate the arrogant inspector. The subdued rivalry between them often takes the form of a flippant banter with a belligerent undercurrent, where the Prefect is frequently outclassed. At the conclusion of one verbal bout between them, heavily interspersed with Dupin's sarcasm, the Prefect laughs, "'Oh, Dupin, you will be the death of me yet!'" (p. 30). Beneath the superficial levity of the remark is the suggestion of ferocity and violence, and a veiled allusion to the more consequential enmity between Dupin and D——.

Second, there is the matter of the reward. We are told by the "Rue Morgue" narrator that Dupin is a man deprived of his fortune by a "variety of untoward events" and allowed to subsist only "by courtesy of his creditors."[5] The Prefect repeatedly mentions the prize offered for the return of the letter, and each time stresses that it is "enormous" —"I don't like to say how much, precisely" (p. 38). The vagueness of the amount of course augments its value to the hearer. Dupin employs the letter for his own financial intrigue. He promptly demands a large check from the Prefect and withholds the twice stolen document until the sum is paid. Although it may be considered fair recompense, nevertheless Dupin's little machination is a form of extortion and looks very much like one of D——'s habits.

Third, there is the political turmoil unleashed by the affair of the letter. The Minister has taken it to gain political advantage over the unnamed owner and the interests she represents. The power associated with possession of the letter is frequently underlined by the Prefect as he reveals the story of the theft to Dupin. D—— has been wielding this power "for some months past" "to a dangerous extent," by blackmailing its recipient. This political advantage is not lost upon Dupin, who employs the document for that very purpose when he plots the downfall of D—— and the deliverance of the "illustrious personage" from the hold of her enemies: "You know my political prepossessions. In this matter, I act as a partisan of the lady concerned" (p. 51). Hence, Dupin (like D——) uses the letter to obtain influence and (like D——) to further partisan ends. Moreover, even his ostensibly chivalric rescue of the royal lady in distress is not free from moral ambiguity and possibly impropriety since he is, in effect, assisting her to shelter an illicit romance and to deceive the "other personage from whom it was her wish to conceal it" (p. 31).

Finally, there is the motive of personal revenge against the Minister who "once did [him] an evil turn." Dupin has apparently long nurtured a private vendetta against D——; although he depicts the matter as a kind of amicable contest ("I told him, quite good humoredly, that I should remember" [p. 52]), there is an edge of compulsiveness to his vengeance which is intimated by the epigraph attributed to Seneca: "*Nil sapientiae odiosius acumine nimio.*"—"Nothing is so hateful to wisdom as too much sharpness." This implication, that the rivalry is tinged with an element of hate, is reinforced by further evidence of Dupin's vindictiveness, for example, his near glee at the prospect of D——'s downfall and his willingness to expose himself to possible injury, even death, to assure such a consequence:

> "D——," replied Dupin, "is a desperate man, and a man of nerve. His hotel, too, is not without attendants devoted to his interests. Had I made the wild attempt you suggest [seizing the letter openly], I might never have left the Ministerial presence alive." (p. 51)

The extremity of the danger present, and Dupin's unusual daring in the face of it, emphasize the viciousness which underlies the personal competition between them. Furthermore, Dupin feels the need to make himself known conclusively to his victim and to invite further reprisals. He inserts tauntingly into the substitute letter an excerpt from Crébillon's *Atrée*, a play which dramatizes the fatal opposition between two brothers. Dupin's quotation recalls the excessive and bloody retaliation of Atreus against the affronts of his brother Thyestes, and implies the truly malicious quality of the present revenge.

> —Un dessein si funeste,
> S'il n'est digne d'Atrée, est digne de Thyeste.

> —A design so deadly,
> If it's not worthy of Atreus, it's worthy of Thyestes.

The two characters in the play alluded to are paired by their like capacity for malice and brutality and are implicit counterparts of the detective and his adversary.

Dupin pursues his scheme to promote D——'s downfall in part because he believes the Minister to be a "*monstrum horrendum*, an unprincipled man of genius" (p. 52). He sees in D——'s example the hazards which may attend the ascendency of one of exceptional intelligence who uses his talents for unscrupulous ends. But what really differentiates Dupin from his opponent? The two are virtual surrogates. Except for the fact that Dupin is on the side of the established order (and even this is perplexing, since it is not clear whether he represents the "queen" or royal figure *against* her husband, presumably then the "king," or both of them together against common conspirators), his own motives are not less suspect than those of D——, and his methods are as cunning and often as reprehensible as those of his rival. For Dupin, in instigating the overthrow of such a reprobate as D——, becomes an ethical replica of his enemy, a *monstrum horrendum* in his own right.

The pattern of the double suggests further possibilities. There is some implication, for example, that the enigmatic relationship between Dupin and the Minister may be fraternal. A close personal intimacy between them is clearly alluded to several times. Dupin knows D——'s private and official dealings almost better than does the Prefect, who has been following the Minister for several months. It is apparent that the detective has been acquainted with D—— for a considerable time. Dupin remarks specifically upon a prior encounter "at Vienna, once," and others are implied. Moreover, the two men are familiar enough that Dupin's unexpected arrival at D——'s dwelling causes the latter no evident surprise. Dupin relates that he "maintained a most animated discussion with the Minister, upon a topic which I knew well had never failed to interest and excite him" (p. 50). The sleuth knows the idiosyncracies of his rival well; there is ample suggestion that some unusual affinity exists between them. Dupin is so intimate with the workings of D——'s mind that he anticipates the Minister's thoughts with an almost deterministic certainty and intuits D——'s reasoning patterns in their exact order. Dupin is also able to penetrate the Minister's various dissemblings. He perceives that D——'s nightly excursions are calculated "ruses" to fool the police, and he recognizes that the crumpled letter visible in the letter rack is "so inconsistent with the *true* methodical habits of D——" that it must be a disguise for the missing one. This uncanny perceptivity exceeds the kind of shrewdness which is requisite for detective work.

Poe drops several clues that this strong affiliation between the two characters is fraternal. Certainly Dupin's choice of the Crébillon quotation referring to the fatal competition between brothers invites such speculation. The narrator also invokes conjecture that Dupin and D—— may be brothers by his confusion about the reputed accomplishments of the Minister. "'But is this really the poet?' I asked. 'There are two brothers, I know; and both have attained reputation in letters'" (p. 43). Who is the second brother? He is never identified, for Dupin conspicuously fails to acknowledge the remark. The mention of an unnamed relation who mirrors his brother's achievements certainly suggests Dupin. We are also struck by the fact that Monsieur Dupin and Minister D—— share phonetically similar names and surnames which begin with the same letter; the obscurity surrounding the pointedly undisclosed last name invites some inference that it may be "Dupin."

But Poe's persistent duplication suggests yet another possibility: that the two characters somehow constitute a single person. Although biographical details in this story are few, those given do tend to underscore this notion of unanimity. Both men live in relatively secluded quarters. Dupin's lodgings are located in "a retired and desolate portion of the Faubourg St. Germain,"[6] and the Minister, despite his eminence at Court, prefers a solitary apartment and houses his servants "at a distance." Also important is the way that the two characters are counterpoised in time in the story. Dupin, at least in this tale, stays home at night. The Prefect arranges his visits in the evenings, "just after dark," because he knows Dupin prefers to deliberate in the dark. Conversely, the Minister has a habit of being "frequently absent from home all night." In fact, "for three months a night has not passed" that he has not disappeared to some unstated and unknown location. Dupin's only outings in the course of the story (his two visits to D——) both occur in the morning. Significantly, on both occasions he finds the Minister at home, "yawning, lounging and dawdling as usual" (p. 48). One goes out only at night and the other leaves only in the daytime. It is almost as if the two participate co-operatively in some sort of phased existence and one half of the twosome ceases to exist after nightfall. It is notable that the Minister's presence in the tale is related only by hearsay. We are apprised of his activities by the Prefect and by Dupin, but they are *never* directly depicted in the story. There is some implication that D—— may not exist as a separate, independent being at all. D—— figures immediately in only one episode of the plot, and that is reported, after the fact, solely by Dupin. Dupin's account of the meeting is sketchy and suspiciously vague. No dialogue is recorded; for that matter, we are never made to hear any verbatim statement by D——. Dupin's report focuses almost entirely on his own undercover inspection of the apartment. The single reference to D——'s physical appearance is more mystifying than informative: Dupin depicts D—— in a state of pretended languor and then remarks: "He is, perhaps, the most really energetic human being now alive—but that is only when nobody sees him" (p. 48). What does this statement mean? Dupin seems to imply that the Minister is a different person when he is not being observed, a man with a divided identity which changes aspect depending on the viewer. Perhaps the comment by Dupin is a concealed reference to himself. Importantly, the same kind of observation has been made about the detective. The narrator of the "Rue Morgue" tale observes a potential second self resident within the personality of the detective and often "amused [himself] with the fancy of a double Dupin."[7] Hence, like D——, Dupin also has been portrayed as a person of fluctuating identity, and in still another sense is interchangeable with D——. All of these factors, then, tend to interfuse the two figures into one singular character whole and point ultimately to the suggestion that the tale is, in its deepest implications, a study in the oneness of pursuer and pursued.

Poe's use of the double in "The Purloined Letter" is so pervasive that it deserves serious scrutiny. I have attempted to demonstrate that Poe employs the doubling in the tale chiefly to expose a deep affinity between

Dupin and his arch-rival, one which equates them morally and calls into question the customary ethical norms of the detective tale. Further, the emphatic double pattern encourages the inference that Dupin and D——— may be brothers, and suggests finally that the two may constitute a singular composite being. In this ultimate sense, then, "The Purloined Letter" explores the composition of the self, and the double becomes a metaphor for the variant phases—hunter and hunted—of the human mind.

NOTES

1. For example, in her introduction to *The Omnibus of Crime* (New York: Harcourt Brace, 1929), 16, Dorothy L. Sayers praises the story for its contributions to the new detective story genre (the "method of *psychological deduction* and solution by the formula of the *most obvious place*"), but her analysis does not extend much beyond this. Brander Matthews states the commonly held attitude that the tale (and all Poe's detective fiction) is noteworthy for its process of analytical deduction, rather than for any intrinsic interest in the mystery itself. "Poe and the Detective Story," *The Recognition of Edgar Allan Poe,* ed. Eric Carlson (Ann Arbor: University of Michigan Press, 1966), 85. See also Ellery Queen, "Introduction," in Michael Harrison, *The Exploits of the Chevalier Dupin* (Sauk City, Wis.: Arkham House, 1968), ix; T. O. Mabbott in his introduction to *The Selected Poetry and Prose of Edgar Allan Poe* (New York: Modern Library, 1951), xiv; Arthur Hobson Quinn, *Edgar Allan Poe: A Critical Biography* (New York: Appleton-Century, 1941), 421, all of whom evaluate "The Purloined Letter" as Poe's best detective tale, but do little to defend or explain their assessments.

2. *The Letters of Edgar Allan Poe,* ed. John Ward Ostrom, 2d ed. (New York: Gordian Press, 1966), 2:328.

3. Although scholars have frequently observed Poe's propensity for the "double" image in fiction, few have noticed its operation in "The Purloined Letter." Those who mention the idea do little to develop the point. See Howard Haycraft, "Murder for Pleasure," in *The Art of the Mystery Story: A Collection of Critical Essays,* ed. Howard Haycraft (New York: Simon and Schuster, 1946), 174: attempting to identify the historical model for Dupin as one of two illustrious brothers surnamed Dupin, Haycraft comments on the similarity between the fictional Dupin and the Minister D———, and suggests that "in the dual circumstances of Poe's . . . adaptation of the characteristics of the real brothers Dupin," one will readily "scent a highly logical, if possibly unconscious 'transference,'" between hero and foe. See also Alice Chandler, "'The Visionary Race': Poe's Attitude Toward His Dreamers," *Emerson Society Quarterly,* no. 60 (1970), pt. 2, 73–81; Joseph Moldenhauer, "Murder as a Fine Art: Basic Connections Between Poe's Aesthetics, Psychology and Moral Vision," *PMLA* 83 (1968):294; Patrick Quinn in *The French Face of Edgar Poe* (Carbondale: Southern Illinois University Press, 1957), especially 223–56; and Richard Wilbur, "The Poe Mystery Case," *New York Review of Books* (13 July 1967), 16, 25–28. Wilbur deals primarily with "The Murders in the Rue Morgue," which he attempts to explicate as a study in the multiple nature of the personality and accounts for parallels between Dupin and the other main characters "allegorically as elements of one person." He does not extend his study to "The Purloined Letter."

4. "The Purloined Letter," *The Complete Works of Edgar Allan Poe,* ed. James A. Harrison (New York: Crowell, 1902), 6:41. All citations from the text of this story are hereafter included in parentheses and inserted in the main body of the paper after the quotation.

5. *The Complete Works of Edgar Allan Poe,* ed. James A. Harrison, 17 vols. (New York: Crowell, 1902), 4:150. Hereafter cited as *Works.*

6. *Works,* 4:151.

7. *Works,* 4:152.

Interpretation: "A Rose for Emily"

CLEANTH BROOKS *and* ROBERT PENN WARREN

Brooks and Warren consider the ironic relationship between Emily and the community-narrator to answer the question, What does the story mean? If the story is to have merit, they assert, the horror must have "meaning in moral terms." They examine Emily, who is perceived by the townspeople as both idol and scapegoat. Her position suggests that of a tragic hero: because Emily heroically meets the world on her own terms, she arouses the community's admiration and horror.

THIS STORY [WILLIAM FAULKNER's "A Rose for Emily"], like Poe's "The Fall of the House of Usher," is a story of horror. In both stories we have a decaying mansion in which the protaganist, shut away from the world, grows into something monstrous, and becomes as divorced from the human as some fungus growing in the dark on a damp wall. Roderick Usher and Miss Emily Grierson remain in voluntary isolation (or perhaps fettered by some inner compulsion) away from the bustle and dust and sunshine of the human world of normal affairs. As we have seen, Poe closes his story with a melodramatic gesture in which the house falls into the lake, carrying with it its dead master. The ending of Faulkner's story is not so spectacular, but what is found in the upstairs room gives perhaps a sense of more penetrating and gruesome horror than ever Poe has achieved.

It has been indicated that, in the case of Poe, the sense of horror has been conjured up for its own sake. Is this true of Faulkner's story? If it is not, then why has he contrived to insert so much of the monstrous into the story? In other words, does the horror contribute to the theme of Faulkner's story? Is the horror meaningful?

From *Understanding Fiction,* by Cleanth Brooks, Jr., and Robert Penn Warren (New York: Appleton-Century-Crofts, 1943), 410–14. Copyright 1943 by F. S. Crofts & Co., Inc. Reprinted by permission.

In order to answer this question, we shall have to examine rather carefully some of the items earlier in the story. In the first place, why does Miss Emily commit her monstrous act? Is she supplied with a proper motivation—a matter which we concluded was handled rather weakly in "The Fall of the House of Usher." Faulkner has been rather careful to prepare for his dénouement. Miss Emily, it becomes obvious fairly early in the story, is one of those persons for whom the distinction between reality and illusion has blurred out. For example, she refuses to admit that she owes any taxes. When the mayor protests, she does not recognize him as mayor. Instead, she refers the committee to Colonel Sartoris, who, as the reader is told, has been dead for nearly ten years. For Miss Emily, apparently, Colonel Sartoris is still alive. Most specific preparation of all, when her father dies, she denies to the townspeople for three days that he is dead: "Just as they were about to resort to law and force, she broke down, and they buried her father quickly."

Miss Emily is obviously a pathological case. The narrator indicates plainly enough that people felt that she was crazy. All of this explanation prepares us for what Miss Emily does in order to hold her lover—the dead lover is in one sense still alive for her—the realms of reality and appearance merge. But having said this, we have got no nearer to justifying the story: for, if Faulkner is merely interested in relating a case history of abnormal psychology, the story lacks meaning and justification as a story. His interest in this case is as "clinical" as is the interest of Poe in Roderick Usher. If the story is to be justified, there must be what may be called a moral significance, a meaning in moral terms—not merely psychological terms.

Incidentally, it is very easy to misread the story as merely a horrible case history, presented in order to titillate the reader. Faulkner has been frequently judged to be doing nothing more than this in his work.

The lapse of the distinction between illusion and reality, between life and death, is important, therefore, as helping supply the motivation for the story, but a definition of this in itself is not a complete definition of the author's intention. We shall have to go behind it if we are to understand what Faulkner is about.

Suppose we approach the motivation again in these terms: what is Miss Emily like? What are the mainsprings of her character? What causes the distinction between illusion and reality to blur out for her? She is obviously a woman of tremendous firmness of will. In the matter of the taxes, crazed though she is, she is never at a loss. She is utterly composed. She dominates the rather frightened committee of officers who see her. In the matter of her purchase of the poison, she completely overawes the clerk. She makes no pretenses. She refuses to tell him what she wants the poison for. And yet this firmness of will and this iron pride have not kept her from being thwarted and hurt. Her father has run off the young men who came to call upon her, and for the man who tells the story, Miss Emily and her father form a tableau: "Miss Emily a slender figure in white in the background, her father a spraddled silhouette in the foreground, his back to her and clutching a horsewhip, the two of them framed by the back-flung front door." Whether the picture is a remembered scene, or merely a symbolical construct, this is the picture which remains in the storyteller's mind.

We have indicated that her pride is connected with her contempt for public opinion. This comes to the fore, of course, when she rides around about the town with the foreman whom everybody believes is beneath her. And it is her proud refusal to admit an external set of codes, or conventions, or other wills which contradict her own will, which makes her capable at the end of keeping her lover from going away. Confronted with his jilting her, she tries to override not only his will and the opinion of other people, but the laws of death and decay themselves.

But this, still, hardly gives the meaning of the story. For in all that has been said thus far, we are still merely accounting for a psychological aberration—we are still merely dealing with a case history in abnormal psychology. In order to make a case for the story as "meaningful," we shall have to tie miss Emily's thoughts and actions back into the normal life of the community, and establish some sort of relationship between them. And just here one pervasive element in the narration suggests a clue. The story is told by one of the townspeople. And in it, as a constant factor, is the reference to what the community thought of Miss Emily. Continually through the story it is what "we" said, and then what "we" did, and what seemed true to "us," and so on. The narrator puts the matter even more sharply still. He says, in the course of the story, that to the community Miss Emily seemed "dear, inescapable, impervious, tranquil, and perverse." Each of the adjectives is important and meaningful. In a sense, Miss Emily because of her very fact of isolation and perversity belongs to the whole community. She is even something treasured by it. Ironically, because of Emily's perversion of an aristocratic independence of mores and because of her contempt for "what people say," her life is public, even communal. And various phrases used by the narrator underline this view of her position. For example, her face looks "as you imagine a lighthouse-keeper's face ought to look," like the face of a person who lives in the kind of isolation imposed on a lighthouse-keeper, who looks out into the blackness and whose light serves a public function. Or, again, after her father's death, she becomes very ill, and when she appears after the illness, she has "a vague resemblance to those angels in colored church windows—sort of tragic and serene." Whatever we make of these descriptions, certainly the author is trying to suggest a kind of calm and dignity which is super-mundane, unearthly, or "over-earthly," such as an angel might possess.

Miss Emily, then, is a combination of idol and scapegoat for the community. On the one hand, the community feels admiration for Miss

55

Emily—she represents something in the past of the community which the community is proud of. They feel a sort of awe of her, as is illustrated by the behavior of the mayor and the committee in her presence. On the other hand, her queerness, the fact that she cannot compete with them in their ordinary life, the fact that she is hopelessly out of touch with the modern world—all of these things make them feel superior to her, and also to that past which she represents. It is, then, Miss Emily's complete detachment which gives her actions their special meaning for the community.

Miss Emily, since she is the conscious aristocrat, since she is consciously "better" than other people, since she is above and outside their canons of behavior, can, at the same time, be worse than other people; and she *is* worse, horribly so. She is worse than other people, but at the same time, as the narrator implies, she remains somehow admirable. This raises a fundamental question: why is this true?

Perhaps the horrible and the admirable aspects of Miss Emily's final deed arise from the same basic fact of her character: she insists on meeting the world on her own terms. She never cringes, she never begs for sympathy, she refuses to shrink into an amiable old maid, she never accepts the community's ordinary judgments or values. This independence of spirit and pride can, and does in her case, twist the individual into a sort of monster, but, at the same time, this refusal to accept the herd values carries with it a dignity and courage. The community senses this, as we gather from the fact that the community carries out the decencies of the funeral before breaking in the door of the upper room. There is, as it were, a kind of secret understanding that she has won her right of privacy, until she herself has entered history. Furthermore, despite the fact that, as the narrator says, "already we knew that there was one room in that region above stairs which no one had seen in forty years, and which would have to be forced," her funeral is something of a state occasion, with "the very old men—some in their brushed Confederate uniforms—on the porch and the lawn, talking of Miss Emily as if she had been a contemporary of theirs, believing that they had danced with her and courted her perhaps. . . ." In other words, the community accepts her into its honored history. All of this works as a kind of tacit recognition of Miss Emily's triumph of will. The community, we are told earlier, had wanted to pity Miss Emily when she had lost her money, just as they had wanted to commiserate over her when they believed that she had actually become a fallen woman, but she had triumphed over their pity and commiseration and condemnation, just as she had triumphed over all their other attitudes.

But, as we have indicated earlier, it may be said that Miss Emily is mad. This may be true, but there are two things to consider in this connection. First, one must consider the special terms which her "madness" takes. Her madness is simply a development of her pride and her refusal to submit to ordinary standards of behavior. So, because of this fact, her "madness" is meaningful after all. It involves issues which in themselves are really important and have to do with the world of conscious moral choice. Second, the community interprets her "madness" as meaningful. They admire her, even if they are disappointed by her refusals to let herself be pitied, and the narrator, who is a spokesman for the community, recognizes the last grim revelation as an instance of her having carried her own values to their ultimate conclusion. She would marry the common laborer, Homer Barron, let the community think what it would. She would not be jilted. And she would hold him as a lover. But it would all be on her own terms. She remains completely dominant, and contemptuous of the day-to-day world.

It has been suggested by many critics that tragedy implies a hero who is completely himself, who insists on meeting the world on his own terms, who wants something so intensely, or lives so intensely, that he cannot accept any compromise. It cannot be maintained that this story is comparable to any of the great tragedies, such as *Hamlet* or *King Lear,* but it can be pointed out that this story, in its own way, involves some of the same basic elements. Certainly, Miss Emily's pride, isolation, and independence remind one of factors in the character of the typical tragic hero. And it can be pointed out that, just as the horror of her deed lies outside the ordinary life of the community, so the magnificence of her independence lies outside their ordinary virtues.

Flannery O'Connor's "Revelation"

DOROTHY T. McFARLAND

New Criticism sees poetic images as concrete universals, that is, as things important in themselves which also connote other levels of reality. Because images have a dual nature, they can embody the contradictions structuring human existence. McFarland suggests that the pig images in "Revelation" symbolize the tension between the human and the divine and so enable the story to resolve meaningfully.

MRS. TURPIN, THE protagonist of "Revelation," is convinced of her own goodness. Mrs. Turpin is a good Christian woman who looks after

From chapter 3, "Everything That Rises Must Converge" in *Flannery O'Connor,* by Dorothy T. McFarland (New York: Frederick Ungar, 1976), 43–44; 60–63. Copyright © 1976 by Frederick Ungar Publishing Co., Inc. Reprinted by permission of Frederick Ungar Publishing Co.

the poor, works for the church, and thanks Jesus effusively for making her what she is—and not "a nigger or white trash or ugly." Mrs. Turpin's failure of charity, despite her works of charity, is obvious as she sums up the other patients in the doctor's waiting room in which the story opens. Sizing up a "stylish lady" as one of her own kind and striking up a conversation with her, Mrs. Turpin reveals, through her words and thoughts, her interior judgments on the others present. Her veiled racism and social snobbery, her cheerful complacency, and her unabashed pride in her good disposition are too much for the stylish lady's daughter, a fat, scowling girl who has obviously had to suffer much of the same sort of thing from her mother. The girl responds to Mrs. Turpin's remarks with ugly looks until finally, provoked beyond endurance, she flings a book at Mrs. Turpin's head and lunges at her throat. "Go back to hell where you came from, you old wart hog," the girl whispers to her fiercely.

Hog imagery has already been introduced in the conversation between Mrs. Turpin and the stylish lady. Mrs. Turpin mentioned the hogs she raises in a concrete-floored pig parlor. Responding to an unwelcome interruption by a "white-trash woman," who declares hogs to be "Nasty stinking things, a-gruntin and a-rootin all over the place," Mrs. Turpin coldly replied that her hogs are washed down every day with a hose and are "cleaner than some children I've seen." ("Cleaner by far than that child right there," [the "white-trash" woman's child] she added to herself.)

O'Connor uses hogs in this story (and elsewhere) as symbols of unredeemed human nature. As no amount of external cleanliness can fundamentally change hog nature, so no amount of external goodness can fundamentally change human nature, which, in O'Connor's view, is contaminated with evil—whether it be the consciously chosen evil of Johnson or the more subtle evil of pride and self-righteousness displayed by Sheppard and Mrs. Turpin.

Evil seems a strong word to apply to a character like Mrs. Turpin, who, for all her pride and complacency, is surely not a "bad" woman. Yet O'Connor obviously felt that Mrs. Turpin's belief in her own goodness was, if anything, more of an obstacle to the salvation of her soul than an outright commitment to evil. Thomas Merton reflects on this paradox: "Truly the great problem is the salvation of those who, being good, think they have no further need to be saved and imagine their task is to make others 'good' like themselves."[1]

Mrs. Turpin is at first shocked and indignant at the injustice of what has happened to her. Why should she, a hard-working, respectable, church-going woman, be singled out for such a message when there was "trash in the room to whom it might justly have been applied"? At the same time, however, Mrs. Turpin senses that the girl "knew her in some intense and personal way, beyond time and place and condition," and the message, unpleasant as it is, has for her the force of divine revelation.

After pondering the girl's words with increasing wrath and indignation all afternoon, Mrs. Turpin marches down to the pig parlor on her farm and contemplates her hogs. "What do you send me a message like that for?" she demands of God. "How am I a hog and me both? How am I saved and from hell too?" She rails at God with increasing sarcasm until, with a final surge of fury, she roars, "Who do you think you are?" An echo of her own words comes back to her, like an answer, out of the silence.

Who does she think she is? The imagery surrounding this scene suggests that Mrs. Turpin considers herself the equal of God. The sun, that perennial symbol of God in O'Connor's fiction, seems comically obedient to Mrs. Turpin's presumption, and hangs over the tree line in an attitude almost exactly imitative of her own position on the fence of the pig parlor: "The sun was behind the wood, very red, looking over the paling of trees like a farmer inspecting his own hogs." While this image embodies Mrs. Turpin's assumption of the equality between her and God, it also suggests that the true relation between them is that God is the farmer, the world is His farm, and Mrs. Turpin is one of the "hogs"—humanity—at which He is gazing. His gaze—His light, symbolically the infusion of His grace into the world—is transforming; in the light of the setting sun the pigs are suffused with a red glow, and appear to "pant with a secret life." Mrs. Turpin, too, is touched by this transforming light, and life flows into her. "Like a monumental statue coming to life," she bends her head and gazes, "as if through the very heart of mystery, down into the pig parlor at the hogs."

The mystery of humanity, as O'Connor saw it, is that it is rooted in earth, yet bathed in God's light that fills it with secret life, the life of grace that is in no way dependent on worthiness or on the scale of human values Mrs. Turpin cherishes. The irrelevance of social values in the sphere of grace is manifested in the vision that is given to her as she lifts her eyes from the pigs and gazes at the purple streak in the sky left like a trail by the setting sun:

> She saw the streak as a vast swinging bridge extending upward from the earth through a field of living fire. Upon it a vast horde of souls were rumbling toward heaven. There were whole companies of white-trash, clean for the first time in their lives, and bands of black niggers in white robes, and battalions of freaks and lunatics shouting and clapping and leaping like frogs. And bringing up the end of the procession was a tribe of people whom she recognized at once as those who, like herself and Claud [her husband], had always had a little of everything and the God-given wit to use it right. . . . They were marching behind the others with great dignity, accountable as they had always been for good order and common sense and respectable behavior. They alone were on key. Yet she could see by their shocked and altered faces that even their virtues were being burned away.

For her to rise, to follow even at the end of the heaven-bound procession, it is necessary for her virtues to be burned away, for her to see herself as no more worthy of God's grace than the Negroes and white trash and freaks and lunatics she habitually looks down upon. Good works, in O'Connor's view, do not redeem; they only prevent Mrs. Turpin from seeing that she shares in the poverty and limitation and evil proclivities common to all humanity. She is not capable of lifting herself out of this condition by her own efforts; indeed, her efforts to do so only compound evil by making her think herself superior to others and thus reinforcing social inequality, pride, and complacency. "Rising" comes about by grace, and by Mrs. Turpin's response of openness to it. Appropriately enough, the instrument of grace—the ugly girl who hurled a book at Mrs. Turpin's head and declared that lady's kinship with hogs and hell—is named Mary Grace.

NOTE

1. Thomas Merton, *Conjectures of a Guilty Bystander* (Garden City, N.Y.: Doubleday, 1968), 170.

New Critical Provocateurs

1. On what grounds might one challenge and defend the New Critical tenets that a poem must be unified to be effective and that the critic's job is to interpret this unity, or meaning?

2. Anderson's and Brooks's close readings of "Sailing to Byzantium" explore how a poem's formal elements (its words, metrics, tone, and imagery) express and resolve the poem's central tensions. These tensions appear in the poem as ironies, paradoxes, ambiguities, antinomies, and antitheses. Perform a New Critical close reading by applying their terms and strategy to another poem such as Dickinson's "You constituted Time—" quoted at the end of Anderson's essay.

3. Compare your first experience upon reading "Sailing to Byzantium" to your subsequent rereadings and to your colleagues' readings. Do the differences contest the New Critical theory of the "innocent" reader (i.e., that close reading allows us all to experience the central meaning in the poem)?

4. In her stylistic analysis of the Byzantium poems, Perloff argues that rhyme relates to meaning. To study this relationship, she purports to move from physical evidence (types of rhymes) to semantic interpretation. Examine the basis of her distinctions between irony and antithesis; between metonymy and metaphor (what she calls "symbol"). Could these rhymes be categorized differently? Would a different categorization of the rhymes change the interpretation of the poem's meaning?

5. Sociological critics claim that by divorcing a poem from its histori-

cal context, as Brooks and Warren seem to do in their interpretation of "The Birthmark," the New Critics are really perpetuating certain unexamined ideological values. What values might these be? How might a contemporary feminist answer this question? a contemporary Marxist?

6. What is the difference between Heilman's analysis of the "great theme" in "The Birthmark" and Brooks's and Warren's discussion of the story's moral significance"?

7. How do Babener's close reading strategies justify her assertion that "The Purloined Letter" questions the morality of the detective story?

8. While New Critics analyzing poetry discuss "voice," "persona," and tone, New Critics examining prose consider "point-of-view" and narrator. Brooks and Warren, in their critique of "A Rose for Emily," assume that the narrator, the voice of the townspeople, is reliable. However, later critics, including Brooks himself, have become more wary; they call the narrator an unreliable busybody. How does the possibility that the narrator is unreliable affect Brooks's and Warren's conclusion that Miss Emily is a kind of tragic hero, a "combination of idol and scapegoat for the community"?

9. New Critics see the literary work as an ontological whole, complete in itself; therefore, the critic need not "go outside" the poem itself to interpret it. To what degree, however, might McFarland's reading of hogs as "symbols of unredeemed nature" depend upon her extrinsic knowledge that O'Connor was a deeply committed Christian?

CHAPTER 2

Phenomenological Criticism

PHENOMENOLOGICAL CRITICS try to overcome the division between subjective self and objective world in order to recoup the unified sense of lived reality. They do this by appealing to consciousness. Consciousness, they argue, is always awareness of some thing (phenomenon); in other words, consciousness dissolves the divisions between our inside self (subject) and the outside (object). To use examples from literary studies, a book *is* to be read, a story *is* to be heard. The reading of a book or the hearing of a story, then, mutually implicates both subject and object. In such acts, phenomenologists claim, we experience the unified "is-ness" of existence.

The varied literary criticisms called "phenomenological" draw largely on the philosophical methods of Edmund Husserl. He urged that we focus only on objects—a poem or a story is an object—as they appear to us (phenomena) in consciousness and describe them. Everything else, such as presuppositions or judgments of good or bad, are to be bracketed off as unknowable. Now, a literary work is both an object and a form of consciousness because it arises from and preserves the authorial act of consciousness (the "intentionality") which brought it into being. The critic's job is to describe the work's (author's) consciousness, or intentionality. To do this, phenomenological critics "open themselves" to the work; they identify with it. Husserlian critics aim at recording what the author had in mind. Those phenomenological critics who draw also on Martin Heidegger's philosophy aim at seeing how the text's poetic language conceals existence and so reveals the existential character of 'being.' In general, phenomenological critics are receptive to images and themes of time and space since these best display the author's structures of consciousness, his sense of being in the world. As important, phenomenological critics try to be neutral, or "innocent" interpreters; they feel they should divest themselves of bias and self interests. Only then, they say, will they be able to describe accurately the form of consciousness that is the literary work.

Poe's Detective Tales

DAVID HALLIBURTON

In the preface to *Edgar Allan Poe: A Phenomenological View,* Halliburton tells us that he discovers the authorial intentionality in a story by identifying with the main character. He points out, however, that the protagonist is not identical with the author's creating consciousness but is a product of that consciousness. Yet a character—Dupin, for example—is at the same time a product that possesses a subjectivity of his own, a subjectivity which is one of the objective elements in the story. Halliburton says, "When I interpret I identify with this character, not in order to burden him with my conscience but to assume the weight of him." By coming close to Dupin, then, Halliburton feels that the boundaries between subject and object are dissolved.

Halliburton's interpretation of Poe's detective tales emphasizes the parallelism between how an interpreter reads a text and how Dupin identifies with, or thinks like, his opponents. In both instances, the interpreter (critic or Dupin) creates an interactive set of polarities which broach inside (subject) and outside (object) barriers.

Halliburton has been examining tales in which transcendent women like Berenice, Ligeia, and Eleonora overpower the male narrators. According to Halliburton, the chambers and tombs in these tales provide a spatial component for the narrator's constricted consciousness.

THE CIRCUMSCRIPTION OF PERSONS that we have seen in the poems and the tales about women is a given of the detective tales as well. Like the ladies and their lovers, Dupin and his companion live in cloistered intimacy: "Our seclusion was perfect. We admitted no visitors. . . . We existed ourselves alone" (4:151).[1] The pair create an atmosphere for dreaming, their main pastime during the day, by blocking out the sunlight and reading, writing, or talking until nightfall, when they go out

From David Halliburton, *Edgar Allan Poe: A Phenomenological View.* Copyright © 1973 by Princeton University Press. Excerpts, pp. 237–45 reprinted by permission of Princeton University Press.

into the city. These forays merely lengthen the dreaming period, for the two are alone together even in the streets, where their sole concern is "that infinity of mental excitement which quiet observation can afford" (4:152). The inner life in the shuttered house and the outer life in the busy city are thus, at the same time, polarities and complements. There is a similar doubleness in Dupin himself. Noticing how differently Dupin acts when possessed by one of his ratiocinative moods, the narrator speculates "upon the old philosophy of the Bi-Part Soul," and amuses himself "with the fancy of a double Dupin—the creative and resolvent" (4:152). The pattern extends to Dupin's modes of detection as well. There are, on the one hand, "inductions" (4:172), corresponding respectively with the "*à posteriori*" [*sic*] approach (4:174) that Dupin mentions, and the a priori that he does not refer to by name but frequently employs. To the two "conditions" of "Eleonora" (4:236)—that of lucid reason, associated with the past, and that of shadow and doubt, associated with the present—"The Murders in the Rue Morgue" thus responds with a complete binary system:

inner	outer
dream	observation
deduction	induction
a priori	a posteriori
creative	resolvent

These pairs are not "hateful contraries" but rather, like Dupin and the narrator, coequal partners; the relationship is a reciprocity in which each member works with and for its complement. While reserving perfect reciprocity—in which cause and effect are completely interchangeable—for God, Poe recognized that a lower, more contingent reciprocity was characteristic of human life (8:272). A thoroughgoing reciprocity, such as we find in "The Murders in the Rue Morgue," relates the paired elements so intimately to one another that they all but merge. This can be seen, for instance, in the pairing of dream and observation. The superiority of the analytical mind, says the narrator, "lies not so much in the validity of the inference as in the quality of the observation" (4:148). With Dupin, the greater intellect of the two, observation becomes "'a species of necessity'" (4:155). This is not to equate Dupin with Berenice's Egaeus, who stares obsessively and intensely at objects of no interest. But there is in both men, Dupin and Egaeus, a strong imaginative element. Dupin's reflective moods are trances (4:152); at such times he is, for all practical purposes, a man possessed. The narrator, furthermore, cites imagination as one of Dupin's great virtues, and concludes "that the ingenious are always fanciful, and the *truly* imaginative never otherwise than analytic" (4:150). It is misleading to contend, as [Edward H.] Davidson does, that "the ratiocinative exercise of the detective is simply an allegory of how the mind may impose its interior logic on exterior circumstances."[2] What the story demonstrates, on the contrary, is that "exterior circumstance" has a logic of its own that the human mind is able to comprehend. Dupin's mind operates *in* the world, not *on* it. Observation, far from being incompatible with imagination, works with it in a partnership as close as the partnership of the narrator and Dupin. For an investigator like Dupin there is no way to see facts but imaginatively. If he is a seer he is a seer of circumstance.

The second sight Dupin seems to possess is only a higher form of insight. To have *in*sight is literally to see in—to enter the interiority of another through an act of identification. Interpreters share this faculty with writers: "Indeed the author of Crusoe must have possessed, above all other faculties, what has been termed the faculty of *identification*— that dominion exercised by volition over imagination which enables the mind to lose its own, in a fictitious individuality. This includes, in a very great degree, the power of abstraction . . ." (8:170). The narrator of "The Murders in the Rue Morgue" illustrates the process by showing how the interpreter would play a game of draughts in which only four kings remain on the board: "It is obvious that here the victory can be decided (the players being at all equal) only by some *recherché* movement, the result of some strong exertion of the intellect. Deprived of ordinary resources, the analyst throws himself into the spirit of his opponent, identifies himself therewith, and not unfrequently sees thus, at a glance, the sole methods . . . by which he may seduce into error or hurry into miscalculation" (4:147–48). This process of analysis differs in no material way from the process by which an interpreter analyses a text. If it is a cipher-text, as in "The Gold-Bug," the interpreter's first job is "'to divide the sentence into the natural division intended by the cryptographist'" (5:137). If it is a literary text (such as, for example, Dickens' *Barnaby Rudge*) the procedure remains the same: ". . . *the intention once known,* the *traces* of the design can be found upon every page" (11:49). Identification with the intention of a writer leads the interpreter back, full circle, to an even earlier identification: "While on this topic we may as well offer an ill-considered opinion of our own as to the *intention of the poet* in the delineation of the Dane. It must have been well known to Shakespeare, that a leading feature in certain more intense classes of intoxication . . . is an almost irresistible impulse to counterfeit a farther degree of excitement than actually exists. Analogy would lead any thoughtful person to suspect the same impulse in madness. . . . This, Shakespeare *felt*—not thought. He felt it through his marvellous power of *identification* with humanity at large . . ." (12:227). The power of identification, then, is something shared by the author and the interpreter, whether his "text" happens to be words on a page or events in the everyday world. In the exercise of this power the interpreter thus follows the lead of Friedrich Schleiermacher, the founder of modern hermeneutics, who held that we comprehend a text by going back into the consciousness that made it, in order to relive its signifying acts. There is no reason to believe that Poe read Schleiermacher, or that he had to. As a reader and a reviewer he was in contact with developments in the rising, related disciplines of Biblical and grammatical study, and could comment, in his review of [John Lloyd] Stephens' *Arabia Petraea*, on "the vast importance of critical and philological research in dissipating the obscurities and determining the exact sense of the Scriptures . . ." (10:1). In order to understand a prophetic text, Poe argues, the interpreter must focus on the literal meaning of the words. But interpretation is a to-and-fro process. Consequently the hermeneutist must not only move very close to the page, as it were, but far away from it; if the words he studies are prophetic he must view them against the horizon of the future:

> We mean to say that, in *all* instances, the most strictly literal interpretation will apply. There is, no doubt, much unbelief founded upon the *obscurity* of the prophetic expression. . . . That many prophecies are absolutely unintelligible should not be denied—it is a part of their essence that they should be. The obscurity, like the apparently irrelevant detail, has its object in the providence of God. Were the words of inspiration, affording insight into the events of futurity, *at all times* so pointedly clear that he who runs might read, they would in many cases . . . afford a rational ground for unbelief in the inspiration of their authors . . . for it would be supposed that these distinct words, exciting union and emulation among Christians, had thus been merely the means of working out their own accomplishment. It is for this reason that most of the predictions become intelligible only when viewed from the proper point of observation—the period of fulfilment. (10:10)

The interpreter—whether he is reading the faces of an opponent in a game or lines in a text—creates a *figure* and a *ground,* the latter being the general field in which an object appears, the former being the object itself. In his interpretation of *Hamlet,* Poe presents the figure of Hamlet— the concrete, individual phenomenon as given in the play—against the ground, or general field of common experience. He asks, in effect: What do most people know about certain kinds of intoxication? Narrowing down to a smaller group (thoughtful persons), he then asks whether a member of such a group would see an analogy between the behavior of an intoxicated person and the behavior of a mad one.

In "The Mystery of Marie Rogêt" Dupin combines these techniques in order to recreate the consciousness, motivation, and probable behavior of the girl's murderer, of a theoretical gang, and of the girl herself. Employing the third-person, Dupin reconstructs the thinking of the hypothetical killer from a moment just after the murder to the moment he decides to flee: "'The sounds of life encompass his path. A dozen times he hears or fancies the step of an observer. Even the very lights from the city bewilder him. . . . His sole thought is immediate escape. He turns his back *forever* upon those dreadful shrubberies, and flees as from the wrath to come'" (5:55). Dupin reasons that a gang of men, by their very numbers, would not have felt the terror of the lone criminal, and, having the advantage of manpower, would have cleaned up any telltale evidence. Since such evidence was found, the involvement of a gang becomes an improbable inference, and Dupin concludes that the murder was the act of an individual. In his reconstruction of the victim's behavior, Dupin identifies through use of the first-person:

> We may imagine her thinking thus—"I am to meet a certain person for the purpose of elopement, or for certain other purposes known only to myself. It is necessary that there be no chance of interruption. . . . I will give it to be understood that I shall visit and spend the day with my aunt at the Rue des Drômes—I will tell St. Eustache not to call for me until dark. . . . Now, if it were my design to return *at all* . . . it would not be my policy to bid St. Eustache call; for, calling, he will be *sure* to ascertain that I have played him false—a fact of which I might keep him for ever in ignorance, by leaving home without notifying him of my intention, by returning before dark, and by then stating that I had been to visit my aunt in the Rue des Drômes. But, as it is my design *never* to return . . . the gaining of time is the only point about which I need give myself any concern." (5:44−45)

In this account Dupin connects "intention" with "design" just as Poe did in his reading of Dickens. The association is not casual for the two terms are used in tandem throughout the criticism,[3] designating, on the one hand, the aims of authors, and on the other the aims of the characters they create. For Dupin as for Poe, every language-using being—a man on the street, an author, a character, or God Himself—is endowed with intentionality. Thus Dupin uses the same methods in reconstructing the thoughts of Marie Rogêt as in determining the aims of the newspapermen whose articles, throughout much of the narrative, are his texts:

> The first aim of the writer is to show, from the brevity of the interval between Marie's disappearance and the finding of the floating corpse, that this corpse cannot be that of Marie. The reduction of this interval to its smallest possible dimension, becomes thus, at once, an object with the reasoner. . . . The paragraph beginning "It is folly to suppose that the murder, etc.," however it appears as printed in L'Etoile, may be imagined to have existed actually *thus* in the brain of its inditer—"It is folly to suppose that the murder . . . could have been committed soon enough to have enabled her murderers to throw the body into the river before midnight . . . and to suppose at the same time . . . that the body was *not* thrown in until *after* midnight"—a sentence sufficiently inconsequential in itself, but not so utterly preposterous as the one printed. (5:22−23)

Dupin perceives a discrepancy between intention and achievement and, instead of merely labelling it, demonstrates it through an improvised monologue. Such tactics are common in these stories, which are concerned with solutions to practical and more or less urgent problems. In "The Purloined Letter" Dupin draws an implicit parallel between himself and a schoolboy who was skilled at a certain guessing game. Surmising that the boy was able to identify with the playmate who decided whether the marbles would be "odd" or "even," Dupin asks him to explain his technique: "'When I wish to find out how wise, or how stupid, or how good, or how wicked is any one, or what are his thoughts at the moment, I fashion the expression of my face, as accurately as possible, in accordance with the expression of his, and then wait to see what thoughts or sentiments arise in my mind and heart, as if to match or correspond with the expression'" (6:41). The schoolboy, like Rameau's nephew, is a plastic, "physical" mimic who enters into the very gesture and body of the other. The older, more pensive Dupin, being less concerned with tactics than with the interpretation of a complex circumstantial design, is more "detached." When the reflective mood is upon him he is indeed, as we have seen, a man possessed: "His manner at these moments was frigid and abstract; his eyes were vacant in expression; while his voice, usually a rich tenor, rose into a treble which would have sounded petulantly but for the deliberateness and entire distinctness of the enunciation" (4:152). That might be a description of Roderick Usher as his consciousness tunes itself to the harmonies of a world beyond the gulf, or of Vankirk, the character in "Mesmeric Revelation" who communicates with that world and reports on it to the man who has placed him in the mesmeric state. This is one way in which the "beyond" gets into the tales of detection. It also enters through the notion of design, which embraces not only everyday reality and literary creation but the divine creation as well. In his literary application of the idea of design, Dupin anticipates the procedures of Martin Heidegger, who views a statement against a horizon of expression that it fails to reach. The interpreter, in such a case, "fills in" what he perceives to be missing in when intention is compared with achievement: "'The sentence in question has but one meaning, as it stands; and this meaning I have fairly stated: but it is material that we go behind the mere words, for an idea which these words have obviously intended, and failed to convey. It was the design of the journalist to say that . . . it was improbable that the assassins would have ventured to bear the corpse to the river before midnight'" (5:23). The narrator of "The Mystery of Marie Rogêt," more consciously concerned with the beyond, begins his story with a quotation from Novalis, who saw both a "real" and an "ideal" series of events (5:2), and ends with an examination of coincidence in light of the "Calculus of Probabilities" (5:65) and the intentions of God. The idea here is that there are two kinds of design, the human and the divine, but that the connections between them are problematic. That such considerations enter such a work at all affirms once again Poe's tendency to see every phenomenon in relation to something greater than itself. That these considerations are carried no further than they are indicates Poe's recognition that the detective tale had boundaries that it could not cross without becoming another kind of work.

NOTES

1. All quotations from the prose are to *The Complete Works of Edgar Allan Poe*, the "Virginia Edition," ed. James A. Harrison, 17 vols. (New York, 1902), cited by volume and page.

2. Davidson, *Poe: A Critical Study* (Cambridge, Mass.: Harvard University Press, Belknap Press, 1957), 221. Cf. Robert Daniel, "Poe's Detective God," *Furioso* 6 (1951): 45–52, and John F. Lynen, *The Design of the Present: Essays on Time and Form in American Literature* (New Haven: Yale University Press, 1969), 237ff.

3. See, for example, Poe's discussion of Hawthorne's *Twice-Told Tales*, in *Works*, 11:108–9; also, 8:208; 10:117, 118, 127, 131; 11:45–61.

A Woman—White:
Emily Dickinson's Yarn of Pearl

SANDRA M. GILBERT

The subtitle of *The Madwoman in the Attic: The Woman Writer and the Nineteenth-Century Literary Imagination* by Gilbert and Susan Gubar emphasizes their concern with the existence of an essentially female imagination (or mind). Phenomenological criticism has been called, at different times, criticism of consciousness, of subjectivity, of identification. It could be asserted that, being women, Gilbert and Gubar are better able than males to identify with female writers. These critics contend that to escape the confines of patriarchal conditions, nineteenth-century female writers resorted to certain aesthetic strategies such as obsessive use of spatial metaphors. By being open and receptive to these tropes, sympathetic critics can perceive the poem's true meaning; they can intuit what the author had "in mind."

Gilbert and Gubar combine a feminist perspective, New Criti-

From *The Madwoman in the Attic: The Woman Writer and the Nineteenth-Century Literary Imagination*, by Sandra M. Gilbert and Susan Gubar (New Haven and London: Yale University Press, 1979), 606–10. Copyright © 1979 by Yale University Press. Reprinted by permission.

cal close reading, and phenomenological methodology in their study of female writers' consciousness. This chapter on Emily Dickinson describes the poet's sense of psychological constriction and of female powerlessness engendered by a nineteenth-century patriarchal culture. Trapped in her father's house, Dickinson played the part of a child who was subject to the powerful male Other. Gilbert shows how Dickinson's poems express both agoraphobia (the desire for walls, for reassurance, for love and certainty) and claustrophobia (the fear of prisonlike walls and locks).

FOR A SELF-AWARE and volcanic talent like Dickinson's, however, as for Brontë's or Fuller's, no imprisonment could be permanent. Her claustrophobia alternated (as John Cody has suggested) with agoraphobia— or, rather, the two were necessary complements.[1] Beyond this, however, hers was a soul whose "Bandaged moments" were frequently supplanted by "moments of Escape" when, violently transcending sexual limits, "it" danced "like a Bomb, abroad," fleeing from the shadowy enclosure of female submission, passivity, and self-abnegation to the virile self-assertion of "Noon, and Paradise" (J. 512).* And, as we shall see, the poet's strategies for such escape were as varied and inventive as the masks of her defeat had been. In many cases, in fact, the masks of defeat were transformed into the faces of victory.

Though Dickinson's child mask, for instance, helped imprison her in the unadmitted wound of her own life, it did at the same time save her from the unconsciousness that she saw as sealing the soul of the honorably eclipsed wife. Mothered by Awe, the childish little Pilgrim might sometimes abase herself to her distant Master in a fever of despair, but she could also transform him into a powerful muse who served *her* purposes. "Captivity is Consciousness, / So's Liberty," she noted in one poem (J. 384), and for her this was true because even in her most claustrophobic moments of defeat she refused to abandon her "first Prospective" on things. Thus in "I have a King, who does not speak" (J. 103) or "My Life had stood—a Loaded Gun" (J. 754) she celebrates the poetic inspiration her distant stately lover provides. Though he is withdrawn during the day, and though in a poem like "Why make it doubt—it hurts it so" she could not speak *to* him, in "I have a King" she triumphs by encountering him in dreams where she "peep[s]" into regal "parlors, shut by day." In "To My small Hearth His fire came" (J. 638), moreover, she describes the doorless house of "Doom"—the house of the locked-in child—transfigured by inspiration: "all my House aglow / Did fan and rock, with sud-

---

*Citation refers to *The Poems of Emily Dickinson*, ed. Thomas H. Johnson (Cambridge, Mass.: Harvard University Press, Belknap Press, 1955).—ED.

den light—" she exclaims, in a poem that transmutes emotional defeat into spiritual victory through a depiction of the poetic process. For in the light of the Master/Muse's sacred fire "Twas Noon—without the News of Night—"—what theologians would call eternity. And energized by such immortal fire, Dickinson at times sloughs off her child mask entirely and confesses—in, say, "My Life had stood—a Loaded Gun—"—that she actually speaks *for* her fiery but silent Master/Muse, her "King who does not speak." And she speaks with Vesuvian intensity.

If Dickinson's Master is silent while she speaks, however, who is really the master and who the slave? Here her self-effacing pose as Nobody suggests levels of irony as intricately layered as the little bundles of speech that lay hidden all her life in her bureau drawer. It is of course these booklets of poetry which were the real playthings of her life, the ones she refused to drop, no matter what Requirements were imposed upon her. Our awareness of her refusal must qualify our reading of her anguished addresses to Nobodaddy, the man of noon. "Have you the little chest to put the Alive in?" she asks in the second Master letter,[2] and the childlike question is at least in part an ironic one, for it was Dickinson herself who had a modest chest full of live poems. But doesn't a little girl who "plays" by creating a whole garden of verses secretly triumph over the businesslike world of fathers and teachers and households? If so, is not the little girl really, covertly an adult, one of the Elect, even an unacknowledged queen or empress?

At times, confronting the tension between her helpless and dependent child-self (that old fashioned little girl named "Daisy") and her "Adequate—Erect" queenly self (the "woman—white" she once entitled the "Empress of Calvary") Dickinson meditated quietly upon her obscure triumph:

> And then—the size of this "small" life
> The Sages—call it small—
> Swelled—like Horizons—in my vest—
> And I sneered—softly—"small"!

(J. 271)

At other times, however, her almost inaudible sneers were replaced by angry fantasies of more thunderous speech. In "My Life had stood—a Loaded Gun—," for instance, the murderous energy of which the Gun/speaker boasts is at least as significant as the fact that she (or "it") speaks for a silent Master.

> My Life had stood—a Loaded Gun—
> In Corners—till a Day
> The Owner passed—identified—
> And carried Me away—

And now We roam in Sovereign Woods—
And now We hunt the Doe—
And every time I speak for Him—
The Mountains straight reply—

And do I smile, such cordial light
Upon the Valley glow—
It is as a Vesuvian face
Had let its pleasure through—

And when at Night—Our good Day done—
I guard My Master's Head—
'Tis better than the Eider-Duck's
Deep Pillow—to have shared—

To foe of His—I'm deadly foe—
None stir the second time—
On whom I lay a Yellow Eye—
Or an emphatic Thumb—

Though I than He—may longer live
He longer must—than I—
For I have but the power to kill,
Without—the power to die—

(J. 754)

Certainly there is a suggestion of autonomous power in the fierce but courtly braggadocio of this smiling Gun/speaker's "Vesuvian face," and in the sinister wit of her understated "None stir the second time— / On whom *I* lay a Yellow Eye— / Or an emphatic Thumb—."

This Gun clearly is a poet, and a Satanically ambitious poet at that. In fact, it seems here as if the muselike Master or "Owner" may be merely a catalyst in whose presence the deadly vocabulary of the Gun/poet is activated. The irony of the riddling final quatrain, moreover, hints that it is the gun and not the Master, the poet and not her muse, who will have the last word. For, enigmatic though these lines are, they do imply that in his humanity the Master is subject to necessities which do not control the Gun's existence. The Master, being human, *must* live, for instance, whereas the Gun, living only when "it" speaks/kills, may or may not be obliged to "live." And in his fleshliness, of course, the Master has the "power" (for which read "weakness," since power in this line means not strength but capacity) to die, while the Gun, inhumanly energized by rage and flame, has "but the power to kill"—only, that is, the immortality conferred by "its" own Vesuvian fury.

The indecorous, Satanic ferocity of this poem is illuminated when we consider the work's relationship to a verse that may possibly have been one of its sources: Sir Thomas Wyatt's "The Lover Compareth His Heart to the Overcharged Gun."

The furious gun, in his most raging ire,
When that the bowl is rammed in too sore,
And that the flame cannot part from the fire,
Cracks in sunder, and in the air do roar
The shevered pieces. So doth my desire,
Whose flame encreaseth ay from more to more;
Which to let out I dare not look nor speak;
So inward force my heart doth all to-break.[3]

Here, too, the conceit of the passionate self-as-gun has volcanically and angrily sexual connotations. The gun is a phallus; its explosion implies orgasm; its sexual energy is associated with "raging ire." But, interestingly enough, in Wyatt's verse the gun's fury is turned against itself. "Overcharged" (as the poem's title indicates), its "flame encreaseth ay from more to more," and eventually it becomes akin to an "inward force [which] my heart doth all to-break."

For Dickinson, on the other hand, the Gun's Vesuvian smile is directed outward, impartially killing the timid doe (a female who rose to patriarchal Requirements?), all the foes of the Muse/Master, and perhaps even, eventually, the vulnerably human Master himself. Dancing "like a Bomb" abroad, exploding out of the "sod gown," the "frame" of darkness to which her life had been "shaven and fitted," the enraged poet becomes her own weapon, her instrumentality transferred from "His Requirements" to her own needs. In a sense, the Master here is no more than the explanation or occasion for the poet's rage. Her voice, we realize, speaks sentences of death that she herself conceives. Like George Eliot's Armgart, she carries her "revenges in [her] throat," and in uttering death, dealing out "words like blades" and laying the "emphatic Thumb" of power on her Master's foes, she attains, herself, a masculine authority or, to use Simone de Beauvoir's existentialist terminology, a kind of "transcendence."[4] De Beauvoir has perceptively commented that in those primitive societies upon which modern patriarchal civilization is still patterned "the worse cure that was laid upon woman was that she should be excluded from [the] warlike forays [of the men, since] superiority has been accorded in humanity not to the sex that brings forth but to that which kills."[5] And in this connection, in a brilliant analysis of "My Life had stood," Albert Gelpi has pointed out the intricate parallels between Dickinson's Gun and the Keatsian Romantic poet who—as in, for example, the "Ode on a Grecian Urn"—"kills" life into art.[6] Taken together, his comments and de Beauvoir's suggest that there are many ways in which this enigmatically powerful poem is an astounding assertion of "masculine" artistic freedom.

NOTES

1. See Cody, *After Great Pain: The Inner Life of Emily Dickinson* (Cambridge, Mass.: Harvard University Press, Belknap Press, 1971), 52.

2. *The Letters of Emily Dickinson*, ed. Thomas H. Johnson and Theodora Ward (Cambridge, Mass.: Harvard University Press, 1958), 2 : 375.

3. We are indebted to Celeste Turner Wright for calling this poem to our attention.

4. George Eliot, *Armgart*, in *The Writings of George Eliot: Poems* (Boston: Houghton Mifflin, Riverside Press Cambridge, 1908). 92.

5. Simone de Beauvoir, *The Second Sex*, trans. H. M. Parshley (New York: Knopf, 1953), 58.

6. Albert Gelpi, "Emily Dickinson and the Deerslayer" (reprinted below, in Chapter 3).

Hawthorne, Heidegger, and the Holy: The Uses of Literature

BENITA A. MOORE

Working from the Heideggerian view that poetic language "presences Being" (names the holy), Moore compares Hawthorne's sense of being in the world with Heidegger's *Dasein*. As the title of Heidegger's famous work *Sein und Zeit (Being and Time)* indicates, for him existence is bound up with temporality. Human existence is a movement projecting itself toward the future (Being-toward-Death) in order to determine its authentic past and authentic present. The awareness (Dread) of both time and death manifests itself in Care, the fundamental structure of human being. In other words, for Heidegger, existence involves emotion, moods, and the nonrational modes of consciousness. Moore relates these concerns to Hawthorne's spiritual understanding of existence. You will notice that she frames both Hawthorne's and Heidegger's writings within a Christian hermeneutics.

MARTIN HEIDEGGER OFFERED a fruitful line of inquiry for the interpretation and appreciation of literature when he wrote in his Postscript to "What Is Metaphysics?": "The thinker utters Being. The poet names

From "Hawthorne, Heidegger, and the Holy: The Uses of Literature," by Benita A. Moore, *Soundings* 64 (Summer 1981): 170–73; 176–82; 188–94. Copyright 1981 by *Soundings*. Reprinted by permission.

what is holy."[1] Ultimately, there is a connection between the two types of speaking which Heidegger himself pursued, especially regarding the poetry of Friedrich Hölderlin. Extending the definition of poetry to include imaginative prose of poetic intent, Heidegger's line of inquiry may usefully be applied to the writing of Nathaniel Hawthorne.[2] Heidegger's insight helps lay bare the source of a certain wonder-provoking unfathomability which the attentive reader feels in Hawthorne's work prior to critical reflection on why one should feel that quality. In turn, aspects of Hawthorne's work illustrate the meaning and justice of such Heideggerian formulations as: rescuing the question of Being from oblivion, the nature of language as naming the holy, and the experience of Nothingness.

The analysis which follows seeks to demonstrate how insights from two such diverse writers, separated by time, nationality, culture, and mode of discourse, nonetheless converge where they touch the depths of human experience. A selective process of comparison and juxtaposition can illuminate the similarity of the thought of the two authors as well as their common subject matter—the human person encountering "the other" in experience.

There is, of course, no attempt to suggest direct causal connection between the work of Heidegger and that of Hawthorne (passing over one of those odd coincidences which delight wordsmiths—to borrow a coinage from Nabokov—namely, that one of Hawthorne's best-known stories is "Dr. Heidegger's Experiment"). Both authors do, however, belong to the same universe of discourse in that both are legatees of the Western intellectual tradition, responding to further ramifications of the break-up of the "medieval synthesis"—the steady decline of the centrality of consensus religion and the increasing dominance of science at the heart of culture. Both belong to the era of refined, post-Reformation debates and to the large movement of Romanticism, Hawthorne relating to its flowering in America, Heidegger to its decline in Europe. In that sense, there is historical connection, as well as a connection in a special Heideggerian sense which this essay will explore.

The major claims made here are two: first, that Hawthorne's fulfillment of the mission of the poet, as that mission is formulated by Heidegger, provides a clue to much of the delight afforded by Hawthorne's "style" in all its celebrated ambiguity, as well as an indication of the reason why we turn to literature at all—to enter the presence of the sacred; and secondly, that Heidegger, anticipated by Hawthorne, has contributed to our understanding of human nature, language, poetry, and the sacred.

There is another underlying purpose at work in this comparison and that is to show that there is some ultimate relationship between literature and philosophy, which *could* be pursued to a third stage—theology. That is to say, these three disciplines, involving different contents, methods, and languages, coalesce around a single endeavor, showing the same things from different perspectives. Working from the same referential material, the poet names, the philosopher analyzes, and the theologian refers to a given religious standpoint. As cultural products, the works of each become common property, entering a circle of mutual influence. Put another way, the poet conveys the presence of Being in experience through an artistically evoked immediacy, while the philosopher deals with the same theme at the abstract level of reflection, presenting the structures of reality conceptually. At a still further remove from experience stands the theologian, who seeks to explain the meaning of a religious standpoint in terms adapted to contemporary thought patterns by using philosophically formulated structures which reflect those patterns. (Theology is dealt with in the present essay only by way of suggestion, though it would be quite possible—even necessary for the sake of completeness—to carry the discussion through to this third stage.[3]) Poetry, then, stands at the head of the process as the "prolepsis" or anticipation of the other modes of thought. As Heidegger says in "Hölderlin and the Essence of Poetry," poetry is the inaugural act" (*EB*, 287).

Perhaps a cautionary disclaimer should be entered at the outset. It may well be the case that the insights achieved by Heidegger and Hawthorne can only occur in context—through the cracks, as it were, of the specific language events they have created. Both use language in an idiosyncratic way precisely calculated to cause such insightful disclosure. The present essay hopes merely to indicate several striking points of convergence; it may well only be possible to test my hypotheses at their sources.

Four points where Heidegger and Hawthorne appear to converge will be examined as aspects of a single process, leading toward the duty of those charged with the "care of the word" (Heidegger; *EB*, 360): to name the holy, to utter Being. First, both Hawthorne and Heidegger are concerned with the loss of the sacred in culture, with "the gods that have fled" (Heidegger; *EB*, 289). Second, both authors sense that recovery of the sacred has to do with man's capacity for language. Third, both writers offer evidence that before that language appears which will reveal the sacred, the poet/philosopher (and perhaps Everyman, in some sense) must courageously and actively confront the mood of Dread which brings about the experience of Nothingness. And finally, both point to the fact that in the experience of Nothingness "beings" emerge in their otherness and reveal the Holy/Being. At this juncture, newly disclosive utterance can take place. In both Hawthorne and Heidegger, these four points overlap. That is, they are not disjunctive but are rather "moments" in one process. My discussion will seek to trace a line of continuity in the thought of each of the writers, leading in one and the same direction for both despite the fact that the insights cited as evidence are scattered throughout the corpus of each author's work. The thread of continuity thus discerned is predicated on the belief that in some sense an author's "works" constitute one "work," published one "chapter" at a time, to be sure, but all a part of one unfolding thought-world.

My method will be to present Hawthorne under the four Heideggerian rubrics mentioned above to show how Hawthorne rather tentatively (perhaps because he was aware of just how "new" what he was saying really was) but artfully describes in experiential terms something Heidegger later would proclaim boldly with the heavy artillery of analytic discourse. By offering Heidegger's explanation after Hawthorne's description, chronological accuracy is preserved and the force of poetic language as "proleptic" is more adequately demonstrated. . . .

[Moore shows that Hawthorne's critiques of nineteenth-century religion and Heidegger's raising the question of Being were their ways of decrying the loss of the sacred in their cultures.]

The second point of convergence between Hawthorne and Heidegger is found in the process of reawakening the sense of the holy in culture through language. The very term "fled gods" is embedded in Heidegger's discussion of poetry and language. Before returning to his explication, let us look at how Hawthorne anticipates this insight.

In the opening essay of *Mosses from an Old Manse*, Hawthorne alludes once again to the desiccation he perceives in clerical religion, but here he moves on to point toward the evocative or "Being"-property of living words, in contrast to religiously dead words which no longer call forth the sacred from its hiding place. On an early page of the essay "The Old Manse," Hawthorne says that one of the things he hoped residence in the Old Manse would inspire him to write would be "a layman's unprofessional and therefore unprejudiced views of religion."[4] Later in the essay he writes of rummaging about in the garret among the volumes left by previous ministerial occupants, inheritors of the New England Puritan tradition:

> The rain pattered upon the roof and the sky gloomed through the dusty garret windows while I burrowed among these venerable books *in search of any living thought* which should burn like a coal of fire, or *glow like an inextinguishable gem,* beneath the dead trumpery that had long hidden it. But I found no such treasure; *all was dead alike;* and I could not but muse deeply and wonderingly upon the humiliating fact that the works of man's intellect decay like those of his hands. Thought grows mouldy. *What was good and nourishing food for the spirits of one generation affords no sustenance for the next.* Books of religion, however, cannot be considered a fair test of the *enduring and vivacious properties of human thought,* because *such books seldom really touch their ostensible subject,* and have therefore, so little business to be written at all. So long as an unlet-

tered soul can attain to saving grace, there would seem to be no deadly error in *holding theological libraries to be accumulations of, for the most part, stupendous impertinence*. . . . *In fine, of this whole dusty heap of literature, I tossed aside all the sacred part, and felt myself none the less a Christian for eschewing it.* (*Tales*, 387–88) (Italics added.)

Hawthorne thus clearly describes how the religious language of yesteryear fails to evoke the sacred: it has become commonplace, a dead letter. If such language ever possessed a living "Being"-character, which he seems to doubt, it had no "permanence"—it will not reveal the holy for a later age, a different culture.

Hawthorne goes on, however, to describe what he *did* find of living value in the "dusty heap" and that was the picture of daily life afforded by old newspapers and almanacs. Why, he asks, had the ministers "been able to produce nothing half so real as these newspaper scribblers and almanac makers had thrown off in the effervescence of a moment"? His answer:

It is the age itself that writes newspapers and almanacs, which, therefore, have a distinct purpose and meaning at the time, and a *kind of intelligible truth for all times;* whereas most other works . . . are likely to possess little significance when new, and none at all when old. *Genius indeed melts many ages into one, and thus effects something permanent, yet still with a similarity of office to that of the more ephemeral writer. A work of genius is but the newspaper of a century, or perhaps of a hundred centuries.* (*Tales*, 388) (Italics added.)

In this passage, Hawthorne approaches the insight Heidegger will later go far toward nailing down conceptually in the Hölderlin essay, where he asks: "Who lays hold of something permanent in ravenous time and fixes it in the word? . . . [The poet, because] poetry is the establishing of being by means of the word" (*EB*, 280–81). Hawthorne shows that the religious language of sermons in the mouths of ministers who have not personally bared their breasts to "the divine lightning" (to anticipate Heidegger once again) will not summon the divine presence. A nearer approximation to the living word is offered by old newspapers whose details conjure up real life, things (beings, in philosophical language) in which the sheen of "Being" glimmers. Nearest of all to the living word, which Hawthorne quite clearly associates with the living God, is the work of Genius, i.e., real poetry which, more surely than old newspapers, captures the permanent out of the flux of time.

In the paragraph following the one quoted above, Hawthorne elaborates on his insight that the living holy or "the truth of Being"[5] somehow resides in "the word":

Lightly as I have spoken of these old books, there yet lingers with me a superstitious *reverence for literature of all kinds.* A bound volume has a charm in my eyes similar to what scraps of manuscript possess for the good Mussulman. He imagines that these wind-wafted records are perhaps hallowed by some sacred verse; and I, that *every new book or antique one may contain the "open sesame"—the spell to disclose treasures hidden in some unsuspected cave of Truth.* (*Tales,* 389) (Italics added.)

Heidegger, it seems to me, takes the basic insight Hawthorne describes and reduces it to process. What Hawthorne *felt* to be occurring in words—almost intuitively and pre-critically, in the sense that he lacked the philosophical machinery Heidegger would later supply to make possible thinking of experience in this particular critical way—Heidegger analyzed into its several stages. Read in Heidegger himself, the analysis possesses conceptual clarity and virtual indisputability, though even then the clarity is of the now-you-see-it-now-you-don't variety. However, there is nothing mystical about Heidegger's account, if "mystical" is taken to mean something supra-rational. Rather, Heidegger gives a rational explanation of what occurs, what *must* occur, in language and how. (This is not to say that there is nothing further to be understood about language, but rather that Heidegger carried the explanation of *Dasein** and *Dasein's* language to new levels of understanding.)

The account which follows articulates the process of just how "the holy" resides in living words. Insofar as possible, a common-sense terminology, based on my own interpretation, will be used, entailing the aforementioned risk of draining the account of real meaning. The task is rendered even more difficult by the fact that in the essays on poetry Heidegger's language is itself poetic, metaphorical, and evocative, rather than strictly conceptual and philosophical, though Heidegger himself eventually links the two modes of utterance.

To get at Heidegger's analysis of words naming the gods which have fled, we may begin with two Heideggerian propositions which seem circular, but which in fact do shed light on each other. Stated summarily, these propositions are: the essence of poetry is language, and the essence of language is poetry. To understand how poetry achieves its power of evoking the holy, one must get at our language-making ability at its very roots. Conversely, our language-making ability is fundamentally poetic—evoking the holy by naming. Put another way, if one begins with the experienced capability of poetic language to awe, to reveal the sacred, the search for the explanation for this potential leads to the exploration of language in general. If one begins at the other end by trying to explain

---

*Moore has defined *Dasein* earlier as "the 'being-there' of the individual person, 'the entity which each of us is himself and which includes inquiring as one of the possibilities of its being' (Heidegger, *Being and Time*)."—Ed.

the nature of human beings through their language, one is led to the nature of poetry, for language is fundamentally poetic and metaphorical. Heidegger chooses the poetry of Hölderin for his analysis of poetry and language because of its character as "meta-poetry," i.e., a poetry above all about the act of poetry-making itself.

If I hear correctly what Heidegger is saying (and in my effort to "hear" I have been influenced more than a little by Walker Percy's essays on language in *The Message in the Bottle*), the process goes something like this: At some moment, lost from present historical view, a hominoid, or some hominoids, discovered that vocal sounds could be used not only as signs, or indicators for behavior, but as symbols to be shared—i.e., when I say "chair," it is a chair for you as well as for me, requiring no further action from us, whereas a sound-*sign* used in a pre-human or non-human animal species indicates or directs behavior.[6] In that decisive moment of discovery, several things happened simultaneously: human beings appeared, time began, and history began.

Humans appeared. A part of genus hominoid became species homo sapiens, the specific difference being the ability of humans to make word-symbols. In Heidegger's words: "We—mankind—are a conversation. The being of men is founded in language" (*EB*, 277). "Conversation" is "the act of speaking with others about something," "the process of coming together, . . . the ability to speak and the ability to hear" being "equally fundamental" (*EB*, 278). The existence of humans qua humans is fundamentally relational in language, requiring one person to utter a symbol and another to hear and share it, and vice versa.

Time began. Out of the flux of events, words give a quality of permanence to *things*. With words to preserve it, experience becomes accessible to memory and further conversation. As Heidegger says: "Language has the task of making manifest in its work the existent [a something], and of preserving it as such" (*EB*, 275). Time is no longer mere succession—verbalized experience comes into view as now, before now, or after now.

History began. Experience thus revealed as taking place *in time* can be recalled and reflected on in words which can eventually be written down and subjected to further recall, reflection, and interpretation in a continual process of conversing with others of our species. Heidegger puts the matter of *Dasein*, time, and history this way: "Since when have we been a conversation? . . . We have been a single conversation since the time when it 'is time.' . . . Both—existence as a *single* conversation and historical existence—are alike ancient, they belong together and are the same thing" (*EB*, 278–79).

Humans, time, and history were born together in the advent of "the word," in *Dasein*'s ongoing openness to Being.

In the moment that human beings discovered that they were able to take up a position opposite to "what-is-in-totality" ("On the Essence of Truth," *EB*, 311), to receive into themselves that which is "manifest" all around them and to utter some of it in words which can be shared, they became *Da-sein*—the one who is "there" to *Sein*, to the Being of beings. "Beings" can be expressed in words, but behind or in them stands Being as permanently expressing itself. Put another way, in the process of naming in words (of course, something more than labels for noun-type objects is meant here), or singling particular things out from the previously unnamed all-that-is and preserving them in symbols, the permanent Being of all-that-is stands revealed anew as it yields up this new particular. Every inaugural naming is poetry as such, for poetry means nothing else but the new revelation of Being, a new shining forth in time of that which is one and the same in all beings—the permanent: "Only after 'ravenous time' has been riven into present, past and future, does the possibility arise of agreeing on something permanent" (*EB*, 279). In "The Way Back into the Ground of Metaphysics," Heidegger puts it this way: "Beings as beings appear in the light of Being" (Kaufmann, 206). The essay "On the Essence of Truth" relates the inaugural encounter of the "essential word" (*EB*, 278) to the notions of "truth" and "freedom," as appears from the following related statements: "The essence of truth is freedom. . . . Freedom reveals itself as the 'letting-be' of what is. . . . Truth is the unconcealment and revealment of what is" (*EB*, 303, 305, 309).

The following summary may serve as a further gloss on these texts: only when human nature, time, and history appear together in the beginning of our "conversation" do humans as such begin to ex-ist—i.e., to stand apart from other beings as *Dasein*, the one open in freedom to the revelation of the permanent, the true, the Being of beings. Each such revelation is awe-inspiring, filling us with wonder at "the holy"—at the mystery that there is indeed anything at all.

Heidegger's meditations on Hölderlin, which issued in the foregoing explanation of the origin of language/poetry, led to further meditations centering on the "holy" in the later essay, "Remembrance of the Poet," which links Being and the holy, albeit suggestively rather than analytically. In this essay, he speaks of "the essence of the holy being, which is invoked in this poem" and "that which the poet in his poethood invokes ('the Holy')" (*EB*, 233). At other points, he makes "holy being" appear to be synonymous with "the highest," "the high one," "the Joyous," "the Joyous One," and "the Serene." However named, Being is there to be unconcealed and *Dasein* wants to receive the revelation, as this line of Hölderlin's indicates: "That which thou seekest is near, and already coming to meet thee" (*EB*, 244). Such revelation is the only thing that brings man true joy.

It appears, however, that the Joyous High One (Being) cannot be revealed directly, but only in beings or things as "the heralds" of Being, "the angels" (*EB*, 248). These heralds seem to crowd the poet, asking to be named, so that Being in all its wonder may again appear. This is how

Heidegger interprets Hölderlin's "angels of the house" (space) and "angels of the year" (time). The angels are "the first to draw near," and "appear only if there are any who are composing" (*EB*, 248–50); i.e., only if there is a poet able to receive new beings/Being and name them. In yet another way, then, these metaphors point to the fact that it is only in the particulars of one's space-time relation with the earth that Being, the serene and joyous permanent, breaks through.

"To write poetry is to make a discovery," writes Heidegger (*EB*, 247). It is to discover that one has come "home" to the source—to know with the joy of the first time what one has already known, at least in some inchoate fashion, to know "that which has already been given and is yet at the same time withheld . . . because [human beings] . . . are not yet ready for it" (*EB*, 245); i.e., not yet ready for the new revelation of Being.

In this connection, Heidegger initiates the notion of the "fled gods" which he will elaborate in the subsequent Hölderlin essay. The poet, he says, "without fear of the appearance of godlessness . . . must remain near the failure of the god, and wait long enough in the prepared proximity of the failure, until out of the proximity of the failing god the initial word is granted, which names the High One" (*EB,* 265). But even non-poets, who do not share the poet's vocation of "care of poetic speech," the people who make use of previous "essential words," now de-poetized as common words, have the responsibility "to become hearers," and are therefore kindred to the poet (*EB*, 265–66). These "slow ones" linger conservingly at some distance from the new revelation, content with old words. (One thinks of Hawthorne's Mr. Frost here.) Old messages from the gods—"essential words"—need time to become ordinary so that all may use such words. As Heidegger would subsequently explain: "Poetry is the inaugural naming of being and of the essence of all things—not just any speech, but that particular kind which for the first time brings out into the open all that which we then discuss and deal with in everyday language" (*EB*, 283). But common use finally obscures the real import of these "essential words" and new messages are needed. That is, words appropriated in the act of a poet, of a *Dasein* with special poetic gifts, become the common property of mankind, and then through common usage, sink into "everydayness"—the revelation of Being that accompanied the inaugural naming is forgotten.[7] Being falls once again into oblivion.

A cycle is thus set up: the poet speaks the essential, poetic word, but the people resist the new. Finally they listen and in their widespread use the word becomes ordinary before the people fully realize it. The poet, the first to sense the "failure of the god," goes back to the mountaintop, lingers in proximity to the Holy one, and through the "heralds" brings the new word/revelation to the people. They resist, and the cycle begins again. Conceived thus, abstractly and structurally, the process appears to be simpler and neater than is the actual case in a complex culture. The lines of such a structure can be discerned in cultural history, however.

In any event, it is clear that poetry is far from being "that most innocent of all occupations" (*EB*, 270), a game, a diversion, a harmless ornament of culture (*EB*, 283), as practical persons of the world or any of the "slow ones" might see it. It is the very basis of language, of the shared world of the human species, the sacred precinct for divine revelation. Just as "poetry is the primitive language of a historical people" (*EB*, 283), so it is poetry which continues to push forward the human enterprise in its single, cyclic conversation, utilizing the primary cultural form—language. Poetry is the very locus of Being, of the new and living. As such, it is a continual menace to the everyday, the old and dead.

In his gently ironic way, Hawthorne pointed to the same misunderstanding of the poet's calling on the part of the "slow ones" when he wrote in "The Custom House," prefacing *The Scarlet Letter,* of the disapprobation his stern Puritan ancestors would hold for such a "positively disgraceful" vocation as his: "'What is he?' murmurs one gray shadow of my forefathers to the other. 'A writer of storybooks! What kind of business in life—what mode of glorifying God, or being serviceable to mankind in his day and generation—may that be? Why, the degenerate fellow might as well have been a fiddler!'"[8]

To sum up regarding this second point of convergence, it appears that Hawthorne accurately discerned the difference between living and dead language, between the "essential word" and the everyday, and that he rightly suspected that the locus of the holy, the permanent, the spiritually refreshing, occurred somewhere en route from the one to the other. Heidegger spelled out just how this is so, using the philosophical notion of the *Dasein* "whose Being is distinguished by the open-standing standing-in in the unconcealedness of Being" (Kaufmann, 214)—by that truly amazing capacity for language. . . .

[According to Moore, Hawthorne's and Heidegger's writings show that before language revealing the sacred can appear, the poet-philosopher must first confront the mood of Dread which brings about the experience of Nothingness.]

The final point of convergence, then, is the emergence of beings/ Being out of the experience of Nothing empowering newly revelatory language on the part of the poet/philosopher. We again begin with Hawthorne.

In light of the discussion thus far, it may now be asserted more confidently that a good part of the wizardry of Hawthorne's "style" lies in his ability to render objects in themselves as present in their "strangeness" (a favorite word of Hawthorne's), their mystery, their otherness, their separation from the general chaos of "being-in-the-world." Many examples of his responsiveness to "the voice of Being" in "things" could be drawn from his mature fiction, keeping in mind the earlier disclaimer: torn from their contexts, the words cited may not provide the disclosure of Being that occurs when they are encountered in their proper settings, where in the leisurely unfolding of Hawthorne's narration, objects suddenly appear with the unexpectedness of revelation. But perhaps if we remember that it is in the management of language itself in the work of art that the poet brings "the divine gift" to the people, another brief look at parts of his text will be worthwhile.

"The Custom House" preface to *The Scarlet Letter* provides one example emphasizing the strangeness of "things" in sudden overtness. In a meditative mood, the author looks around his "familiar room" and suddenly "sees." The moonlight, "falling so white upon the carpet, and showing all its figures so distinctly—making every object so minutely visible, yet so unlike a morning or noontide visibility," makes the objects of the "domestic scenery" appear as if for the first time. At the same time, the "things" tend to disappear into their ground:

> All these details, so completely seen, are so spiritualized by the unusual light, that they seem to lose their actual substance, and become things of intellect. Nothing is too small or trifling to undergo this change, and acquire dignity thereby. A child's shoe; the doll, seated in her little wicker carriage; the hobby-horse—whatever, in a word, has been used or played with during the day is now invested with a quality of strangeness and remoteness. (*SL*, 33)

In this experience, the author and reader are filled with wonder. The "thing" thus perceived reveals anew the awe-ful truth that there is indeed something and not nothing. The "overtness" of beings points to their marvelous background, Being-itself.

Perhaps richest of all Hawthorne's works in reverence for "things"— and interestingly enough, Hawthorne's own favorite—is *The House of the Seven Gables*. Henry James put his finger on it when he called this novel "a large and generous production, pervaded with that vague hum, that indefinable echo, of the whole multitudinous life of man."[9] From such wealth, it is difficult to choose one passage: the descriptions of the house itself, the street scenes, or perhaps the cookie muncher, Ned Higgins. But the description of a June afternoon in the Pyncheon garden may serve best to demonstrate Hawthorne's "care of the word."

Enclosed by wooden fences and outbuildings of other houses, the garden contains, among other things, a decaying summerhouse, a plashing fountain, and a coop of remarkable chickens. But it is the soil itself which first claims attention: "The black, rich soil had fed itself with the decay of a long period of time; such as fallen leaves, the petals of flowers, and the stalks and seed-vessels of vagrant and lawless plants, more useful after their death than ever while flaunting in the sun."[10] The soil is very real, but it also points beyond itself as a symbol.

Phoebe, the fictional viewer of the garden, notices evidence of human tending and calls attention to the interplay of human cultivation and vagrant Nature itself while she names the various items of vegetation:

> The white double rose-bush had evidently been propped up anew. . . . There were also a few species of antique and hereditary flowers, in no very flourishing condition, but scrupulously weeded. . . . The remainder of the garden presented a well-selected assortment of esculent vegetables, in a praiseworthy state of advancement. Summer squashes, almost in their golden blossom; cucumbers, now evincing a tendency to spread away from the main stock, and ramble far and wide; two or three rows of string-beans, and as many more that were about to festoon themselves on poles; tomatoes, occupying a site so sheltered and sunny that the plants were already gigantic, and promised an early and abundant harvest. . . . Phoebe found an unexpected charm in this little nook of grass, and foliage, and aristocratic flowers, and plebian vegetables. The eye of Heaven seemed to look down into it pleasantly, and with a peculiar smile, as if glad to perceive that nature, elsewhere overwhelmed, and driven out of the dusty town, had here been able to retain a breathing-place. (*House,* 74–75)

This garden in words is as real in pointing beyond itself to something permanent and universal as many another sunny June afternoon in a garden, remembered in tranquility.

Hawthorne later apologizes for the meticulous description, suggesting that "the author needs great faith in his reader's sympathy" to tolerate "details so minute, and . . . so trifling" (*House,* 130). Behind this self-effacing remark, the perceptive reader can discern an author who knows precisely the ontological, thematic point of his lengthy description. But he rather offhandedly explains that the reason for lingering "too long, no doubt, beside this paltry rivulet of life" is that the "mean incidents and poor delights" of the garden helped Clifford's return to "health and substance," for they "had the earth-smell in them" (*House,* 133). There we have it: it is the "earth-smell" of real things which gives to the *Dasein* self and world in integrity. Here again Hawthorne's convergence with Heidegger is remarkable. In the essay on Hölderlin, Heidegger says: "Man is *he* who *is,* precisely in the affirmation of his own existence. . . . But what must he affirm? That he belongs to the earth" (*EB,* 274).

In other examples of Hawthorne's garden imagery, things of earth take on more directly mythic levels of meaning. The baby chick which gave Phoebe "a sagacious wink" when she held it in her hand was more than a chick: "It was a feathered riddle; a mystery hatched out of an egg" (*House,* 132). But first it was a real chick. The garden itself was indeed a real garden, but it was also "the Eden of a thunder-smitten Adam [Clifford], who had fled for refuge thither out of the same dreary and perilous wilderness into which the original Adam was expelled" (*House*, 130). This "new Eden," or the real material earth, is the locus of another possibility to Being, in that a new Adam and Eve—Holgrave and Phoebe—first find intimations of love in this very garden. Again Hawthorne finds the paradox at every turn: the mythic scene of the fall of man is the very occasion for a new ascent. It is in the world of quotidian reality that human beings find "the holy" and their proper relation to it.

In fact the whole progress of *The House of the Seven Gables* is structured toward this paradox of hopeful affirmation, a theme which reappears constantly in Hawthorne's work. This novel shows clearly the movement from inner isolation, symbolized by the dark inner precincts of the house, into love and human fellowship pursued in communion with the great world under the light of day, symbolized by the garden and the street outside the house. Mysteriously, it is knowledge of the "inner precincts" which makes possible "coming forth," only now with newly attained depth. Hawthorne shows this by offering, just before the "coming forth" which is the resolution of the novel, a long unflinching meditation on death, occasioned by the unattended corpse of Judge Pyncheon. Can anyone not feel the dread the author portrays? "There is no window! There is no face! An infinite, inscrutable blackness has annihilated sight! Where is our universe? All crumbled away from us; and we, adrift in chaos, may hearken to the gusts of homeless wind, that go singing and murmuring about, in quest of what was once a world! . . . Would that we were not an attendant spirit here! It is too awful!" (*House*, 241–42). The very majesty of Hawthorne's utterance at this point helps redeem life from any unwarranted triviality. Further, it opens deep ground for hope in the omnipresence of life: "Tomorrow! Tomorrow! Tomorrow! We that are alive, may arise betimes tomorrow. As for him that has died to-day, his morrow will be resurrection morn" (*House*, 241). In showing Being emerging from the terror of nihilation (and anticipating Heidegger's "Being-towards-death," which is necessary to undergird "authentic existence" [*EB*, 61–64]), Hawthorne shows death, accepted, as the springboard to the novel's resolution. In a chapter significantly entitled "The Flower of Eden," Hawthorne has Holgrave and Phoebe come to full realization of their love *in* the house, in the very presence of awful death thus lingered over. The Evil causing the isolation of the house's inhabitants has been opened up and dispelled. In the very precincts of death, love is not unfittingly born:

> And it was in this hour, so full of doubt and awe, that the one miracle was wrought, without which every human existence is a blank. The bliss which makes all things true, beautiful, and holy shone around this youth and maiden. They were conscious of nothing sad nor old. They

transfigured the earth, and made it Eden again, and themselves the first dwellers in it. . . . "Now let us meet the world!" said Holgrave. (*House*, 269)

WITH THE HELP OF several of Heidegger's statements from "Hölderlin and the Essence of Poetry," it is now possible to sum up the four "moments" in the process we have been examining, here reordered historically:

Moment 1 (Original naming of the gods/beings, revealing, in language, the Holy/*Sein* over against the *Dasein;* humans appear): "Since we have been a conversation—man has learnt much and named many of the holy ones. Since language really became actual as conversation, the gods have acquired names and a world has appeared. . . . The presence of the gods and the appearance of the world are not merely a consequence of the actualization of language, they are contemporaneous with it. . . . It is precisely in the naming of the gods, and in the transmutation of the world into word, that real conversation, which we ourselves are, consists" (*EB*, 279).

Moment 2 (The essence of shared language is poetry, and poetry is original revelation/naming of Being): "The poet names the gods and names all things in that which they are" (*EB*, 281).

Moments 3 and 4 (When language has fallen into everydayness, when Being has fallen into oblivion, when there is need for recovery of the sacred, the poet in the experience of Nothing is enabled to rename the Holy/Being): "[The poet] first determines a new time. It is the time of the gods that have fled *and* of the god that is coming. It is the time of *need*, because it lies under a double lack and a double Not: the No-more of the gods that have fled and the Not-yet of the god that is coming" (*EB*, 289).

The poet is one who penetrates the accepted surfaces of discourse. Seeing something for the first time in its own whatness, separating it out from its state of being unnoticed or taken for granted, and giving it a name in language, the poet shocks us anew with amazement at why there should be something, anything at all, and not nothing. He thus points again to the teeming fruitfulness of Being and makes us see the Holy, precisely where we had been previously unobservant and unaware.

Heidegger made a signal contribution to our understanding of man, language, poetry, and the sacred; he was able to "utter Being." Hawthorne, presenting his vision of man in the world artistically, anticipated the several moments in the process Heidegger would articulate philosophically. Sensing a loss of the sacred in culture, Hawthorne fulfilled the mission of the poet—to "name the holy" and to proclaim "the new time." He criticized Transcendentalism, and perhaps more broadly, Protestant Liberalism, for slighting much of life's dark seriousness, a criticism that was to pick up tempo as the nineteenth century gave way to the twentieth. Were there space to pursue it, it could readily be shown that his preoccupation with sin and guilt and his treatment of it in his fiction amounts to a transvaluation of the Calvinistic doctrine of total human depravity, encompassing the radical guilt of the human situation on its ontological roots, as a modern philosopher or theologian might put it.[11] Also, he anticipated the concerns of a later age in his insistence on the possibility of overcoming isolation and estrangement from self and world, at least partially, through "theonomous" relations of love and compassionate human fellowship. In showing the "strangeness" of beings/Being emerging from Nothing in Time, he ushers his readers into the presence of the awe-inspiring sacred. He shows his concern for the real word that gives life, as opposed to the counterfeit that deadens. In giving back to the reader some of life's splendor and sadness, Hawthorne offers joy and hope, for it is more meaningful to encounter the presence of the holy than to say the word "God."

So THE SPIRAL OF human thought—its "single conversation" in encounter with the world and other persons—goes on. Artists of the future, having appropriated the discoveries of literature, philosophy, and theology, will confront the world in new openness and uncover yet more of the unfathomable mystery of Being. Heidegger, in his reclusive life in the Black Forest, and Hawthorne—the proto-existentialist—in his lonely years in Salem, both looked at human beings and the world, swaying dizzily between Being and Nothing, and concluded reverently: "There is indeed something rather than nothing! Thank God!" "What is more enigmatic: that beings are, or that Being is?" asks Heidegger (Kaufmann, 221). The individual existents, temporary condensations of the flux of historicity, are themselves real, but they point beyond themselves to something permanent yet ever-changing in its face. In the recesses of one's being, the dark caverns where no outsider can be finally admitted, the authentic person knows this: "It is holy ground where the shadow falls" (*House*, 155).

NOTES

1. Heidegger, "Postcript" to "What Is Metaphysics?" in *Existence and Being*, ed. Werner Brock (Chicago: Regnery, 1959; Gateway Edition, 1970), 360. Cited in the text as *EB*.

2. See Q. D. Leavis, "Hawthorne as Poet," *Sewanee Review* 59 (April, June 1951): 179–205, and 59 (July, September 1951): 426–58. See also Hyatt H. Waggoner, *Hawthorne: A Critical Study* (Cambridge, Mass.: Harvard University Press, 1963), 105–6.

3. For example, the Catholic theologian Karl Rahner and the Protestant theologian Paul Tillich make extensive use of Heidegger in their theologizing, to name but two.

4. Nathaniel Hawthorne, "The Old Manse," in *Selected Tales and Sketches*, with a Revised Introduction by Hyatt H. Waggoner (New York: Holt, Rinehart and Winston, 1967), p. 374. Cited in the text as *Tales*.

5. [Martin Heidegger, "The Way Back into the Ground of Metaphysics," in *Existentialism from Dostoevsky to Sartre*, ed. Walter Kaufmann (New York: World, 1956; Meridian Books, 1965), 217. Cited in text as Kaufmann.]

6. Walker Percy, *The Message in the Bottle* (New York: Farrar, Straus and Giroux, 1954), 282.

7. Walker Percy also makes use of the concept of "everydayness." For example, in his novel *The Moviegoer* (New York: Knopf, 1961), Binx is concerned at many points with the problem of being thrust by "everydayness" into an inert life, stripped of wonder, of the possibility of breakthrough, and of ability to really *see* things.

8. Nathaniel Hawthorne, *The Scarlet Letter* (New York: Airmont Books, 1962), 14. Cited in the text as *SL*.

9. Henry James, *Hawthorne* (Ithaca, New York: Cornell University Press, 1956), p. 103. Granting the justice of this characterization, James was wide of his own mark in summarily dismissing Hawthorne's *Notebooks:* "The reader says to himself that when a man turned thirty gives a place in his mind—and his ink-stand—to such trifles as these it is because nothing else of superior importance demands admission" (35–36). Rather, it would seem that Hawthorne's respect for "things" in their "inwardness" is clarified in his *Notebooks*. He often worked such details into his fiction after articulating their form initially in the *Notebooks*. That this was a conscious procedure may be surmised from his 1840 letter to Longfellow: "I have seen so little of the world that I have nothing but thin air to concoct my stories of, and it is not easy to give a life-like semblance to such shadowy stuff. Sometimes, through a peephole, I have caught a glimpse of the real world, and the two or three articles in which I have portrayed these glimpses please me better than the others" (James, *Hawthorne*, 43). In terms of what he could see by minutely perceiving objects, Hawthorne invites comparison with a Zen Buddhist.

10. Nathaniel Hawthorne, *The House of the Seven Gables* (New York: Holt, Rinehart and Winston, 1957), 74. Cited in the text as *House*.

11. In light of Heidegger's analysis, it is not necessary to suppose that concern with guilt, nothingness, blackness, sin, etc., bespeaks a somewhat demented morbidity in Hawthorne. Even a valuable study like Frederick C. Crews' *The Sins of the Fathers: Hawthorne's Psychological Themes* (New York: Oxford University Press, 1966), which shows the relevance of reading Hawthorne through Freud's eyes, does not necessarily constitute the final word on Hawthorne. As thinkers try to give new accounts or theories of human experience, they frequently turn to art for examples. Such new theories can bring to consciousness aspects of works of art which eluded previous perceptions. An art as complex as Hawthorne's cannot be reduced to the psychological level alone. Even if one has "psycho-analyzed" Hawthorne and his characters, pointing out what he and they should have done to adapt themselves to "reality," one has not exhausted his work of all other possible meanings. Hawthorne's maladapted characters—or even the authorial persona—may reveal more about human existence than could better adapted characters and authors. The "tragic" vision of life is more than a psychological accident.

The Parables of Flannery O'Connor

JOHN R. MAY

Literary interpreters who draw on the existential or hermeneutical phenomenology of Martin Heidegger try to describe how the text's language reveals the essential character of Being. According to Heidegger, our sense of being-in-the-world (*Dasein*) is constituted both by time and by language; indeed, only where there is language is there *human* existence. Moreover, poetic language can unconceal Being. Thus the Heideggerian critic, engaged in a mutual interaction with the poem, works to describe how the poem's language does this.

Heideggerian critics often refer to their approach as the "New Hermeneutics." According to this, hermeneutics—a general term for interpreting textual truths or meanings—becomes *newly* empowered through Heideggerian insights. For example, here May develops the Heideggerian emphasis on the ability of poetic language to make apparent the existential character of Being. Referring to O'Connor's parables, May writes that the New Hermeneutical understanding of "word" as interpreter of human existence startles us by providing us with a glimpse of the sacred (Being) in the midst of our ordinary life.

THE AESTHETIC PRINCIPLE that orchestrates the whole of O'Connor's fiction while allowing the individual works to appear in their maximum uniqueness is to be found, I propose, in the New Hermeneutic's understanding of "word" as interpreter of human existence. Whereas O'Connor's own literary theory is principally concerned with the relationship between the work of art and external reality (which, for her, is ultimately "mystery"), her fiction achieves its distinctive dramatic impact through the power of language to interpret its listener rather than through its need to be interpreted by him. The word of revelation spoken or the gesture of judgment seen constitutes the dramatic core of O'Connor's narratives and articulates their meaning for the reader.

The word-orientation of O'Connor's fiction, moreover, is basically scriptural in inspiration and parabolic in effect. The specific New Testament literary form that her art imitates is the parable, where religious meaning is structured in terms of human conflict symbolizing man's rela-

From *The Pruning Word: The Parables of Flannery O'Connor*, by John R. May (Notre Dame, Ind., and London: University of Notre Dame Press, 1976), xxiv–xxv; 12–14; 113–16. Copyright, 1976, by the University of Notre Dame Press, Notre Dame, Indiana 46556.

tionship with God. For what the parables of Jesus reveal to the listener is that life is gained or lost in the midst of everyday existence. Thus, the problem of art and belief in O'Connor is resolved, at least on the level of interpretation, when the reader-critic realizes that the often harsh, specifically Christian theology of O'Connor's fiction constitutes its countryside (the literal level) whereas its true country (the level of meaning) employs the hermeneutic word of radical human respect for mystery. The reader has no choice but to hear the universal language of homo religiosus spoken by her contemporary parables, and no valid interpretation of them can avoid at least the literary analogues of their basic religious language—poverty, possibility, and judgment.

Moreover, as a structural aesthetic principle that varies from narrative to narrative, the interpreting word permits each short story and novel to mediate its own specific insight into the mystery of existence and thus preserves perfectly the uniqueness of the individual text. If in the final analysis the overall configuration of meaning that the parables produce suggests rather than states a religious view that is Christian, each story is no more integrally Christian in meaning than the parables of Jesus taken singly. The prophetic voice that O'Connor dares to imitate—with acknowledged success—speaks with eschatological urgency, yet with simplicity, of the poverty of man. Audacious enough to judge the modern world with her own "pruning word," she reluctantly but realistically accepted the probability that her work—like the parables of Jesus—would be rejected. The reader should, however, understand precisely what he is rejecting—not orthodox Christian theology in its fullness but a single-minded revelation of human limitation and possibility in the face of mystery. . . .

. . . The question of [O'Connor's] world view, so well known from her lectures in theory and her defense of the Catholic writer, is significant only to the extent it reveals itself in the dramatic structure of the story. For word as understood in the New Hermeneutic is radically human—and therefore possibly religious rather than specifically Christian—inasmuch as it mediates all reality, even mystery, to the listener. As word the stories can illumine the reader's existence; that is the power of language itself. They at least challenge him to respond.

O'Connor's short story "Revelation" is prototypical of the hermeneutical function of language and of a literary text, and brief reference to it here will no doubt help to illustrate this new understanding of language and to set the stage for the following chapters. The protagonist, Mrs. Turpin, is a good woman whose one shortcoming apparently is that she has constructed an artificial hierarchy of social classes in which she can place anyone she meets. She pities white-trash and Negroes, who are obviously less well off than she is, because they cannot seem to make anything of themselves or do anything with what is given to them. The conflict in the story results from the confrontation of her condescending social philosophy with the revealing word of judgment spoken to her by Mary Grace, who calls her an "old wart hog" and tells her to go back to hell where she came from. Mary Grace, as her name itself suggests, announces the time of repentance. Ruby Turpin is thus suspended between word and response, between judgment and acceptance. The word of judgment interprets her because it clearly places her where she has placed white-trash and Negroes—last! Before she can accept the judgment leveled against her, she goes through the tortures of a self-righteous Job. But she does eventually respond; the word effects her acceptance of a new vision of reality and the ordering of classes. The authentic language of judgment is spoken to her, and it brings forth new life by announcing its possibility. Her encounter with Mary Grace is event and promise.

Although Mrs. Turpin tries initially to interpret the word, to remove its sting, she eventually allows it to interpret her, to shatter her illusions of superiority to "trashy" people—the folly of her social condescension based on material possessions. Flannery O'Connor has given brilliant contemporary expression to Jesus' teaching that the first shall be last and the last first. But we have until now discussed only the hermeneutical function of the word *within* the story. The story itself speaks this word of judgment to the reader. It interprets as well the folly of our own human tendency to determine—rather than discover—reality's order, to consider ourselves superior to others, to impose our ways on others. It forces us, through the shared experience of Mrs. Turpin's ordeal, to accept the fact that the word must interpret us, not we the word.

To specify precisely *how* O'Connor's stories work, in the light of the New Hermeneutic, we must appeal to the literary form of the Word in Scripture which most closely approximates, if not adequately corresponds to, the fictional form she uses. That scriptural form is of course the parable. Meaning in O'Connor's fiction like meaning in the parables of Jesus is accurately expressed only in terms of universal human experience. If their meaning is fundamentally religious, it is because they confront man with his radical poverty in the face of reality. They startle him with the suddenness of the sacred in the midst of the ordinary. . . .

Ruby Turpin's dramatic conflict in "Revelation" is a prototype of the hermeneutic structure of Flannery O'Connor's stories. If the title of the story were not sufficient indication, Ruby herself—"a respectable, hardworking, church-going woman"—is portrayed as being immediately certain about the source of, if not the reason for, her encounter with the young psychology major in the doctor's waiting room. She is dumbfounded that "she had been singled out for *the message,* though there was trash in the room to whom it might justly have been applied" (italics added). The ultimate cause of the power of the human word that interprets the lives of O'Connor's protagonists, though explicit here, is always at least by implication divine. The root meaning of "revelation" is "to draw back the veil"; thus the New Testament Book of Revelation claims to disclose the ultimate mystery of God's plan operating in the world. It is appropriate that the only story of O'Connor's that lays bare the religious dynamics of her hermeneutic core is itself called "Revelation"—an observation that contributes some additional support, I think, to Forrest Ingram's thesis that the cycle of stories in the second collection properly ends with this one.[1] As reassuring as this unveiling may be, the essential point that I have been trying to make remains true: the hermeneutic structure stands dramatically as a saving dialogue *among men:* it nevertheless illumines existence at its very core. Such is the effect of O'Connor's tales analogous to the parables of Jesus.

Characteristic of the exposed dynamism of the story is the blatantly indicative name given to the Wellesley girl, reading the "thick blue book . . . entitled *Human Development*" and listening painfully to Mrs. Turpin's social commentary. What is unexpected is that Mary Grace, a fat, ugly girl, "blue with acne," is a budding intellectual—utterly unique in Flannery O'Connor's world where intellectuals are typically judged by others, rather than the ones judging. When she throws the book at Ruby and sinks her fingers quickly into Ruby's neck, the latter is jolted violently from the secure moorings of her social hierarchy and forced to reassess her vision. Mary Grace whispers the word of revelation to the dazed Ruby Turpin: "Go back to hell where you came from, you old wart hog!" Then the deranged girl is carried away quickly by ambulance to a hospital.

By external standards Ruby is a "good" woman, "grateful" to God for all her material blessings and her "good disposition" and trying "to help anybody out that [needs] it," yet she tends to take back with her mind what her hands have offered. Even though she does help "trashy" people, she is convinced deep down of the futility of it: "Help them you must, but help them you couldn't." She is grateful for what she has, but her sense of dependence has not prevented her from thinking "that you had to *have* certain things before you could *know* certain things." Her stratification of society on the basis of possessions has placed her precariously close to the top. She occupies herself at night "naming the classes of people": "On the bottom of the heap were most colored people, not the kind she would have been if she had been one, but most of them; then next to them—not above, just away from—were the white-trash; then above them were the home-owners, and above them the home-and-land-owners, to which she and Claud belonged. Above she and Claud were people with a lot of money and much bigger houses and much more land."

Despite the onslaught of grace, Ruby begrudges every inch of self she must yield to reevaluation. While taking out her wrath on her pigs with the spray from a hose, she directs her questions with the fury of a latter-day Job at the acknowledged source of the revelation: "How am I a hog and me both? . . . How am I a hog? . . . Exactly how am I like them?"[2] The answer comes back to Ruby in the form of a double vision.

"As if through the very heart of mystery," she looks down into the pig parlor where the frightened hogs have settled in one corner, seeming "to pant with a secret life." Then, turning to the sunset, she sees a purple streak in the sky, an extension of the nearby highway, as "a vast swinging bridge extending upward from the earth through a field of living fire," on which "a vast horde of souls were rumbling toward heaven." The "life-giving knowlege" that identification with hogs, even her clean ones, has brought her is projected onto the sunset. Ruby realizes that the actual order of salvation has nothing to do with possessions, because at the head of the procession are "whole companies of white-trash, clean for the first time in their lives," and bringing up the rear are people like herself and Claud, who own a home and some land. She can see "by their shocked and altered faces that even their virtues [are] being burned away." Those who exalt themselves will indeed be humbled. As she returns to the house, the new vision of reality is firmly planted in her mind, replacing the old order that she had so carefully but foolishly constructed. Ruby Turpin truly believes now that the first will be last and the last first.[3]

Ruby has allowed herself to be cut down to size by the word. The story is artfully framed by images of her in relation to the world that confirm her acceptance of the revelation. Our first impression of Ruby is of a "very large" woman "looming" over the other patients in a ridiculously small waiting room; she "[makes] it look even smaller by her presence." At the end of the story, Ruby is alone, "bent" over the side of her pig pen, staring into the heart of mystery, dwarfed by the cosmic dimensions of the apocalyptic sunset. Moreover, Ruby's ability to classify people by looking at their feet is ironic foreshadowing of her realization of her actual level in creation's order. And the very cause of her pride in possessions—the immaculate pig parlor—suggests a biblical indictment of her as "unclean" of heart. The meaning of the story is more precise therefore than Carter Martin implies when he appropriates in this context Robert Drake's general comment about O'Connor's world ("There is, finally, no salvation in *works*, whatever form they may take, or in *self*").[4] Ruby Turpin did not think either who she was or what she did would be her salvation; like the servant who received one talent, she unhappily confused what she was given with her final reward.

NOTES

1. Forrest L. Ingram, "O'Connor's Seven-Story Cycle," *The Flannery O'Connor Bulletin* 2 (1973): 19–28.

2. As explicit as the story is about the source of its "revelation," not every critic has been willing to take its allusions at face value. In view of the quality of Ruby's final vision, her emphasis on gratitude to God, the simile that has her "defending her innocence to invisible guests who were like the comforters of Job,"

and the repeated though noncapitalized references to "you" in Ruby's monologue, Josephine Hendin seems unnecessarily reserved in saying that Ruby "shouts . . . to her fields," rather than at God as she actually does (Hendin, *The World of Flannery O'Connor* [Bloomington: Indiana University Press, 1970], 119).

3. A few deft changes to the conclusion of the story once again demonstrate how O'Connor's revisions repeatedly strengthened the interpretive structure of her stories and clarified the nature of the protagonist's response. In an earlier version of "Revelation," Ruby returns to the house *before* her vision; the last paragraph of that version follows:

> Until the sun slipped finally behind the tree line she remained there with her gaze bent to them. Then she got down and turned off the faucet and made her way on the darkening path to the house. By the time she reached her back door and looked behind her, there was only a purple streak in the sky, like an extension of the highway leading into the night, but a visionary light had settled in her eyes. She saw the streak as a vast swinging bridge extending upward from the earth. Upon it a hoard of souls rumbled toward heaven. There were whole companies of white-trash, clean for the first time in their lives, and bands of black niggers in white robes, and battalions of freaks and lunatics shouting and clapping and leaping like frogs. And coming behind all of them was a tribe of people whom she recognized at once as those who, like herself and Claud, had always had a little of everything and the God-given wit to use it right. They were marching behind the others with great dignity, *driving them, in fact, ahead of themselves*, still responsible as they had always been for good order and common sense and respectable behavior. *They walked upright as they had done in life, their eyes small but fixed unblinkingly on what lay ahead.* And the whole hoard was shouting halleluja. (An earlier version of the published MS, 27–28, O'Connor Collection.) (Italics added.)

Although Ruby's "tribe" is bringing up the rear of the procession, their appearance is far less subdued than in the final version (note italicized portions), and their eyes rather than Ruby's are "fixed unblinkingly on what lay ahead." The published version emphasizes the relationship between the vision and Ruby's status as "wart hog" by having her remain at the pig parlor during the revelation and return "to the house" only after the "abysmal life-giving knowledge" has been "absorbed."

4. Carter W. Martin, *The True Country: Themes in the Fiction of Flannery O'Connor* (Nashville: Vanderbilt University Press, 1969), 130.

Phenomenological Provocateurs

1. Phenomenological critics have been faulted for being a-historical and essentialist. Consider these charges in light of the phenomenological essays in this text.

2. Would it be possible for a phenomenological critic to describe the ego, or mind, of an author like Luis Borges or Alain Robbe-Grillet who deliberately attempts to erase any personal psychological trace in his writings?

95

3. Halliburton identifies with the protagonist Dupin and the narrator throughout Poe's detective tales. Why these characters only? Could it be argued that to read a story, we must identify not only with all the characters—major and minor, good and bad—but also with all the elements in the story—the settings, events, symbols, and so on? If one could make this case, does this invalidate, or at least contest, Halliburton's phenomenological approach?

4. Although Gilbert and Gubar would not deny that male critics can identify with female authors, their descriptions of female writers describe a gendered consciousness, or imagination, more easily accessible to women than to men. Might the same reasoning hold that black female critics should interpret black female authors? Hispanic male critics interpret Hispanic male authors?

5. While Halliburton and Gilbert see literature as a kind of embodiment of the author's consciousness, their strategies for describing this consciousness vary considerably. Discuss the differences.

6. Phenomenological critics strive for neutrality, a kind of personal transparency. However, how could May's previous knowledge of Flannery O'Connor's deep commitment to Catholic faith *not* have biased his choice of parables as an interpretive strategy? Is it possible for critics to rid themselves of presuppositions? of ways of understanding words? of personal interest?

7. The privileged position of language, of "the word," is evident in both May's and Moore's hermeneutics. Both would agree that the power of the word interprets its listener rather than vice versa. Yet May asserts that the "word as understood in the New Hermeneutic is radically human," while Moore follows Heidegger's dictum that "the poet names what is holy." Based on your reading of these two essays, do you think Moore and May agree or disagree on what the word reveals?

CHAPTER 3

Archetypal and Genre Criticism

ARCHETYPAL OR MYTH critics—the terms are used interchangeably—
hold that literature is structured by widespread, communal thought patterns (archetypes). These critics differ somewhat, however, about what
these archetypes are, where they come from, and how they function. For
example, literary scholars who draw upon psychologist C. G. Jung's theories believe that archetypes reside in the deepest part of the shared human psyche, the collective unconscious. Since this unconscious acts as a
communal inheritance, even cultures separated by time and space see reality through such patternings as chaos and order, light and dark, sky
father and earth mother, the hero, up and down, the mandala, and
so on. These patterns, then, allow critics to understand the literary discourses of different societies. Jungian critics also explore archetypes in
individual authors' works. As you will see when you read Albert Gelpi's
essay, they use Jung's archetypes of the psyche—persona, soul-mate, and
shadow—to interpret an author's meaning.

Other myth critics turn to culture, not to the psyche, as the locus and
transmitter of archetypal patterns. Drawing on various anthropological
studies, these critics tend to see literature as versions of social practices
or of earlier religious rituals which bond human society to "natural" vegetation cycles. Although Northrop Frye, one of the most influential arche-
typalist critics, does not make this causal connection, he does assert that
the order of words parallels the order of nature. According to Frye, the
order of words is shaped by archetypes—fundamental psychic movements which structure literature into comedy, romance, irony, and tragedy. These archetypal movements, then, can be seen to correspond with
daily and annual natural cycles in this manner: comedy-dawn-spring,
romance-zenith-summer, tragedy-sunset-fall, irony-dark-winter. Frye
uses these organizing concepts to outline a critical system that he hopes
will encompass, and so interrelate, the whole of Western literature.

Like archetypal criticism, genre study classifies literature according to patterns; but instead of thought patterns, genre emphasizes formal or rhetorical ones. Indeed, Northrop Frye's critical theory includes genre as another way of conceiving literature, a way which brings out many relationships that would otherwise go unnoticed. At least as far back as Aristotle, literary artifacts have been classified in overlapping groups according to their forms (e.g., drama, poetry, prose) or to their techniques (e.g., realism, romanticism) or to their subject matter (e.g., westerns, mysteries). Today, these critics, along with their more traditional role of describing the borders between literary kinds explore genres as systems of continual transformation. Thus, genre study might be described as a cross between literary history and general poetics.

Emily Dickinson and the Deerslayer
ALBERT GELPI

Gelpi uses Jungian archetypes, the manifestations of psychic tendencies all humans share, to interrelate Dickinson's individual psyche with cultural patterns. Gelpi maintains that the poet empowered herself poetically by identifying with the masculine aspect of her psyche, what Jung calls the "animus." (Men would identify with their "anima," or feminine aspect.) According to Jungian theory, the psyche's inherited structural components can be thought of as the persona, the anima (or animus), and the shadow—symbolized in melodrama as hero, heroine, and villain. To be an independent, whole person, one must recognize the negative (shadow) as well as the positive parts of oneself. Because Dickinson did, she could align herself with the American pioneer myth—man achieves manhood by confronting and subduing the wilderness (Mother Nature). Gelpi makes further use of archetypal qualities of transpersonality, or universality, to interpret the difficult final quatrain of Dickinson's poem and to set her poetry within the wider social context of nineteenth-century society.

IN NINETEENTH-CENTURY AMERICA there were many women poets—or, I should better say, lady poets—who achieved popular success and quite lucrative publishing careers by filling newspaper columns, gift books, and volumes of verse with the conventional pieties concerning

From *Shakespeare's Sisters: Feminist Essays on Women Poets*, edited with an introduction by Sandra M. Gilbert and Susan Gubar, © 1979 by Sandra M. Gilbert and Susan Gubar. Reprinted by permission of Indiana University Press.

mortality and immortality; most especially they enshrined the domestic role of wife and mother in tending her mortal charges and conveying them to immortality. Mrs. Lydia Sigourney, known as "the Sweet Singer of Hartford," is the type, and Mark Twain's Emmeline Grangerford is the parodic, but barely parodic re-creation. Emily Dickinson was not a lady poet, but she was the only major American woman poet of the nineteenth century—in fact, a poet of such great consequence that any account of women's experience in America must see her as a boldly pioneering and prophetic figure.

In the Dickinson canon the poem which has caused commentators the most consternation over the years is "My Life had stood—a Loaded Gun—." It figures prominently and frequently in *After Great Pain,* John Cody's Freudian biography of Dickinson, and more recently Robert Weisbuch prefaces his explication in *Emily Dickinson's Poetry* with the remark that it is "the single most difficult poem Dickinson wrote," "a riddle to be solved." The poem requires our close attention and, if possible, our unriddling because it is a powerful symbolic enactment of the psychological dilemma facing the intelligent and aware woman, and particularly the woman artist, in partriarchal America. Here is the full text of the poem, number 754 in the Johnson variorum edition,[1] without, for the moment, the variants in the manuscript:

My Life had stood—a Loaded Gun—
In Corners—till a Day
The Owner passed—identified—
And carried Me away—

And now We roam in Sovereign Woods—
And now We hunt the Doe—
And every time I speak for Him—
The Mountains straight reply—

And do I smile, such cordial light
Upon the Valley glow—
It is as a Vesuvian face
Had let its pleasure through—

And when at Night—Our good Day done—
I guard My Master's Head—
'Tis better than the Eider-Duck's
Deep Pillow—to have shared—

To foe of His—I'm deadly foe—
None stir the second time—
On whom I lay a Yellow Eye—
Or an emphatic Thumb—

Though I than He—may longer live
He longer must—than I—
For I have but the power to kill,
Without—the power to die—

Despite the narrative manner, it is no more peopled than the rest of Dickinson's poems, which almost never have more than two figures: the speaker and another, often an anonymous male figure suggestive of a lover or of God or of both. So here: I and "My Master," the "Owner" of my life. Biographers have tried to sift the evidence to identify the "man" in the central drama of the poetry. Three draft-"letters" from the late 1850s and early 1860s, confessing in overwrought language her passionate love for the "Master" and her pain at his rejection, might seem to corroborate the factual basis for the relationship examined in this poem, probably written in 1863. However, as I have argued elsewhere,[2] the fact that biographers have been led to different candidates, with the fragmentary evidence pointing in several directions inconclusively, has deepened my conviction that "he" is not a real human being whom Dickinson knew and loved and lost or renounced, but a psychological presence or factor in her inner life. Nor does the identification of "him" as an image symbolic of certain aspects of her own personality, qualities and needs and potentialities which have been identified culturally and psychologically with the masculine, and which she consequently perceived and experienced as masculine.

Carl Jung called this "masculine" aspect of the woman's psyche her "animus," corresponding to the postulation of an "anima" as the "feminine" aspect of the man's psyche. The anima or animus, first felt as the disturbing presence of the "other" in one's self, thus holds the key to fulfillment and can enable the man or woman to suffer through the initial crisis of alienation and conflict to assimilate the "other" into an integrated identity. In the struggle toward wholeness the animus and the anima come to mediate the whole range of experience for the woman and the man: her and his connection with nature and sexuality on the one hand and with spirit on the other. No wonder that the animus and the anima appear in dreams, myths, fantasies, and works of art as figures at once human and divine, as lover and god. Such a presence is Emily Dickinson's Master and Owner in the poem.

However, for women in a society like ours which enforces the subjection of women in certain assigned roles, the process of growth and integration becomes especially fraught with painful risks and traps and ambivalences. Nevertheless, here, as in many poems, Dickinson sees the chance for fulfillment in her relationship to the animus figure, indeed in her identification with him. Till he came, her life had known only inertia, standing neglected in tight places, caught at the right angles of walls: not just *a* corner, the first lines of the poem tell us, but corners, as though wherever she stood was thereby a constricted place. But all the time she knew that she was something other and more. Paradoxically, she attained her prerogatives through submission to the internalized masculine principle. In the words of the poem, the release of her power depended on her being "carried away"—rapt, "raped"—by her Owner and Master. Moreover, by further turns of the paradox, a surrender of womanhood transformed her into a phallic weapon, and in return his recognition and adoption "identified" her.

Now we can begin to see why the serious fantasy of this poem makes her animus a hunter and woodsman. With instinctive rightness Dickinson's imagination grasps her situation in terms of the major myth of the American experience. The pioneer on the frontier is the version of the universal hero myth indigenous to our specific historical circumstances, and it remains today, even in our industrial society, the mythic mainstay of American individualism. The pioneer claims his manhood by measuring himself against the unfathomed, unfathomable immensity of his elemental world, whose "otherness" he experiences at times as the inhuman, at times as the feminine, at times as the divine—most often as all three at once. His link with landscape, therefore, is a passage into the unknown in his own psyche, the mystery of his unconscious. For the man the anima is the essential point of connection with woman and with deity.

Eric
de Beauvoir

But all too easily, sometimes all too unwittingly, connection—which should move to union—can gradually fall into competition, then contention and conflict. The man who reaches out to Nature to engage his basic physical and spiritual needs finds himself reaching out with the hands of the predator to possess and subdue, to make Nature serve his own ends. From the point of view of Nature, then, or of woman or of the values of the feminine principle the pioneer myth can assume a devastating and tragic significance, as our history has repeatedly demonstrated. Forsaking the institutional structures of patriarchal culture, the woodsman goes out alone, or almost alone, to test whether his mind and will are capable of outwitting the lures and wiles of Nature, her dark children and wild creatures. If he can vanquish her—Mother Nature, Virgin Land—then he can assume or resume his place in society and as boon exact his share of the spoils of Nature and the service of those, including women and the dark-skinned peoples, beneath him in the established order.

In psychosexual terms, therefore, the pioneer's struggle against the wilderness can be seen, from [that] viewpoint, to enact the subjugation of the feminine principle, whose dark mysteries are essential to the realization of personal and social identity but for that reason threaten masculine prerogatives in a patriarchal ordering of individual and social life. The hero fights to establish his ego-identity and assure the linear transmission of the culture which sustains his ego-identity, and he does so by maintaining himself against the encroachment of the Great Mother. Her rhythm is the round of Nature, and her sovereignty is destructive to the independent individual because the continuity of the round requires that she devour her children and absorb their lives and consciousness back into her teeming womb, season after season, generation after generation. So the pioneer who may first have ventured into the woods to discover the otherness which is the clue to identity may in the end find himself maneuvering against the feminine powers, weapon in hand, with mind and will as his ultimate weapons for self-preservation. No longer seeker or lover, he advances as the aggressor, murderer, rapist.

As we have seen, in this poem Emily Dickinson accedes to the "rape," because she longs for the inversion of sexual roles which, from the male point of view, allows a hunter or a soldier to call his phallic weapon by a girl's name and speak of it, even to it, as a woman. Already by the second stanza "I" and "he" have become "We": "And now We roam in Sovreign Woods— / And now We hunt the Doe—," the rhythm and repetition underscoring the momentous change of identity. However, since roaming "in Sovreign Woods—," or, as the variant has it, roaming "the—Sovreign Woods—" is a contest of survival, it issues in bloodshed. "To foe of His— I'm deadly foe," she boasts later, and here their first venture involves hunting the doe. It is important that the female of the deer is specified, for Dickinson's identification of herself with the archetype of the hero in the figure of the woodsman seems to her to necessitate a sacrifice of her womanhood, explicitly the range of personality and experience as sexual and maternal woman. In just a few lines she has converted her "rape" by the man into a hunting-down of Mother Nature's creatures by manly comrades—Natty Bumppo and Chingachgook in *The Last of the Mohicans*, Natty Bumppo and Hurry Harry in *The Deerslayer*.

Nor are we imposing a psychosexual interpretation on the naive innocence of an early Romantic idyll; the implications of the myth are all there in Cooper. Here is the first appearance of Natty and Hurry Harry in Chapter 1 of *The Deerslayer*. They hack their way out of "the tangled labyrinth" of the Great Mother's maw or belly. The description acknowledges the awesome solemnity of the "eternal round" of the Great Mother's economy but acknowledges as well the threat to the individual snared in her dark and faceless recesses and unable to cut his way free. Initially there is no sign of human life; then from her timeless and undifferentiated "depths" emerge first two separate voices "calling to each other" and at last two men, "liberated" and "escaped" into lighted space where they can breathe. The passage reads:

> Whatever may be the changes produced by man, the eternal round of the seasons is unbroken. Summer and winter, seed-time and harvest, return in their stated order, with a sublime precision, affording to man one of the noblest of all the occasions he enjoys of proving the high powers of his far-reaching mind, in compassing the laws that control their exact uniformity, and in calculating their never-ending revolutions. Centuries of summer suns had warmed the tops of the same noble oaks and pines, sending their heats even to the tenacious roots, when voices were heard calling to each other in the depths of the forest, of which the leafy surface lay bathed in the brilliant light of a cloudless day in June, while the trunks of the trees rose in gloomy grandeur in the shades beneath. The calls were in different tones, evidently pro-

ceeding from two men who had lost their way, and were searching in different directions for their path. At length a shout proclaimed success, and presently a man of gigantic mould broke out of the tangled labyrinth of a small swamp, emerging into an opening that appeared to have been formed partly by the ravages of the wind, and partly by those of fire. This little area, which afforded a good view of the sky, although it was pretty well filled with dead trees, lay on the side of one of the high hills, or few mountains, into which nearly the whole of the adjacent country was broken.

"Here is room to breathe in!" exclaimed the liberated forester, as soon as he found himself under a clear sky, shaking his huge frame like a mastiff that had just escaped from a snow-bank. "Hurray, Deerslayer, here is daylight at last, and yonder is the lake."

Man "proves" "the high powers of his far-reaching mind" by "compassing" and "calculating" (that is, by comprehending and thus holding within bounds in the mind) the cycle of generation. From an elevated perspective above the woods "the brilliant light of a cloudless day in June" may grace "the leafy surface," but "in the shades beneath," where the men "had lost their way," was the oppressive gloom of the tree-trunks and "the tenacious roots." The two "gigantic" men emerge into an area cleared by wind and fire, the lighter and more spiritual elements, from the "small swamp," compounded of mud and water, the heavier elements conventionally associated with the feminine matrix.

True to the archetypal meaning of the situation, the first conversation between Hurry Harry and Natty turns on the question of proving one's manhood. The immediate victim is the doe, slain by Natty's rifle, Killdeer, but soon the real contention becomes clear. As the moral and sensitive woodsman, Natty finds himself defending his brother Delawares, arguing with the coarse Hurry Harry that they are not "women," as Hurry charges, but "heroes," despite the fact that they are dark children of the Great Mother. The conversation begins as follows:

"Come, Deerslayer, fall to, and prove that you have a Delaware stomach, as you say you have had a Delaware edication," cried Hurry, setting the example by opening his mouth to receive a slice of cold venison steak that would have made an entire meal for a European peasant; "fall to, lad, and prove your manhood on this poor devil of a doe, with your teeth, as you've already done with your rifle."

"Nay, nay, Hurry, there's little manhood in killing a doe, and that too out of season; though there might be some in bringing down a painter or a catamount," returned the other, disposing himself to comply. "The Delawares have given me my name, not so much on account of a bold heart, as on account of a quick eye and an actyve foot. There may not be any cowardyce in overcoming a deer, but, sartin it is, there's no great valor."

"The Delawares themselves are no heroes," muttered Hurry through his teeth, the mouth being too full to permit it to be fairly opened, "or they never would have allowed them loping vagabonds, the Mingoes, to make them women."

"That matter is not rightly understood—has never been rightly explained," said Deerslayer, earnestly, for he was as zealous a friend as his companion was dangerous as an enemy; "the Mengwe fill the woods with their lies, and misconstruct words and treaties. I have now lived ten years with the Delawares, and know them to be as manful as any other nation, when the proper time to strike comes."

"Harkee, Master Deerslayer, since we are on the subject, we may as well open our minds to each other in a man-to-man way; answer me one question: you have had so much luck among the game as to have gotten a title, it would seem; but did you ever hit anything human or intelligible? Did you ever pull trigger on an inimy that was capable of pulling one upon you?"

Not yet; but the subtitle of the book is *The First War-Path,* and in the course of the action Natty spills human blood for the first time, all of it Indian. Natty may be a doeslayer with a difference, but even his unique combination of the best qualities of civilization and nature does not exempt him from the conflicts and contradictions of the pioneer myth. Though a man of the woods, roaming the realm of the Great Mother, he must remain unspotted from complicity with her dark and terrible aspect, just as his manhood has to be kept inviolate from the advances of Judith Hutter, the dark and sullied beauty in *The Deerslayer,* and from his own attraction to Mabel Dunham in *The Pathfinder.*

In the psychological context of this archetypal struggle Emily Dickinson joins in the killing of the doe without a murmur of pity or regret; she wants the independence of will and the power of mind which her allegiance with the woodsman makes possible. Specifically, engagement with the animus unlocks her artistic creativity; through his inspiration and mastery she becomes a poet. The variant for "power" in the last line is "art," and the irresistible force of the rifle's muzzle-flash and of the bullet are rendered metaphorically in terms of the artist's physiognomy: his blazing countenance ("Vesuvian face"), his vision ("Yellow Eye"), his shaping hand ("emphatic Thumb"), his responsive heart ("cordial light"). So it is that when the hunter fires the rifle, "I speak for Him—." Without his initiating pressure on the trigger, there would be no incandescence; but without her as seer and craftsman there would be no art. From their conjunction issues the poem's voice, reverberant enough to make silent nature echo with her words.

In Hebrew the word "prophet" means to "speak for." The prophet translates the wordless meanings of the god into human language. Whitman defined the prophetic function of the poet in precisely these terms: "it means one whose mind bubbles up and pours forth as a fountain from inner, divine spontaneities revealing God. . . . The great matter is to reveal and outpour the God-like suggestions pressing for birth in the soul."[3] Just as in the male poetic tradition such divine inspiration is characteristically experienced as mediated through the anima and imaged as the poet's muse, so in this poem the animus figure functions as Dickinson's masculine muse. Where Whitman experiences inspiration as the gushing flux of the Great Mother, Dickinson experiences it as the Olympian fire: the gun-blast and Vesuvius. In several poems Dickinson depicts herself as a smoldering volcano, the god's fire flaring in the bosom of the female landscape. In her first conversation with the critic Thomas Wentworth Higginson, Dickinson remarked: "If I feel physically as if the top of my head were taken off, I know *that* is poetry. . . . Is there any other way."[4]

But why is the creative faculty also destructive, Eros inseparable from Thanatos? To begin with, for a woman like Dickinson, choosing to be an artist could seem to require denying essential aspects of herself and relinquishing experience as lover, wife, and mother. From other poems we know Dickinson's painfully, sometimes excruciatingly divided attitude toward her womanhood, but here under the spell of the animus muse she does not waver in the sacrifice. Having spilled the doe's blood during the day's hunt, she stations herself for the night ("Our good Day done—") as stiff, soldierly guard at "My Master's Head," scorning to enter the Master's bed and sink softly into "the Eider-duck's / Deep Pillow." Her rejection of the conventional sexual and domestic role expected of women is further underscored by the fact that the variant for "Deep" is "low" ("the Eider-Duck's / Low Pillow") and by the fact that the eiderduck is known not merely for the quality of her down but for lining her nest by plucking the feathers from her own breast. No such "female masochism" for this doeslayer; she is "foe" to "foe of His," the rhyme with "doe" effecting the grim inversion.

Moreover, compounding the woman's alternatives, which exact part of herself no matter how she chooses, stands the essential paradox of art: that the artist kills experience into art, for temporal experience can only escape death by dying into the "immortality" of artistic form. The fixity of "life" in art and the fluidity of "life" in nature are incompatible. So no matter what the sex of the deer, it must be remade in the artist's medium; the words of the poem preserve the doe and the buck in an image of their mortality. These ironies have always fascinated and chilled artists. Is the vital passion of the youthful lovers on Keats's "Grecian Urn" death or immortality? In Eudora Welty's "A Still Moment" Audubon shoots the exquisite white bird so that he can paint it. In John Crowe Ransom's "Painted Head" the artist betrays the young man he has painted by shrinking him into an image. It seems a death's head now, yet this painted head of a now-dead man radiates unaltered health and happiness. No wonder Audubon is willing to shoot the bird. No wonder a poet like Emily Dickinson will surrender to painful self-sacrifice. The loss of a certain range of experience might allow her to preserve what remained; that sacrifice might well be her apotheosis, the only salvation she might know.

Both the poet's relation to her muse and the living death of the art-work lead into the runic riddle of the last quatrain. It is actually a double riddle, each two lines long connected by the conjunction "for" and by the rhyme:

> Though I than He—may longer live
> He longer must—than I—
> For I have but the power to kill,
> Without—the power to die—

In the first rune, why is it that she *may* live longer than he but he *must* live longer than she? The poet lives on past the moment in which she is a vessel or instrument in the hands of the creative animus for two rea-sons—first, because her temporal life resumes when she is returned to one of life's corners, a waiting but loaded gun again, but also because on another level she surpasses momentary possession by the animus in the poem she has created under his inspiration. At the same time, he *must* transcend her temporal life and even its artifacts because, as the arche-typal source of inspiration, the animus is, relative to the individual, transpersonal and so in a sense "immortal."

The second rune extends the paradox of the poet's mortality and survival. The lines begin to unravel and reveal themselves if we read the phrase "Without—the power to die—" not as "lacking the power to die" but rather as "except for the power to die," "unless I had the power to die." The lines would then read: unless she were mortal, if she did not have the power to die, she would have only the power to kill. And when we straighten out the grammatical construction of a condition-contrary-to-fact to conform with fact, we come closer to the meaning: with mor-tality, if she does have the power to die—as indeed she does—she would not have only the power to kill. What else or what more would she then have? There are two clues. First, the variant of "art" for "power" in the last line links "the power to die," mortality, all the more closely with "the power to kill," the artistic process. In addition, the causal conjunction "for" relates the capacity for death in the second rune back to the capac-ity for life in the first rune. Thus, for her the power to die is resolved in the artist's power to kill, whereby she dies into the hypostasized work of art. The animus muse enables her to fix the dying moment, but it is only her human capabilities, working in time with language, which are able to translate the fixed moment into the words on the page. The artistic act is, therefore, not just destructive but in the end self-creative. In a myste-rious way the craftsmanship of the doomed artist recues her exalted mo-ments from oblivion and extends destiny beyond "dying" and "killing."

Now we can grasp the two runes together. The poet's living and dying permit her to be an artist; impelled by the animus, she is empowered to kill experience and slay herself into art. Having suffered mortality, she "dies into life," as Keats's phrase in *Hyperion* has it; virgin as the Grecian urn and the passionate figures on it, her poetic self outlasts temporal process and those climactic instants of animus possession, even though in the process of experience she knows him as a free spirit independent of her and transcendent of her poems. In different ways, therefore, each survives the other: she mortal in her person but timeless in her poems, he transpersonal as an archetype but dependent on her transitory experience of him to manifest himself. The interdependence through which she "speaks for" him as his human voice makes both for her dependence and limitations and also for her triumph over dependence and limitation.

Nevertheless, "My Life had stood—a Loaded Gun—" leaves no doubt that a woman in a patriarchal society achieves that triumph through a blood sacrifice. The poem presents the alternatives unsparingly: be the hunter or the doe. She can refuse to be a victim by casting her lot with the hunter, but thereby she claims herself as victim. By the rules of the hunter's game, there seems no escape for the woman in the woods. Emily Dickinson's sense of conflict within herself and about herself could lead her to such a desperate and ghastly fantasy as the following lines from poem 1737:

> Rearrange a "Wife's" affection!
> When they dislocate my Brain!
> Amputate my freckled Bosom!
> Make me bearded like a man!

The violent, exclamatory self-mutilation indicates how far we have come from the pieties of Mrs. Sigourney and her sisters.

Fortunately for Dickinson the alternatives did not always seem so categorical. Some of her most energetic and ecstatic poems—those supreme moments which redeemed the travail and anguish—celebrate her experience of her womanhood. The vigor of these dense lyrics matches in depth and conviction Whitman's sprawling, public celebration of his manhood. At such times she saw her identity not as a denial of her feminine nature in the name of the animus but as an assimilation of the animus into an integrated self. In that way "he" is not a threat but a force—and a source. As part of herself, "he" initiates her into the mysteries of experience which would otherwise remain "other"; "his" mind and will summon her to consciousness—not the fullness of manhood but the completion of her womanhood. There, in the privacy of her psyche, withdrawn from the world of men and even of family, she would live out all the extremes of feeling and response, all the states of mind which fall under the usual rubrics of love, death, and immortality.

Poem 508, probably composed a year or so before "My Life had stood—a Loaded Gun—," describes her psychological metamorphosis in terms of two baptisms which conferred name and identity: the first the sacramental baptism in the patriarchal church when she was an unknowing and helpless baby; the second a self-baptism into areas of personality conventionally associated with the masculine, an act of choice and will undertaken in full consciousness, or, perhaps more accurately, into full consciousness. Since Emily Dickinson was not a member of the church and had never been baptized as child or adult, the baptism is a metaphor for marking stages and transitions in self-awareness and identity. The poem is not a love poem or a religious poem, as its first editors thought in 1890, but a poem of sexual or psychological politics enacted in the convolutions of the psyche:

> I'm ceded—I've stopped being Their's—
> The name They dropped upon my face
> With water, in the country church
> Is finished using, now,
> And They can put it with my Dolls,
> My childhood, and the string of spools,
> I've finished threading—too—
>
> Baptized, before, without the choice,
> But this time, consciously, of Grace—
> Unto supremest name—
> Called to my Full—The Crescent dropped—
> Existence's whole Arc, filled up,
> With one small Diadem.
>
> My second Rank—too small the first—
> Crowned—Crowing—on my Father's breast—
> A half unconscious Queen—
> But this time—Adequate—Erect,
> With Will to choose, or to reject,
> And I choose, just a Crown—

Some of the manuscript variants emphasize the difference between the two states of being. The variants for "Crowing" in "Crowned—Crowing—on my Father's breast—" are "whimpering" and "dangling," as contrasted with "Adequate" and "Erect" later. The variants in the phrase "A half unconscious Queen—" are "too unconscious" and "insufficient." As the poet comes to consciousness in the second and third stanzas, she assumes, as in the previous poem, something of the phallicism and privileges of the masculine. "Power" is the variant for "Will" in the second-to-last line, but now the power of will is the Queen's. She has displaced the Father, the crown he conferred replaced by her round diadem; she calls herself by her "supremest name."

Dickinson wrote several "Wife" poems on the same theme. Poem

199, written a little earlier than the one above, probably in 1860, sums the situation up:

> I'm "wife"—I've finished that—
> That other state—
> I'm Czar—I'm "Woman" now—
> It's safer so—
>
> How odd the Girl's life looks
> Behind this soft Eclipse—
> I think that Earth feels so
> To folks in Heaven—now—
>
> This being comfort—then
> That other kind—was pain—
> But why compare?
> I'm "Wife"! Stop there!

The passage from virgin girlhood to "wife" and "Woman" is again accomplished through the powerful agency of the animus, in this poem the "Czar." The "wife" and "Czar" couple into the androgynous completion of her woman's Self. However, for Dickinson it is a womanhood reached at heavy cost, a wifehood consummated on peculiarly private terms withdrawn from the risks and dangers of contact with actual men in a man-dominated culture. Only alone and in secret could this royal pair wed and be joined in the hierogamy, or mystic marriage, of identity. As the poem warns us, "It's safer so—."

Until recently, women poets since Emily Dickinson have found themselves caught in the same quandary, and, in exchange for more public recognition, have chosen to repress the "feminine" or the "masculine" aspects of themselves. Some, such as Marianne Moore and Elizabeth Bishop, tended to obscure or deflect passion and sexuality in favor of fine discriminations of perceptions and ideas. Others, such as Edna St. Vincent Millay and Elinor Wylie, took as their woman's strain precisely the thrill of emotion and tremor of sensibility which rendered them susceptible to the threats of the masculine "other." In the isolation of her upstairs bedroom, Emily Dickinson refused finally to make that choice; but in the first half of the century perhaps only H.D., especially in the great poems and sequences of her old age, committed head and heart, sexuality and spirit to the exploration of her womanhood: a venture perhaps made possible only through an expatriation from American society more complete than Gertrude Stein's or Eliot's or Pound's. During the last decade or two, however, in the work of poets as different as Sylvia Plath and Denise Levertov, Muriel Rukeyser and Robin Morgan and Jean Valentine, and most importantly, I think, in the work of Adrienne Rich, women have begun exploring that mystery, their own mystery, with a new sense of calling and community. Sometimes ecstatically, sometimes angrily, sometimes in great agony of body and spirit, but always now with the sustaining knowledge that they are not living and working alone, that more and more women and a growing number of men are hearing what they say, listening to them and with them. Such a realization makes a transforming and clarifying difference in the contemporary scene. And it is an important aspect of Emily Dickinson's enormous achievement that she pursued the process of exploration so far and so long on her own.

NOTES

1. *The Poems of Emily Dickinson*, ed. Thomas H. Johnson (Cambridge, Mass.: Harvard University Press, Belknap Press, 1955).

2. Albert Gelpi, *The Tenth Muse: The Psyche of the American Poet* (Cambridge, Mass.: Harvard University Press, 1975), 247ff.; see also Albert Gelpi, *Emily Dickinson: The Mind of the Poet* Cambridge, Mass.: Harvard University Press, 1965), 109–15.

3. *Prose Works 1892*, ed. Floyd Stovall (New York: New York University Press, 1963), 1:250.

4. *The Letters of Emily Dickinson*, ed. Thomas H. Johnson and Theodora Ward (Cambridge, Mass.: Harvard University Press, 1958), 2:474. For volcano poems, see *Poems*, 3:1141, 1153, and 1174.

The Archetypes of Literature

NORTHROP FRYE

Northrop Frye attempts to provide a self-conscious critical system which can coherently order the whole body of literary and critical knowledge. Frye's "new poetics" contests the New Critical assertion that criticism is a second-rate discourse, a transparent parasite on the first-rate discourse of literature. Frye contends instead that literature is an object and that whenever we talk, teach, or critique literature we always do so from a point of view; we never "innocently" interpret literature as the New Critics suppose. Our interpretation is always a form of criticism. What we need then, Frye contends, is a theoretical understanding of the various critical approaches we use in discussing literature.

Frye, in his *Anatomy of Criticism* (1957), classifies these approaches as historical, ethical, archetypal, and rhetorical. As a pluralist, Frye holds that different interpretations are inevitable since we each 'see' from different positions. He gives this example. When we stand close to a painting, we notice its brush strokes (rhetorical criticism), but when we stand far off we see the overall structural patterns (archetypal criticism). Frye himself stands far enough back to view the whole of literature simultaneously; he sees a self-contained verbal structure, a product of civilization, embodying "the total dream of man."

According to Frye, the critic should describe and account for this verbal structure, not evaluate it. To help accomplish this scientific task, Frye supplies us with various analytical tools, one of which is archetypal criticism with its theory of "mythos." The "mythos" is the narrative or plot form (comic, romantic, tragic, and ironic) of the four archetypal movements. As we saw above, these four archetypal patterns correspond to the natural daily and yearly cycles (comedy-dawn-spring, romance-zenith-summer, and so on). When you read the following essay, you will note that romance, not comedy, is allied with dawn and spring. In his later expanded version of this essay in *Anatomy of Criticism,* Frye switches this order and parallels comedy with spring, romance with summer. The shift causes few major changes in Frye's schema. The switch does, however, emphasize the centrality of the romance genre with its mythos of the hero a-quest in the land of heart's desire.

EVERY ORGANIZED BODY OF KNOWLEDGE can be learned progressively; and experience shows that there is also something progressive about the learning of literature. Our opening sentence has already got us into a semantic difficulty. Physics is an organized body of knowledge about nature, and a student of it says that he is learning physics, not that he is learning nature. Art, like nature, is the subject of a systematic study, and has to be distinguished from the study itself, which is criticism. It is therefore impossible to "learn literature": one learns about it in a certain way, but what one learns, transitively, is the criticism of literature. Similarly, the difficulty often felt in "teaching literature" arises from the fact that it cannot be done: the criticism of literature is all that can be directly taught. So while no one expects literature itself to behave like a science, there is surely no reason why criticism, as a systematic and organized study, should not be, at least partly, a science. Not a "pure" or "exact" science, perhaps, but these phrases form part of a nineteenth century cosmology which is no longer with us. Criticism deals with the arts and may well be something of an art itself, but it does not follow that it must be unsystematic. If it is to be related to the sciences too, it does not follow that it must be deprived of the graces of culture.

Certainly criticism as we find it in learned journals and scholarly monographs has every characteristic of a science. Evidence is examined scientifically; previous authorities are used scientifically; fields are investigated scientifically; texts are edited scientifically. Prosody is scientific in structure; so is phonetics; so is philology. And yet in studying this kind of critical science the student becomes aware of a centrifugal movement carrying him away from literature. He finds that literature is the central division of the "humanities," flanked on one side by history and on the other by philosophy. Criticism so far ranks only as a subdivision of literature; and hence, for the systematic mental organization of the subject, the student has to turn to the conceptual framework of the historian for events, and to that of the philosopher for ideas. Even the more centrally placed critical sciences, such as textual editing, seem to be part of a "background" that recedes into history or some other non-literary field. The thought suggests itself that the ancillary critical disciplines may be related to a central expanding pattern of systematic comprehension which has not yet been established, but which, if it were established, would prevent them from being centrifugal. If such a pattern exists, then criticism would be to art what philosophy is to wisdom and history to action.

Most of the central area of criticism is at present, and doubtless always will be, the area of commentary. But the commentators have little sense, unlike the researchers, of being contained within some sort of scientific discipline: they are chiefly engaged, in the words of the gospel hymn, in brightening the corner where they are. If we attempt to get a more comprehensive idea of what criticism is about, we find ourselves wandering over quaking bogs of generalities, judicious pronouncements of value, reflective comments, perorations to works of research, and other consequences of taking the large view. But this part of the critical field is so full of pseudo-propositions, sonorous nonsense that contains no truth and no falsehood, that it obviously exists only because criticism, like nature, prefers a waste space to an empty one.

The term "pseudo-proposition" may imply some sort of logical positivist attitude on my own part. But I would not confuse the significant proposition with the factual one; nor should I consider it advisable to muddle the study of literature with a schizophrenic dichotomy between subjective-emotional and objective-descriptive aspects of meaning, considering that in order to produce any literary meaning at all one has to ignore this dichotomy. I say only that the principles by which one can distinguish a significant from a meaningless statement in criticism are not clearly defined. Our first step, therefore, is to recognize and get rid of meaningless criticism: that is, talking about literature in a way that cannot help to build up a systematic structure of knowledge. Casual value-judgments belong not to criticism but to the history of taste, and reflect, at best, only the social and psychological compulsions which prompted their utterance. All judgments in which the values are not based on literary experience but are sentimental or derived from religious or political prejudice may be regarded as casual. Sentimental judgments are usually based either on non-existent categories or antitheses ("Shakespeare studied life, Milton books") or on a visceral reaction to the writer's personality. The literary chit-chat which makes the reputations of poets boom and crash in an imaginary stock exchange is pseudo-criticism. That wealthy investor Mr. Eliot, after dumping Milton on the market, is now buying him again; Donne has probably reached his peak and will begin to taper off; Tennyson may be in for a slight flutter but the Shelley stocks are still bearish. This sort of thing cannot be part of any systematic study, for a systematic study can only progress: whatever dithers or vacillates or reacts is merely leisure-class conversation.

We next meet a more serious group of critics who say: the foreground of criticism is the impact of literature on the reader. Let us, then, keep the study of literature centripetal, and base the learning process on a structural analysis of the literary work itself. The texture of any great work of art is complex and ambiguous, and in unravelling the complexities we may take in as much history and philosophy as we please, if the subject of our study remains at the center. If it does not, we may find that in our anxiety to write about literature we have forgotten how to read it.

The only weakness in this approach is that it is conceived primarily as the antithesis of centrifugal or "background" criticism, and so lands us in a somewhat unreal dilemma, like the conflict of internal and external relations in philosophy. Antitheses are usually resolved, not by picking one side and refuting the other, or by making eclectic choices between them, but by trying to get past the antithetical way of stating the problem. It is right that the first effort of critical apprehension should take the form of a rhetorical or structural analysis of a work of art. But a purely structural approach has the same limitation in criticism that it has in biology. In itself it is simply a discrete series of analyses based on the mere existence of the literary structure, without developing any explanation of how the structure came to be what it was and what its nearest relatives are. Structural analysis brings rhetoric back to criticism, but we need a new poetics as well, and the attempt to construct a new poetics out of rhetoric alone can hardly avoid a mere complication of rhetorical terms into a sterile jargon. I suggest that what is at present missing from literary criticism is a coordinating principle, a central hypothesis which, like the theory of evolution in biology, will see the phenomena it deals with as parts of a whole. Such a principle, though it would retain the centripetal perspective of structural analysis, would try to give the same perspective to other kinds of criticism too.

The first postulate of this hypothesis is the same as that of any science: the assumption of total coherence. The assumption refers to the science, not to what it deals with. A belief in an order of nature is an inference from the intelligibility of the natural sciences; and if the natural sciences ever completely demonstrated the order of nature they would presumably exhaust their subject. Criticism, as a science, is totally intelligible; literature, as the subject of a science, is so far as we know, an inexhaustible source of new critical discoveries, and would be even if new works of literature ceased to be written. If so, then the search for a limiting principle in literature in order to discourage the development of criticism is mistaken. The assertion that the critic should not look for more in a poem than the poet may safely be assumed to have been conscious of putting there is a common form of what may be called the fallacy of premature teleology. It corresponds to the assertion that a natural phenomenon is as it is because Providence in its inscrutable wisdom made it so.

Simple as the assumption appears, it takes a long time for a science to discover that it is in fact a totally intelligible body of knowledge. Until it makes this discovery it has not been born as an individual science, but remains an embryo within the body of some other subject. The birth of physics from "natural philosophy" and of sociology from "moral philosophy" will illustrate the process. It is also very approximately true that the modern sciences have developed in the order of their closeness to mathematics. Thus physics and astronomy assumed their modern form in the Renaissance, chemistry in the eighteenth century, biology in the nineteenth and the social sciences in the twentieth. If systematic criticism, then, is developing only in our day, the fact is at least not an anachronism.

We are now looking for classifying principles lying in an area between two points that we have fixed. The first of these is the preliminary effort of criticism, the structural analysis of the work of art. The second is the assumption that there is such a subject as criticism, and that it makes, or could make, complete sense. We may next proceed inductively from structural analysis, associating the data we collect and trying to see larger patterns in them. Or we may proceed deductively, with the consequences that follow from postulating the unity of criticism. It is clear, of course, that neither procedure will work indefinitely without correction from the other. Pure induction will get us lost in haphazard guessing; pure deduction will lead to inflexible and over-simplified pigeon-holing. Let us now attempt a few tentative steps in each direction, beginning with the inductive one.

II

The unity of a work of art, the basis of structural analysis, has not been produced solely by the unconditioned will of the artist, for the artist is only its efficient cause: it has form, and consequently a formal cause. The fact that revision is possible, that the poet makes changes not because he likes them better but because they are better, means that poems, like poets, are born and not made. The poet's task is to deliver the poem in as uninjured a state as possible, and if the poem is alive, it is equally anxious to be rid of him, and screams to be cut loose from his private memories and associations, his desire for self-expression, and all the other navel-strings and feeding tubes of his ego. The critic takes over where the poet leaves off, and criticism can hardly do without a kind of literary psychology connecting the poet with the poem. Part of this may be a psychological study of the poet, though this is useful chiefly in analysing the failures in his expression, the things in him which are still attached to his work. More important is the fact that every poet has his private mythology, his own spectroscopic band or peculiar formation of symbols, of much of which he is quite unconscious. In works with characters of their own, such as dramas and novels, the same psychological analysis may be extended to the interplay of characters, though of course literary psychology would analyse the behavior of such characters only in relation to literary convention.

There is still before us the problem of the formal cause of the poem, a problem deeply involved with the question of genres. We cannot say much about genres, for criticism does not know much about them. A good many critical efforts to grapple with such words as "novel" or "epic" are chiefly interesting as examples of the psychology of rumor. Two conceptions of the genre, however, are obviously fallacious, and as they are opposite extremes, the truth must lie somewhere between them. One is the pseudo-Platonic conception of genres as existing prior to and independently of creation, which confuses them with mere conventions of form like the sonnet. The other is that pseudo-biological conception of them as evolving species which turns up in so many surveys of the "development" of this or that form.

We next inquire for the origin of the genre, and turn first of all to the social conditions and cultural demands which produced it—in other words to the material cause of the work of art. This leads us into literary history, which differs from ordinary history in that its containing categories, "Gothic," "Baroque," "Romantic," and the like are cultural categories, of little use to the ordinary historian. Most literary history does not get as far as these categories, but even so we know more about it than about most kinds of critical scholarship. The historian treats literature and philosophy historically; the philosopher treats history and literature philosophically; and the so-called history of ideas approach marks the beginning of an attempt to treat history and philosophy from the point of view of an autonomous criticism.

But still we feel that there is something missing. We say that every poet has his own peculiar formation of images. But when so many poets use so many of the same images, surely there are much bigger critical problems involved than biographical ones. As Mr. Auden's brilliant essay *The Enchaféd Flood* shows, an important symbol like the sea cannot remain within the poetry of Shelley or Keats or Coleridge: it is bound to expand over many poets into an archetypal symbol of literature. And if the genre has a historical origin, why does the genre of drama emerge from medieval religion in a way so strikingly similar to the way it emerged from Greek religion centuries before? This is a problem of structure rather than origin, and suggests that there may be archetypes of genres as well as of images.

It is clear that criticism cannot be systematic unless there is a quality in literature which enables it to be so, an order of words corresponding to the order of nature in the natural sciences. An archetype should be not only a unifying category of criticism, but itself a part of a total form, and it leads us at once to the question of what sort of total form criticism can see in literature. Our survey of critical techniques has taken us as far as literary history. Total literary history moves from the primitive to the sophisticated, and here we glimpse the possibility of seeing literature as a complication of a relatively restricted and simple group of formulas that can be studied in primitive culture. If so, then the search for archetypes is a kind of literary anthropology, concerned with the way that literature is informed by pre-literary categories such as ritual, myth and folk tale. We next realize that the relation between these categories and literature is by no means purely one of descent, as we find them reappearing in the greatest classics—in fact there seems to be a general tendency on the part of great classics to revert to them. This coincides with a feeling that we have all had: that the study of mediocre works of art, however energetic, obstinately remains a random and peripheral form of critical experience, whereas the profound masterpiece seems to draw us to a point at which we can see an enormous number of converging patterns of significance. Here we begin to wonder if we cannot see literature, not only as complicating itself in time, but as spread out in conceptual space from some unseen center.

This inductive movement towards the archetype is a process of backing up, as it were, from structural analysis, as we back up from a painting if we want to see composition instead of brushwork. In the foreground of the grave-digger scene in *Hamlet,* for instance, is an intricate verbal texture, ranging from the puns of the first clown to the danse macabre of the Yorick soliloquy, which we study in the printed text. One step back, and we are in the Wilson Knight and Spurgeon group of critics, listening to the steady rain of images of corruption and decay. Here too, as the sense of the place of this scene in the whole play begins to dawn on us, we are in the network of psychological relationships which were the main interest of Bradley. But after all, we say, we are forgetting the genre: *Hamlet* is a play, and an Elizabethan play. So we take another step back into the Stoll and Shaw group and see the scene conventionally as part of its dramatic context. One step more, and we can begin to glimpse the archetype of the scene, as the hero's *Liebestod* and first unequivocal declaration of his love, his struggle with Laertes and the sealing of his own fate, and the sudden sobering of his mood that marks the transition to the final scene, all take shape around a leap into and return from the grave that has so weirdly yawned open on the stage.

At each stage of understanding this scene we are dependent on a certain kind of scholarly organization. We need first an editor to clean up the text for us, then the rhetorician and philologist, then the literary psychologist. We cannot study the genre without the help of the literary social historian, the literary philosopher and the student of the "history of ideas," and for the archetype we need a literary anthropologist. But now that we have got our central pattern of criticism established, all these interests are seen as converging on literary criticism instead of receding from it into psychology and history and the rest. In particular, the literary anthropologist who chases the source of the Hamlet legend from the pre-Shakespeare play to Saxo, and from Saxo to nature-myths, is not running away from Shakespeare: he is drawing closer to the archetypal form which Shakespeare recreated. A minor result of our new perspective is that contradictions among critics, and assertions that this and not that critical approach is the right one, show a remarkable tendency to dissolve into unreality. Let us now see what we can get from the deductive end.

III

Some arts move in time, like music; others are presented in space, like painting. In both cases the organizing principle is recurrence, which is called rhythm when it is temporal and pattern when it is spatial. Thus we speak of the rhythm of music and the pattern of painting; but later, to show off our sophistication, we may begin to speak of the rhythm of painting and the pattern of music. In other words, all arts may be conceived both temporally and spatially. The score of a musical composition may be studied all at once; a picture may be seen as the track of an intricate dance of the eye. Literature seems to be intermediate between music and painting: its words form rhythms which approach a musical sequence of sounds at one of its boundaries, and form patterns which approach the hieroglyphic or pictorial image at the other. The attempts to get as near to these boundaries as possible form the main body of what is called experimental writing. We may call the rhythm of literature the narrative, and the pattern, the simultaneous mental grasp of the verbal structure, the meaning or significance. We hear or listen to a narrative, but when we grasp a writer's total pattern we "see" what he means.

The criticism of literature is much more hampered by the representational fallacy than even the criticism of painting. That is why we are apt to think of narrative as a sequential representation of events in an outside "life," and of meaning as a reflection of some external "idea." Properly used as critical terms, an author's narrative is his linear movement; his meaning is the integrity of his completed form. Similarly an image is not merely a verbal replica of an external object, but any unit of a verbal structure seen as part of a total pattern or rhythm. Even the letters an author spells his words with form part of his imagery, though only in special cases (such as alliteration) would they call for critical notice. Narrative and meaning thus become respectively, to borrow musical terms, the melodic and harmonic contexts of the imagery.

Rhythm, or recurrent movement, is deeply founded on the natural cycle, and everything in nature that we think of as having some analogy with works of art, like the flower or the bird's song, grows out of a profound synchronization between an organism and the rhythms of its environment, especially that of the solar year. With animals some expressions of synchronization, like the mating dances of birds, could almost be called rituals. But in human life a ritual seems to be something of a voluntary effort (hence the magical element in it) to recapture a lost rapport with the natural cycle. A farmer must harvest his crop at a certain time of year, but because this is involuntary, harvesting itself is not precisely a ritual. It is the deliberate expression of a will to synchronize human and natural energies at that time which produces the harvest songs, harvest sacrifices and harvest folk customs that we call rituals. In ritual, then, we may find the origin of narrative, a ritual being a temporal sequence of acts in which the conscious meaning or significance is latent: it can be seen by an observer, but is largely concealed from the participators themselves. The pull of ritual is toward pure narrative, which, if there could be such a thing, would be automatic and unconscious repetition. We should notice too the regular tendency of ritual to become encyclopedic. All the important recurrences in nature, the day, the phases of the moon, the seasons and solstices of the year, the crises of existence from birth to death, get rituals attached to them, and most of the higher religions are equipped with a definitive total body of rituals suggestive, if we may put it so, of the entire range of potentially significant actions in human life.

Patterns of imagery, on the other hand, or fragments of significance, are oracular in origin, and derive from the epiphanic moment, the flash of instantaneous comprehension with no direct reference to time, the importance of which is indicated by Cassirer in *Myth and Language*. By the time we get them, in the form of proverbs, riddles, commandments and etiological folk tales, there is already a considerable element of narrative in them. They too are encyclopedic in tendency, building up a total structure of significance, or doctrine, from random and empiric fragments. And just as pure narrative would be unconscious act, so pure significance would be an incommunicable state of consciousness, for communication begins by constructing narrative.

The myth is the central informing power that gives archetypal significance to the ritual and archetypal narrative to the oracle. Hence the myth *is* the archetype, though it might be convenient to say myth only when referring to narrative, and archetype when speaking of significance. In the solar cycle of the day, the seasonal cycle of the year, and the organic cycle of human life, there is a single pattern of significance, out of which myth constructs a central narrative around a figure who is partly the sun, partly vegetative fertility and partly a god or archetypal human being. The crucial importance of this myth has been forced on literary critics by Jung and Frazer in particular, but the several books now available on it are not always systematic in their approach, for which reason I supply the following table of its phases:

1. The dawn, spring and birth phase. Myths of the birth of the hero, of revival and resurrection, of creation and (because the four phases are a cycle) of the defeat of the powers of darkness, winter and death. Subordinate characters: the father and the mother. The archetype of romance and of most dithyrambic and rhapsodic poetry.

2. The zenith, summer, and marriage or triumph phase. Myths of apotheosis, of the sacred marriage, and of entering into Paradise. Subordinate characters: the companion and the bride. The archetype of comedy, pastoral and idyll.

3. The sunset, autumn and death phase. Myths of fall, of the dying god, of violent death and sacrifice and of the isolation of the hero. Subordinate characters: the traitor and the siren. The archetype of tragedy and elegy.

4. The darkness, winter and dissolution phase. Myths of the triumph of these powers; myths of floods and the return of chaos, of the defeat of the hero, and Götterdämmerung myths. Subordinate characters: the ogre and the witch. The archetype of satire (see, for instance, the conclusion of *The Dunciad*).

The quest of the hero also tends to assimilate the oracular and random verbal structures, as we can see when we watch the chaos of local legends that results from prophetic epiphanies consolidating into a narrative mythology of departmental gods. In most of the higher religions this in turn has become the same central quest-myth that emerges from ritual, as the Messiah myth became the narrative structure of the oracles of Judaism. A local flood may beget a folk tale by accident, but a comparison of flood stories will show how quickly such tales become examples of the myth of dissolution. Finally, the tendency of both ritual and epiphany to become encyclopedic is realized in the definitive body of myth which constitutes the sacred scriptures of religions. These sacred scriptures are consequently the first documents that the literary critic has to study to gain a comprehensive view of his subject. After he has understood their structure, then he can descend from archetypes to genres, and see how the drama emerges from the ritual side of myth and lyric from the epiphanic or fragmented side, while the epic carries on the central encyclopedic structure.

Some words of caution and encouragement are necessary before literary criticism has clearly staked out its boundaries in these fields. It is part of the critic's business to show how all literary genres are derived from the quest-myth, but the derivation is a logical one within the science of criticism: the quest-myth will constitute the first chapter of whatever future handbooks of criticism may be written that will be based on enough organized critical knowledge to call themselves "introductions" or "outlines" and still be able to live up to their titles. It is only when we try to expound the derivation chronologically that we find ourselves writing pseudo-prehistorical fictions and theories of mythological contract. Again, because psychology and anthropology are more highly developed sciences, the critic who deals with this kind of material is bound to appear, for some time, a dilettante of those subjects. These two phases of criticism are largely undeveloped in comparison with literary history and rhetoric, the reason being the later development of the sciences they are related to. But the fascination which *The Golden Bough* and Jung's book on libido symbols have for literary critics is not based on dilettantism, but on the fact that these books are primarily studies in literary criticism, and very important ones.

In any case the critic who is studying the principles of literary form has a quite different interest from the psychologist's concern with states of mind or the anthropologist's with social institutions. For instance: the mental response to narrative is mainly passive; to significance mainly active. From this fact Ruth Benedict's *Patterns of Culture* develops a distinction between "Apollonian" cultures based on obedience to ritual and "Dionysiac" ones based on a tense exposure of the prophetic mind to epiphany. The critic would tend rather to note how popular literature which appeals to the inertia of the untrained mind puts a heavy emphasis on narrative values, whereas a sophisticated attempt to disrupt the connection between the poet and his environment produces the Rimbaud type of *illumination,* Joyce's solitary epiphanies, and Baudelaire's conception of nature as a source of oracles. Also how literature, as it develops from the primitive to the self-conscious, shows a gradual shift of the poet's attention from narrative to significant values, this shift of attention being the basis of Schiller's distinction between naive and sentimental poetry.

The relation of criticism to religion, when they deal with the same documents, is more complicated. In criticism, as in history, the divine is always treated as a human artifact. God for the critic, whether he finds him in *Paradise Lost* or the Bible, is a character in a human story; and for the critic all epiphanies are explained, not in terms of the riddle of a possessing god or devil, but as mental phenomena closely associated in their origin with dreams. This once established, it is then necessary to say that nothing in criticism or art compels the critic to take the attitude of ordinary waking consciousness towards the dream or the god. Art deals not with the real but with the conceivable; and criticism, though it will eventually have to have some theory of conceivability, can never be justified in trying to develop, much less assume, any theory of actuality. It is necessary to understand this before our next and final point can be made.

We have identified the central myth of literature, in its narrative aspect, with the quest-myth. Now if we wish to see this central myth as a pattern of meaning also, we have to start with the workings of the subconscious where the epiphany originates, in other words in the dream. The human cycle of waking and dreaming corresponds closely to the natural cycle of light and darkness, and it is perhaps in this correspondence that all imaginative life begins. The correspondence is largely an antithesis: it is in daylight that man is really in the power of darkness, a prey to frustration and weakness; it is in the darkness of nature that the "libido" or conquering heroic self awakes. Hence art, which Plato called a dream for awakened minds, seems to have as its final cause the resolution of the antithesis, the mingling of the sun and the hero, the realizing of a world in which the inner desire and the outward circumstance coincide. This is the same goal, of course, that the attempt to combine human and natural power in ritual has. The social function of the arts, therefore, seems to be closely connected with visualizing the goal of work in human life. So in terms of significance, the central myth of art must be the vision of the end of social effort, the innocent world of fulfilled desires, the free human society. Once this is understood, the integral place of criticism among the other social sciences, in interpreting and systematizing the vision of the artist, will be easier to see. It is at this point that we can see how religious conceptions of the final cause of human effort are as relevant as any others to criticism.

The importance of the god or hero in the myth lies in the fact that such characters, who are conceived in human likeness and yet have more power over nature, gradually build up the vision of an omnipotent personal community beyond an indifferent nature. It is this community which the hero regularly enters in his apotheosis. The world of this apotheosis thus begins to pull away from the rotary cycle of the quest in which all triumph is temporary. Hence if we look at the quest-myth as a pattern of imagery, we see the hero's quest first of all in terms of its fulfillment. This gives us our central pattern of archetypal images, the vision of innocence which sees the world in terms of total human intelligibility. It corresponds to, and is usually found in the form of, the vision of the unfallen world or heaven in religion. We may call it the comic vision of life, in contrast to the tragic vision, which sees the quest only in the form of its ordained cycle.

We conclude with a second table of contents, in which we shall attempt to set forth the central pattern of the comic and tragic visions. One essential principle of archetypal criticism is that the individual and the universal forms of an image are identical, the reasons being too complicated for us just now. We proceed according to the general plan of the game of Twenty Questions, or, if we prefer, of the Great Chain of Being:

1. In the comic vision the *human* world is a community, or a hero who represents the wish-fulfillment of the reader. The archetype of images of symposium, communion, order, friendship and love. In the tragic vision the human world is a tyranny or anarchy, or an individual or isolated man, the leader with his back to his followers, the bullying giant of romance, the deserted or betrayed hero. Marriage or some equivalent consummation belongs to the comic vision; the harlot, witch and other varieties of Jung's "terrible mother" belongs to the tragic one. All divine, heroic, angelic or other superhuman communities follow the human pattern.

2. In the comic vision the *animal* world is a community of domesticated animals, usually a flock of sheep, or a lamb, or one of the gentler birds, usually a dove. The archetype of pastoral images. In the tragic vision the animal world is seen in terms of beasts and birds of prey, wolves, vultures, serpents, dragons and the like.

3. In the comic vision the *vegetable* world is a garden, grove or park, or a tree of life, or a rose or lotus. The archetype of Arcadian images, such as that of Marvell's green world or of Shakespeare's forest comedies. In the tragic vision it is a sinister forest like the one in *Comus* or at the opening of the *Inferno,* or a heath or wilderness, or a tree of death.

4. In the comic vision the *mineral* world is a city, or one building or temple, or one stone, normally a glowing precious stone—in fact the whole comic series, especially the tree, can be conceived as luminous or fiery. The archetype of geometrical images: the "starlit dome" belongs here. In the tragic vision the mineral world is seen in terms of deserts, rocks and ruins, or of sinister geometrical images like the cross.

5. In the comic vision the *unformed* world is a river, traditionally fourfold, which influenced the Renaissance image of the temperate body with its four humors. In the tragic vision this world usually becomes the sea, as the narrative myth of dissolution is so often a flood myth. The combination of the sea and beast images gives us the leviathan and similar water-monsters.

Obvious as this table looks, a great variety of poetic images and forms will be found to fit it. Yeats's "Sailing to Byzantium," to take a famous example of the comic vision at random, has the city, the tree, the bird, the community of sages, the geometrical gyre and the detachment from the cyclic world. It is, of course, only the general comic or tragic context that determines the interpretation of any symbol: this is obvious with relatively neutral archetypes like the island which may be Prospero's island or Circe's.

Our tables are, of course, not only elementary but grossly over-simplified, just as our inductive approach to the archetype was a mere hunch. The important point is not the deficiencies of either procedure, taken by itself, but the fact that, somewhere and somehow, the two are clearly going to meet in the middle. And if they do meet, the ground plan of a systematic and comprehensive development of criticism has been established.

Flannery O'Connor and the Catholic Grotesque

GILBERT H. MULLER

In this selection, Muller frames O'Connor's fiction within the historical and cross-cultural genre of the grotesque. He asserts that this genre provides a method for investigating certain philosophical problems that envision an alienated world, a world in which we sense the radical discontinuity of things. He defines the grotesque genre both by its subject matter—visions of horror—and by its technique—comic treatment of characters. As a fictive character in this grotesque and absurd world who is blind to her own spiritual estrangement, Ruby Turpin is both foolish and unsympathetic. This special combination of the ludicrous and the horrible characterizes the grotesque genre. It also gives O'Connor's stories their singular complexity of tone.

FLANNERY O'CONNOR ONCE REMARKED that the most memorable event in her life prior to the publication of *Wise Blood* was the featuring of a bantam chicken which she had trained to walk backwards by Pathé newsreels. Mary Flannery was six years old at the time, attending parochial school in Savannah, Georgia. Later, while enrolled in Peabody High School in Milledgeville, where the family had moved in 1938, she confounded her home economics teacher by outfitting another bantam hen

Reprinted from *Nightmares and Visions: Flannery O'Connor and the Catholic Grotesque*, by Gilbert H. Muller, by permission of the University of Georgia Press. Copyright © 1972 by The University of Georgia Press.

in a white piqué coat and striped trousers which she had designed and sewn to specification. Up to the time of her death in 1964 at the age of thirty-nine, Miss O'Connor retained this fondness for domestic fowl, especially those varieties which were eccentric rather than normative. She even confessed to favoring barnyard birds "with one green eye and one orange or with overlong necks and crooked combs. I wanted one with three legs or three wings but nothing in that line turned up."[1]

Unable to locate her ideal grotesque among God's humbler creatures, Miss O'Connor turned to her fellow human beings. And here she discovered a Goyaesque assortment of deformed individuals which she made as unique and imperishable as her bantam hens. In dealing with these human grotesques, the author was writing from personal and drastic experience; she lived in a region where Bible Belt values strongly affected both culture and the human will. Moreover, Miss O'Connor's own affliction, which she carried with her during the major part of her literary career, forced a certain austerity upon her fiction; inevitably she transferred personal agony and suffering to her work. Yet in dealing with her characters' agonies, and in sustaining her own, Flannery O'Connor was sardonic rather than sentimental. She wielded a literary hatchet rather than a handkerchief; she realized that only a stern intellect, an adamant faith, and an accretion of humor which usually shaded into the grotesque could confront suffering, violence, and evil in this world.

In the fictive landscape which she created, Flannery O'Connor's grotesques—deformed in body and soul alike—wrangle with ultimate problems which also must have beset their creator. Her use of the grotesque to establish the moral and aesthetic climate of a work is pronounced, but it is not, as William Van O'Connor has suggested, a peculiarly modern method.[2] Actually the tradition of the grotesque has many antecedents. Viewed historically, the aesthetic is older than its designation: the noted German art historian Wolfgang Kayser cites presences of the grotesque in the convolutions of early Roman art, despite the fact that the term, *la grottesca*, was not applied to these manifestations until the late fifteenth century.[3] Properly speaking, however, the grotesque first became prominent during the Middle Ages. A grotesque perspective was frequently offered by church art, which revealed to a contemporary of these times, Saint Bernard of Clairvaux, "a wonderful sort of hideous beauty and beautiful deformity."[4] Moreover, numerous analogies to the grotesque can be found in medieval graphic art, where comedy is often allied with the more somber aspects of the fantastic, the hallucinatory, and the terrible.

When Gothic form (which should not be confused with the later literary development of Gothic romance) replaced its Romanesque predecessor in the twelfth century, the evolution of the grotesque actually became unavoidable; with fixed proportions destroyed and replaced by spatial distortions and increasingly complex forms, the groundwork had been established for an art of the grotesque. Most importantly, High Gothic form reveals a profound sense of contrast and contradiction in impulses and relationships, as though things are always on the verge of disintegration. As Erwin Panofsky accurately describes it, the key to this period is found in an "ACCEPTANCE AND ULTIMATE RECONCILIATION OF CONTRADICTORY POSSIBILITIES."[5] In viewing the proliferation of contradictory aspects in fourteenth-century art—in roof bosses, stained glass, wood carving, wall painting, and the marginalia of manuscripts—we can readily perceive that High Gothic form, characterized by this juxtaposition of extremes, nurtured in itself an aesthetic which eventually found expression in the pure grotesque.

The late fourteenth century produced one of the foremost artists of the pure grotesque, a figure extremely relevant to this inquiry, because the eschatological themes of Hieronymus Bosch, concerned with Heaven and Hell, the Last Judgment, and the Deadly Seven, are similar in many respects to the main literary preoccupations of Flannery O'Connor. In fact, Bosch's most famous painting, the *Millennium* triptych, provides a gloss on what Miss O'Connor termed her "stories of original sin." Reading from left to right, the three panels of the *Millennium* show how evil came into the world, how it spread through Creation, and how it inevitably leads to Hell. Yet when the panels are closed, one is presented with an ordered view of the universe on the third day of Creation. Like Bosch, Flannery O'Connor creates a landscape wherein life is already hellish, and where men are possessed by demons and devils who completely control their souls and who subject them to excruciating torment. Her own Millennium canvas, dominated by the unexpected and disconnected, the malformed and the estranged, projects what is perhaps the most consistently grotesque body of work in our time. What both Bosch and Miss O'Connor present, in a style that is pointed and precise, is a violation of the limits which have been laid down by God for man. Thus, for these two artists, the grotesque does not function gratuitously, but in order to reveal underlying and essentially theological concepts.

The contemporary grotesque has predecessors not only in the visual arts but in literature as well, for the popular verbal fun and macabre wit which we encounter in Rabelais and Swift, the demented souls and retarded fools in many of Shakespeare's plays, the Dickensian caricatures and Dostoevskian madmen who populate late nineteenth- and twentieth-century fiction are facets in a continuous and rather pervasive literary aesthetic which scholars have yet to define adequately. Within the restricted province of American literature the grotesque has been an informing principle. It has its genesis in the autobiographical writing of the colonial period, where gross exaggeration of flora and fauna, as well as absurd contortions of faith, are casually remarked. There are aspects of the grotesque in the fiction of Charles Brockden Brown and Poe, writers who generally rely on the trappings of Gothic romance but who, in revealing a merging of categories, a preoccupation with subjective states of being, and a comic tone in face of the terrible, create a tension more readily associated with the grotesque. The grotesque also provides a dark current in an astonishing body of southwestern humor which extends from the 1830s well into the Genteel Age, where it was picked up by writers like Ambrose Bierce and carried into the twentieth century. In the opening decades of the twentieth century Sherwood Anderson gave the grotesque a certain poetic substance, and F. Scott Fitzgerald, in parts of *The Great Gatsby* and in the middle section of *The Vegetable,* recognized excrescences of it in the Jazz Age. Among the major writers of the thirties the grotesque was a seminal impulse in the fiction of Faulkner and Nathanael West; and it continues to pervade the best contemporary fiction, for to examine such writers as Vladimir Nabokov, John Barth, James Purdy, John Hawkes, and Thomas Pynchon—all of whom emphasize the personal vagaries of insanity and the contradictory impulses of identity in conflict with a world that is essentially chaotic and absurd—is to realize that these writers accept the grotesque as a matter of course.[6]

Essentially the grotesque in literature is a method of investigating certain metaphysical problems through fictive constructions. In other words the grotesque projects a world vision that is framed by distinct techniques: in the best grotesque art, vision and technique must function congruently. The vision itself presents existence as deprived of meaning. All traces of natural order are willfully subverted so as to produce an alienated world, a world in which man, sensing the radical discontinuity of things, is estranged from his environment. This division between man and his environment is what actually produces the grotesque, or the absurd, wherein man discovers that in a universe which is disjointed and senseless, which is contradictory in every aspect, he is something less than what he should be. Camus correctly calls this division between man and his world, a "divorce," underscoring the concept by remarking that "the feeling of absurdity does not spring from the mere scrutiny of a fact or an impression, but it . . . bursts from the comparison of a bare fact and a certain reality, between an action and the world that transcends it."[7]

To the extent that both words refer to the alienated world, we can say that the grotesque and the absurd are synonymous. Wolfgang Kayser, whose definition still remains the best in modern criticism, states that the grotesque is predicated upon this alienated vision, upon what he terms

THE ESTRANGED WORLD. . . . Suddenness and surprise are essential elements. . . . We are so strongly affected and terrified because it is our world which ceases to be reliable, and we feel that we would be unable to live in this changed world. The grotesque instills the fear of life rather than the fear of death. Structurally, it presupposes that the categories which apply to our world view become inapplicable. We have observed the progressive dissolution . . . the fusion of realms which we know to be separated, the abolition of the law of statics, the loss of identity, the distortion of "natural" size and shape, the suspension of the category of objects, the destruction of the personality, and the fragmentation of the historical order. . . . THE GROTESQUE IS A PLAY WITH THE ABSURD. . . . AN ATTEMPT TO INVOKE AND SUBDUE THE DEMONIC ASPECTS OF THE WORLD.[8]

Kayser's analysis suggests that the grotesque is a literature of extreme situation, and indeed mayhem, chaos, and violence seem to predominate in the genre, causing characters to be projected in curious ways. As the world disintegrates and categories merge, these characters frequently become burlesque figures whose actions mime the grotesque world which they inhabit.

The grotesque character therefore is one who either exerts himself against the absurd or who is a part of the absurd. This character frequently assumes recognizable postures: guilt, obsession, and madness are among his peculiarities, and at his best he is simultaneously a rebel, rogue, and victim. He can also be prankster, saint, demonist, fanatic, clown, moron, or any combination of these; or at the more mundane level the grotesque can be reflected in an absurd family group. All these types appear in Flannery O'Connor's gallery of grotesques—and others as well, for as Miss O'Connor was fond of remarking, we are all grotesques in one aspect or another, although we might not realize it; since what most people consider to be normal is actually grotesque, whereas the grotesque itself, because of its pervasiveness, is merely reality.

The grotesque character is a comic figure. It is impossible to sympathize with him, despite his agonies, because we view him from a detached perspective, and when we are not emotionally involved in his suffering, we are amused. Martin Esslin, in examining the theater of the absurd, stresses this principle when he writes:

> Characters with whom the audience fails to identify are inevitably comic. If we identified with the figure of farce who loses his trousers, we should feel embarrassment and shame. If, however, our tendency to identify has been inhibited by making such a character grotesque, we laugh at his predicament. We see what happens to him from the outside, rather than from his own point of view.[9]

As with the grotesque character the entire technique of the grotesque is also essentially comic, for we always view the grotesque from a vantage point. To be certain, the subject matter of the grotesque—the raw material which creates the vision—is always potentially horrible, but the treatment of this material is comic: this explains the peculiar complexity of tone, combining both horror and the ludicrous, which characterizes the grotesque as an art form. Pure horror, of course, cannot produce a grotesque effect: as subject matter it is unrelieved horror and nothing more. But the grotesque, through the interjection of humor, releases the terror and makes it understandable. It is perhaps legitimate to speak of a comic grotesque as distinguished from a "black" grotesque, but it is more precise to say that the grotesque is always a source of humor. (Baudelaire's definition of the grotesque as "the absolute comic" stresses this criterion.) And usually the final equilibrium of the grotesque consists of amused introspection, although to qualify Esslin, we are prevented from laughing at the characters with an easy conscience because of the grotesque's deliberate play upon matters of life and death. . . .

. . . The true cultural grotesques are the invariably well-mannered members of the community who ignore the spiritual foundations of their culture. Miss O'Connor sees the South as struggling to preserve this spiritual identity, not only against the Raybers and the Sheppards, but also against those numerous members of the community who substitute sanctimoniousness for true Christian virtue. This insight into human nature applies especially well to her earth mothers—to Mrs. May in "Greenleaf," to Mrs. McIntyre in "The Displaced Person," to Mrs. Cope in "A Circle in the Fire," and to Mrs. Turpin in "Revelation." These women traipse their fields, pastures, and woods with a singleminded sense of righteous proprietorship that prevents them from recognizing a fundamentally spiritual estrangement from their surroundings, an estrangement rooted in their inability to act charitably toward their neighbors. Unaware of their alienation, these ordinary individuals are extremely vulnerable to extraordinary events which test their harshness and rigidity of spirit.

One of the most remarkable of these cultural grotesques is Ruby Turpin, the protagonist of Flannery O'Connor's short story, "Revelation." Unlike many writers whose energies atrophy in middle age, Miss O'Connor had talents that were constantly improving, and a story as nearly flawless as "Revelation" (which won a posthumous first prize in the O'Henry competitions) is a poignant testament to a talent thwarted by death. First published in the *Sewanee Review* in 1964, it is a fable of God's providence operating in a doctor's office and in a pig pen. A triumph of the comic grotesque, the story opens in a doctor's waiting room, where an extraordinary collection of patients who form a miniature society— a ship of fools—awaits examination. Assembled in this almost claustrophobic office are representative diseases of the body, the mind, and the spirit: the crippled bodies of the aged, the maimed intelligences of the poor and the neuroses of the intellectually gifted, and the defective souls of the self-righteous. Their illnesses represent the maladies of society, and the traits of this society are progressively revealed to a point where the absurdity implicit in the characters' behavior must explode.

Ruby Turpin, who self-indulgently speculates about the blessings bestowed on her by the Lord, unconsciously turns the story into a punitive fable on arrogance, hypocrisy, and pride. She gradually emerges as a high-toned Christian lady whose sense of social and moral superiority and whose extreme self-absorption and pride border on narcissism. Negative aspects of her character are progressively revealed and thrown into grotesque perspective, and each brushstroke fills in a canvas that is unrelieved by any redeeming qualities. Mindless of her faults, she establishes herself as a type of white culture heroine, aligned with a pitiful minority against the encroachments of Negroes, poor-white trash, and the baser elements of humanity. Because of her obsessions and her spiritual deformities she is inherently grotesque; her thoughts and her actions reveal her as a negative moral agent, unaware of her own absurdity because she is so attached to an inauthentic existence.

It is relevant that Miss O'Connor plots this story at a pace that is discernibly slower than most of her short fiction and that Ruby's unbearable self-righteousness is gradually reinforced to the point of the reader's exasperation. The lack of any physical action, counterpointed by Ruby's constant speculation on the mysteries of creation and by the mechanical conversation of the patients, creates a repressed narrative pace wherein the slightest disruption in movement could have the unusual effect of releasing tensions which lie just beneath the surface of the story. Thus the dramatic escalation which occurs abruptly after Ruby thanks the Lord for having created in her such a fine creature is so unanticipated that the shocking impact creates one of the revelations to which the title of the story alludes. As the Wellesley girl strikes Ruby Turpin in the eye with a hurled book and pounces on her in a frenzy, the astonishing disclosure of the girl's imprecation is not only authoritative in moral terms, but approximates, as perfectly as the literary medium can, the actual force of revelation.

The execration which the girl hurls at Ruby Turpin is both shocking and convincing, for it calls Ruby's self-contained egocentric existence into question. Ruby tries to rebel against this revelation, which in theological terms is a manifestation of God's providence, and which in emotional terms is cathartic. Because of this revelation she becomes an inhabitant of a world which suddenly appears estranged to her. Her initial revelation—that she is, in the girl's words, a wart-hog from hell—is at first incomprehensible and then outrageous, and the remainder of the story traces the process whereby she painfully learns obedience, which is a prerequisite of true faith and of salvation.

Ruby's failure to present a suitable defense of herself shifts from outrage to hatred and bitterness toward God, and the image of this woman marching out to the pig parlour to wage battle with the Lord is a brilliant and hilarious picture of the false believer journeying to meet her apocalypse. Still actively engaged in an attempt to reconstruct the world in her own image, she subsumes any conception of God to her own blueprint, an act that constitutes absolute heresy. This is her central crisis—and the crisis of all of Flannery O'Connor's cultural grotesques: as the landscape transforms itself from the brightness of late afternoon to a deepening and mysterious blue, the reality of this crisis begins to catch up with her.

Ruby Turpin is one of the author's countless grotesques who are largely the creations of themselves. Their own misconception of self and of social laws places them in opposition to a higher justice which assures the ultimate triumph of their opposites—the humble and the meek. Assuredly the lame shall enter first, while the superior citizen, conducting his life for his own sake, shall suffer a humiliation even more acute than total damnation.

Conscious elaboration of the cultural grotesque was merely a part of Flannery O'Connor's incisive depiction of degeneracy at all social levels. All her characters are susceptible to defects in nature and spirit, and these deficiencies are what estrange them from the community and from God. Whether it is Haze Motes trying nihilistically to overturn his culture, or Ruby Turpin attempting to preserve it, Miss O'Connor ridicules pride and hypocrisy wherever she finds it. She unmasks her grotesques by exposing their perversity, affectation, and vanity, and she frequently reduces them to impotence through satire. For O'Connor it is the grotesque which underlies all forms of failure. Revealing the dilemmas in the quest for human identity, she shows how the lack of an integrated society—which for the author would be a Christian society—prevents the possibility of an integrated personality. All her grotesques eventually come to the realization of the fact that they are aspiring toward illusory points in a secular world. This defect in vision, epitomized by Haze Motes, whose very name suggests his confused condition, creates an abnormality which is not easily cured.

The grotesques of Flannery O'Connor are individuals who cannot erase the horrors of their obsessions. Few images of peace and beauty populate their world, few are the interludes of order. Implicit in their behavior are all the conventions of the grotesque—the nightmare world, the perversion, the satanic humor. These people wear their deficiencies of spirit as scars—as emblems of a world without order, meaning, or sense of continuity. In an attempt to transcend their painful condition, to rise above that which is alienated and estranged, Miss O'Connor's protagonists invariably descend into the demonic. Obsessed with their own sins, with weakness, evil, and suffering, they turn inward upon themselves and act out their agonies in extraordinary ways. Because O'Connor's grotesques are—to paraphrase T. S. Eliot in his essay on Baudelaire—men enough to be saved or damned, their actions in this world become reflections of the interior life of the soul. It is one of the triumphs of Flannery O'Connor's art—and a mark of her vital faith— that she is willing to write about all types of malefactors who, utterly out of harmony with the world and with Creation, risk exile and damnation for their disbelief.

NOTES

1. Flannery O'Connor, "The King of Birds," in *Mystery and Manners*, ed. Sally Fitzgerald and Robert Fitzgerald (New York: Farrar, Straus & Giroux, 1969), 4. This essay, which first appeared in *Holiday* (September 1961), should be read carefully, for it reveals significant aspects of Miss O'Connor's art and the form in which she cast it.

2. William Van O'Connor, "The Grotesque: An American Genre," *The Grotesque and Other Essays* (Carbondale: Southern Illinois University Press, 1962), 1–19. Aside from a certain looseness in definition, this essay is one of the few incisive analyses of the grotesque in American literature.

3. Kayser, *The Grotesque in Art and Literature*, trans. Ulrich Weisstein (Bloomington: Indiana University Press, 1963), 19. Although literary critics have largely ignored the grotesque as a genre or art form, a considerable amount of spade work has been performed by art historians such as Kayser. In this connection, books by Erwin Panofsky (*Gothic Architecture and Scholasticism*, [Latrobe, Pa.: Archabbey Press, 1951]), Emile Mâle (*The Gothic Image*, [New York: Harper, 1958]), and Otto von Simson (*The Gothic Cathedral*, [New York: Harper, 1956]) are most useful in exploring the medieval foundations of the grotesque. As for the art of the grotesque during the past two centuries, Kayser's book remains the most intelligent investigation of the subject. This study may be profitably supplemented by Arthur Clayborough's *The Grotesque in English Literature* (Oxford: Clarendon Press, 1965); by Lee Jennings's *The Ludicrous Demon* (Berkeley: University of California Press, 1963); and by the first chapter in Alfred Appel, Jr.'s *A Season of Dreams* (Baton Rouge: Louisiana State University Press, 1965).

4. T. Tindall Wildridge, *The Grotesque in Church Art* (London: W. Andrews, 1899), 23.

5. Panofsky, *Gothic Architecture and Scholasticism*, 64.

6. This brief summary scarcely does justice to a major tradition in American fiction. Either in pure or hybrid form, the grotesque appears in the work of most of our major writers. What we might term the theological grotesque is evident in Hawthorne (but only in those stories—for instance "My Kinsman, Major Molineux"—where there is an inordinate amount of demonic laughter), in certain works by Melville (notably *The Confidence-Man*), in Nathanael West, Djuna Barnes, Robert Penn Warren, J. F. Powers, and of course Miss O'Connor. The secular grotesque can be traced from the southwestern humorists to most contemporary fiction writers like Purdy and Hawkes. Moreover with our most complex novelists—for example Melville and Nabokov—the grotesque merges with the art of involution, in which the reader himself is drawn into the writer's absurd vision.

7. Camus, *The Myth of Sisyphus and Other Essays*, trans. Justin O'Brien (New York: Knopf, 1961), 22.

8. Kayser, *The Grotesque in Art and Literature*, 184, 185, 187, 188.

9. Esslin, *The Theatre of the Absurd* (London: Hubert Wilson, 1962), 300. Esslin uses the words "grotesque" and "absurd" interchangeably, a procedure which is—as I have tried to demonstrate in this chapter—quite proper. Mr. Esslin's final two chapters, in which he traces the evolution of the absurd in European drama, provide superlative commentary on this genre.

Archetypal and Genre Provocateurs

1. Both archetypal criticism and genre criticism offer ways to categorize and interrelate literature. In so doing, they emphasize similarities, not differences, among texts. What are some of the strengths and weaknesses of this emphasis for individual texts?

2. Gelpi situates a literary work and the social myth it expresses within historical time and place. In contrast, Frye sees the quest myth as a universal pattern spanning Western civilization. Each approach has advantages and disadvantages. Find out what some of these are by considering Aylmer's quest for perfection ("The Birthmark") from Gelpi's point of view, then from Frye's.

3. Why might Frye, who sees literature as imitating "the total dream of man," dismiss realistic literature as "conventional" and nonliterary?

4. What objections would a New Critic make to Muller's crossing of cultural disciplines to interrelate literature, architecture, and painting?

CHAPTER 4

Structuralist-Semiotic Criticism

FROM THE 1960S ON, structuralism as a new way of thinking has had a revolutionary effect on most disciplines, including literary studies. Its theories of language challenge our commonsense view that words are merely transparent labels we pin to our pre-existent thoughts and feelings, to our experiences, and to objects. As I indicated in the Con-Text, structuralism claims that language is a self-enclosed system so powerful that it shapes us and our world. Accordingly, structuralist logic forces us to radically revise our traditional notions of literary theory. It makes us examine the very nature of literary studies.

This self-examination was actuated by the insights of Swiss linguist Ferdinand de Saussure and, to a lesser extent, by those of the American philosopher Charles S. Peirce. Saussure was concerned with the general structure and laws of language (*langue*) more than with its individual utterances (*parole*). In his view, languages are systems made up of signs; "sign" meant a unit composed of a signifying sound-image (signifier) and a signified concept. He likened the sign to a sheet of paper which has two sides yet is an inseparable unit. Imagine, he suggested, prelinguistic experience as two continuous streams—one of confused sounds, the other of confused ideas—which language cross-cuts, or articulates, into sections (signs or words). We see then that languages of different cultures section off differently: for example, the Latin word *mus* includes the concepts not only of mouse, but also of rat, marten, sable, and ermine. In some cultures orange and yellow are called by the same name and hence seen as one color; in other cultures, gray and blue. Indeed, some cultures divide the color spectrum into four colors, not eight, as we do. Language can be seen as structuring reality in other ways, too. Some societies identify nouns by gender, others do not construct sentences out of nouns and verbs, and so on. Thus Saussure inferred language systems are arbitrary and vary with cultural conventions. Therefore, he concluded, there is no immutable bond between words (signs) and things in the 'real' world. Instead, the bond is arbitrary and conventional.

As important, Saussure pointed out that in language there are only differences without positive terms. These differences operate through a relational system. For example, we recognize "mouse" because English distinguishes the written image *from* related images like "mousse," "mousakka," "louse," and so on. Similarly, on the conceptual plane, you—not being an ancient Roman—know that I mean mouse and not rat when I write "mouse" because English differentiates between these concepts. Thus meaning does not inhere essentially *in* objective things or *in* the psychology of the subject, but is produced by the relational structures of language (the *langue*).

What has this to do with literary studies? A great deal. Because the very material of literature is language, structuralists infer that literature and language are similar in form and function (homologous). Thus literature, too, is to be analyzed as a self-enclosed, relational system with its own rules, a system that does not depend on outside 'reality' for validity. One result of this view, then, is to see so-called realistic literature not as a reflection of 'the real world' but as a system of discursive conventions. Further, if outside reality can not be accepted as the authority for literature, neither can the author or the reader. In what is called "decentering of the subject," structuralism argues that language is its own referent, its own authority.

While structuralists, or semioticians (the terms are generally interchangeable), assert that language acts as its own authority, they assert also that language is produced and constrained by social systems. (Recall *mus* as rat and mouse and ermine?) Yet many of the systems governing text production and reception are not apparent to most of us and so go unnoticed. Therefore, semioticians like Robert Scholes expose the hidden constraints and conventions that guide readers' understanding by calling attention to the text's gaps, or incompleteness. Semioticians like Roland Barthes apply structuralist analyses to other discourses besides literature—ideology, institutional structures, media, psychoanalysis, styles, and so on. They describe the covert and overt codes, or systems, that make us perceive something as 'natural'. Post-structuralist semioticians like Hebdige who argue that signifiers refer to other signifiers that refer to still other signifiers, ad infinitum, question the very possibility of meaning. Whatever their particular focus, semioticians in general are concerned not with meaning but with how meaning is produced.

Sign, Structure, and Self-Reference in W. B. Yeats's "Sailing to Byzantium"

ANTHONY L. JOHNSON

Using structural linguistics, Johnson analyzes how various discourse levels (referential, semantic, structural, signic) intercede one with another to construct "Sailing to Byzantium." He argues that the poem's plane of expression (its imagistic and signic levels) works against the thought level which is structured by simple oppositions—Time/Eternity, Youth/Age, Art/Self, Body/Soul. These binary oppositions are subverted by the semantically complex bird images as well as the signic "I" which condenses many contradictory meanings. Finally, by fusing the poetic "I" with the bird-song to constitute "the artifice of Eternity," the poem provides a model of the transforming creative act.

OF ALL YEATS'S POEMS, none seems to have attracted more discussion or interpretation than "Sailing to Byzantium" (written September 26, 1926) and "Byzantium" (September, 1930), usually called "the Byzantine poems." This paper aims to offer some pointers toward a signic, structural and semiotic reading of the first of these two poems.[1] At many levels, especially that of poetic substance, this poem appears to offer a richness unsurpassed, and perhaps unequalled, by its sequel. In fact, it seems no exaggeration to say that the difficulty of "unwind[ing] the winding path" of the material of thought in "Byzantium"—its obdurate resistance to glossing—has been erected by some critics into a patent of aesthetic merit. The greater directness, vigour and structural solidity of "Sailing to Byzantium" may reveal levels of "organised complexity" so far neglected by critical intellect:

Sailing to Byzantium

1 That is no country for old men. The young
2 In one another's arms, birds in the trees
3 —Those dying generations—at their song,
4 The salmon-falls, the mackerel-crowded seas,
5 Fish, flesh, or fowl, commend all summer long
6 Whatever is begotten, born, and dies.
7 Caught in that sensual music all neglect
8 Monuments of unageing intellect.

9 An aged man is but a paltry thing,
10 A tattered coat upon a stick, unless

From *Annali della Scuola normale superiore di Pisa, Classe di lettere e filosofia* 8 (1978): 213–47. Reprinted by permission.

11 Soul clap its hands and sing, and louder sing
12 For every tatter in its mortal dress,
13 Nor is there singing school but studying
14 Monuments of its own magnificence;
15 And therefore I have sailed the seas and come
16 To the holy city of Byzantium

17 O sages standing in God's holy fire
18 As in the gold mosaic of a wall,
19 Come from the holy fire, perne in a gyre,
20 And be the singing-masters of my soul.
21 Consume my heart away; sick with desire
22 And fastened to a dying animal
23 It knows now what it is; and gather me
24 Into the artifice of eternity.

25 Once out of nature I shall never take
26 My bodily form from any natural thing,
27 But such a form as Grecian goldsmiths make
28 Of hammered gold and gold enamelling
29 To keep a drowsy Emperor awake;
30 Or set upon a golden bough to sing
31 To lords and ladies of Byzantium
32 Of what is past, or passing, or to come.

Here, to a degree perhaps unique in Yeats's poetry, there is a clear-cut semantic articulation which coincides with the division into verses. The four verses display four stages or situations, as if we were to study four panels in a pictorial rendering of a temporally ordered panorama of the human predicament.

Yeats was, of course, strongly fascinated by—and wished to believe in—reincarnation and life after death (in *A Vision* he dismisses F. H. Bradley as "an arrogant, sapless man" for believing "that he could stand by the death-bed of wife or mistress and not long for an immortality of body and soul").[2] Thus his panorama of human existence here requires eternity, symbolised by "the holy city of Byzantium," verses 3 and 4.

TIME VERSUS ETERNITY

Verse 1 shows unselfconscious youth, and verse 2 self-conscious age, so revealing the two faces of TIME. The first gives *satisfied youth* (in bodily vigour) and the second *dissatisfied age* (in bodily decay). In verse 1, the dialectical struggle between BODY and SOUL works wholly in BODY's favor, so that ART is neglected. Verse 2 displays the tearing of a body which is now "10 A tattered coat upon a stick"—a Neoplatonic garment of "flesh" which has become frightening. It is, in fact, pictured as a *scarecrow* which will *frighten* the "birds" of verse 1, and stop the "sensual music" of "their song." In verse 1, FLESH makes FLESH; in verse 2, SOUL must make *itself,* by creating a non-bodily music of "clapped hands" (another "bird-frightening" sound). To create such music, it must receive instruction from ART's "14 Monuments."

Verses 3 and 4 display the two faces of ETERNITY. First, in verse 3, the poetic "I" appeals to the "17 sages" to "19 Come from the holy fire." They must descend to carry the soul up to the level of eternity. The whole of the second half of the poem relies on a sense-expanding ambiguity—a use of language as *interface*—between Byzantium as an "existential" (historical) reality and as an artistic (timeless) one. Such a situation is characteristic of Yeats's later poetry, where "the superhuman" ("Byzantium") is sought, but is constantly interpreted through, or perceived in terms of, artistic moduli. Yeats called on many artistic disciplines to convey the experience of "Heaven blazing into the head" ("Lapis Lazuli")—including mosaic work, painting and fresco-painting, sculpture, rhetoric, landscape gardening, and many forms of drama, song and dance. . . .

[Johnson here provides more examples of how the poem's images, especially that of the golden bird, work against a simple referential opposition.]

ETERNITY'S DILEMMA: SCORNFUL SPIRITUALITY OR REINCARNATION

Insufficient attention has been directed in the literature to the last clause in the poem, "30–32 *to sing* / To lords and ladies of Byzantium / *Of what is past, or passing, or to come.*" The earlier syntagma on which this is modelled, "6 Whatever is begotten, born, and dies" has as its third, phonically dissimilar but climactic term "dies"—the seal of *subjection to time,* while here the third, phonically dissimilar and climactic term is "to come"—the seal of *freedom from subjection to time.*

The lexeme *come* ties up the whole poem by acting as climax to another triple series:

(a) 15 . . . and *come*
       16 To the holy city of Byzantium.
(b) 17 O sages standing in God's holy fire
       19 *Come* from the holy fire . . .
(c) 30 . . . to sing
       32 Of what is past, or passing, or *to come.*

This series, through rhetorically effective shifts in meaning conveyed through the same sign, marks out the three stages in the spiritual journey of the poetic "I":

(a)   COME → already *completed* journey to a spirituality located
                    in the *past;*
(b)   COME → appeal, set in the *present,* to be gathered into an
                    eternity which is "present";

(c) TO COME → a *future* intention ("I shall take") to become a
bird whose knowledge will extend to the *future*
(so making the final objective: superiority to
time + participation in it).

Thus the lexeme *come* not only, in its third modulation, assures us
that a higher knowledge can be won, but also presents its poetic simulacrum, artificial birdsong, as interface between temporal and atem-
poral, between TIME and ETERNITY.

Yeats's poetry advanced from its earlier staticity to its later dynamism
by learning to create such an art-mediated friction—by showing the
creatures of time Platonically in love with eternity; or eternity, and its
symbols, Blakeanly in love with the creatures of time. Here the bird's
"superhuman" knowledge derives from eternity—it is prophetically able
to sing about "what is . . . to come" but its subject is the world of events
and living creatures. Once "25 out of nature," Yeats's symbols for spiritually may choose to "live their deaths"[3] through participation in life—
here, the return towards life involved in the last four lines; or they can
choose to remain at the "top of the tree,"[4] "disdain[ing] / All that man
is" —the situation represented by the dome in "Byzantium."

The third verse of "Byzantium," in fact, presents the two choices one
after another, enlarging on the figure of the golden bird inaugurated by
the earlier poem:

17 Miracle, bird or golden handiwork,
18 More miracle than bird or handiwork,
19 Planted on the star-lit golden bough,
20 Can like the cocks of Hades crow,
21 Or, by the moon embittered, scorn aloud
22 In glory of changeless metal
23 Common bird or petal
24 And all complexities of mire and blood.

On reflection, however, we may see that the choice (certainly in "Sailing
to Byzantium") is unbalanced—it is biased in favour of a return to life.
Whichever choice is made—reincarnation (line 20 in "Byzantium") or
scornful self-sufficiency (21–24),[5] the "Miracle, bird or golden handiwork" is given an unsurpassably *artistic* form in the poem. It is evidently
made to be seen; it contains an immanent teleology of artistic communication. Both Yeats's Byzantine poems, in fact, offer an abundant experience
of poetic perception of his symbol—it is resoundingly displayed through
image, sound and rhetoric. Once again, then, we find the substance of
Yeats's poetry—its rhythmic power, its imagery and the splendour of that
imagery—dragging values away from the referential levels. These seem
to dictate an equality of choice in "Byzantium"—or even, it might be argued, a clear epiphanic preference for the life-refusing choice, which

gets four lines against the single line displaying the life-accepting choice; and they trenchantly announce that the soul is now "out of nature" at the start of verse 4 in "Sailing to Byzantium." But in looking deeply into the golden bird image in each, and into the last lines in "Byzantium" dedicated to the "sea" of life, we feel the pull of a powerful semantic undertow towards a final option for life.

Significantly, Yeats was stimulated to write "Byzantium" by a letter from Sturge Moore (written on 16 April 1930), which protested that:

> Your "Sailing to Byzantium," magnificent as the first three stanzas are, lets me down in the fourth, as such a goldsmith's bird is as much nature as a man's body, especially if it only sings like Homer and Shakespeare of what is past or passing or to come to Lords and Ladies.[6]

If we leave aside Moore's rather pedantic quibble about the sheer materiality of the bird, his letter may be said to pinpoint the contradiction between the avowed renunciation of life and nature, and the life-oriented song of the bird, which Moore comprehensibly imagines as being modelled on the works of two of the most life-loving of all "makars," Homer and Shakespeare.

What changes between the two poems is that in "Sailing to Byzantium" the poetic "I" still seems to belong *outside* Byzantium; "15 I have sailed the seas and come / 16 To the holy city of Byzantium," and the city is actually seen (rather than imagined), if at all—"18 *As in* the gold mosaic of a wall," with an outsider's eyes. Certainly, the thought of eternity is projected into an indefinite future, "25 *Once* out of nature I *shall* . . . ," and the vitality springing from both halves of the poem seems to reduce the real difference between time and eternity to a threshold of joyous rebirth to a *new kind of life*. In "Byzantium," the poetic "I" is already located in the holy city, and it looks outwards *from the city* to "40 That dolphin-torn, that gong-tormented sea" which beats beyond the walls. The city itself, in sympathy with the I's predicament, has taken on the midnight pallor and hushed silence of death, and the mood sums to an anguished desire for a reprieve from perhaps imminent death—a desire itself torn by images of suffering and of a longing to be free of it.[7] (Seven years after writing it, two years before his death, Yeats went so far as to tell "his wife that it was harder for him to live than to die."[8])

We may say, then, that the singing of the golden bird in "Sailing to Byzantium" is presented as symbolising a state of spiritual purification, but it is displayed in a way which offers its listeners—both *within* the poem and *outside* it—a particularly gratifying image of sensuous delight (the eyes and ears enjoy their own "sensual music"!); its function as entertainer of the Byzantine lords and ladies amounts to an attribution to it of a virtual yearning after a sensual form of existence, or, at least, after a communicative contact with life. Thus a parallel but opposite movement is produced to the speaker's yearning for spirituality in verse 3. On a higher plane, the continual dwelling on images of sensual satisfaction of artistic type ends up by englobing the whole "journey into eternity" in an experience of ecstasy peculiar to art. . . .

[The omitted section discusses how the two types of magnificence—"Monuments of unageing intellect" and "Monuments of its own magnificence"—correspond, respectively, to Yeats's views of Eastern and Western art. Johnson proposes that Yeats's dynamic conception of Byzantium synthesizes these conflicting views.]

THE PARADOX OF ART

The paradox of art has fully emerged from our comparison between the two types of "monument" and of "magnificence." The artist can only learn from the past, and its achievements. He therefore calls on the "sages" to "20 be the singing-masters of my soul"; but he does so only to reject—to transform—that achievement, spurred by the need not just to copy or appreciate "8 Monuments of unageing intellect," but to create anew, to sing a new song. This model of the artistic act (significantly, it is found embedded in the poem, not declared outright) sounds remarkably modern today. It has a structural and typological orientation, so that it sounds as if it had absorbed the views of a series of writers stretching from Shklovsky and Tynyanov on to Mukařovský and Lotman, though there is no reason to suppose that Yeats knew the work even of those contemporary with him.[9]

The self-negating, self-renewing quality of art, which requires cyclical renewal to counter self-absorption, and calls for simultaneous *acceptance* and *refusal* of the older model, leads us to an insight in another line in "Sailing to Byzantium."

The danger of "self-defeating success," as we may call it, is extended to the whole range of human ambition—love, art and power—in the second of the "Two Songs from a Play," published in the same collection as "Sailing to Byzantium" (*The Tower*):

9 Everything that man esteems
10 Endures a moment or a day.
11 Love's pleasure drives his love away,
12 *The painter's brush consumes his dreams;*
13 The herald's cry, the soldier's tread
14 Exhaust his glory and his might:
15 Whatever flames upon the night
16 Man's own resinous heart has fed.

Characteristically, it is the *painter's* experience which is powerfully concrete, while those of love, herald and soldier seem, by comparison, vague and generalised. This poem not only uses the same verb as "Sailing to Byzantium," "21 *Consume* my heart away," but ends with an equivalence between the fulfilment of all such human dreams and the consumption of the heart in *flames.*

The consuming fire (whose burning corresponds to the artist's "ecstatic suffering," and whose ultimate source is probably the holy fire seen by Moses as a sign of God's power—a fire which burned but did not physically "consume[ ]" the bush)[10] is the instrument by which painter or poet may become a great artist as his "heart" is figuratively "Consume[d] . . . away." Similarly, the fourth, "purgatorial" verse of "Byzantium" displays the purification of "blood-begotten spirits" in *"flames* begotten of *flame,"* and the destruction of "complexities of fury" in "32 An agony of *flame that cannot singe a sleeve."*

That the artist's transfiguration from a creature of time into a creature of eternity is equivalent to an apprenticeship to ART, and to the ARTistic process, is revealed by a passage in *Mythologies*[11] which offers the syntagma "gather us into eternity"—minimally transformed here into "23 *gather me / Into* the artifice of *eternity"*:

> . . . ; and terror and content, birth and death, love and hatred, and the fruit of the tree, are but instruments for that *supreme art* which is to win us from life and *gather us into eternity* like doves into their dove-cots.

In this passage too the transfigured selves are seen as birds.

Structural Modelling in "Sailing to Byzantium"

The basic oppositional conflicts ruling over the construction of "Sailing to Byzantium" can now be given diagrammatic form:

VERSE	EPIPHANY	TIME/ ETERNITY	YOUTH/AGE	RELATION TO ART AND SELF	FORM OF SONG AND WISDOM	STATE OF BODY AND SOUL
1	Youth	Time	Youth only (Y+ A−)	Neglect of art: absorption in self	Natural bird-song: absence of wisdom	Body satisfied
2	Age	Time	Age only (Y− A+)	Quest for art: repudiation of self	Human song: quest for wisdom	Body dissatisfied
3	Life → Art	Eternity	Neither age nor youth (Y− A−)	Learning of art: consumption of self (sensuality spiritualised)	Sage's song: gift of wisdom	Soul dissatisfied
4	Art → Life	Eternity	Age and youth (Y+ A+)	Achievement of art: disappearance of self (spirituality sensualised)	Artificial bird-song: restitution of wisdom to life	Soul satisfied

The partly implicit, partly explicit Yeatsian views of eternity as being imaginable or perceivable only in terms of art, and of culture as necessarily centring on art, are perhaps the most consistent features of Yeats's peculiar system. In fact, the constancy with which this line of thought is applied is "excessive," in the sense that it gives rise to consequences which appear unrealistic. Within the ambit of "Sailing to Byzantium," however,—whatever we may think in "philosphical" terms about Yeats's system, it is undeniable that the rooting in *art* of all existence's four basic Yeatsian phases, corresponding to verses 1–4, supplies the poem with a marvelous coherence. The four stages of the journey—from full display of youth (verse 1), to full display of age (verse 2), to an image of *ascesis* towards a timeless state (verse 3), to an image of descent back towards contact with life prefiguring possible reincarnation (verse 4)—are all rendered in terms of artistically—or at least aesthetically—gratifying experience.

The abundant forms of life centring on sexual consummation in verse 1 correspond to a celebration (self-celebration) of life in song:

5 Fish, flesh, or fowl, commend all summer long
6 Whatever is begotten, born, and dies.

In fact, SONG is the thread which leads through the bewildering wealth of Yeats's poem, uniting all four verses—"3 SONG"—"11 SING, and louder SING," "20 SINGING-masters"—"30 set upon a golden bough to SING." If verse 1 offers a celebration of presence, verse 2 presents a "singing" of absence, with the desire for a new presence—the consciousness of eternity, or unity of being. It is this "perfected song" which is taught by the "singing-masters" identified as "sages standing in God's holy fire" in verse 3. In the final phase, of willing descent down the gyre towards nature, the golden bird "sing[s]" to the Byzantine court, offering a "restitution" of nature to itself through the reformulation of "26 natural thing[s]" into immortal song. This could be called the "wisdom of art."

The final state of achieved art is the most "tormented" by Byzantium's double status. The singing can be imagined as occurring either within historical Byzantium (even if only as the image of a wish), or as an imaginative "reconstruction" of eternal joy. Even on the latter reading, however, the implicit doctrine of "things below are copies" (as "Ribh Denounces Patrick" was to say)—here seen in blatantly reversed form, in the sense that the artificial bird proudly outdoes the *natural* birds of verse 1 [12]—assures us that a return to life is contemplated. Such a return is a "built-in feature" of the sensuousness and sensory pleasure of the birdsong appreciated by the noble audience; it is guaranteed by the moduli of art itself—its desire and need to communicate.

This tacit turning towards life through the perfection of artistic experience is enhanced by the "play within a play" effect of ending the poem here, with its cunningly timed suspension of "suspension of disbelief." We are given back to a consciousness of having heard a poem in a way which makes our condition strictly parallel to that of Emperor, lords and ladies. Have we too not been privileged listeners—temporarily withdrawn from consciousness of time to a timeless sphere—to that impersonal I's "artificial birdsong"? . . .

[Johnson discusses how the poem's use of the poetic "I" incorporates Yeats's theory that the individual artist must continually transform himself.]

"MAGNIFICENCE" IN THOUGHT AND EXPRESSION

Sturge Moore's letter quoted above [Moore approved of the first three stanzas of "Sailing" but felt let down by the fourth stanza because the goldsmith's bird is as much nature as a man's body] offers an intriguing example of the "contagion" of the appreciation of art by the substance and sign of the art work; Sturge Moore finds the first three verses "magnificent"—and this, as we know already, is a key sign in the poem. In addition, it gives a name to the type of phonic substance—what Ellmann refers to as "*magnificence of tone*" [13]—which is the hallmark of Yeats's poetic display here. This adds another level of self-reference to the poem; the poet has disappeared in the poem. He has been "gather[ed]" into the "eternity"—the "holy fire" of the poetic act, so transforming the "magnificence" he saw in Byzantine art into the "magnificence" of his own poetry. And now, "How can we know the dancer from the dance?"

The prevalence of art over its "existential" subject-matter—even where this happens to be "eternity"—and of the plane of expression over that of thought, with the covert interpretation of immortality in terms of the "immortal" status of the art work, is made signically and semantically flagrant by the last lines of verse 3:

23 . . . and gather me
24 Into the ARTifice of eternity.

Here eternity is presented in opposition to the unthinking abundance and self-dependence of nature as something constructed "alchemically," in a convergent, anagogic movement (spiralling up towards the top of the gyre) from the multiplicity of "Fish, flesh, or fowl" to the "oneness"—the goldenness which unites all the artistic objects seen in Byzantium (verses 3 and 4).

THE ANAGOGIC URGE IN NATURE

This urge upwards from NATURE to ART and from the MAKING of nature to the MAKING of art, is present from the first verse. The display in 4–6:

4 The salmon-falls, the mackerel-crowded seas,
5 Fish, flesh, or fowl, commend all summer long
6 Whatever is begotten, born, and dies.

begins with the two kinds of fish and dwells most specifically on them. They occupy the lowest level—below ground—and the triad "Fish, flesh, or fowl" moves from below ground level to ground level to above ground level—to air, the medium for flight. Functionally, the salmon present nature's sheer *power* and the mackerel represent its sheer *abundance*[14]—indeed, we find a perfectly ordered anagram of MAKE, the poem's key verb, in "MAcKErEl."

Yet, just as "3 dying generations" presented nature's wasteful contradictoriness, the simultaneity of its dying with its living and self-reproduction, so Yeats not only chooses the salmon as his emblem of nature's power—a fish whose death coincides with its act of fecundation, but he also uses a phrase, "salmon-falls," which offers a type of oxymoron closely parallel to "dying generations." The latter gives DEATH + LIFE (in the act of REPRODUCTION), with life made dominant by its being thus "raised to the second power," while the first points to nature's capacity to RISE against the stream in leaping the FALLS—or, we might say, in "flying" upwards through falling water. Here the flight of erotic desire is seen conquering the entropy of inanimate nature, and this is confirmed phonosymbolically, by the dominance of initial [f], symbolising flight, together with an admixture of the joyous-aggressive male phonemes [r, k].[15] The presence of death appears phonosymbolically, too, however, in the melancholy-passive phonemes [l, m], so setting up, on another plane, the cohabitation of eros and thanatos, of the life and death principles, in nature:

> The salmon-falls, the mackerel-crowded seas,
>   [m f l   m k r lkr]
> Fish, flesh, or fowl, commend all summer long
> [f fl (r)f l k m   l m (r)l]

Male (active) phonemes: [f] = 4; [r] = 4; [k] = 3; *total* = 11, of which 6 are lexemically initial.

Female (passive) phonemes: [l] = 6; [m] = 4; *total* = 10, of which 2 are lexemically initial.

This internal conflict within nature, and the need for life to RISE against the tendency of the individual organism to FALL to inanimate matter, correspond to the pain of the struggle between the two principles seen at the end of "Byzantium," "40 That *dolphin*-torn, that *gong*-tormented *sea*," where the *sea* of life feels the agony of the impulse towards sublimation; the *dolphin*, like the salmon, displays an astonishing capacity to jump out of its medium, its Platonic *hyle*, while the *gong* is that of the "4 great cathedral" of Holy Wisdom (Hagia Sophia).

Clearly, Yeats's whole presentation in "Sailing to Byzantium" points to a secret alliance between artistic creativity—a process of sublimation—and erotic desire—a process of sensualisation, and these two may be seen antiphonally in verses 3 and 4. Verse 3 shows sensuality being "spiritualised," and verse 4 shows spirituality being "sensualised."

Two Kinds of Making

There are thus two types of making—nature's making through reproduction, already seen inscribed in "4 MACKErEl, or the making of art, which is seen by Yeats as "24 ARTifice," and as offering the substance of "eternity."

If ARTIFICE is divided into the two segments, ART[α:t] + IFICE [ifis], the first is found to represent the self-referential subject of the poem, and the second the central portion, including the stressed vowel, of MAG-NIFICENCE [mæg′nifisəns] (→ IFICE [ifis])—the quality which best defines Yeats's "holy city." Etymologically, in fact, ARTIFICE offers the combination "MAKING of ART," and MAGNIFICENCE offers "MAKING of GREATNESS." In both words the segment -FICE- derives from Latin *facere*, "to make."

Nature, then, offers a self-regarding, self-reproducing type of beauty and of making, whereas art offers an other-regarding, other-producing type of beauty and making in which the self ("21 my heart") is "fire-consumed" in something greater than itself. Paradoxically, it is only the "spiritualising" of sensuality into a timeless contemplation of truth, and that spirituality's return through a descent into the sensual beauty of art (and hence of nature as "32 what is past, or passing, or to come") which offer a "restitution" of nature to itself, in a synthesis of timeless (immortal) form with time-bound ("12 mortal") content. This synthesis depends aesthetically on that comparison between a *natural* base with an *artificial* apex ("2 birds" with golden bird) which distinguished the form and the song of the Byzantine bird. The golden bird thus emblemises art as the emulation of nature—a supersession given back to nature for its contemplation.

Signic Alchemy: God in Gold

The anagogic transmutation of matter into art points towards alchemy's emblem for immortality and divinity—GOLD. In fact, GOD appears just once in "17 God's holy fire," and is afterward supplanted or substituted by the concreteness of GOLD(EN). Phonically and graphically, GOLD perfectly condenses "GOD[god]" + "HOLY[ˈhəuli]." GOLD(EN) appears no less than five times, with subtle variations in its syntactic, semantic and rhymthic roles:

18 As in the GOLD mosaic of a wall,
27 But such a form as Grecian GOLDsmiths make
28 Of hammered GOLD and GOLD enamelling
30 Or set upon a GOLDEN bough to sing

The poem's artistic synaesthesia reaches its climax in the last verse, where the golden bird delights not only sight and touch, but hearing too. The living are given "intellectual" life by the perfection of an artistic construct; Emperor, lords and ladies are kept awake and entertained by a GOLDEN ART, which entrances the senses without tiring or consuming any of them. Here Yeats's pattern is chiasmically circular—the "lords and ladies" (satisfied YOUTH + AGE)[16] of the *one-but-last* line answer "the young / In one another's arms" of the *first two* lines. The love felt for a work of art which delights the senses without consuming them is superior to the "sensual music" of self-consuming bodily gratification. In the same way, line 7's "sensual music" is answered almost symmetrically, first by art's "outworking"[17] of nature in "gold mosaic," and then by "goldsmiths make" in the sixth-last line:

SENSUAL	MUSIC	['mju:zik]
GOLD	MOSAIC	[məu'zeiik]
GOLDSMITHS	MAKE	[meik]

What is "sensual" is excelled by what is "golden"; and so is the "music" by the "mosaic" and by the "goldsmiths[']" ability to "make" (cf. the Scottish name for poet, "makar"). The achieved beauty of the "gold mosaic" leads into an image for the active *making* ("make" is in the present tense) of a "super-natural" (ambiguously *above* nature and *outdoing* nature) self for the "I." MUSIC → MOSAIC → MAKE are linked phonically and graphically, most clearly by initial M[m] and final [k]. All three involve a making—the first a bodily making (a begetting), the second the making of an ideal image, and the third of a simulacrum for a poem without a poet, slightly displaced as a "song without a singer." The golden bird is a subtle image for the impersonality of a great artwork. As Yeats wrote about Byzantine art:

> The painter, the mosaic worker, the worker in gold and silver, the illuminator of sacred books, were *almost impersonal*, almost perhaps without the consciousness of individual design, *absorbed in their subject-matter* and that the vision of a whole people. (*A Vision*, 279–80)

In other words, instead of verse 1's bodily making, with intense sensual joy given by coitus, verse 4 shows the making of a "bodily form" which is self-sufficient—an "end in itself"; here a higher form of sensual pleasure is given by art. Thus Yeats's poetic parallelism cleverly models art as a "spiritual begetting." For Yeats, even pure spirit needs its "26 bodily form," and he gave an explicit reminder in *A Vision* (212) that "all the symbolism of this book applies to *begetting and birth*." . . .

[These sections assert that the poem's greatest paradox lies in the resurgence of life and nature through its poetic images. Such poetic forms provide the only way of synthesizing temporal and eternal, sensual and spiritual.]

SEMANTIC AND SIGNIC BINDING

The sharpness of the semantic breaks between the four verses of "Sailing to Byzantium" is accompanied by a variety of techniques for binding the four units together again. In particular, the first lines of verses 2, 3 and 4 display double or triple links with previous verses; they are also anchored to the last one or two lines of the previous verse, and, via these, to the first line of the poem, which must thus be considered the poem's signic and semantic foundation-stone:

  1 That is no country for OLD MEN. . . .
   . . . .
  7 Caught in that sensual music all neglect
  8 Monuments of UNAGEING intellect

  9 An AGED MAN is but a paltry thing
   . . . .
 15 And therefore I have sailed the seas and come
 16 To the HOLY city of BYZANTIUM.

 17 O SAGES standing in God's HOLY fire
   . . . .
 23 . . . gather me
 24 Into the ARTIFICE of ETERNITY.

 25 Once OUT OF NATURE I shall never take
 26 My bodily form from any NATURAL thing,
 27 But [as a golden bird]
 30 . . . sing
 31 To lords and ladies of BYZANTIUM
 32 Of what is PAST, OR PASSING, OR TO COME.

In lines included in the script for a programme of his work for the B.B.C. (Belfast, 8 September, 1931), but omitted from the actual broadcast, Yeats wrote:

> Now I am trying to write about the state of my soul, for it is *right for an* OLD MAN *to make his soul*, and some of my thoughts upon that subject I have put into a poem called "Sailing to Byzantium." (Italics and capitals added.)

The poem's central concern, and primary generative principle, is this need for an OLD MAN to MAKE his soul (note the choice of verb in "27 such a form as Grecian goldsmiths MAKE"). There is an immediate juxtaposition between the antonymous terms "OLD MEN" and "The YOUNG" in line 1.[18] It is the apparently idyllic nature of "That . . . country," where, we might say, "soul is bruised to pleasure body," that leads to neglect of "Monuments of UNAGEING intellect." Besides anticipating "16 holy city of Byzantium," this sets up a clear contrast between "1 old men" and "8 unageing." When youth's "5 summer" is over, "1 The Young" will realize they are ageing.

Line 9's "aged ['eidʒid]" reverses 8's "unageing [ʌn'eidʒiŋ]," so returning to equivalence with line 1: "old men" ≡ "An aged man"; differentiation comes through age's *absence* in 1 and its *presence* in 8, and through the plural diffuseness of the first, and the singular (poignant) compactness of the second. The poet's predicament is now displayed. If the aged man is to "make his soul," the tragic gaiety of "clapping hands" is a harsh necessity, but it also offers a joyful salvation. More specifically, this verse rejects possible soul-construction through philosophy or religion; the only prospect it allows is that of art taught and learnt as "self-enclosed" quest (which is what Yeats's poem is): "sing, and louder sing" → "singing school" → "Monuments of its own magnificence."

Verse 3 begins: "O sages ['seidʒiz]," which contains "AGE [eidʒ]" phonically and graphically. The sages are seen "in God's holy fire." Thus "sages" not only links up with lines 9 and 1, but their "HOLY fire" mirrors the "16 HOLY city" which gives verse 2 its climax.

As to the links straddling the gap between verses 3 and 4, "25 out of *nature*" is flexed against "24 *artifice* of *eternity*." This repeats the modulus of line 1; there, "old men" clashed with "The young," but the first were absent or rejected, and the second present or accepted. Here the first element, "eternity," is present or accepted, and the second, "nature," is absent or rejected (in the sense that the "voyage to Byzantium" is devised as an escape from it). This split between ETERNITY and NATURE arranges the first as a positive future (which artistic ecstasy makes available as a perpetual present), and the second as a negative past. As in verse 1, the verse-*incipit* models a mental reality on exclusion of a possibility:

    1 That is *no* country for old men [NEGATION OF AGE]
    25 Once out of nature I shall *never* take [FLIGHT FROM NATURE]
    26 My bodily form from *any* natural thing, [NEGATION OF NATURE]

Signically, the "*artifice* of eternity" yields Yeats's antinomic contrast with "any *natural* thing." As already glimpsed, however, there is a strong "return of the repressed" —or, to be more exact, "return of the suppressed." Nature's forms are *already* present here as paradigms to be absorbed and superseded, while the "31 lords and ladies of Byzantium" are similarly modelled on, and supersede "1 – 2 The young / In one another's arms."[19] The "sensual music" of nature in verse 1, in fact, is self-directed (open to youth only), whereas the art of verse 4 is other-directed (open to all age-groups and all ages); but being other-directed, art must surreptitiously readmit nature, both as a principle of artistic construction (bird, tree, song) and as its opposite term in the communicative process (living audience which must be "kept awake").

YEATS'S THREE "TRINITIES"

A still more striking "return of suppressed nature" is found in the lexical and syntactic "trinities." This modulus is first seen—twice—in verse 1, and it is powerfully reawoken, with an implicit "display of all time and all nature," as the subject-matter of the unageing song, in the last line of the poem:

> 5 Fish, flesh, or fowl . . . [WHOLE OF NATURAL LIFE]
> 6 Whatever is begotten, born, and dies. [ITS TRANSIENCE]
>
> 32 Of what is past, or passing, or to come. [WHOLE CONTENT OF TIME]

The "trinities" of lines 6 and 32 (unlike that of line 5) show third terms differentiated from the other two; these share "b-n [b-n]" in 6 and "pas-[pɑ:s]" in 32. The first ends: "dies" [DEATH], whereas the second ends: "TO COME," which truculently introduces a future *with respect to* eternity; this may be read as a cunningly oblique but unmistakeable hint at reincarnation. In fact, Yeats gets a fine irony out of having his lords and ladies—who, under one aspect, are inhabitants of eternity—learn about the future from a mechanical bird; this effect anticipates that of Yeats's later title, "News for the Delphic Oracle."

Thus Yeats's "immortal bird" is actually displayed singing of the whole of life. It has supernatural access to the future (and did not Yeats's *A Vision* aim to sing "Of what is past, or passing, or to come?"), but the words and form of the last line recall the abundance of the country of the young. The summit of the Byzantine hierarchy—its emblem of perfection—the "Emperor," is, rather like Blake's "god in the sun,"[21] "drowsy"—in danger of falling asleep. He, like "the pale unsatisfied ones" with "ancient faces" in "The Magi," who search for divinity "on the bestial floor," is seen attracted towards his antithetical opposite. In his perfect "oneness," he wishes to hear the varied multiplicity of mortal events celebrated.

THE TRANSMUTATION OF HUMANITY INTO ART

Line 28, "Of hammered gold and gold enamelling," shows what Yeats's golden bird is made of. It simultaneously offers a signic transmutation. We find a perfect mirror-image reversal of "9 aged MAN [mæn]" (it-self re-expressing "1 OLD MEN") in the stressed syllable of "ENAMelling [i'næməliŋ]"; and the first two elements, MA [æ], are found again, simi-larly reversed, in "HAMMered ['hæmə(r)d]." In between we find that the key lexeme "OLD [əuld]" has been chiasmically absorbed whole in the twice iterated "GOLD [gəuld]":[22]

	Of	HAMMered	GOLD	ANd	GOLD	ENAMellinng
	[əv	'hæmə(r)d	gəuld	ənd	gəuld	i'næməliŋ]
Signic			OLD		OLD	
OLD [əuld]:			[əuld]		[əuld]	

Signic MAN→	AMM	AN	NAM	N
NAM [næem]:	[æm]	[n]	[næm]	[n]

Thus the signic "alchemy" of the human element occurs through the reversal of MAN [mæn] into NAM [næm], and this appears in the flanking (protective) segments which surround the two compact instances of GOLD (which has "absorbed" OLD), the alchemical symbol for perfection, value and immortality.

This reading is reinforced by the graphic and phonic content of the poem's twice-iterated word "MONUMENts," which offers "M-N-MEN-" graph-ically and [m-n-m-n-] phonically. In retrospect, we may in fact say that "MONUMENts," whose presence is so important in verses 1 and 2, antici-pates and leads into the nature of Yeats's Byzantium. Semantically, it con-denses the meanings, "mentally creative *constructs*" (→ works of ART) with "objectively magnificent *constructions*" (making up a CITY famous for its architecture and art). And these two valencies are exactly those Yeats gives his "holy city of Byzantium" in both Byzantine poems—here in the *other* two verses, 3 and 4. The "M-N-MEN" anagrammatic content of the word secretly highlights the fact that not only works of art, but cities too, are a direct product of human thought—of "MEN," a typically Yeatsian thesis. (*Both* key words in 14 contain ordered anagrams of MEN: "MONUMENts," "MagNificeNce," and another, compact one is found in "5 coMMENd").

CONCLUSION: ETERNITY AS ARTIFICE

Yeats's subordination of eternity to ART is strikingly revealed in an-other way when we see how he transformed his source (or his memory of it) for his golden bird. The problem of which source(s) Yeats really drew on has been the subject of lively and fascinating debate[23]; what is certain is that Yeats's own note in his *Collected Poems* reads, "I have read some-where that in the Emperor's palace at Byzantium was a tree made of gold and silver, and *artificial* birds that sang" (532). In "Sailing to Byzantium" we see Yeats using an artificial bird as a symbol of eternity *communicating with life;* Stallworthy's interpretation here looks one-sided or incomplete, because it seems to treat Yeats's Byzantium as little more than a "city of the mind," as if the historical city could be overlooked. Thus he goes so far as to say that Yeats's "'lords & ladies of Byzantium' can only be the spirits of the noble dead!"[24]

But this is not all; Yeats takes the lexeme "artificial" away from its original referent in memory, the birds, and daringly displaces it on to eternity itself, making "artifice" his key word in characterising that time-less state. The provocativeness of Yeats's reworking is strengthened by the prominent position given to "artifice" (at the start of verse 3's last line) and by its rhythmic power; its first syllable, "ART [ɑ:t]," carries the strongest stress in the line, whose climactic prominence is increased by its brevity.

In practice, Yeats uses his bird's artificial beauty as a "justification" or "motivation" of his desire to be "gathered into eternity," rather than the reverse (the traditional justification of art as "changeless" which is found in verse 3 of "Byzantium"). Ellmann states that "'artifice' has unpleasant connotations" which Yeats "does not entirely disavow" because "the natu-ral world still holds some attraction for him."[25] Thus Ellmann presents "artifice" as displaying a compromise between conflicting principles. Now Ellmann is almost alone in not drastically underestimating the at-traction felt for nature at the end of the poem, but his account fails to explain part of the power of "Into the *artifice* of eternity." Yeats is, I would say, strongly exploiting the culturally accepted negativity of "ar-tifice" to challenge his readers, and create a *conflict against expectation.* By opting for "the artifice of eternity," the poem's "I" is swimming against the current of "linguistic prejudice"—a device often used brilliantly by him, as, for instance, in the last line of "After Long Silence," "Young we loved each other and were *ignorant.*" It was this willingness to be advo-cate for the "wrong" side and "give it its say" which gave his poetry its depth and completeness, its "higher sincerity." It is the final "return of suppressed nature" which is the poem's undeclared undertow, its rebel-lion against the reckless championing of artifice and eternity.

The originality of Yeats's model for thought in "Sailing to Byzantium" lies here. There is no shortage of believers in immortality, but how many have believed in it because they saw it as the perfect sphere for an *ar-tificial* art—Nature's antithetical rival? Yeats's cunningest twist was to di-rect this supposedly "anti-natural" art back to an audience of sensually demanding people. This also offered a subtle and disturbing challenge to his readers, who are tacitly compared with "drowsy Emperor" and "lords and ladies of Byzantium." Thus Yeats ends up by "creat[ing] mar-vellous drama out of [his] own li[fe]"; he theatrically casts himself as a lifeless bird in an eternity of Art, trying to communicate with a "drowsy" or entertainment-hungry élite who expect their poet to know all the se-crets of time and eternity. The bird-poet is "set upon a golden bough to sing," as an amusing toy whose supernatural truths are inseparable from the aesthetic pleasure they give.

NOTES

1. This essay is chiefly indebted to the following discussions of "Sailing to Byzantium": Richard Ellmann, *Yeats: The Man and the Masks* (London, 1961 [1949]): 256–60, and *The Identity of Yeats*, 1964 (1965): xxii, 10, 165, 237; Jon Stallworthy, *Between the Lines: Yeats's Poetry in the Making* (London, 1963), chap. 5, 87–112; A. Norman Jeffares, *A Commentary on the Collected Poems of W. B. Yeats* (London, 1968), 251–57, and "The Byzantine Poems of W. B. Yeats," *Review of English Studies* 22, no. 85 (1946): 44–52; Curtis Bradford, "Yeats's Byzantine Poems," *PMLA* 75, no. 1 (1960): 110–25; F. A. C. Wilson, *W. B. Yeats and Tradition* (London, 1958), 82, 231–32, and *Yeats's Iconography* (London, 1969 [1960]), 284–85, 305; F. L. Gwynn, "Yeats's Byzantium and Its Sources," *Philological Quarterly* 32, no. 1 (1953): 9–21; M. Praz, *The Romantic Agony* (London, 1933), chaps. 4 and 5; Giorgio Melchiori, *The Whole Mystery of Art* (London, 1960), 200–234; Agostino Lombardo, *La poesia inglese dall'estetismo al simbolismo* (Rome, 1950), 97–100, 249–88. For a specific bibliography, see James L. Allen, "Charts for the Voyage to Byzantium: An Annotated Bibliography of Scholarship and Criticism on Yeats' Byzantium Poems, 1935–1970," *Bulletin of the New York Public Library* 77, no. 1 (1973): 28–50; see also K. P. S. Jochum, "W. B. Yeats: A Survey of Book Publications, 1966–1972," *Anglia* 92 (1974): 143–71. In this essay all italics in passages of quoted verse or prose are mine.

2. Yeats, *A Vision* (London, 1937), 219; this, the second edition, has been used for all quotations in this essay. The first—and shorter—edition, subtitled: *An Explanation of Life founded upon the Writings of Giraldus and upon Certain Doctrines attributed to Kusta Ben Luka* was published in London in 1925, before "Sailing to Byzantium" was written.

3. Yeats's favourite Heraklitean fragment, "Men and Gods die each other's life, live each other's death" (Thomas Taylor, *A Dissertation* [Amsterdam, 1790], 7) was absorbed into his system as an expression of the antithetical interdependence of the two spheres of time and eternity. In *A Vision* this thought appears at least four times (pp. 68, 197, 271, 275 in the 1937 ed.), and it is also found—even if given a Coleridgean formulation—in "Byzantium": "15 I hail the superhuman; / 16 I call it death-in-life and life-in-death" (cf. Wilson, *W. B. Yeats and Tradition*, 59).

4. Wilson, *W. B. Yeats and Tradition*, 238: "As [Yeats] does, the Kabbalistic writers symbolise the whole of life by a diagram of a single tree, at whose apex the purified soul is placed. . . ." Wilson's scholarship is usually impeccable and his readings sensitive, but his attachment to Neoplatonic and, in general, Traditional beliefs leads him to overlook questions which do not arise at the level of the material of thought, so that his analyses tend to be cramped by being restricted to the level of glossing.

5. See the excellent discussion on this point by Wilson, in ibid., 238–39, and Ellmann, *Yeats: The Man*, 274–75.

6. Quoted by Stallworthy, *Between the Lines*, 115.

7. As Stallworthy (ibid., 90) notes, "At the time of writing ["Sailing to Byzantium," Yeats] was over sixty and conscious of the presence of death. In November 1924 bad health and high blood-pressure had driven him from Ireland to Italy and the Mediterranean." The thought of death had penetrated much deeper by the time "Byzantium" was written. Yeats himself wrote in the notes to his *Collected Poems* (537), "ill again, I warmed myself back into life with 'Byzantium' and 'Veronica's Napkin,' looking for a theme that might befit my years." Stallworthy adds, "He had been perilously near death from Malta fever at Rapallo during the autumn of 1929 . . ." (115).

8. Ellmann, *Yeats: The Man*, 288. "Byzantium" was written in September, 1930, Ellmann dates Yeats's remark as made in 1937, and Yeats died on January 28, 1939.

9. Yeats came to realise that the systematic features of *A Vision* were "stylistic arrangements of experience comparable to the cubes in the drawing of Wyndham Lewis and to the ovoids in the sculpture of Brancusi" (introd. to 1937 ed., 25); as Melchiori has pointed out, these arrangements are "what we would nowadays . . . call semiotic schemata." (*L'uomo e il potere* [Turin, 1973], 205, my trans.).

10. *Exodus* 3 : 2.

11. London 1959, 300−301 (originally in *The Tables of the Law* [London, 1897]).

12. Cf. Ellmann, "the bird is . . . irrevocably dependent upon the nature which it affects to spurn" (*The Identity*, xxii).

13. Ellmann, *The Identity*, 246. So too J. Crowe Ransome, in "The Irish, the Gaelic, the Byzantine," *Southern Review* 7 (1941−42): 521−22, first declares that it is hard to absorb "all this *magnificence* at once" and then that "its *magnificence* is a little bit forced."

14. Jeffares (*A Commentary*, 254−55) offers useful biographical material on the associations salmon and mackerel had for Yeats.

15. On these phonosymbolic values, see Ivan Fónagy's excellent paper, *Il linguaggio poetico: forma e funzione* in AA.VV., *I problemi attuali della linguistica* (Milan, 1968), 85−135, esp. 88−94.

16. Cf. ending of *I see Phantoms of Hatred* . . . , "38−40 The abstract joy, / The half-read wisdom of daemonic images, / Suffice the *ageing man as once the growing boy*."

17. Cf. *Antony and Cleopatra*, 2.2.201.

18. The drafts show that Yeats was tempted at one stage to model his "country of the young" on the Platonic "Saturnine" country: "Here all is young, & grows young day by day" (Stallworthy, *Between the Lines*, 91). The definitive verse 1 shows a country where only the young are happy, and that happiness lasts only a "long summer"—a "season" of life.

19. The "lords and ladies" are bound consonantally—"l-d(-)s [l-d(-)z]," and the "young / In one another's arms" vocalically by the three stressed [ʌ]s, and also by the five nasale consonants [ŋ, n, n, n, m]—one for each word.

20. For the sexual valency of such trinities in Yeats, and the anti-Christian polemic they imply, see my "Actantial modelling of the love relationship in W. B. Yeats: from 'He wishes for the Cloths of Heaven' to 'Leda and the Swan,'" *Linguistica e letteratura* 1 (1977): 155−79.

21. Kathleen Raine, in *Blake and Tradition* (Princeton, 1968), points out that

one of Blake's engravings for *Job* contains a "drowsy figure of God" (1 : 95), while one of the illustrations for *Jerusalem* contains a similar figure of a drowsy God (2 : 227). In describing the Arlington Court Painting (Yeats could not have known this directly, as it was rediscovered in 1949), she notes that "in the car [the chariot of the sun], the god is sunk in sleep or deep drowsiness"; Blake is here interpreting fundamental doctrines in the Tradition, primarily "Porphyry's treatise on Homer's *Cave of the Nymphs*" (extensively drawn on by Yeats for "News for the Delphic Oracle," as shown by Wilson, *W. B. Yeats*, 222–23), and secondarily "details from the *Odyssey* and from Platonic sources" (1 : 75). The fact that "the sun-god . . . is sunk in profound sleep" suggests "the contrasting states of life in this world as death in the other; or, in this case, the waking of the one as the sleep of the other" (1 : 96). This, of course, is how Yeats interpreted the Heraklitean dictum discussed in n. 3 above. Thus Yeats's "29 To keep a drowsy Emperor awake" implies that if the human imagination is excited by divine images of eternity, the divine imagination is excited by human images of time—the product of human artifice which, as here, ultimately turns back to nature. Here again, a symmetrical situation is devised.

22. For the other, "GOD-HOLY" valency of the sign GOLD, see above, p. 145.

23. See esp. Jeffares, *A Commentary*, 257, "The Byzantime Poems," 48–49, and "Yeats's Byzantine Poems and the Critics," *English Studies in Africa* 5 (1962): 1–27; T. L. Dume, "Yeats's Golden Tree and Birds in the Byzantine Poems," *Modern Language Notes* 67 (1952): 404–7; E. Schanzer, "'Sailing to Byzantium,' Keats and Anderson," *English Studies* 41 (1960): 376–80; M. Praz, "L'usignolo d'oro," in *Cronache letterarie anglosassoni* (Rome, 1966), 4 : 75–76.

24. Stallworthy, *Between the Lines*, 101.

25. Ellmann, *The Identity*, 144.

William Faulkner's "A Rose for Emily"

NIKOLAUS HAPPEL

Happel's essay can be considered an example of narratology, a branch of structuralist poetics dealing with the homology between language and narrative. Narratologists explore the relation between how the story is narrated (the "discourse") and what is narrated (the "story"). Linguistically, "story" is roughly analogous to *langue,* and "discourse" to *parole.* Since narration has to do with events in time, narratologists often contrast the narrator's reordering of events (discourse time) with the chronological, cause-effect order of events (story time). Happel points

From *William Faulkner: "A Rose for Emily"*, ed. M. Thomas Inge (Columbus, Ohio: Charles E. Merrill, 1970), 68–72. Translated from the German by Alfred Kolb for *William Faulkner: "A Rose for Emily"* and reprinted by permission, from the complete essay in *Die Neueren Sprachen*, no. 9 (1962): 396–404.

out how the ambiguous role of the narrator (the "we") in "A Rose for Emily" adds to the reader's uncertainty about what really happens. By enabling Faulkner to excise such events as the "smell" affair and the "drugstore" scene from the chronological sequence, the ("we") narrator instills a sense of mystery, complexity, and comic tension in the story. The excerpt here follows Happel's summary of the plot of "A Rose for Emily" as it moves forward and backward in time.

THE PERSPECTIVE OF presentation in "A Rose for Emily" is not centralized. Althought the event is quite objectively recorded by the narrator, he often relinquishes the objective point of view and becomes a participant in the story's action. He doesn't emerge as an "I" in the foreground, but he places himself as the "we" within the circle of the townspeople, and becomes a participatory witness and observer. By means of the directness of the experience, the presentation receives a heightened credibility and intensity. But just who is included in the circle of the "we," however, is not clearly delineated. Here too uncertainty dominates, as it does in several other aspects of the story. From the first sentence the collective "we" is disclosed by the possessive form of "our town," but then the narrative tone becomes objective until the second chapter; at the end of which it is again replaced by the subjective "we." At first the narrator's circle of participants seems to be designated by the "we," for it appears next to "people," "the ladies," and "older people" (but later, with the benefit of hindsight, this idea seems no longer tenable). Then the feelings and observations of the "we" group so completely blend with those of the other people that the impression of a larger collective emerges, a collective group which includes most of the townspeople.

At another time the whole of the town, originally termed as "our," is clearly referred to as "we." The subjectively weak "our town," which still invests the narrator with a certain aloofness from the group, gives way to the "our" which allows the narrator to merge entirely with the collective: "The day after his death all the ladies prepared to call at the house and offer condolence and aid, *as is our custom.*" The participation in the event grows ever more intensive, and the group of participants becomes a community in which the individual loses his identity. To begin with, the unity of the many is presented through the "we all"; then this unity takes on an almost personal character. It is only when it is said of Miss Emily that "she carried her head high" that the unified reaction is interrupted and the collective recedes. "Some ladies" act independently, in order to give additional impetus to the occurrence. Thereafter the collective "we" again comes to the fore; the general interest is thus heightened and receives more attention.

Later the town administration, which at the outset was introduced in the third person as "mayors and aldermen" of the "next generation," is absorbed in the "we." Narrator and townspeople identify themselves with the city administration; the imposing mass stands in contrast to Miss Emily and lets her appear in lonely isolation: "Each December *we* sent her a tax notice, which would be returned by the post office a week later, unclaimed." Even the story's end brings no unequivocal clarification of the concept, for who can be meant by the "we," to which yet another dark "they" is attached? "Already *we* knew that there was one room in that region above stairs which no one had seen in forty years, and which would have to be forced. *They* waited until Miss Emily was decently in the ground before *they* opened it." At first certainly the townspeople, but then no longer, for it says ". . . for a long while *we* just stood there [in the open door of the room], looking down at the profound and fleshless grin" of Homer Barron's corpse.

The "we" remains obscure; it eludes any clear definition or bounds and thereby leaves the reader in uncertainty. Only conjecture and pre-sentiment which here underscore the specific criteria limit the weakly circumscribed concept of the "we." One thing however becomes clear: the narrator is involved in the event; the depicted reality and the world of the narrator coalesce. His being is a part of the viable whole of the town; he participates in the events of this community and pulls the reader into this participation. Strangely enough, nowhere in the story is there mention of a rose. In the course of her life, Miss Emily never re-ceived a rose. But her casket was decorated with flowers: Miss Emily rested "beneath a mass of bought flowers." These flowers cannot express real sympathy. If anyone took Miss Emily's part, then it was Captain Sartoris and the members of the older generation who still had respect for the aristocratic tradition. Their attitude, however, can also not be viewed in terms of sincere human support. If any connection of the title can be made with the "bought flowers" (in the reader's awareness this is conveyed through the disclosure of the "bought flowers" near the end of the story), then it must be construed as irony, as irony which is directed against the lovelessness of the townsfolk, as irony which above all impli-cates the "ladies sibilant and macabre" and exposes them to ridicule. In the irony-laden title the narrator preserves his separateness from the at-titude of the people who ordered the flowers for the burial. There ap-pears to be a premeditated distance, kept in respect to the narrator's ironic intent. Nonetheless, the narrator cannot absolutely dissociate him-self, for he was himself—as the description from the perspective of the "we" indicates—included in the group of the "townspeople" and fre-quently shared their sentiments. Thus the perplexity of the narrator, which finds its support in the title, is understandable. Through the title and thence through the story, the narrator strives to demonstrate his genuine sympathy for Miss Emily and to make up, so to speak, for his neglect of her during her lifetime. The narrator feels sympathy and probably also guilt and attempts to reach some understanding of Miss Emily through his tale. He defends Miss Emily, for her fate was sealed by powers and forces against which she could not contend.

The meaning of the story's title—as the titles of several other Faulknerian works, for example, *Wild Palms, Light in August*—is ambivalent, and this peculiarity permits the disclosure of an essential aspect of Faulkner's narrative mode. It remains, as do many other concepts, complicated and multiplex and eludes any absolute interpretation.

A powerful tension is evident in the aspect of the odd, for it is here bound up with the tragic and macabre. One such oddity is of course the "smell" that one can detect around Miss Emily's house, the smell whose origin still remains a mystery: ". . . the smell. That was two years after her father's death and a short time after her sweetheart—the one we believed would marry her—had deserted her." The smell remains a mystery until, at the end of the story, it is resolved by the horrendous sight of Homer Barron's cadaver. In this manner, through hindsight, according to his reading of the tale, the relation of the macabre and the comic becomes manifest for the reader; this relation grows out of the town administration's deference for the aristocratic lady. As the "smell" in the neighborhood becomes more of a nuisance, and something simply has to be done about it, the Mayor, Judge Stevens (eighty years old), observes to a younger generation "alderman" who presses for action: "Dammit, sir, . . . will you accuse a lady to her face of smelling bad?" The odd effect of the statement is that an attribute is connected with the idea of "lady" which cannot, in the essence of the concept, be permitted; and further, this connection is essentially not intended—"smell" should not be directly applicable to that person. Even the decision to allay the "smell" becomes an odd, spectral procedure: "So the next night, after midnight, four men crossed Miss Emily's lawn and *slunk* about the house *like burglars, sniffing* along the base of the brickwork and at the cellar openings *while one of them performed a regular sowing motion* with his hand out of a sack slung from his shoulder. They broke open the cellar door and sprinkled lime there, and in all the outbuildings. . . . They *crept* quietly across the lawn and into the shadow of the locusts that lined the street." By considering the feelings of the "lady," these individuals are forced to assume a behavioral mode, that, through its particular movements and gestures (slink, sniff, creep), seem animal-like. People slink around and sniff like beasts because it is unseemly to call a "lady's" attention to a "smell" for which she is essentially to blame. The druggist dares not ask Miss Emily a second time what use she intended to make of the arsenic she requested. Here too the peculiar effect of consideration or deference for the "lady" is evident. The druggist suspects something, for he lets the

"Negro delivery boy" bring Miss Emily the bottle; and he has himself labeled the bottle, as Miss Emily later observes at home, "for rats." "The Negro delivery boy brought her the package; the druggist didn't come back. When she opened the package at home there was written on the box, under the skull and bones: '*For rats.*'" The comic effect inheres in the sudden mental transposition of the person for whom the poison could be intended with the idea of "rats." The knowledge of impending tragedy makes the comic element possible here. Comic and tragic aspects are even connected with Miss Emily's attitude. For example, some comic effects are evidenced in her behavior, vis-à-vis the "aldermen"; her refusal to pay taxes; the attempt not to accept the death of her father; the observation "She carried her head high"; her bearing in the drugstore, etc.; in fact, her entire manner insofar as it carries the mark of a certain rigidity and fanaticism. [Henri] Bergson's description in *Laughter* of the comic type underscores the comic aspect of her behavior: "In Moliere's plays how many comic scenes can be reduced to this simple type: *a character following up his one idea,* and continually recurring to it in spite of incessant interruptions! The transition seems to take place imperceptibly from the man who will listen to nothing to the one who will see nothing, and from this latter to the one who sees only what he wants to see. A stubborn spirit ends by adjusting things to its own way of thinking, instead of accommodating its thoughts to the things."

Effective artistic possibilities reside in Faulkner's configuration of time. Particularly through the juxtapositions of several strictly chronological sequences of events can a few intimations of the tension be glimpsed. The event in the first segment of "A Rose for Emily" is, in the light of the following sections, already past. Only at the conclusion of the story's second section, at the disclosure of Miss Emily's father's death, is there an attempt at a generally normal chronological account. Previously, mention is made of the "smell," which appeared "after her sweetheart . . . had deserted her," but its puzzling source comes to light only at the conclusion, through the discovery of Homer Barron's body. By means of excising events from their chronological sequence, the "smell" affair and the "drugstore" scene are imbued with the character of mystery. Upon these factors a major part of the tension, unique to the story, is based, in that they are accented in their connection with the comic. This tension is of course resolved at story's end by the discovery, after Miss Emily's funeral, of Homer Barron's corpse; however, this resolution is not intended for the reader, for it forces him to glance back and reflect anew upon the event and its suggestive leitmotifs and images. The reader is shaken, as the narrator too is deeply moved, by the sight of Homer Barron; one feels the necessity to re-examine the life of Miss Emily and her milieu. One theorizes about the motives for Miss Emily's action. And in the process of this re-evaluation one will seek to comprehend the title of the story and will again experience the suggestiveness and complexity of individual concepts as well as the many contrasts, images, allusions, and relationships, that merge with the elements of the comic, tragic, and ironic.

What Novels Can Do That Films Can't (and Vice Versa)

SEYMOUR CHATMAN

As a narratologist, Chatman draws on theories of transformational generative linguistics which posit a deep-structure, or story, level to narratives. It is this structure which allows narratives to be transposed into different media. Here, however, Chatman is less interested in story than in its expression, or discourse. He asserts that narratology can also highlight the different expressive strengths of various media. In the first part of his essay, reprinted here, he demonstrates his point by contrasting the differences between written and filmic modes of description.

THE STUDY OF NARRATIVE has become so popular that the French have honored it with a term—*la narratologie*. Given the escalating and sophisticated literature on the subject, its English counterpart, "narratology," may not be as risible as it sounds. Modern narratology combines two powerful intellectual trends: the Anglo-American inheritance of Henry James, Percy Lubbock, E. M. Forster, and Wayne Booth; and the mingling of Russian formalist (Viktor Shklovsky, Boris Eichenbaum, Roman Jakobson, and Vladimir Propp) with French structuralist approaches (Claude Lévi-Strauss, Roland Barthes, Gérard Genette, and Tzvetan Todorov). It's not accidental that narratology has developed during a period in which linguistics and cinema theory have also flourished. Linguistics, of course, is one basis for the field now called semiotics—the study of all meaning systems, not only natural language. Another basis is the work of the philosopher Charles S. Peirce and his continuator, Charles W. Morris. These trees have borne elegant fruit: we read fascinating semiotic analyses of facial communication, body language, fashion, the circus, architecture, and gastronomy. The most vigorous, if controversial, branch of cinema studies, the work of Christian Metz, is also semiotically based.

One of the most important observations to come out of narratology is

From *Critical Inquiry* 7, no. 1 (Autumn 1980): 121–33. © 1980 by The University of Chicago Press. Reprinted by permission of The University of Chicago Press.

that narrative itself is a deep structure quite independent of its medium. In other words narrative is basically a kind of text organization, and that organization, that schema, needs to be actualized: in written words, as in stories and novels; in spoken words combined with the movements of actors imitating characters against sets which imitate places, as in plays and films; in drawings; in comic strips; in dance movements, as in narrative ballet and in mime; and even in music, at least in program music of the order of *Till Eulenspiegel* and *Peter and the Wolf*.

A salient property of narrative is double time structuring. That is, all narratives, in whatever medium, combine the time sequence of plot events, the time of the *histoire* ("story-time") with the time of the presentation of those events in the text, which we call "discourse-time." What is fundamental to narrative, regardless of medium, is that these two time orders are independent. In realistic narratives, the time of the story is fixed, following the ordinary course of a life: a person is born, grows from childhood to maturity and old age, and then dies. But the discourse-time order may be completely different: it may start with the person's deathbed, then "flashback" to childhood; or it may start with childhood, "flashforward" to death, then end with adult life. This independence of discourse-time is precisely and only possible because of the subsumed story-time. Now of course *all* texts pass through time: it takes x number of hours to read an essay, a legal brief, or a sermon. But the internal structures of these *non*-narrative texts are not temporal but logical, so that their discourse-time is irrelevant, just as the viewing time of a painting is irrevelant. We may spend half an hour in front of a Titian, but the aesthetic effect is as if we were taking in the whole painting at a glance. In narratives, on the other hand, the dual time orders function independently. This is true in any medium: flashbacks are just as possible in ballet or mime or opera as they are in a film or novel. Thus, in theory at least, any narrative can be actualized by any medium which can communicate the two time orders.

Narratologists immediately observed an important consequence of this property of narrative texts, namely, the translatability of a given narrative from one medium to another: *Cinderella* as verbal tale, as ballet, as opera, as film, as comic strip, as pantomime, and so on. This observation was so interesting, so much in keeping with structuralist theory, and so productive of further work in narrative analysis that it tended to concentrate attention exclusively on the constancies in narrative structure across the different media at the expense of interesting differences. But now the study of narrative has reached a point where the differences can emerge as objects of independent interest.

In the course of studying and teaching film, I have been struck by the sorts of changes typically introduced by screen adaptation (and vice versa in that strange new process "novelization," which transforms already exhibited films into novels). Close study of film and novel versions of the same narrative reveals with great clarity the peculiar powers of the two media. Once we grasp those peculiarities, the reasons for the differences in form, content, and impact of the two versions strikingly emerge. Many features of these narratives could be chosen for comparison, but I will limit myself to only two: description and point of view.

Critics have long recognized that descriptive passages in novels are different somehow in textual *kind* from the narrative proper. They have spoken of "blocks" or "islands" or "chunks" of description in early fiction and have noted that modern novels shy away from blatantly purple descriptive passages. Joseph Conrad and Ford Madox Ford formulated theories of what they called "distributed" exposition and description, in which the described elements were insinuated, so to speak, into the running narrative line. What has not emerged very clearly until recently, however, is a genuine theoretical explanation of novelistic description. The emphasis has been on the pictorial, the imaged. We read in typical handbooks like Thrall and Hibbard: "Description . . . has as its purpose the picturing of a scene or setting." But that is only part of the story; such a definition eliminates inter alia the description of an abstract state of affairs, or of a character's mental posture, or, indeed, of anything not strictly visual or visualizable. Narratologists argue that a more correct and comprehensive account of description rests on temporal structure. As we have already noted, narrative proper requires a double and independent time ordering, that of the time line of the story and that of the time line of the discourse. Now what happens in description is that the time line of the story is interrupted and frozen. Events are stopped, though our reading- or discourse-time continues, and we look at the characters and the setting elements as at a tableau vivant.

As an example of this process, consider a bit of the short story which underlies a film by Jean Renoir, Maupassant's "Une Partie de campagne" [A Country Excursion].[1] The story opens with a summary of events which clearly establishes story-time: "For five months they had been talking of going to lunch at some country restaurant. . . . They had risen very early that morning. Monsieur Dufour had borrowed the milkman's cart, and drove himself [on avait projeté depuis cinq mois d'aller déjeuner aux environs de Paris. . . . Aussi . . . s'était-on levé de fort bonne heure ce matin-là. M. Dufour, ayant emprunté la voiture du latier, conduisait lui-même]" (p. 63). There are three events, and, as we note from the use of the past perfect with "had," they predate the opening moment of the story proper, the moment of story-now, so to speak, which is the moment named by the expression "and drove himself." The story proper begins with the family en voyage, already in the midst of their excursion. The story sequence is *naturally* ordered: at some point in that past before the story proper began, someone first mentioned going to lunch in the country (let's call that event A); the family continued this discussion, thus event A was iterated (let's call that A sub-n since we don't know how many times the topic came up during those five months); next, Monsieur

Dufour borrowed the milkman's cart, presumably the Saturday night before the trip (event B); then they arose early on Sunday morning (event C); and finally, here they are, driving along the road (event D). Notice, incidentally, the disparity between the story order and discourse order: story order is A, B, C, D; discourse order is A, C, B, D.

This first sentence, then, is straight narration which takes us out of the expository past into the narrative present. Now the very next sentence is clearly of a different order: ". . . it [the cart] had a roof supported by four iron posts to which were attached curtains, which had been raised so that they could see the countryside [. . . elle avait un toit supporté par quatre montants de fer où s'attachaient les rideaux qu'on avait relevés pour voir le paysage]" (63). This is, of course, unadulterated description. Story-time stops as the narrator characterizes a story object, a prop. The sentence reflects the static character of the passage. The verb "to have" is clearly equivalent to the typical copula of description: it is not a verb of action and communicates no sense of an event but simply evokes the quality of an object or state of affairs. Maupassant could have—and more recent writers probably would have—avoided direct description by writing something like "The cart, its roof supported by four iron posts, rolled merrily down the road." This active syntax would have kept story-time going and would have eased in the characterization of the cart. Maupassant's prose provokes, rather, the start-and-stop effect customary to early fiction, a fashion now somewhat dated. Not that the surface verb, the verb in the actual verbal medium, *needs* to be the copula "to be." It could be a perfectly active verb in the strict grammatical sense and still evoke the descriptive copula at the deep narrative level, as in the sentence that immediately follows: "The curtain at the back . . . fluttered in the breeze like a flag [celui de derrière, seul, flottait au vent, comme un drapeau]." "Fluttered" is an active verb, but from the textual point of view, the sentence is pure description; it is not tied into the event chain. The sentence could as easily be phrased, "In the back there *was* a curtain fluttering in the breeze like a flag."

The paragraph continues with a brief description of Mme. Dufour and makes references to the grandmother, to Henriette, and to a yellow-haired youth who later becomes Henriette's husband. Paragraphs immediately thereafter continue the narrative by citing events: the passing of the fortifications at Porte Maillot; the reaching of the bridge of Neuilly; the pronouncement by M. Dufour that at last they have reached the country, and so on.

Let's consider the opening scene of Jean Renoir's 1936 film version of this story, also entitled *Une Partie de campagne*. (Ideally, you would watch the film as you read this essay, but something of the effect, I hope, can be communicated by the following illustrations.*) The whole sequence intro-

---

*Not reproduced here.—ED.

ducing the Dufours takes only a minute of viewing time, so we don't have much time to remark the details of their borrowed cart. But looking at a single frame enables us to examine it at our leisure.

We note, for instance, that the cart is absurdly small, has only two wheels, bears the name of the owner, "Ch. Gervais," painted on the side, and has a railing on the roof. There is no flapping curtain at the back but instead some kind of sun shield, and so on. Now these details are appartently of the same order as those in the story—remember the reference to the roof, the four iron posts, and the rolled up curtains. But there are some vital differences. For one thing, the number of details in Maupassant's sentence is limited to three. In other words, the selection among the possible number of details evoked was absolutely determined: the author, through his narrator, "selected" and named precisely three. Thus the reader learns only those three and can only expand the picture imaginatively. But in the film representation, the number of details is indeterminate, since what this version gives us is a simulacrum of a French carriage of a certain era, provenance, and so on. Thus the number of details that we could note is potentially large, even vast. In practice, however, we do not register many details. The film is going by too fast, and we are too preoccupied with the meaning of this cart, with what is going to happen next, to dwell upon its physical details. We simply label: we say to ourselves, "Aha, a cart with some people in it." We react that way because of a technical property of film texts: the details are not asserted as such by a narrator but simply presented, so we tend, in a pragmatic way, to contemplate only those that seem salient to the plot as it unrolls in our minds (in what Roland Barthes calls a "hermeneutic" inquiry). Now if you think about it, this is a rather odd aesthetic situation. Film narrative possesses a plenitude of visual details, an excessive particularity compared to the verbal version, a plenitude aptly called by certain aestheticians visual "over-specification" (*überbestimmtheit*), a property that it shares, of course, with the other visual arts. But unlike those arts, unlike painting or sculpture, narrative films do not usually allow us time to dwell on plenteous details. Pressure from the narrative component is too great. Events move too fast. The contemplation of beautiful framing or color or lighting is a pleasure limited to those who can see the film many times or who are fortunate enough to have access to equipment which will allow them to stop the frame. But watching a movie under normal circumstances in a cinema is not at all like being in a gallery or art museum. The management wants us up and out of the theater so that the 10:30 patrons can take our seats. And even sophisticated moviegoers who call a film "beautiful" are more likely to be referring to literary than to visual components. Indeed, there are movies (like Terence Malick's recent *Days of Heaven*) which are criticized because their visual effects are too striking for the narrative line to support. Narrative pressure is so great that the interpretation of even non-narrative films is sometimes affected by it—at least for a time, until the audience gets its bearings. For example, there is a film which presents a sequence of frozen frames, on the basis of which the audience is prompted to construct a story. Then, after the last frame, the camera pulls away to reveal that the frames were all merely part of a collage of photographs organized randomly. This last shot "denarrativizes" the film.

Narrative pressure similarly affects the genre of film that André Bazin writes about in his essay "Painting and Cinema," the kind in which the camera moves around close-up details of a single painting. An example of this genre is Alain Resnais' film on Picasso's *Guernica*. No less a personage than the Inspector General of Drawing of the French Department of Education complained: "However you look at it the film is not true to the painting. Its dramatic and logical unity establishes relationships that are chronologically false." The inspector was speaking about the relationships and chronology in the implied narrative of Picasso's development as an artist, but he might as well have been speaking of the relationships and chronology implicit in a narrative hypothecated on the visual details of *Guernica* itself. By controlling the viewer's order and duration of perceiving, a film scanning a painting might imply the double time structure of narrative texts. For example, if the camera wandering over *Guernica* were first focused on the head and lantern-bearing arm sweeping in through the window, then shifted to the screaming horse, then to the body on the ground with the broken sword and flower in its hand, the audience might read into the painting a story sequence which Picasso did not intend: first the alarm was heard, then the horse whinnied as the bombs fell, then one victim died.

The key word in my account of the different ways that visual details are presented by novels and films is "assert." I wish to communicate by that word the force it has in ordinary rhetoric: an "assertion" is a statement, usually an independent sentence or clause, that something is in fact the case, that it is a certain sort of thing, that it does in fact have certain properties or enter into certain relations, namely, those listed. Opposed to asserting there is mere "naming." When I say, "The cart was tiny; it came onto the bridge," I am asserting that certain property of the cart of being small in size and that certain relation of arriving at the bridge. However, when I say "The green cart came onto the bridge," I am asserting nothing more than its arrival at the bridge; the greenness of the cart is not asserted but slipped in without syntactic fuss. It is only named. Textually, it emerges by the way. Now, most film narratives seem to be of the latter textual order: it requires special effort for films to assert a property or relation. The dominant mode is presentational, not assertive. A film doesn't say, "This *is* the state of affairs," it merely shows you that state of affairs. Of course, there could be a character or a voice-over commentator asserting a property or relation; but then the film would be using its sound track in much the same way as fiction uses assertive syntax. It is not cinematic description but merely description by literary assertion transferred to film. Filmmakers and critics traditionally show disdain for verbal commentary because it explicates what, they feel, should be implicated visually. So in its essential visual mode, film does not describe at all but merely presents; or better, it *depicts*, in the original etymological sense of that word: renders in pictorial form. I don't think that this is mere purism or a die-hard adherence to silent films. Film attracts that component of our perceptual apparatus which we tend to favor over the other senses. Seeing is, after all, believing.

That the camera depicts but does not describe seems confirmed by a term often used by literary critics to characterize neutral, "non-narrated" Hemingwayesque fiction—the *camera eye* style. The implication of "camera eye" is that no one recounts the events of, for example, "The Killers": they are just *revealed,* as if some instrument—some cross between a video tape recorder and speech synthesizer—had recorded visually and then translated those visuals into the most neutral kind of language.

Now, someone might counterargue: "You're forgetting obvious cinematic devices whose intention is arguably descriptive. What about the telling close-up? What about establishing shots?" But the close-ups that come immediately to mind seem introduced for plot unravelling, for hermeneutic purposes. Think of Hitchcock's famous close-ups: the villain's amputated little finger in *The Thirty-Nine Steps;* the poisoned coffee cup in *Notorious;* Janet Leigh's horribly open eye in the bloody shower in *Psycho.* For all their capacity to arrest our attention, these close-ups in no way invite aesthetic contemplation; on the contrary, they function as extremely powerful components in the structure of the suspense. They present, in the most dramatic fashion, that abiding narrative-hermeneutic question: "My God," they cry out, "what next?" Of course, a real description in a novel may also serve to build suspense. We curse Dickens for stopping the action at a critical moment to describe something. "Keep still," shouts the sudden, terrifying figure to Pip at the beginning of *Great Expectations,* "or I'll cut your throat." And then, as we dangle in suspense, a whole paragraph describes the man: the iron on his leg, his broken shoes, the rag tied around his head, and so on. Yes, we curse Dickens—and love every second of it. But in the movie version, the sense of continuing action could not stop. Even if there were a long pause to give us a chance to take in the fearsome details of Magwitch's person, we would still feel that the clock of story-time was ticking away, that that pause was *included* in the story and not just an interval as we perused the discourse. We might very well infer that the delay means something, perhaps that Magwitch was trying to decide what to do with Pip, or, in a supersophisticated "psychological" version, that Pip's own time scale had somehow been stretched out because of his great terror. In either case, the feeling that we were sharing time passage with a character would be a sure clue that not only our discourse-time but their story-time was continuing to roll. And if it is the case that story-time necessarily continues to roll in films, and if description entails precisely the arrest of story-time, then it is reasonable to argue that films do not and cannot describe.

Then what about establishing shots? An establishing shot, if you're not up on movie jargon, is defined as follows (in Ernest Lindgren's *The Art of Film*): "A long shot introduced at the beginning of a scene to establish the interrelationship of details to be shown subsequently in nearer shots." Standard examples are the bird's-eye shots that open *The Lady Vanishes* and *Psycho*. In *The Lady Vanishes*, the camera starts high above a Swiss ski resort, then moves down, and in the next shot we're inside the crowded hotel; in *Psycho*, the camera starts high above Phoenix, then glides down into a room where a couple are making love. It is true that both of these shots are in a certain sense descriptive or at least evocative of place; but they seem to enjoy that status only because they occur at the very beginning of the films, that is to say, before any characters have been introduced. Now narrative in its usual definition is a causal chain of events, and since "narrative event" means an "action performed by or at least of some relevance to a character," we can see why precisely the absence of characters endows establishing shots with a descriptive quality. It is not that story-time has been arrested. It is just that it has not yet begun. For when the same kind of shot occurs in the middle of a film, it does not seem to entail an arrest or abeyance of story-time. For example, recall the scene in the middle of *Notorious* just at the moment when Cary Grant and Ingrid Bergman are flying into Rio de Janeiro. We see shots of the city from the air, typical street scenes, and so on. Yet our sense is not of a hiatus in the story-time but rather that Rio is down there waiting for Cary and Ingrid to arrive. All that street activity is felt to be transpiring while the two go about their business, the business of the plot, which because of its momentarily mundane character—landing, clearing customs, and so on—is allowed to happen off screen.

Even the literal arrest of the picture, the so-called freeze-frame, where the image is reduced to a projected still photograph, does not automatically convey a description. It was popular a dozen years ago to end films that way, in medias res. Remember how Truffaut's young hero Antoine Doinel was frozen on the beach in *The Four Hundred Blows*? Truffaut has continued to follow the Doinel character in an interesting way, as the actor Jean-Pierre Léaud has himself aged, but I for one had no idea when I originally saw *The Four Hundred Blows* that there would be sequels; for me the sense of the frozen ending was that Doinel was trapped in a fugitive way of life. I perceived not a description but a kind of congealed iteration of future behavior.

Why is it that the force of plot, with its ongoing march of events, its ticking away of story-time, is so hard to dispel in the movies? That's an interesting question, but a psychologist or psychologically oriented aesthetician will have to answer it. I can only hazard a guess. The answer may have something to do with the medium itself. Whereas in novels, movements and hence events are at best constructions imaged by the reader out of words, that is, abstract symbols which are different from them in kind, the movements on the screen are so iconic, so like the real life movements they imitate, that the illusion of time passage simply cannot be divorced from them. Once that illusory story-time is established in a film, even dead moments, moments when nothing moves, will be felt to be part of the temporal whole, just as the taxi meter continues to run as we sit fidgeting in a traffic jam.

Let's try these ideas out on a longer and more challenging passage of Maupassant's story, the third paragraph:

[1] Mademoiselle Dufour was trying to swing herself standing up, but she could not succeed in getting a start. [2] She was a pretty girl of about eighteen; [3] one of those women who suddenly excite your desire when you meet them in the street, and who leave you with a vague feeling of uneasiness and of excited senses. [4] She was tall, had a small waist and large hips, with a dark skin, very large eyes, and very black hair. [5] Her dress clearly marked the outlines of her firm, full figure, which was accentuated by the motion of her hips as she tried to swing herself higher. [6] Her arms were stretched over her head to hold the rope, so that her bosom rose at every movement she made. Her hat, which a gust of wind had blown off, was hanging behind her, [7] and as the swing gradually rose higher and higher, she showed her delicate limbs up to the knees at each time. . . . (p. 66)[2]

The first narrative unit, "Mademoiselle Dufour was trying to swing herself" and so on, refers to an event. The second, "She was a pretty girl of about eighteen," seems on the face of it a straightforward description; but look at it from the point of view of a filmmaker. For one thing, "pretty" is not only descriptive but evaluative: one person's "pretty" may be another person's "beautiful" and still a third person's "plain." There will be some interesting variations in the faces selected by directors across cultures and even across time periods: Mary Pickford might be just the face for the teens and twenties, while Tuesday Weld may best represent the sixties. Renoir chose the face of Sylvie Bataille. The interesting theoretical point to be made about evaluative descriptions in verbal narrative is that they can invoke visual elaboration in the reader's mind. If he or she requires one, each reader will provide just the mental image to suit his or her own notions of prettiness. But the best a film (or theater) director can hope for is some degree of consensus with the spectator's ideal of prettiness. Even with the luckiest choice, some patrons will mutter, "I didn't think she was pretty at all." A similar point could be made about age; Sylvie Bataille's Henriette seems closer to thirty than eighteen, but that may be because of the costume she's wearing. The more serious point is that visual appearance is only a rough sign of age. Again the author's task is easier: correct 'attribution can be insured by simply naming the attribute. The filmmaker, on the other hand, has to depend on the audience's agreement to the justice of the visual clues.

Still another point to be made about this piece of description concerns the word "about" and the whole of the next descriptive bit in the third unit. These not only refine and add to the description but also make salient the voice of a narrator. "*About* eighteen" stresses that the narrator himself is guessing. And, "one of those women who suddenly excite your desire" tells us even more: the narrator is a man responsive to female charms, perhaps a roué, at least a man-about-town. Such is the character of speech: it usually tells us something about the speaker. Long ago I. A. Richards labeled this function "tone." The camera, poor thing, is powerless to invoke tone, though it can present some alternatives to it. In this case, as we shall see, Renoir's sense of the need to show Henriette's innocent seductiveness seems to have prompted several amusing reaction shots which compensate for the camera's sexless objectivity.

The adjectives in our fourth segment are easier for film to handle: height, girth, skin, and hair color are features that film can communicate reliably. (The communication, of course, is always comparative, scalar: a character is tall relative to other people and objects in the film.) The motion of her hips bears a double function: the movement itself is an event, but it also contributes to the description of a part of Henriette's anatomy that the narrator finds quite absorbing. The same double role is played by the bosom and falling hat in segment six. As movements, these of course are simple for the film to convey; Henriette's voluptuousness, however, is not asserted but only suggestively depicted.

In the seventh segment, an odd ambiguity is introduced. The text says that as the swing rose, "she showed her delicate limbs up to the knees [montrant à chaque retour ses jambes fines jusqu'au genou]." The camera is certainly capable of presenting the requisite portion of anatomy. But what about the implications of "showed"? In both story and film, Henriette is generally represented as innocent; conscious exhibitionism does not go with her character, her family situation, or the times. The answer is perhaps an equivoque on the verb "to show": the definition of that word neither excludes nor includes conscious intention. And it is precisely an ambiguity that would go with the coquetry of a nineteenth-century maiden: to show but not *necessarily* to be conscious of showing. The camera, again, would seem unable to translate that verbal innuendo.

But see what Renoir makes of this problem. He elects to present Henriette first from the point of view of one of the two young boat men—not Henri, who is later to fall in love with her, but his comrade, Rodolphe. The term "point of view" means several things, but here I am using it in the strictly perceptual sense. Because the camera is behind Rodolphe's back as he looks out onto the garden through the window he's just opened, the camera, and hence the narrative point of view, identifies with him. It conspires, and invites us to conspire, with his voyeurism. Point of view is a complex matter worthy of a whole other discussion, but one theoretical observation is worth making here. The fact that most novels and short stories come to us through the voice of a narrator gives authors a greater range and flexibility than filmmakers. For one thing, the visual point of view in a film is always *there:* it is fixed and determinate precisely because the camera always needs to be placed *somewhere.* But in verbal fiction, the narrator may or may not give us a visual bearing. He may let us peer over a character's shoulder, or he may represent something from a generalized perspective, commenting indifferently on the front, sides, and back of the object, disregarding how it is possible to see all these parts in the same glance. He doesn't have to account for his physical position at all. Further, he can enter solid bodies and tell what things are like inside, and so on. In the present case, Maupassant's narrator gives us a largely frontal view of Henriette on the swing, but he also casually makes observations about her posterior. And, of course, he could as easily have described the secret contents of her heart. The filmmaker, with his bulky camera, lights, tracks, and other machinery, suffers restrictions. But the very limitations, as Rudolf Arnheim has shown so eloquently, encourage interesting artistic solutions. Renoir uses precisely the camera's need for placement to engage the problem of communicating the innocent yet seductive quality of Henriette's charms. Since seductiveness, like beauty, is in the eye of a beholder, Renoir requisitions Rodolphe's point of view to convey it. It is not Henriette so much as Rodolphe's reaction to Henriette, even on first seeing her, that shall establish her seductiveness and not only in his mind but in ours, because we cannot help but look on with him. Small plot changes help to make the scene plausible. Henri, disgusted with the Parisians invading his fishing sanctuary, does not even care to see what this latest horde looks like. It is Rodolphe who opens the window, flooding sunlight into the gloomy dining room and making a little stage in the deep background against which Henriette and her mother move like cute white puppets. . . .

NOTES

1. Guy de Maupassant, "Une Partie de campagne," *Boule de Suif* (Paris, n.d.), 63–78; all further references will be cited parenthetically in the text; my translations.

2. "Mlle Dufour essayait de se balancer debout, toute seule, sans parvenir à se donner un élan suffisant. C'était une belle fille de dix-huit à vingt ans; une de ces femmes dont la rencontre dans la rue vous fouette d'un désir subit, et vous laisse jusqu'à la nuit une inquiétude vague et un soulèvement des sens. Grande,

mince de taille et large des hanches, elle avait le peau très brune, les yeux très grands, les cheveux très noirs. Sa robe dessinait nettement les plénitudes fermes de sa chair qu'accentuaient encore les efforts des reins qu'elle faisait pour s'enlever. Ses bras tendus tenaient les cordes au-dessus de sa tête, de sorte que sa poitrine se dressait, sans une secousse, à chaque impulsion qu'elle donnait. Son chapeau, emporté par un coup de vent, était tombé derrière elle; et l'escarpolette peu à peu se lançait, montrant à chaque retour ses jambes fines jusqu'au genou. . . ."

Decoding Papa: "A Very Short Story" as Work and Text*

ROBERT SCHOLES

For semioticians like Scholes, literary texts are networks of social codes that enable us to read fiction as fiction. Some of these codes are apparent, some are hidden. Scholes decodes by analyzing fictional narrative as "text" (words) and "diegesis" (what the words allow readers to create as a fiction). We read a narrative by translating the words into organized events, characters, and scenes. The cultural codes that we have internalized both enable and constrain this reading process (diegesis). By analyzing the dialogue between text and diegesis in Hemingway's "A Very Short Story," Scholes explores how textual strategies interact with social codes to determine meaning.

THE SEMIOTIC STUDY of a literary text is not wholly unlike traditional interpretation or rhetorical analysis, nor is it meant to replace these other modes of response to literary works. But the semiotic critic situates the text somewhat differently, privileges different dimensions of the text, and uses a critical methodology adapted to the semiotic enterprise. Most interpretive methods privilege the "meaning" of the text. Hermeneutic critics seek authorial or intentional meaning; the New Critics seek the ambiguities of "textual" meaning; the "reader response" critics allow readers to make meaning. With respect to meaning the semiotic critic is

From *Semiotics and Interpretation* (New Haven and London: Yale University Press, 1982), 110–26. Copyright © 1982 by Yale University Press. Reprinted by permission.

*Because of [Hemingway's] restrictions against reprinting "A Very Short Story" as a whole in any work other than a volume made up exclusively of his own work, the full text of the story has not been included here. The reader is requested to consult the text of "A Very Short Story" in Hemingway's *In Our Time* or *The Short Stories of Ernest Hemingway* (New York: Charles Scribner's Sons, The Scribner Library, 19.) before reading this [essay]. My apologies for the inconvenience.

situated differently. Such a critic looks for the generic or discursive structures that enable and constrain meaning.

Under semiotic inspection neither the author nor the reader is free to make meaning. Regardless of their lives as individuals, as author and reader they are traversed by codes that enable their communicative adventures at the cost of setting limits to the messages they can exchange. A literary text, then, is not simply a set of words, but (as Roland Barthes demonstrated in *S/Z*, though not necessarily in just that way) a network of codes that enables the marks on the page to be read as a text of a particular sort.

In decoding narrative texts, the semiotic method is based on two simple but powerful analytical tools: the distinction between story and discourse, on the one hand, and that between text and events on the other. The distinction between story and discourse is grounded in a linguistic observation by Emile Benveniste to the effect that some languages (notably French and Greek) have a special tense of the verb used for the narration of past events. (See "The Correlations of Tense in the French Verb," chapter 19 of *Problems in General Linguistics*. See also Seymour Chatman, *Story and Discourse*.[1]) This tense, the aorist or *passé simple*, emphasizes the relationship between the utterance and the situation the utterance refers to, between the narration and the events narrated. This is par excellence the mode of written transcriptions of events: *histoire* or "story." Benveniste contrasts this with the mode of *discours* or "discourse," in which the present contact between speaker and listener is emphasized. Discourse is rhetorical, and related to oral persuasion. Story is referential and related to written documentation. Discourse is now; story is then. Story speaks of he and she; discourse is a matter of you and me, I and thou.

In any fictional text, then, we can discern certain features that are of the story: reports on actions, mentions of times and places, and the like. We can also find elements that are of the discourse: evaluations, reflections, language that suggests an authorial or at least narratorial presence who is addressing a reader or narratee with a persuasive aim in mind. When we are told that someone "smiled cruelly," we can detect more of story in the verb and more of discourse in the adverb. Some fictional texts, those of D. H. Lawrence for example, are highly discursive. To read a Lawrence story is to enter into a personal relationship with someone who resembles the writer of Lawrence's private correspondence. Hemingway, on the other hand, often seems to have made a strong effort to eliminate discourse altogether—an effort that is apparent in "A Very Short Story."

The distinction between story and discourse is closely related to another with which it is sometimes confused, and that is the distinction between the *récit* and *diégésis* of a narrative. In this case we are meant to distinguish between the whole text of a narration as a text, on the one hand, and the events narrated as events on the other. We can take over the Greek term, diegesis, for the system of characters and events, and simply anglicize the other term as recital; or just refer to the "text" when we mean the words and the "diegesis" for what they encourage us to create as a fiction.

The text itself may be analyzed into components of story and discourse, but it may also be considered in relation to the diegesis. One of the primary qualities of those texts we understand as fiction is that they generate a diegetic order that has an astonishing independence from its text. To put it simply, once a story is told it can be recreated in a recognizable way by a totally new set of words—in another language, for instance—or in another medium altogether. The implications of this for analysis are profound. Let us explore some of them.

A fictional diegesis draws its nourishment not simply from the words of its text but from its immediate culture and its literary tradition. The magical words "once upon a time" in English set in motion a machine of considerable momentum which can hardly be turned off without the equally magical "they lived happily ever after" or some near equivalent. The diegetic processes of "realistic" narrative are no less insistent. "A Very Short Story," by its location in Hemingway's larger text (*In Our Time*), and a few key words—Padua, carried, searchlights, duty, operating, front, armistice—allows us to supply the crucial notions of military hospital, nurse, soldier, and World War I that the diegesis requires.

This process is so crucial that we should perhaps stop and explore its implications. The words on the page are not the story. The text is not the diegesis. The story is constructed by the reader from the words on the page by an inferential process—a skill that can be developed. The reader's role is in a sense creative—without it, no story exists—but it is also constrained by rules of inference that set limits to the legitimacy of the reader's constructions. Any interpretive dispute may be properly brought back to the "words on the page," of course, but these words never speak their own meaning. The essence of writing, as opposed to speech, is that the reader speaks the written words, the words that the writer has abandoned. A keen sense of this situation motivates the various sorts of "envoi" that writers supplied for their books in the early days of printing. They felt that their books were mute and would be spoken by others.

In reading a narrative, then, we translate a text into a diegesis according to codes we have internalized. This is simply the narrative version of the normal reading process. As E. D. Hirsch has recently reminded us (in the *Philosophy of Composition* [Chicago, 1977], 122–23), for almost a century research in reading (Binet and Henri in 1894, Fillenbaum in 1966, Sachs in 1967, Johnson-Laird in 1970, Levelt and Kampen in 1975, and Brewer in 1975—specific citations can be found in Hirsch) has shown us that memory stores not the words of texts but their concepts, not the signifiers but the signifieds. When we read a narrative text, then, we process it as a diegesis. If we retell the story, it will be in our own words. To the extent that the distinction between poetry and fiction is a useful one, it is based on the notion of poetry as monumental, fixed in the words of the text and therefore untranslatable; while fiction has proved highly translatable because its essence is not in its language but in its diegetic structure. As fiction approaches the condition of poetry, its precise words become more important; as poetry moves toward narrative, its specific language decreases in importance.

In reading fiction, then, we actually translate from the text to a diegesis, substituting narrative units (characters, scenes, events, and so on) for verbal units (nouns, adjectives, phrases, clauses, etc.) And we perform other changes as well. We organize the material we receive so as to make it memorable, which means that we systematize it as much possible. In the diegetic system we construct, time flows at a uniform rate; events occur in chronological order; people and places have the qualities expected of them—unless the text specifies otherwise. A writer may relocate the Eiffel Tower to Chicago but unless we are told this we will assume that a scene below that tower takes place in Paris—a Paris equipped with all the other items accorded it in our cultural paradigm.

Places and other entities with recognizable proper names (Napoleon, Waterloo, Broadway) enter the diegesis coded by culture. The events reported in a narrative text, however, will be stored in accordance with a syntactic code based on a chronological structure. The text may present the events that compose a story in any order, plunging in medias res or following through from beginning to end, but the diegesis always seeks to arrange them in chronological sequence. The text may expand a minute into pages or cram years into a single sentence, for its own ends, but the minutes and years remain minutes and years of diegetic time all the same. In short, the text may discuss what it chooses, but once a diegesis is set in motion no text can ever completely control it. "How many children had Lady Macbeth?" is not simply the query of a naive interpreter but the expression of a normal diegetic impulse. Where authors and texts delight in equivocation, the reader needs certainty and closure to complete the diegetic processing of textual materials. From this conflict of interests comes a tension that many modern writers exploit.

The semiotician takes the reader's diegetic impulse and establishes it as a principle of structuration. The logic of diegetic structure provides a norm, a benchmark for the study of textual strategies, enabling us to explore the dialogue between text and diegesis, looking for points of stress, where the text changes its ways in order to control the diegetic material for its own ends. The keys to both affect and intention may be found at these points. Does the text return obsessively to one episode of diegetic history? Does it disturb diegetic order to tell about something important to its own discursive ends? Does it omit something that diegetic inertia deems important? Does it change its viewpoint on diegetic events? Does it conceal things? Does it force evaluations through the rhetoric of its discourse? The calm inertia of diegetic process, moved by the weight of culture and tradition and the needs of memory itself, offers a stable background for the mapping of textual strategies. And our most esthetically ambitious texts will be those that find it most necessary to put their own stamp on the diegetic process.

Hemingway's "A Very Short Story" presents itself as exceptionally reticent. The familiar Hemingway style, which Gérard Genette has called "behaviorist," seems to efface itself, to offer us a pure diegesis. Boy meets girl—a "cute meet," as they used to say in Hollywood—they fall in love, become lovers, plan to marry, but the vicissitudes of war separate them, and finally forces that are too strong for them bring about their defeat. This is the story, is it not: a quasi-naturalistic slice of life that begins almost like a fairy tale ("Once upon a time in another country . . ."—and ends with the negation of the fairy-tale formula ("and they lived unhappily ever after")—a negation that proclaims the text's realistic or naturalistic status? But there is already a tension here, between the open form of the slice of life and the neat closure of the fairy tale, which emerges most clearly if we compare the progress of diegetic time with the movement of the text. We can do this in a crude way by mapping the hours, days, and weeks of diegetic time against the paragraphs of the text. The slowest paragraphs are the first: one night; and the third: one trip to the Duomo. The fastest are the fourth: his time at the front; the sixth: Luz's time in Pordenone; and the seventh or last: which carries Luz to the point of infinity with the word "never." The narrative thus increases its speed throughout, and achieves its effect of culmination by the use of the infinite terms in the last paragraph. The text might easily have contented itself with recounting the fact that the major did not marry Luz in the spring, but it feels obliged to add "or any other time," just as it is obliged to use the word "never" in the next sentence. Something punitive is going on here, as the discourse seems to be revenging itself upon the character. Why?

Before trying to answer that question we would do well to consider some other features of the text/diegesis relationship. From the first paragraph on, it is noticeable that one of the two main characters in the diegesis has a name in the text while the other is always referred to by a pronoun. Why should this be? The answer emerges when we correlate this detail with other features of the text/diegesis relationship. The text, as we have observed, is reticent, as if it, too, does not want to "blab about anything during the silly, talky time." But it is more reticent about some things than others. In the first paragraph, the male character is introduced in the first sentence. Luz appears in the fifth. When she sits on the bed we are told, "she was cool and fresh in the hot night." Why this information about her temperature? She is the nurse, after all, and he the patient. In fact it is not information about how she feels at all, but about how she appears to him. The text is completely reticent about how he feels himself, though the implication is that he finds her coolness attractive. How he seems to her or how she feels about him are not considered relevant. This is a selective reticence. Our vision is subjectively with him (as the personal pronoun implies), while Luz is seen more objectively (as the proper name implies). The final implication of paragraph 1 is that they make love right then and there. But the reticent text makes the reader responsible for closing that little gap in the diegesis.

This matter of the point of view taken by the text can be established more clearly with the use of a sort of litmus test developed by Roland Barthes. If we rewrite the text substituting the first-person pronoun for the third, we can tell whether or not we are dealing with what Barthes calls a "personal system," a covert, first-person narration (see "Introduction to the Structural Analysis of Narratives," in *Image-Music-Text* [ed. S. Heath (London: William Collins PLC, Fontana–Flamingo, 1977)], 112). In the case of "A Very Short Story," where we have two third-person characters of apparently equal consequence, we must rewrite the story twice to find out what we need to know. Actually, the issue is settled conclusively after the first two paragraphs, which are all I will present here:

The first two paragraphs of "A Very Short Story" rewritten—"he" transposed to "I":

> One hot evening in Padua they carried me up onto the roof and I could look out over the top of the town. There were chimney swifts in the sky. After a while it got dark and the searchlights came out. The others went down and took the bottle with them. Luz and I could hear them below on the balcony. Luz sat on the bed. She was cool and fresh in the hot night.
>
> Luz stayed on night duty for three months. They were glad to let her. When they operated on me she prepared me for the operating table; and we had a joke about friend or enema. I went under the anaesthetic holding tight on to myself so I would not blab about anything during the silly, talky time. After I got on crutches I used to take the temperatures so Luz would not have to get up from the bed. There were only a few patients, and they all knew about it. They all liked Luz. As I walked back along the halls I thought of Luz in my bed.

The same paragraphs—"Luz" transposed to "I":

> One hot evening in Padua they carried him up onto the roof and he could look out over the top of the town. There were chimney swifts in the sky. After a while it got dark and the searchlights came out. The others went down and took the bottle with them. He and I could hear

them below on the balcony. I sat on the bed. I was cool and fresh in the hot night.

I stayed on night duty for three months. They were glad to let me. When they operated on him I prepared him for the operating table; and we had a joke about friend or enema. He went under the anaesthetic holding tight on to himself so he would not blab about anything during the silly, talky time. After he got on crutches he used to take the temperatures so I would not have to get up from the bed. There were only a few patients, and they all knew about it. They all liked me. As he walked back along the halls he thought of me in his bed.

"He" transposes to "I" perfectly, but "Luz" does not. In the second rewriting the first person itself enters the discourse with a shocking abruptness, since the earlier sentences seem to have been from the male patient's point of view. The stress becomes greater in the last sentence of the first paragraph, which has been constructed to indicate how she appeared to him, not how she seemed to herself. But the last two sentences of the second paragraph in the second rewriting are even more ludicrous, with the first-person narrator informing us of how well liked she was, and finally describing his thoughts about her. In this rewriting there is simply too great a tension between the angle of vision and the person of the voice. The discourse loses its coherence. But the first rewriting is completely coherent because in it voice and vision coincide. It is really his narrative all the way. The third-person narration of the original text is a disguise, a mask of pseudo-objectivity worn by the text for its own rhetorical purposes.

The discourse of this text, as I have suggested, is marked by its reticence, but this reticence of the text is contrasted with a certain amount of talkativeness in the diegesis. He, of course, doesn't want to "blab," but *they* want "every one to know about" their relationship. Implication: *she* is the one who wants the news spread. There is absolutely no direct discourse in the text, but there are two paragraphs devoted to letters and one to recounting a quarrel. Here, too, we find reticence juxtaposed to talkativeness. Luz writes many letters to him while he is at the front. But the text does not say whether he wrote any to her. Hers are clearly repetitive and hyperbolic. The style of the discourse becomes unusually paratactic—even for Hemingway—whenever her letters are presented. "They were all about the hospital, *and how* much she loved him *and how* it was impossible to get along without him *and how* terrible it was missing him at night" (italics added). The repetitive "how"s, the hyperbolic "impossible" and "terrible," and all the "and"s suggest an unfortunate prose style even without direct quotation. Above all, they indicate an ominous lack of reticence.

The quarrel is not represented in the text but the "agreement" that causes it is summarized for us, at least in part. It takes the form of a series of conditions that *he* must fulfill in order to be rewarded with Luz's hand in marriage. Curiously, the conditions are represented not only as things it is "understood" that he will and will not do but also as things he wants and does not want to do. He does not "want to see his friends or any one in the States. Only to get a job and be married." It is not difficult to imagine a man being willing to avoid his friends, to work, and to stay sober in order to please a woman, but it is hard to imagine any human being who does not "*want* to see his friends or *anyone*." Not *want* to? Not *anyone*? The text seems to be reporting on the diegesis in a most curious way here. This is not simply reticence but irony. There is a strong implication that he is being coerced, pushed too far, even having his masculinity abused. If there are any conditions laid upon Luz, we do not hear of them.

Finally, the final letter arrives. In reporting it the text clearly allows Luz's prose to shine through once again, complete with repetition of the horrible phrase about the "boy and girl" quality of their relationship and the splendidly hyperbolic cacophony of "expected, absolutely unexpectedly." Her behavior belies her words. Her true awfulness, amply suggested earlier by the reticent text, blazes forth here as her hideous discourse perfectly complements her treacherous behavior.

But how did *he* behave while she was discovering the glories of Latin love? *Nihil dixit.* The text maintains what we can now clearly see as a specifically manly reticence. Did he drink? Did he see his friends? Or anyone? Did he want to? We know not. We do know, however, of his vehicular indiscretion in Lincoln Park and its result. The text is too generous and manly to say so, of course, but we know that this, too, is Luz's fault. She wounded him in the heart and "a short time after" this salesgirl got him in an even more vital place. The discourse leaves them both unhappy, but it clearly makes Luz the agent of the unhappiness.

And what does it make him? Why, the patient, of course. He is always being carried about, given enemas, operated on, sent to the front, sent home, not wanting anything, reading letters. He is wounded at the beginning and wounded at the end. The all-American victim: polite, reticent, and just waiting for an accident to happen to him. Who is to blame if his accidents keep taking the form of women? Who indeed? Whose discourse is this, whose story, whose diegesis, whose world? It is Papa's, of course, who taught a whole generation of male readers to prepare for a world where men may be your friends but women are surely the enema.

The story quite literally leaves its protagonist wounded in his sex by contact with a woman. From the bed in Padua to the back seat in Lincoln Park our Hero is carried from wound to wound. We never hear the accents of his voice or the intonations of his prose. We do not have to. The text speaks for him. Its voice is his. And its reticence is his as well. In this connection we should look once again at a passage in the second paragraph: ". . . they had a joke about friend or enema. He went under the anaesthetic holding tight on to himself so he would not. . . ." Up to this point in the second sentence we are not aware that there has been a change of topic from that which closed the earlier sentence. The language of oral retentiveness coincides neatly with that of anal retentiveness. Logorrhea and diarrhea are equally embarrassing. Enemas are enemies and to "blab about anything during the silly, talky time" (to finish the sentence) would be as bad as to discharge matter freely from the opposite end of the alimentary canal. As Hemingway put it on another occasion: "If you talk about it, you lose it."

The point of this discussion is that the text reveals the principle behind its reticent prose style through an impartial and equal distress at the idea of excessive discharge of either verbal or fecal matter. It is an anal retentive style, then, in a surprisingly literal way. And through this style the text presents us with a lesson about women. Luz first gives our retentive hero a literal enema and then she metaphorically emasculates him by making him renounce alcohol, friends, and all the pleasures of life. The salesgirl from the loop merely administers the literal coup de grace to his already figuratively damaged sexuality.

Having come this far with a semiotic analysis, we can begin to distinguish it more precisely from New Critical exegesis. In doing so, we must begin by admitting that the two approaches share a certain number of interpretive gestures. We must also recognize that no two semiotic analyses or New Critical exegeses are likely to be identical. The major differences in the two critical approaches can be traced to their different conceptions of the object of study: for New Criticism, the work; for semiotics, the text. As a work, "A Very Short Story" must be seen as complete, unified, shaped into an aesthetic object, a verbal icon. The pedagogical implications of this are important.

The student interpreting "A Very Short Story" as a "work" is put into an interesting position. Like many of Hemingway's early stories, this one presents a male character favorably and a female unfavorably. In fact, it strongly implies favorable things about masculinity and unfavorable things about femininity. It does this, as our semiotic analysis has shown, by mapping certain traits on to a value structure. The good, loyal, reticent male character is supported by the discourse, through its covert first-person perspective and the complicity of its style with those values. The bad, treacherous, talkative female is cast out. Even the carefully established point of view is violated in the last paragraph so that the narrator can track Luz through eternity and assure us that she never married her major "in the spring, or any other time." But for the most part Hemingway's control over his text is so great that the anger at the root of the story is transformed into what we may take as the cool, lapidary prose of the pure, impersonal artist.

And there definitely is an anger behind this story, to which we shall soon turn our attention. For the moment we must follow a bit further the situation of the student faced with this story in the form of a "work" to be interpreted. The concept of "the student" is one of those transcendental abstractions that we accept for convenience's sake and often come to regret. We can begin to break it down by reminding ourselves that students come in at least two genders. Actual students read this story in different ways. Most male students sympathize with the protagonist and are very critical of Luz—as, indeed, the discourse asks them to be. Many female students try to read the story as sympathetic to Luz, blaming events on the "weakness" of the young man or the state of the world. This is a possible interpretation, but it is not well supported by the text. Thus the female student must either "misread" the work (that is, she must offer the more weakly supported of two interpretations) or accept one more blow to her self-esteem as a woman. Faced with this story in a competitive classroom, women are put at a disadvantage. They are, in fact, in a double bind.

By New Critical standards the narrator is impersonal and reliable. The words on the page are all we have, and they tell us of a garrulous, faithless woman who was unworthy of the love of a loyal young man. But semiotic analysis has already suggested alternatives to this view. Seen as a text that presents a diegesis, this story is far from complete. There are gaps in the diegesis, reticences in the text, and a highly manipulative use of covert first-person narrative. There are signs of anger and vengefulness in the text, too, that suggest not an omniscient impersonal author but a partial, flawed human being—like the rest of us—behind the words on the page. . . .

NOTE

1. [Benveniste, *Problems in General Linguistics*, trans. Mary Elizabeth Meek (Coral Gables, Fla.: University of Miami Press, 1971). Chatman, *Story and Discourse: Narrative Structure in Fiction and Film* (Ithaca, N.Y.: Cornell University Press, 1978).]

Striptease

ROLAND BARTHES

In the preface to the 1970 edition of *Mythologies*, Roland Barthes recounts how, after reading Ferdinand de Saussure, he wanted not only to unmask semiotically the language of mass culture but also to "account *in detail* for the mystification which transforms petit-bourgeois culture into a universal nature." Thus, Barthes's lively essays on everything from wrestling/boxing to Garbo films explore how ideological myths covertly reinforce common assumptions about ourselves and 'reality'.

Although "ideology" is variously defined, Barthes and most of the critics here use it to mean the largely unconscious and unquestioned conditions of our existence in the world—the things that "go without saying." Because ideology is inscribed in our signifying practices, it works to hide contradictions within discourse systems and to preserve the status quo as truth. Just as we seem to see through words to 'things out-there', so we are made to feel that that is the way the world "naturally" is. In "Striptease," Barthes challenges our usual ideological assumptions by contrasting the differing discursive strands of this X-rated amusement.

STRIPTEASE—AT LEAST PARISIAN striptease—is based on a contradiction: Woman is desexualized at the very moment when she is stripped naked. We may therefore say that we are dealing in a sense with a spectacle based on fear, or rather on the pretence of fear, as if eroticism here went no further than a sort of delicious terror, whose ritual signs have only to be announced to evoke at once the idea of sex and its conjuration.

It is only the time taken in shedding clothes which makes voyeurs of the public; but here, as in any mystifying spectacle, the decor, the props and the stereotypes intervene to contradict the initially provocative intention and eventually bury it in insignificance: evil is *advertised* the better to impede and exorcize it. French striptease seems to stem from what I have earlier called "Operation Margarine," a mystifying device which consists in inoculating the public with a touch of evil, the better to plunge it afterwards into a permanently immune Moral Good: a few particles of eroticism, highlighted by the very situation on which the show is based, are in fact absorbed in a reassuring ritual which negates the flesh as surely as the vaccine or the taboo circumscribe and control the illness or the crime.

There will therefore be in striptease a whole series of coverings placed upon the body of the woman in proportion as she pretends to strip it bare. Exoticism is the first of these barriers, for it is always of a petrified kind which transports the body into the world of legend or romance: a Chinese woman equipped with an opium pipe (the indispensable symbol of "Sininess"), an undulating vamp with a gigantic cigarette-holder, a Venetian decor complete with gondola, a dress with panniers and a singer of serenades; all aim at establishing the woman *right from the start* as an object in disguise. The end of the striptease is then no longer to drag into the light a hidden depth, but to signify, through the shedding of an incongruous and artificial clothing, nakedness as a *natural* vesture of woman, which amounts in the end to regaining a perfectly chaste state of the flesh.

The classic props of the music-hall, which are invariably rounded up here, constantly make the unveiled body more remote, and force it back into the all-pervading ease of a well-known rite: the furs, the fans, the gloves, the feathers, the fishnet stockings, in short the whole spectrum of adornment, constantly makes the living body return to the category of luxurious objects which surround man with a magical decor. Covered with feathers or gloved, the woman identifies herself here as a stereotyped element of music-hall, and to shed objects as ritualistic as these is no longer a part of a further, genuine undressing. Feathers, furs and gloves go on pervading the woman with their magical virtue even once removed, and give her something like the enveloping memory of a luxurious shell, for it is a self-evident law that the whole of striptease is given in the very nature of the initial garment: if the latter is improbable, as in the case of the Chinese woman or the woman in furs, the nakedness which follows remains itself unreal, smooth and enclosed like a beautiful slippery object, withdrawn by its very extravagance from human use: this is the underlying significance of the G-String covered with diamonds or sequins which is the very end of striptease. This ultimate triangle, by its pure and geometrical shape, by its hard and shiny material, bars the way to the sexual parts like a sword of purity, and definitively drives the woman back into a mineral world, the (precious) stone being here the irrefutable symbol of the absolute object, that which serves no purpose.

Contrary to the common prejudice, the dance which accompanies the striptease from beginning to end is in no way an erotic element. It is probably quite the reverse: the faintly rhythmical undulation in this case exorcizes the fear of immobility. Not only does it give to the show the alibi of Art (the dances in strip-shows are always "artistic"), but above all it constitutes the last barrier, and the most efficient of all: the dance, consisting of ritual gestures which have been seen a thousand times, acts on movements as a cosmetic, it hides nudity, and smothers the spectacle under a glaze of superfluous yet essential gestures, for the act of becoming bare is here relegated to the rank of parasitical operations carried out in an improbable background. Thus we see the professionals of striptease wrap themselves in the miraculous ease which constantly clothes them, makes them remote, gives them the icy indifference of skilful practitioners, haughtily taking refuge in the sureness of their technique: their science clothes them like a garment.

All this, this meticulous exorcism of sex, can be verified *a contrario* in the "popular contests" (*sic*) of amateur striptease: there, "beginners" undress in front of a few hundred spectators without resorting or resorting very clumsily to magic, which unquestionably restores to the spectacle its erotic power. Here we find at the beginning far fewer Chinese or Spanish women, no feathers or furs (sensible suits, ordinary coats), few disguises as a starting point—gauche steps, unsatisfactory dancing, girls constantly threatened by immobility, and above all by a "technical" awkwardness (the resistance of briefs, dress or bra) which gives to the gestures of unveiling an unexpected importance, denying the woman the alibi of art and the refuge of being an object, imprisoning her in a condition of weakness and timorousness.

And yet, at the *Moulin Rouge*, we see hints of another kind of exorcism, probably typically French, and one which in actual fact tends less to nullify eroticism than to tame it: the compère tries to give striptease a reassuring petit-bourgeois status. To start with, striptease is a *sport*: there is a Striptease Club, which organizes healthy contests whose winners come out crowned and rewarded with edifying prizes (a subscription to physical training lessons), a novel (which can only be Robbe-Grillet's *Voyeur*), or useful prizes (a pair of nylons, five thousand francs). Then, striptease is identified with a *career* (beginners, semi-professionals, professionals), that is, to the honourable practice of a specialization (strippers are skilled workers). One can even give them the magical alibi of work: *vocation*; one girl is, say, "*doing well*" or "*well on the way to fulfilling her promise*," or on the contrary "*taking her first steps*" on the arduous path of striptease. Finally and above all, the competitors are socially situated: one is a salesgirl, another a secretary (there are many secretaries in the Striptease Club). Striptease here is made to rejoin the world of the public, is made familiar and bourgeois, as if the French, unlike the American public (at least according to what one hears), following an irresistible tendency of their social status, could not conceive eroticism except as a household property, sanctioned by the alibi of weekly sport much more than by that of a magical spectacle: and this is how, in France, striptease is nationalized.

Subculture: The Meaning of Style

DICK HEBDIGE

Hebdige's semiotic analysis can be called "post-structuralist" because it calls into question the very possibility of meaning. He analyzes a third discursive level which subverts the meanings generated on the informational and symbolic discursive levels. This third level has to do with the continuous play of signifiers.

From *Subculture: The Meaning of Style* by Dick Hebdige (London: Methuen, 1979). Copyright 1979 by Dick Hebdige. Reprinted by permission.

As Charles S. Peirce had argued long ago, every sign must be interpreted by another sign: signifiers slide into signifiers, not signifieds. They produce an infinity of possible meanings. From this perspective, discourse is seen as open, in process, and "polysemic" (having multiple meanings).

The selection below forms part of a larger discussion of ways to read, or interpret, subcultures. According to Hebdige, the increasing fragmentation and polarization accompanying Britain's social and economic decline has heightened tensions between dominant middle-class and subordinate working-class groups. These tensions are encoded in subversive styles that can be read as signs (objects invested with meaning) communicating difference as well as group identity. For example, we can read the punk styles of revolt, or revolting styles, as signifying practices that undermine traditional norms by juxtaposing two apparently incompatible realities such as flag:jacket; hole:tee shirt; comb:weapon.

In this section, Hebdige explains how Lévi-Strauss's concept of "homology" can be used to read punk subculture as a third level of discourse. Punk style "deconstructs" itself by representing the experience of class contradictions in the form of visual puns, bondage, ripped tee shirts, and the like. In linguistic terms, these stylistic signifiers of sex and class refer to other signifiers, not to signifieds. As a result, punk styles become a "dislocated, ironic, and self-aware" third-level discourse signaling the values of contradiction, disruption, and process.

STYLE AS HOMOLOGY

THE PUNK SUBCULTURE, then, signified chaos at every level, but this was only possible because the style itself was so thoroughly ordered. The chaos cohered as a meaningful whole. We can now attempt to solve this paradox by referring to another concept originally employed by Lévi-Strauss: homology.

Paul Willis first applied the term "homology" to subculture in his study of hippies and motor-bike boys using it to describe the symbolic fit between the values and life-styles of a group, its subjective experience and the musical forms it uses to express or reinforce its focal concerns.[1] In *Profane Culture*, Willis shows how, contrary to the popular myth which presents subcultures as lawless forms, the internal structure of any particular subculture is characterized by an extreme orderliness: each part is organically related to other parts and it is through the fit between them that the subcultural member makes sense of the world. For instance, it was the homology between an alternative value system ("Tune in, turn on, drop out"), hallucinogenic drugs and acid rock which made the hippy culture cohere as a "whole way of life" for individual hippies. In *Resistance Through Rituals,* Hall et al. crossed the concepts of homology and *bricolage* to provide a systematic explanation of why a particular subcultural style should appeal to a particular group of people. The authors asked the question: "What specifically does a subcultural style signify to the members of the subculture themselves?"[2]

The answer was that the appropriated objects reassembled in the distinctive subcultural ensembles were "made to reflect, express and resonate . . . aspects of group life." The objects chosen were, either intrinsically or in their adapted forms, homologous with the focal concerns, activities, group structure and collective self-image of the subculture. They were "objects in which (the subcultural members) could see their central values held and reflected" (Hall et al.).

The skinheads were cited to exemplify this principle. The boots, braces and cropped hair were only considered appropriate and hence meaningful because they communicated the desired qualities: "hardness, masculinity and working-classness." In this way "The symbolic objects—dress, appearance, language, ritual occasions, styles of interaction, music—were made to form a *unity* with the group's relations, situation, experience" (Hall et al.).

The punks would certainly seem to bear out this thesis. The subculture was nothing if not consistent. There was a homological relation between the trashy cut-up clothes and spiky hair, the pogo and amphetamines, the spitting, the vomiting, the format of the fanzines, the insurrectionary poses and the "soulless," frantically driven music. The punks wore clothes which were the sartorial equivalent of swear words, and they swore as they dressed—with calculated effect, lacing obscenities into record notes and publicity releases, interviews and love songs. Clothed in chaos, they produced Noise in the calmly orchestrated Crisis of everyday life in the late 1970s—a noise which made (no)sense in exactly the same way and to exactly the same extent as a piece of avant-garde music. If we were to write an epitaph for the punk subculture, we could do no better than repeat Poly Styrene's famous dictum: "Oh Bondage, Up Yours!" or somewhat more concisely: the forbidden is permitted, but by the same token, nothing, not even these forbidden signifiers (bondage, safety pins, chains, hair-dye, etc.) is sacred and fixed.

This absence of permanently sacred signifiers (icons) creates problems for the semiotician. How can we discern any positive values reflected in objects which were chosen only to be discarded? For instance, we can say that the early punk ensembles gestured towards the signified's "modernity" and "working-classness." The safety pins and bin liners signified a relative material poverty which was either directly experienced and exaggerated or sympathetically assumed, and which in turn was made to stand for the spiritual paucity of everyday life. In other words, the safety pins, etc. "enacted" that transition from real to symbolic scarcity which Paul Piccone has described as the movement from "empty stomachs" to "empty spirits—and therefore an empty life notwithstanding [the] chrome and the plastic . . . of the life style of bourgeois society."[3]

We could go further and say that even if the poverty was being parodied, the wit was undeniably barbed; that beneath the clownish make-up there lurked the unaccepted and disfigured face of capitalism; that beyond the horror circus antics a divided and unequal society was being eloquently condemned. However, if we were to go further still and describe punk music as the "sound of the Westway," or the pogo as the "high-rise leap," or to talk of bondage as reflecting the narrow options of working-class youth, we would be treading on less certain ground. Such readings are both too literal and too conjectural. They are extrapolations from the subculture's own prodigious rhetoric, and rhetoric is not self-explanatory: it may say what it means but it does not necessarily "mean" what it "says." In other words, it is opaque: its categories are part of its publicity. [In the words of J. Mepham], "The true text is reconstructed not by a process of piecemeal decoding, but by the identification of the generative sets of ideological categories and its replacement by a different set."[4]

To reconstruct the true text of the punk subculture, to trace the source of its subversive practices, we must first isolate the "generative set" responsible for the subculture's exotic displays. Certain semiotic facts are undeniable. The punk subculture, like every other youth culture, was constituted in a series of spectacular transformations of a whole range of commodities, values, common-sense attitudes, etc. It was through these adapted forms that certain sections of predominantly working-class youth were able to restate their opposition to dominant values and institutions. However, when we attempt to close in on specific items, we immediately encounter problems. What, for instance, was the swastika being used to signify?

We can see how the symbol was made available to the punks (via Bowie and Lou Reed's "Berlin" phase). Moreover, it clearly reflected the punks' interest in a decadent and evil Germany—a Germany which had "no future." It evoked a period redolent with a powerful mythology. Conventionally, as far as the British were concerned, the swastika signified "enemy." None the less, in punk usage, the symbol lost its "natural" meaning—fascism. The punks were not generally sympathetic to the parties of the extreme right. On the contrary, the conflict with the resurrected teddy boys and the widespread support for the anti-fascist movement (e.g., the Rock against Racism campaign) seem to indicate that the punk subculture grew up partly as an antithetical response to the reemergence of racism in the mid-70s. We must resort, then, to the most obvious of explanations—that the swastika was worn because it was guaranteed to shock. (A punk asked by *Time Out* [17–23 December 1977] why she wore a swastika, replied: "Punks just like to be hated.") This represented more than a simple inversion or inflection of the ordinary meanings attached to an object. The signifier (swastika) had been wilfully detached from the concept (Nazism) it conventionally signified, and although it had been re-positioned (as "Berlin") within an alternative subcultural context, its primary value and appeal derived precisely from its lack of meaning: from its potential for deceit. It was exploited as an empty effect. We are forced to the conclusion that the central value "held and reflected" in the swastika was the communicated absence of any such identifiable values. Ultimately, the symbol was as "dumb" as the rage it provoked. The key to punk style remains elusive. Instead of arriving at the point where we can begin to make sense of the style, we have reached the very place where meaning itself evaporates.

STYLE AS SIGNIFYING PRACTICE

We are surrounded by emptiness but it is an emptiness filled with signs.
—Lefebvre, *Everyday Life in the Modern World*

It would seem that those approaches to subculture based upon a traditional semiotics (a semiotics which begins with some notion of the "message"—of a combination of elements referring unanimously to a fixed number of signifieds) fail to provide us with a "way in" to the difficult and contradictory text of punk style. Any attempt at extracting a final set of meanings from the seemingly endless, often apparently random, play of signifiers in evidence here seems doomed to failure.

And yet, over the years, a branch of semiotics has emerged which deals precisely with this problem. Here the simple notion of reading as the revelation of a fixed number of concealed meaning is discarded in favour of the idea of *polysemy* whereby each text is seen to generate a potentially infinite range of meanings. Attention is consequently directed towards that point—or more precisely, that level—in any given text where the principle of meaning itself seems most in doubt. Such an approach lays less stress on the primacy of structure and system in language ("langue"), and more upon the *position* of the speaking subject in discourse ("parole"). It is concerned with the *process* of meaning-construction rather than with the final product.

Much of this work, principally associated with the *Tel Quel* group in France, has grown out of an engagement with literary and filmic texts. It involves an attempt to go beyond conventional theories of art (as mimesis, as representation, as a transparent reflection of reality, etc.) and to introduce instead "the notion of art as 'work,' as 'practice,' as a particular *transformation* of reality, a version of reality, an account of reality."[5]

One of the effects of this redefinition of interests has been to draw critical attention to the relationship between the means of representation and the object represented, between what in traditional aesthetics have been called respectively the "form" and "content" of a work of art. According to this approach, there can no longer be any absolute distinction between these two terms and the primary recognition that the *ways* in which things are said—the narrative structures employed—impose quite rigid limitations on *what* can be said is of course crucial. In particular, the notion that a detachable content can be inserted into a more or less neutral form—the assumption which seems to underpin the aesthetic of realism—is deemed illusory because such an aesthetic "denies its own status as articulation. . . . [in this case] the real is not articulated, *it is*."[6]

Drawing on an alternative theory of aesthetics, rooted in modernism and the avant-garde and taking as its model Brecht's idea of an "epic theatre,"[7] the *Tel Quel* group sets out to counter the prevailing notion of a transparent relation between sign and referent, signification and reality, through the concept of *signifying practice*. This phrase reflects exactly the group's central concerns with the ideological implications of form, with the idea of a positive construction and deconstruction of meaning, and with what has come to be called the "productivity" of language. This approach sees language as an active, transitive force which shapes and positions the "subject" (as speaker, writer, reader) while always itself remaining "in process" capable of infinite adaptation. This emphasis on signifying practice is accompanied by a polemical insistence that art represents the triumph of process over fixity, disruption over unity, "collision" over "linkage"[8]—the triumph, that is, of the signifier over the signified. It should be seen as part of the group's attempt to substitute the values of "fissure" and contradiction for the preoccupation with "wholeness" (i.e. the text "conceived as a closed structure"),[9] which is said to characterize classic literary criticism.

Although much of this work is still at a tenative stage, it does offer a radically different perspective on style in subculture—one which assigns a central place to the problems of reading which we have encountered in our analysis of punk. Julia Kristeva's work on signification seems particularly useful. In *La Revolution du Langage Poetique* she explores the subversive possibilities within language through a study of French symbolist poetry, and points to "poetic language" as the "place where the social code is destroyed and renewed."[10] She counts as "radical" those signifying practices which negate and disturb syntax—"the condition of coherence and rationality"[11]—and which therefore serve to erode the concept of "actantial position" upon which the whole "Symbolic Order,"* [12] is seen to rest.

---

*The "symbolic order" to which I have referred throughout should not be confused with Kristeva's "Symbolic Order" which is used in a sense derived specifically from Lacanian psychoanalysis. I use the term merely to designate the apparent unity of the dominant ideological discourses in play at any one time.

Two of Kristeva's interests seem to coincide with our own: the creation of subordinate groups through *positioning in language* (Kristeva is specifically interested in women), and the disruption of the process through which such positioning is habitually achieved. In addition, the general idea of signfying practice (which she defines as "the setting in place and cutting through or traversing of a system of signs")[13] can help us to rethink in a more subtle and complex way the relations not only between marginal and mainstream cultural formations but between the various subcultural styles themselves. For instance, we have seen how all subcultural style is based on a practice which has much in common with the "radical" collage aesthetic of surrealism and we shall be seeing how different styles represent different signifying practices. Beyond this I shall be arguing that the signifying practices embodied in punk were "radical" in Kristeva's sense: that they gestured towards a "nowhere" and actively *sought* to remain silent, illegible.

We can now look more closely at the relationship between experience, expression and signification in subculture; at the whole question of style and our reading of style. To return to our example, we have seen how the punk style fitted together homologically precisely through its lack of fit (hole:tee-shirt::spitting:applause::bin-liner:garment::anarchy:order)—by its refusal to cohere around a readily identifiable set of central values. It cohered, instead, *elliptically* through a chain of conspicuous absences. It was characterized by its unlocatedness—its blankness—and in this it can be contrasted with the skinhead style.

Whereas the skinheads theorized and fetishized their class position, in order to effect a "magical" return to an imagined past, the punks dislocated themselves from the parent culture and were positioned instead on the outside: beyond the comprehension of the average (wo)man in the street in a science fiction future. They played up their Otherness, "happening" on the world as aliens, inscrutables. Though punk rituals, accents and objects were deliberately used to signify working-classness, the exact origins of individual punks were disguised or symbolically disfigured by the make-up, masks and aliases which seem to have been used, like Breton's art, as ploys "to escape the principle of identity."[14]

This working-classness therefore tended to retain, *even in practice, even in its concretized forms,* the dimensions of an idea. It was abstract, disembodied, decontextualized. Bereft of the necessary details—a name, a home, a history—it refused to make sense, to be grounded, "read back" to its origins. It stood in violent contradiction to that other great punk signifier—sexual "kinkiness." The two forms of deviance—social and sexual—were juxtaposed to give an impression of multiple warping which was guaranteed to disconcert the most liberal of observers, to challenge the glib assertions of sociologists no matter how radical. In this way, although the punks referred continually to the realities of school, work, family and class, these references only made sense at one remove:

they were passed through the fractured circuitry of punk style and re-presented as "noise," disturbance, entropy.

In other words, although the punks self-consciously mirrored what Paul Piccone calls the "pre-categorical realities"[15] of bourgeois society—inequality, powerlessness, alienation—this was only possible because punk style had made a decisive break not only with the parent culture but with its own *location in experience*. This break was both inscribed and re-enacted in the signifying practices embodied in punk style. The punk ensembles, for instance, did not so much magically resolve experienced contradictions as *re-present* the experience of contradiction itself in the form of visual puns (bondage, the ripped tee shirt, etc.). Thus while it is true that the symbolic objects in punk style (the safety pins, the pogo, the ECT hairstyles) were "made to form a '*unity*' with the group's relations, situations, experience" (Hall et al.) this unity was at once "ruptural" and "expressive," or more precisely it expressed itself through rupture.

This is not to say, of course, that all punks were equally aware of the disjunction between experience and signification upon which the whole style was ultimately based. The style no doubt made sense for the first wave of self-conscious innovators at a level which remained inaccessible to those who became punks after the subculture had surfaced and been publicized. Punk is not unique in this: the distinction between originals and hangers-on is always a significant one in subculture. Indeed, it is frequently verbalized (plastic punks or safety-pin people, burrhead rastas or rasta bandwagon, weekend hippies, etc. versus the "authentic" people). For instance, the mods had an intricate system of classification whereby the "faces" and "stylists" who made up the original coterie were defined against the unimaginative majority—the pedestrian "kids" and "scooter boys" who were accused of trivializing and coarsening the precious mod style. What is more, different youths bring different degrees of commitment to a subculture. It can represent a major dimension in people's lives—an axis erected in the face of the family around which a secret and immaculate identity can be made to cohere—or it can be a slight distraction, a bit of light relief from the monotonous but none the less paramount realities of school, home and work. It can be used as a means of escape, of total detachment from the surrounding terrain, or as a way of fitting back in to it and settling down after a week-end or evening spent letting off steam. In most cases it is used, as Phil Cohen suggests, magically to achieve both ends. However, despite these individual differences, the members of a subculture must share a common language. And if a style is really to catch on, if it is to become genuinely popular, it must say the right things in the right way at the right time. It must anticipate or encapsulate a mood, a moment. It must embody a sensibility, and the sensibility which punk style embodied was essentially dislocated, ironic and self-aware.

Just as individual members of the same subculture can be more or less conscious of what they are saying in style and in what ways they are saying it, so different subcultural styles exhibit different degrees of rupture. The conspicuously scruffy, "unwholesome" punks obtruded from the familiar landscape of normalized forms in a more startling fashion than the mods, tellingly described in a newspaper of the time as ". . . pinneat, lively and clean," although the two groups had none the less engaged in the same signifying practice (i.e. self-consciously subversive *bricolage*).

This partly explains or at least underpins internal subcultural hostilities. For example, the antagonism between the teddy boy revivalists and the punk rockers went beyond any simple incompatibility at the level of "content"—different music, dress, etc.—beyond even the different political and racial affiliations of the two groups, the different relationships with the parent community, etc., and was inscribed in the very way in which the two styles were constructed: the way in which they communicated (or refused to communicate) meaning. Teddy boys interviewed in the press regularly objected to the punks' symbolic "plundering" of the precious 50s wardrobe (the drains, the winklepickers, quiffs, etc.) and to the ironic and impious uses to which these "sacred" artefacts were put when "cut up" and reworked into punk style where presumably they were contaminated by association (placed next to "bovver boots" and latex bondage-wear!).[16] Behind punk's favored "cut ups" lay hints of disorder, of breakdown and category confusion: a desire not only to erode racial and gender boundaries but also to confuse chronological sequence by mixing up details from different periods.

As such, punk style was perhaps interpreted by the teddy boys as an affront to the traditional working-class values of forthrightness, plain speech and sexual puritanism which they had endorsed and revived. Like the reaction of the rockers to the mods and the skinheads to the hippies, the teddy boy revival seems to have represented an "authentic" working-class backlash to the proletarian posturings of the new wave. *The way in which it signified,* via a magical return to the past, to the narrow confines of the community and the parent culture, to the familiar and the legible, was perfectly in tune with its inherent conservatism.[17] Not only did the teds react aggressively to punk objects and "meanings," they also reacted to the way in which those objects were presented, those meanings constructed and dismantled. They did so by resorting to an altogether more primitive "language": by turning back, in George Melly's words, to a "'then' which was superior to 'now'" which, as Melly goes on to say, is "a very anti-pop concept."[18]

We can express the difference between the two practices in the following formula: one (i.e. the punks') is kinetic, transitive and concentrates attention on *the act of transformation* performed upon the object: the other (i.e. the teds') is static, expressive, and concentrates attention on the *objects-in-themselves.* We can perhaps grasp the nature of this dis-

tinction more clearly if we resort to another of Kristeva's categories—
"*signifiance*." She has introduced this term to describe the work of the
signifier in the text in contrast to signification which refers to the work of
the signified. Roland Barthes defines the difference between the two operations thus:

> Signifiance is a *process* in the course of which the "subject" of the text,
> escaping (conventional logic) and engaging in other logics (of the sig-
> nifier, of contradiction) struggles with meaning and is deconstructed
> ("lost"); signifiance—and this is what immediately distinguishes it from
> signification—is thus precisely a work; not the work by which the (intact
> and exterior) subject might try to master the language . . . but that radi-
> cal work (leaving nothing intact) through which the subject explores—
> entering not observing—how the language works and undoes him or
> her. . . . Contrary to signification, signifiance cannot be reduced there-
> fore, to communication, representation, expression: it places the sub-
> ject (of writer, reader) in the text not as a projection . . . but as a "loss," a
> "disappearance." [19]

Elsewhere, in an attempt to specify the various kinds of meaning
present in film, Barthes refers to the "moving play" of signifiers as the
"third (obtuse) meaning" (the other two meanings being the "informational" and the "symbolic" which, as they are "closed" and "obvious" are
normally the only ones which conern the semiotician). The third meaning works against ("exceeds") the other two by "blunting" them—round-
ing off the "obvious signified" and thus causing "the reading to slip."
Barthes uses as an example a still from Eisenstein's film *Battleship Pot-
emkin* which shows an old woman, a headscarf pulled low over her fore-
head, caught in a classical, grief-stricken posture. At one level, the level
of the obvious meaning, she seems to typify "noble grief" but, as Barthes
observes, her strange headdress, and rather "stupid" fish-like eyes cut
across this typification in such a way that "there is no guarantee of intentionality." [20] This, the third meaning, flows upstream as it were, against
the supposed current of the text, preventing the text from reaching its
destination: a full and final closure. Barthes thus describes the third
meaning as "a gash rased [*sic*] of meaning (of the desire for meaning) . . .
it outplays meaning—subverts not the content but the whole practice of
meaning."

The ideas of "signifiance" and "obtuse meaning" suggest the presence in the text of an intrinsically subversive component. Our recognition of the operations performed within the text at the level of the
signifier can help us to understand the way in which certain subcultural
styles seem to work against the reader and to resist any authoritative interpretation. If we consider for a moment it becomes clear that not all
subcultural styles "play" with language to the same extent: some are more
"straightforward" than others and place a higher priority on the con-

struction and projection of a firm and coherent identity. For instance, if we return to our earlier example, we could say that whereas the teddy boy style says its piece in a relatively direct and obvious way, and remains resolutely committed to a "finished" meaning, to the signified, to what Kristeva calls "signification," punk style is in a constant state of assemblage, of flux. It introduces a heterogeneous set of signifiers which are liable to be superseded at any moment by others no less productive. It invites the reader to "slip into" "signifiance" to lose the sense of direction, the direction of sense. Cut adrift from meaning, the punk style thus comes to approximate the state which Barthes has described as "a *floating* (the very form of the signifier); a floating which would not destroy anything but would be content simply to disorientate the Law."[21]

The two styles, then, represent different signifying practices which confront the reader with quite different problems. We can gauge the extent of this difference (which is basically a difference in the degree of *closure*) by means of an analogy. In *The Thief's Journal*, Genet contrasts his relationship to the elusive Armand with his infatuation with the more transparent Stilittano in terms which underline the distinction between the two practices: "I compare Armand to the expanding universe. . . . Instead of being defined and reduced to observable limits, Armand constantly changes as I pursue him. On the other hand, Stilittano is already encircled."[22]

The relationship between experience, expression and signification is therefore not a constant in subculture. It can form a unity which is either more or less organic, striving towards some ideal coherence, or more or less ruptural, reflecting the experience of breaks and contradictions. Moreover, individual subcultures can be more or less "conservative" or "progressive," integrated *into* the community, continuous with the values of that community, or extrapolated *from* it, defining themselves *against* the parent culture. Finally, these differences are reflected not only in the objects of subcultural style, but in the signifying practices which represent those objects and render them meaningful.

NOTES

1. Willis, *Profane Culture* (New York: Routledge and Kegan Paul, 1978).

2. S. Hall; J. Clarke; T. Jefferson; and B. Roberts, eds., "Subculture, Culture, and Class," in *Resistance Through Rituals*, ed. Hall et al. (London: Hutchinson, 1976). Cited in the text as Hall et al.

3. Piccone, "From Youth Culture to Political Praxis," *Radical America* 15 November 1969.

4. Mepham, "The Theory of Ideology in 'Capital,'" W.P.C.S.ᵉ (University of Birmingham) 1974, no. 6.

5. Sylvia Harvey, *May 68 and Film Culture* (British Film Institute, 1978). This is an extremely lucid introduction to the notoriously difficult work of the "second wave" semioticians (much of which has yet to be translated into English).

Harvey traces the development of radical film theory in France from the appro-priation of Russian formalism by the journals *Cahiers* and *Cinétique* in the early seventies to the beginnings of "a science of the signifier" as developed by the *Tel Quel* group in Paris.

6. C. MacCabe, "Notes on Realism," *Screen* 15, no. 2 (1974). See MacCabe, "Theory and Film: Principles of Film and Pleasure," *Screen* 17, no. 3 (1975), for another representative critique of realism.

7. Brecht intended that his "epic theatre" should let the audience "in" on the "secret" of its own construction through the celebrated "alienation tech-niques" which have the effect of distancing the spectator from the spectacle and, theoretically at least, making him or her reflect on the social relations depicted in the play and on his or her *position* on (rather than "in") the text. By preventing audience identification with character, and by avoiding plot continuity, resolu-tion, etc., epic theatre is supposed to jar the audience into the recognition that "reality is alterable" (see *Brecht on Theatre* [Willett, 1978]). Brecht's preoccupation with formal techniques and their role in the politicization of theatre has proved extremely influential in the formation of the new film theory (see Harvey, *May 68*).

8. As part of his attempt to break down the traditional unity of narrative, Eisenstein based his theory of montage (the juxtaposition of shots in film) on the principle of "collision" rather than "linkage" (see Harvey, *May 68, 65*).

9. H. Lackner and D. Matias, "John Ford's *Young Mister Lincoln*," *Screen* 13, no. 3 (1972); originally published in *Cahiers* 1970, no. 233.

10. Kristeva, "The Speaking Subject and Poetical Language," paper pre-sented at Cambridge University, 1975.

11. A. White, "L'eclatement du sujet: The Theoretical Work of Julia Kris-teva," paper available from University of Birmingham.

12. I can only refer the reader to A. White's critique (ibid.) for an explica-tion of Kristeva's use of terms like the "symbolic" and of the dialectic between unity and process, the "symbolic" and the "semiotic" which forms the thematic core of her work:

> The symbolic is . . . that major part of language which names and relates things, it is that unity of semantic and syntactic competence which allows com-munication and rationality to appear. Kristeva has thus divided language into two vast realms, the *semiotic*—sound, rhythm and movement anterior to sense and linked closely to the impulses (Triebe)—and the *symbolic*—the semantico-syntactic function of language necessary to all rational communication about the world. The latter, the *symbolic*, usually "takes charge of" the semiotic and binds it into syntax and phonemes, but it can only do so on the basis of the sounds and movements presented to it by the semiotic. The dialectic of the two parts of language form the *mise en scène* of Kristeva's description of poetics, subjectivity and revolution.

(See also G. Nowell-Smith's introduction to "Signifying Practice and Mode of Production" in the *Edinburgh '76 Magazine*, no. 1).

13. The setting in place, or constituting of a system of signs requires the iden-tity of a speaking subject in a social institution which the subject recognises as the support of its identity. The traversing of the system takes place when the speaking subject is put in process and cuts across, at an angle as it were, the

social institutions in which it had previously recognised itself. It thus coincides with the moment of social rupture, renovation and revolution (Kristeva, "Signifying Practice and Mode of Production," *Edinburgh '76 Magainze*, no. 1).

Again, Kristeva is specifically concerned with positing a notion of the *subject in process* against the traditional conception of the single, unified subject, and she uses the terms "signifiance," "symbolic," "semiotic" and "imaginary" in the context of Jacques Lacan's theory of psychoanalysis. Her definition of "signifying practice" none the less still holds when transplanted to the quite different context of the analysis of style in subculture.

14. "Who knows if we are not somehow preparing ourselves to escape the principle of identity?" (A. Breton, Preface to the 1920 Exhibition of Max Ernst).

15. Piccone, "From Youth to Political Praxis."

16. See, for instance, *Melody Maker*, 30 July 1977, and *Evening Standard*, 5 July 1977. The teddy boys interviewed typically complained of the punks' lack of stylistic integrity and accused them of trying to be "clever."

17. ". . . it is the *way in which* the semiotic relates to and disfigures the symbolic, as well as the *way in which* the symbolic reasserts its unifying control of the semiotic, which gives us the basis of subjectivity as a process" (White, "L'éclatement du sujet"). Similarly, it is the way in which subordinate groups relate to and disfigure the symbolic order which gives us the basis of subculture as a mode of resistance.

18. Melly, *Revolt into Style* (Harmondsworth, U.K.: Penguin, 1972).

19. S. Heath, ed., *Image, Music, Text* (London: (William Collins PLC, Fontana—Flamingo, 1977).

20. Barthes, "The Third Meaning," in *Image, Music, Text*, ed. S. Heath.

21. Barthes, "Writers, Intellectuals, Teachers," in *Image, Music, Text*, ed. S. Heath.

22. J. Genet, *The Thief's Journal* (Harmondsworth, U.K.: Penguin, 1967).

Structuralist-Semiotic Provocateurs

1. Structuralists have been accused of endangering literature by "decentering" the text, by insisting that a text's language, not its author, produces meaning*s*, not meaning. Discuss.

2. What substantiation does Johnson offer for his claim that "Sailing to Byzantium" is structured by certain binary oppositions? or for his claim that the poetic "I" becomes identified with the golden bird?

3. Using Happel's method as a model, distinguish between *how* the story of "The Purloined Letter" is told and *what* story is told. Does paying attention to the role of the narrator shed any new light on the tale?

4. In a critique of Chatman's essay and of narratology in general, Barbara Herrnstein Smith questions whether Maupassant's work and Renoir's film are both versions of another deep-structure story to which they are each independently related as Chatman contends, or whether Renoir's is an adaptation, a retelling, of Maupassant's story (*Critical Inquiry* 7 [1980]: 213–36). Discuss.

5. According to Scholes, an analysis of the diegetic fiction (the story constructed by the reader's inferential process from the words on the page and from the cultural context) of a realistic, or "objective," text by Hemingway's would differ from an analysis of a discursive text by D. H. Lawrence. (By "discursive" Scholes means texts that suggest an authorial presence who evaluates and persuades the reader.) What might be some of these differences? Would the same contrast between realistic and discursive texts obtain between O'Connor's "Revelation" and Poe's "The Purloined Letter"?

6. What middle-class (petit-bourgeois) ideology does Barthes unmask in "Striptease"? Using his essay as a model, analyze the covert ideology implicit in other mass-culture erotica, such as X-rated films, rock album covers, or "sexy" TV jean advertisements.

7. Punk style, which Hebdige describes as "subculture," has now become fashionable and popular. What does that suggest about dominant cultural codes and their power of appropriation?

CHAPTER 5

Sociological Criticism: Historical, Marxist, Feminist

SOCIOLOGICAL CRITICS PLACE LITERARY DISCOURSE within the context of a larger social reality of historical time and cultural space. Although these critics have different theories and methodologies about social reality, all are concerned with the interaction of society and literature.

Earlier historical critics like John Heath-Stubbs and William York Tindall tend to locate a work within the context of a literary movement (e.g., romanticism) and a genre (e.g., lyric poetry). They may describe how an author's governing ideas reflect the *zeitgeist* (world view) of their era, or they may focus on extrinsic factors affecting the author or text such as publication, editions, or reviews. More recently, the "new historicism," demonstrated here by Jerome McGann's essay, examines literature as a complex process also involving readers and critics. Indeed, "reception theory" now covers a growing group of historically minded critics interested in the reader's interpretive role (see George Dillon's "Styles of Reading" in Reader-Response Criticism, Chapter 7).

Marxists and feminist critics are also concerned with the reader-text-world interaction. However, unlike the literary historians, Marxist and feminist critics actively work to change this interaction by revealing literature's classism, racism, and sexism. Because Marxist critics see social reality in terms of historical struggles among antagonistic socioeconomic classes, they work to delineate the mechanisms that keep class hegemony, or domination, in place. Because feminist critics see society as a patriarchal structure, they work to expose the gender asymmetry that perpetuates "masculine" dominance over "feminine."

Both Marxist and feminist critics are political in the sense that they want to redistribute society's power (knowledge is seen as a form of power). This accounts for their growing interest in ideology—the collective body of ideas and desires, conscious and unconscious, which "goes without saying" and which seems to be obvious or "natural." As false representation, ideology depends upon a discrepancy between actual experience and knowledge. This complex concept is explored in various ways: Barthes, as you have seen, equates it with certain semiotic practices; Brecht with dramatic conventions that "naturalize" our world and so benumb our responses.

Transcendentalism and W. B. Yeats

WILLIAM YORK TINDALL

As a historical critic, Tindall situates Yeats's "Sailing to Byzantium" within the romantic tradition, especially as that tradition draws upon Oriental and occult sources. Here Tindall disclaims Yeats's account that daemons dictated the private mythological system recorded in *The Vision* through the automatic writing of the poet's wife. Instead, Tindall proposes that certain Eastern transcendental ideas influenced *The Vision*. This emphasis on the shaping power of certain concepts characterizes a critical approach called the History of Ideas.

IF THIS ELABORATE SYSTEM [Yeats's *The Vision*] was dictated by daemons there is nothing more to say except perhaps for a word of astonishment or awe. But it is possible that Yeats was deceiving or deceived and that the work is his own synthesis of more or less Asiatic wisdom.

Multiplied by four, his system resembles the spiral chain of reincarnation around seven planets as taught by Sinnett in *Esoteric Buddhism* and by Blavatsky in *The Secret Doctrine*. Their authority seems to have been the Buddhist wheel of destiny around which spirits move until they escape from time into nirvana. But the Buddhist wheel does not involve the moon, which Yeats could have found in the bright and dark fortnights of the *Upanishads*. Yeats frequently cites these Hindu fortnights as parallels lending authority to his own; but what he cited as parallel may be source. It would not be difficult to impose Hindu moon upon Buddhist wheel. For the states of soul between incarnations Yeats could have found what he wanted in the *Upanishads* or in treatises on yoga. But the

From "Transcendentalism in Contemporary Literature," by William York Tindall, in *The Asian Legacy and American Life*, ed. Arthur E. Christy (New York: Harper & Row, John Day). Copyright 1942, 1943, 1945 by Harper & Row, Publishers, Inc. Reprinted by permission of Harper & Row Publishers, Inc.

conflict of opposites and the alternating cycles of history which also turn upon Yeats's wheel seem to owe less to Asia. They come perhaps from Plato, Empedocles, Hegel, Vico, and Spengler, with all of whom Yeats was on familiar terms.

Though Occidental in origin, Yeats's philosophy of history has an Oriental bearing. In his system two opposite civilizations, the antithetical and the primary or the spiritual and the secular, alternate every two thousand years. At present Europe is nearing the end of a primary period, beginning with Christ, and characterized by materialism, democracy, and heterogeneity. Asia, on the other hand, and by Asia here he meant the Near East, is aristocratic and spiritual. Yeats looked hopefully toward the begetting by Asia on Europe of a new spiritual era in Europe to begin about the year 2000. By his wheel of history Yeats explained to himself, since few readers now dared to invade his privacy, his dissatisfaction with the modern Europe which had imposed privacy and occultism upon him. And by his wheel Yeats explained his love for an Asia which seemed to represent his dreams of aristocracy and religion or Europe's opposite. The synthesis of West and East in Yeats's system, with its emphasis upon the East, epitomizes the destined union of those conflicting opposites.

Meanwhile questions occur to the Western mind. One may ask how a poet could produce a system so formidable and abstract as this. But Yeats had a gift for abstractions, which he detested; and he admits that he wrote *A Vision* to purge his mind of abstractions, leaving it free to create poems. If one asks how seriously Yeats, a man of high intelligence, took his synthetic doctrine and what purpose it served, one may recall his own answer to these questions. He says somewhere that although his critical mind mocked, he was delighted. He felt that a poet needs a philosophy, a religion, or a myth in order to excite his passions, and, failing to discover a suitable myth in modern Europe, he turned inventor. His system was to him what theology was to Dante, opium to Coleridge, or alcohol to Poe. Poe may have been a drunkard because he liked to drink but Yeats was an occultist for the sake of art. The dictating daemon who said, "We have come to give you metaphors of your poetry," knew what he was talking about. Many of Yeats's best poems, the best poems of our time, were inspired by his system; and whatever has that effect, though it may pass our understanding, compels, if not adherence, our most genial applause.

That memorable poem "Sailing to Byzantium" was so inspired. Byzantium, situated between East and West, is Yeats's image for the aristocratic and spiritual place of his desires. The lords and ladies to whom he will sing bear little resemblance to the English or Irish audience. His song of "what is past or passing or to come" cannot but suggest a phase in Yeats's own translation of the *Mandookya Upanishad:* "Past, present, future—everything is Om." The sages who "perne in a gyre" are Asiatic masters, spiritual advisers to Yeats and his aristocrats. The nature from which Yeats will be free is not only his senility but Europe and the cycle of time and destiny. Byzantium is a poetic equivalent of nirvana, shaped to the needs of a modern European. "Two Songs from a Play," an equally distinguished poem, is based upon the wheel of history as suggested by Plato's "Timaeus," Vergil's Messianic eclogue, and Shelley's chorus from *Hellas*. The poem tells of the transition from the Asiatic, antithetical period, symbolized by "Babylonian starlight," Plato, and "Doric discipline," to the new order of Europe, symbolized by Christ. Pythagoras, who appears in several of the later poems, symbolizes the Orphic sage, half Asiatic and half Greek. If romanticism is the pursuit of a spiritual ideal in unpropitious times, these poems are romantic in theme. But in manner they are what we have come to associate with the classics. The language, unlike Wordsworth's, is general. The order of words is natural. The manner is as grand as Gibbon's. Nothing of our time approaches more closely the feeling of Ben Jonson and Racine. It is both pleasing and odd that the Oriental and the occult, which have served romantics so faithfully, should have inspired these classical poems.

Beyond Aestheticism: W. B. Yeats

JOHN HEATH-STUBBS

Heath-Stubbs places Yeats in a 1930s European historical context by linking the "violence and hardness" of his Byzantium poems, expressive of the poet's reactionary aristocratic aestheticism, to European fascism. Heath-Stubbs warns democratic humanists that they must learn how to respond to an aesthetic vision like Yeats's which fuses violence and oppression in the "cause of Beauty."

   Heath-Stubbs has been arguing against critics who claim that the great qualities of Yeats's later verse result from the poet's repudiation of Aestheticism for realism. In contrast, Heath-Stubbs suggests that Yeats struggled to modify and enlarge his aesthetic scheme to include the political crisis of Irish Nationalism. Yeats's struggle resulted in his rediscovery of the concrete and, as Heath-Stubbs explains below, further poetic findings.

BUT IN HIS LATER YEARS, Yeats's pursuit of aesthetic experience led him to further discoveries. He came to find once more the actual *beauty*

From *The Darkling Plain: A Study of the Later Fortunes of Romanticism in English Poetry from George Darley to W. B. Yeats,* by John Heath-Stubbs (London: Eyre & Spottiswoode, 1950). Reprinted by permission.

of hard intellectual system, and of the commonplace—a knowledge the poets had steadily been losing sight of since the seventeenth century, and which the aesthetic poets had wholly set aside. In a late play, *The Words upon the Window Pane,* in which the spirit of Swift manifests itself at a séance in modern Dublin, the eighteenth century is represented as the period when the human intellect reached its greatest heights. In many poems of his later years Yeats celebrates Swift, Berkeley, Goldsmith, and Burke as types of the great Protestant Irish tradition of which he himself was the last representative.

The Aesthetic philosophy which had taken the place of morals in art, Yeats began to apply to life. He became increasingly conscious of the sheer beauty of the life of the individual, untrammelled by social or ethical considerations. Men reached their highest stature in moments of proud defiance:

> A great man in his pride,
> Confronting murderous men.

Hence he found it necessary, in contradiction to Christian values, to exalt Pride above all other moral qualities, and in his latest poems—beginning with the "Crazy Jane" sequence—he exalted Lust in like manner. This was the logical conclusion of the neo-paganism which had entered English poetry with Keats and Landor, but it must necessarily be shocking not only for Christians—but still more for those to whom it has never occurred to dispute the liberal humanitarian code (the legitimate child of Puritanism) of the nineteenth century.

Yeats confused aesthetics with morals, and magic with religion. The Symbolists had laid stress upon the incantatory power of words. The poem became a "charm," in the magical sense, and the poet a magician. The earlier Romantics had tended to see him as a prophet. Victor Hugo, whom Yeats admired, and who also dabbled, in his later years, in occult philosophy, is a prime example of this. Among the successors of the Symbolists the tendency was for the poet to become a mystagogue, the priest of a private religion. This role Yeats in Ireland, and, far more consistently and seriously, Stefan George in Germany, both adopted. Poetry became for them a means of self-exaltation, a method of obtaining spiritual power over others.

At the back of Yeats's poetry lies a philosophy of Power, not unakin to that of Nietzsche, who was also primarily an aesthetic thinker, and whom Yeats came greatly to admire. Such ideas were widespread in European culture at the time, and their connection with the genesis of Fascism—on however much of a lower level that political movement actually took shape—must not be glossed over.

That element is in Yeats's poetry, and it is more than skin deep. He had a romantic belief in aristocracy, and a contempt for "the butcher, the baker, the candlestick-maker"; he was embittered by his experience of the Irish revolution and its sequel. But, besides this, in his quest for an aesthetic synthesis, he came to exalt violence, and even cruelty, the instinctive and animal, over the human. When he envisaged the ideal state of the future he frankly enumerated the phenomenon of "great wealth in the hands of a few men" as among its characteristics. His poem "The Second Coming" has been interpreted as a prophecy of the advent of Fascism; but it is not clear that in this wonderful poem the "rough beast" which "slouches towards Bethlehem to be born" is regarded as an enemy—rather it is looked upon as a new Redeemer who comes to inaugurate an era of violence and inhumanity, which the poet himself accepts and even welcomes.

Left wing or Liberal critics have either shut their eyes to this element in Yeats's poetry, or have been rendered very uneasy by it. They would like to deny to Yeats, as a "reactionary," his just place as the greatest of modern poets in the English language. But this is impossible; no honest critic of any sensibility can fail to mark his superiority, not only in his own generation, but over any poet who has so far succeeded him.

In the two poems, "Byzantium" and "Sailing to Byzantium," that imperial city becomes the symbol of Yeats's other world of aesthetic experience, to which, after death, his soul is to go, taking the form of a gold mechanical singing bird in the Emperor's garden—"a work of art producing works of art," as has been well remarked. The sensuous island paradise, derived from Celtic legend, which appears in the early poems—such as "The Happy Townland"—has given place to this great image. Everything in Byzantium suggests hardness or violence. The sages standing in the fire, in the gold mosaic of a wall, the blood-begotten spirits, the Emperor's drunken soldiery,

That dolphin-torn, that gong-tormented sea

—all these, at the same time as they evoke the static beauty of a world of perfected art. This is the ideal existence to which Yeats is so strongly drawn, and in terms of life it implies a deliberate and heartless regime of oppression in the cause of beauty.

It is difficult for those who have inherited no tradition but that of nineteenth-century bourgeois Liberalism to understand the strength of the temptation which the vision of Byzantium represents. They cannot realize how often democratic ideals have blurred the vision of beauty which the artist apprehends, or sacrificed it to inadequate moral considerations. They do not understand how much beauty there is, even in human violence and cruelty.

Instead of treating Yeats's poetry with reserve or hostility, these critics should submit themselves in spirit to his vision. They should be grateful to the poet who can show them the terrible image of Byzantium, and the power of its attraction. It was because the intellectual and emotional scope of their own philosophy was not wide enough, that so many were unexpectedly stampeded into the unreasoning reaction of Fascism. The progressive must realize the power and extent of pure aesthetic hunger in the soul of man. Unless, in the world they are striving for, that hunger can also have satisfaction, Byzantium will persist as a potential enemy of the Just City.

The Text, the Poem, and the Problem of Historical Method

JEROME J. McGANN

According to McGann, the historical critical act, "occurring in a self-conscious present," looks at a poem and its texts "not as fixed objects but as the locus of certain past human experiences." He claims that seeing the work this way emphasizes what is most particular and distinctive about it. This selection follows McGann's introductory remarks, which raise the problem of the historical method or what he also calls "the scandal of referentiality." That is, should we continue to approach a poem intrinsically, as a self-subsistent verbal system or text—the approach that has been the most influential literary criticism over the past fifty years—or can we also benefit from approaching a poem extrinsically as a historical object?

In his essay, McGann suggests that the problem of the historical method can best be approached by making more careful distinctions between such terms as "poem," "text," and "poetical work." By clarifying the distinction between a poem and its various texts, McGann's example from Byron's *Don Juan*, which discusses how various modes of publication produce different poems, reveals the value of a systematic theory of historical criticism. In addition, at the level of practical criticism, McGann's example from Dickinson demonstrates how intrinsic assumptions about a poem's universality blind critics both to the poem's and their own ideological presuppositions.

THIS IDEA OF THE POEM as verbal object is so commonplace in modern criticism that we may seem perverse to question it. Still we must do

From "The Text, the Poem, and the Problem of Historical Method" in *New Literary History* 12 (1981): 274–76; 277–85. Copyright © 1981 by *New Literary History*, The University of Virginia. Reprinted by permission of the Johns Hopkins University Press.

so, for the "problem of historical method"—whether we approach it from an "intrinsic" or an "extrinsic" point of view—will never be opened to solutions until we see one of the signal failures of modern criticism: its inability to distinguish clearly between a concept of the *poem* and a concept of the *text*. Indeed, when we recover this essential analytic distinction, we will begin to reacquire some other, equally crucial distinctions which have fallen into disuse: for example, the distinction between concepts of *poem* and of *poetical work*. For the present I will concentrate on the first of these distinctions, and my analysis will proceed through a series of illustrative examples.[1]

WHEN BYRON SENT THE MANUSCRIPT of *Don Juan* cantos 1 and 2 to his publisher John Murray late in 1818, the poet was not only, with Goethe, the most famous writer in the Western world, his works were the most salable products on the English literary market. He was not an author Murray wanted to lose. But this new work set Murray back on his heels. He was filled with wonder at its genius and with loathing at its immorality—at its obscenity, its blasphemy, its libelous attacks upon the poet laureate, and its seditious attitude toward the English government's policies at home and abroad.[2]

In the struggle that ensued, Murray and his London circle (which included some of Byron's best and oldest friends) pressed the poet either to withdraw the poem altogether or to revise it drastically and remove its objectionable parts. Byron agreed to some revisions, but his final line of retreat still seemed a fearful one to his publisher. When Byron threatened to take his poem elsewhere, Murray agreed to publish; he did not, however, tell his celebrated author precisely *how* he would publish.

For Murray, the problem was how to issue this inflammatory work without provoking a legal action against himself either by the government directly or by the notorious Society for the Suppression of Vice. His plan of action was ingenious but, in the end, self-defeating. Murray decided to issue a short run (1,500 copies) of the poem in a sumptuous quarto edition and to print it without either Byron's name as author or even his own as publisher. The price—£1 11s. 6d.—was set high in order to ensure a circulation limited alike in numbers and in social class.

The immediate effect of this maneuver was successful, for *Don Juan* stole into the world without provoking any moral outcry. The earliest reviewers were generally quite favorable, even from entrenched conservative quarters like *The Literary Gazette*.

But Murray's plan for avoiding the censors failed, in the end, because it was, in the words of Hugh J. Luke, Jr., "a contradictory one."[3] Murray avoided prosecution for issuing *Don Juan*, but his method of publication ensured a widespread piratical printing of the poem in the radical press. Thousands of copies of *Don Juan* were issued in cheap pirated editions, and as the work received wider celebrity and distribution, so the moral outcry against it was raised, and spread.

The significance which this story holds for my present purposes—i.e., for my aim to elucidate the problematics of the "text"—is neatly explained by an anonymous article (possibly by Southey) printed in the conservative *Quarterly Review* in April 1822. In its quarto form, the reviewer notes, *Don Juan* "would have been confined by its price to a class of readers with whom its faults might have been somewhat compensated by its merits; with whom the ridicule, which it endeavours to throw upon virtue, might have been partially balanced by that with which it covers vice, particularly the vice to which the class of readers to whom we are alluding are most subject—that which pleads romantic sensibility, or ungovernable passion; to readers, in short, who would have turned with disgust from its indecencies, and remembered only its poetry and its wit."[4] But the poem was issued in numerous cheap piracies and therein lay the mischief, "some publishing it with obscene engravings, others in weekly numbers, and all in a shape that brought it within the reach of purchasers on whom its poison would operate without mitigation—who would search its pages for images to pamper a depraved imagination, and for a sanction for the insensibility to the sufferings of others, which is often one of the most unhappy results of their own." In short, as the reviewer says so well: "'Don Juan' in quarto and on hot-pressed paper would have been almost innocent—in a whity-brown duodecimo it was one of the worst of the mischievous publications that have made the press a snare."

Several important conclusions follow from this eventful narrative. In the first place, the example illustrates how different texts, in the bibliographical sense, embody different poems (in the aesthetic sense) despite the fact that both are linguistically identical. In the second place, the example also suggests that the method of printing or publishing a literary work carries with it enormous cultural and aesthetic significance for the work itself. Finally, we can begin to see, through this example, that the essential character of a work of art is not determined *sui generis* but is, rather, the result of a process involving the actions and interactions of a specific and socially integrated group of people.[5]

The contemporary fashion of calling literary works "texts" carries at least one unhappy critical result: it suggests that poems and works of fiction possess their integrity *as poems and works of fiction* totally aside from the events and materials describable in their bibliographies. In this usage we are dealing with "texts" which transcend their concrete and actual textualities. This usage of the word *text* does not at all mean anything written or printed in an actual physical state; rather, it means the opposite: it points to an Ur-poem or meta-work whose existence is the Idea that can be abstracted out of all concrete and written texts which have ever existed or which ever will exist.[6] All these different texts are what can be called—Ideally—"The Text."

This Ideal Text is the object of almost all the critical scrutiny produced in the New Critical and post–New Critical traditions, whether formal, stylistic, or structural.[7] To arrive at such a Text, however, the critic normally obligates himself to make certain that his physical text is "correct," which is to say that it corresponds, linguistically, to the author's final intentions about what editors call his work's substantive and accidental features. By meeting this obligation the critic pays his dues to the philological traditions of the last three hundred years. At the same time, the critic places himself in a position from which he can treat the literary work as if it were a timeless object, unconnected with history. The Text is viewed *sub specie aeternitatis,* and modern criticism approaches it much as the precritical scholar of Sacred Scripture approached the Word of God.

But in fact not even a linguistic uniformity sanctioned by philology can deliver over to us a final, definitive Text which will be the timeless object of critical interpretation and analysis. The example from Byron suggests this, clearly, but that case is merely paradigmatic. No literary work is definable purely in linguistic terms, and the illustration from Byron could easily be replaced by examples from any writer one might choose. . . .

The illustration from Byron is especially illuminating because it brings to our attention another crucial productive figure (anterior to the audience of consumers) who participates in the artistic process initiated by the artist: I mean, of course, the reviewer (or critic), who is the final mediating force between author and audience. It is the function of the (contemporary) reviewer and (subsequent) critic to make explicit the lines of interpretation which exist *in potentia* in their respective audiences. Critics and reviewers—to adapt a phrase from Shelley—imagine what students and audiences already know about the works they are to read.

AT THIS POINT, IN THE ANALYSIS, though we have, I believe, established the generic functional usefulness of preserving distinctions among texts, poems, and poetical works, the specific value of such distinctions for literary criticism is still unclear. Are these the sort of distinctions which, in the end, make no difference?

In the example which follows I mean to illustrate two related points: first (on the negative side), that the failure to maintain these distinctions creates a procedural error which necessarily threatens any subsequent practical criticism with disaster; and second (on the positive side), that the pursuit and elucidation of such distinctions sharply increases our understanding of poetry and poems in both the theoretical and the practical spheres. This second aspect of the demonstration will return us to the "problem of historical method" which was raised at the outset. By framing these historically self-conscious demonstrations along the traditional "intrinsic" lines of formal and thematic analysis, I propose to show: (1) that poems are, by the nature of the case (or, as Kant might say, "transcendentally"), time- and place-specific; (2) that historical analysis is, therefore, a necessary and essential function of any advanced practical criticism.

The case I propose to consider is Allen Tate's famous interpretation of Emily Dickinson's poem "Because I could not Stop for Death."[8] His discussion raises, once again, the whole range of unresolved problems which lie in wait for any critical method which cannot make serious distinctions between texts and poems.

Tate begins by quoting the poem in full and declaring it to be "one of the greatest in the English language" and "one of the perfect poems in English." His argument for these judgments rests upon T. S. Eliot's famous discussion of the "dissociation of sensibility." Dickinson's poem is "perfect" because it displays a perfect "fusion of sensibility and thought": "The framework of the poem is, in fact, the two abstractions, mortality and eternity, which are made to associate in equality with the images; she sees the ideas, and thinks the perceptions. She did, of course, nothing of the sort; but we must use the logical distinctions, even to the extent of paradox, if we are to form any notion of this rare quality of mind" (p. 161). Tate argues for this general position by instancing what he sees as the poem's precision and tight structure of rhythm, image, and theme. The poem has nothing to excess; it is marked throughout by "a restraint that keeps the poet from carrying" her dramatic images too far. As for the poem's ideas, they are something altogether different from "the feeble poetry of moral ideals that flourished in New England in the eighties":

> The terror of death is objectified through this figure of the genteel driver, who is made ironically to serve the end of Immortality. This is the heart of the poem: she has presented a typical Christian theme in its final irresolution, without making any final statements about it. There is no solution to the problem; there can be only a presentation of it in the full context of intellect and feeling. A construction of the human will, elaborated with all the abstracting powers of the mind, is put to the concrete test of experience: the idea of immortality is confronted with the fact of physical disintegration. We are not told what to think; we are told to look at the situation. (p. 161)

In evaluating this criticism we begin with the text quoted by Tate. When he calls the poem "The Chariot," as he does at the beginning of his discussion, he tells us what his text shows: Tate is reading the work printed in 1890 by Todd and Higginson. But of course, "The Chariot" is not what Dickinson wrote, at any time; rather, it is a text which her first editors produced when they carefully worked over the (untitled) text written by the author. Among other, less significant changes, an entire stanza was removed (the fourth) and several lines underwent major alterations.[9] Since Tate's argument for the greatness of the poem depends heavily upon his view of its linguistic perfection, we are faced with a rather awkward situation. Under the circumstances, one would not find it very difficult to embarrass Tate's reading by subjecting it to an ironical inquisition on the subject of textual criticism.

Of course, Tate had no access to the text Dickinson actually wrote. Nevertheless, his critical judgment ought to have been warned that textual problems existed since he did have available to him another—and, as it happens, more accurate—text of Dickinson's work. This text appeared in Martha Dickinson Bianchi's 1924 edition of *The Complete Poems*, and it is the one cited by Yvor Winters in the critique of Tate's essay first published by Winters in *Maule's Curse*.[10] But Tate's critical method could not prepare him to deal with problems in textual criticism. Indeed, he could not even *see* such problems, much less analyze their critical relevance. In this case, the impoverished historical sense of his general critical method appears as an inability to make critical judgments about poetic texts, to make distinctions between poems and their texts, and to relate those judgments and distinctions to the final business of literary criticism.

We have no call, nor any desire, to ridicule Tate's essay on this matter. Nevertheless, the issue must be faced squarely, for the problems raised by Tate's lack of textual scrupulousness appear at other points, and in other forms, in his discussion, and his example typifies the sort of problems that remain widespread in Western modes of formal, stylistic, structural, and poststructural procedures. We may observe the congruence of his critical practice—the symmetry between his disinterest in textual matters and his general interpretive approach—by examining his remarks on the poem's thematic concerns. We shall notice two matters here: first, a tendency to overread the poem at the linguistic level; and second, a reluctance to take seriously, or even notice, either the fact or the importance of the poem's ideological attitudes. In each case we are dealing with something fundamental to Tate's literary criticism and to twentieth-century interpretive approaches generally: their attempt to lift the poem out of its original historical context and to erase the distance between that original context and the immediate context of the critical act.

In this next phase of my analysis, then, I am proposing to extend the discussion from its specific interest in "the problem of the text" to the more general issue which that problem localizes. Critics who do not or cannot distinguish between the different concrete texts which a poem assumes in its historical passage are equally disinclined to study the aesthetic significance of a poem's topical dimensions, or its didactic, ethical, or ideological materials. Poems that have no textual histories have, at the thematic level, only those meanings and references which "transcend" the particulars of time and place. The poetry of poems, in this view, is a function not of specific ideology or topical matters but of "universal" themes and references—and the *most* universal of these universals are a poem's formal, stylistic, or structural excellences. The ultimate consequence of such approaches is that the present critic loses altogether his awareness that his own criticism is historically limited and time-bound in very specific ways. Losing a critical sense of the past, the interpreter necessarily loses his ability to see his own work in a critical light.

Let me return to Tate's analysis and the Dickinson poem, however, where we can study these problems as they emerge in concrete forms. When Tate says, for example, that the poem presents "the idea of immortality . . . confronted with the fact of physical disintegration," we observe a critical move characteristic of twentieth-century criticism: that is, the habit of dealing with poetry's substantive concerns at the most abstract and generalized thematic levels. I will have more to say about this sort of critical abstraction in a moment. For now we want most to query Tate's interpretation of the thematic aspects of the Dickinson poem. When he argues, for example, that the poem does not treat "moral ideas," and that its takes a noncommittal ("unresolved") stance toward a serious intellectual problem, we are surely justified in demurring. The civil kindliness of Death is of course ironically presented, but the irony operates at the expense of those who—foolishly, the poem implies— regard Death as a fearful thing and who give all their attention to their mortal affairs ("My labor, and my leisure too") either because of their fear or as a consequence of it. Like the poem's speaker before Death "stopped" for her, the readers of the poem are assumed to be fearful of Death and too busy with the affairs of their lives to "stop" for him.[11] The poem does indeed have "a moral," and it appears in an unmistakable form in the final stanza:

> Since then—'tis Centuries—and yet
> Feels shorter than the Day
> I first surmised the Horses Heads
> Were toward Eternity—

"We are not told what to think" by the poem, Tate asserts, but his position is only technically correct. Of course the poems does not *tell* us what to think, but its message about the benevolence of Death is plain enough. This message, however, like the poem which carries it, is no simple-minded pronouncement; the message is rich and affecting because it is delivered in human rather than abstract space. Dickinson's poem locates a set of relationships in which Dickinson, her fictive speaker, and her invited readers engage with each other in various emotional and intellectual ways.[12] The focus of these engagements is the poem's commonplace Christian theme: that people who are too busily involved with their worldly affairs give little serious thought to Death and the Afterlife. Criticizing such thoughtlessness, the poem encourages its readers to ponder Death and the Afterlife in a positive way. Its procedure for doing so involves the assumption of another thematic commonplace—that people fear to think about Death—and then undermining its force by a play of wit.

The wit appears most plainly in the rhetorical structure of the poem, which pretends to be spoken by a person already dead. Like some Christian Blessed Damozel from New England, Dickinson's speaker addresses this world from the other side, as it were, and lets us know that Death leads us not to oblivion but to "Eternity" and "Immortality." [13] But the wit goes deeper, for Dickinson does not present her fiction as anything *but* fiction. The playfulness of the poem—which is especially evident in the final stanza, whose quiet good humor has been remarked upon frequently—is the work's most persuasive argument that Death can be contemplated not merely without fear but—more positively—with feelings of civilized affectionateness. The kindliness and civility of the carriage driver are qualities we recognize in the *voice* of the poem's speaker and in the *wit* of its maker.

When we speak of the poem's wit, however, we should not lose ourselves in a hypnotic fascination with its verbal reality alone. The wit is at least as much a function of Dickinson's perspicuous observations of, and comments upon, social reality as it is of her facility with language. We may see this more clearly if we recall the standard critical idea that the figure of Death in this poem is—in the words of a recent critic—a "gentlemanly suitor." [14] Tate seems to have initiated this reading when he spoke of the driver as "a gentleman taking a lady out for a drive," and when he proceeded to notice the "erotic motive" associated with "this figure of the genteel driver." His commentary shows an acute awareness of one of the poem's subtlest and least explicit aspects, but it also displays a failure to see a more obvious but no less important fact about the driver.

This man is not a suitor but an undertaker, as we see quite clearly in the penultimate line's reference to "Horses Heads." [15] This small matter of fact has considerable importance for anyone wishing to develop an accurate critical account of the poem. It forces us to see, for example, that the journey being presented is not some unspecified drive in the country, but a funeral ride which is located quite specifically in relation to Emily Dickinson and her Amherst world. The hearse in the poem is on its way out Pleasant Street, past Emily Dickinson's house, to the cemetery located at the northern edge of the town just beyond the Dickinson homestead. [16] Of course, these details are not verbalized into the Dickinson poem as explicit description. They are only present implicitly, as an originally evoked context which we—at our historical remove—can (and must) reconstitute if we wish to focus and explain the special emotional character of the work.

Consider once again, for example, the undertaker who appears in the poem. The behavior of this man—his correctness, his rather stiff but kindly formality, his manner of driving the carriage—defines a character-type well known in nineteenth-century culture, and a favorite one with contemporary caricaturists.[17] Behind the civility and kindly formal behavior of Emily Dickinson's undertaker lies a tradition which saw in this man a figure of grotesque obsequiousness, as we know from Mark Twain's memorable scene in *Huckleberry Finn*. Indeed, I do not see how one could fully appreciate the finesse of what Tate calls the "erotic motive" without also seeing just how the poem plays with it, and how Dickinson's poetic style both *re*presents and quietly modifies the contemporary stereotype of this important social functionary so well known to the inhabitants of towns like Amherst. The poem's general ideology, as a work of Christian consolation, would be merely religious claptrap without these "poetic"[18] elements; and such elements can only escape the critical method which does not seek to grasp the poem at a level more comprehensive than a merely linguistic one.

The power of the poem, then, rests in its ability to show us not merely the thoughts and feelings of Dickinson and her fictive speaker, but the attitudes of her implied readers as well. For all her notorious privacy, Emily Dickinson is, like every poet, a creator of those structures of social energy which we call poems. "Because I could not Stop for Death" locates not merely an expressive lyrical act, but a significant relationship between the poet and her readers which we, as still later readers, are meant to recognize, enter into, and (finally) extend. Our sympathy with the poem may not be the same as that felt by a Christian reader, whether contemporary with the poem or not; nevertheless, it is *continuous* with the sympathy of such readers (who are consciously and explicitly assumed by the poem) because it takes those readers as seriously as it takes Emily Dickinson and her fictive speaker. Indeed, it must do this, for all are part of the poem in question. Later readers may not share the ideologies of the people represented by this poem, but they cannot read it without recognizing and respecting those ideologies—without, in fact, perpetuating them in a critical human memory whose sympathetic powers are drawn from a historical consciousness.

Having discussed the "ideological set" of this poem—its poetically rendered "message"—let us return to Allen Tate's essay, where an absence of ideological commitments is imputed to Dickinson's work. We return to ask why Tate should insist upon "misreading" the poem as he has done.

The reason emerges when we ponder carefully Tate's use of T. S. Eliot. Tate's interpretation shows that he shares Eliot's ideas about how moral concepts should appear in verse (not "didactically" but dramatically); that he prizes Eliot's views on Metaphysical verse and its excellences; and that he is anxious to deliver his praise of Dickinson's poem in critical terms that will draw her into the company of those poets who illustrate Eliot's standards. In short, Tate reads Emily Dickinson in the same spirit that Eliot read Donne and the Metaphysicals. *Why* Tate, and Eliot before him, should have taken such a position toward the moral aspects of poetry—and especially of Christian poetry in its various forms—is beyond the scope of this analysis, though scholars recognize that the answer lies in the historical factors which generated modernism and its various ideologies.[19]

I have not dwelt upon Tate's discussion in order to debunk it, but rather in order to show how consonant his interpretation of the Emily Dickinson poem is with his ignorance of its textual problems. Tate's eye is no more focused upon Dickinson's poem than it is on the 1890 text of "The Chariot." Rather, Tate has "taken 'The Chariot' for his text," as we might say of one who delivers a sermon or a moral lesson. "The Chariot" is the occasion for his ideological polemic on behalf of certain aesthetic criteria.

One important lesson to be drawn from this investigation of Tate's essay is that literary criticism—and even the analysis of poems—is not fundamentally a study of verbal structure per se. The very existence of Tate's influential and justly admired essay demonstrates that fact. Literary criticism must study poetic texts—the "verbal structures" of poems—but the analysis of these verbal structures does not comprehend a poetic analysis. This paradox of critical method emerges forcibly in Tate's essay, which dramatizes, in its very limitations, the distinction between text and poem—a distinction, indeed, which Tate's analysis is incapable of making. Yet the distinction must be made—and textual criticism, in the traditional sense, must be revived among literary critics—if our received works of literature are to regain their full human resources—that is to say, if the entire history of poetry and all the potential of specific poems are to be made known and available to each new generation. Poetry and poems are, in this sense, trans-historical, but they acquire this perpetuity by virtue of the particular historical adventures which their texts undergo from their first appearance before their author's eyes through all their subsequent constitutions.

The textual histories of poems, in other words, are paradigm instances of the historically specific character of all poetry. By clarifying the distinction between a poem and its various texts, the examples from Byron and Blake illustrate the need for a systematic theory and method of historical criticism. On the other hand, the example from Dickinson argues, at the level of practical criticism, the specific critical powers inherent in a historical method. These powers appear as a special capacity for elucidating, in a systematic way, whatever in a poem is most concrete, local and particular to it. Criticism cannot analyze poems, or reveal their special characteristics and values, if it abstracts away from their so-called accidental features. Attending merely to the formal or linguistic phenomena of poems constitutes an initial and massive act of abstraction from what are some of the most crucial particulars of all poems.

Facing the poem and its texts, then, historical criticism tries to define what is most peculiar and distinctive in specific poetical works. Moreover, in specifying these unique features and sets of relationships, it transcends the concept of the-poem-as-verbal-object to reveal the poem as a special sort of communication event. This new understanding of poems takes place precisely because the critical act, occurring in a self-conscious present, can turn to look upon poems created in the past not as fixed objects but as the locus of certain past human experiences. Some of these are dramatized *in* the poems, while others are preserved *through* the poetical works, which embody various human experiences *with* the poems, beginning with the author's own experiences. In this way does a historical criticism define poetry not as a formal structure or immediate event but as a continuing human process. That *act* of definition is the fundamental *fact* of literary criticism.

The new fact about *historical* criticism, however, is that it systematically opposes its own reification. Being first of all an *act* of definition rather than a *set* of definitions, historical criticism calls attention to the time-specific and heuristic character of its abstractions. Like the poetry it studies, criticism is always tendentious because it always seeks to define and preserve human values. One of the special values of historical criticism, to my view at any rate, lies in its eagerness to specify and examine its polemical positions. This self-critical aspect of a historical approach seems to be a direct function of its basic method, for in attempting to specify historical distinctions, we set a gulf between our past and our present. It is this gulf which enables us to judge and criticize the past, but it is equally this gulf which enables the past—so rich in its achievements—to judge and criticize us. Thus in our differences do we learn about, and create, a community.

NOTES

1. Literary criticism in general would benefit if certain clear distinctions were preserved when using words (and concepts) like *text, poem,* and *poetical work.* In the present essay, the word *text* is used as a purely bibliographical concept which means to deal with the material of poetry in a purely physical or impersonal frame of reference. The term deliberately abstracts away the critic's or the reader's immediate (social) point of view. Poetry is a social phenomenon, but the concept of *text* withholds from consideration all matters that relate to the involvement of reader or audience in the reproduction of the work. It does so, of course, for analytic purposes, and *only provisionally.* I propose that we use the term *text* when we deal with poems as they are part of a productive (or reproductive) process, but when we are withholding from consideration all matters that

relate to the process of consumption. *Poem,* on the other hand, is the term I will use to refer to the work as it is the locus of a specific process of production (or reproduction) and consumption. *Poetical work* is my term for the global history of some particular work's process of production/reproduction and consumption. I use the term *poetry* to refer generically to imaginative literary works without respect to any specific social or historical factors. The terms *text* and *Ideal Text* also appear in this essay, and these refer to various (nonhistorical and nonsociological) twentieth-century critical concepts.

I hope it is clear that these distinctions mean to counter the semiological approach to the concepts of *text* and *textuality.* A paradigm example of the latter approach will be found in Roland Barthes's famous essay "From Work to Text," reprinted in *Textual Strategies,* edited with an introduction by Josué V. Harari (Ithaca, N.Y., 1979), 73–81.

2. See *Don Juan: A Variorum Edition,* ed. T. G. Steffan and W. W. Pratt (Austin, Tex., 1957), 1:11–32, and 4:293–308.

3. "The Publishing of *Don Juan,*" *PMLA* 80 (June 1965):200.

4. Quotations from the *Quarterly Review* appear in "The Publishing of *Don Juan,*" ibid., 202.

5. Cf. Levin Schüking, *The Sociology of Literary Taste* (London, 1966).

6. Poststructural critiques of their own (formalist) tradition have been widespread during the past ten years and have contributed to the breakup of the academic consensus which developed between 1935 and 1965. See John Fekete, *The Critical Twilight* (London, 1978). The attacks upon the New Criticism have tended to accuse it of an arrogant and technocratic empiricism, with its insistence upon taking the poem as *sui generis.* These attacks—see Richard Palmer, *Hermeneutics* (Evanston, 1969), for example—charge the New Criticism with a crude theory of the poem as "object" or "thing." This sort of attack is deeply misguided and misses entirely the fundamental Idealism of both the New Criticism in particular and its larger Formalist context in general. A revisionist commentator like Gerald Graff has been able to see the mistake in such critiques and to suggest what is in fact the case: that New Criticism and its bourgeois inheritors (including many of its recent antagonists) are part of a single tradition (*Literature Against Itself* [Chicago, 1979], chap. 5). As Graff notes, New Criticism was marked throughout by contradictions along an Ideal/Empirical fault line; nor could it have been otherwise with a fundamentally Idealist theory which was seeking to establish its authority in a scientific, rational, and technological world. Graff's views have been anticipated by a number of trenchant critiques put out from relatively orthodox Marxist writers: see, e.g., Robert Weimann, "Past Significance and Present Meaning in Literary History," in *New Directions in Literary History,* ed. Ralph Cohen (Baltimore, 1974), esp. 43–50.

7. That an Ideal Text is the object of contemporary "textual" interpreters is patent; see also Tony Bennett, *Formalism and Marxism* (London, 1979), 70–71. And see nn. 1 and 6 above, where I argue that the case is little different for critics in earlier twentieth-century formalist traditions.

8. This is poem no. 712 in *The Poems of Emily Dickinson,* ed. Thomas H. Johnson (Cambridge, Mass., 1955), 2:546–47. For Tate's discussion, see his "New England Culture and Emily Dickinson," in *The Recognition of Emily Dickinson,* ed. C. E. Blake and C. F. Wells (Ann Arbor, 1968), 153–67, esp. 160–62, from which the quotations below are taken.

9. See *Poems by Emily Dickinson,* ed. Mabel Loomis Todd and Thomas W. Higginson (Boston, 1890). Also see Johnson's edition, where the textual issues are succinctly presented.

10. Winters's essay is reprinted in *The Recognition of Emily Dickinson;* see esp. 192–93.

11. This motif is an ancient one in the tradition of Christian art and poetry. For its biblical sources see Matt. 24:43 and 1 Thess. 5:2–4. An excellent contemporary example is to be found in Alan Dugan's "Tribute to Kafka for Someone Taken."

12. See V. N. Volosinov, "Discourse in Life and Discourse in Art," in *Freudianism: A Marxist Critique,* trans. I. R. Titunik (New York, 1976), where Volosinov distinguishes among the author, the reader, and the figure he calls "the hero" or the "third participant."

13. In adopting this rhetorical model, Dickinson was following a literary practice that had grown extremely popular in the nineteenth century. See Ann Douglas, "Heaven Our Home: Consolation Literature in the Northern United States 1830–1880," in *Death in America,* ed. Daniel Stannard (Philadelphia, 1974); see esp. 58–59, 61–62. But the procedure is deeply traditional; see also Rosemary Woolf, *English Religious Lyric in the Middle Ages* (Oxford, 1963), chap. 9 passim.

14. Robert Weisbuch, *Emily Dickinson's Poetry* (Chicago, 1972), 114.

15. That is to say, a suitor's carriage would have had only one horse.

16. The hearse's journey to the Amherst cemetery—one of the new, so-called rural cemeteries—must have been appallingly familiar to Emily Dickinson. The mortality rate in Amherst was high, and Emily Dickinson's room overlooked the cemetery route. See Millicent Todd Bingham, *Emily Dickinson's Home* (New York, 1955), the map facing p. 62 and pp. 179–80; also Jay Leyda, *The Years and Hours of Emily Dickinson* (New Haven, 1960), 2:2–3. Emily Dickinson's bedroom was the best vantage in the house for observing the stately procession of the funeral hearse as it moved out Pleasant Street to the cemetery. The special location of the Dickinson house meant that the funeral hearse would always pass by, no matter where the deceased person had lived in town. One should also note that the poem's references to the "School" and the "Fields of Gazing Grain" are precise. In point of fact, "Because I could not Stop for Death" narrates the imagined (not imaginary) journey of the hearse from somewhere in the central part of Amherst out along Pleasant Street, past the schoolhouse on the left, and out to the beginning of the "Fields of Gazing Grain," at which point the undertaker would have turned to the right and driven past more fields to the gravesite. For a general discussion of the rural cemetery see Neil Harris, "The Cemetery Beautiful," in *Passing: The Vision of Death in America,* ed. Charles O. Jackson (Westport, 1977), 103–11.

17. See Alfred Scott Warthen, "The Period of Caricature" and "The Modern Dance of Death," in *The Physician of the Dance of Death* (New York, 1934). Twain was fond of presenting the undertaker from a comic point of view. See *Huckleberry Finn,* chap. 27, and his essay "The Undertaker's Chat."

18. What makes them "poetic" is their ability to dramatize the relationships which exist between specific social realities and a complex set of related—and often antagonistic—ideological attitudes and formations.

19. See Richard Ohmann, "Studying Literature at the End of Ideology," in

The Politics of Literature, ed. Louis Kampf and Paul Lauter (New York, 1973), esp. 134–59; Renato Poggioli, *The Theory of the Avante-Garde,* trans. Gerald Fitzgerald (New York, 1971); and see nn. 1 and 6 above.

Theatre for Pleasure or Theatre for Instruction

BERTOLT BRECHT

Marxist playwright Bertolt Brecht was more interested in the pragmatic than in the theoretical aspects of literary discourse. He wanted to create revolutionary art and wrote "epic dramas" of the type he here defends. However, his ideas, such as the need to alienate (distance) spectators in order to reveal certain ideological assumptions, were widely influential in literary circles. "When something seems 'the most obvious thing in the world'" Brecht commented on ideology, "it means that any attempt to understand the world has been given up." Brecht wanted people to understand so they would change their world for the better.

A FEW YEARS BACK, anybody talking about the modern theatre meant the theatre in Moscow, New York and Berlin. He might have thrown in a mention of one of Jouvet's productions in Paris or Cochran's in London, or *The Dybbuk* as given by the Habima (which is to all intents and purposes part of the Russian theatre, since Vakhtangov was its director). But broadly speaking there were only three capitals so far as modern theatre was concerned.

Russian, American and German theatres differed widely from one another, but were alike in being modern, that is to say in introducing technical and artistic innovations. In a sense they even achieved a certain stylistic resemblance, probably because technology is international (not just that part which is directly applied to the stage but also that which influences it, the film for instance), and because large progressive cities in large industrial countries are involved. Among the older capitalist countries it is the Berlin theatre that seemed of late to be in the lead. For a period all that is common to the modern theatre received its strongest and (so far) maturest expressions there.

The Berlin theatre's last phase was the so-called epic theatre, and it showed the modern theatre's trend of development in its purest form.

Whatever was labelled "*Zeitstück*" or "*Piscatorbühne*" or "*Lehrstück*" belongs to the epic theatre.

THE EPIC THEATRE

Many people imagine that the term "epic theatre" is self-contradictory, as the epic and dramatic ways of narrating a story are held, following Aristotle, to be basically distinct. The difference between the two forms was never thought simply to lie in the fact that the one is performed by living beings while the other operates via the written word; epic works such as those of Homer and the medieval singers were at the same time theatrical performances, while dramas like Goethe's *Faust* and Byron's *Manfred* are agreed to have been more effective as books. Thus even by Aristotle's definition the difference between the dramatic and epic forms was attributed to their different methods of construction, whose laws were dealt with by two different branches of aesthetics. The method of construction depended on the different way of presenting the work to the public, sometimes via the stage, sometimes through a book; and independently of that there was the "dramatic element" in epic works and the "epic element" in dramatic. The bourgeois novel in the last century developed much that was "dramatic," by which was meant the strong centralization of the story, a momentum that drew the separate parts into a common relationship. A particular passion of utterance, a certain emphasis, on the clash of forces are hallmarks of the "dramatic." The epic writer Döblin provided an excellent criterion when he said that with an epic work, as opposed to a dramatic, one can as it were take a pair of scissors and cut it into individual pieces, which remain fully capable of life.

This is no place to explain how the opposition of epic and dramatic lost its rigidity after having long been held to be irreconcilable. Let us just point out that the technical advances alone were enough to permit the stage to incorporate an element of narrative in its dramatic productions. The possibility of projections, the greater adaptability of the stage due to mechanization, the film, all completed the theatre's equipment, and did so at a point where the most important transactions between people could no longer be shown simply by personifying the motive forces or subjecting the characters to invisible metaphysical powers.

To make these transactions intelligible the environment in which the people lived had to be brought to bear in a big and "significant" way.

This environment had of course been shown in the existing drama, but only as seen from the central figure's point of view, and not as an independent element. It was defined by the hero's reactions to it. It was seen as a storm can be seen when one sees the ships on a sheet of water unfolding their sails, and the sails filling out. In the epic theatre it was to appear standing on its own.

The stage began to tell a story. The narrator was no longer missing, along with the fourth wall. Not only did the background adopt an attitude to the events on the stage—by big screens recalling other simultaneous events elsewhere, by projecting documents which confirmed or contradicted what the characters said, by concrete and intelligible figures to accompany abstract conversations, by figures and sentences to support mimed transactions whose sense was unclear—but the actors too refrained from going over wholly into their role, remaining detached from the character they were playing and clearly inviting criticism of him.

The spectator was no longer in any way allowed to submit to an experience uncritically (and without practical consequences) by means of simple empathy with the characters in a play. The production took the subject-matter and the incidents shown and put them through a process of alienation: the alienation that is necessary to all understanding. When something seems "the most obvious thing in the world" it means that any attempt to understand the world has been given up.

What is "natural" must have the force of what is startling. This is the only way to expose the laws of cause and effect. People's activity must simultaneously be so and be capable of being different.

It was all a great change.

The dramatic theatre's spectator says: Yes, I have felt like that too— Just like me—It's only natural—It'll never change—The sufferings of this man appall me, because they are inescapable—That's great art; it all seems the most obvious thing in the world—I weep when they weep, I laugh when they laugh.

The epic theatre's spectator says: I'd never have thought it—That's not the way—That's extraordinary, hardly believable—It's got to stop— The sufferings of this man appall me, because they are unnecessary— That's great art: nothing obvious in it—I laugh when they weep, I weep when they laugh.

THE INSTRUCTIVE THEATRE

The stage began to be instructive.

Oil, inflation, war, social struggles, the family, religion, wheat, the meat market, all became subjects for theatrical representation. Choruses enlightened the spectator about facts unknown to him. Films showed a montage of events from all over the world. Projections added statistical material. And as the "background" came to the front of the stage so people's activity was subjected to criticism. Right and wrong courses of action were shown. People were shown who knew what they were doing, and others who did not. The theatre became an affair for philosophers, but only for such philosophers as wished not just to explain the world but also to change it. So we had philosophy, and we had instruction. And where was the amusement in all that? Were they sending us back to school, teaching us to read and write? Were we supposed to pass exams, work for diplomas?

Generally there is felt to be a very sharp distinction between learning and amusing oneself. The first may be useful, but only the second is pleasant. So we have to defend the epic theatre against the suspicion that it is a highly disagreeable, humourless, indeed strenuous affair.

Well: all that can be said is that the contrast between learning and amusing oneself is not laid down by divine rule; it is not one that has always been and must continue to be.

Undoubtedly there is much that is tedious about the kind of learning familiar to us from school, from our professional training, etc. But it must be remembered under what conditions and to what end that takes place.

It is really a commercial transaction. Knowledge is just a commodity. It is acquired in order to be resold. All those who have grown out of going to school have to do their learning virtually in secret, for anyone who admits that he still has something to learn devalues himself as a man whose knowledge is inadequate. Moreover the usefulness of learning is very much limited by factors outside the learner's control. There is unemployment, for instance, against which no knowledge can protect one. There is the division of labour, which makes generalized knowledge unnecessary and impossible. Learning is often among the concerns of those whom no amount of concern will get any forwarder. There is not much knowledge that leads to power, but plenty of knowledge to which only power can lead.

Learning has a very different function for different social strata. There are strata who cannot imagine any improvement in conditions: they find the conditions good enough for them. Whatever happens to oil they will benefit from it. And: they feel the years beginning to tell. There can't be all that many years more. What is the point of learning a lot now? They have said their final word: a grunt. But there are also strata "waiting their turn" who are discontented with conditions, have a vast interest in the practical side of learning, want at all costs to find out where they stand, and know that they are lost without learning; these are the best and keenest learners. Similar differences apply to countries and peoples. Thus the pleasure of learning depends on all sorts of things; but none the less there is such a thing as pleasurable learning, cheerful and militant learning.

If there were not such amusement to be had from learning the theatre's whole structure would unfit it for teaching.

Theatre remains theatre even when it is instructive theatre, and in so far as it is good theatre it will amuse.

THEATRE AND KNOWLEDGE

But what has knowledge got to do with art? We know that knowledge can be amusing, but not everything that is amusing belongs in the theatre.

I have often been told, when pointing out the invaluable services that modern knowledge and science, if properly applied, can perform for art and specially for the theatre, that art and knowledge are two estimable but wholly distinct fields of human activity. This is a fearful truism, of course, and it is as well to agree quickly that, like most truisms, it is perfectly true. Art and science work in quite different ways: agreed. But, bad as it may sound, I have to admit that I cannot get along as an artist without the use of one or two sciences. This may well arouse serious doubts as to my artistic capacities. People are used to seeing poets as unique and slightly unnatural beings who reveal with a truly godlike assurance things that other people can only recognize after much sweat and toil. It is naturally distasteful to have to admit that one does not belong to this select band. All the same, it must be admitted. It must at the same time be made clear that the scientific occupations just confessed to are not pardonable side interests, pursued on days off after a good week's work. We all know how Goethe was interested in natural history, Schiller in history: as a kind of hobby, it is charitable to assume. I have no wish promptly to accuse these two of having needed these sciences for their poetic activity; I am not trying to shelter behind them; but I must say that I do need the sciences. I have to admit, however, that I look askance at all sorts of people who I know do not operate on the level of scientific understanding: that is to say, who sing as the birds sing, or as people imagine the birds to sing. I don't mean by that that I would reject a charming poem about the taste of fried fish or the delights of a boating party just because the writer had not studied gastronomy or navigation. But in my view the great and complicated things that go on in the world cannot be adequately recognized by people who do not use every possible aid to understanding.

Let us suppose that great passions or great events have to be shown which influence the fate of nations. The lust for power is nowadays held to be such a passion. Given that a poet "feels" this lust and wants to have someone strive for power, how is he to show the exceedingly complicated machinery within which the struggle for power nowadays takes place? If his hero is a politician, how do politics work? If he is a business man, how does business work? And yet there are writers who find business and politics nothing like so passionately interesting as the individual's lust for power. How are they to acquire the necessary knowledge? They are scarcely likely to learn enough by going round and keeping their eyes open, though even then it is more than they would get by just rolling their eyes in an exalted frenzy. The foundation of a paper like the *Völkischer Beobachter* or a business like Standard Oil is a pretty complicated affair, and such things cannot be conveyed just like that. One important field for the playwright is psychology. It is taken for granted that a poet, if not an ordinary man, must be able without further instruction to discover the motives that lead a man to commit murder; he must be

able to give a picture of a murderer's mental state "from within himself."
It is taken for granted that one only has to look inside oneself in such a
case; and then there's always one's imagination. . . . There are various
reasons why I can no longer surrender to this agreeable hope of getting
a result quite so simply. I can no longer find in myself all those motives
which the press or scientific reports show to have been observed in
people. Like the average judge when pronouncing sentence, I cannot
without further ado conjure up an adequate picture of a murderer's
mental state. Modern psychology, from psychoanalysis to behaviourism,
acquaints me with facts that lead me to judge the case quite differently,
especially if I bear in mind the findings of sociology and do not overlook
economics and history. You will say: but that's getting complicated. I have
to answer that it *is* complicated. Even if you let yourself be convinced,
and agree with me that a large slice of literature is exceedingly primitive,
you may still ask with profound concern: won't an evening in such a theatre be a most alarming affair? The answer to that is: no.

Whatever knowledge is embodied in a piece of poetic writing has to
be wholly transmuted into poetry. Its utilization fulfils the very pleasure
that the poetic element provokes. If it does not at the same time fulfil
that which is fulfilled by the scientific element, none the less in an age of
great discoveries and inventions one must have a certain inclination to
penetrate deeper into things—a desire to make the world controllable—
if one is to be sure of enjoying its poetry.

Is the Epic Theatre Some Kind of "Moral Institution"?

According to Friedrich Schiller the theatre is supposed to be a moral
institution. In making this demand it hardly occurred to Schiller that by
moralizing from the stage he might drive the audience out of the theatre. Audiences had no objection to moralizing in his day. It was only
later that Friedrich Nietzsche attacked him for blowing a moral trumpet.
To Nietzsche any concern with morality was a depressing affair; to Schiller
it seemed thoroughly enjoyable. He knew of nothing that could give
greater amusement and satisfaction than the propagation of ideas. The
bourgeoisie was setting about forming the ideas of the nation.

Putting one's house in order, patting oneself on the back, submitting
one's account, is something highly agreeable. But describing the collapse
of one's house, having pains in the back, paying one's account, is indeed a
depressing affair, and that was how Friedrich Nietzsche saw things a century later. He was poorly disposed towards morality, and thus towards
the previous Friedrich too.

The epic theatre was likewise often objected to as moralizing too
much. Yet in the epic theatre moral arguments only took second place.
Its aim was less to moralize than to observe. That is to say it observed,
and then the thick end of the wedge followed: the story's moral. Of

course we cannot pretend that we started our observations out of a pure passion for observing and without any more practical motive, only to be completely staggered by their results. Undoubtedly there were some painful discrepancies in our environment, circumstances that were barely tolerable, and this not merely on account of moral considerations. It is not only moral considerations that make hunger, cold and oppression hard to bear. Similarly the object of our inquiries was not just to arouse moral objections to such circumstances (even though they could easily be felt—though not by all the audience alike; such objections were seldom for instance felt by those who profited by the circumstances in question) but to discover means for their elimination. We were not in fact speaking in the name of morality but in that of the victims. These truly are two distinct matters, for the victims are often told that they ought to be contented with their lot, for moral reasons. Moralists of this sort see man as existing for morality, not morality for man. At least it should be possible to gather from the above to what degree and in what sense the epic theatre is a moral institution.

CAN EPIC THEATRE BE PLAYED ANYWHERE?

Stylistically speaking, there is nothing all that new about the epic theatre. Its expository character and its emphasis on virtuosity bring it close to the old Asiatic theatre. Didactic tendencies are to be found in the medieval mystery plays and the classical Spanish theatre, and also in the theatre of the Jesuits.

These theatrical forms corresponded to particular trends of their time, and vanished with them. Similarly the modern epic theatre is linked with certain trends. It cannot by any means be practised universally. Most of the great nations today are not disposed to use the theatre for ventilating their problems. London, Paris, Tokyo and Rome maintain their theatres for quite different purposes. Up to now favourable circumstances for an epic and didactic theatre have only been found in a few places and for a short period of time. In Berlin Fascism put a very definite stop to the development of such a theatre.

It demands not only a certain technological level but a powerful movement in society which is interested to see vital questions freely aired with a view to their solution, and can defend this interest against every contrary trend.

The epic theatre is the broadest and most far-reaching attempt at large-scale modern theatre, and it has all those immense difficulties to overcome that always confront the vital forces in the sphere of politics, philosophy, science and art.

["Vergnügungstheater oder Lehrtheater?" from
Schriften zum Theater, 1957]

Power and Law in Hawthorne's Fictions

ERIC MOTTRAM

Mottram draws on the work of recent Marxist theorists who attempt to combine Marxist theories with a Lacanian version of Freud to answer the question, Why do people desire their own oppression? These critics seek a politico/psychic fusion because the older dialectical theory—that class conflicts generate revolution—does not account for the seeming stability of certain "oppressive" socio-economic systems. The Marxist-Freudian analyses employ, in various ways, psychoanalytic theories relating desire and repression. For example, Gilles Deleuze aligns desire (unconscious human wants) with productive forces. (For Marx, the contradiction between productive forces and the relations of production generates class conflict.) Thus, as consciousness represents the repression of our libidinal desires, so ideology channels the repression of our social relations.

FRANKENSTEIN CREATES A MONSTER and becomes himself monstrous; the two figures are popularly taken as one. Aylmer becomes monstrous by manipulating his wife before the laughing "underworker," the shaggy, smoky and earthy Aminadab. Hawthorne writes guardedly of the possibility that "the Eve of Powers" might be converted to "a monster." Intellectuality and sexuality are shown in dubious relationship as the Aylmer house is turned into a laboratory, as other fictional nineteenth-century houses are turned into asylums or houses of correction or assignation. The wife becomes a patient first, and then a victim murdered for scientific curiosity and erotic self-satisfaction. The repressed returns in the disguise of science, and the professional gets away with it once again: it is the continual theme of Hawthorne's fictions of professionals. Here and in "Rappaccini's Daughter" the Renaissance seventeenth-century scientist returns as the nineteenth-century inventor manipulating energy, human and nonhuman, for and against the social, ambivalently a figure of exploitation and enterprise (the business man is not fully used until Dreiser's Cowperwood). The scientist inventor, supposedly the generative centre of technological progress and trade, is morally negated. The relationships of desire to production, of desire to public and private interests, and therefore to law, are repeatedly proposed in Hawthorne's fictions. But in both "The Birthmark" and "Rappaccini's Daughter" the

From "Power and Law in Hawthorne's Fictions" in *Nathaniel Hawthorne: New Critical Essays*, ed. A. Robert Lee (London: Vision Press Ltd; Totowa, N.J.: Barnes & Noble Books, 1982). Copyright 1982 by Vision Press Ltd. Reprinted by permission.

victim is a woman. Hawthorne's contemporary, Karl Marx, wrote in the 1844 *Economic and Philosophic Manuscripts:*

> The direct, natural and necessary relation of person to person is the relation of man to woman. . . . It therefore reveals the extent to which man's natural behaviour has become human . . . the extent to which man's need has become a human need; the extent to which, therefore, the other person as a person has become for him a need—the extent to which he in his individual existence is at the same time a social being.[1]

Hawthorne repeatedly collapses and reinstates, sometimes in variable forms, male dominance figures parallel to the partial emergence, and sometimes the total suppression, of female figures. Obedience and disobedience between men and women fascinate him; for him, the cannibal and vampire steal energy, take over, expropriate wherever the class structure permits it. But his sense of the inevitable action of predatory will is that it cannot be halted, let alone eradicated, because it is "evil." He asks the crucial questions: What is control, what is counter-control, and who operates their system? What values conflict? What is the nature of alienation and its relations with isolation and community? But he asks them in a particular structure of actual and imagined inheritance, still thinking of the production of relationships as a theological theatre rather than a political factory. "Historical fixatives" control his ethics or "traditional bonds"; he feels bound to confront the American seventeenth-century origins with mid-nineteenth century industrial capitalist democracy in terms of an unchanging, unchangeable manichean battle.[2] Deleuze and Guattari put the force of the secular instances in such fictions in post-Reichian terms:

> The strength of Reich consists in having shown how psychic repression depended on social repression . . . social repression needs psychic repression precisely in order to form docile subjects and ensure the reproduction of the social formation, including its repressive structures . . . civilization must be understood in terms of a social repression inherent in a given form of social production.[3]

Hawthorne comes near to asking his questions of repression within the crucial question—particularly in *The Scarlet Letter* and *The Marble Faun*— how does it come about that we desire our own repression? But his questions are taken up with a constant reminder that Americans are helpless, that Emerson's characteristic dicta of self-reliance are mistaken. Helplessness is a main source for gothic, horror and science fiction systems, the oscillations between voluntary and involuntary behaviours. Seventeenth-century New England society can be used as the instance of a group which knows it is corrupt but knows, too, that, short of prayer, penitence and Jeremiads, it is condemned to the manichean battlefield, the prior inhuman system of God and Devil. Life polarized into punishment and blessing, confession and concealment, marks the presence of the repressed in continuous dialectic with the public surfaces, partly euphoric drive and partly exhausting depression. "Confidence in America" could be the endlessly punning title of the history of New World fictions. Confidence is undermined in Hawthorne's contribution by his fast conviction that the Unpardonable Sin is utterly wrong and inevitable. His work is therefore a criticism of *all* manipulative power between human beings. Since religion and capitalism [imply] manipulation, his work has to be a criticism of the American structure itself (in 1981, we have President Reagan attacking Communists for not believing in an afterlife). So that the inevitability of America as a euphoric prophecy, reaching fulfilment in the mid-nineteenth century, is confronted with the regressiveness of the manichean permanence. Hawthorne moves out from concepts he hardly changes; it is both a strength and an inhibition. His characters are liable to be obliterated by an ideological scheme in which they have to be exemplary. This is his peculiar legalism, his own totalitarian pattern, which, curiously and especially in *The Marble Faun*, needs the Unpardonable Sin just as he defined it in his *American Notebooks*—"want of love and reverence for the Human Soul; in consequence of which the investigator pried into its dark depths, not with a hope or purpose of making it better, but from a cold philosophical curiosity . . . the separation of the intellect from the heart." But what exactly are the risks? The desires of the heart are notoriously as possibly cruel as the desires of intellect may be beneficent. Hawthorne's framework of enquiry initiates but clings to a prohibitive social ethos. The preface to his children's *Wonder-Book* (1851) asks "Is not the human heart deeper than any system of philosophy?" But what does "deeper" [imply] as value? A spatialization of ethical images does not make the differentiations any the more "natural." "System" apparently must be a surface action in its artifice. It is a fatal and mistaken separation, since theory and coherence are as "deep" a need as automatic feeling, and both are equally liable to be programmatic.

But Hawthorne properly resists an over-interiorization of behaviour motivations and sequences. He knows that the so-called individual is, as Marx postulates it, "a social product (as is even the language in which the thinker is active): my *own* existence *is* social activity. . . . The Individual's manifestations of life—even if they may not appear in the direct form of *communal* manifestations of life carried out in association with others—*are* therefore an expression and confirmation of social life."[4] But the effect of using "Puritan seventeenth-century New England" (his own artefact, in fact) as an exemplary field of events, images and explanations through which to compose nineteenth-century fictions is to universalize that field by dehistoricizing it—as if the theocratic state were *the* archetype: just as Freud creates a universal Law of the Father out of parts of an Oedipus story in one ancient Greek writer, refusing to describe "the unconscious" as an historically determined phenomenon, variable in different societies with differing modes of production. Dehistoricization is mystification. Hawthorne resorts to an onward-going explanatory scheme—in effect, an ideology—of good and evil which is a manichean structure beyond dialectical change, a diachrony carried forward in a vocabulary of inheritance and inevitability, partly Christian, partly medieval, and partly heretical. It is hardly surprising that the nineteenth-century and the seventeenth-century intervention into this scheme is the woman who will not submit to male usage, unlike Aylmer's Georgiana and Rappaccini's Beatrice. Psychological analysis is a politics rather than a science. The anxiety over Mesmerism everywhere in Hawthorne has to be poised between fear of hypnotic domination and submission from one man (a singular source of energy control) and a sense that something beneficial might come from it.

Mesmerism is the type of all procedures that control subliminally, whether through religion or education or psychological persuasion within desire and the erotic. Hawthorne is well aware that interference with another self [implies] the presence of the Unpardonable Sin immediately the process becomes sheer usage for production—a perverse desire to move in on someone's life and use it, perhaps to use it up. The popular seventeenth-century context for Ethan Brand is male witchcraft. But Brand himself believes that the Devil can only use "half-way sinners." His full sin is to have sacrificed everything to the claims of "an intellect," "a high state of enthusiasm" (Hawthorne uses the term in the late seventeenth-century and Augustan usage). A girl, Esther (from the same source as Hester), is "made the subject of a psychological experiment" through which she is "wasted, absorbed and perhaps annihilated"—or, as William Burroughs would say, "assimilated." Brand's "powers," his "star-lit eminence" in the intellectual world, are detached from that "moral nature" which is the basis of "brotherhood." But Hawthorne withdraws from the actual processes of experimental control. The fiction remains visual and theoretical, a discourse on an abstract theme. The erotic desire at its centre is barely hinted. But at least the story reaches towards a point where we can say "psychoanalysis is a soul murder."[5] The detective story, like science fiction and fantastic fiction, must be a book of philosophy.[6]

Hawthorne is haunted by a further seventeenth-century image-event—the ability of Comus to change men into beasts in "the forest" (his name means "revelry" and he is the son of Bacchus or Dionysus, the enemy of Christ, and Circe), a figure of Control by total transformation. But Hawthorne's mode is not Milton's (the redemptive Lady channel is not available to him) but a different enquiry into the verbal and visual forms and the political-religious dogmas of Control. The manner of transformation may be visually symbolic but, like the burning A and its several interpretations, its effects are concrete enough. Hawthorne explores how much and what should be repressed by oppression to produce a society, and asks long before *Civilization and its Discontents*. "Young Goodman Brown" proposes that Christ and the Devil may control equally well in terms of daily co-ordinated moral living in a town, and that dogmatic exclusivity may produce deadly isolation. The Mars/Indian leader at the head of the rebel Comus rout looks directly at Robin, and his gaze is the challenge of counter-control from revolt in the State. The rout may be docile, but it is the American future. Power operates on the frontier crossings of legality, crime and sin. Transgression and innovation move together. In the words of Deleuze and Guattari (*Anti-Oedipus*):

> We docile subjects say to ourselves: so that's what I wanted! Will it ever be suspected that the law discredits—and has an interest in discrediting and disgracing—the person it presumes to be guilty, the person the law wants to be guilty and wants to be made to feel guilty? One acts as if it were possible to conclude directly from psychic repression the nature of the repressed, and from the prohibition the nature of what is prohibited . . . what really takes place is that the law prohibits something that is perfectly fictitious in the order of desire or of the "instincts," so as to persuade its subjects that they had this intention corresponding to this fiction. This is indeed the only way the law has of getting a grip on intention, of making the unconscious guilty.

This is the casual plot of Hester Prynne's obedience and disobedience between the law of marriage and transcendental law of erotic desire, with "a consecration of its own" (chapter 17). Hawthorne is further to dramatize the transmission of repression, from the seventeenth century to the nineteenth, from Europe to New England, in the palimpsest of his Rome, in *Blithedale* with its Fourierism and Mesmerism and Benthamite panopticon, in all those who use "natural science" to tamper with the human body and soul. The Devil is the repressed working through the ages and needs human souls, and working especially in the utopian ambivalences of Westervelt and Hollingsworth, the classic double figure of repression/oppression in *The Blithedale Romance*. Woody Allen's self-lacerating comedy takes up guilt and neurosis into an anti-intellectual series of routines; his standard figures are sceptical and paralyzed into indecision and endless verbalizations. Hawthorne's professionals are decisive in control but still neurotic, and equally cut off from the masses. The ritual sacrifice of intellectuals and artists lies well within the traditions of the Paleface, in Rahv's terms, and the celebrated thin pale face of the American intellectual.[7]

In fact the repressed returns in Hawthorne's fictions largely if not altogether through the Comus intellectual with or without his rout, or her dark erotic pressures. And there is an accurate sense that energies are repressed in American as in any other western culture, at least since the Salem witch-hunts. Sexual energy, and its transference into creativity, is repressed towards the ideal which haunts nineteenth-century American fiction: the robot, the automaton, the slave without human limitations which interfere with productivity, who is so totally balanced that he can be used as an it. The woman is repressed towards subordinate passivity and away from assertion, creativity and organizational responsibility. Children's impishness is interpreted as devilry and educated out, for future labour usefulness. In America the repressed appears as the Indian, the Black Man in the forest, wilderness and wildness, the Devil, uncontrolled libido in any form—so that religious and capitalist relationships can be imposed. Sects flourish but they are rarely liberatory. Hawthorne can easily use the seventeenth century as a continuous present in which the repressed returns, since what is feared continually is the coherence of a particularly thrustful energy imaged as the Adversary. Certain salient sections of that past are given key powers, certain events become metonymic instances. The resulting fiction is employed to analyze the nineteenth-century lacks and suppressions, especially the deterioration of professionals in law, science, the church, and so on, which erodes confidence in society. What thrusts past the censor, what threatens normality, is presented as monstrous, a villain, the natural threatening state forms. The overwhelming emphasis on self-reliance, individual enterprise and personal aggressiveness is countered by the chances of being transformed in this process into a criminal, a sinner, a monster or a deprived recluse at the very moment of self-realization. Brand commits suicide in the Devil's fire, and Clifford Pyncheon emerges from false imprisonment as an enfeebled eccentric. A man may live with a snake in his body or facially concealed beneath a long black veil. A woman may be turned into an adulteress just as a black woman is turned into a negress. Innocence is everywhere emergent as experience because of the determinate need to conquer energy. Women and sexuality are nervously shown by Hawthorne moving against their relegation in Christian capitalist society to the utilitarian and subordinate, to the reality principle which devours pleasure. Pearl's position proposes that the innocence of children may no longer be assumed (the educational system had long ago given up such a belief). "Possession" haunts Hawthorne's pages as a challenge to both reason and innocence and is signalled by displays of intellectual and physical passion. It is "Rome" in *The Marble Faun* to such an extent that "New England" becomes a shadowy place for the chastened American lovers to return to. In Hawthorne's fictions heroes and heroines have all but vanished as figures of dominant revolutionary apparatus. Threats to the State and to the family, the nucleus of the State, have to be put down as "Merry England," maypoles and garlanded lords of misrule are put down. But the threats remain. All Endicott can do is have the May Lord's hair cropped and throw a wreath of roses over his head.

Some of the reasons are clear. The creative/subversive must somehow be given permission: the dilemma of the State. Within Hawthorne's critique of the exceptional man or woman lies a fear that the masses may produce nothing new, do not produce through disobedience or breaking laws. The power of the social group in "My Kinsman, Major Molineux" and "The Artist of the Beautiful" is clear: the rout may have destructive leadership. Lonely work is fearful to the mob, but that is a major source of change. The rout's leader in "Molineux" is the figure of choice in law-breaking to which Robin is invited to contribute his energy for a new stage in social production—in effect, the future of New England and of the United States lies with the Mars/Indian at the head of a lynch mob. And here the tar-and-feathering is laid on the governor rather than Southern blacks or the keepers in "The System of Doctor Tarr and Professor Fether." Nostalgia for a feudal order in hierarchy, a class-structured unity, confronts the new, the forward movement in revolt. Within the writing confidence of the tale, the author is puzzled by the possibility of two orders of control in conflict which seems to be inevitable. But he finely shows how they lie on either side of the moment where the paradigm is forcibly changing. The fiction is generated from and generates the question so frequently posed in Hawthorne's career: where does change come from? The individual and the masses conflict precisely here. Hawthorne's thought is not evolutionary, as Whitman's is, nor is it an organicist longing for the unity in which "the everlasting universe of Things/Flows through the Mind . . . from secret springs."[8]

So he works within fictional methods which are voyeuristic and manichean. An obsessive basis in the visual, the placing of crucial events within the single perception, demands a voyeuristic mode, and the fiction becomes spectatorist. The complete oeuvre is an equivalent of a panopticon, with Hollingsworth, the author, at its centre, gazing into each cell holding its captive. Or Henry Ford dreaming of being able to survey each assembly-line operative, and then follow him home. Hollingsworth the egotistic reformer has to be defeated and converted to love of a passive woman. Following a leader almost certainly means you yield to him or her. The continuing power of this programme, within the manichean control system, is still highly valid in the polarizations of Mailer's *Why Are We in Vietnam?* in 1967, where the plot includes, essentially, the reaches of cosmic energy, still imaged as the divine or the satanic into the human brain, "in the deep of its mysterious unwindings" "the deep mystery which is whatever is electricity." This is no great distance from that Poe-like entry in the *American Notebooks:* "questions as to unsettled points of History, and Mysteries of Nature, to be asked of a mesmerized person." Like Mailer, Hawthorne grasped the need of the fantastic mode in order to work in these interfaces between possibility, probability and the present:

> In a world which is indeed our world, the one we know, a world without devils, sylphides, or vampires, there recurs an event which cannot be explained by the laws of this same familiar world. The person who

experiences the event must opt for one of two possible solutions: either he is the victim of an illusion of the senses, of a product of the imagination—and laws of the world then remain what they are; or else the event has indeed taken place, it is an integral part of reality—but then this reality is controlled by laws unknown to us. Either the devil is an illusion, an imaginary being; or else he really exists, precisely like the other living beings—with this reservation, that we encounter him infrequently.

The fantastic occupies the duration of this uncertainty. Once we choose one answer or the other, we leave the fantastic for a neighbouring genre, the uncanny or the marvellous. The fantastic is that hesitation experienced by a person who knows only the laws of nature confronting an apparently supernatural event.[9]

But in fact it may be possible, and Hawthorne certainly found it possible, to oscillate between a secular and a theological usage of what Todorov calls "illusion," "supernatural." Inside these defining procedures lies, therefore, a further decision: the writer may hesitate or he may not, and his reader may hesitate or not, according to prior belief, knowledge and experience. Science fiction and science non-fiction may be experienced as possible or improbable or probable accordingly. The "fantastic" uses "the laws of nature" to extrapolate a fiction from scientific hypotheses as well as scientific discovery. The writer may compose to a formulaic procedure which produces money-spinners out of tidy moral plots or shiver-causing plots of indecision. In the nineteenth century, the nature of already rapidly accelerating cultural change could frequently be experienced as "fantastic"—and the decision to place it theologically or not would have to follow. Ignorance and indecision are made within apparent knowledge and decisions. Fictional products imitate. "The wonderful world around us in harmony" of the Romantics may be poisonous and incurably so, or at least governed, as Rappaccini's garden is, by the Roman god of change (and Hawthorne uses the language of "adultery" for the hybrids there—"no longer of God's making, but the monstrous offspring of man's depraved fancy, glowing with only an evil mockery of beauty"). Legalistic Nature is the fiction of the Law of the State. Fallout kills Lucy in Cumbria. The apparently inexplicable may be an apparent killer in the real world, and without "hesitation." Explanations may "hesitate" but existential and manmade events happen to real people. You have to believe it, as today's Americans say, to counter the fantastic. Laws kill in the hands of class, caste and intellect or brute force. The victim's innocence may be proved later by other laws. The event is not fantastic unless you believe in singular god-permitted control which is infallible everywhere and at all times—so that you can shift between centuries without shifting gear.

Who in fact "hesitates" between descriptions of events? Todorov gives the formula which sums up the spirit of the fantastic as "I nearly reached the point of believing."[10] Total faith or total incredulity would lead beyond the fantastic: it is hesitation that sustains life, he says. Or in Kuhn's terms, the paradigmatic closure is penetrated, and only then generates. But Hester Prynne's risk in sexuality is fantastic only to the unpassionate and the timid, the forever obedient and the academic in whatever class of caste, the utterly law-abiding. Decisions about her action lie between reading fiction and the reader's life praxis. He who hesitates may well be lost, as Miles Coverdale is, rather than sustained. And sustained where? In *The Scarlet Letter* Hester survives in an Atlantic shore cottage—"within the verge of the peninsular, but not in close vicinity to any other habitation"—in order to become a new social power in a tired and hesitant community. But the penalty would have otherwise been worse—Edmund Wilson quotes Sophocles in his essay on the "Philoctetes": "Everything becomes disgusting when you are false to your own nature and behave in an unbecoming way." The hero with a suppurating wound is abandoned on his peninsular—"exacerbated by hardship and chagrin"—but becomes sacred, acquires superhuman powers and "is destined to be purged of his guilt." And Gide's version says: "I have come to know more of the secrets of life than my masters had ever revealed to me."[11]

So the monster created by a society or by and through its invented gods—and this is a major basis of all fiction since Defoe, and cuts across the genres—elicits sympathy because he or she or it is the form of the repressed and oppressed. The illegal becomes a category of necessity and therefore strangely legal.

Fear in the legal citizen relates to power, control, authority, the State, the gods, all forms of the One and its agents and agencies. The practical counter is in the matter-of-factness of Mistress Hibbins, who knows what Hester has been up to. In one of the few comic scenes in the book (chapter 22):

> "Fie, woman, fie!" cried the old lady, shaking her finger at Hester. "Dost think I have been to the forest so many times, and have yet no skill to judge who else has been there? . . . Thou wearest (the token) openly; so there need be no question about that. But this minister! Let me tell thee, in thine ear! When the Black Man sees one of his own servants, signed and sealed, so shy of owning to the bond as is the Reverend Mr. Dimmesdale, he hath a way of ordering matters so that the mark shall be disclosed in open daylight to the eyes of all the world!"

So Arthur's A may be psychosomatic or it may be diabolic. But more important is that this passage indicates another judge, outside the law and inside the community. What is more, it is a woman to whom Hawthorne gives central words on the way the repressed inevitably returns. And she speaks without hesitation. If, as Todorov believes, quoting Lovecraft, "a tale is fantastic if the reader experiences an emotion of profound fear and terror, the presence of unsuspected worlds and powers," Mistress

Hibbins partly allays those fears in her familiarity with "the forest" as a daily pattern, as daily as the Church, and she certainly is not perplexed.

Hawthorne understood something of how laws exemplify active ideology—in Colin Sumner's terms:

> As the (passive) reflections of certain social relations, ideologies can become embodied in laws which, when applied, involve their intrinsic ideologies as (active) determinants of other social relations. The legal process also admirably illustrates the theoretical point that, once embodied, ideologies do not *necessarily* (re-)structure our practice; sometimes they need reinforcement to make them effective. . . . New ideologies, new uses for old ideologies, old ideologies—all are thoroughly social products.[12]
>
> A legal enactment is a hybrid form combining power and ideology; an ideological formation sanctioned, according to fixed and hallowed procedures for the creation of Law, by the instituted executors of social power. . . . An ideology of legality develops which celebrates and elevates The Law to an exalted status as the expression of unity in the nation.[13]

Curiously, Hawthorne felt the need to "establish a theatre, a little removed from the highway of ordinary travel, where the creatures of his brain may play their phantasmagorical antics, without exposing them to too close a comparison with the actual events of real lives." In fact, his patterns of guilt, shame, power and law dramatize the real. . . .

NOTES

1. Karl Marx, *Economic and Philosophic Manuscripts of 1844* (London: Lawrence and Wishart, 1961), 101.

2. G. Deleuze and F. Guattari, *Anti-Oedipus* (New York: Viking Press, 1977), 256.

3. Ibid., 118.

4. K. Marx and F. Engels, *Collected Works*, vol. 3 (London: Lawrence and Wishart, 1975), 298–99.

5. G. Deleuze, "Four Perspectives On Psychoanalysis," *Language, Sexuality and Subversion*, ed. P. Foss and M. Morris (Darlington, Australia, 1978). Working Papers Collection, 138.

6. Colin Gordon, "The Subtracting Machine," *I & C: Power and Desire—Diagrams of the Social*, no. 8 (Oxford: I & C Publications, 1981), 34.

7. Philip Rahv, "Paleface and Redskin," *Image And Idea* (New York: New Directions, 1957).

8. Shelley, "Mont Blanc."

9. Tzvetan Todorov, *The Fantastic: A Structural Approach to a Literary Genre* (Ithaca, New York: Cornell University Press, 1975), 25.

10. Ibid., 31.

11. Edmund Wilson, *The Wound and the Bow* (London: Methuen, 1961), 254–55.

12. Colin Sumner, *Reading Ideologies* (London, New York and San Francisco: Academic Press, 1979), 22–23.

13. Ibid., 293.

Ideology and Literary Form: W. B. Yeats

TERRY EAGLETON

Using Marxist perspectives, Eagleton contends that Yeats's interest in the ancient Irish aristocracy was a move to counter middle-class hegemony. As a bourgeois Protestant Anglo-Irishman, however, Yeats's Irish nationalism was contradictory. Yet, according to Eagleton, it was Yeats's awareness of this contradiction that called forth his best poetry.

WHILE ELIOT, POUND, T. E. HULME and the Imagists are turning in England from the dwindling resources of Romantic individualism towards forms of classical or symbolist impersonality, W. B. Yeats reaches back in Ireland to Celtic mythology and the early English Romantic heritage, defiantly opposing style, passion and personality to the "hot-faced bargainers and the money-changers," the encroaching world of the Irish bourgeoisie. Whereas in England Romantic individualism is an ideological component of a long-established bourgeois class, that class in imperially subjugated Ireland is still nascent; Yeats therefore has to hand, in his struggle against bourgeois hegemony, the resources of an *aristocratic* Romanticism long since moribund in bourgeois England—the idealised cavalier, ceremonious lineage of the Anglo-Irish Ascendancy.

Yet Yeats's relation to that heritage, and through it to Irish society as a whole, is markedly contradictory. He belonged by birth not to the Ascendancy class but to the Protestant bourgeoisie; and as such he was doubly dislocated within Irish society, both from the class with whom he identified and from the Catholic nationalist movement whose poetic mythologer he attempted to become. As the leader of the cultural wing of the nationalist movement in the 1890s, Yeats recoiled from the very Catholic bourgeoisie who formed the nationalist movement's mass social basis; the Land League, with its strategy of transferring economic power from Protestant to emergent Catholic bourgeoisie by organised boycott, had weakened the influence of both Yeats's own class and the Ascendancy to which he spiritually belonged. Yeats accordingly committed himself to the Romantic nationalism of John O'Leary's Fenian Brotherhood, which

From *Criticism and Ideology: A Study in Marxist Literary Theory*, by Terry Eagleton (London: Verso/NLB, 1978). Copyright Terry Eagleton 1975, 1976. Reprinted by permission.

rejected the Land League's agrarian agitational tactics, and so refused one of the most effective weapons against English imperialism. Yeats's cultural project was to replace the threadbare patriotic jargon of the Young Ireland poetic movement with a richer symbology of nationalist aspirations, nurtured by aristocratic Romanticism and traditional mythology; yet that commitment to the Anglo-Irish Ascendancy, who had never occupied a role of active popular leadership, threw him into contradiction with the real history and basis of the nationalist movement. His cultural nationalism, itself a displacement and appropriation of the political energies temporarily diffused by the Parnell affair, moves into deepening conflict with the realities of nationalist politics—a conflict poetically focused in Maud Gonne, for Yeats at once symbol of Ireland's eternal beauty and rancorous political demagogue. The oxymoronic double-vision of "Easter 1916" reveals well enough Yeats's difficulties in trying to reconcile the Romantic heroism of the uprising with the despised ideology and social class of its leaders.

Yeats's consciousness of his social disinheritance is precisely what fuels the process of his poetic maturation, as his poetry turns in the early years of this century from narcotic fantasy to the stripped, toughened forms of a bitter yet defiant disillusion. Fin-de-siècle languour is transformed into combative oratory as the historical contradictions sharpen, forcing the progressively displaced Yeats into a compensatory ideology of aggressive poetic activism. The theory of the poetic mask is accordingly developed, as a projection of Romantic "personality" into impersonal, socially representative form; the mask protects the poet within a spiritually alien society, but also enacts the organic unity of personal identity and social function which that society has destroyed. Similarly, Yeats moves his poetry closer to common speech at the very point where his aristocratic values are being most scornfully flouted by bourgeois philistinism, and in doing so reactivates a crucial contradiction of early Romanticism—the poet's need to claim centrally "representative" status at precisely the point where he is being relegated to an historically peripheral role.

It is to that early English Romanticism that Yeats returns, in his attempt to mediate turbulent individualism into historically "representative" terms. In his drive to "hammer (his) thoughts into unity," to counter bourgeois power with a cohesive, elaborate symbology less vulnerable to collapse than the vagaries of purely individualist impulse, Yeats reaches back to rework and relive the massive symbolic totalities of that earlier mythologer of bourgeois revolution, William Blake, whose poetry he edits in the early 1890s. Blake, too, marks an ideological conjuncture at which Romantic individualism must be raised to an elaborate mythological system if it is to survive and illuminate the real history which produces it. And as Yeats must come to terms with Blake, so Blake, in his major poem "Milton," must engage in turn with his own bourgeois revolutionary predecessor. All three poets construct "cosmic" symbologies which, in mythologising bourgeois revolution, can assess its historical limitations from the visionary vantage-point of an absolute idealism. The culmination of that process in the case of Yeats is the extraordinary cosmology of "A Vision," the first draft of which was completed in 1917 in the throes of Irish nationalist and world imperialist crisis. The esoteric theosophical symbolism of that work, with its image of reality as a cyclical interpenetration of antinomies, signifies Yeats's most ambitious attempt to "resolve the deep enmity between man and his destiny"—to reduce the contingencies of a recalcitrant history to the controlling order of myth.

From the outset, Yeats's search was for a mythology which would restore the organic unity of Irish society ("Have not all races had their first unity from a mythology, which marries them to rock and hill?"[1]). The organising symbols of his verse—tree, dancer, tower—are the poetic nodes of such organic wholeness. As that ideal unity became progressively unrealisable in bourgeois Ireland, it was forced into the political mould of fascism. His admiration for Mussolini and the extreme right-wing Free State Senator Kevin O'Higgins, his commitments to O'Duffy's Irish fascist movement in the 1930s, his advocation of "force and marching men" to break the "reign of the mob," his dream of a new European civilisation based on despotic élitist rule—in these political doctrines of the ageing Yeats, one destination of the organic ideal in literature stands starkly revealed.

NOTE

1. Yeats, *Autobiographies* (London, 1966), 194.

The Cinema After Babel: Language, Difference, Power

ELLA SHOHAT *and* ROBERT STAM

In this selection from a longer essay, Shohat and Stam examine how American and European films that are translated into other languages become colonizing vehicles disseminating Western culture. These critics draw on the theories of Russian writer Mikhail Bakhtin and his group, who hold each language to be a set of intersecting idioms of classes, races, generations, gender,

These selections are reprinted from "The Cinema After Babel: Language, Difference, Power," by Ella Shohat and Robert Stam in *Screen* 26 (May–August 1985): 35–36; 48–58. Reprinted by permission.

and locales ("heteroglossia") which socially constitute the person. Thus the general dissemination of Western films into other languages erases differences within and between cultures and establishes Western ideology as the norm.

THE REALITY OF LANGUAGE DIFFERENCE, the world-wide babble of mutually incomprehensible tongues and idioms, entails consequences for the cinema which have yet to be explored. While contemporary theoretical work has concerned itself with film *as* language, little attention has been directed to the role of language and language difference *within* film. Working out of the tradition of Saussure-derived linguistics, cine-semioticians have examined the analogies and disanalogies between "natural language" and film as a discursive practice, but they have not delineated the impact on the cinema of the prodigality of tongues in which it is produced, spoken and received. Our purpose here will be to explore, in a necessarily speculative fashion, the myriad ways in which the sheer fact of linguistic diversity impinges on film as a signifying practice and on the cinema as an "encratic" institution deeply embedded in multiform relations of power.

By language, we refer, first of all, to the clearly distinct idioms— English, French, Russian, Arabic—recognised as linguistic unities by grammars and lexicons. We refer as well, however, to the multiple "languages" inhabiting a single culture or a single speech-community, at least insofar as these intra-linguistic differences bear on questions of inter-cultural film reception. Here we follow the thought of Mikhail Bakhtin, for whom the "crude" boundaries separating natural languages ("polyglossia") represent only one extreme on a continuum. For Bakhtin, every apparently unified linguistic community is also characterised by "heteroglossia," or "many-languagedness," in which the idioms of different generations, classes, races, genders, locales compete for ascendancy. For Bakhtin, language is the arena for the clash of differently oriented social accents; each word is subject to conflicting pronunciations, intonations and allusions. Every language is a set of languages, and every speaking subject opens onto a multiplicity of languages. All communication entails an apprenticeship in the language of the other, a kind of translation or coming to terms with meaning on the boundaries of one's own set of languages and those of another. Thus inter-linguistic translation has as its counterpart the *intra*-linguistic "translation" required for dialogue between diverse individuals and between diverse communities.[1]

Contemporary thought has been haunted by the idea of language. Central to the project of thinkers as diverse as Russell, Wittgenstein, Cassirer, Heidegger, Merleau-Ponty, and even Derrida, is the idea that language so completely structures our grasp of the world that "reality" can be seen as an effect of linguistic convention. According to the Sapir-Whorf hypothesis, language *is* culture, and those who "inhabit" different languages might be said to inhabit different worlds. The grammatical and semantic fields of a language, indeed its entire conceptual framework, install speakers in habitual grooves of perception and expression which predispose them to experience the world in culturally specific ways. This linguistic "relativity principle" has as its corollary the view of all languages as fundamentally equal. For contemporary linguistics, languages do not exist in a hierarchy of value. The notion of "primitive" languages, rooted in the evolutionary assumption that the complex develops from the simple, here lacks pertinence since every language is perfectly suited to the cultural needs and cultural reality of its speakers.

But if all languages are created equal, some are made "more equal than others." Inscribed within the play of power, languages are caught up in artificial hierarchies rooted in cultural hegemonies and political oppression. English, for example, as a function of its colonising status, became the linguistic vehicle for the projection of Anglo-American power, technology and finance. Hollywood, especially, came to incarnate a linguistic hubris bred of empire. Presuming to speak for others in *its* native idiom, Hollywood proposed to tell the story of other nations not only to Americans, but also for the other nations themselves, and always in English. In Cecil B. De Mille epics, both the ancient Egyptians and the Israelites spoke English, and so, for that matter, did God. In Hollywood, the Greeks of *The Odyssey,* the Romans of *Ben Hur,* Cleopatra of Egypt, Madame Bovary of France, Count Vronsky of Russia, Helen of Troy and Jesus of Nazareth all had as their *lingua franca* the English of Southern California. Hollywood both profited from and itself promoted the universalisation of the English language as *the* idiom of speaking subjects, thus contributing indirectly to the subtle erosion of the linguistic autonomy of other cultures. By virtue of its global diffusion, Hollywood became an agent in the dissemination of Anglo-American cultural hegemony.[2] . . .

SOUND AND LANGUAGE DIFFERENCE: POST-SYNCHRONISATION

The choice of post-synchronisation as opposed to subtitling has significant consequences. Post-synchronisation, or "dubbing," can be defined for our purposes as the technical procedure by which a voice, whether of the original performer or another, is "glued" to a visible speaking figure in the image. With dubbing, the original and adopted texts are homogenous in their material of expression: what was phonetic in the original remains phonetic in the translation, unlike subtitles, where the phonetic original becomes graphological in the translation. With subtitles, the difference in material of expression allows for the juxtaposition of two parallel texts, one aural and the other written, and thus for the possibility of comparison. Errors become potentially "visible," not only to privileged spectators familiar with the languages in question, but also to the general viewer conscious of small inconsistencies: a disproportion in duration between spoken utterance and written translation, for example, or the failure of subtitles to register obvious linguistic disturbances such as a lisp or a stutter. The single-track nature of dubbing, in contrast, makes comparison impossible. Without the original script or version, there is simply nothing with which to compare the dubbed rendition.[3] Given our desire to believe that the heard voices actually emanate from the actors/characters on the screen, we repress all awareness of the possibility of an incorrect translation; in fact, we forget that there has been any translation at all.

While subtitling resembles a kind of summary prose translation, dubbing is more comparable to the complex juggling of sense, rhythm and technical prosody involved in poetic translation. Subtitles can concentrate meaning, transforming redundant into more efficient language, or, on the other hand, they might (although this possibility is rarely explored) explicate a punning reference or offer contextual footnotes. With dubbing, in contrast, each visible sign of speech activity must be somehow rendered; words or sounds must be fitted to the moving mouth. Dubbing, in this sense, poses immense *technical* as well as *linguistic* challenges. Interlingual dubbing substitutes a separate and new sound recording in a second language for the original text. The newly recorded dialogue, separated out from the noise and music tracks, must be carefully matched with the articulatory movements and the audible speech results in what István Fodor calls, on the analogy of "phoneme" and "morpheme," a "dischroneme," i.e., the minimal unit of non-coincidence of speech and movement, in contrast with the "synchroneme" or successful matching of dubbed voice and articulatory movement.[4] This matching is diversely articulated with specific cinematic codes such as angle, scale, lighting and so forth, with exigencies varying according to whether a shot is close-up or *plan américain*, profile or frontal, well or dimly lit. Direct address at close camera range—the extreme close-up of Kane's "Rosebud" or the disembodied lips mouthing the lyrics of the initial song in *The Rocky Horror Picture Show*—poses the greatest challenge because it amplifies attention to speech movement. A long or darkly-lit shot, meanwhile, can blur the distinctive visual features of speech production, and the noise and music tracks can divert attention from the speech organs. Even screen format affects our experience of synchronous matching; wide-screen splays out the speech organs and thus poses more difficult challenges than standard format.

Along with phonetic synchrony, dubbers also strive for what Fodor calls "character synchrony," that is, the skilful match between the timbre, volume, tempo and style of the speech of the acoustic personifier (the dubber) and the physical gestures and facial expressions of the screen actor. As with any translation, the rendering can never be fully "faithful"; the chameleonism of dubbing is always partial. While words are socially shared and therefore more-or-less translatable, voices are as irreducibly individual as fingerprints. The same word pronounced by a Marlene Dietrich, a Woody Allen or an Orson Welles is in a sense no longer the same word; each voice imprints a special resonance and colouring. The practice of dubbing can lead to a number of anomalous situations. When the target audience is aware, from other films, of the voice and acting style of a given player, the dubbed voice is often an irritant. Those familiar with Jean-Pierre Léaud, for example, are likely to be annoyed by the dubbed English version of Truffaut's *Day for Night*. The memory of the "real" voice provokes a kind of resistance to the substitute. In international co-production, meanwhile, a multi-lingual player might dub him/herself into a second or even a third language for foreign versions; so that each linguistic situation results in a new dubbing configuration. At times, the dubbers themselves achieve a certain status and notoriety. In the '30s in Germany, according to Jay Leyda, dubbers earned salaries in proportion to the stars they were dubbing (since audiences insisted on hearing the same voice), resulting in a kind of parasitic star system. In India, meanwhile, stardom is "bifurcated," as imaged stars share popularity with the unseen "playback singers" whose voices they borrow.

The Italian situation as regards dubbing calls for special comment. Post-synchronisation has been a feature of Italian cinema since fascism, but forms part of a process of cultural levelling which dates back to the unification of Italy. Since most Italian actors speak "dialect" rather than the "official" Tuscan, they are made to speak an artificial language uttered in studios by a specialised corps of dubbers. While well-known actors (Gassman, Mastroianni, Vitti) dub themselves, many lesser-known actors have never been heard in their own voice. The dubbing of foreign films, meanwhile, results in Italians seeing bastardised versions in which cultural specificities are flattened. Within the specialised linguistic code developed for translating the Western, for example, as Geoffrey Nowell-Smith points out, the Union and the Confederacy are rendered as "*nordista*" and "*sudista*," geographical terms with precise connotations in Italy (evoking the tension between "feudal" South and developing capitalist North), so that the Civil War is read in "terms of the Risorgimento." Such abuses led in 1967 to an angry manifesto, signed by Antonioni, Bellocchio, Bertolucci, Pasolini, Rosi and others, denouncing obligatory post-synchronisation: "Contemporary developments in theoretical studies on the sound film imply the need to take up a position at the outset against the systematic abuse of dubbing, which consistently compromises the expressive values of the film." Post-synchronisation and the dubbing-translation of foreign films, the authors conclude, "are the two equally absurd and unacceptable sides of one and the same problem. . . ."[5]

Post-synchronisation exploits our naive faith in cinematic reality, our belief that the temporal coincidence of moving lips with phonetic sounds points to a causal and existential connection. Buñuel subverts this faith in *Cet Objet Obscur du Désir* (1977) by having two actresses, dubbed by a third voice, play the same role. Split in the image, the character regains a semblance of unity through the soundtrack. Post-synchronisation also forms part of the film's elaboration of the themes of Frenchness and Spanishness: a film by a Spaniard who has lived in France, adapting a French novel about Spain (*La Femme et le Pantin*) whose Spanish protagonist is transformed by Buñuel into a Frenchman, but played by a Spaniard (Fernando Rey) and dubbed by a well-known French actor (Michel Piccoli). Other film-makers deploy more explicitly disruptive strategies to highlight the factitious nature of post-synchronisation. Godard in *Tout Va Bien* (1972) and Hanoun in *Une Simple Histoire* deliberately misdub in order to sabotage the fictive unity of voice and image. A Brazilian film, significantly entitled *Voz do Brasil* ("Voice of Brazil") after a widely-detested official radio news broadcast, shows an American film being dubbed in a Brazilian sound studio. As the film loop of an emotionally-charged sequence passes on the screen, the dubbing technicians do their work and exchange trivialities. We are struck by the disjunction between the passionate drama on the screen and the apparent boredom in the studio, as well as by the contrast between the glamorous star and the ordinary-looking woman lending her voice. Film dubbers usually remain, to borrow Pierre Schaeffer's term, *acousmatique*, their voices are heard but the real source of the enunciation remains invisible. The provocation of *Voz do Brasil* is to reveal the hidden face of these normally acousmatic dubbers and thus render visible the effaced labour of a particular cinematic process.

The marriage of convenience that weds a voice from one language and culture to an imaged speaker coming from another often triggers a kind of battle of linguistic and cultural codes. Linguistic communication is multi-track; every language carries with it a constellation of corollary features having to do with oral articulation, facial expression and bodily movement. Certain locutions are regularly accompanied, often without the speaker's awareness, by codified gestures and automatic motions. The norms of physical expressiveness, moreover, sharply vary from culture to culture; extroverted peoples accompany their words with a livelier play of gesticulations than more introverted peoples. Michael Anderson's *Around the World in Eighty Days* contrasts the expressive codes of the phlegmatic Englishman Phineas Fogg with those of the vehemently gesticulating Frenchman Passepartout. In *Trouble in Paradise* (1932), Lubitsch humorously counterpoints the speech manners of southern and northern Europeans. Recounting a robbery to the Italian police, the Edward Everett Horton character speaks in English (posited as putative French) while the Italian interpreter ferries his words over to the police. Horton's speech is unemotional, efficient and gestureless, while the interpreter's is flamboyant and animated with lively facial expressions and emphatic Italianate gestures. In a single long-take, Lubitsch recurrently pans with the shuttling translator, alternately placing with Horton or the police but never *with* the police, thus further underlining the linguistic and cultural gulf between them.

To graft one language, with its own system of linking sound and gesture, onto the visible behaviour associated with another, then, is to foster a kind of cultural violence and dislocation. Relatively slight when the languages and cultures closely neighbour, this dislocation becomes major when they are more distant, resulting in a clash of cultural repertoires. Brazilian television, like many in the Third World, for example, constantly programmes American films and television series in which American media stars speak fluent dubbed Portuguese. The match of the moving mouths of Kojak, Colombo and Starsky and Hutch with the sounds of Brazilian Portuguese, however, results in a kind of monstrosity, a collision between the cultural codes associated with Brazilian Portuguese (strong affectivity, a tendency toward hyperbole, lively gestural accompaniment of spoken discourse) and those associated with police-detective English (minimal affectivity, understatement, controlled gestures, a cool, hard, tough demeanour). A Brazilian avant-garde film, Wilson Coutinho's *Cildo Meireles* (1981), exploits this gap to satiric effect by matching the image of John Wayne on horseback to incongruous discourse in Portuguese. Wayne's moving lips, in this case, are made to articulate contemporary theories of *différance* and deconstruction. When his antagonists resist his intellectual claims, our hero guns the heretics down.

Language and Power

Although languages as abstract entities do not exist in hierarchies of value, languages as lived operate within hierarchies of power. Language and power intersect not only in obvious conflicts concerning official tongues, but wherever the question of language difference becomes involved with asymmetrical political arrangements. As a potent symbol of collective identity, language is the focus of fierce loyalties existing at the razor edge of national difference. In South Africa, blacks protest the imposition of Afrikaans as the official language of education; in the United States, Hispanics struggle for bilingual education and examinations. What are the implications of this language/power intersection for the cinema? What is the linguistic dimension of an emerging cinema within a situation of "unstable bilingualism" such as that of Quebec? How many of the estimated five thousand languages currently in use are actually spoken in the cinema? Are there major languages completely lacking in cinematic representation? How many appear briefly in an ethnographic film and as quickly disappear? How many films are never subtitled due to insufficient funds and therefore never distributed internationally? What about anti-colonialist films (Pontecorvo's *Burn*) artificially made to speak a hegemonic language to guarantee geographic distribution and economic survival?

The penetration of a hegemonic language often helps clear the path for cinematic domination. In the aftermath of World War II, English became what George Steiner has called the "vulgate" of Anglo-American power. Countless films in the post-war period, as a consequence, reflect the prestige and projection of English and the axiomatic self-confidence of its speakers. The producer Prokosch, in Godard's *Contempt*, embodies the self-importance and linguistic arrogance of the industrial managers of American cinema; while he is more or less monolingual, his European collaborators move more easily from language to language. In *Der Amerikanische Freund* (*The American Friend*, 1977), Wim Wenders calls attention to the lack of linguistic reciprocity between American and European. The major non-American characters all speak English along with their native language, while the American friend Tom, the "cowboy in Hamburg," speaks only English. Jonathon's last sentence to the Swiss doctor— "It hurts in any language"—echoes another filmic demonstration of linguistic non-reciprocity: Miguel/Michael's response in *Touch of Evil* to Quinlan's insistence that he speak English and not Spanish. "I think it will be unpleasant in any language." Like many New German films, *The American Friend* critically foregrounds the widespread dissemination of English and of American popular culture, thus illustrating the ways that "the Yanks," as another Wenders character puts it in *Kings of the Road*, "have colonised our subconscious."[6]

One could speak as well, in this context, of any number of metaphorical "colonisations" having to do with region, class, race and gender. Human beings do not enter simply into language as a master code; they participate in it as socially constituted subjects. Where there is no true communality of interest, power relations determine the conditions of social meeting and linguistic exchange. Even monolingual societies are characterised by heteroglossia; they englobe multiple "languages" or "dialects" which both reveal and produce social position, each existing in a distinct relation to the hegemonic language. The "word," in Bakhtin's sense, is a sensitive barometer of social pressure and dynamics. In many British New Wave films, upper-class English is worn like a coat of arms, an instrument of exclusion, while working-class speech is carried like a stigmata. A cynical reincarnation of Eliza Doolittle, the protagonist of Clive Donner's *Nothing But the Best* (1964), gradually sheds his working class speech in favour of Oxbridge English in order to scale the social heights. In Perry Henzell's *The Harder They Come* (1973), similarly, the singer-protagonist's lower-class status is marked by his speaking Jamaican "dialect" while the upper-class figures more closely approximate "standard" English, thus positing a homology between class and linguistic hegemony. (A dialect, it has been said, is only a "language without an army," or, we might add, without economic or political powers.[7]) Issues of race also intersect with questions of language, power, and social stratification. Black English in the United States was often called "bad" English because linguists failed to take into account the specific African-historical roots and imminent logical structure of black speech. Not un-like women, blacks developed internal codes of communication and defence, a coded language of resistance.[8] One of the innovations of Melbin Van Peebles' *Sweet Sweetback's Baadaas Song* (1971)—whose very title resonates with black intonations—was to abandon Sidney Poitier just-like-white-people middle-class diction in order to get down and talk black.

The interest of Sembène's *Black Girl* lies in having the film's female protagonist stand at the point of convergence of multiple oppressions—as maid, as black, as woman, as African—and in conveying her oppression specifically through language. Diouana, who the spectator knows to be fluent in French, overhears her employer say of her: "She under-stands French . . . by instinct . . . like an animal." The colonialist, who, according to Fanon, cannot speak of the colonised without resorting to the bestiary, here transforms the most defining human character-istic—the capacity for language—into a sign of animality. The gap of knowledge between the spectator, aware of Diouana's fluency, and her unknowing French employers, serves to expose the colonialist habit of linguistic nonreciprocity. This typically colonialist asymmetry (Diouana knows their language but they do not know hers) distinguishes colo-nial bilingualism from ordinary linguistic dualism. For the coloniser, as Memmi points out, the language and culture of the colonised are de-graded and unworthy of interest, while for the colonised mastery of the coloniser's tongue is both means for survival and a daily humiliation. The colonised language exercises no power and enjoys no prestige in every-day life; it is not used in government offices or the court system, and even street signs make the native feel foreign in his/her own land. Pos-session of two languages is not here a matter of having two tools, but rather entails participation in two conflicting psychic and cultural realms. Through a long apprenticeship in unequal dialogue, the colonised be-comes simultaneously self and other. The mother tongue, which holds emotional impact and in which tenderness and wonder are expressed, is precisely the one least valued.[9]

For the coloniser, to be human is to speak *his* language. In countless films, linguistic discrimination goes hand in hand with condescending characterisation and distorted social portraiture. The Native Americans of Hollywood westerns, denuded of their own idiom, mouth pidgin English, a mark of their inability to master the "civilised" language. In many films set in the Third World, the language of the colonised is re-duced to a jumble of background noises while the "native" characters are obliged to meet the coloniser on the latter's linguistic turf. In films set in North Africa, Arabic exists as an indecipherable murmur, while the "real" language is the French of Jean Gabin in *Pépé le Moko* or the English of Bogart and Bergman in *Casablanca*. Even in David Lean's *Lawrence of Arabia* (1962), pretentiously, even ostentatiously, sympathetic to the

Arabs, we hear almost no Arabic but rather English spoken in a motley of accents almost all of which (Omar Sharif's being the exception) have little to do with Arabic. The Arabs' paralinguistic war cries, meanwhile, recall the "barbaric yawp" of the "Indians" of countless westerns. The caricatural representation of Arabic in the cinema prolongs the Eurocentric "orientalist" tradition in both linguistics and literature. Ernst Renan invented the contrast, flattering to Europe's self-image, between the "organic" and "dynamic" Indo-European languages, and the "inorganic" Semitic languages—"arrested, totally ossified, incapable of self-regeneration." [10] For romantics such as Lamartine, Nerval and Flaubert, meanwhile, the Orient served as a mirror for their Western narcissism, when it was not a backdrop for the pageant of their sensibilities. Lamartine saw his trip to the Orient as "un grand acte de ma vie intérieure" ("a great act in my interior life") and discoursed with supreme confidence on the subject of Arabic poetry despite his total ignorance of the language. [11] Twentieth-century film-makers, in certain respects, have inherited the attitudes of the nineteenth-century philological tradition (so ably anatomised by Said), pointing out "defects, virtues, barbarisms, and shortcomings in the language, the people and the civilization." [12]

Colonising cinema, meanwhile, committed its own "barbarisms" in relation to the languages of the colonised. One of the Italian directors who dominated the early history of film-making in Egypt, Osato, outraged the Islamic community in his *El Zouhour el Katela* (*Fatal Flowers*, 1918) by garbling well-known phrases from the Koran. A similarly cavalier attitude toward linguistic sensitivities led to the misattribution of major languages. Mervyn Leroy's *Latin Lovers* (1953), for example, mistakenly suggests that the national language of Brazil is Spanish. Although Carmen Miranda was called the "Brazilian bombshell," the names given her characters (such as Rosita Conchellas in *A Date with Judy*, 1948), were more Hispanic than Brazilian. [13] Although she reportedly spoke excellent English, she was prodded to speak in her distinctive caricatural manner (the linguistic correlative of her Tutti-Frutti hat), thus reflecting one of many ways that Latins were ridiculed by Hollywood cinema. The dubbed version of Marcel Camus' *Orfeu Negro* (*Black Orpheus*, 1959), finally, substitutes a variety of Caribbean accents in English for the Brazilian Portuguese of the original, thus placing diverse Third World communities under what Memmi calls "the mark of the plural": "They are all the same."

The existing global distribution of power makes the First World nations of the West cultural "transmitters" while it reduces Third World nations to "receivers." Given this unidirectional flow of sounds, images and information, Third World countries are constantly inundated with North American cultural products—from television series and Hollywood films to best-sellers and top-forty hits. The omnipresence of English phrases in Brazil, for example, can be seen as a linguistic symptom of neo-colonialism. A carnival samba penned shortly after the arrival of American sound films already lamented the widespread currency of English phrases: "Goodbye, goodbye boy / Quit your mania for speaking English / It doesn't become you. . . ." One stanza explicitly links the dissemination of English to the economic power of the Anglo-American electricity monopoly "Light"; "It's no longer *Boa Noite* or *Bom Dia* / Now it's Good Morning and Good Night / And in the *favelas* they scorn the kerosene lamp / and only use the light from Light." Hollywood, meanwhile, became the beacon toward which the Third World looked, the model of "true" cinema. The linguistic corollary of domination was the assumption that some languages were inherently more "cinematic" than others. The English "I love you," Brazilian critics argued in the twenties, was infinitely more beautiful and cinematic than the Portuguese "Eu te amo." The focus on the phrase "I love you" is in this case highly overdetermined, reflecting not only the lure of a romantic model of cinema projecting glamour and beautiful stars, but also an intuitive sense of the erotics of linguistic colonialism—i.e. that the colonising language exercises a kind of phallic power. Behind the preference as well was the notion that there are "beautiful" and "ugly" languages, a notion which came to pervade countries with a colonised complex of inferiority.[14] It was in the face of this prejudice that Brazilian film-maker Arnaldo Jabor defiantly entitled his recent film *Eu Te Amo* (1981) and insisted that the title remain in Portuguese even when distributed abroad.

It is against this same backdrop that we must understand the linguistic duality of Carlos Diegues' *Bye Bye Brazil*. Precisely because of the widespread dissemination of English, the film was titled in English even in Brazil. The theme song by Chico Buarque features English expressions like "bye bye" and "night and day" and "OK" as an index of the Americanisation (and multinationalisation) of a world where tribal chiefs wear designer jeans and backwoods rock groups sound like the Bee Gees. Even the name of the travelling entertainment troupe—"Caravana Rolidei"—a phonetic transcription of the Brazilian pronunciation of the English "holiday"—reflects this linguistic colonisation. A typical colonial ambivalence operates here: on the one hand, sincere affection for an alien tongue, and on the other, the penchant for parody and creative distortion, the refusal to "get it straight."

Many Third World films ring the changes on the subject of linguistic colonialism. Youssef Chahine's *Alexandria Why?*, a reflexive film about an aspiring Egyptian film-maker who entertains Hollywood dreams, explores the linguistic palimpsest that was Egypt at the time of the Second World War. Chahine offers an Egyptian perspective on Western cultural products and political conflicts. From the protagonist's point of view, we watch his adored American musical comedies, subtitled in Arabic, and European newsreels with Arabic voice-over. (At certain points, in a linguistic Chinese box effect, the Arabic subtitles of the American film-within-the-film are enclosed within the English subtitles of *Alexandria Why?* itself.) In another sequence, an Egyptian theatre production pokes fun at the occupying powers. Each European power is reduced to a stereotypical cultural emblem: Hitler's moustache, Churchill's cigar, a French chef, an Italian pizza. In a reversal of traditional representation, it is now the colonised who consciously caricature the coloniser. As representatives of the Allied and the Axis powers chaotically pursue each other across the stage, each mumbling their own idiom, the Egyptian characters remain seated, spectators of an alien war on their land. Irrationality, a feature insistently projected by the West onto Arabs and their language, here boomerangs against the Europeans.

Language is a social battleground, the place where political struggles are engaged both comprehensively and intimately. In *Xala* (1975), Sembène again inter-articulates questions of language, culture and power. The protagonist, El Hadji, a polygamous Senegalese businessman who becomes afflicted with *xala*—a religiously-sanctioned curse of impotence—embodies neo-colonised attitudes of the African elite so vehemently denounced by Fanon. Sembène structures the film around the opposition of Wolof and French as the focal point of conflict. While the elite make public speeches in Wolof and wear African dress, they speak French among themselves and reveal European suits beneath their African garb. Many of the characterisations revolve around the question of language. El Hadji's first wife, Adja, representing a pre-colonial African woman, speaks Wolof and wears traditional clothes. The second wife, Oumi, representing the colonised imitator of European fashions, speaks French and wears wigs, sunglasses and low-cut dresses. El Hadji's daughter, Rama, finally, representing a progressive synthesis of Africa and Europe, knows French but insists on speaking Wolof to her francophile father. Here again conflicts involving language are made to carry with them a strong charge of social and cultural tension.

The title of Glauber Rocha's *Der Leone Have Sept Cabeças* subverts the linguistic positioning of the spectator by mingling the languages of five of Africa's colonisers. Rocha's Brechtian fable animates emblematic figures representing the diverse colonisers, further suggesting an identity of roles among them by having an Italian speaker play the role of the American, a Frenchman play the German and so forth. Another polyglot fable, Raul Ruiz' *Het Dak Van de Walvis* (*The Top of the Whale*, 1981) also focuses on the linguistic aspect of oppression. The point of departure for the film, according to Ruiz, was his discovery that certain tribes in Chile, due to their traumatising memory of genocide, spoke their own language only among themselves and never in front of a European.[15] The resulting tale, about a French anthropologist's visit to the last surviving members of an Indian tribe whose language has defied all attempts at interpretation, is turned by Ruiz into a sardonic demystification of the colonialist undergirdings of anthropology.

The intonation of the same word, Bakhtin argues, differs profoundly between inimical social groups. "You taught me language," Caliban tells Prospero in *The Tempest*, "and my profit on it is, I know how to curse. The red plague rid you for learning me your language." In the social life of the utterance as a concrete social act, we began by saying, each word is subject to rival pronunciations, intonations and allusions. While the discourse of Power strives to officialise a single language, one dialect among many, into *the* Language, in fact language is the site of heteroglossia, open to historical process. There is no political struggle, according to Bakhtin, that does not also pass through the word. Languages can serve to oppress and alienate, but also to liberate. We have tried to question the presumption of the masters of language. The "system" of language so dear to the Saussureans, we have implicitly suggested, is subject to what Bakhtin calls centripetal and centrifugal forces; it is always susceptible to subversion. By shifting attention from the abstract system of *langue* to the concrete heterogeneity of *parole,* we have tried to stress the dialogic nature of language in the cinema, its constantly changing relationship to power, and thus point to the possibility of reappropriating its dynamism in the world.

NOTES

1. For Bakhtin's ideas concerning language, see *Problems of Dostoevski's Poetics* (Ann Arbor: Ardis, 1973); *Rabelais and His World,* (Cambridge, Mass.: MIT Press, 1968); and *The Dialogic Imagination* (Austin: University of Texas Press, 1981). See also V. N. Volosinov, *Marxism and the Philosophy of Language* (New York: Seminar Press, 1973). The authorship of this last is disputed; there is considerable evidence that Bakhtin wrote substantial portions or at least worked in extremely close collaboration with Volosinov. See also "Forum on Mikhail Bakhtin," a special issue of *Critical Inquiry* (10, no. 2 [December 1983]) devoted to Bakhtin, as well as the *Revue de l'Université d'Ottawa/University of Ottawa Review* 53, no. 1 (January/March 1983).

2. One might easily posit an analogy here between English as *the* international language, and dominant cinema as *the* film language, with alternative idioms being reduced to the status of "dialects."

3. A partial exception to this rule occurs in the case of that hybrid form, common in documentaries and in newscasts, which combines the dubbed voice of a translator simultaneously with the original voices, at low volume, in the background.

4. See István Fodor, *Film Dubbing: Phonetic, Semiotic, Esthetic and Psychological Aspects* (Hamburg: Buske Verlag, 1976). Fodor's book is thorough and useful, but limited by an underlying assumption of the ultimate possibility of a virtually total adequation between original and dubbed version. The book also limits itself to European languages.

5. See Geoffrey Nowell-Smith, "Italy Sotto Voce," in *Sight and Sound* 37, no. 3 (Summer 1968): 145–47.

6. The wide dissemination of American cultural forms accounts for the frequent nontranslation into German of American film titles: *Easy Rider, Ameri-*

can Graffiti, Taxi Driver, Hair, Apocalypse Now and *Reds* were all left untranslated for German exhibition. In other cases, titles were changed into *different* English titles: *Being There* became *Welcome, Mr. Chance.* Or an original English title is supplemented by a German addition: *The Fog* becomes: *The Fog: Der Nebel des Grauen* (The fog of horror).

7. The use of the term "dialect" apparently dates back to the early colonial era, when it was assumed that verbal communication systems unaccompanied by extensive written literature were somehow unworthy of the term "language." Thus, Europe speaks languages while Africa, for example, speaks "dialects." In fact, a country like Nigeria speaks hundreds of *languages*, i.e. fully developed linguistic systems which, unlike dialects, are not mutually intelligible.

8. A study of the relation between sexual difference and language difference in the cinema would necessarily touch on the play of gender in films whose diegesis features multiple languages (e.g. the association of Catherine in *Jules and Jim* with the German neuter and androgyny); and the implications for film of the fact that different languages "see" gender differently.

9. For Memmi on colonial bilingualism, see *The Colonizer and the Colonized* (Boston: Beacon Press, 1967).

10. See Edward Said, *Orientalism* (New York: Pantheon, 1978), 142.

11. Ibid., 177–78.

12. Ibid., 142.

13. Stanley Donen's *Blame It on Rio* continues this tradition of Hispanicising Brazilian names.

14. Israel, interestingly, offers a similar phenomenon. Many members of the film milieu considered Hebrew as intrinscially noncinematic and an "obstacle" to "good" dialogue, implicitly suggesting a kind of shame about speaking a Semitic rather than a European language. The protagonist of a seventies TV series, *Hedva ve Ani* (Hedva and I) complained that it is impossible to say "Ani Ohev Otach" (Hebrew for "I love you") because unlike "I love you" or "Je t'aime," it is "ugly."

15. See "Entretien avec Raoul Ruiz," *Cahiers du Cinéma*, March 1983.

Vesuvius at Home: The Power of Emily Dickinson

ADRIENNE RICH

Rich's feminist essay not only locates Dickinson in specific time and space (note Rich's emphasis on the actual house and room) but uses that contextualization to revaluate, or re-vision, Dickinson. Rich discovers a powerful woman who survived by translating nineteenth-century patriarchal society into her own poetic terms. Speaking in her own voice, Rich acknowledges her inter-

Reprinted from "Vesuvius at Home: The Power of Emily Dickinson," in *On Lies, Secrets, and Silence: Selected Prose, 1966–1978*, by Adrienne Rich, by permission of the author and the publisher, W. W. Norton & Company, Inc. Copyright © 1979 by W. W. Norton & Company, Inc.

est as a poet and as a woman in Dickinson. This stance typifies the feminist position that since there is no such thing as complete objectivity and all criticism is value-laden, critics should be forthright about their own interests and values.

I AM TRAVELING at the speed of time, along the Massachusetts Turnpike. For months, for years, for most of my life, I have been hovering like an insect against the screens of an existence which inhabited Amherst, Massachusetts, between 1830 and 1886. The methods, the exclusions, of Emily Dickinson's existence could not have been my own; yet more and more, as a woman poet finding my own methods, I have come to understand her necessities, could have been witness in her defense.

"Home is not where the heart is," she wrote in a letter, "but the house and the adjacent buildings." A statement of New England realism, a directive to be followed. Probably no poet ever lived so much and so purposefully in one house; even, in one room. Her niece Martha told of visiting her in her corner bedroom on the second floor at 280 Main Street, Amherst, and of how Emily Dickinson made as if to lock the door with an imaginary key, turned and said: "Matty: here's freedom."

I am traveling at the speed of time, in the direction of the house and buildings.

Western Massachusetts: the Connecticut Valley: a countryside still full of reverberations: scene of Indian uprisings, religious revivals, spiritual confrontations, the blazing-up of the lunatic fringe of the Puritan coal. How peaceful and how threatened it looks from Route 91, hills gently curled above the plain, the tobacco-barns standing in fields sheltered with white gauze from the sun, and the sudden urban sprawl: ARCO, MacDonald's, shopping plazas. The country that broke the heart of Jonathan Edwards, that enclosed the genius of Emily Dickinson. It lies calmly in the light of May, cloudy skies breaking into warm sunshine, light-green spring softening the hills, dogwood and wild fruit-trees blossoming in the hollows.

From Northampton bypass there's a four-mile stretch of road to Amherst—Route 9—between fruit farms, steakhouses, supermarkets. The new University of Massachusetts rears its skyscrapers up from the plain against the Pelham Hills. There is new money here, real estate, motels. Amherst succeeds on Hadley almost without notice. Amherst is green, rich-looking, secure; we're suddenly in the center of town, the crossroads of the campus, old New England college buildings spread around two village greens, a scene I remember as almost exactly the same in the dim past of my undergraduate years when I used to come there for college weekends.

Left on Seelye Street, right on Main; driveway at the end of a yellow picket fence. I recognize the high hedge of cedars screening the house, because twenty-five years ago I walked there, even then drawn toward the spot, trying to peer over. I pull into the driveway behind a generous nineteenth-century brick mansion with wings and porches, old trees and green lawns. I ring at the back door—the door through which Dickinson's coffin was carried to the cemetery a block away.

For years I have been not so much envisioning Emily Dickinson as trying to visit, to enter her mind, through her poems and letters, and through my own intimations of what it could have meant to be one of the two mid-nineteenth-century American geniuses, and a woman, living in Amherst, Massachusetts. Of the other genius, Walt Whitman, Dickinson wrote that she had heard his poems were "disgraceful." She knew her own were unacceptable by her world's standards of poetic convention, and of what was appropriate, in particular, for a woman poet. Seven were published in her lifetime, all edited by other hands; more than a thousand were laid away in her bedroom chest, to be discovered after her death. When her sister discovered them, there were decades of struggle over the manuscripts, the manner of their presentation to the world, their suitability for publication, the poet's own final intentions. Narrowed down by her early editors and anthologists, reduced to quaintness or spinsterish oddity by many of her commentators, sentimentalized, fallen-in-love-with like some gnomic Garbo, still unread in the breadth and depth of her full range of work, she was, and is, a wonder to me when I try to imagine myself into that mind.

I have a notion that genius knows itself; that Dickinson chose her seclusion, knowing she was exceptional and knowing what she needed. It was, moreover, no hermetic retreat, but a seclusion which included a wide range of people, of reading and correspondence. Her sister Vinnie said, "Emily is always looking for the rewarding person." And she found, at various periods, both women and men: her sister-in-law, Susan Gilbert, Amherst visitors and family friends such as Benjamin Newton, Charles Wadsworth, Samuel Bowles, editor of the Springfield *Republican* and his wife; her friends Kate Anthon and Helen Hunt Jackson, the distant but significant figures of Elizabeth Barrett, the Brontës, George Eliot. But she carefully selected her society and controlled the disposal of her time. Not only the "gentlewomen in plush" of Amherst were excluded; Emerson visited next door but she did not go to meet him; she did not travel or receive routine visits; she avoided strangers. Given her vocation, she was neither eccentric nor quaint; she was determined to survive, to use her powers, to practice necessary economies.

Suppose Jonathan Edwards had been born a woman; suppose William James, for that matter, had been born a woman? (The invalid seclusion of his sister Alice is suggestive.) Even from men, New England took its psychic toll; many of its geniuses seemed peculiar in one way or another, particularly along the lines of social intercourse. Hawthorne, until he married, took his meals in his bedroom, apart from the family. Thoreau insisted on the values both of solitude and of geographical restriction, boasting that "I have travelled much in Concord." Emily Dickinson—viewed by her bemused contemporary Thomas Higginson as "partially cracked," by the twentieth century as fey or pathological—has increasingly struck me as a practical woman, exercising her gift as she had to, making choices. I have come to imagine her as somehow too strong for her environment, a figure of powerful will, not at all frail or breathless, someone whose personal dimensions would be felt in a household. She was her father's favorite daughter though she professed being afraid of him. Her sister dedicated herself to the everyday domestic labors which would free Dickinson to write. (Dickinson herself baked the bread, made jellies and gingerbread, nursed her mother through a long illness, was a skilled horticulturalist who grew pomegranates, calla lilies, and other exotica in her New England greenhouse.)

Upstairs at last: I stand in the room which for Emily Dickinson was "freedom." The best bedroom in the house, a corner room, sunny, overlooking the main street of Amherst in front, the way to her brother Austin's house on the side. Here, at a small table with one drawer, she wrote most of her poems. Here she read Elizabeth Barrett's "Aurora Leigh," a woman poet's narrative poem of a woman poet's life; also George Eliot; Emerson; Carlyle; Shakespeare; Charlotte and Emily Brontë. Here I become, again, an insect, vibrating at the frames of windows, clinging to panes of glass, trying to connect. The scent here is very powerful. Here in this white-curtained, high-ceilinged room, a redhaired woman with hazel eyes and a contralto voice wrote poems about volcanoes, deserts, eternity, suicide, physical passion, wild beasts, rape, power, madness, separation, the daemon, the grave. Here, with a darning-needle, she bound these poems—heavily emended and often in variant versions—into booklets, secured with darning-thread, to be found and read after her death. Here she knew "freedom," listening from above-stairs to a visitor's piano-playing, escaping from the pantry where she was mistress of the household bread and puddings, watching, you feel, watching ceaselessly, the life of sober Main Street below. From this room she glided downstairs, her hand on the polished banister, to meet the complacent magazine editor, Thomas Higginson, unnerve him while claiming she herself was unnerved. "Your scholar," she signed herself in letters to him. But she was an independent scholar, used his criticism selectively, saw him rarely and always on *her* premises. It was a life deliberately organized on her terms. The terms she had been handed by society—Calvinist Protestantism, Romanticism, the nineteenth-century corseting of women's bodies, choices, and sexuality—could spell insanity to a woman genius. What this one had to do was retranslate her own unorthodox, subversive, sometimes volcanic propensities into a dialect called metaphor: her native language. "Tell all the Truth—but tell it Slant—." It is always what is under pressure in us, especially under pressure of concealment—that explodes in poetry.

The women and men in her life she equally converted into metaphor. The masculine pronoun in her poems can refer simultaneously to many aspects of the "masculine" in the patriarchal world—the god she engages in dialogue, again on *her* terms; her own creative powers, unsexing for a woman, the male power-figures in her immediate environment—the laywer Edward Dickinson, her brother Austin, the preacher Wadsworth, the editor Bowles—it is far too limiting to trace that "He" to some specific lover, although that was the chief obsession of the legend-mongers for more than half a century. Obviously, Dickinson was attracted by and interested in men whose minds had something to offer her; she was, it is by now clear, equally attracted by and interested in women whose minds had something to offer her. There are many poems to and about women, and some which exist in two versions with alternate sets of pronouns. Her latest biographer, Richard Sewall, while rejecting an earlier Freudian biographer's theory that Dickinson was essentially a psycho-pathological case, the by-product of which happened to be poetry, does create a context in which the importance, and validity, of Dickinson's attachments to women may now, at last, be seen in full. She was always stirred by the existences of women like George Eliot or Elizabeth Barrett, who possessed strength of mind, articulateness, and energy. (She once characterized Elizabeth Fry and Florence Nightingale as "holy"—one suspects she merely meant, "great.")

But of course Dickinson's relationships with women were more than intellectual. They were deeply charged, and the sources both of passionate joy and pain. We are only beginning to be able to consider them in a social and historical context. The historian Carroll Smith-Rosenberg has shown that there was far less taboo on intense, even passionate and sensual, relationships between women in the American nineteenth-century "female world of love and ritual," as she terms it, than there was later in the twentieth century. Women expressed their attachments to other women both physically and verbally; a marriage did not dilute the strength of a female friendship, in which two women often shared the same bed during long visits, and wrote letters articulate with both physical and emotional longing. The nineteenth-century close woman friend, according to the many diaries and letters Smith-Rosenberg has studied, might be a far more important figure in a woman's life than the nineteenth-century husband. None of this was condemned as "lesbianism."[1] We will understand Emily Dickinson better, read her poetry more perceptively, when the Freudian imputation of scandal and aberrance in women's love for women has been supplanted by a more informed, less misogynistic attitude toward women's experiences with each other.

But who, if you read through the seventeen hundred and seventy-five poems—who—woman or man—could have passed through that imagination and not come out transmuted? Given the space created by her in that corner room, with its window-light, its potted plants and work-table, given that personality, capable of imposing its terms on a household, on a whole community, what single theory could hope to contain her, when she'd put it all together in that space?

"Matty: here's freedom," I hear her saying as I speed back to Boston along Route 91, as I slip the turnpike ticket into the toll-collector's hand. I am thinking of a confined space in which the genius of the nineteenth-century female mind in America moved, inventing a language more varied, more compressed, more dense with implications, more complex of syntax, than any American poetic language to date; in the trail of that genius my mind has been moving, and with its langauge and images my mind still has to reckon, as the mind of a woman poet in America today. . . .

Much energy has been invested in trying to identify a concrete, flesh-and-blood male lover whom Dickinson is supposed to have renounced, and to the loss of whom can be traced the secret of her seclusion and the vein of much of her poetry. But the real question, given that the art of poetry is an art of transformation, is how this woman's mind and imagination may have used the masculine element in the world at large, or those elements personified as masculine—including the men she knew; how her relationship to this reveals itself in her images and language. In a patriarchal culture, specifically the Judeo-Christian, quasi-Puritan culture of nineteenth-century New England in which Dickinson grew up, still inflamed with religious revivals, and where the sermon was still an active, if perishing, literary form, the equation of divinity with maleness was so fundamental that it is hardly surprising to find Dickinson, like many an early mystic, blurring erotic with religious experience and imagery. The poem [#315, "He fumbles at your Soul"] has intimations of both seduction and rape merged with the intense force of a religious experience. But are these metaphors for each other, or for something more intrinsic to Dickinson? Here is another:

He put the Belt around my Life—
I heard the buckle snap—
And turned away, imperial,
My lifetime folding up—
Deliberate, as a Duke would do
A Kingdom's Title Deed
Henceforth, a Dedicated sort—
Member of the Cloud.

Yet not too far to come at call—
And do the little Toils
That make the Circuit of the Rest—
And deal occasional smiles
To lives that stoop to notice mine—
And kindly ask it in—
Whose invitation, know you not
For Whom I must decline?

(#273)

These two poems are about possession, and they seem to me a poet's poems—that is, they are about the poet's relationship to her own power, which is exteriorized in masculine form, much as masculine poets have invoked the female Muse. In writing at all—particularly an unorthodox and original poetry like Dickinson's—women have often felt in danger of losing their status as women. And this status has always been defined in terms of relationship to men—as daughter, sister, bride, wife, mother, mistress, Muse. Since the most powerful figures in patriarchal culture have been men, it seems natural that Dickinson would assign a masculine gender to that in herself which did not fit in with the conventional ideology of womanliness. To recognize and acknowledge our own interior power has always been a path mined with risks for women; to acknowledge that power and commit oneself to it as Emily Dickinson did was an immense decision.

Most of us, unfortunately, have been exposed in the schoolroom to Dickinson's "little-girl" poems, her kittenish tones, as in "I'm Nobody! Who Are You?" (a poem whose underlying anger translates itself into archness) or

I hope the Father in the skies
Will lift his little girl—
Old fashioned—naughty—everything
Over the stile of "Pearl."

(#70)

or the poems about bees and robins. One critic—Richard Chase—has noted that in the nineteenth century "one of the careers open to women was perpetual childhood." A strain in Dickinson's letters and some—though by far a minority—of her poems was a self-diminutization, almost as if to offset and deny—or even disguise—her actual dimensions as she must have experienced them. And this emphasis on her own "littleness," along with the deliberate strangeness of her tactics of seclusion, have been, until recently, accepted as the prevailing character of the poet: the fragile poetess in white, sending flowers and poems by messenger to unseen friends, letting down baskets of gingerbread to the neighborhood children from her bedroom window; writing, but somehow naively. John Crowe Ransom, arguing for the editing and standardization of Dickinson's punctuation and typography, calls her "a little home-keeping person" who, "while she had a proper notion of the final destiny of her poems . . . was not one of those poets who had advanced to that later stage of operations where manuscripts are prepared for the printer, and the poet's diction has to make concessions to the publisher's style-book." (In short, Emily Dickinson did not wholly know her trade, and Ransom believes a "publisher's style-book" to have that last word on poetic diction.) He goes on to print several of her poems, altered by him "with all possible forbearance." What might, in a male writer—a Tho-

reau, let us say, or a Christopher Smart or William Blake—seem a legitimate strangeness, a unique intention, has been in one of our two major
poets devalued into a kind of naiveté, girlish ignorance, feminine lack of
professionalism, just as the poet herself has been made into a sentimental object. ("Most of us are half in love with this dead girl," confesses Ar-
chibald MacLeish. Dickinson was fifty-five when she died.)

It is true that more recent critics, including her most recent biographer, have gradually begun to approach the poet in terms of her
greatness rather than her littleness, the decisiveness of her choices
instead of the surface oddities of her life or the romantic crises of her
legend. But unfortunately anthologists continue to plagiarize other anthologies, to reprint her in edited, even bowdlerized versions; the popular image of her and of her work lags behind the changing consciousness
of scholars and specialists. There still does not exist a selection from her
poems which depicts her in her fullest range. Dickinson's greatness cannot be measured in terms of twenty-five or fifty or even five hundred
"perfect" lyrics; it has to be seen as the accumulation it is. Poets, even, are
not always acquainted with the full dimensions of her work, or the sense
one gets, reading in the one-volume complete edition (let alone the
three-volume variorum edition) of a mind engaged in a lifetime's musing
on essential problems of language, identity, separation, relationship, the
integrity of the self; a mind capable of describing psychological states
more accurately than any poet except Shakespeare. I have been surprised at how narrowly her work, still, is known by women who are writing poetry, how much her legend has gotten in the way of her being
re-possessed, as a source and a foremother.

I know that for me, reading her poems as a child and then as a
young girl already seriously writing poetry, she was a problematic figure.
I first read her in the selection heavily edited by her niece which appeared in 1937; a later and fuller edition appeared in 1945 when I was
sixteen, and the complete, unbowdlerized edition by Johnson did not appear until fifteen years later. The publication of each of these editions
was crucial to me in successive decades of my life. More than any other
poet, Emily Dickinson seemed to tell me that the intense inner event, the
personal and psychological, was inseparable from the universal; that
there was a range for psychological poetry beyond mere self-expression.
Yet the legend of the life was troubling, because it seemed to whisper that
a woman who undertook such explorations must pay with renunciation,
isolation, and incorporeality. With the publication of the *Complete Poems*,
the legend seemed to recede into unimportance beside the unquestion-
able power and importance of the mind revealed there. But taking possession of Emily Dickinson is still no simple matter.

The 1945 edition, entitled *Bolts of Melody*, took its title from a poem
which struck me at the age of sixteen and which still, thirty years later,
arrests my imagination:

I would not paint—a picture—
I'd rather be the One
Its bright impossibility
To dwell—delicious—on—
And wonder how the fingers feel
Whose rare—celestial—stir
Evokes so sweet a Torment—
Such sumptuous—Despair—

I would not talk, like Cornets—
I'd rather be the One
Raised softly to the Ceilings—
And out, and easy on—
Through Villages of Ether
Myself endured Balloon
By but a lip of Metal
The pier to my Pontoon—

Nor would I be a Poet—
It's finer—own the Ear—
Enamored—impotent—content—
The License to revere,
A privilege so awful
What would the Dower be,
Had I the Art to stun myself
With Bolts of Melody!

(#505)

This poem is about choosing an orthodox "feminine" role: the receptive rather than the creative; viewer rather than painter; listener rather than musician; acted-upon rather than active. Yet even while ostensibly choosing this role she wonders "how the fingers feel / Whose rare—celestial—stir / Evokes so sweet a Torment—" and the "feminine" role is praised in a curious sequence of adjectives: "Enamored—*impotent*—content—." The strange paradox of this poem—its exquisite irony—is that it is about choosing not to be a poet, a poem which is gainsaid by no fewer than one thousand seven hundred and seventy-five poems made during the writer's life, including itself. Moreover, the images of the poem rise to a climax (like the Balloon she evokes) but the climax happens as she describes, not what it is to be the receiver, but the maker and receiver at once: "A privilege so awful / What would the Dower be, / Had I the Art to stun myself / With Bolts of Melody!"—a climax which recalls the poem: "He fumbles at your soul / As Players at the Keys / Before they drop full Music on—." And of course, in writing those lines she possesses herself of that privilege and that "dower." I have said that this is a poem of exquisite ironies. It is, indeed, though in a very different mode, related to Dickinson's "little-girl" strategy. The woman who feels herself to be Vesuvius at home has need of a mask, at least, of innocuousness and of containment.

> On my volcano grows the Grass
> A meditative spot—
> An acre for a Bird to choose
> Would be the General thought—
>
> How red the Fire rocks below—
> How insecure the sod
> Did I disclose
> Would populate with awe my solitude.

(#1677)

Power, even masked, can still be perceived as destructive.

> A still—Volcano—Life—
> That flickered in the night—
> When it was dark enough to do
> Without erasing sight—
>
> A quiet—Earthquake style—
> Too subtle to suspect
> By natures this side Naples—
> The North cannot detect
>
> The Solemn—Torrid—Symbol—
> The lips that never lie—
> Whose hissing Corals part—and shut—
> And Cities—ooze away—

(#601)

Dickinson's biographer and editor Thomas Johnson has said that she often felt herself possessed by a demonic force, particularly in the years 1861 and 1862 when she was writing at the height of her drive. There are many poems besides "He put the Belt around my Life" which could be read as poems of possession by the daemon—poems which can also be, and have been, read, as poems of possession by the deity, or by a human lover. I suggest that a woman's poetry about her relationship to her daemon—her own active, creative power—has in patriarchal culture used the language of heterosexual love or patriarchal theology. Ted Hughes tells us that

> the eruption of [Dickinson's] imagination and poetry followed when she shifted her passion, with the energy of desperation, from [the] lost man onto his only possible substitute,—the Universe in its Divine aspect. . . . Thereafter, the marriage that had been denied in the real world, went forward in the spiritual . . . just as the Universe in its Divine aspect became the mirror-image of her "husband," so the whole religious di-

lemma of New England, at that most critical moment in its history, became the mirror-image of her relationship to him, of her "marriage" in fact.[2]

This seems to me to miss the point on a grand scale. There are facts we need to look at. First, Emily Dickinson did not marry. And her non-marrying was neither a pathological retreat as John Cody sees it, nor probably even a conscious decision; it was a fact in her life as in her contemporary Christina Rossetti's; both women had more primary needs. Second: unlike Rossetti, Dickinson did not become a religiously dedicated woman; she was heretical, heterodox, in her religious opinions, and stayed away from church and dogma. What, in fact, *did* she allow to "put the Belt around her Life"—what *did* wholly occupy her mature years and possess her? For "Whom" did she decline the invitations of other lives? The writing of poetry. Nearly two thousand poems. Three hundred and sixty-five poems in the year of her fullest power. What was it like to be writing poetry you knew (and I am sure she did know) was of a class by itself—to be fueled by the energy it took first to confront, then to condense that range of psychic experience into that language; then to copy out the poems and lay them in a trunk, or send a few here and there to friends or relatives as occasional verse or as gestures of confidence? I am sure she knew who she was, as she indicates in this poem:

Myself was formed—a carpenter—
An unpretending time
My Plane—and I, together wrought
Before a Builder came—

To measure our attainments
Had we the Art of Boards
Sufficiently developed—He'd hire us
At Halves—

My Tools took Human—Faces—
The Bench, where we had toiled—
Against the Man—persuaded—
We—Temples Build—I said—

(#488)

This is a poem of the great year 1862, the year in which she first sent a few poems to Thomas Higginson for criticism. Whether it antedates or postdates that occasion is unimportant; it is a poem of knowing one's measure, regardless of the judgments of others. . . .

There is one poem which is the real "onlie begetter" of my thoughts here about Dickinson; a poem I have mused over, repeated to myself, taken into myself over many years. I think it is a poem about possession by the daemon, about the dangers and risks of such possession if you are

257

a woman, about the knowledge that power in a woman can seem destructive, and that you cannot live without the daemon once it has possessed you. The archetype of the daemon as masculine is beginning to change, but it has been real for women up until now. But this woman poet also perceives herself as a lethal weapon:

> My Life had stood—a Loaded Gun—
> In Corners—till a Day
> The Owner passed—identified—
> And carried Me away—
>
> And now We roam in Sovereign Woods—
> And now We hunt the Doe—
> And every time I speak for Him—
> The Mountains straight reply—
>
> And do I smile, such cordial light
> Upon the Valley glow—
> It is as a Vesuvian face
> Had let its pleasure through—
>
> And when at Night—Our good Day done—
> I guard My Master's Head—
> 'Tis better than the Eider-Duck's
> Deep Pillow—to have shared—
>
> To foe of His—I'm deadly foe—
> None stir the second time—
> On whom I lay a Yellow Eye—
> Or an emphatic Thumb—
>
> Though I than He—may longer live
> He longer must—than I—
> For I have but the power to kill,
> Without—the power to die—

(#754)

Here the poet sees herself as split, not between anything so simple as "masculine" and "feminine" identity but between the hunter, admittedly masculine, but also a human person, an active, willing being, and the gun—an object, condemned to remain inactive until the hunter—the *owner*—takes possession of it. The gun contains an energy capable of rousing echoes in the mountains and lighting up the valleys; it is also deadly, "Vesuvian"; it is also its owner's defender against the "foe." It is the gun, furthermore, who *speaks for him.* If there is a female consciousness in this poem it is buried deeper than the images: it exists in the ambivalence toward power, which is extreme. Active willing and creation in women are forms of aggression, and agression is both "the power to kill" and punishable by death. The union of gun with hunter embodies the danger of identifying and taking hold of her forces, not least that in so doing she risks defining herself—and being defined—as aggressive, as unwomanly ("and now We hunt the Doe"), and as potentially lethal. That which she experiences in herself as energy and potency can also be experienced as pure destruction. The final stanza, with its precarious balance of phrasing, seems a desperate attempt to resolve the ambivalence; but, I think, it is no resolution, only a further extension of ambivalence.

> Though I than He—may longer live
> He longer must—than I—
> For I have but the power to kill,
> Without—the power to die—

The poet experiences herself as loaded gun, imperious energy; yet without the Owner, the possessor, she is merely lethal. Should that possession abandon her—but the thought is unthinkable: "He longer *must*—than I." The pronoun is masculine; the antecedent is what Keats called "The Genius of Poetry."

I do not pretend to have—I don't even wish to have—explained this poem, accounted for its every image; it will reverberate with new tones long after my words about it have ceased to matter. But I think that for us, at this time, it is a central poem in understanding Emily Dickinson, and ourselves, and the condition of the woman artist, particularly in the nineteenth century. It seems likely that the nineteenth-century woman poet, especially, felt the medium of poetry as dangerous, in ways that the woman novelist did not feel the medium of fiction to be. In writing even such a novel of elemental sexuality and anger as *Wuthering Heights,* Emily Brontë could at least theoretically separate herself from her characters; they were, after all, fictitious beings. Moreover, the novel is or can be a construct, planned and organized to deal with human experiences on one level at a time. Poetry is too much rooted in the unconscious; it presses too close against the barriers of repression; and the nineteenth-century woman had much to repress. It is interesting that Elizabeth Barrett tried to fuse poetry and fiction in writing "Aurora Leigh"—perhaps apprehending the need for fictional characters to carry the charge of her experience as a woman artist. But with the exception of "Aurora Leigh" and Christina Rossetti's "Goblin Market"—that extraordinary and little-known poem drenched in oral eroticism—Emily Dickinson's is the only poetry in English by a woman of that century which pierces so far beyond the ideology of the "feminine" and the conventions of womanly feeling. To write it at all, she had to be willing to enter chambers of the self in which

> Ourself behind ourself, concealed—
> Should startle most—

and to relinquish control there, to take those risks, she had to create a relationship to the outer world where she could feel in control. . . .

NOTES

1. Carroll Smith-Rosenberg, "The Female World of Love and Ritual: Relations Between Women in 19th Century America." *Signs: Journal of Women in Culture and Society* 1 (1975).

2. *A Choice of Emily Dickinson's Verse,* ed. Ted Hughes (London: Faber & Faber, 1969), 11.

Women Beware Science: "The Birthmark"

JUDITH FETTERLEY

In *The Resisting Reader,* Fetterley asserts that American literature is male and calls for a feminist rereading of our literary canon. She argues that our traditional literature reflects the values of a patriarchal society which include misogyny ("the quintessential American experience is betrayal by a woman") and certain sexist assumptions about power (man = human = universal; women = other). She writes, "To be male, to be universal, to be American—is to be not female." As a result, women are excluded from a positive reading experience and instead internalize self-doubt and self-hatred. To counter this, and so empower female consciousness, Fetterley urges women to become "resisting" readers.

Fetterley asserts that on one level "The Birthmark" is a study of sexual politics: it exposes the mechanics whereby patriarchal society disguises hatred as love, neurosis as science, murder as idealization, and success as failure. It is about a man's desire to perfect himself, an idealization that leads to his wife's death. Feminists suggest that one way to test for sexism is by reversing male-female roles. As Fetterley points out, we cannot imagine "The Birthmark" in reverse.

THE SCIENTIST AYLMER IN Nathaniel Hawthorne's "The Birthmark" provides another stage in the psychological history of the American protagonist. Aylmer is Irving's Rip and Anderson's boy discovered in that

From *The Resisting Reader: A Feminist Approach to American Fiction,* by Judith Fetterley (Bloomington and London: Indiana University Press, 1978). Copyright 1978 by Judith Fetterley. Reprinted by permission.

middle age which Rip evades and the boy rejects. Aylmer is squarely confronted with the realities of marriage, sex, and women. There are compensations, however, for as an adult he has access to a complex set of mechanisms for accomplishing the great American dream of eliminating women. It is testimony at once to Hawthorne's ambivalence, his seeking to cover with one hand what he uncovers with the other; and to the pervasive sexism of our culture that most readers would describe "The Birthmark" as a story of failure rather than as the success story it really is—the demonstration of how to murder your wife and get away with it. It is, of course, possible to read "The Birthmark" as a story of misguided idealism, a tale of the unhappy consequences of man's nevertheless worthy passion for perfecting and transcending nature; and this is the reading usually given it.[1] This reading, however, ignores the significance of the form idealism takes in the story. It is not irrelevant that "The Birthmark" is about a man's desire to perfect his wife, nor is it accidental that the consequence of this idealism is the wife's death. In fact, "The Birthmark" provides a brilliant analysis of the sexual politics of idealization and a brilliant exposure of the mechanisms whereby hatred can be disguised as love, neurosis can be disguised as science, murder can be disguised as idealization, and success can be disguised as failure. Thus, Hawthorne's insistence in his story on the metaphor of disguise serves as both warning and clue to a feminist reading.

Even a brief outline is suggestive. A man, dedicated to the pursuit of science, puts aside his passion in order to marry a beautiful woman. Shortly after the marriage he discovers that he is deeply troubled by a tiny birthmark on her left cheek. Of negligible importance to him before marriage, the birthmark now assumes the proportions of an obsession. He reads it as a sign of the inevitable imperfection of all things in nature and sees in it a challenge to man's ability to transcend nature. So nearly perfect as she is, he would have her be completely perfect. In pursuit of this lofty aim, he secludes her in chambers that he has converted for the purpose, subjects her to a series of influences, and finally presents her with a potion which, as she drinks it, removes at last the hated birthmark but kills her in the process. At the end of the story Georgiana is both perfect and dead.

One cannot imagine this story in reverse—that is, a woman's discovering an obsessive need to perfect her husband and deciding to perform experiments on him—nor can one imagine the story being about a man's conceiving such an obsession for another man. It is woman, and specifically woman as wife, who elicits the obsession with imperfection and the compulsion to achieve perfection, just as it is man, and specifically man as husband, who is thus obsessed and compelled. In addition, it is clear from the summary that the imagined perfection is purely physical. Aylmer is not concerned with the quality of Georgiana's character or with the state of her soul, for he considers her "fit for heaven without tasting death." Rather, he is absorbed in her physical appearance, and perfection for him is equivalent to physical beauty. Georgiana is an exemplum of woman as beautiful object, reduced to and defined by her body. And finally, the conjunction of perfection and nonexistence, while reminding us of Anderson's story in which the good girl is the one you never see, develops what is only implicit in that story: namely, that the only good woman is a dead one and that the motive underlying the desire to perfect is the need to eliminate. "The Birthmark" demonstrates the fact that the idealization of women has its source in a profound hostility toward women and that it is at once a disguise for this hostility and the fullest expression of it.

The emotion that generates the drama of "The Birthmark" is revulsion. Aylmer is moved not by the vision of Georgiana's potential perfection but by his horror at her present condition. His revulsion for the birthmark is insistent: he can't bear to see it or touch it; he has nightmares about it; he has to get it out. Until she is "fixed," he can hardly bear the sight of her and must hide her away in secluded chambers which he visits only intermittently, so great is his fear of contamination. Aylmer's compulsion to perfect Georgiana is a result of his horrified perception of what she actually is, and all his lofty talk about wanting her to be perfect so that just this once the potential of Nature will be fulfilled is but a cover for his central emotion of revulsion. But Aylmer is a creature of disguise and illusion. In order to persuade this beautiful woman to become his wife, he "left his laboratory to the care of an assistant, cleared his fine countenance from the furnace smoke, washed the stains of acid from his fingers." Best not to let her know who he really is or what he really feels, lest she might say before the marriage instead of after, "You cannot love what shocks you!" In the chambers where Aylmer secludes Georgiana, "airy figures, absolutely bodiless ideas, and forms of unsubstantial beauty" come disguised as substance in an illusion so nearly perfect as to "warrant the belief that her husband possessed sway over the spiritual world." While Aylmer does not really possess sway over the spiritual world, he certainly controls Georgiana and he does so in great part because of his mastery of the art of illusion.

If the motive force for Aylmer's action in the story is repulsion, it is the birthmark that is the symbolic location of all that repels him. And it is important that the birthmark is just that: a birth *mark*, that is, something physical; and a *birth* mark, that is, something not acquired but inherent, one of Georgiana's givens, in fact equivalent to her.[2] The close connection between Georgiana and her birthmark is continually emphasized. As her emotions change, so does the birthmark, fading or deepening in response to her feelings and providing a precise clue to her state of mind. Similarly, when her senses are aroused, stroked by the influences that pervade her chamber, the birthmark throbs sympathetically. In his efforts to get rid of the birthmark Aylmer has "administered agents powerful enough to do aught except change your entire physical system," and these have failed. The object of Aylmer's obsessive revulsion, then, is Georgiana's "physical system," and what defines this particular system is the fact that it is female. It is Georgiana's female physiology, which is to say her sexuality, that is the object of Aylmer's relentless attack. The link between Georgiana's birthmark and her sexuality is implicit in the birthmark's role as her emotional barometer, but one specific characteristic of the birthmark makes the connection explicit: the hand which shaped Georgiana's birth has left its mark on her in *blood*. The birthmark is redolent with references to the particular nature of female sexuality; we hardly need Aylmer's insistence on seclusion, with its reminiscences of the treatment of women when they are "unclean," to point us in this direction. What repels Aylmer is Georgiana's sexuality; what is imperfect in her is the fact that she is female; and what perfection means is elimination.

In Hawthorne's analysis the idealization of women stems from a vision of them as hideous and unnatural; it is a form of compensation, an attempt to bring them up to the level of nature. To symbolize female physiology as a blemish, a deformity, a birthmark suggests that women are in need of some such redemption. Indeed, "The Birthmark" is a parable of woman's relation to the cult of female beauty, a cult whose political function is to remind women that they are, in their natural state, unacceptable, imperfect, monstrous. Una Stannard in "The Mask of Beauty" has done a brilliant job of analyzing the implications of this cult:

> Every day, in every way, the billion-dollar beauty business tells women they are monsters in disguise. Every ad for bras tells a woman that her breasts need lifting, every ad for padded bras that what she's got isn't big enough, every ad for girdles that her belly sags and her hips are too wide, every ad for high heels that her legs need propping, every ad for cosmetics that her skin is too dry, too oily, too pale, or too ruddy, or her lips are not bright enough, or her lashes not long enough, every ad for deodorants and perfumes that her natural odors all need disguising, every ad for hair dye, curlers, and permanents that the hair she was born with is the wrong color or too straight or too curly, and lately ads for wigs tell her that she would be better off covering up nature's mistake completely. In this culture women are told they are the fair sex, but at the same time that their "beauty" needs lifting, shaping, dyeing, painting, curling, padding. Women are really being told that "the beauty" is a beast.[3]

The dynamics of idealization are beautifully contained in an analogy which Hawthorne, in typical fashion, remarks on casually: "But it would be as reasonable to say that one of those small blue stains which some-times occur in the purest statuary marble would convert the Eve of Pow-ers to a monster." This comparison, despite its apparent protest against just such a conclusion, implies that where women are concerned it doesn't take much to convert purity into monstrosity; Eve herself is a classic ex-ample of the ease with which such a transition can occur. And the transi-tion is easy because the presentation of woman's image in marble is essentially an attempt to disguise and cover a monstrous reality. Thus, the slightest flaw will have an immense effect, for it serves as a reminder of the reality that produces the continual need to cast Eve in the form of purest marble and women in the molds of idealization.

IN EXPLORING THE SOURCES of men's compulsion to idealize women Hawthorne is writing a story about the sickness of men, not a story about the flawed and imperfect nature of women. There is a hint of the nature of Aylmer's ailment in the description of his relation to "mother" Nature, a suggestion that his revulsion for Georgiana has its root in part in a jeal-ousy of the power which her sexuality represents and a frustration in the face of its impenetrable mystery. Aylmer's scientific aspirations have as their ultimate goal the desire to create human life, but "the latter pur-suit, however, Aylmer had long laid aside in unwilling recognition of the truth—against which all seekers sooner or later stumble—that our great creative Mother, while she amuses us with apparently working in the broadest sunshine, is yet severely careful to keep her own secrets, and, in spite of her pretended openness, shows us nothing but results. She per-mits us, indeed, to mar, but seldom to mend, and, like a jealous patentee, on no account to make." This passage is striking for its undercurrent of jealousy, hostility, and frustration toward a specifically female force. In the vision of Nature as playing with man, deluding him into thinking he can acquire her power, and then at the last minute closing him off and allowing him only the role of one who mars, Hawthorne provides an-other version of woman as enemy, the force that interposes between man and the accomplishment of his deepest desires. Yet Hawthorne locates the source of this attitude in man's jealousy of woman's having something he does not and his rage at being excluded from participating in it.

Out of Aylmer's jealousy at feeling less than Nature and thus less than woman—for if Nature is woman, woman is also Nature and has, by virtue of her biology, a power he does not—comes his obsessional pro-gram for perfecting Georgiana. Believing he is less, he has to convince himself he is more: "and then, most beloved, what will be my triumph when I shall have corrected what Nature left imperfect in her fairest work! Even Pygmalion, when his sculptured woman assumed life, felt not greater ecstasy than mine will be." What a triumph indeed to upstage and outdo Nature and make himself superior to her. The function of the fantasy that underlies the myth of Pygmalion, as it underlies the myth of

Genesis (making Adam, in the words of Mary Daly, "the first among history's unmarried pregnant males"[4]), is obvious from the reality which it seeks to invert. Such myths are powerful image builders, salving man's injured ego by convincing him that he is not only equal to but better than woman, for he creates in spite of, against, and finally better than nature. Yet Aylmer's failure here is as certain as the failure of his other "experiments," for the sickness which he carries within him makes him able only to destroy, not to create.

If Georgiana is envied and hated because she represents what is different from Aylmer and reminds him of what he is not and cannot be, she is feared for her similarity to him and for the fact that she represents aspects of himself that he finds intolerable. Georgiana is as much a reminder to Aylmer of what he is as of what he is not. This apparently contradictory pattern of double-duty is understandable in the light of feminist analyses of female characters in literature, who frequently function this way. Mirrors for men, they serve to indicate the involutions of the male psyche with which literature is primarily concerned, and their characters and identities shift accordingly. They are projections, not people; and thus coherence of characterization is a concept that often makes sense only when applied to the male characters of a particular work. Hawthorne's tale is a classic example of the woman as mirror, for, despite Aylmer's belief that his response to Georgiana is an objective concern for the intellectual and spiritual problem she presents, it is obvious that his reacion to her is intensely subjective. "Shocks you, my husband?" queries Georgiana, thus neatly exposing his mask, for one is not shocked by objective perceptions. Indeed, Aylmer views Georgiana's existence as a personal insult and threat to him, which, of course, it is, because what he sees in her is that part of himself he cannot tolerate. By the desire she elicits in him to marry her and possess her birthmark, she forces him to confront his own earthiness and "imperfection."

But it is precisely to avoid such a confrontation that Aylmer has fled to the kingdom of science, where he can project himself as a "type of the spiritual element." Unlike Georgiana, in whom the physical and the spiritual are complexly intertwined, Aylmer is hopelessly alienated from himself. Through the figure of Aminadab, the shaggy creature of clay, Hawthorne presents sharply the image of Aylmer's alienation. Aminadab symbolizes that earthly, physical, erotic self that has been split off from Aylmer, that he refuses to recognize as part of himself, and that has become monstrous and grotesque as a result: "With his vast strength, his shaggy hair, his smoky aspect, and the indescribable earthiness that incrusted him, he seemed to represent man's physical nature; while Aylmer's slender figure, and pale, intellectual face, were no less apt a type of the spiritual element." Aminadab's allegorical function is obvious and so is his connection to Aylmer, for while Aylmer may project himself as objective, intellectual, and scientific and while he may pretend to be totally unrelated to the creature whom he keeps locked up in his dark room to do his dirty work, he cannot function without him. It is Aminadab, after all, who fires the furnace for Aylmer's experiments; physicality provides the energy for Aylmer's "science" just as revulsion generates his investment in idealization. Aylmer is, despite his pretenses to the contrary, a highly emotional man: his scientific interests tend suspiciously toward fires and volcanoes; he is given to intense emotional outbursts; and his obsession with his wife's birthmark is a feeling so profound as to disrupt his entire life. Unable to accept himself for what he is, Aylmer constructs a mythology of science and adopts the character of a scientist to disguise his true nature and to hide his real motives, from himself as well as others. As a consequence, he acquires a way of acting out these motives without in fact having to be aware of them. One might describe "The Birthmark" as an exposé of science because it demonstrates the ease with which science can be invoked to conceal highly subjective motives. "The Birthmark" is an exposure of the realities that underlie the scientist's posture of objectivity and rationality and the claims of science to operate in an amoral and value-free world. Pale Aylmer, the intellectual scientist, is a mask for the brutish, earthy, soot-smeared Aminadab, just as the mythology of scientific research and objectivity finally masks murder, disguising Georgiana's death as just one more experiment that failed.

HAWTHORNE'S ATTITUDE TOWARD MEN and their fantasies is more critical than either Irving's or Anderson's. One responds to Aylmer not with pity but with horror. For, unlike Irving and Anderson, Hawthorne has not omitted from his treatment of men an image of the consequences of their ailments for the women who are involved with them. The result of Aylmer's massive self-deception is to live in an unreal world, a world filled with illusions, semblances, and appearances, one which admits of no sunlight and makes no contact with anything outside itself and at whose center is a laboratory, the physical correlative of his utter solipsism. Nevertheless, Hawthorne makes it clear that Aylmer has got someone locked up in that laboratory with him. While "The Birthmark" is by no means explicitly feminist, since Hawthorne seems as eager to be misread and to conceal as he is to read and to reveal, still it is impossible to read his story without being aware that Georgiana is completely in Aylmer's power. For the subject is finally power. Aylmer is able to project himself onto Georgiana and to work out his obsession through her because as woman and as wife she is his possession and in his power; and because as man he has access to the language and structures of that science which provides the mechanisms for such a process and legitimizes it. In addition, since the power of definition and the authority to make those definitions stick is vested in men, Aylmer can endow his illusions with the weight of spiritual aspiration and universal truth.

The implicit feminism in "The Birthmark" is considerable. On one level the story is a study of sexual politics, of the powerlessness of women and of the psychology which results from that powerlessness. Hawthorne dramatizes the fact that woman's identity is a product of men's responses to her: "It must not be concealed, however, that the impression wrought by this fairy sign manual varied exceedingly, according to the difference of temperament in the beholders." To those who love Georgiana, her birthmark is evidence of her beauty; to those who envy or hate her, it is an object of disgust. It is Aylmer's repugnance for the birthmark that makes Georgiana blanch, thus causing the mark to emerge as a sharply-defined blemish against the whiteness of her cheek. Clearly, the birthmark takes on its character from the eye of the beholder. And just as clearly Georgiana's attitude toward her birthmark varies in response to different observers and definers. Her self-image derives from internalizing the attitudes toward her of the man or men around her. Since what surrounds Georgiana is an obsessional attraction expressed as a total revulsion, the result is not surprising: continual self-consciousness that leads to a pervasive sense of shame and a self-hatred that terminates in an utter readiness to be killed. "The Birthmark" demonstrates the consequences to women of being trapped in the laboratory of man's mind, the object of unrelenting scrutiny, examination, and experimentation.

In addition, "The Birthmark" reveals an implicit understanding of the consequences for women of a linguistic system in which the word "man" refers to both male people and all people. Because of the conventions of this system, Aylmer is able to equate his peculiarly male needs with the needs of all human beings, men and women. And since Aylmer can present his compulsion to idealize and perfect Georgiana as a human aspiration, Georgiana is forced to identify with it. Yet to identify with his aspiration is in fact to identify with his hatred of her and his need to eliminate her. Georgiana's situation is a fictional version of the experience that women undergo when they read a story like "Rip Van Winkle." Under the influence of Aylmer's mind, in the laboratory where she is subjected to his subliminal messages, Georgiana is co-opted into a view of herself as flawed and comes to hate herself as an impediment to Aylmer's aspiration; eventually she wishes to be dead rather than to remain alive as an irritant to him and as a reminder of his failure. And as she identifies with him in her attitude toward herself, so she comes to worship him for his hatred of her and for his refusal to tolerate her existence. The process of projection is neatly reversed: he locates in her everything he cannot accept in himself, and she attributes to him all that is good and then worships in him the image of her own humanity.

Through the system of sexual politics that is Aylmer's compensation for growing up, Hawthorne shows how men gain power over women, the power to create and kill, to "mar," "mend," and "make," without ever having to relinquish their image as "nice guys." Under such a system there need be very few power struggles, because women are programmed to deny the validity of their own perceptions and responses and to accept male illusions as truth. Georgiana does faint when she first enters Aylmer's laboratory and sees it for one second with her own eyes; she is also aware that Aylmer is filling her chamber with appearances, not realities; and she is finally aware that his scientific record is in his own terms one of continual failure. Yet so perfect is the program that she comes to respect him even more for these failures and to aspire to be yet another of them.

Hawthorne's unrelenting emphasis on "seems" and his complex use of the metaphors and structures of disguise imply that women are being deceived and destroyed by man's system. And perhaps the most vicious part of this system is its definition of what constitutes nobility in women: "Drink, then, thou lofty creature," exclaims Aylmer with "fervid admiration" as he hands Georgiana the cup that will kill her. Loftiness in women is directly equivalent to the willingness with which they die at the hands of their husbands, and since such loftiness is the only thing about Georgiana which does elicit admiration from Aylmer, it is no wonder she is willing. Georgiana plays well the one role allowed her, yet one might be justified in suggesting that Hawthorne grants her at the end a slight touch of the satisfaction of revenge: "'My poor Aylmer,' she repeated, with a more than human tenderness, you have aimed loftily; you have done nobly. Do not repent that with so high and pure a feeling, you have rejected the best the earth could offer.'" Since dying is the only option, best to make the most of it.

NOTES

1. See, for example, Cleanth Brooks and Robert Penn Warren, *Understanding Fiction* (New York: Appleton-Century-Crofts, 1943), 103–6 [reprinted, above, in Chapter 1]: "We are not, of course, to conceive of Aylmer as a monster, a man who would experiment on his own wife for his own greater glory. Hawthorne does not mean to suggest that Aylmer is depraved and heartless. . . . Aylmer has not realized that perfection is something never achieved on earth and in terms of mortality"; Richard Harter Fogle, *Hawthorne's Fiction: The Light and the Dark*, rev. ed. (Norman, Okla.: University of Oklahoma Press, 1964), 117–31; Robert Heilman, "Hawthorne's 'The Birthmark': Science as Religion," *South Atlantic Quarterly* 48 (1949): 575–83: "Aylmer, the overweening scientist, resembles less the villain than the tragic hero: in his catastrophic attempt to improve on human actuality there is not only pride and a deficient sense of reality but also disinterested aspiration"; F. O. Matthiessen, *American Renaissance* (New York: Oxford University Press, 1941), 253–55; Arlin Turner, *Nathaniel Hawthorne* (New York: Holt, Rinehart, and Winston, 1961), 88, 98, 132: "In 'The Birthmark' he applauded Aylmer's noble pursuit of perfection, in contrast to Aminadab's ready acceptance of earthiness, but Aylmer's achievement was tragic failure because he had not realized that perfection is not of this world." The major variation in

these readings occurs as a result of the degree to which individual critics see Hawthorne as critical of Aylmer. Still, those who see Hawthorne as critical locate the source of his criticism in Aylmer's idealistic pursuit of perfection—e.g., Millicent Bell, *Hawthorne's View of the Artist* (New York: State University of New York, 1962), 182–85: "Hawthorne, with his powerful Christian sense of the inextricable mixture of evil in the human compound, regards Aylmer as a dangerous perfectibilitarian"; William Bysshe Stein, *Hawthorne's Faust* (Gainesville: University of Florida Press, 1953), 91–92: "Thus the first of Hawthorne's Fausts, in a purely symbolic line of action sacrifices his soul to conquer nature, the universal force of which man is but a tool." Even Simon Lesser (*Fiction and the Unconscious* [1957; reprint, New York: Vintage-Random, 1962], 87–90 and 94–98) [see Chapter 6, below], who is clearly aware of the sexual implications of the story, subsumes his analysis under the reading of misguided idealism and in so doing provides a fine instance of phallic criticism in action:

> The ultimate purpose of Hawthorne's attempt to present Aylmer in balanced perspective is to quiet our fears so that the wishes which motivate his experiment, which are also urgent, can be given their opportunity. Aylmer's sincerity and idealism give us a sense of kinship with him. We see that the plan takes shape gradually in his mind, almost against his conscious intention. We are reassured by the fact that he loves Georgiana and feels confident that his attempt to remove the birthmark will succeed. Thus at the same time that we recoil we can identify with Aylmer and through him act out some of our secret desires. . . . The story not only gives expression to impulses which are ordinarily repressed; it gives them a sympathetic hearing—an opportunity to show whether they can be gratified without causing trouble or pain. There are obvious gains in being able to conduct tests of this kind with no more danger and no greater expenditure of effort than is involved in reading a story.

The one significant dissenting view is offered by Frederick C. Crews, *The Sins of the Fathers: Hawthorne's Psychological Themes* (New York: Oxford University Press, 1966), whose scattered comments on the story focus on the specific form of Aylmer's idealism and its implication for his secret motives.

2. In the conventional reading of the story Georgiana's birthmark is seen as the symbol of original sin—see, for example, Heilman, "Hawthorne's 'The Birthmark,'" 579; Bell, *Hawthorne's View of the Artist*, 185. But what this reading ignores are, of course, the implications of the fact that the symbol of original sin is female and that the story only "works" because men have the power to project that definition onto women.

3. Vivian Gornick and Barbara K. Moran, eds., *Women in Sexist Society: Studies in Power and Powerlessness* (New York: New American Library, 1971), 192.

4. Daly, *Beyond God the Father: Toward a Philosophy of Women's Liberation* (Boston: Beacon Press, 1973), 195. It is useful to compare Daly's analysis of "Male Mothers" with Mary Ellmann's discussion of the "imagined motherhood of the male" in *Thinking About Women* (New York: Harcourt Brace Jovanovich, 1968), 15ff. It is obvious that this myth is prevalent in patriarchal culture, and it would seem reasonable to suggest that the patterns of co-optation noticed in "Rip Van Winkle" and "I Want to Know Why" are minor manifestations of it. *An American Dream* provides a major manifestation, in fact a tour de force, of the myth of male motherhood.

A Rose for "A Rose for Emily"

JUDITH FETTERLEY

According to Fetterley, the grotesque genre is created when our "natural" expectations of gender are reversed. Thus, we are shocked because a "lady" turns out to be a necrophiliac and a murderer. Fetterley argues that Faulkner was deliberately writing a feminist story about sexual conflict and about the patriarchy of North and South.

In "A Rose for Emily" the grotesque reality implicit in Aylmer's idealization of Georgiana becomes explicit. Justifying Faulkner's use of the grotesque has been a major concern of critics who have written on the story. If, however, one approaches "A Rose for Emily" from a feminist perspective, one notices that the grotesque aspects of the story are a result of its violation of the expectations generated by the conventions of sexual politics. The ending shocks us not simply by its hint of necrophilia; more shocking is the fact that it is a woman who provides the hint. It is one thing for Poe to spend his nights in the tomb of Annabel Lee and another thing for Miss Emily Grierson to deposit a strand of iron-gray hair on the pillow beside the rotted corpse of Homer Barron. Further, we do not expect to discover that a woman has murdered a man. The conventions of sexual politics have familiarized us with the image of Georgiana nobly accepting death at her husband's hand. To reverse this "natural" pattern inevitably produces the grotesque.

Faulkner, however, is not interested in invoking the kind of grotesque which is the consequence of reversing the clichés of sexism for the sake of a cheap thrill; that is left to writers like Mickey Spillane. (Indeed, Spillane's ready willingness to capitalize on the shock value provided by the image of woman as killer in *I, the Jury*, suggests, by contrast, how little such a sexist gambit is Faulkner's intent.) Rather, Faulkner invokes the grotesque in order to illuminate and define the true nature of the conventions on which it depends. "A Rose for Emily" is a story not of a conflict between the South and the North or between the old order and the new; it is a story of the patriarchy North and South, new and old, and of the sexual conflict within it. As Faulkner himself has implied,[1] it is a story of a woman victimized and betrayed by the system of sexual politics, who nevertheless has discovered, within the structures that victimize her, sources of power for herself. If "The Birthmark" is the story of how to murder your wife and get away with it, "A Rose for Emily" is the story of

From *The Resisting Reader: A Feminist Approach to American Fiction*, by Judith Fetterley (Bloomington and London: Indiana University Press, 1978). Copyright 1978 by Judith Fetterley. Reprinted by permission.

how to murder your gentleman caller and get away with it. Faulkner's story is an analysis of how men's attitudes toward women turn back upon themselves; it is a demonstration of the thesis that it is impossible to oppress without in turn being oppressed, it is impossible to kill without creating the conditions for your own murder. "A Rose for Emily" is the story of a *lady* and of her revenge for that grotesque identity.

"When Miss Emily Grierson died, our whole town went to her funeral." The public and communal nature of Emily's funeral, a festival that brings the town together, clarifying its social relationships and revitalizing its sense of the past, indicates her central role in Jefferson. Alive, Emily is town property and the subject of shared speculation; dead, she is town history and the subject of legend. It is her value as a symbol, however obscure and however ambivalent, of something that is of central significance to the identity of Jefferson and to the meaning of its history that compels the narrator to assume a communal voice to tell her story. For Emily, like Georgiana, is a man-made object, a cultural artifact, and what she is reflects and defines the culture that has produced her.

The history the narrator relates to us reveals Jefferson's continuous emotional involvement with Emily. Indeed, though she shuts herself up in a house which she rarely leaves and which no one enters, her furious isolation is in direct proportion to the town's obsession with her. Like Georgiana, she is the object of incessant attention; her every act is immediately consumed by the town for gossip and seized on to justify their interference in her affairs. Her private life becomes a public document that the town folk feel free to interpret at will, and they are alternately curious, jealous, spiteful, pitying, partisan, proud, disapproving, admiring, and vindicated. Her funeral is not simply a communal ceremony; it is also the climax of their invasion of her private life and the logical extension of their voyeuristic attitude toward her. Despite the narrator's demurral, getting inside Emily's house is the all-consuming desire of the town's population, both male and female; while the men may wait a little longer, their motive is still prurient curiosity: "Already we knew that there was one room in that region above stairs which no one had seen in forty years, and which would have to be forced. They waited until Miss Emily was decently in the ground before they opened it."

In a context in which the overtones of violation and invasion are so palpable, the word "decently" has that ironic ring which gives the game away. When the men finally do break down the door, they find that Emily has satisfied their prurience with a vengeance and in doing so has created for them a mirror image of themselves. The true nature of Emily's relation to Jefferson is contained in the analogies between what those who break open that room see in it and what has brought them there to see it. The perverse, violent, and grotesque aspects of the sight of Homer Barron's rotted corpse in a room decked out for a bridal and now faded and covered in dust reflects back to them the perverseness of their

271

own prurient interest in Emily, the violence implicit in their continued invasions of her life, and the grotesqueness of the symbolic artifact they have made of her—their monument, their idol, their lady. Thus, the figure that Jefferson places at the center of its legendary history does indeed contain the clue to the meaning of that history—a history which began long before Emily's funeral and long before Homer Barron's disappearance or appearance and long before Colonel Sartoris' fathering of edicts and remittances. It is recorded in that emblem which lies at the heart of the town's memory and at the heart of patriarchal culture: "We had long thought of them as a tableau, Miss Emily a slender figure in white in the background, her father a spraddled silhouette in the foreground, his back to her and clutching a horsewhip, the two of them framed by the back-flung front door."

The importance of Emily's father in shaping the quality of her life is insistent throughout the story. Even in her death the force of his presence is felt; above her dead body sits "the crayon face of her father musing profoundly," symbolic of the degree to which he has dominated and shadowed her life, "as if that quality of her father which had thwarted her woman's life so many times had been too virulent and too furious to die." The violence of this consuming relationship is made explicit in the imagery of the tableau. Although the violence is apparently directed outward—the upraised horsewhip against the would-be suitor—the real object of it is the woman-daughter, forced into the background and dominated by the phallic figure of the spraddled father whose back is turned on her and who prevents her from getting out at the same time that he prevents them from getting in. Like Georgiana's spatial confinement in "The Birthmark," Emily's is a metaphor for her psychic confinement: her identity is determined by the constructs of her father's mind, and she can no more escape from his creation of her as "a slender figure in white" than she can escape his house.

What is true for Emily in relation to her father is equally true for her in relation to Jefferson: her status as a lady is a cage from which she cannot escape. To them she is always *Miss* Emily; she is never referred to and never thought of as otherwise. In omitting her title from his, Faulkner emphasizes the point that the real violence done to Emily is in making her a "Miss"; the omission is one of his roses for her. Because she is *Miss* Emily *Grierson*, Emily's father dresses her in white, places her in the background, and drives away her suitors. Because she is Miss Emily Grierson, the town invests her with that communal significance which makes her the object of their obsession and the subject of their incessant scrutiny. And because she is a lady, the town is able to impose a particular code of behavior on her ("But there were still others, older people, who said that even grief could not cause a real lady to forget *noblesse oblige*") and to see in her failure to live up to that code an excuse for interfering in her life. As a lady, Emily is venerated, but veneration results in the more telling emotions of envy and spite: "It was another link between the gross, teeming world and the high and mighty Griersons"; "People . . . believed that the Griersons held themselves a little too high for what they really were." The violence implicit in the desire to see the monument fall and reveal itself for clay suggests the violence inherent in the original impulse to venerate.

The violence behind veneration is emphasized through another telling emblem in the story. Emily's position as a hereditary obligation upon the town dates from "that day in 1894 when Colonel Sartoris, the mayor—he who fathered the edict that no Negro woman should appear on the streets without an apron on—remitted her taxes, the dispensation dating from the death of her father on into perpetuity." The conjunction of these two actions in the same syntactic unit is crucial, for it insists on their essential similarity. It indicates that the impulse to exempt is analogous to the desire to restrict, and that what appears to be a kindness or an act of veneration is in fact an insult. Sartoris' remission of Emily's taxes is a public declaration of the fact that a lady is not considered to be, and hence not allowed or enabled to be, economically independent (consider, in this connection, Emily's lessons in china painting; they are a latter-day version of Sartoris' "charity" and a brilliant image of Emily's economic uselessness). His act is a public statement of the fact that a lady, if she is to survive, must have either husband or father, and that, because Emily has neither, the town must assume responsibility for her. The remission of taxes that defines Emily's status dates from the death of her father, and she is handed over from one patron to the next, the town instead of husband taking on the role of father. Indeed, the use of the word "fathered" in describing Sartoris' behavior as mayor underlines the fact that his chivalric attitude toward Emily is simply a subtler and more dishonest version of her father's horsewhip.

The narrator is the last of the patriarchs who take upon themselves the burden of defining Emily's life, and his violence toward her is the most subtle of all. His tone of incantatory reminiscence and nostalgic veneration seems free of the taint of horsewhip and edict. Yet a thoroughgoing contempt for the "ladies" who spy and pry and gossip out of their petty jealousy and curiosity is one of the clearest strands in the narrator's consciousness. Emily is exempted from the general indictment because she is a *real* lady—that is, eccentric, slightly crazy, obsolete, a "stubborn and coquettish decay," absurd but indulged; "dear, inescapable, impervious, tranquil, and perverse"; indeed, anything and everything but human.

Not only does "A Rose for Emily" expose the violence done to a woman by making her a lady; it also explores the particular form of power the victim gains from this position and can use on those who enact this violence. "A Rose for Emily" is concerned with the consequences of violence for both the violated and the violators. One of the most striking aspects of the story is the disparity between Miss Emily Grierson and the Emily to whom Faulkner gives his rose in ironic imitation of the chivalric behavior the story exposes. The form of Faulkner's title establishes a camaraderie between author and protagonist and signals that a distinction must be made between the story Faulkner is telling and the story the narrator is telling. This distinction is of major importance because it suggests, of course, that the narrator, looking through a patriarchal lens, does not see Emily at all but rather a figment of his own imagination created in conjunction with the cumulative imagination of the town. Like Ellison's invisible man, nobody sees *Emily*. And because nobody sees *her*, she can literally get away with murder. Emily is characterized by her ability to understand and utilize the power that accrues to her from the fact that men do not see her but rather their concept of her: "'I have no taxes in Jefferson. Colonel Sartoris explained it to me. . . . Tobe! . . . Show these gentlemen out.'" Relying on the conventional assumptions about ladies who are expected to be neither reasonable nor in touch with reality, Emily presents an impregnable front that vanquishes the men "horse and foot, just as she had vanquished their fathers thirty years before." In spite of their "modern" ideas, this new generation, when faced with Miss Emily, are as much bound by the code of gentlemanly behavior as their fathers were ("They rose when she entered"). This code gives Emily a power that renders the gentlemen unable to function in a situation in which a lady neither sits down herself nor asks them to. They are brought to a "stumbling halt" and can do nothing when confronted with her refusal to engage in rational discourse. Their only recourse in the face of such eccentricity is to engage in behavior unbecoming to gentlemen, and Emily can count on their continuing to see themselves as gentlemen and her as a lady and on their returning a verdict of helpless noninterference.

It is in relation to Emily's disposal of Homer Barron, however, that Faulkner demonstrates most clearly the power of conventional assumptions about the nature of ladies to blind the town to what is going on and to allow Emily to murder with impunity. When Emily buys the poison, it never occurs to anyone that she intends to use it on Homer, so strong is the presumption that ladies when jilted commit suicide, not murder. And when her house begins to smell, the women blame it on the eccentricity of having a man servant rather than a woman, "as if a man—any man—could keep a kitchen properly." And then they hint that her eccentricity may have shaded over into madness, "remembering how old lady Wyatt, her great aunt, had gone completely crazy at last." The presumption of madness, that preeminently female response to bereavement, can be used to explain away much in the behavior of ladies whose activities seem a bit odd.

But even more pointed is what happens when the men try not to explain but to do something about the smell: "'Dammit, sir,' Judge Stevens said, 'will you accuse a lady to her face of smelling bad?'" But if a lady cannot be told that she smells, then the cause of the smell cannot be discovered and so her crime is "perfect." Clearly, the assumptions behind the Judge's outraged retort go beyond the myth that ladies are out of touch with reality. His outburst insists that it is the responsibility of gentlemen to make them so. Ladies must not be confronted with facts; they must be shielded from all that is unpleasant. Thus Colonel Sartoris remits Emily's taxes with a palpably absurd story, designed to protect her from an awareness of her poverty and her dependence on charity, and to protect him from having to confront her with it. And thus Judge Stevens will not confront Emily with the fact that her house stinks, though she is living in it and can hardly be unaware of the odor. Committed as they are to the myth that ladies and bad smells cannot coexist, these gentlemen insulate themselves from reality. And by defining a lady as a subhuman and hence sublegal entity, they have created a situation their laws can't touch. They have made it possible for Emily to be extra-legal: "'Why, of course,' the druggist said, 'If that's what you want. But the law requires you to tell what you are going to use it for.' Miss Emily just stared at him, her head tilted back in order to look him eye for eye, until he looked away and went and got the arsenic and wrapped it up." And, finally, they have created a situation in which they become the criminals: "So the next night, after midnight, four men crossed Miss Emily's lawn and slunk about the house like burglars." Above them, "her upright torso motionless as that of an idol," sits Emily, observing them act out their charade of chivalry. As they leave, she confronts them with the reality they are trying to protect her from: she turns on the light so that they may see her watching them. One can only wonder at the fact, and regret, that she didn't call the sheriff and have them arrested for trespassing.

Not only is "A Rose for Emily" a supreme analysis of what men do to women by making them ladies; it is also an exposure of how this act in turn defines and recoils upon men. This is the significance of the dynamic that Faulkner establishes between Emily and Jefferson. And it is equally the point of the dynamic implied between the tableau of Emily and her father and the tableau which greets the men who break down the door of that room in the region above the stairs. When the would-be "suitors" finally get into her father's house, they discover the consequences of his oppression of her, for the violence contained in the rotted corpse of Homer Barron is the mirror image of the violence represented in the tableau, the back-flung front door flung back with a vengeance. Having been consumed by her father, Emily in turn feeds off Homer Barron, becoming, after his death, suspiciously fat. Or, to put it another way, it is as if, after her father's death, she has reversed his act of incorporating her by incorporating and becoming him, metamorphosed from the slender figure in white to the obese figure in black whose hair is "a vigorous iron-gray, like the hair of an active man." She has taken into herself the violence in him which thwarted her and has reenacted it upon Homer Barron.

THAT FINAL ENCOUNTER, however, is not simply an image of the reciprocity of violence. Its power of definition also derives from its grotesqueness, which makes finally explicit the grotesqueness that has been latent in the description of Emily throughout the story: "Her skeleton was small and spare; perhaps that was why what would have been merely plumpness in another was obesity in her. She looked bloated, like a body long submerged in motionless water, and of that pallid hue. Her eyes, lost in the fatty ridges of her face, looked like two small pieces of coal pressed into a lump of dough." The impact of this description depends on the contrast it establishes between Emily's reality as a fat, bloated figure in black and the conventional image of a lady—expectations that are fostered in the town by its emblematic memory of Emily as a slender figure in white and in us by the narrator's tone of romantic invocation and by the passage itself. Were she not expected to look so different, were her skeleton not small and spare, Emily would not be so grotesque. Thus, the focus is on the grotesqueness that results when stereotypes are imposed upon reality. And the implication of this focus is that the real grotesque is the stereotype itself. If Emily is both lady and grotesque, then the syllogism must be completed thus: the idea of a lady is grotesque. So Emily is metaphor and mirror for the town of Jefferson; and when, at the end, the town folk finally discover who and what she is, they have in fact encountered who and what they are.

Despite similarities of focus and vision, "A Rose for Emily" is more implicitly feminist than "The Birthmark." For one thing, Faulkner does not have Hawthorne's compulsive ambivalence; one is not invited to misread "A Rose for Emily" as one is invited to misread "The Birthmark." Thus, the interpretation of "The Birthmark" that sees it as a story of misguided idealism, despite its massive oversights, nevertheless *works;* while the efforts to read "A Rose for Emily" as a parable of the relations between North and South, or as a conflict between an old order and a new, or as a story about the human relation to Time, don't work because the attempt to make Emily representative of such concepts stumbles over the fact that woman's condition is not the "human" condition.[2] To understand Emily's experience requires a primary awareness of the fact that she is a woman.

But, more important, Faulkner provides us with an image of retaliation. Unlike Georgiana, Emily does not simply acquiesce; she prefers to murder rather than to die. In this respect she is a welcome change from the image of woman as willing victim that fills the pages of our literature, and whose other face is the ineffective fulminations of Dame Van Winkle. Nevertheless, Emily's action is still reaction. "A Rose for Emily" exposes the poverty of a situation in which turnabout is the only possibility and in which one's acts are neither self-generated nor self-determined but are simply a response to and a reflection of forces outside oneself. Though Emily may be proud, strong, and indomitable, her murder of

Homer Barron is finally an indication of the severely limited nature of the power women can wrest from the system that oppresses them. Aylmer's murder of Georgiana is an indication of men's absolute power over women; it is an act performed in the complete security of his ability to legitimize it as a noble and human pursuit. Emily's act has no such context. It is possible only because it can be kept secret; and it can be kept secret only at the cost of exploiting her image as a lady. Furthermore, Aylmer murders Georgiana in order to get rid of her; Emily murders Homer Barron in order to have him.

Patriarchal culture is based to a considerable extent on the argument that men and women are made for each other and on the conviction that "masculinity" and "feminity" are the natural reflection of that divinely ordained complement. Yet, if one reads "The Birthmark" and "A Rose for Emily" as analyses of the consequences of a massive differentiation of everything according to sex, one sees that in reality a sexist culture is one in which men and women are not simply incompatible but murderously so. Aylmer murders Georgiana because he must at any cost get rid of woman; Emily murders Homer Barron because she must at any cost get a man. The two stories define the disparity between cultural myth and cultural reality, and they suggest that in this disparity is the ultimate grotesque.

NOTES

1. See *Faulkner in the University: Class Conferences at the University of Virginia 1957–1958*, edited by Frederick L. Gwynn and Joseph L. Blotner (Charlottesville: University of Virginia Press, 1959), 87–88; *Faulkner at Nagano*, edited by Robert A. Jeliffe (Toyko: Kenkyusha, 1956), 71.

2. For a sense of some of the difficulties involved in reading the story in these terms, I refer the reader to the collection of criticism edited by M. Thomas Inge, *A Rose for Emily* (Columbus, Ohio: Merrill, 1970).

Sociological Provocateurs

1. In what ways do the sociological critics' views of the relation between literature and life differ from the New Critics' views? from the phenomenological critics' views?

2. How might Tindall answer a Marxist argument that the History of Ideas approach separates mind from matter and, in effect, distorts history by privileging ideas above material actuality?

3. Heath-Stubbs seems to be addressing those critics who deny "greatness" to Yeats's poetry on the grounds that Yeats held reactionary, some would say fascist, beliefs. Yet Heath-Stubbs does not argue this from the New Critical position (literature is nonpolitical and should be judged solely on its artistic merit). From what position does he reason?

4. McGann contends that Allen Tate's New Critical reading of Dickinson's poems carries hidden ideological values and interests. What are these? What might an analysis of McGann's reading of Tate's interpretation disclose about McGann's values and interests?

5. Brecht, among other Marxists, has challenged and condemned the seemingly transparent style of so-called realistic literature which purports to be an accurate reflection of an actual world. Brecht would argue that realistic literature demonstrates how middle-class ideology, as a collective representation of ideas and experience, dulls us to actual experience. What might Brecht say about such "realistic" genres as newspapers? TV docu-dramas? Andy Warhol's paintings of Campbell soup cans?

6. How might Brecht respond to the statement of genre critic Gilbert Muller (Chapter 3, "Flannery O'Connor and the Catholic Grotesque") that "the grotesque character is a comic figure. It is impossible to sympathize with him, despite his agonies, because we view him from a detached perspective."?

7. Explore class and race relations in O'Connor's "Revelation" by using some of the key concepts of Marxist-psychoanalytic theory which Mottram employs: Psychic repression depends on social repression; The production of relationships results from the political (power distribution) context; Master narratives structure our political unconscious.

8. What identifies Eagleton's "Ideology and Literary Form: W. B. Yeats" as an example of Marxist criticism?

9. Consider the foreign films you have seen in the light of Shohat's and Stam's essay. Did you experience any jarring, or sense of dislocation, between the screen images and the translated words?

10. Rich's essay embodies the feminist maxim, "The personal is political." How does she do this? Do you find this strategy effective?

11. Feminist and Marxist critics urge that we test certain common assumptions about what we take to be "natural." We can do this by imaginatively reversing the positions of commonly paired opposites such as white/black, man/woman, boss/worker. This reversal allows us to see that what we took for natural is often socially conditioned. Fetterley suggests we do this with "The Birthmark": Think of scientist Georgiana seeking perfection by striving to remove a blemish from the cheek of her husband who, alas, dies in her noble but misguided attempt. The plot becomes absurd and cruel. Try applying this man/woman reversal to Poe's "The Purloined Letter" or perhaps to some currently popular films.

12. Fetterley's essays come from her book *The Resisting Reader*. In these essays, what exactly is she asking us, as readers, to resist?

CHAPTER 6

Psychoanalytic Criticism

EVER SINCE SIGMUND FREUD'S *The Interpretation of Dreams* (1900) called attention to the repressive power of the Unconscious, literary critics have drawn on the psychological sciences—especially on psychoanalysis. Over the years critics have generally shifted their interests from author, to text, to reader, to the interaction among these. For example, earlier or classical critics like Marie Bonaparte apply psychoanalysis to literature as a way to reveal the author's "id," Freud's term for the dynamic system of repressed instinctual drives. These early critics were less interested in the manifest or formal aspects of literature than in the latent, hidden meaning in literature because only at the "deeper" level is the author's psyche revealed.

Around mid-century, many American psychoanalytic critics began to turn their attention from unconscious id to conscious ego and, concomitantly, from author to text and reader. Contributing to this redirection were I. A. Richards's work with the reader and close reading, the New Critics' focus on form, and psychoanalysts' concern with transference and countertransference, which seemed to provide a possible model for the reader/text relationship. Critics like Simon O. Lesser began relating artistic forms to ego work. They suggested that, like dream work, the ego's defense mechanisms of condensation and displacement operate through metaphor and metonymy to disguise and so make presentable our libidinal desires. They claimed that by releasing tensions, literature acts therapeutically to make us "whole."

More recent psychoanalytic theorists, however, have claimed such emphasis on ego control weakens and distorts psychoanalysis. Perhaps in response to this critique as well as to structuralism, critics are again re-reading and re-visioning Freud's writings. Harold Bloom reframes poets and their poetic forefathers within the contestatory father/son Oedipal struggle. Jacques Lacan explodes the traditional notion of reading and of subjectivity. His "reading" of Poe's story demonstrates that both texts and ourselves are constituted by language and, as a result, are continuously in-process.

"The Purloined Letter"

MARIE BONAPARTE

In *The Life and Works of Edgar Allan Poe* (1933), psychoanalyst Marie Bonaparte applies Freudian analysis to literature. In these classical psychoanalytic interpretations, Poe's writings serve as a case history to reveal the poet's unconscious motivating fantasy: his desire for his dead mother. This repressed desire, along with its attendant fear of castration, dominates his writing. As a result, his poetic images, like a neurotic's symptoms, are disguised and "over-determined"—they metaphorically condense many covert meanings into one image.

Bonaparte includes "The Purloined Letter" within a group of Poe's tales she calls "Tales About Mother." She has just finished analyzing "The Black Cat," whose main theme of castration anxiety is supplemented by one of guilt anxiety. She suggests that the "gaping aperture of the chimney recall[s] the dread cloaca of the mother," a spatial symbolization that recurs in the Dupin tales.

OTHER TALES BY POE also express, though in different and less aggressive fashion, regret for the missing maternal penis, with reproach for its loss. First among these, strange though it seem, is "The Purloined Letter."[1]

The reader will remember that, in this story, the Queen of France, like Elizabeth Arnold,* is in possession of dangerous and secret letters, whose writer is unknown. A wicked minister, seeking a political advantage and to strengthen his power, steals one of these letters under the Queen's eyes, which she is unable to prevent owing to the King's presence. This letter must at all costs be recovered. Every attempt by the police fails. Fortunately Dupin is at hand. Wearing dark spectacles with which he can look about him, while his own eyes are concealed, he makes

---

From *The Life and Works of Edgar Allen Poe: A Psycho-Analytic Interpretation,* by Marie Bonaparte, trans. John Rodker (London: Imago Publishing Co., 1933; 1949), 483–85. Reprinted by permission of Chatto & Windus.

*Elizabeth Arnold, Poe's actress mother who died when Poe was three years old, left behind a packet of letters—practically her only legacy to her son.—ED.

an excuse to call on the minister, and discovers the letter openly displayed in a card-rack, hung "from a little brass knob just beneath the middle of the mantelpiece."

By a further subterfuge, he possesses himself of the compromising letter and leaves a similar one in its place. The Queen, who will have the original restored to her, is saved.

Let us first note that this letter, very symbol of the maternal penis, also "hangs" over the fireplace, in the same manner as the female penis, if it existed, would be hung over the cloaca which is here represented— as in the foregoing tales—by the general symbol of fireplace or chimney. We have here, in fact, what is almost an anatomical chart, from which not even the clitoris (or brass knob) is omitted. Something very different, however, should be hanging from that body!

The struggle between Dupin and the minister who once did Dupin an "ill turn"—a struggle in which the latter is victorious—represents, in effect, the Oedipal struggle between father and son, though on an archaic, pregenital and phallic level, to seize possession, not of the mother herself, but of a part; namely, her penis.

We have here an illustration of that "partial love" and desire, not for the whole of the loved being but for an organ, which characterises one stage of infantile libidinal development.[2]

Yet though the minister, impressive father-figure and "man of genius" as he is, is outwitted by the ratiocinatory and so more brilliant son, he presents one outstanding characteristic which recalls that very "son" for he, too, is a poet! He is a composite figure, combining characteristics of the two "wicked" fathers; first of Elizabeth Arnold's unknown lover, her castrator in the child's eyes, and then of John Allan.

For did not John Allan, too, appear to the child as the ravisher castrator of a woman, Frances, Edgar's beloved and ailing "Ma"?* More still, had he not impugned his true mother's virtue and injured her reputation, as the blackmailing minister planned to do with the Queen's?

The minister also reminds us of John Allan by his unscrupulous ambition. And it was John Allan again, who, to Poe as a child, represented that "*monstrum horrendum*—an unprincipled man of genius," not far removed from the "criminal" of "vast intelligence" figured in "The Man of the Crowd." So does the father often appear to the small boy, at once admired and hated.

Most striking of all, the minister exhibits Poe's outstanding feature, his poetic gift. And here Poe, in fact, identifies himself with the hated though admired father by that same gift of identification whose praises he sings in "The Purloined Letter" as being the one, supremely effective way of penetrating another's thoughts and feelings.

Poe, impotent and a poet, could never so wholly identify himself with

---

*John and Frances Allan adopted the young Edgar after his mother's death.—ED.

the Orang-Outang in "The Murders in the Rue Morgue," for there the father conquers the mother only by reason of his overwhelming strength. But, in his unconscious, Poe could achieve this with the minister for, though the latter, once more, triumphs by superior strength, this time it is of the intellect.

As to the King whom the Queen deceives, he must again be David Poe, Elizabeth's husband. Small wonder that Dupin, embodying the son, should declare his "political sympathies" with the lady! Finally, in return for a cheque of 50,000 francs, leaving to the Prefect of Police the fabulous reward, Dupin restores the woman her symbolic letter or missing penis. Thus, once more, we meet the equation gold = penis. The mother gives her son gold in exchange for the penis he restores.

So too, in "The Gold Bug," the treasure would seem to be bestowed by the mother, on the son, in return for the penis he restores to her. In our analysis of the tale it was too soon to emphasize the equivalence gold = penis: the point had not been reached at which we could offer an explanation. But now that we know the unconscious significance of the hanging-theme, we will recall the strange means devised by Captain Kidd to lead to his treasure. A plumb-line, *hung* through a hollow eye-socket, gives the position from which measurements should be made to reveal its presence. This is, indeed, strangely reminiscent of the gouged-out eye, symbolising castration, and the hanging theme, symbolising re-phallisation. Both relate to the dead mother, whose skull thus, clearly, guards the treasure.

This theme of the castrated mother, so familiar to infantile ways of thinking and the unconscious throughout life, though far removed from consciousness and adult ways of thought, is thus found at the root of some of Poe's best-known tales.

IT IS TIME, HOWEVER, to leave these tales which revolve round so many avatars of the mother. As was to be expected, in almost all the tales we have so far analysed, the son's relation to the mother is the main theme. Nevertheless, in some—as in the Marchese Mentoni on his palace steps, old Berlifitzing in his castle, or Mr. Windenough and the surgeon in "Loss of Breath"—we already catch fleeting glimpses of the father. In "The Murders in the Rue Morgue," the father, killer and castrator, as the anthropoid ape is, even, the main character. But it is in "The Man of the Crowd" that, for the first time in Poe's work, the father's figure fills the stage in all his tragic grandeur. Even the mother and victim remains hid in the mystery shrouding the crime. Indeed, we might well be asked why we included this tale in the "Tales of the Mother" at all, were it not that the deeper logic of Poe's inspiration determined that place, since its main theme, in fact, is the father's relation *to the mother*.

The tales which now remain to be studied are almost all variants on another main theme: that of the son's relation to the father. We shall now see these two protagonists at grips; hate being uppermost first, then love.

NOTES

1. *The Purloined Letters: The Gift*, 1845.
2. Cf. Abraham, *A Short Study of the Development of the Libido.*

Fiction and the Unconscious: "The Birthmark"

SIMON O. LESSER

Lesser asks, Why do we read fiction? and answers, Because it is good for us. By harmonizing the contradictory claims of our id-ego-superego, fiction strengthens our sense of identity. Fiction does this by acting as a "compromise formation" which embodies both our unconscious desires and our defenses against them. In this view, the id provides the raw materials or content of fiction, the ego its form. Like dreams, fiction becomes a process of production: just as the vital secondary revisioning of dream work reorders images into narrative, so ego work transforms unconscious materials into fictional forms. Lesser, like Bonaparte, sees texts as disguised messages from the repressed unconscious. But unlike Bonaparte he is less interested in what the story reveals about the author than in how it becomes accessible to the reader.

THE MATERIALS OF FICTION

We are already acquainted with the factor primarily responsible for our tendency to disregard certain considerations and falsify matters when we weigh our own problems: it is repression, or, more basically, the underlying anxiety which stirs this mechanism into activity. In a general way we also know the kind of things we prefer not to take into account: they are things which would make us anxious, for example, ideas which would arouse feelings of self-reproach or jeopardize an adjustment to life which we fear to upset even though it leaves us unhappy.

What may surprise us is the range of the ideas which can arouse anxiety. Of course we do not wish to be reminded of impulses we find it difficult to cope with or of selfish and malicious motives. But we may be no more willing to face anything which will remind us of relatively trivial shortcomings, of peevishness, let us say, or stinginess. Even ideas which it might be expected we would welcome, or at any rate regard with indifference, may be rejected because in some roundabout way they mobilize anxiety. For example, we may try to discount some generous and idealistic action because, to excuse our own corruption, we are trying to convince ourselves that no one acts unselfishly. Or we may try to disavow feelings of revulsion toward life because they call for a more searching examination of our own situation or our society than we feel prepared to make.

Under the most favorable conditions there are many facets of human experience, many kinds of situations, many surmises about why people act and feel as they do, which we are unable to consider objectively. When we are involved in a conflict which could disrupt our life, the situation is still worse. A certain degree of blindness and a certain amount of distortion are almost inevitable. It is worth illustrating this, although any example, presented in expository terms, must seem sketchy and crude.

Let us take a case which arises frequently enough in life and will also suggest parallel instances in fiction—the case of a man involved in a serious extramarital relationship. How likely is he to see either the relationship or any of the people involved in it with any clarity? He may not even admit that a problem exists, however unhappy everyone may be, for any resolution of the situation involves danger and possible loss. What is more certain is that, to justify his own conduct or to escape the full force of the conflict, he will alter the facts this way or that. He may try to disparage his mistress and his feeling for her, acknowledging only those qualities in her about which he is ambivalent, such as her physical beauty, and denying that he is drawn to her by anything but sexual attraction. In keeping with this he may pretend that his marriage is better than it is and stifle complaints against his wife he would be justified in making. Alternatively, he may endow his mistress with qualities which she does not possess and deny his wife her own virtues.

It is our fears, obviously, which lead us to evade and falsify our problems. *But in reading fiction we do not have to be afraid;* there honesty is possible and welcome. We turn to fiction because we know that there we will find our problems imaged in their full intensity and complexity, everything faithfully shown, the desires and fears we have slighted drawn as distinctly as anything else. Unconsciously we want to see justice done to those neglected considerations—they are a part of us too.

We value fiction in part because it redresses balances. It tries to annihilate the unctuous lies we live by—the lies which other forms of communication, incidentally, from newspaper editorials to political oratory, tire us by trying to sustain. It exposes, sometimes, of course, too indecorously, the backside of life.[1] In the words in which the hero of Dostoevsky's *Notes from Underground* seeks to justify himself, it carries to an extreme what we have not dared to carry halfway, and it does not mistake cowardice for good sense or tolerate self-deception. A phrase Edward Bullough uses to describe art in general seems particularly applicable to fiction: it gives us a "sudden view of things from their reverse, usually unnoticed side."[2]

In terms of content this means most obviously that fiction makes restitution to us for some of our instinctual deprivations. It emphasizes "sex" to augment the meager satisfactions available through sanctioned channels and to allay our guilt feelings about our frequent transgressions of those sanctions, either in deed or in desire. It gives expression and outlet to aggressive tendencies which we are expected to hold in strict leash though they are covertly encouraged by our competitive culture. The present vogue of detective stories and melodramas has here its explanation. It is equally important to realize that fiction provides an outlet for idealistic and contemplative tendencies thwarted in our daily experience; in a phrase of Kenneth Burke's, it is a "corrective of the practical." "A great work of art," writes Louise Rosenblatt, "may provide us the opportunity to feel more profoundly and more generously, to perceive more fully the implications of experience, than the hurried and fragmentary conditions of life permit."[3] This is certainly the case, though generosity and contemplation have even more formidable enemies than the ones Rosenblatt names, notably the pressures upon us to live prudently and even selfishly.

Fiction, then, makes good certain omissions in our lives. It serves as a devil's advocate for tendencies in ourselves we may be afraid to defend; it depicts precisely those aspects of experience our fears cause us to scant. Out of the vast body of fiction available to us, from the past and the present, we choose those works which we believe will best perform this service for us, and our search is no less purposive because in large part it is pursued unconsciously.[4]

In its zeal to do justice to our repressed tendencies fiction is in constant danger of overstating the case for them. Particularly if it does this too directly, with a minimum of disguise and control—we think at once of such a writer as Henry Miller—it is likely to arouse aversion rather than pleasure. But it is not always easy to say whether a work of fiction or a reader is responsible for a failure of this sort. A work which in the perspective of time may seem well balanced may cause us to recoil because it insists on telling us more of the truth, above all more of the truth about ourselves, than we are prepared to accept. As Havelock Ellis declares in the passage of *The Dance of Life* from which I have already quoted, certain books "may have to knock again and again at the closed door of our hearts. 'Who is there?' we carelessly cry, and we cannot open the door; we bid the importunate stranger, whatever he may be, to go away; until, as in the apologue of the Persian mystic, at last we seem to hear the voice outside saying: 'It is thyself.'"

In emphasizing the tendency of fiction to plead the cause of impulses we ourselves might hesitate to defend, we have perhaps done it a disservice. For admirable as that tendency is, it is no more than one aspect of a more general—but far more elusive—characteristic. This is the tendency to see a problem from every possible point of view, to balance demands, to harmonize claims and counter-claims. It is this characteristic which we must now examine more closely. It lies close to the very heart of fiction. More than any trait connected with content rather than form, it explains fiction's capacity to deal with our problem in a manner which leaves us satisfied. . . .

Many additional examples of the same general character will immediately occur to any reader of fiction—Cervantes' treatment of Don Quixote, Richardson's incapacity to deny Lovelace and his most persuasive heroine, Clarissa, their vitality and appeal. "That complicated balance of elements which is necessary for good fiction," writes Joseph Wood Krutch, "seems usually to have been achieved by the imagination of a writer whose mind was to some extent divided against itself." [5] All the examples given so far would tend to suggest that the balance stems from a conflict between the conscious intention of the writer and his unconscious sympathies. But we do not know, nor does it matter, whether the balance always arises in this fashion. Probably a great deal of conscious vacillation helped determine Shakespeare's attitude toward his tragic heroes, Tolstoy's toward Anna Karenina, James's toward Isabel Archer, Joyce's toward Gabriel Conroy. What is certain is that these characters are presented to us from many different, and opposed, points of view. When a single viewpoint predominates, particularly if it is a conscious and narrowly moralistic one, the fiction writer is likely, in Krutch's phrase, to win "a lugubrious triumph over his own art." [6]

The most passionate affirmations of literature, it appears, show an awareness of all the considerations which can be urged against them. The awareness may be implicit rather than explicit, sketched in rather than developed—in Shakespeare's Sonnet 116 it is crowded into a single cry, "O, no!"; but unless the awareness is there a work will lack tension and excitement and its affirmations will carry little conviction. The characterizations, the value systems of great literature, certainly of great narrative art, are all pervaded by what I like to think of as *a sense of the opposite.* The underlying attitude is one of poised and sustained ambivalence.

LET US SEE HOW this attitude manifests itself in a particular story, using for purposes of illustration "The Birthmark" by Nathaniel Hawthorne. This is not a simple story, for Hawthorne was not a simple man, yet [Cleanth] Brooks and [Robert Penn] Warren seem justified in calling it a parable—a kind of story, according to their definition, "which makes an obvious point or has a rather obvious symbolic meaning."[7] Hawthorne himself says that the tale has "a deeply impressive moral."

"The Birthmark" is the story of a brilliant scientist, Aylmer, who became obsessed with the idea of removing a birthmark, which rather resembles a tiny crimson hand, from the cheek of his beautiful young wife, Georgiana. Aware of her husband's abhorrence of this flaw, of his desire to have her perfect, Georgiana agrees to let him attempt to remove the birthmark, an attempt which he feels is certain to succeed. But it develops that the crimson stain, superficial as it seems, has clutched its grasp into Georgiana's being with a strength of which Aylmer had no conception. Nevertheless, he persists, and develops a draught which to his "irrepressible ecstasy" removes the birthmark from his wife's cheek. But his ecstasy lasts but for a second, for "as the last crimson tint of the birthmark—that sole token of human imperfection" fades from Georgiana's cheek, she dies. "The fatal hand had grappled with the mystery of life, and was the bond by which an angelic spirit kept itself in union with a mortal frame."

The most obvious meaning of "The Birthmark," the "deeply impressive moral," is implicit in the story, but so that we cannot possibly fail to see it, is heavily underscored. We cannot have perfection. Georgiana's birthmark represents "the fatal flaw of humanity which Nature, in one shape or another, stamps ineffaceably on all her productions, either to imply that they are temporary and finite, or that their perfection must be wrought by toil and pain." By refusing to resign himself to "the limitations and imperfections of nature"[8] Aylmer rejects, in the words of his dying wife, "the best the earth could offer."

The story has a second meaning, which is also so heavily emphasized that it is hard to believe that it was not consciously intended.[9] What can be the specific symbolic significance of this crimson mark, which sometimes called to mind a tiny bloody hand—a mark which some of Georgiana's lovers had found attractive and which Aylmer, more spiritual than they, only became aware of after his marriage? Hawthorne does not leave us in much doubt. "The crimson hand expressed the ineludible gripe in which mortality clutches the highest and purest of earthly mould, degrading them into kindred with the lowest, and even with the very brutes, like whom their visible frames return to dust." The crimson mark symbolizes sexuality,[10] and Aylmer is one of those men, described by Freud,[11] who sharply disassociate heavenly and earthly love, the tender and the sensual. Such men strive "to keep their sensuality out of contact with the objects they love."[12] Just so, Aylmer rejects his wife's sexuality, ultimately with physical revulsion; and she regards his attitude as an affront.

What sort of man is this, who in his pride insists on perfection and in his refinement recoils from his wife's femininity? In reaching a judgment it might seem helpful to get outside the frame of the story for a minute and, accepting the story as a true account, try to imagine in what terms Aylmer's character and conduct would have been described by the gossips of the town. But we do not have to do this; the adverse judgments appear in the story itself. Aylmer's laboratory assistant, Aminadab, who, "with his vast strength, his shaggy hair . . . and the indescribable earthiness that incrusted him . . . seemed to represent man's physical nature" declares that if Georgiana were his wife he would "never part with that birthmark." And Georgiana herself, though docile and unembittered, bitingly indicts her husband's restless spirit. She could not, she says, hope to satisfy him for "longer than one moment . . . for his spirit was ever on the march, ever ascending, and each instant required something that was beyond the scope of the instant before."

These viewpoints are present in the story, *but they are not the only viewpoints and they are not Hawthorne's.* They are kept in poised tension with other viewpoints which show, as Brooks and Warren put it, that "The author is sympathetic to [Aylmer], and obviously sees in his ruinous experiment a certain nobility."[13] The very speech of Georgiana's from which I have already quoted contains other statements that, though not without a tinge of irony, predominantly express understanding and admiration of her idealistic husband. "Her heart exulted, while it trembled, at his honorable love—so pure and lofty that it would accept nothing less than perfection nor miserably made itself contented with an earthlier nature than he had dreamed of." It is clear, furthermore, as Brooks and Warren also point out, that if Aminadab provides a sort of measuring stick for Aylmer's folly he provides one also for his nobility. Despite his shortcomings, Aylmer, the intellectual and spiritual man, is the hero of the tale. It is difficult to resist the surmise that he represents certain aspects of his creator. Perhaps Hawthorne, too, found it hard to accept sensuality in woman. We may be sure in any case that he knew what it meant to strive for perfection and find himself miserably thwarted. There are unmistakable autobiographical allusions in the story. "Perhaps every man of genius in whatever sphere might recognize the image of his own experience in Aylmer's journal."

But Hawthorne does not attempt to excuse the folly of Aylmer's course either; on the contrary, he mercilessly exposes it and shows its disastrous consequences. His attitude is not a condemnatory one, but neither is it indulgent. If it were, we may be sure, we would not be pleased: we would regard the story as a form of special pleading, perhaps for some weakness of Hawthorne's, acknowledged or unacknowledged.

IT IS CLEAR ENOUGH that Hawthorne was both attracted and repelled by Aylmer; his attitude reflects a delicate balance. But why we should place a high value upon such an attitude is not immediately clear. There is still something a little puzzling about the attitude itself.

In life itself, it immediately occurs to us, the kind of interested impartiality which is indigenous to fiction is extremely rare. By a very indirect route the greatest religious and moral leaders—Hosea, for example, and Jesus—achieve judgments which are no less perfectly balanced. Aware of tendencies in themselves over which they have triumphed, they refuse, even when those tendencies have spent their force, to condemn those who succumb to them. But the attitude of fiction is not a judging attitude at all. It has so little in common with the kind of moral evaluations one commonly encounters that, in trying to describe it, one is tempted to search for some antonym of the word "moral." But then the attitude is uncommon in every area of our experience. It represents a balance of forces which is evidently extremely hard to achieve or maintain. When there is a narcissistic investment in another person, we tend to overestimate his virtues and capacities and deny or minimize his faults. When we are antagonistic, we do just the opposite—overlook good qualities and exaggerate weaknesses. We are correct in assuming that the kind of exposure of a person's failings which is characteristic of fiction is usually in the service of aggression.

In trying to clarify my understanding of the balanced attitude of fiction, I kept returning again and again, at first without perceiving why, to what is perhaps the most beautiful of all Freud's papers, the six-page note on "Humour."[14] In that special form of the comic called humor, which Freud distinguishes sharply from wit, the humorist, he suggests, "[adopts] toward the other the attitude of an adult toward a child, recognizing and smiling at the triviality of the interests and sufferings which seem to the child so big."[15] The humorist identifies himself to some extent with the father. In that very important form of humor "in which a man adopts a humorous attitude towards himself in order to ward off possible suffering,"[16] the situation is not so very different: the superego, the internal representative of the parental function, strives to comfort the ego. "'Look here!'" it says in effect, "'This is all that this seemingly dangerous world amounts to. Child's play—the very thing to jest about!'"[17]

In fiction no such comforting takes place, nor is there usually any attempt to minimize the issues, but all the same we sense some sort of parallel. It is evident, in the first place, that the same two institutions of the mind are concerned: the ego and superego share an interest in the remorseless facing of truth which fiction insists upon, and it is, of course, the superego which requires that transgressions be punished. We suspect, too, that some sort of communication is taking place between the superego and the ego. Only one thing prevents us from divining its nature immediately: our tendency to think of the superego as stern and punitive. But the example of humor reminds us that the superego inherits the kindly as well as the harsh aspects of the parents.[18] Once we realize this, we can readily reconstruct the nature of the intrapsychic interchange which the attitude of fiction stimulates: it is a kind of confession based upon acceptance and love. The ego withholds nothing and it asks for nothing, neither for extenuation of punishment nor even for forgiveness. The superego voluntarily gives the ego something it evidently values even more than these, understanding and the assurance of continued love. It notes the strivings of the ego which have gotten it into difficulty, but without revulsion or censure. Like a fond parent, the superego assures the ego: "I see your faults very clearly. But I do not condemn you. And I love you still." . . .

The Appeals to the Parts of the Psyche

Narrative art, then, deals with and attempts to resolve our emotional conflicts in a way which does full justice to all the factors which are relevant. In trying to understand why we place such a high value on this characteristic, we have perhaps described those factors too exclusively in one set of terms. Fiction mirrors, we have said, the struggle between the kind of considerations to which we give obeisance in our daily living and the kind we tend to disregard and even repress. But it also mirrors the struggle between id, ego and superego, and between the pleasure principle and the reality principle—between our wishes and the forces, internal and external, opposed to their fulfilment. To some extent these are overlapping categories, but each of them may contribute something a little different to our understanding of fiction. Sometimes it is advantageous to approach the same story from more than one point of view.

For example, the aspect of "The Birthmark" on which we have focussed our attention thus far, the skill with which Hawthorne has presented Aylmer and his experiment in a balanced light, functions as "means" rather than as "end": it is a device to insure our neutrality while a portentous drama is played out. This drama centers around the clash between two deep-seated wishes and our defenses against them. Without identifying the forces on each side, we could not fully account for our response to "The Birthmark."

The more buried of the wishes is a variant of the desire that the mother be virginal; here the wish is that the wife, who we may suspect is to some extent a mother-surrogate, should be free of the "stain" of sexuality. The wish which emerges more clearly may seem quite foreign to us in the form in which it is expressed. Do we have any desire to achieve perfection or to make those around us perfect? Perhaps not; perhaps few of us have impulses as unreasonable as this. On the other hand, it is a commonplace that we may be unduly sensitive about the faults—perhaps we are not always even justified in calling them that—of members of our family and others close to us. Cannot this sensitivity be readily equated with the desire to have them different in this or that respect? Frequently enough we even express our dissatisfaction, in effect goading them to change. Aylmer's desire to make his wife perfect represents no more than an extension of a tendency present to some degree in nearly everyone. The extension facilitates our understanding of the tendency. It is justified, too, perhaps, because the tendency is particularly likely to assert itself without check toward those whose relation to us may involve some degree of subordination—toward women and children. Every parent and teacher has probably experienced the impulse to mold a child this way or that—an impulse not easy to subdue even when one senses that the changes desired are not in accord with the child's natural bent. We are, of course, more cautious about trying to influence adults, but, particularly if we have a wife as tractable as Georgiana, we may find ways of letting her know which of her personality traits endear her to us and which ones we would like her to efface.

However, our defenses against the wishes dealt with in "The Birthmark" are as powerful as the wishes themselves. The wishes arouse anxiety—so much anxiety that, instead of being approached from the point of view of the impulses it seeks to satisfy, the story could be regarded as an attempt to examine and reinforce certain dim but intense fears. The impulse to overspiritualize love or woman is opposed to our knowledge of reality, which tells us that any such attempt is foredoomed to failure. Fears that are more indistinct, but no less strong, warn us against tampering with the personality of others. We have some premonition—perhaps we know from experience—that good and bad are intermingled and that efforts to change a person, even when successful, may have calamitous consequences we had not foreseen; we may chasten a child only to find that at the same time we have made him less joyous, less enterprising and less creative. We know, too, that attempts to change people can lead to a kind of death—death of their love for us. We may be deterred by still vaguer dreads—feelings that in seeking to change another we are arrogating to ourselves a God-like function, which we have neither the right nor the wisdom to assume. The human personality and the human body are ringed by a sacred sheath, which we fear to violate.

So powerful are these fears that our dominant reaction in life to the kind of experiment Aylmer undertakes would probably be one of abhorrence. The ultimate purpose of Hawthorne's attempt to present Aylmer in balanced perspective is to quiet our fears so that the wishes which motivate his experiment, which are also urgent, can be given their opportunity. Aylmer's sincerity and idealism give us a sense of kinship with him. We see that the plan takes shape gradually in his mind, almost against his conscious intention. We are reassured by the fact that he loves Georgiana and feels confident that his attempt to remove the birthmark will succeed. Thus at the same time that we recoil we can identify with Aylmer and through him act out some of our secret desires.

Those desires are frustrated—or we should say, to be faithful to the story, fulfilled only momentarily and at a tragic cost. Behind this resolution we can discern narrative art's respect for the reality principle. Regularly in fiction—perhaps more regularly than in life—mistakes and transgressions are punished. The punishments satisfy not only the superego but the ego; they assure it that fiction is not tempted to disregard the dearly bought knowledge that sooner or later we are likely to be called to account for our misdeeds and our mistakes. . . .

. . . It may appear that the claims of the pleasure principle are being scanted. But closer examination reveals that even such a story as "The Birthmark" affords us more gratification than may at first be apparent. The story not only gives expression to impulses which are ordinarily repressed; it gives them a sympathetic hearing—an opportunity to show whether they can be gratified without causing trouble or pain. There are obvious gains in being able to conduct tests of this kind with no more danger and no greater expenditure of effort than is involved in reading a story. Furthermore, even though the resolution of "The Birthmark" is negative, it affords us satisfaction. It confirms the wisdom of the ego in keeping a rein on the impulses to which Aylmer succumbed; this, perhaps, must be scored as a victory for the reality principle. But in another way the outcome of the story satisfies the pleasure principle as well, or perhaps we should say the entire personality. Hawthorne has carefully prepared us for the probability that Aylmer's experiment will fail. The ending of the story satisfies certain emotional expectations, like a note for which our ears are waiting.

The example reminds us that narrative art has, as it were, certain internal resources it can exploit for our pleasure even when, in terms of external reference, the satisfactions it can offer are limited. How rich those resources are we shall perhaps better appreciate after we have completed our consideration of form. But in terms of content, also, fiction strives to give us as much pleasure as it can without resorting to falsehoods; the satisfaction of our desires is the propelling impulse, the reality principle is the restraining one. Fiction endeavors to gratify as many of our longings as possible, but the very effort to teach us how they can be reconciled with one another and with reality compels it to take cognizance of the ineluctable limits of the human situation.[19]

We fail to realize how much wish fulfilment occurs in narrative art because the wishes underlying many stories escape conscious notice. We are, of course, aware of the extent to which popular fiction satisfies erotic or ambitious desires. But, as the example of "The Birthmark" may suggest, in the greatest fiction wishes are ordinarily disguised with subtle care.

NOTES

1. This is most obviously true of the novel, which, as D. H. Lawrence pungently maintains, is the most difficult of all media to fool. "Somehow, you

sweep the ground a bit too clear in the poem or the drama, and you let the human Word fly a bit too freely. Now in a novel there's always a tom-cat, a black tom-cat that pounces on the white dove of the Word, if the dove doesn't watch it; and there is a banana-skin to trip on; and you know there is a water-closet on the premises. All these things help to keep the balance." "The Novel," *The Later D. H. Lawrence* (New York: Knopf, 1952), 191.

2. "'Psychical Distance' as a Factor in Art and an Esthetic Principle," *A Modern Book of Esthetics*, ed. Melvin M. Rader (New York: Holt, 1935), 318. Cf. Havelock Ellis: ". . . when we think of a book proper, in the sense that a Bible means a book, we mean . . . a revelation of something that had remained latent, unconscious, perhaps even more or less intentionally repressed, within the writer's own soul, which is, ultimately, the soul of mankind." Preface to *The Dance of Life* (London: Constable, 1923).

3. Rosenblatt, *Literature as Exploration* (New York, Appleton, 1948), 45.

4. Of course the choice of books is governed by other considerations also. [Cf. Lesser, *Fiction and the Unconscious*, chap. 8.]

5. Krutch, *Five Masters* (New York: Jonathan Cape & Harrison Smith, 1930), 165.

6. Ibid., 166.

7. Brooks and Warren, *Understanding Fiction* (New York: Appleton-Century-Crofts, 1943), 607.

8. Ibid., 104.

9. Needless to say, however, so long as the meaning is demonstrably present, it does not matter whether Hawthorne was conscious of putting it there.

10. More specifically still, it may represent female sexuality—that is, be a castration symbol. I am indebted to Dr. Charles Fisher for this suggestion.

11. Freud, "The Most Prevalent Form of Degradation in Erotic Life," *Collected Papers*, vol. 4.

12. Ibid., 207.

13. Brooks and Warren, *Understanding Fiction*, 105.

14. Freud, *Collected Papers*, vol. 5.

15. Ibid., 218.

16. Ibid., 218.

17. Ibid., 220.

18. Freud's paper predicts that other ways in which these kindly aspects assert themselves would be discovered.

19. I am aware that this formulation somewhat resembles I. A. Richards'; e.g., "The experiences of the artist, those at least which give value to his work, represent conciliations of impulses which in most minds are still confused, intertrammelled and conflicting. His work is the ordering of what in most minds is disordered. . . ." There can be no more important service than this, Richards believes, for "the conduct of life is throughout an attempt to organise impulses so that success is obtained for the greatest number or mass of them, for the most important and the weightiest set. . . ." While some sacrifices may be necessary in the interest of stability, a systematization must be judged "by the extent of the loss, the range of impulses thwarted or starved. . . . That organisation which is least wasteful of human possibilities is . . . the best." *Principles of Literary Criticism* (New York: Harcourt, Brace, 1934), 61 and passim. I believe that these insights, which underlie Richards' entire theory, are valid and extremely valuable. Unfortunately, Richards lacked a psychology which would enable him to specify in suf-

ficient detail how they apply to literature. His language sometimes suggests, too, that the achievement of a better systematization is a more rational and conscious endeavor than I conceive it to be.

Fantasy and Defense in Faulkner's "A Rose for Emily"

NORMAN N. HOLLAND

Over the years Norman Holland's critical interest has shifted from concern about how stories make meaning (*The Dynamics of Literary Response*, 1975) to how readers make meaning (*5 Readers Reading*, 1975). Nevertheless, analysis of literary works as the interaction of unconscious fantasies and conscious defenses—be they the author's, the character's, or the reader's—has remained his central concern. In this early essay he analyzes the "objective" patterns in "A Rose for Emily," namely, the defense strategies of incorporation and denial, and relates them to stages in Miss Emily's ego development. The selection below follows Holland's summary of the story and of its various critical interpretations. He contends that the sociological critics, who stress the conflict between new North and old South, and the New Critics and myth critics, who emphasize the contrast between past time and a present time that denies change, are accentuating different levels óf the same central conflict, a conflict best explored at the unconscious levels of fantasy and defense mechanisms. Holland's concluding section, omitted here, looks forward to his reader-oriented criticism: he writes that no matter how elaborate his model, all he can "really do is set up a matrix of possibilities which will finally find their reality as some reader makes them his own."

> Many experiences such as this lead me to assert
> that the dream-work is under some kind of
> necessity to combine all the sources which have
> acted as stimuli for the dream into a single
> unity in the dream itself.
> —[S. Freud], *The Interpretation of Dreams*

Excerpted from "Fantasy and Defense in Faulkner's 'A Rose for Emily,'" *Hartford Studies in Literature* 4 (1972): 1–35. Copyright 1972 Norman N. Holland. Reprinted by permission of *Hartford Studies in Literature*.

> My experience in the clearing-up of hysterical
> symptoms has shown that it is not necessary for
> the various meanings of a symptom to be compatible
> with one another, that is, to fit together into
> a connected whole. It is enough that the unity
> should be constituted by the subject matter which
> has given rise to all the various phantasies.
>
> —[S. Freud], "Fragment of an Analysis
> of a Case of Hysteria"

WHEN WE TURN TO THE unconscious themes that underlie those conscious ones, we find that something in turn "stands for" Miss Emily: her house. The symbolism is familiar and well known, but even so, the story spells it out. In "what had once been our most select street," "only Miss Emily's house was left, lifting its stubborn and coquettish decay above the cotton wagons and the gasoline pumps." The adjectives, Professor [Ray B.] West notes, "make the house reflect" what Miss Emily has herself become: "stubborn in her attempt to thwart the passage of time, coquettish in her refusal to admit that she had grown old." "Both Emily and the house are, 'monuments of the past' set in the present," says Professor [William O.] Hendricks.[1] Twice the story calls Miss Emily "impervious," an adjective that could apply equally well to a house that no white person has entered for years, that has not even a mailbox or a number. Judge Stevens makes the equation quite explicit, when the younger generation complains about the smell around the house. "'Dammit, sir,' Judge Stevens said, 'will you accuse a lady to her face of smelling bad?'"

Another symbolism may have relevance here: the genital meaning of the "rose" of the title, on which Professor [George] Snell comments, "Miss Emily's 'rose' is bequeathed and discovered and becomes a charnel-house flower all in a breath,"[2] or in the four astonishingly abrupt last paragraphs, anyway. Professor [William T.] Going wittily suggests that, given Faulkner's "subtle and gruesome treatment of odors in the story and the importance of the Grierson name, the title may well refer to Shakespeare's familiar lines from another tragedy of lovers:

What's in a name? That which we call a rose
By any other name would smell as sweet.[3]

Both the symbolism of the house and of the rose suggest that the story concerns a feminine body with a nasty secret inside it, dust and darkness and, most strongly, smells: "a close, dank smell," "a thin, acrid pall," a "dust dry and acrid in the nostrils." "It smelled of dust and disuse." The smell "was another link between the gross, teeming world and the high and mighty Griersons," and the adjective "high" may even conceal a particularly sardonic pun.

This imagery of dust, dirt, and smell suggests that the story, at an unconscious level, is dealing with an anal character or anal fantasy or at least that Freud's anal triad might be relevant. Orderliness, parsimony, and obstinacy all derive from holding on or letting go the feces in response to outer demands. We find the orderliness reversed with Miss Emily, not cleanliness but uncleanliness: the smells, dirt, and dust, "which no other woman of her standing would have permitted," Professor [C. W. M.] Johnson notes. The non-psychoanalytic explicators have singled out (in Johnson's phrase) Miss Emily's "obstinate refusal to submit to, or even to concede, the inevitability of change," her "attempting, almost by force of will alone, to halt the natural process of decay," as West puts it. Professors [Cleanth] Brooks and [Robert Penn] Warren sum the matter up: "She is obviously a woman of tremendous firmness of will," and their word, "firmness," like the other phrasing ("the inevitability of change," "the natural process") contains the faintest hint of the body "holding on" against the irresistible excretory pressure to "let go," which must be the unconscious core of the story.[4]

For Emily is nothing if not retentive—Brooks and Warren see her crime as "what Miss Emily does in order to hold her lover." Professor West points to her final belief "that she could retain her lover by . . . holding his body prisoner," Professor Johnson to her inability to stand his "slipping out of her life." In Japan, Faulkner himself said simply, "She had had something and she wanted to keep it." Recognizing the anal theme explains one of the story's more startling images, a description of the aged Miss Emily: "she looked bloated, like a body long submerged in motionless water." "Motionless," Professor West points out, links her to the absence of change, but more specifically to the kind of stasis that swells a body up. This is a story—at one level—about the difficulty prized things have in going into and out of a certain house (or body).[5]

Given the familiar symbols for feces, it is no surprise that some of what goes in and out is money: "the old thrill and the old despair of a penny more or less." Miss Emily does not pay money out in taxes. Instead, she defies the authorities who demand that she do so. "She gave lessons in china-painting"—one could hardly find a more obsessional or anal pastime. Further, to learn this art, "the daughters and granddaughters of Colonel Sartoris' contemporaries were sent to her with the same regularity and in the same spirit that they were sent to church on Sundays with a twenty-five-cent piece for the collection plate." Freud, as early as 1907, had pointed out the similarity between religious practices and obsessive actions, even before he had brought out the special connection between anal erotism and obsessional behavior and, indeed, of painting as a possible sublimation of coprophilia.[6] Thus, religious images play a part in establishing the level of unconscious fantasy on which the story builds: Miss Emily as "a tradition, a duty, and a care," resembling "those angels in colored church windows," "an idol," "an idol in a niche," and after her death "a fallen monument."

I do not, however, wish to give the impression that the unconscious content of the story is all anal—certainly not with a father like Miss Emily's. He is shown as penniless, violent, angry, having fallen out with the Griersons' only relatives. "We had long thought of them as a tableau, Miss Emily a slender figure in white in the background, her father a spraddled silhouette in the foreground, his back to her and clutching a horsewhip." With such a father, there must be an oedipal component to the story. Obviously, he dominates Emily, driving her suitors away with his horsewhip, and he continues his power, somehow, after his death. Even after hers, there was "the crayon face of her father musing profoundly above the bier."

In this oedipal and anal view the very center of the story is the narrator's remark: "We knew that with nothing left, she would have to cling to that which had robbed her, as people will." But Emily does more than cling to her father's body. After Homer Barron has apparently deserted her, she isolates herself, "as if," the narrator comments, "that quality of her father which had thwarted her woman's life so many times had been too virulent and too furious to die." He goes on to describe her hair as a "vigorous iron-gray, like the hair of an active man." She is described as a "lighthouse-keeper," as having "vanquished them [the town government], horse and foot, just as she had vanquished their fathers thirty years before." Appropriately enough for a woman with great force of will, she is buried among soldiers. Thus, Professor West concludes, "In the picture of Emily and her father together . . . we have a reversal of the contrast that is to come later." Perhaps Professor Irving Malin is correct when he says, "Her passionate, almost sexual relationship with her dead father forces her to distrust the living body of Homer and to kill him so that he will resemble the dead father she can never forget."[7] Or, perhaps it suffices to say Miss Emily identifies with her father, taking on his iron will, his strength, and his brutality, regressing from the little girl's oedipal wish to *have* her father to the pre-oedipal, phallic wish to *be* her father.

In this context, despite the objections of the townsfolk ("'A Grierson would not think seriously of a Northerner, a day laborer'"), her degraded choice of Homer Barron becomes almost inevitable. He is tabooed, a substitute for her father, the original, incestuously forbidden lover. The disapproval tempts by re-enacting that first, disapproved love, even as it guarantees the lover is no parent. As Freud says, "The condition of forbiddenness in the erotic life of women is, I think, comparable to the need on the part of men to debase their sexual object," both being ways of seeking "only objects which do not recall the incestuous figures forbidden" in childhood, although, "These new objects will still be chosen on the model . . . of the infantile ones."[8]

Thus, Emily keeps Homer's body as she tried to keep her father's. At the same time, her vengeful murder of Homer is just the kind of thing her father would do and suggests the degree to which she has incorporated in herself her father's brutality. There is, in effect, a man in Emily's house—or body—or mind. Even Faulkner tended to masculinize Emily in his description of the story to the students at Virginia: "the conflict of conscience with glands, with the Old Adam." "The conflict was in Miss Emily," including, apparently, Old Adam's glands.

By contrast, the town outside Emily's house sharply distinguishes men from women. Indeed, the long opening sentence establishes just that: sexes are markedly different in this town, but Emily's house involves a kind of peculiar combination of man and woman: "When Miss Emily Grierson died, our whole town went to her funeral: the men through a sort of respectful affection for a fallen monument, the women mostly out of curiosity to see the inside of her house, which no one save an old man-servant—a combined gardener and cook—had seen in at least ten years." Similarly, in the remission of Miss Emily's taxes, "Only a man of Colonel Sartoris' generation and thought could have invented [the story], and only a woman could have believed it." Colonel Sartoris was the one who "fathered the edict that no Negro woman should appear on the streets without an apron," but in Miss Emily's house the servant is a male cook. The narrator repeatedly insists on calling her supervising relatives, "the two female cousins," and, in general, it falls to the ladies to keep up standards in the town. "'Just as if a man—any man—could keep a kitchen properly,' the ladies said; so they were not surprised when the smell developed." It is the ladies who get the Baptist minister to remonstrate with Emily about her relationship with Homer. The day after the father's death, "all the ladies prepared to call at the house and offer condolence and aid, as is our custom."

In effect, the town, by sharply differentiating the sexes, recapitulates the kind of outside control Miss Emily had when her father was alive and before she had incorporated his masculinity into herself. Although Faulkner himself, as well as many readers, retained a vivid image of the delicately feminine Miss Emily, she actually appears in only one phrase, "a slender figure in white." Most of the time, we see Emily as she appears to the druggist, "cold, haughty black eyes in a face the flesh of which was strained across the temples and about the eyesockets as you imagine a lighthouse-keeper's face ought to look." "She carried her head high enough," driving with Homer Barron, and the word is applied at least two more times to the Griersons as a family. "Miss Emily with her head high"—her body, again, matches the house itself, "lifting its stubborn and coquettish decay above" its sordid surroundings.

"The anal character," notes Karl Abraham,

> sometimes seems to stamp itself on the physiognomy of its possessor. It seems particularly to show itself in a morose expression. [Such persons] tend to surliness as a rule. A constant tension of the line of the nostril together with a slight lifting of the upper lip seem to me significant fa-

cial characteristics of such people. In some cases this gives the impression that they are constantly sniffing at something. Probably this feature is traceable to their coprophilic pleasure in smell.[9]

One could equally well trace it to controlling, "keeping a grip on" oneself.

Certainly control is a basic issue of the story, not only for Miss Emily, but also in the town from whose point of view we see her. Repeatedly, we hear about the forces of law in the town, and such writers as [Erik H.] Erickson have shown the close link between law as that which "apportions to each his privileges and his limitations, his obligations and his rights" and the "sense of rightfully delimited autonomy in the parents" at the anal stage so involved with retention and elimination, with holding on and letting go, with shame and autonomy, control and will. All these things are important in "A Rose for Emily," particularly in view of what West calls "the conflicting demands of the past and the present."[10]

In the more modern period of the story, law takes the form of institutions or groups: "the post office," "them," "the sheriff's office," "the city authorities," "the town." It is the government of laws, not men. If there are men, they act on behalf of the law, as the mayor and the aldermen and the druggist do. In the older period of the story, it is a government of men, not laws, as government must appear to a child. It is Judge Stevens or Colonel Sartoris who controls, and this style of government is closely associated with Miss Emily's father. Thus, in describing the remission of her taxes, Faulkner uses the word three times: "Colonel Sartoris, the mayor—he who fathered the edict that no Negro woman should appear on the streets without an apron—remitted her taxes, the dispensation dating from the death of her father . . . [and] invented an involved tale to the effect that Miss Emily's father had loaned money to the town."

In many ways, as the "edict" suggests, this kind of law is more like unlawfulness, like her father's horsewhip or like justice in the American South even today. Thus, Professor [Austin] Wright finds the story showing a peculiar combination of violence and "the weakness of the society in enforcing its laws and principles" against Emily. When Judge Stevens gets the Board of Aldermen to take the law into their own hands, "the next night, after midnight, four men . . . slunk about like burglars." Similarly, her father is described as "that which had robbed her." Then, if we think of the tenacity with which the South has clung to the "peculiar institution" which has cost the South so much, we can find still another dimension in the story's key clause: "With nothing left, she would have to cling to that which had robbed her, as people will."

Predictably, it is this kind of being "above the law" that Miss Emily adopts as her own life-style once her father has died. She refuses to pay her taxes. Her house smells enough to be a public nuisance. She refuses to give up her father's body or to tell the druggist what she wants the poison for or to let the town put street numbers and a mailbox on her house. And she commits murder. Miss Emily puts the person above the law, as when she refuses to recognize the sheriff's authority—"'Perhaps he considers himself the sheriff'"—or the Board of Alderman's. Instead, "'See Colonel Sartoris. I have no taxes in Jefferson.'" "Colonel Sartoris had been dead almost ten years"—like her father.

Such a government counts on the pride and dignity of its Sartorises, Griersons, and Stevenses. It punishes by the opposite of pride and dignity—like the aprons the Negro women must wear as a badge of servitude. Shame is a visual thing. Again, in discussing the anal phase of development, Erikson says, "Shame supposes that one is completely exposed and conscious of being looked at." "One is visible and not ready to be visible; which is why we dream of shame as a situation in which we are stared at in a condition of incomplete dress, in night attire, 'with one's pants down.'"[11] Presumably, the control through shame provides the occasion for the many, many references to watching in the story, mostly references to the peeping, whispering, gossiping townspeople as they comment on Emily's actions.

Emily seems unaffected by this watching. Indeed she takes on a symbolic role as a result of it: "As they recrossed the lawn, a window that had been dark was lighted and Miss Emily sat in it, the light behind her, and her upright torso motionless as that of an idol. Now and then we would see her in one of the downstairs windows—she had evidently shut up the top floor of the house—like the carven torso of an idol in a niche, looking or not looking at us, we could never tell which." She becomes the lighthouse-keeper, watching and watched, visible symbol of the old "tradition" with its hard training heavily based on shame, like the educational systems of certain primitive peoples.

As Erikson notes, "Visual shame precedes auditory guilt," has more of the primitive about it, just as the Sartorises' and Stevenses' system of government does, and Emily, ultimately, is not a well-governed person. The very act of letting her father be buried was "out of character," notes Professor Johnson. "Social pressure had been too great, but she learned from that incident the necessity for concealment. The story is a success story—of success in maintaining an untenable position." "Too much shaming," notes Erikson, "does not lead to genuine propriety but to a secret determination to try to get away with things, unseen—if, indeed, it does not result in defiant shamelessness." Emily is both, shameless with Homer alive, secret with him dead. "Already we knew that there was one room in that region above stairs which no one had *seen* in forty years," and the participle I have [italicized] is psychologically exact.

Control, particularly control based on shaming, plays an important part in the anal stage of development, in adults with predominantly anal characters, and in this story. Yet, as in Freud's original formulation, the most central issue of all is possessing or, in Erikson's phrase, "holding on and letting go." In this story, to love is to possess someone, as one would possess a thing. Emily holds on to Homer's body as, earlier, she had held on to her father's body. Homer, too, signifies his careless love by the way he doesn't even own his horses but has to rent them from the livery stable. Emily takes possession of him by gifts: a nightshirt, a toilet set, and, evidently, at least the promise of herself. Conversely, to be loved is to become a gift, to be possessed like an object. Thus, the language of the story links love and death in "the tomb . . . decked and furnished as for a bridal," in "the long sleep that outlasts love . . . [that] had cuckolded him." To die—to give up something precious or dirty—is to love and become something precious or dirty.

Always, in this story, to understand it fully, one must keep in mind the picture of a parental figure (Emily's father, the narrator, the town) presiding over what goes into and out of Miss Emily's house—or body. Erikson calls it the "battle for autonomy."

If outer control by too rigid or too early training persists in robbing the child of his attempt gradually to control his bowels and other functions willingly and by his free choice. . . . [among other outcomes, he may] pretend an autonomy and an ability to do without anybody's help which he has by no means really gained. This stage, therefore, becomes decisive for the ratio between loving good will and hateful self-insistence, between cooperation and willingness, and between self-expression and compulsive self-restraint or meek compliance.[12]

Miss Emily, like a child being trained, vacillates between shameless defiance of that authority (when it is the town) or totally introjecting its demands and complying with them (when it is her father). Towards the parent trying to regulate the feces that come from its body, Dr. Spock notes the way the child is "apt to fight in rage and terror, as if he thought he was going to remove a very part of his body," or at least will become "worried to see this object, which he considers part of himself, snatched away."[13] This is another sense in which we must understand the key statement in the story: "With nothing left, she would have to cling to that which had robbed her, as people will." It is more than just a bad pun to say Miss Emily is a possessive woman. Miss Emily had "incorporated" or "introjected" the harsh controls based on pride and shame that her father embodied. Holding his body and Homer's, retaining them inside her house or body, is the outward sign of an inward adaptation. So also, I would guess, is her becoming obese a sign of oral incorporation as well as anal retention.

This highly special reading of the story gets confirmation from an odd detail—Faulkner's handling of the voices. [Otto] Fenichel sums up some psychoanalytic thinking about speech: "The function of speech is frequently connected unconsciously with the genital function, particularly with the male genital function. To speak means to be potent; inability to speak means castration." Thus, virile Homer is associated with "a lot of laughing," was "a big, dark, ready man, with a big voice." "The little boys would follow in groups to hear him cuss the niggers."

By contrast, "Her voice was dry and cold," and, as for the Negro manservant, "He talked to no one, probably not even to her, for his voice had grown harsh and rusty, as if from disuse." Fenichel gives one way of interpreting their silence:

> The anal-erotic nature of speech is seen best when, in analysis, a specific situation, which either provokes or accentuates stuttering, proves to be an anal temptation. Unconsciously, speech in general or in certain situations is thought of as a sexualized defecation. The same motives which in childhood were directed against pleasurable playing with feces make their appearance again in the form of inhibitions of the pleasure of playing with words. The expulsion and retention of words means the expulsion and retention of feces, and actually the retention of words, just as previously the retention of feces, may be either a reassurance against possible loss or a pleasurable autoerotic activity.

Clearly, it is the first of these two for Miss Emily. The story, however, shows even a third significance Fenichel gives for speech: "In dreams, to speak is the symbol of life, and to be mute the symbol of death." [14] Thus, in a marvellously chosen adjective, we see Homer's "two mute shoes" in the sealed bedroom.

These references to speech and the voice—though only a small series of images in the story—nevertheless trace out its pattern. The issue is one of going in or coming out, in both a phallic and an anal sense. That is, Miss Emily's father restricts the suitors who can enter her house and thus her body. Deprived, Miss Emily, and the story as a whole, regress to the anal stage. She will hold on to what she has: first her father; then her father's tradition, and style; finally, Homer Barron, the man who would have robbed her. (There may even be a play on "robber barron.") In contrast, then, to big-voiced Homer, who puts out sound freely, Miss Emily's silent house signifies the attempt to hold things in. He represents the new freedom from the North, she, the attempt to keep things as they are in the South, to stop process and change—a kind of social constipation.

We have already seen many of the regular explicators of the story call Emily's resistance to change the central theme, whether one regards change in the specific context of the American South or in a larger, more philosophical way. In psychoanalytic terms, they are saying Miss Emily is using a specific defense mechanism or adaptive strategy (maladaptive, really), *denial.* "She denies Time, even to the point of ignoring . . . Death." She refused "to comply with the requirements of the law, because for her they did not exist." "The distinction between reality and illusion has blurred out."[15] Miss Emily simply acts as though the "next generation," "newer generation," "rising generation," did not exist. She lives where she does despite the change in the street. She writes on "paper of an archaic shape." She becomes fixed like "the carven torso of an idol," and "Thus she passed from generation to generation." She becomes "a tradition, a duty, and a care."

Thus, the town by accepting her, incorporates this idol in a miniature version of Miss Emily's more drastic incorporations—one way the story generalizes into "Southernness." The town mirrors Miss Emily. She keeps in her house the crayon portrait of her father, while the townspeople "had long thought of [both Miss Emily and her father] as a tableau." Miss Emily had her mythic dimension: the colors of the triple goddess; Homer disappearing or her holding onto her father's body for the canonical three days. These Persephonic images become the feebly feminine religion of the "ladies" in the town, even to their gaucherie in sending the Baptist minister to admonish Episcopalian Emily.

In the same way, the town goes along—up to a point—with Miss Emily's denial of her father's death. "We did not say that she was crazy then. We believed she had to do that." Similarly, the townsfolk accept her becoming a recluse "as if that quality of her father which had thwarted her woman's life so many times had been too virulent and too furious to die"—a miniature version of Miss Emily's denial of his death. The townsfolk believe, "'They are married,'" then become curiously silent on the subject when Homer disappears—again, they use a less mad version of her own denial, as do "the old" generally in the richly Faulknerian clause some readers of the story have seen as its center: "the old . . . to whom all the past is not a diminishing road but, instead a huge meadow which no winter ever quite touches, divided from them now by the narrow bottleneck of the most recent decade of years." The image conveys, on the one hand, denial of change by the assertion of timelessness, but also the incorporation of fantasy in the memory, so that they can be "talking of Miss Emily as if she had been a contemporary of theirs, believing that they had danced with her and courted her perhaps, confusing time"— and again, the participle is exact. Mrs. Ruth Sullivan has shown how the narrator matches Emily: his opening sentence about entering her house matches the final breaking into the sealed bedroom. Many phrasings in the story suggest he is a kind of oedipal child committing necrophilia on Emily just as she committed necrophilia on her oedipal love object.[16]

In effect we are seeing what Ludwig Jekels long ago called "the duplicated expression of psychic themes." Both the town-narrator and Emily use a combination of two defense mechanisms: denial and incorporation. The problem they must deal with is change. Emily (and, in a more muted way, the town) deal with it in one of two ways. If denial, she will say there is no "new thing" in external reality. The taxes. The mailbox. Her murder of Homer, which serves, in a way, to deny that she is really unmarried. It also shows the other defensive mode, incorporation.

In external reality, the old is passing and being replaced by the new. Her denials, however, say there is no new thing in external reality, while her incorporations say, I still have the old thing inside me (in my mind or in my house or in my body). This defense takes its most drastic form in Miss Emily's keeping her father or Homer in her house, less drastically in her treating marriage as a possession or keeping the crayon portrait of her father. The townsfolk share this defense by themselves passing Miss Emily on from generation to generation and in their interest in what they take to be something precious or secret in the house, to be watched or approached "like burglars."

These two defensive strategies, denial and incorporation, correspond remarkably neatly to the fantasy at the root of the story. We have said, for example, that the story builds on several levels of libidinally satisfying fantasy: oedipally having the father or the tabooed lover; a woman's acquiring masculine, phallic force; anally retaining something precious or valued; orally taking valued things into oneself, as Miss Emily incorporates Homer or the South, Miss Emily. Clearly, all these are forms of incorporation. In the same way, the story builds on several levels of aggressively satisfying fantasy; at an oedipal level, defeating the taboo on a forbidden lover, having and destroying him; at the phallic level, not only not being overcome by a strong male, but overcoming him; anally defying (by withholding) outer authority and control; orally devouring and eviscerating a loved person. Equally clearly, these are all forms of aggressive attack on an outside force felt as coercive or controlling, as denial sometimes is. By denying the requirements of the law, she destroys them.

Two defensive strategies, several levels of unconscious fantasy, three ways of stating the conscious theme of the story—such variety calls for as clear an exposition as I can give. With appropriate reservations, I think a chart of these various types and levels of unity would help:

Putting within yourself and so controlling . . .	*Something that is outside where it cannot be controlled but seeks to control you.*
Conscious themes:	
Intellectual-aesthetic:	
"She would have to cling . . . as people will."	"to that which had robbed her"
Denial of change	Inevitability of change
Social	
The South and fixed traditions	The North and change

Mythic
  The Persephonic idol   Forces of change
                                                  [Conscious]

Defensive modes: [Unconscious]

  Incorporation   Denial
    I will take and keep the   There is no new thing in
    old thing inside me.   external reality.

Fantasy modes:

  Oedipal
    Identification with the   Destroying the tabooed lover
    regressive father

  Phallic
    Becoming a strong   Being overcome by a strong
    progressive male   male

  Anal
    Keeping the precious-dirty   Defiance of outer authority
    thing inside   and control; refusing the inner
                                    inexorability of excretion

  Primal scene
    The reader-townsfolk   Stillness, quiet
      imagine the violent sexual
      scene

  Oral
    Being in the matrix of   Being outside the matrix of
    tradition   tradition
    Obesity (inviscerating)   The skeleton (eviscerating)

In effect, the chart itself is a spine or skeleton that spreads through the whole story at every level. As many regular explicators have said, "A Rose for Emily" pivots on the issue of change and resistance to change, or, if we take into account the rich variety of unconscious themes, perceiving change as robbery and resisting that robbery by taking into oneself the outer being that seeks to force you to change. One conscious component of such a theme is the historical issue of South and North. Another is Miss Emily as the Persephonic goddess, traditionally both creator and destroyer, but lifeless in this story, a motionless monument or idol pitted against social and industrial forces of progress.

Just as central, I think, is the story's own statement that "with nothing left," that is, with realities denied, people will "cling to"—incorporate—"that which had robbed" them, that is, the outer forces seeking to control and force them. *I will cling in fantasy to that which has robbed me of reality*—almost a direct statement of the interaction of the story's defensive modes of incorporation and denial as well as the various libidinal levels of fantasy. Oedipally, Emily becomes like her father just as she destroys the tabooed lover's external reality and incorporates him in the house of her body. She becomes strong and phallic and masculine and conquers the father-lover who seeks to overcome her. She retains, anally, the precious contents of her life despite external pressures to let them go. At an oral level, her body grows fat as she incorporates, while Homer's body is eviscerated. The sealed bedroom is depleted. It holds a dusty stillness and quiet, while the townspeople—and the reader—are left to create in themselves the sights and sounds of the sex and the death-agony on the night of Homer's death. . . .

NOTES

The following notes are for reference only.

I have used only one abbreviation: *The Standard Edition of the Complete Psychological Works of Sigmund Freud* (translated by James Strachey, Anna Freud, Alix Strachey, and Alan Tyson), edited by James Strachey, 24 vols. (London: Hogarth Press and the Institute of Psycho-analysis, 1957–) is referred to simply as *Std. Edn.*

1. Ray B. West, Jr., *Reading the Short Story* (New York: Thomas Y. Crowell, 1968), 83; William O. Henricks, "Linguistics and the Structural Analysis of Literary Texts" (manuscript, Department of English, University of Nebraska, Lincoln), 87.

2. George Snell, *The Shapers of American Fiction* (New York: E. P. Dutton, 1947), 98.

3. Going, "Faulkner's 'A Rose for Emily,'" *Explicator* 16 (1958), item 27.

4. C. W. M. Johnson, "Faulkner'[s] 'A Rose for Emily'" *Explicator* 6 (1948), item 45. Ray B. West, Jr., *The Short Story in America* (Chicago: Henry Regnery Co., 1952), 93. Cleanth Brooks and Robert Penn Warren, *Understanding Fiction*, 2d ed. (New York: Appleton-Century-Crofts, 1959), 352.

5. Brooks and Warren, *Understanding Fiction*, 351. Ray B. West, Jr. (with Robert Wooster Stallman), *The Art of Modern Fiction* (New York: Rinehart and Co., 1949), 275. *Faulkner at Nagano*, edited by Robert A. Jeliffe (Tokyo: Kenkyusha, 1956), 70. West, *Reading the Short Story*, 83.

6. Freud, "Obsessive Actions and Religious Practices" (1907), "Character and Anal Erotism" (1908), *Std. Edn.*, 4:117–27; 169–75.

7. West, *Art of Modern Fiction*, 272. Irving Malin, *William Faulkner: An Interpretation* (Stanford, Calif.: Stanford University Press, 1957), 37.

8. "On the Universal Tendency to Debasement in the Sphere of Love" (1912), *Std. Edn.*, 11:186–87, 182–83, and 181.

9. Abraham, "Contributions to the Theory of the Anal Character" (1921),

in *On Character and Libido Development: Six Essays by Karl Abraham,* edited by Bertram D. Lewin (New York: W. W. Norton, 1966), 186.

10. Erikson, *Identity, Youth and Crisis* (New York: W. W. Norton, 1968), 107–14. West, *Reading the Short Story,* 84.

11. Erikson, *Childhood and Society,* 2d ed. (New York: W. W. Norton, 1963), 252–53.

12. Erikson, *Identity,* 108–9.

13. Benjamin Spock, *Baby and Child Care,* 2d ed. (New York: Pocket Books, 1957), sects. 380, 383.

14. Fenichel, *The Psychoanalytic Theory of Neurosis* (New York: W. W. Norton, 1945), 312–13.

15. West, *Art of Modern Fiction,* 272; Brooks and Warren, *Understanding Fiction,* 351.

16. Sullivan, "The Narrator in 'A Rose for Emily,'" *Journal of Narrative Technique* 1 (1971): 159–78.

A Psychoanalytic Study: "Sailing to Byzantium"

BRENDA S. WEBSTER

Webster compares the golden bird in "Sailing to Byzantium" to a transitional object of the poet's psyche. Although she does not here cite psychoanalyst D. W. Winnicott, who developed object relations theory in his work with children, Webster and other critics use his account of these objects to analyze poetic images. Winnicott tells us that "transitional objects designate the intermediate area of experience between the thumb and the teddy bear, between the oral eroticism and the true object-relationship."* Like the metaphors of the metaphysical poets, transitional objects emphasize a paradoxical relationship and so work to maintain psychic balance.

"SAILING TO BYZANTIUM" has traditionally been read as an affirmation of the spirit over the life of the body. Elder Olson, long one of the most influential exponents of this view, sees the old man of the poem as freed by age from sensual passion and thus able "to rejoice in the liberation of the soul."[1] In contrast, Simon Lesser has recently observed that

Reprinted from *Yeats: A Psychoanalytic Study,* by Brenda S. Webster, with the permission of the publishers, Stanford University Press. © 1973 by the Board of Trustees of the Leland Stanford Junior University.

**Playing and Reality* (London: Tavistock, 1971), 2.

far from being an affirmation of spirit, the poem is a "cry of agony."[2] The old man is tormented by sexual desire and envy of the young; in Lesser's view it is the tension between desire and his aging body that sets the old man moving toward Byzantium, rather than an appreciation of the superior value of spirit. Lesser suggests that Olson's blindness to the old man's tortured sexuality is symptomatic of a general tendency among critics to concentrate so exclusively on a poem's intellectual framework and formal structure that they lose sight of its emotional content. He finds it impossible to justify emotionally Olson's conclusion that the old man's transformation into a golden bird represents a triumph, that the bird somehow becomes a haven for the old man's free and happy soul. To Lesser, the golden bird is merely an automaton, "a bitter, tinselly travesty of what the 'I' of the poem values . . . and would want of an afterlife."

Olson's very avoidance of the emotional issues, however, leaves him in a better position than Lesser to react appropriately to the symbol of the golden bird. The bird functions as a defense against anxieties unconsciously raised by the poem—not just the fear of aging and thwarted sexuality noted by Lesser, but the overarching fear of a loss of integrity. The old man's anguish at being excluded from the pleasures of the young is so great not only because of sexual frustration, but because Yeats associates loss of potency with other terrifying threats to his integrity—passivity, castration, and disintegration. An old man is but "a tattered coat upon a stick." Olson's unconscious reaction both to these threats and to the bird's defensive role can be sensed in his description of the golden bird. Within the bird, the old man's soul is "free to act in its own supremacy and in full cognizance of its own excellence, incorruptible and secure" from all the ills of the flesh; his soul, that is, is active rather than passive, narcissistically gratified rather than depressed by impotence, and secure against disintegration. As Norman Holland puts it, a work of art is "a complex dialectic of impulse and defense."[3]

To appreciate the full complexity of the bird's defensive function, it is necessary to distinguish in the poem two competing but coalescing themes. The old man's frustrated sexual desire is the visible strand in what we shall see is a submerged theme or fantasy of union with the mother. Merging this fantasy with the theme of aging and death was possible for Yeats because of his masochistic attitude toward both. As we have seen, in the works by Yeats that embody incestuous fantasies, the hero is often symbolically castrated or mutilated by the mother figure before he can be loved. In "Sailing to Byzantium" Yeats endows the aging process itself with the threatening qualities of a cruel mother. Now it is age that sexually frustrates the old man and threatens him with disintegration and loss of self. In the Ribh poems Yeats fought similar fears of disintegration by stressing sexual vitality and thus intactness. This particular defensive maneuver was made easier by Yeats's Steinach operation, which increased his sense of sexual vitality. "Sailing" was written before that operation, after a spate of illnesses that undoubtedly intensified the 61-year-old Yeats's fear of death; in "Sailing" Yeats turns to another instrument of psychic defense, the talismanic object.

In studying the golden bird, one is struck by its resemblance to a transitional object or to a fetish (fetish is used here in the sense of a symbolic object with phallic significance that offers protection against fears of castration). Like both the transitional object and the fetish, the bird is used to maintain psychic balance and a sense of self. Like the transitional object it is something onto which the self is projected, something partly self and partly other; Olson's feeling that the bird is an "insouled monument" expresses this double quality. The bird is also basically a "good object," one that reassures its owner and banishes feelings of sadness and inadequacy. The bird's phallic significance and its role as a defense against fears and fantasies of castration emerge clearly when the bird is compared to objects in other works that more obviously represent the phallus. . . .

[Webster discusses Yeats's "The Cap and the Bells" and his drama *A Full Moon in March,* which also "embody Yeats's fantasies of submitting to a cruel mother."]

In "Sailing to Byzantium" Yeats, in order to banish sadness, makes use of both a good object that banishes bad objects—the precious golden bird—and a good feeling (this includes denial, the thought that man survives in his work, but also contains many other elements), gaiety, that banishes bad feelings. In "Sailing" it is his gaiety that keeps the old man from being merely tatters. Though the contrast is intended to be one of bodily tatters versus the singing soul, the ultimate emotional message is that if the old man sings loudly enough, he will not disintegrate physically.

The reader will recall a similar "gay" reaction to death, expressed in similar imagery, in *Oisin;* the extent to which Yeats transcends his masochism in "Sailing" is underscored if we compare the resolutions of the two poems. When St. Patrick taunts Oisin with death and damnation, Oisin responds with defiant song:

> . . . I go to the Fenians, O cleric, to chaunt
> The war-songs that roused them of old; they will rise . . .
> Innumerable, singing, exultant.
>
> $(3.201-3)$ [4]

Patrick reacts with increased severity to Oisin's defiance: "kneel and wear out the flags and pray for your soul that is lost" (3.215). Overwhelmed by Patrick's threats, Oisin loses his gaiety, and it becomes clear that the gaiety is defending against a feeling of disintegration. Like the tattered protagonist of "Among School Children" Oisin is broken with age, a "show unto children" (3.218). In an image that suggests the tattered coat of "Sailing," he feels "All emptied . . . as a beggar's cloak in the rain" (3.219). The poem ends with this complete deflation of the hero. It is significant that in the drafts of "Sailing," the "I" takes a penitential position similar to the one St. Patrick urges upon Oisin. The "I" prays for death from the God who threatened Oisin, and wonders if "God's love will refuse"

> When prostrate on the marble step I fall
> And cry aloud. . . .[5]

Yeats deleted these masochistic lines—and all other Christian references—for images of his own synthesis. Throughout his work Yeats saw the Christian God as playing a punitive part in the struggle between impulsive forces (e.g., Oisin) and repression (e.g., St. Patrick), and in "Sailing to Byzantium" Yeats wanted to portray transformation, not simply destruction. In *Oisin* the hero, deformed by age and blindness, "lies on the anvil of the world" (2.203–4). The smith who strikes the sinner is of course God. In "Sailing to Byzantium" the act of hammering becomes part of the process of making an artifact. Yeats identifies both with the artificer who destroys in order to create and with the material that is transformed. In his youth he wrote: "My life has been in my poems. To make them I have broken my life in a mortar."[6] The destructive god who batters Oisin with age becomes a Grecian goldsmith who gives the "I" a permanent, invulnerable form.

As we have seen, one of Yeats's main concerns in "Sailing to Byzantium" is the translation of the body into an invulnerable form. F. A. C. Wilson, like Olson preoccupied by the soul-body dichotomy in the poem, calls the golden bird "the soul's image,"[7] but it is certainly the body's image as well. In the drafts, thoughts of the body clearly predominate over thoughts of the spirit. Byzantium is a place where the body is immortalized in art. The art that Yeats chooses for his Holy City is one that specifically celebrates the human body, the sculpture of Phidias. Compare two parallel passages, the first from *Oisin* and the second from the drafts of "Sailing":

> a countless flight
> Of moonlit steps glimmered; and right and left
> Dark statues glimmered over the pale tide
> Upon dark thrones.
>
> (2. 34–37)

> Statues of Phidias
> . . . .
> Mirrored in water
> . . . .
> Statues of bronze over a marble stair.[8]

The first passage has a disembodied quality characterized by the vague, glimmering moonlight. Forty years later, Yeats brings out the potential hardness and precise outlines of the statues. Classical sculpture was well adapted to becoming one of Yeats's hard, valuable, essentially phallic, symbolic objects that glorify the body and magically preserve it from destruction.

The golden bird is perhaps the finest example of the Yeatsian symbol whose phallic nature and talimanic qualities make it comparable in function to the fetish and the transitional object. Another group of images and symbols, less detachable from their context but identifiable nonetheless, are basically womb symbols, which come to represent a place of safety or source of sustenance that often includes a talismanic object. In *Oisin*, the reader will recall, Yeats uses a stair over which moisture continually flows, and a dome to represent the interior of the female body. The domed cavern's similarity to a womb is increased by Oisin's exit through a tiny door next to a stream. Both stair and dome reappear in the early drafts of "Sailing to Byzantium," but they have lost their natural qualities and are specifically connected with art. The sea-slime of *Oisin*'s stair has been transformed into cold marble, and the rocky dome filled with shadowy faces into the mosaic-filled dome of St. Sophia. This change represents a process of repudiation, a "cleaning up" of bodily images to remove what is ephemeral, disgusting, or dangerous.

Though the "I" longs to see the dome of St. Sophia in early drafts, explicit mention of the dome has disappeared from the final draft. Its vestigial presence is definitely felt, however. Figures are described descending a gold mosaic wall in a spiral movement that Yeats, in previous works, has associated with a dome. Giorgio Melchiori has pointed out the descent of similar gyrating figures from a dome in "Rosa Alchemica,"[9] but there is an earlier and equally significant allusion to the dome in *Oisin*, where the gyrating motion is represented by the hero's circling the floor before he exits. The dome in *Oisin* is even filled with shadowy faces (similar to the blurred figures of the later "Rosa Alchemica") "loaded with the memory of days / Buried and mighty." The concept of a dome filled with memories is an obvious prototype of Yeats's concept of the Great Memory, *Anima Mundi*, and is echoed in the drafts of "Sailing to Byzantium" by the dome of St. Sophia, which, as Yeats delightedly remarks elsewhere, was called the "Holy Wisdom."[10]

In the revisions of "Sailing" the dome's benign wisdom is embodied by the sages. This final version differs in an important way from earlier versions, in which the sages were saints and Yeats prayed to them to make him like themselves:

> Consume this heart & make it what you were
> Rigid, abstracted, and fanatical.[11]

The saints were never important to Yeats in a Christian sense as certain critics seem to think. They were important because of their toughness and indestructibility. In this respect, they resemble other hard defensive objects and Yeats is drawn to them. He repudiates and replaces them, however, because of other, less pleasant associations. Like politicians and critics, the saints, in Yeats's view, are castrated by envy and fanaticism and are hostile to both creativity and sexuality. To become like them is to suffer castration.

In revision, Yeats turn the saints into the less threatening sages. Oisin's experience within the domed cavern of the Isle of Fears illuminates the sages' function. It is within the cavern, the reader will recall, that Oisin receives the gift of the word sword, with which to fight the demon. Yeats always thought of *Anima Mundi* both as a repository of poetic images and as the place to go for "answers" when in difficulty. In "Sailing," the sages assume the dome's function as a repository of wisdom, and thus become helpful rather than castrating. The sages in Yeats's final version will not deprive the "I" of anything: they will be his "singing-masters."

NOTES

1. As cited by Simon Lesser in his article, "'Sailing to Byzantium': Another Voyage, Another Reading," *College English* 28 (1967): 293.

2. Ibid.

3. Holland, *Psychoanalysis and Shakespeare* (New York: McGraw-Hill, 1964), 53.

4. [All quotations from *The Wanderings of Oisin* are from *The Variorium Edition of the Poems of W. B. Yeats*, ed. Peter Allt and Russell K. Alspach (New York: Macmillan, 1957); references are to stanza and line.]

5. Stallworthy, *Between the Lines: Yeats's Poetry in the Making* (London, 1963), 98.

6. Yeats, *Letters of W. B. Yeats*, ed. Alan Wade (New York: Macmillan, 1955), 84.

7. Wilson, *Yeats's Iconography* (London: Gollancz, 1960), 285.

8. Stallworthy, *Between the Lines*, 95.

9. Giorgio Melchiori, *The Whole Mystery of Art: Pattern into Poetry in the Work of W. B. Yeats* (London: Routledge & Kegan Paul, 1960), 221–23.

10. [*A Vision* (New York: Macmillan Paperbacks, 1966), 280.]

11. Stallworthy, *Between the Lines*, 100.

Yeats and "Sailing to Byzantium"

HAROLD BLOOM

Bloom's well-known "anxiety of influence" paradigm employs Freudian strategies to defend humanist values of individualism.

Bloom theorizes that each poet composes in an anxiety-laden relation to his poetic forefathers, or precursors. This Oedipal situation (son: father :: poet: precursor poet) requires each poet to rename or rework previous poems to make room for himself. In this patriarchal order, not only can each poet be seen contending with the great poets preceding him, but each major poem can be seen as a "mis-reading" or "mis-prisoning" (a sort of critical revisioning) of earlier influential poems. By valorizing the poet's individual will as it struggles against the "wealth of tradition," Bloom seems to be upholding an individualistic humanism in the face of what he takes to be the nihilistic threat of deconstruction.

INTRODUCTION*

Dr. Johnson, despite his profound understanding of the relations between poets, was too involved in his own relation to Milton to understand fully that particular case of poetic influence. Except for the Founder, Freud, we do not expect any doctor of the mind to analyze his own case, or even necessarily to see that he constitutes a case. Even so, when a poet is also a gifted critic, we rightly do not expect him to know or describe accurately what his relation to his precursors is. We need to be warier than we have been in contemplating such a poet-critic's portraits of his precursors, for the portraits necessarily show us not what the precursors were, but what the poet-critic needed them to have been.

The most remarkable such portrait in poetic history that I know is the cosmic one rendered of Milton by Blake throughout his work, but particularly in the "brief epic" called "Milton." Blake's Milton is the Poet proper, the heroic Bard whose inspiration is absolute, and whose achievement stands as a second Scripture, all but as sacred as Scripture itself. Blake, in *The Marriage of Heaven and Hell,* entered upon a massive re-interpretation of Milton that almost every modern scholar has judged to be a misinterpretation. So I suppose it is, as all significant reading of one creator by another must be. Poets, or at least strong poets, do not read one another even as the strongest of critics read poetry. Poetic influence is a labyrinth that our criticism scarcely begins to exlore. Borges, the scholar of labyrinths, has given us the first principle for the investigation of poetic influence:

> In the critics' vocabulary, the word "precursor" is indispensable, but it should be cleansed of all connotation of polemics or rivalry. The fact is that every writer *creates* his own precursors. His work modifies our conception of the past, as it will modify the future. In this correlation the identity or plurality of the men involved is unimportant.[1]

*This section is from chapter 1, *Introduction.*—ED.

Though the theory of poetic influence I pursue swerves sharply from Borges, it accepts the poet's *creation* of his precursors as starting point. But the relation of ephebe or new poet to his precursors cannot be cleansed of polemics or rivalry, noble as the aesthetic idealism of Borges is, because the relation is not clean. Poetic influence, to many critics, is just something that happens, a transmission of ideas and images, and whether or not influence causes anxiety in the later poet is regarded as a problem of temperament or circumstance. But the ephebe cannot be Adam early in the morning. There have been too many Adams, and they have named everything. The burden of unnaming prompts the true wars fought under the banner of poetic influence, wars waged by the perversity of the spirit against the wealth accumulated by the spirit, the wealth of tradition. . . .* Yeats's immediate tradition could be described as the internalization of quest romance, and Yeats's most characteristic kind of poem could be called the dramatic lyric of internalized quest, the genre of "Sailing to Byzantium," "Vacillation," and many of the "Supernatural Songs," and indeed of most of Yeats's major works.

Poetic influence, as I conceive it, is a variety of melancholy or an anxiety-principle. It concerns the poet's sense of his precursors, and of his own achievement in relation to theirs. Have they left him room enough, or has their priority cost him his art? More crucially, where did they go wrong, so as to make it possible for him to go right? In this revisionary sense, in which the poet creates his own precursors by necessarily misinterpreting them, poetic influence forms and malforms new poets, and aids their art at the cost of increasing, finally, their already acute sense of isolation. Critics of a Platonizing kind (in the broad sense, which would include such splendid critics as Borges, [Northrop] Frye, Wilson Knight) refuse to see poetic influence as anxiety because they believe in different versions of what Frye calls the Myth of Concern: "We belong to something before we are anything, nor does growing in being diminish the link of belonging." So, a poet's reputation and influence, that is, what others think he is, is his real self. Milton is what he creates and gives. I urge the contrary view, for the melancholy only the strongest of poets overcome is that they too much belong to something before they are anything, and the link is never diminished. As scholars we can accept what grieves us as isolate egos, but poets do not exist to accept griefs. Freud thought all men unconsciously wished to beget themselves, to be their own fathers in place of their phallic fathers, and so "rescue" their mothers from erotic degradation. It may not be true of all men, but it seems to be definitive of poets *as poets*. The poet, if he could, would be his own precursor, and so rescue the Muse from her degradation. In this sense,

---

*The author explains that in parts of this essay not reprinted here, and elsewhere in his book, he will discuss "the problem of poetic influence" and "the particular kind of Romantic tradition within which Yeats was influenced."—ED.

poetic influence is analogous to Romantic love; both processes are illuminated by Patmore's egregious remarks: "What a Lover sees in the Beloved is the projected shadow of his own potential beauty in the eyes of God." This is certainly what the ephebe or potential poet sees in his precursor, and is akin to Valéry's observations: "One only reads well when one reads with some quite personal goal in mind. It may be to acquire some power. It can be out of hatred for the author."

Reading well, for a strong or potentially strong poet, is necessarily to read as a revisionist. This is particularly true in a tradition like the Romantic, where the poet becomes so haunted by himself, that he begins to present himself as the unique problem. As strength increases, the poet can read only himself, for he contains his own antagonist, a blocking agent or element in his creativity that has gone over to restriction and hardness. . . .

"Sailing to Byzantium" *

"Sailing to Byzantium" was written in August–September 1926, four years before the writing of "Byzantium." F. L. Gwynn was the first, I believe, to indicate a crucial difference between the historical vision of the two poems.[1] The first Byzantium is that praised in "A Vision," the city of Justinian, about A.D. 550, while the city of the second poem is as it was "towards the end of the first Christian millennium." The cities are both of the mind, but they are not quite the same city, the second being at a still further remove from nature than the first.

[Giorgio] Melchiori, in an intricate study of the poem, showed that "Sailing to Byzantium" recalls Yeats's early story, "Rosa Alchemica," and so there is no reason to doubt that the poem is a finished version of Yeats's kind of alchemical quest.[2] The highest claim yet made for "Sailing to Byzantium" is that of Whitaker, who says of this poem and "Among School Children" that "in them is created a new species of man who—unbeknownst to himself, as it were—*is* his contrary."[3] Yeats would have delighted in this claim, but that the poem justifies it is open to some question.

Yeats's first intention in "Sailing to Byzantium" was not to speak in his own proper person, but as "a poet of the Middle Ages." A medieval Irish poet, seeking to make his soul, sets sail for the center of European civilization. But, as Curtis Bradford demonstrates, this persona gradually is eliminated from successive drafts of the poem, and the speaker in the final version may be taken as Yeats himself, a Yeats seeking his *daimon* at the center of Unity of Being, a city where the spiritual life and the creation of art merge as one.[4]

The great example of such a visionary city in English poetry is of course Blake's version of the New Jerusalem, Golgonooza, the city of Los

*This section is from chapter 19, *The Tower*.—Ed.

the artificer. There are Blakean elements in both Byzantium poems, but Yeats's city is emphatically not Blake's, and Blake would have disliked birds (however artificial) and dolphins as final emblems of imaginative salvation. The forms walking the streets of Yeats's city are images, but they are not the Divine Image or Human Form Divine that Blake insisted upon in his vision of last things. The vision of both Byzantium poems is more Shelleyan than Blakean, and the repudiation of nature in both poems has a Shelleyan rather than Blakean twist.

I would guess the ultimate literary source of Yeats's Byzantium to be in Shelley's longest poem, the allegorical epic, "The Revolt of Islam," a poem that Yeats read early, and remembered often. It is not today among the more admired of Shelley's longer poems, and rightly stands below "Alastor," which preceded it, and "Prometheus Unbound," which came after. But it has considerable though uneven power, and it is a worthy companion to "Endymion," having been composed in competition to Keats's longest poem. Most of the poem is an idealized account of left-wing revolution, not likely to move Yeats at any time in his life. But the first and final cantos are almost purely visionary, and they had considerable effect upon Yeats, who cites them in his major essay upon Shelley.

In canto 1 of Shelley's poem, there is a voyage to an immortal Temple:

> . . . likest Heaven, ere yet day's purple stream
>   Ebbs o'er the western forest, while the gleam
> Of the unrisen moon among the clouds
>   Is gathering. . . .

Shelley's starlit dome is surrounded by "marmoreal floods," and reveals itself to us only through the arts, and then only in part:

> Like what may be conceived of this vast dome,
>   When from the depths which thought can seldom pierce
> Genius beholds it rise, his native home,
>   Girt by the deserts of the Universe;
>   Yet, nor in painting's light, or mightier verse,
> Or sculpture's marble language, can invest
>   That shape to mortal sense—[5]

Within the Temple, which is lit by its own radiance, brighter than day's, are paintings wrought by Genii in a winged dance, and also the forms of departed sages, set against the background of fire. It seems only a step from this to Byzantium.

"I fly from nature to Byzantium," reads one canceled line of Yeats's poem, and another canceled phrase salutes the city as the place "where nothing changes." The poet is asking for transfiguration, though at the expense of being made "rigid, abstracted, and fanatical / Unwavering, indifferent." For his need is great, his function as poet being done:

All that men know, or think they know, being young
Cry that my tale is told my story sung. . . .[6]

Yeats seeks the Condition of Fire, as Blake sought it in Golgonooza,
or as Shelley's Adonais attained it, but his motive here is very different
from Blake's or even Shelley's. Byzantium is not attained after:

Mystery's tyrants are cut off & not one left on Earth,
And when all Tyranny was cut off from the face of
Earth. . . .[7]

Nor does the soul of Yeats, after reaching the Holy City, serve as a
beacon, "burning through the inmost veil of heaven," guiding others to
the Eternal. Yeats's Condition of Fire is neither a criticism of life, as
Blake's and Shelley's are, nor is it a manifestation of a freedom open
to all who would find it, nor indeed is it a state of imaginative liberty at
all. It is "extreme, fortuitous, personal," like the moments of visionary
awakening in Wallace Stevens, though it does not present itself honestly
as being such. It is also a state, ironically like the "sweet golden clime"
sought by Blake's Sun-Flower, in which the human image must subside
into the mechanical or merely repetitively natural, unless it is willing to
start out upon its quest again. For Byzantium is no country for men,
young *or* old, and the monuments it contains testify to aspects of the
soul's magnificence that do not support humanistic claims of any kind
whatsoever. Keats, standing in the shrine of Saturn, stands in Byzantium, and is told by the scornful Moneta that those to whom the miseries
of the world *are* misery do not come into that shrine. Yeats would have
found this irrelevant, for his Byzantium does not admit the "sentimen-
talist," the *primary* man, at all. We need not find this excessively relevant,
but we might hold it in mind as we read "Sailing to Byzantium," for the
limitations of the poem's ideal ought to be our concern also.

"God's holy fire" in this poem, is not a state where the creator and his
creation are one, as in Blake, but rather a state where the creator has
been absorbed into his creation, where the art work or "artifice of eternity" draws all reality into itself. Yeats's too-palpable ironies in the last
stanza of the poem are redundant and, as Sturge Moore remarked, the
poet is unjustified in asserting that he is "out of nature."[8] He is where he
always was, poised before his own artifact, and so less accurate than the
Keats who contemplated the Grecian urn, knowing always his own separation from the world wrought upon it.

I am suggesting that "Sailing to Byzantium" belies its title, and is
a rather static poem, and a peculiarly evasive one. The poem that did
not get written is, in this case, more impressive than the final text. If
Mrs. Yeats and Jon Stallworthy were right, then the poem began as a
prose fragment exploring again that tragedy of sexual intercourse which

is the perpetual virginity of the soul.[9] A man past sixty, in early autumn, broods on the loves of his lifetime, and decides that "now I will take off my body" even as "for many loves have I taken off my clothes." As once his loves "longed to see" but could not be enfolded by his soul, perhaps his soul now can cease to be virgin. The line of a later verse draft, "I fly from nature to Byzantium," would then be a wholly dualistic sentiment, abandoning sexual for spiritual love. That is hardly characteristic of Yeats, early or late, and shows only a mood, however powerful. The prose fragment says "I live on love," which is not very characteristic either. In the drafts of the opening stanza a significant change from the simplistic dualism, and the tense concern for love, is quickly manifested. The contrast presented is between the Christ child, smiling upon his mother's knee, and the old gods in the Irish hills, with whom the poet identifies. He is Oisin again, finding no place in the Ireland of St. Patrick, and so he sails to Byzantium.[10]

The flight then is not so much from nature as from a new dispensation of the young. The old poet of the old faith is doubly alienated, and this complex estrangement is the double root of the poem. As a poet, Yeats voyages to find a new faith; as a man, his quest is away—not from the body so much as from the decrepitude of the body. Byzantium is the state of being of "the thing become," as one of the drafts puts it, "and ageless beauty where age is living." In the final draft of the poem's first stanza, much of this richness of the quest-motive is gone, and age alone seems to impel the poet of his journey.[11]

Much else dropped out of the final poem, including both a prophetic and a purgatorial element. The final line—"Of what is past, or passing, or to come"—is severely qualified by the rest of the last stanza, but in the drafts it is presented without irony:

> And set in golden leaves to sing
> Of present past and future to come
> For the instruction of Byzantium. . . .[12]

There is an echo of Blake here, not of the voice of the Bard of Experience, but of the purged prophet Los in "Jerusalem," crying out in triumph that he beholds all reality in a single imagining:

> I see the Past, Present & Future, existing all at once
> Before me; O Divine Spirit sustain me on thy wings!
> That I may awake Albion from his long & cold repose.[13]

Blake-Los affirms his mission in the context of experience, the "long & cold repose" of man, while Yeats seeks his function in the context of a reality beyond experience, but the affinity is clear nevertheless. So is the necessity of purgation, of being made free of the Spectre or Selfhood, if the prophetic role is to be assumed, evident both in Blake and the Yeats of the drafts, but not of the final text, where only the heart, natural passion, is to be consumed away. Yeats, in one draft attempts to mount the purgatorial stairs as Dante does, or Keats in "The Fall of Hyperion," but fails:

> When prostrate on the marble step I fall
> And cry amid my tears—
> And cry aloud—"I sicken with desire
> Though/and fastened to a dying animal
> Cannot endure my life—O gather me
> Into the artifice of eternity."[14]

This does not match the incisiveness gained when Yeats says of his heart: "It knows not what it is," in the final text, but something valuable is lost also, the consciousness that an experiential purgatory must still be borne if a humanizing prophecy is to be uttered. Yeats, as always, knew very well what he was doing as a reviser, and he finds intensity through simplification in the final text. What "Sailing to Byzantium" lacks is just the reverse, the simplification through intensity that sometimes does take Yeats into the Condition of Fire.

NOTES

Chapter 1. *Introduction*

1. Jorge Luis Borges, "Kafka and His Precursors," *Labyrinths* (New York: New Directions, 1964), 201.

Chapter 19. *The Tower*

1. Gwynn, "Yeats's *Byzantium* and Its Sources," *Philological Quarterly* 32 (1953): 9–21.

2. Melchiori, *The Whole Mystery of Art: Pattern into Poetry in the Work of W. B. Yeats* (London: Routledge & Kegan Paul, 1960), 218–25.

3. Thomas Whitaker, *Swan and Shadow: Yeats's Dialogue with History* (Chapel Hill: University of North Carolina Press, 1964), 260–62.

4. Bradford, "Yeats's Byzantium Poems: A Study of Their Development," in *Yeats*, ed. John Unterecker (Englewood Cliffs, N.J.: Prentice-Hall, 1963), 93–130.

5. Shelley, *Poetical Works*, ed. Thomas Hutchinson (London: Oxford University Press, 1943), 51.

6. Bradford, "Yeats's Byzantium Poems," 98.

7. *The Poetry and Prose of William Blake*, ed. David V. Erdman (New York, 1965), 373.

8. *W. B. Yeats and T. Sturge Moore, Their Correspondence, 1901–1937*, ed. Ursula Bridge (New York, 1953), 162.

9. Stallworthy, *Between the Lines, Yeats's Poetry in the Making* (Oxford, 1963), 89–90.

10. A fuller study than this book can be, of Yeats's place in the tradition of

displaced or internalized quest-romance, would relate the "sailing" of this lyric not only to *The Wanderings of Oisin* and *The Shadowy Waters,* and their source in *Alastor,* but to the many versions of sea-quest in later nineteenth-century poetry. Yeats had read many more minor poets of the generation just before his own than most of his scholars have.

11. Bradford, "Yeats's Byzantium Poems," 111.
12. Ibid., 102.
13. Erdman, *Blake,* 157.
14. Bradford, "Yeats's Byzantium Poems," 101.

Seminar on "The Purloined Letter"

JACQUES LACAN

As Jeffrey Mehlman's Introductory Note (see below) points out, Lacan's essay does not present another interpretation of "The Purloined Letter" but instead it offers "a new way to read a text," and, we might add, a new way to read ourselves. Lacan's psychoanalytic structural analysis actually demonstrates how language (by which he means signifiers sliding into signifiers ad infinitum) constructs and controls our reading as well as our subjectivity. In Lacan's words, Poe's story "offers to a reader able to analyze it, a *knowledge,* albeit displaced, of the laws of both its own and the reader's (contradictory) construction."

Lacan calls our construction, or subjectivity, "contradictory" because he views the human being as divided into an egocentric conscious self ("I") and an unconscious ("it"). This division comes into being simultaneously with our advent into language. Lacan here draws on Ferdinand de Saussure's insight that identities arise only through differences. Thus the child only identifies himself or herself as "self" when he or she distinguishes the "I" from the not-me, the other ("you," "it"). Lacan designates the "not-me" or "it" repressed by the ego as the unconscious. In a sense, what Lacan does is to transpose the Oedipal relationship into language terms. For it is at the Oedipal stage that the child's awareness of sexual differences brings about repression of sexual desires. This primary repression of desire, which makes us what we are, is analogous to the repression of signifieds under signifiers. Repressed desire, or want, invests the signifier with meaning, yet we can never grasp that desire, we can never say exactly what we mean, we can never admit what we are. As a re-

From *Yale French Studies* no. 48 (special issue, *French Freud: Structural Studies in Psychoanalysis,* 1972): 39–72. Translated by Jeffrey Mehlman. Copyright 1972 by *Yale French Studies.*

sult, our conscious self is subverted continuously by the unconscious as signifiers are displaced continuously by more signifiers. According to this view, the self, or subject, is dispersed along a chain of signifiers. Thus, although the ego works to depict itself as fixed, unified, and in control, in actuality the self is constantly in process, fragmented, and displaced. Lacan's reading of "The Purloined Letter" explores this overlapping of signification and subjectivity.

Lacan hinges his analysis upon the ambiguity of "letter." A letter, Lacan reminds us, is not only an epistle but also a typographical character, or signifier. As such it functions as a unit of difference which has no meaning in itself yet allows for the possibility of meaning. Metaphorically, the story's purloined letter is just such a signifier; it signifies unconscious desire (the unattainable signified). For example, if we follow the path of the stolen letter—from Queen to Minister to Dupin to Police and back again to Queen—we see that the letter does not communicate a single message (or signified). Instead it signifies an openness or absence—a purloining of fixed meaning. Indeed, we never learn the contents (meaning) of the letter. In this way, then, the letter's route symbolizes, on one hand, the chaining of signifiers as they continually slip, not into signifieds, but into other signifiers, and, on the other hand, the continual undermining of the conscious self by unconscious desires.

Although Lacan reads "The Purloined Letter" on several levels—as an allegory of the reading process, of psychoanalysis, of the nature of fiction—he is concerned basically with how language (what he calls "the symbolic order") constitutes ourselves as subjects. We can only understand this process, however, if we can see its structures, or patterns, which are perceptible only when repeated. According to Lacan, "The Purloined Letter" presents such an opportunity. The story's two key scenes are structured by a three-way relationship in which the characters' positions are fixed by their connection to the letter. Even though characters exchange positions in the second scene, the triadic structure stays the same. As Lacan makes clear, the first, or "primal" scene takes place in the Queen's boudoir. The Queen, concealing the fateful letter from the unobservant King, is seen by the Minister who then boldly steals it. This triadic positioning recurs in the second scene in the Minister's parlour, with the characters displacing one another in a kind of musical chairs. In the replay, the Minister (in the Queen's position), concealing the letter from the unobservant Police (King's position), is seen by Dupin (Minister's position) who then boldly retrieves it.

As we watch each possessor of the purloined letter replaying the symbolic situation, we can begin to understand how this triangulated signifying chain both controls and conceals. Lacan likens these three positions, or "glances," structuring both scenes to the points of an imaginary isosceles triangle. At the apex, he suggests, we have the blind King (or Police) who sees nothing. Lacan calls this state "pure objectivity": the King thinks he knows the Truth, the real meaning, and so misses everything. At another angle, we have the Queen (later, the Minister) who sees that the King does not see the letter but fails to notice that the Minister does. Lacan equates this state to "pure subjectivity": the Queen sees that someone else does not see; therefore, she feels secure in the possession of the truth. Finally, at the third angle, we have the Minister (or Dupin) whose position can be described as understanding. He understands that one's subjectivity (conscious self/unconscious) is a complex of many subject positions. To cite Lacan again, this third position symbolizes "*knowledge*, albeit displaced, of the laws of both its own and the reader's (contradictory) construction."

Lacan's new way of reading "The Purloined Letter" opens many doors. For example, critic Shoshona Felman in "On Reading Poetry" suggests we could envision these three positions as superego (the King's place, "blindness of the Law"), ego (the Queen's position, "looking at oneself in the other's eyes"), and id (the linguistic Id, associated with the unconscious).* Elizabeth Wright, tracing Lacan's analysis of the story as an allegory of reading, suggests that the King's position compares to that of the authorial ego which claims its intention establishes the text's true meaning; the Queen's to the competent reader who, aware of conventions and codes, yet would find a stable meaning; and the Minister-Dupin's to the deconstructionist reader who, like Lacan, is aware of the problematic relationships among language, author, reader, and text.† As Wright suggests, a deconstructionist reading decenters the text in much the same way as Lacan decenters the subject: the single authority, be it self, author, or transcendental Truth is revealed to be in-process, unstable, dispersed along a chain of signifiers. In short, a Lacanian reading discloses Authority to be a kind of Wizard of Oz in the hire of the unconscious structures of desire.

If we as readers are fortunate enough to be in the right position as was Dupin, we can glimpse the workings of these unconscious structures, this slippage into signifiers. We can glimpse

*Felman, "On Reading Poetry: Reflections on the Limits and Possibilities of Psychoanalytical Approaches," in *The Literary Freud: Mechanisms of Defense and the Poetic Will*, ed. Joseph H. Smith (New Haven: Yale University Press, 1980).

†"Modern Psychoanalytic Criticism," in *Modern Literary Theory: A Comparative Introduction*, ed. Ann Jefferson and David Robey (Totowa, N.J.: Barnes and Noble Books, 1982).

how "that sign of contradiction and scandal constituted by the letter," as Lacan asserts, functions as "the source of the divided, contradictory subject." Unfortunately, most of the time, like the Queen who cannot publicly acknowledge the loss of the letter, we cannot admit the wants, or lacks, of the unconscious, "the discourse of the Other." Instead, we think "we" send and receive messages, seldom realizing that what we get back are unconscious desires, our "own message in reverse form."

JEFFREY MEHLMAN'S "INTRODUCTORY NOTE" TO "SEMINAR ON 'THE PURLOINED LETTER'"

[The following note from the editor and translator of Lacan's "Seminar" appeared in *Yale French Studies* 48 (1972): 38–39.]

If "psychoanalytic criticism" is an effort to bring analytic categories to bear in the solution of critical problems, Lacan's text is certainly not an example of that discipline. One has the feeling that, on the contrary, in the confrontation between analysis and literature, the former's role for Lacan is not to solve but to open up a new kind of textual problem. The Poe text then is in many ways a pretext, an exemplary occasion for Lacan to complicate the question of *Beyond the Pleasure Principle*. It is indeed a "purloined letter."

The crux of the problem is in the ambiguity of the term *letter* in Lacan's analysis. It may mean either typographical character or epistle. Why?

a) As typographical character, the letter is a unit of signification without any meaning in itself. In this it resembles the "memory trace," which for Freud is never the image of an event, but a term which takes on meaning only through its differential opposition to other traces. It is a particular arrangement of "frayings." The striking image of this situation in the tale is that we never know the *contents* of the crucial letter. Here then is a psychoanalysis indifferent to deep meanings, concerned more with a latent organization of the manifest than a latent meaning beneath it. In its refusal to accord any "positive" status to linguistic phenomena, this might be viewed as Lacan's Saussurean side (see n. 24).

b) As epistle, the letter allows Lacan to play on the intersubjective relations which expropriate the individual. ("To whom does a letter belong?") It is Lévi-Strauss (and Mauss) who are no doubt at the source of this effort to think of the Oedipus complex in terms of a structure of *exchange* crucial to the "fixation" of unconscious "memory traces."

These losses—of the plenitude of meaning and the security of (self-)possession—are thus the principal modes of the Lacanian *askesis* in this parable of analysis. To which we may add a third: that of metalanguage. By which we mean: (1) that the Prefect is already repeating the "events" he recounts at the moment he pretends to view them objectively; (2) even Dupin (as analyst) is trapped in the fantasmatic circuit (repetitive structure, mobile scenario . . .) at the moment of his rage against the Minister. The difference between the Prefect (trapped in the transference) and Dupin (counteracting the countertransference) is that the latter is intermittently aware of his loss.

In translating the text, we found that a large measure of its difficulty was a function of Lacan's idiosyncratic use of prepositions. As result, the reader has to play with various possibilities of subordination in a number of sentences in order to determine the "proper" one(s). For better or worse, in English we have (necessarily) chosen to normalize the use of prepositions. We have thus occasionally been obliged to chart a course through Lacan's labyrinth rather than reproduce that labyrinth whole. There has no doubt been a concomitant loss (in syntactical richness) and gain (in clarity).

The notes we have added to the text (signed "—ED. [Mehlman]") are, on the whole, explanations of allusions or clarifications of particularly oblique points.

This text was originally written in 1956 and—along with an introductory postface—is the opening text of the *Ecrits*.

[Lacan's "Seminar" immediately follows, below.]

> Und wenn es uns glückt,
> Und wenn es sich schickt,
> So sind es Gedanken.

OUR INQUIRY HAS LED US to the point of recognizing that the reptition automatism (*Wiederholungszwang*) finds its basis in what we have called the *insistence* of the signifying chain.[1] We have elaborated that notion itself as a correlate of the *ex-sistence* (or: eccentric place) in which we must necessarily locate the subject of the unconcious if we are to take Freud's discovery seriously.[2] As is known, it is in the realm of experience inaugurated by psychoanalysis that we may grasp along what imaginary lines the human organism, in the most intimate recesses of its being, manifests its capture in a *symbolic* dimension.

The lesson of this essay is intended to maintain that these imaginary incidences, far from representing the essence of our experience, reveal only what in it remains inconsistent unless they are related to the symbolic chain which binds and orients them.

We realize, of course, the importance of these imaginary impregnations (*Prägung*) in those partializations of the symbolic alternative which give the symbolic chain its appearance. But we maintain that it is the specific law of that chain which governs those psychoanalytic effects that are decisive for the subject: such as foreclosure (*Verwerfung*), repression (*Verdrängung*), denial (*Verneinung*) itself—specifying with appropriate emphasis that these effects follow so faithfully the displacement (*Entstellung*) of the signifier that imaginary factors, despite their inertia, figure only as shadows and reflections in the process.

But this emphasis would be lavished in vain, if it served, in your opinion, only to abstract a general type from phenomena whose particularity in our work would remain the essential thing for you, and whose original arrangement could be broken up only artificially.

Which is why we have decided to illustrate the truth which may be drawn from that moment in Freud's thought under study—namely, that it is the symbolic order which is constitutive for the subject—by demonstrating in a story the decisive orientation which the subject receives from the itinerary of a signifier.

It is that truth, let us note, which makes the very existence of fiction possible. And in that case, a fable is as appropriate as any other narrative for bringing it to light—at the risk of having the fable's coherence put to the test in the process. Aside from that reservation, a fictive tale even has the advantage of manifesting symbolic necessity more purely to the extent that we may believe its conception arbitrary.

Which is why, without seeking any further, we have chosen our example from the very story in which the dialectic of the game of even or odd—occurs.[3] It is, no doubt, no accident that this tale revealed itself propitious to pursuing a course of inquiry which had already found support in it.

As you know, we are talking about the tale which Baudelaire translated under the title: *La lettre volée*. At first reading, we may distinguish a drama, its narration, and the conditions of that narration.

We see quickly enough, moreover, that these components are necessary and that they could not have escaped the intentions of whoever composed them.

The narration, in fact, doubles the drama with a commentary without which no *mise en scène* would be possible. Let us say that the action would remain, properly speaking, invisible from the pit—aside from the fact that the dialogue would be expressly and by dramatic necessity devoid of whatever meaning it might have for an audience:—in other words, nothing of the drama could be grasped, neither seen nor heard, without, dare we say, the twilighting which the narration, in each scene, casts on the point of view that one of the actors had while performing it.

There are two scenes, the first of which we shall straightway designate the primal scene, and by no means inadvertently, since the second may be considered its repetition in the very sense we are considering today.

The primal scene is thus performed, we are told, in the royal boudoir, so that we suspect that the person of the highest rank, called the "exalted personage," who is alone there when she receives a letter, is the Queen. This feeling is confirmed by the embarrassment into which she is plunged by the entry of the other exalted personage, of whom we have already been told prior to this account that the knowledge he might have of the letter in question would jeopardize for the lady nothing less than her honor and safety. Any doubt that he is in fact the King is promptly dissipated in the course of the scene which begins with the entry of the Minister D——. At that moment, in fact, the Queen can do no better than to play on the King's inattentiveness by leaving the letter on the table "face down, address uppermost." It does not, however, escape the Minister's lynx eye, nor does he fail to notice the Queen's distress and thus to fathom her secret. From then on everything transpires like clockwork. After dealing in his customary manner with the business of the day, the Minister draws from his pocket a letter similar in appearance to the one in his view, and having pretended to read it, he places it next to the other. A bit more conversation to amuse the royal company, whereupon, without flinching once, he seizes the embarrassing letter, making off with it, as the Queen, on whom none of his maneuver has been lost, remains unable to intervene for fear of attracting the attention of her royal spouse, close at her side at that very moment.

Everything might then have transpired unseen by a hypothetical spectator of an operation in which nobody falters, and whose *quotient* is that the Minister has filched from the Queen her letter and that—an even more important result than the first—the Queen knows that he now has it, and by no means innocently.

A *remainder* that no analyst will neglect, trained as he is to retain whatever is significant, without always knowing what to do with it: the letter, abandoned by the Minister, and which the Queen's hand is now free to roll into a ball.

Second scene: in the Minister's office. It is in his hotel, and we know—from the account the Prefect of police has given Dupin, whose specific genius for solving enigmas Poe introduces here for the second time—that the police, returning there as soon as the Minister's habitual, nightly absences allow them to, have searched the hotel and its surroundings from top to bottom for the last eighteen months. In vain,—although everyone can deduce from the situation that the Minister keeps the letter within reach.

Dupin calls on the Minister. The latter receives him with studied nonchalance, affecting in his conversation romantic ennui. Meanwhile Dupin, whom this pretense does not deceive, his eyes protected by green glasses, proceeds to inspect the premises. When his glance catches a rather crumpled piece of paper—apparently thrust carelessly in a division of an ugly pasteboard card-rack, hanging gaudily from the middle of the mantelpiece—he already knows that he's found what he's looking for. His conviction is re-enforced by the very details which seem to contradict the description he has of the stolen letter, with the exception of the format, which remains the same.

Whereupon he has but to withdraw, after "forgetting" his snuff-box on the table, in order to return the following day to reclaim it—armed with a facsimile of the letter in its present state. As an incident in the street, prepared for the proper moment, draws the Minister to the window, Dupin in turn seizes the opportunity to snatch the letter while substituting the imitation, and has only to maintain the appearances of a normal exit.

Here as well all has transpired, if not without noise, at least without all commotion. The quotient of the operation is that the Minister no longer has the letter, but, far from suspecting that Dupin is the culprit who has ravished it from him, knows nothing of it. Moreover, what he is left with is far from insignificant for what follows. We shall return to what brought Dupin to inscribe a message on his counterfeit letter. Whatever the case, the Minister, when he tries to make use of it, will be able to read these words, written so that he may recognize Dupin's hand: ". . . *Un dessein si funeste / S'il n'est digne d'Atreé est digne de Thyeste*," whose source, Dupin tells us, is Crébillon's *Atreé*.[4]

Need we emphasize the similarity of these two sequences? Yes, for the resemblance we have in mind is not a simple collection of traits chosen only in order to delete their difference. And it would not be enough to retain those common traits at the expense of the others for the slightest truth to result. It is rather the intersubjectivity in which the two actions are motivated that we wish to bring into relief, as well as the three terms through which it structures them.[5]

The special status of these terms results from their corresponding simultaneously to the three logical moments through which the decision is precipitated and the three places it assigns to the subjects among whom it constitutes a choice.

That decision is reached in a glance's time.[6] For the maneuvers which follow, however stealthily they prolong it, add nothing to that glance, nor does the deferring of the deed in the second scene break the unity of that moment.

This glance presupposes two others, which it embraces in its vision of the breach left in their fallacious complementarity, anticipating in it the occasion for larceny afforded by that exposure. Thus three moments, structuring three glances, borne by three subjects, incarnated each time by different characters.

The first is a glance that sees nothing: the King and the police.

The second, a glance which sees that the first sees nothing and deludes itself as to the secrecy of what it hides: the Queen, then the Minister.

The third sees that the first two glances leave what should be hidden exposed to whomever would seize it: the Minister, and finally Dupin.

In order to grasp in its unity the intersubjective complex thus described, we would willingly seek a model in the technique legendarily attributed to the ostrich attempting to shield itself from danger; for that technique might ultimately be qualified as political, divided as it here is among three partners: the second believing itself invisible because the first has its head stuck in the ground, and all the while letting the third calmly pluck its rear; we need only enrich its proverbial denomination by a letter, producing *la politique de l'autruiche*, for the ostrich itself to take on forever a new meaning.[7]

Given the intersubjective modulus of the repetitive action, it remains to recognize in it a *repetition automatism* in the sense that interests us in Freud's text.

The plurality of subjects, of course, can be no objection for those who are long accustomed to the perspectives summarized by our formula: *the unconscious is the discourse of the Other.*[8] And we will not recall now what the notion of the *immixture of subjects*, recently introduced in our re-analysis of the dream of Irma's injection, adds to the discussion.

What interests us [now] is the manner in which the subjects relay each other in their displacement during the intersubjective repetition.

We shall see that their displacement is determined by the place which a pure signifier—the purloined letter—comes to occupy in their trio. And that is what will confirm for us its status as repetition automatism.

It does not, however, seem excessive, before pursuing this line of inquiry, to ask whether the thrust of the tale and the interest we bring to it—to the extent that they coincide—do not lie elsewhere.

May we view as simply a rationalization (in our gruff jargon) the fact that the story is told to us as a police mystery?

In truth, we should be right in judging that fact highly dubious as soon as we note that everything which warrants such mystery concerning a crime or offense—its nature and motives, instruments and execution; the procedure used to discover the author, and the means employed to convict him—is carefully eliminated here at the start of each episode.

The act of deceit is, in fact, from the beginning as clearly known as the intrigues of the culprit and their effects on his victim. The problem, as exposed to us, is limited to the search for and restitution of the object of that deceit, and it seems rather intentional that the solution is already obtained when it is explained to us. Is *that* how we are kept in suspense? Whatever credit we may accord the conventions of a genre for provoking a specific interest in the reader, we should not forget that "the Dupin tale," this the second to appear, is a prototype, and that even if the genre were established in the first, it is still a little early for the author to play on a convention.[9]

It would, however, be equally excessive to reduce the whole thing to a fable whose moral would be that in order to shield from inquisitive eyes one of those correspondences whose secrecy is sometimes necessary to conjugal peace, it suffices to leave the crucial letters lying about on one's table, even though the meaningful side be turned face down. For that would be a hoax which, for our part, we would never recommend anyone try, lest he be gravely dissapointed in his hopes.

Might there then be no mystery other than, concerning the Prefect, an incompetence issuing in failure—were it not perhaps, concerning Dupin, a certain dissonance we hesitate to acknowledge between, on the one hand, the admittedly penetrating, though, in their generality, not always quite relevant remarks with which he introduces us to his method and, on the other, the manner in which he in fact intervenes.

Were we to pursue this sense of mystification a bit further we might soon begin to wonder whether, from that initial scene which only the rank of the protagonists saves from vaudeville, to the fall into ridicule which seems to await the Minister at the end, it is not this impression that everyone is being duped which makes for our pleasure.

And we would be all the more inclined to think so in that we would recognize in that surmise, along with those of you who read us, the definition we once gave in passing of the modern hero, "whom ludicrous exploits exalt in circumstances of utter confusion." [10]

But are we ourselves not taken in by the imposing presence of the amateur detective, prototype of a latter-day swashbuckler, as yet safe from the insipidity of our contemporary *superman*?

A trick . . . sufficient for us to discern in this tale, on the contrary, so perfect a verisimilitude that it may be said that truth here reveals its fictive arrangement.

For such indeed is the direction in which the principles of that verisimilitude lead us. Entering into its strategy, we indeed perceive a new drama we may call complementary to the first, in so far as the latter was what is termed a play without words whereas the interest of the second plays on the properties of speech. [11]

It is indeed clear that each of the two scenes of the real drama is narrated in the course of a different dialogue, it is only through access to those notions set forth in our teaching that one may recognize that it is not thus simply to augment the charm of the exposition, but that the dialogues themselves, in the opposite use they make of the powers of speech, take on a tension which makes of them a different drama, one which our vocabulary will distinguish from the first as persisting in the symbolic order.

The first dialogue—between the Prefect of police and Dupin—is played as between a deaf man and one who hears. That is, it presents the real complexity of what is ordinarily simplified, with the most confused results, in the notion of communication.

This example demonstrates indeed how an act of communication may give the impression at which theorists too often stop: of allowing in its transmissions but a single meaning, as though the highly significant commentary into which he who understands integrates it, could, because unperceived by him who does not understand, be considered null.

It remains that if only the dialogue's meaning as a report is retained, its verisimilitude may appear to depend on a guarantee of exactitude. But here dialogue may be more fertile than seems, if we demonstrate its tactics: as shall be seen by focusing on the recounting of our first scene.

For the double and even triple subjective filter through which that scene comes to us: a narration by Dupin's friend and associate (henceforth to be called the general narrator of the story)—of the account by which the Prefect reveals to Dupin—the report the Queen gave him of it, is not merely the consequence of a fortuitous arrangement.

If indeed the extremity to which the original narrator is reduced precludes her altering any of the events, it would be wrong to believe that the Prefect is empowered to lend her his voice in this case only by that lack of imagination on which he has, dare we say, the patent.

The fact that the message is thus retransmitted assures us of what may by no means be taken for granted: that it belongs to the dimension of language.

[Elsewhere I have described] the counter case of the so-called language of bees: in which a linguist [12] can see only a simple signaling of the location of objects, in other words: only an imaginary function more differentiated than others.

We emphasize that such a form of communication is not absent in man, however evanescent a naturally given object may be for him, split as it is in its submission to symbols.

Something equivalent may no doubt be grasped in the communion established between two persons in their hatred of a common object: except that the meeting is possible only over a single object, defined by those traits in the individual each of the two resist.

But such communication is not transmissible in symbolic form. It may be maintained only in the relation with the object. In such a manner it may bring together an indefinite number of subjects in a common "ideal": the communication of one subject with another within the crowd thus constituted will nonetheless remain irreducibly mediated by an ineffable relation. [13]

This digression is not only a recollection of principles distantly addressed to those who impute to us a neglect of non-verbal communication: in determining the scope of what speech repeats, it prepares the question of what symptoms repeat.

Thus the indirect telling sifts out the linguistic dimension, and the general narrator, by duplicating it, "hypothetically" adds nothing to it. But its role in the second dialogue is entirely different.

For the latter will be opposed to the first like those poles we have distinguished elsewhere in language and which are opposed like word to speech.

Which is to say that a transition is made here from the domain of exactitude to the register of truth. Now that register, we dare think we needn't come back to this, is situated entirely elsewhere, strictly speaking at the very foundation of intersubjectivity. It is located there where the subject can grasp nothing but the very subjectivity which constitutes an Other as absolute. We shall be satisfied here to indicate its place by evoking the dialogue which seems to us to merit its attribution as a Jewish joke by that state of privation through which the relation of signifier to speech appears in the entreaty which brings the dialogue to a close: "Why are you lying to me?" one character shouts breathlessly. "Yes, why do you lie to me saying you're going to Cracow so I should believe you're going to Lemberg, when in reality you *are* going to Cracow?"[14]

We might be prompted to ask a similar question by the torrent of logical impasses, eristic enigmas, paradoxes and even jests presented to us as an introduction to Dupin's method if the fact that they were confided to us by a would-be disciple did not endow them with a new dimension through that act of delegation. Such is the unmistakable magic of legacies: the witness's fidelity is the cowl which blinds and lays to rest all criticism of his testimony.

What could be more convincing, moreover, than the gesture of laying one's cards face up on the table? So much so that we are momentarily persuaded that the magician has in fact demonstrated, as he promised, how his trick was performed, whereas he has only renewed it in still purer form: at which point we fathom the measure of the supremacy of the signifier in the subject.

Such is Dupin's maneuver when he starts with the story of the child prodigy who takes in all his friends at the game of even and odd with his trick of identifying with the opponent, concerning which we have nevertheless shown that it cannot reach the first level of theoretical elaboration, namely: intersubjective alternation, without immediately stumbling on the buttress of its recurrence.[15]

We are all the same treated—so much smoke in our eyes—to the names of La Rochefoucauld, La Bruyère, Machiavelli and Campanella, whose renown, by this time, would seem but futile when confronted with the child's prowess.

Followed by Chamfort, whose maxim that "it is a safe wager that every public idea, every accepted convention is foolish, since it suits the greatest number," will no doubt satisfy all who think they escape its law, that is, precisely, the greatest number. That Dupin accuses the French of deception for applying the word *analysis* to algebra will hardly threaten our pride since, moreover, the freeing of that term for other uses ought by no means to provoke a psychoanalyst to intervene and claim his rights. And there he goes making philological remarks which should positively delight any lovers of Latin: when he recalls without deigning to say any more that "*ambitus* doesn't mean ambition, *religio*, religion, *homines honesti*, honest men," who among you would not take pleasure in remembering . . . what those words mean to anyone familiar with Cicero and Lucretius. No doubt Poe is having a good time. . . .

But a suspicion occurs to us: might not this parade of erudition be destined to reveal to us the key words of our drama? Is not the magician repeating his trick before our eyes, without deceiving us this time about divulging his secret, but pressing his wager to the point of really explaining it to us without [our] seeing a thing? *That* would be the summit of the illusionist's art: through one of his fictive creations to *truly delude us*.

And is it not such effects which justify our referring, without malice, to a number of imaginary heroes as real characters?

As well, when we are open to hearing the way in which Martin Heidegger discloses to us in the word *aletheia* the play of truth, we rediscover a secret to which truth has always initiated her lovers, and through which they learn that it is in hiding that she offers herself to them *most truly*.

Thus even if Dupin's comments did not defy us so blatantly to believe in them, we should still have to make that attempt against the opposite temptation.

Let us track down [*dépistons*] his footprints there where they elude [*dépiste*] us.[16] And first of all in the criticism by which he explains the Prefect's lack of success. We already saw it surface in those furtive gibes the Prefect, in the first conversation, failed to heed, seeing in them only a pretext for hilarity. That it is, as Dupin insinuates, because a problem is too simple, indeed too evident, that it may appear obscure, will never have any more bearing for him than a vigorous rub of the rib cage.

Everything is arranged to induce in us a sense of the character's imbecility. Which is powerfully articulated by the fact that he and his confederates never conceive of anything beyond what an ordinary rogue might imagine for hiding an object—that is, precisely the all too well known series of extraordinary hiding places: which are promptly catalogued for us, from hidden desk draws to removable table tops, from the detachable cushions of chairs to their hollowed out legs, from the reverse side of mirrors to the "thickness" of book bindings.

After which, a moment of derision at the Prefect's error in deducing that because the Minister is a poet, he is not far from being mad, an error, it is argued, which would consist, but this is hardly negligible, simply in a false distribution of the middle term, since it is far from following from the fact that all madmen are poets.

Yes indeed. But we ourselves are left in the dark as to the poet's superiority in the art of concealment—even if he be a mathematician to boot—since our pursuit is suddenly thwarted, dragged as we are into a thicket of bad arguments directed against the reasoning of mathematicians, who never, so far as I know, showed such devotion to their formulae as to identify them with reason itself. At least, let us testify that unlike what seems to be Poe's experience, it occasionally befalls us—with our friend Riguet, whose presence here is a guarantee that our incursions into combinatory analysis are not leading us astray—to hazard such serious deviations (virtual blasphemies, according to Poe) as to cast into doubt that "x^2 plus px is perhaps not absolutely equal to q," without ever—here we give the lie to Poe—having had to fend off any unexpected attack.

Is not so much intelligence being exercised then simply to divert our own from what had been indicated earlier as given, namely, that the police have looked *everywhere*: which we were to understand—vis-à-vis the area in which the police, not without reason, assumed the letter might be found—in terms of a (no doubt theoretical) exhaustion of space, but concerning which the tale's piquancy depends on our accepting it literally: the division of the entire volume into numbered "compartments," which was the principle governing the operation, being presented to us as so precise that "the fiftieth part of a line," it is said, could not escape the probing of the investigators. Have we not then the right to ask how it happened that the letter was not found *anywhere*, or rather to observe that all we have been told of a more far-ranging conception of concealment does not explain, in all rigor, that the letter escaped detection, since the area combed did in fact contain it, as Dupin's discovery eventually proves.

Must a letter then, of all objects, be endowed with the property of *nullibiety:* to use a term which the thesaurus known as *Roget* picks up from the semiotic utopia of Bishop Wilkins?[17]

It is evident ("a little *too* self-evident") [Lacan's italics] that between *letter* and *place* exist relations for which no French word has quite the extension of the English adjective: *odd. Bizarre*, by which Baudelaire regularly translates it, is only approximate. Let us say that these relations are . . . *singuliers*, for they are the very ones maintained with place by the *signifier*.

. . . [O]ur intention is not to turn them into "subtle" relations, nor is our aim to confuse letter with spirit, even if we receive the former by pneumatic dispatch, and that we readily admit that one kills whereas the other quickens, insofar as the signifier—you perhaps begin to understand—materializes the agency of death.[18] But if it is first of all on the materiality of the signifier that we have insisted, that materiality is *odd* [*singulière*] in many ways, the first of which is not to admit partition. Cut a letter in small pieces, and it remains the letter it is—and this in a completely different sense than *Gestalttheorie* would account for which the dormant vitalism informing its notion of the whole.[19]

Language delivers its judgment to whomever knows how to hear it: through the usage of the article as partitive particle. It is there that spirit—if spirit be living meaning—appears, no less oddly, as more available for quantification than its letter. To begin with meaning itself, which bears our saying: a speech rich with meaning ["plein *de* signification"], just as we recognize a measure of intention ["*de* l'intention"] in an act, or deplore that there is no more love ["plus *d'amour*"]; or store up hatred ["*de la* haine"] and expend devotion ["*du* dévouement"], and so much infatuation ["tant *d'*infatuation"] is easily reconciled to the fact that there will always be ass ["*de la* cuisse"] for sale and brawling ["*du* rififi"] among men.

But as for the letter—be it taken as typographical character, epistle, or what makes a man of letters—we will say that what is said is to be understood *to the letter* [*à la lettre*], that *a letter* [*une lettre*] awaits you at the post office, or even that you are acquainted with *letters* [*que vous avez des lettres*]—never that there is *letter* [*de la lettre*] anywhere, whatever the context, even to designate overdue mail.

For the signifier is a unit in its very uniqueness, being by nature symbol only of an absence. Which is why we cannot say of the purloined letter that, like other objects, it must be *or* not be in a particular place but that unlike them it will be *and* not be where it is, wherever it goes.[20]

Let us, in fact, look more closely at what happens to the police. We are spared nothing concerning the procedures used in searching the area submitted to their investigation: from the division of that space into compartments from which the slightest bulk could not escape detection, to needles probing upholstery, and, in the impossibility of sounding wood with a tap, to a microscope exposing the waste of any drilling at the surface of its hollow, indeed the infinitesimal gaping of the slightest abyss. As the network tightens to the point that, not satisfied with shaking the pages of books, the police take to counting them, do we not see space itself shed its leaves like a letter?

But the detectives have so immutable a notion of the real that they fail to notice that their search tends to transform it into its object. A trait by which they would be able to distinguish that object from all others.

This would no doubt be too much to ask them, not because of their lack of insight but rather because of ours. For their imbecility is neither of the individual nor the corporative variety; its source is subjective. It is the realist's imbecility, which does not pause to observe that nothing, however deep in the bowels of the earth a hand may seek to ensconce it, will ever be hidden there, since another hand can always retrieve it, and that what is hidden is never but what is *missing from its place*, as the call slip puts it when speaking of a volume lost in a library. And even if the book be on an adjacent shelf or in the next slot, it would be hidden there, however visibly it may appear. For it can *literally* be said that something is missing from its place only of what can change it: the symbolic. For the real, whatever upheaval we subject it to, is always in its place; it carries it glued to its heel, ignorant of what might exile it from it.

And, to return to our cops, who took the letter from the place where it was hidden, how could they have seized the letter? In what they turned between their fingers what did they hold but what *did not answer* to their description. "A letter, a litter": in Joyce's circle, they played on the homophony of the two words in English.[21] Nor does the seeming bit of refuse the police are now handling reveal its other nature for being but half torn. A different seal on a stamp of another color, the mark of a different handwriting in the superscription are here the most inviolable modes of concealment. And if they stop at the reverse side of the letter, on which, as is known, the recipient's address was written in that period, it is because the letter has for them no other side but its reverse.

What indeed might they find on its observe? Its message, as is often said to our cybernetic joy? . . . But does it not occur to us that this message has already reached its recipient and has even been left with her, since the insignificant scrap of paper now represents it no less well than the original note?

If we could admit that a letter has completed its destiny after fulfilling its function, the ceremony of returning letters would be a less common close to the extinction of the fires of love's feasts. The signifier is not functional. And the mobilization of the elegant society whose frolics we are following would as well have no meaning if the letter itself were content with having one. For it would hardly be an adequate means of keeping it secret to inform a squad of cops of its existence.

We might even admit that the letter has an entirely different (if no more urgent) meaning for the Queen than the one understood by the Minister. The sequence of events would not be noticeably affected, not even if it were strictly incomprehensible to an uninformed reader.

For it is certainly not so for everybody, since, as the Prefect pompously assures us, to everyone's derision, "the disclosure of the document to a third person, who shall be nameless," (that name which leaps to the eye like the pig's tail twixt the teeth of old Ubu) "would bring in question the honor of a personage of most exalted station, indeed that the honor and peace of the illustrious personage are so jeopardized."

In that case, it is not only the meaning but the text of the message which it would be dangerous to place in circulation, and all the more so to the extent that it might appear harmless, since the risks of an indiscretion unintentionally committed by one of the letter's holders would thus be increased.

Nothing then can redeem the police's position, and nothing would be changed by improving their "culture." *Scripta manent:* in vain would they learn from a *de luxe*-edition humanism the proverbial lesson which *verba volant* concludes. May it but please heaven that writings remain, as is rather the case with spoken words: for the indelible debt of the latter impregnates our acts with its transferences.

Writings scatter to the winds blank checks in an insane charge.[22] And were they not such flying leaves, there would be no purloined letters.[23]

But what of it? For a purloined letter to exist, we may ask, to whom does a letter belong? We stressed a moment ago the oddity implicit in returning a letter to him who had but recently given wing to its burning pledge. And we generally deem unbecoming such premature publications as the one by which the Chevalier d'Éon put several of his correspondents in a rather pitiful position.

Might a letter on which the sender retains certain rights then not quite belong to the person to whom it is addressed? or might it be that the latter was never the real receiver?

Let's take a look: we shall find illumination in what at first seems to obscure matters: the fact that the tale leaves us in virtually total ignorance of the sender, no less than of the contents, of the letter. We are told only that the Minister immediately recognized the handwriting of the address and only incidentally, in a discussion of the Minister's camouflage, is it said that the original seal bore the ducal arms of the S—— family. As for the letter's bearing, we know only the dangers it entails should it come into the hands of a specific third party, and that its possession has allowed the Minister to "wield, to a very dangerous extent, for political purposes," the power it assures him over the interested party. But all this tells us nothing of the message it conveys.

Love letter or conspiratorial letter, letter of betrayal or letter of mission, letter of summons or letter of distress, we are assured of but one thing: the Queen must not bring it to the knowledge of her lord and master.

Now these terms, far from bearing the nuance of discredit they have in *bourgeois* comedy, take on a certain prominence through allusion to her sovereign, to whom she is bound by pledge of faith, and doubly so, since her role as spouse does not relieve her of her duties as subject, but rather elevates her to the guardianship of what royalty according to law incarnates of power: and which is called legitimacy.

From then on, to whatever vicissitudes the Queen may choose to subject the letter, it remains that the letter is the symbol of a pact, and that, even should the recipient not assume the pact, the existence of the letter situates her in a symbolic chain foreign to the one which constitutes her faith. This incompatibility is proven by the fact that the possession of the letter is impossible to bring forward publicly as legitimate, and that in order to have that possession respected, the Queen can invoke but her right to privacy, whose privilege is based on the honor that possession violates.

For she who incarnates the figure of grace and sovereignty cannot welcome even a private communication without power being concerned, and she cannot avail herself of secrecy in relation to the sovereign without becoming clandestine.

From then on, the responsibility of the author of the letter takes second place to that of its holder: for the offense to majesty is compounded by *high treason*.

We say: the *holder* and not the *possessor*. For it becomes clear that the addressee's proprietorship of the letter may be no less debatable than that of anyone else into whose hands it comes, for nothing concerning the existence of the letter can return to good order without the person whose prerogatives it infringes upon having to pronounce judgment on it.

All of this, however, does not imply that because the letter's secrecy is indefensible, the betrayal of that secret would in any sense be honorable. The *honesti homines*, decent people, will not get off so easily. There is more than one *religio*, and it is not slated for tomorrow that sacred ties shall cease to rend us in two. As for *ambitus:* a detour, we see, is not always inspired by ambition. For if we are taking one here, by no means is it stolen (the word is apt), since, to lay our cards on the table, we have borrowed Baudelaire's title in order to stress not, as is incorrectly claimed, the conventional nature of the signifier, but rather its priority in relation to the signified. It remains, nevertheless, that Baudelaire, despite his devotion, betrayed Poe by translating as "la lettre volée" (the stolen letter) his title: the purloined letter, a title containing a word rare enough for us to find it easier to define its etymology than its usage.

To purloin, says the Oxford dictionary, is an Anglo-French word, that is: composed of the prefix *pur-*, found in *purpose, purchase, purport*, and of the Old French word: *loing, loigner, longé*. We recognize in the first element the Latin *pro-*, as opposed to *ante*, in so far as it presupposes a rear in front of which it is borne, possibly as its warrant, indeed even as its pledge (whereas *ante* goes forth to confront what it encounters). As for the second, an old French word: *loigner*, a verb attributing place *au loing* (or, still in use, *longé*), it does not mean *au loin* (far off), but *au long de* (alongside); it is a question then of *putting aside*, or, to invoke a familiar expression which plays on the two meanings: *mettre à gauche* (to put to the left; to put amiss).

Thus we are confirmed in our detour by the very object which draws us on into it: for we are quite simply dealing with a letter which has been diverted from its path; one whose course has been *prolonged* (etymologically, the word of the title), or, to revert to the language of the post office, a *letter in sufferance*.[24]

Here then, *simple and odd*, as we are told on the very first page, reduced to its simplest expression, is the singularity of the letter, which as the title indicates, is the *true subject* of the tale: since it can be diverted, it must have a course *which is proper to it:* the trait by which its incidence as signifier is affirmed. For we have learned to conceive of the signifier as sustaining itself only in a displacement comparable to that found in electric news strips or in the rotating memories of our machines-that-think-like men, this because of the alternating operation which is its principle, requiring it to leave its place, even though it returns to it by a circular path.[25]

This is indeed what happens in the repetition automatism. What Freud teaches us in the text we are commenting on is that the subject must pass through the channels of the symbolic, but what is illustrated here is more gripping still: it is not only the subject, but the subjects, grasped in their intersubjectivity, who line up, in other words our ostriches, to whom we here return, and who, more docile than sheep, model their very being on the moment of the signifying chain which traverses them.

If what Freud discovered and rediscovers with a perpetually increasing sense of shock has a meaning, it is that the displacement of the signifier determines the subjects in their acts, in their destiny, in their refusals, in their blindnesses, in their end and in their fate, their innate gifts and social acquisitions notwithstanding, without regard for character or sex, and that, willingly or not, everything that might be considered the stuff of psychology, kit and caboodle, will follow the path of the signifier.

Here we are, in fact, yet again at the crossroads at which we had left our drama and its round with the question of the way in which the subjects replace each other in it. Our fable is so constructed as to show that it is the letter and its diversion which governs their entries and roles. If *it* be "in sufferance," *they* shall endure the pain. Should they pass beneath its shadow, they become its reflection. Falling in possession of the letter—admirable ambiguity of language—its meaning possesses them.

So we are shown by the hero of the drama in the repetition of the very situation which his daring brought to a head, a first time, to his triumph. If he now succumbs to it, it is because he has shifted to the second position in the triad in which he was initially third, as well as the thief—and this by virtue of the object of his theft.

For if it is, now as before, a question of protecting the letter from inquisitive eyes, he can do nothing but employ the same technique he himself has already foiled: leave it in the open? And we may properly doubt that he knows what he is thus doing, when we see him immediately captivated by a dual relationship in which we find all the traits of a mimetic lure or of an animal feigning death, and, trapped in the typically imaginary situation of seeing that he is not seen, misconstrue the real situation in which he is seen not seeing

And what does he fail to see? Precisely the symbolic situation which he himself was so well able to see, and in which he is now seen seeing himself not being seen.

The Minister acts as a man who realizes that the police's search is his own defence, since we are told he allows them total access by his absences: he nonetheless fails to recognize that outside of that search he is no longer defended.

This is the very *autruicherie* whose artisan he was, if we may allow our monster to proliferate, but it cannot be by sheer stupidity that he now comes to be its dupe.[26]

For in playing the part of the one who hides, he is obligated to don the role of the Queen, and even the attributes of femininity and shadow, so propitious to the act of concealing.

Not that we are reducing the hoary couple of *Yin* and *Yang* to the elementary opposition of dark and light. For its precise use involves what is blinding in a flash of light, no less than the shimmering shadows exploit in order not to lose their prey.

Here sign and being, marvelously asunder, reveal which is victorious when they come into conflict. A man man enough to defy to the point of scorn a lady's fearsome ire undergoes to the point of metamorphosis the curse of the sign he has dispossessed her of.

For this sign is indeed that of woman, in so far as she invests her very being therein, founding it outside the law, which subsumes her nevertheless, originarily, in a position of signifier, nay, of fetish.[27] In order to be worthy of the power of that sign she has but to remain immobile in its shadow, thus finding, moreover, like the Queen, that simulation of mastery in inactivity that the Minister's "lynx eye" alone was able to penetrate.

This stolen sign—here then is man in its possession: sinister in that such possession may be sustained only through the honor it defies, cursed in calling him who sustains it to punishment or crime, each of which shatters his vassalage to the Law.

There must be in this sign a singular *noli me tangere* for its possession, like the Socratic sting ray, to benumb its man to the point of making him fall into what appears clearly in his case to be a state of idleness.[28]

For in noting, as the narrator does as early as the first dialogue, that with the letter's use its power disappears, we perceive that this remark, strictly speaking, concerns precisely its use for ends of power—and at the same time that such a use is obligatory for the Minister.

To be unable to rid himself of it, the Minister indeed must not know what else to do with the letter. For that use places him in so total a dependence on the letter as such, that in the long run it no longer involves the letter at all.

We mean that for that use truly to involve the letter, the Minister, who, after all, would be so authorized by his service to his master the King, might present to the Queen respectful admonitions, even were he to assure their sequel by appropriate precautions,—or initiate an action against the author of the letter, concerning whom, the fact that he remains outside the story's focus reveals the extent to which it is not guilt and blame which are in question here, but rather that sign of contradiction and scandal constituted by the letter, in the sense in which the Gospel says that it must come regardless of the anguish of whomever serves as its bearer. . . .

We will not know why the Minister does not resort to any of these uses, and it is fitting that we don't, since the effect of this non-use alone concerns us; it suffices for us to know that the way in which the letter was acquired would pose no obstacle to any of them.

For it is clear that if the use of the letter, independent of its meaning, is obligatory for the Minister, its use for ends of power can only be potential, since it cannot become actual without vanishing in the process,—but in that case the letter exists as a means of power only through the final assignations of the pure signifier, namely: by prolonging its diversion, making it reach whomever it may concern through a supplementary transfer, that is, by an additional act of treason whose effects the letter's gravity makes it difficult to predict,—or indeed by destroying the letter, the only sure means, as Dupin divulges at the start, of being rid of what is destined by nature to signify the annulment of what it signifies.

The ascendancy which the Minister derives from the situation is thus not a function of the letter, but, whether he knows it or not, of the role it constitutes for him. And the Prefect's remarks indeed present him as someone "who dares all things," which is commented upon significantly: "those unbecoming as well as those becoming a man," words whose pungency escapes Baudelaire when he translates: "ce qui est indigne d'un homme aussi bien que ce qui est digne de lui" (those unbecoming a man as well as those becoming him). For in its original form, the appraisal is far more appropriate to what might concern a woman.

This allows us to see the imaginary import of the character, that is, the narcissistic relation in which the Minister is engaged, this time, no doubt, without knowing it. It is indicated as well as early as the second page of the English text by one of the narrator's remarks, whose form is worth savoring: the Minister's ascendancy, we are told, "would depend upon the robber's knowledge of the loser's knowledge of the robber." Words whose importance the author underscores by having Dupin repeat them literally after the narration of the scene of the theft of the letter. Here again we may say that Baudelaire is imprecise in his language in having one ask, the other confirm, in these words: "Le voleur sait-il? . . ." (Does the robber know?), then: "Le voleur sait . . ." (the robber knows). What? "que la personne volée connaît son voleur" (that the loser knows his robber).

For what matters to the robber is not only that the said person knows who robbed her, but rather with what kind of a robber she is dealing; for she believes him capable of anything, which should be understood as her having conferred upon him the position that no one is in fact capable of assuming, since it is imaginary, that of absolute master.

In truth, it is a position of absolute weakness, but not for the person of whom we are expected to believe so. The proof is not only that the Queen dares to call the police. For she is only conforming to her displacement to the next slot in the arrangement of the initial triad in trusting to the very blindness required to occupy that place: "No more sagacious agent could, I suppose," Dupin notes ironically, "be desired or even imagined." No, if she has taken that step, it is less out of being "driven to despair," as we are told, than in assuming the charge of an impatience best imputed to a specular mirage.

For the Minister is kept quite busy confining himself to the idleness which is presently his lot. The Minister, in point of fact, is not *altogether* mad.[29] That's a remark made by the Prefect, whose every word is gold: it is true that the gold of his words flows only for Dupin and will continue to flow to the amount of the fifty thousand francs worth it will cost him by the metal standard of the day, though not without leaving him a margin of profit. The Minister then is not *altogether* mad in his insane stagnation, and that is why he will behave according to the mode of neurosis. Like the man who withdrew to an island to forget, what? he forgot,—so the Minister, through not making use of the letter, comes to forget it. As is expressed by the persistence of his conduct. But the letter, no more than the neurotic's unconscious, does not forget him. It forgets him so little that it transforms him more and more in the image of her who offered it to his capture, so that he now will surrender it, following her example, to a similar capture.

The features of that transformation are noted, and in a form so characteristic in their apparent gratuitousness that they might validly be compared to the return of the repressed.

Thus we first learn that the Minister in turn has *turned the letter over,* not, of course, as in the Queen's hasty gesture, but, more assiduously, as one turns a garment inside out. So he must proceed, according to the methods of the day for folding and sealing a letter, in order to free the virgin space on which to inscribe a new address.[30]

That address becomes his own. Whether it be in his hand or another, it will appear in an extremely delicate feminine script, and, the seal changing from the red of passion to the black of its mirrors, he will imprint his stamp upon it. This oddity of a letter marked with the recipient's stamp is all the more striking in its conception, since, though forcefully articulated in the text, it is not even mentioned by Dupin in the discussion he devotes to the identification of the letter.

Whether that omission be intentional or involuntary, it will surprise in the economy of a work whose meticulous rigor is evident. But in either case it is significant that the letter which the Minister, in point of fact, addresses to himself is a letter from a woman: as though this were a phase he had to pass through out of a natural affinity of the signifier.

Thus the aura of apathy, verging at times on an affectation of effeminacy; the display of an ennui bordering on disgust in his conversation; the mood the author of the philosophy of furniture[31] can elicit from virtually impalpable details (like that of the musical instrument on the table), everything seems intended for a character, all of whose utterances have revealed the most virile traits, to exude the oddest *odor di femina* when he appears.

Dupin does not fail to stress that this is an artifice, describing behind the bogus finery the vigilance of a beast of prey ready to spring. But that this is the very effect of the unconscious in the precise sense that we teach that the unconscious means that man is inhabited by the signifier: could we find a more beautiful image of it than the one Poe himself forges to help us appreciate Dupin's exploit? For with this aim in mind, he refers to those toponymical inscriptions which a geographical map, lest it remain mute, superimposes on its design, and which may become the object of a guessing game: who can find the name chosen by a partner?—noting immediately that the name most likely to foil a beginner will be one which, in large letters spaced out widely across the map, discloses, often without an eye pausing to notice it, the name of an entire country. . . .

Just so does the purloined letter, like an immense female body, stretch out across the Minister's office when Dupin enters. But just so does he already expect to find it, and has only, with his eyes veiled by green lenses, to undress that huge body.

And that is why without needing any more than being able to listen in at the door of Professor Freud, he will go straight to the spot in which lies and lives what that body is designed to hide, in a gorgeous center caught in a glimpse, nay, to the very place seducers name Sant' Angelo's Castle in their innocent illusion of controlling the City from within it. Look! between the cheeks of the fireplace, there's the object already in reach of a hand the ravisher has but to extend. . . . The question of deciding whether he seizes it above the mantelpiece as Baudelaire translates, or beneath it, as in the original text, may be abandoned without harm to the inferences of those whose profession is grilling.[32]

Were the effectiveness of symbols[33] to cease there, would it mean that the symbolic debt would as well be extinguished? Even if we could believe so, we would be advised of the contrary by two episodes which we may all the less dismiss as secondary in that they seem, at first sight, to clash with the rest of the work.

First of all, there's the business of Dupin's remuneration, which, far from being a closing pirouette, has been present from the beginning in the rather unselfconscious question he asks the Prefect about the amount of the reward promised him, and whose enormousness, the Prefect, however reticent he may be about the precise figure, does not dream of hiding from him, even returning later on to refer to its increase.

The fact that Dupin had been previously presented to us as a virtual pauper in his ethereal shelter ought rather to lead us to reflect on the deal he makes out of delivering the letter, promptly assured as it is by the check-book he produces. We do not regard it as negligible that the unequivocal hint through which he introduces the matter is a "story attributed to the character, as famous as it was excentric," Baudelaire tells us, of an English doctor named Abernethy, in which a rich miser, hoping to sponge upon him for a medical opinion, is sharply told not to take medicine, but to take advice.

Do we not in fact feel concerned with good reason when for Dupin what is perhaps at stake is his withdrawal from the symbolic circuit of the letter—we who become the emissaries of all the purloined letters which at least for a time remain in sufferance with us in the transference? And is it not the responsibility their transference entails which we neutralize by equating it with the signifier most destructive of all signification, namely: money?

But that's not all. The profit Dupin so nimbly extracts from his exploit, if its purpose is to allow him to withdraw his stakes from the game, makes all the more paradoxical, even shocking, the partisan attack, the underhanded blow, he suddenly permits himself to launch against the Minister, whose insolent prestige, after all, would seem to have been sufficiently deflated by the trick Dupin has just played on him.

We have already quoted the atrocious lines Dupin claims he could not help dedicating, in his counterfeit letter, to the moment in which the Minister, enraged by the inevitable defiance of the Queen, will think he is demolishing her and will plunge into the abyss: *facilis descensus Averni*, [34] he waxes sententious, adding that the Minister cannot fail to recognize his handwriting, all of which, since depriving of any danger a merciless act of infamy, would seem, concerning a figure who is not without merit, a triumph without glory, and the rancor he invokes, stemming from an evil turn done him at Vienna (at the Congress?) only adds an additional bit of blackness to the whole. [35]

Let us consider, however, more closely this explosion of feeling, and more specifically the moment it occurs in a sequence of acts whose success depends on so cool a head.

It comes just after the moment in which the decisive act of identifying the letter having been accomplished, it may be said that Dupin already *has* the letter as much as if he had seized it, without, however, as yet being in a position to rid himself of it.

He is thus, in fact, fully participant in the intersubjective triad, and, as such, in the median position previously occupied by the Queen and the Minister. Will he, in showing himself to be above it, reveal to us at the same time the author's intentions?

If he has succeeded in returning the letter to its proper course, it remains for him to make it arrive at its address. And that address is in the place previously occupied by the King, since it is there that it would re-enter the order of the Law.

As we have seen, neither the King nor the Police who replaced him in that position were able to read the letter because that *place entailed blindness.*

Rex et augur, the legendary, archaic quality of the words seems to resound only to impress us with the absurdity of applying them to a man. And the figures of history, for some time now, hardly encourage us to do so. It is not natural for man to bear alone the weight of the highest of signifiers. And the place he occupies as soon as he dons it may be equally apt to become the symbol of the most outrageous imbecility. [36]

Let us say that the King here is invested with the equivocation natural to the sacred, with the imbecility which prizes none other than the Subject.[37]

That is what will give their meaning to the characters who will follow him in his place. Not that the police should be regarded as constitutionally illiterate, and we know the role of pikes planted on the *campus* in the birth of the State. But the police who exercise their functions here are plainly marked by the forms of liberalism, that is, by those imposed on them by masters on the whole indifferent to eliminating their indiscreet tendencies. Which is why on occasion words are not minced as to what is expected of them: "*Sutor ne ultra crepidam,* just take care of your crooks.[38] We'll even give you scientific means to do it with. That will help you not to think of truths you'd be better off leaving in the dark."[39]

We know that the relief which results from such prudent principles shall have lasted in history but a morning's time, that already the march of destiny is everywhere bringing back—a sequel to a just aspiration to freedom's reign—an interest in those who trouble it with their crimes, which occasionally goes so far as to forge its proofs. It may even be observed that this practice, which was always well received to the extent that it was exercised only in favor of the greatest number, comes to [be] authenticated in public confessions of forgery by the very ones who might very well object to it: the most recent manifestation of the pre-eminence of the signifier over the subject.

It remains, nevertheless, that a police record has always been the object of a certain reserve, of which we have difficulty understanding that it amply transcends the guild of historians.

It is by dint of this vanishing credit that Dupin's intended delivery of the letter to the Prefect of police will diminish its import. What now remains of the signifier when, already relieved of its message for the Queen, it is now invalidated in its text as soon as it leaves the Minister's hands?

It remains for it now only to answer that very question, of what remains of a signifier when it has no more signification. But this is the same question asked of it by the person Dupin now finds in the spot marked by blindness.

For that is indeed the question which has led the Minister there, if he be the gambler we are told and which his act sufficiently indicates. For the gambler's passion is nothing but that question asked of the signifier, figured by the *automaton* of chance.

"What are you, figure of the die I turn over in your encounter (*tyché*) with my fortune?[40] Nothing, if not that presence of death which makes of human life a reprieve obtained from morning to morning in the name of meanings whose sign is your crook. Thus did Scheherazade for a thousand and one nights, and thus have I done for eighteen months, suffering the ascendancy of this sign at the cost of a dizzying series of fraudulent turns at the game of even or odd."

So it is that Dupin, *from the place he now occupies,* cannot help feeling a rage of manifestly feminine nature against him who poses such a question. The prestigious image in which the poet's inventiveness and the mathematician's rigor joined up with the serenity of the dandy and the elegance of the cheat suddenly becomes, for the very person who invited us to savor it, the true monstrum horrendum, for such are his words, "an unprincipled man of genius."

It is here that the origin of that horror betrays itself, and he who experiences it has no need to declare himself (in a most unexpected manner) "a partisan of the lady" in order to reveal it to us: it is known that ladies detest calling principles into question, for their charms owe much to the mystery of the signifier.

Which is why Dupin will at last turn toward us the medusoid face of the signifier nothing but whose obverse anyone except the Queen has been able to read. The commonplace of the quotation is fitting for the oracle that face bears in its grimace, as is also its source in tragedy: ". . . Un destin si funeste, / S'il n'est digne d'Atrée, est digne de Thyeste."[41]

So runs the signifier's answer, above and beyond all significations: "You think you act when I stir you at the mercy of the bonds through which I knot your desires. Thus do they grow in force and multiply in objects, bringing you back to the fragmentation of your shattered childhood. So be it: such will be your feast until the return of the stone guest I shall be for you since you call me forth."

Or, to return to a more moderate tone, let us say, . . . we rendered homage to the local password, the signifier's answer to whomever interrogates it is: "Eat your Dasein."

Is that then what awaits the Minister at a rendez-vous with destiny? Dupin assures us of it, but we have already learned not to be too credulous of his diversions.

No doubt the brazen creature is here reduced to the state of blindness which is man's in relation to the letters on the wall that dictate his destiny. But what effect, in calling him to confront them, may we expect from the sole provocations of the Queen, on a man like him? Love or hatred. The former is blind and will make him lay down his arms. The latter is lucid, but will awaken his suspicions. But if he is truly the gambler we are told he is, he will consult his cards a final time before laying them down and, upon reading his hand, will leave the table in time to avoid disgrace.[42]

Is that all, and shall we believe we have deciphered Dupin's real strategy above and beyond the imaginary tricks with which he was obliged to deceive us? No doubt, yes, for if "any point requiring reflection," as Dupin states at the start, is "examined to best purpose in the dark," we may now easily read its solution in broad daylight. It was already implicit and easy to derive from the title of our tale, according to the very formula we have long submitted to your discretion: in which the sender, we tell you, receives from the receiver his own message in reverse form. Thus it is that what the "purloined letter," nay, the "letter in sufferance" means is that a letter always arrives at its destination.

Notes

1. The translation of repetition *automatism*—rather than *compulsion*—is indicative of Lacan's speculative effort to reinterpret Freudian "overdetermination" in terms of the laws of probability. (Chance is *automaton*, a "cause not revealed to human thought," in Aristotle's *Physics*.) Whence the importance assumed by the Minister's passion for gambling later in Lacan's analysis. Cf. Lacan, *Écrits* (Paris: Éditions du Seuil, 1966), 41–61.—Ed.*

2. Cf. Heidegger, *Vom Wesen dar Wahrheit* (Frankfurt am Main: Klostermann, 1949). Freedom, in this essay, is perceived as an "ex-posure." *Dasein* ex-sists, stands out "into the disclosure of what is." It is *Dasein's* "ex-sistent in-sistence" which preserves the disclosure of beings.—Ed.

3. Lacan's analysis of the guessing game in Poe's tale entails demonstrating the insufficiency of an *imaginary* identification with the opponent as opposed to the *symbolic* process of an identification with his "reasoning." See *Écrits*, 59.—Ed.

4. "So infamous a scheme, / If not worthy of Atreus, is worthy of Thyestes." The lines from Atreus's monologue in act 5, scene 5 of Crébillon's play refer to his play to avenge himself by serving his brother the blood of the latter's own son to drink.—Ed.

5. This intersubjective setting which coordinates three terms is plainly the Oedipal situation. The illusory security of the initial *dyad* (King and Queen in the first sequence) will be shattered by the introduction of a *third* term.—Ed.

6. The necessary reference here may be found in "Le Temps logique et l'Assertion de la certitude anticipée," *Écrits*, 197.

7. *La politique de l'autruiche* condenses ostrich (*autruche*), other people (*autrui*), and (the politics of) Austria (*Autriche*).—Ed.

8. Such would be the crux of the Oedipus complex: the assumption of a desire which is originally another's, and which, in its displacements, is perpetually other than "itself."—Ed.

9. The first "Dupin tale" was "The Murders in the Rue Morgue."—Ed.

10. Cf. "Fonction et champ de la parole et du langage" in *Écrits*. Translated by A. Wilden, *The Language of the Self* (Baltimore, 1968).

11. The complete understanding of what follows presupposes a rereading of the short and easily available text of "The Purloined Letter."

12. Cf. Emile Benveniste, "Communication animale et langage humain," *Diogène*, no. 1, and our address in Rome, *Écrits*, 178.

13. For the notion of *ego ideal*, see Freud, *Group Psychology and the Analysis of the Ego* (trans. James Strachey [New York: Liveright, 1951])—Ed.

14. Freud comments on this joke in *Jokes and Their Relation to the Unconscious*

*"—Ed." in these Notes refers to Jeffrey Mehlman.—Ed.

(New York, 1960) 115: "But the more serious substance of the joke is what determines the truth. . . . Is it the truth if we describe things as they are without troubling to consider how our hearer will understand what we say? . . . I think that jokes of that kind are sufficiently different from the rest to be given a special position: What they are attacking is not a person or an institution but the certainty of our knowledge itself, one of our speculative possessions." Lacan's text may be regarded as a commentary on Freud's statement, an examination of the corrosive effect of the demands of an inter-subjective communicative situation on any naive notion of "truth."—ED.

15. Cf. *Ecrits,* 58. "But what will happen at the following step (of the game) when the opponent, realizing that I am sufficiently clever to follow him in his move, will show his own cleverness by realizing that it is by playing the fool that he hås the best chance to deceive me? From then on my reasoning is invalidated, since it can only be repeated in an indefinite oscillation. . . ."

16. We should like to present again to M. Benveniste the question of the antithetical sense of (primal or other) words after the magisterial rectification he brought to the erroneous philological path on which Freud engaged it (cf. *La Psychoanalyse,* 1 : 5 – 16). For we think that the problem remains intact once the instance of the signifier has been evolved. Bloch and Von Wartburg date at 1875 the first appearance of the meaning of the verb *dépister* in the second use we make of it in our sentence.

17. The very one to which Jorge Luis Borges, in works which harmonize so well with the phylum of our subject, has accorded an importance which others have reduced to its proper proportions. Cf. *Les Temps modernes,* June–July 1955, 2135–36, and Oct. 1955, 574–75.

18. The reference is to the "death instinct," whose "death," we should note, lies entirely in its diacritical opposition to the "life" of a naive vitalism or naturalism. As such, it may be compared with the logical moment in Lévi-Strauss's thought whereby "nature" exceeds, supplements, and symbolizes itself: the prohibition of incest.—ED.

19. This is so true that philosophers, in those hackneyed examples with which they argue on the basis of the single and the multiple, will not use to the same purpose a simple sheet of white paper ripped in the middle and a broken circle, indeed a shattered vase, not to mention a cut worm.

20. Cf. [Ferdinand de] Saussure, *Cours de linguistique générale* (Paris, 1969), 166: "The preceding amounts to saying that *in language there are only differences.* Even more: a difference presupposes in general positive terms between which it is established, but in language there are only differences *without positive terms.*"— ED.

21. Cf. *Our Examination Round His Factification for Incamination of Work in Progress,* Shakespeare & Co., 12 rue de l'Odéon, Paris, 1929.

22. The original sentence presents an exemplary difficulty in translation: "Les écrits emportent au vent les traites en blanc d'une cavalerie folle." The blank (bank) drafts (or transfers) are not delivered to their rightful recipients (the sense of *de cavalerie, de complaisance*). That is: in analysis, one finds absurd symbolic debts being paid to the "wrong" persons. At the same time, the mad, driven quality of the payment is latent in *traite,* which might also refer to the day's trip of an insane cavalry. In our translation, we have displaced the "switchword"—joining the financial and equestrian series—from *traite* to *charge.*—ED.

347

23. *Flying leaves* (also fly-sheets) and *purloined letters—feuilles volantes* and *lettres volées*—employ different meanings of the same word in French.—ED.

24. We revive this archaism (for the French: *lettre en souffrance*). The sense is a letter held up in the course of delivery. In French, of course, *en souffrance* means in a state of suffering as well.—ED.

25. See *Ecrits*, 59: ". . . it is not unthinkable that a modern computer, by discovering the sentence which modulates without his knowing it and over a long period of time the choices of a subject, would win beyond any normal proportion at the game of even and odd . . ."

26. *Autruicherie* condenses, in addition to the previous terms, deception (*tricherie*). Do we not find in Lacan's proliferating "monster" something of the *proton pseudos*, the "first lie" of Freud's 1895 *Project:* the persistent illusion which seems to structure the mental life of the patient?—ED.

27. The fetish, as replacement for the missing maternal phallus, at once masks and reveals the scandal of sexual difference. As such it is the analytic object par excellence. The female temptation to exhibitionism, understood as a desire to *be* the (maternal) phallus, is thus tantamount to being a fetish.—ED.

28. See Plato's *Meno:* "Socrates, . . . at this moment I feel you are exercising magic and witchcraft upon me and positively laying me under your spell until I am just a mass of helplessness. If I may be flippant, I think that not only in outward appearance but in other respects as well you are like the flat sting ray that one meets in the sea. Whenever anyone comes into contact with it, it numbs him, and that is the sort of thing you are doing to me now. . . ."—ED.

29. Baudelaire translates Poe's "*altogether* a fool" as "*absolument* fou." In opting for Baudelaire, Lacan is enabled to allude to the realm of psychosis.—ED.

30. We felt obliged to demonstrate the procedure to an audience with a letter from the period concerning M. de Chateaubriand and his search for a secretary. We were amused to find that M. de Chateaubriand completed the first version of his recently restored memoirs in the very month of November 1841 in which the purloined letter appeared in *Chamber's Journal*. Might M. de Chateaubriand's devotion to the power he decries and the honor which that devotion bespeaks in him (*the gift* had not yet been invented), place him in the category to which we will later see the Minister assigned: among men of genius with or without principles?

31. Poe is the author of an essay with this title.

32. And even to the cook herself.—J. L.
The paragraph might be read as follows: analysis, in its violation of the imaginary integrity of the ego, finds its fantasmatic equivalent in rape (or castration, as in the passage analyzed in the previous essay). But whether that "rape" takes place from in front or from behind (above or below the mantelpiece) is, in fact, a question of interest for policemen and not analysts. Implicit in the statement is an attack on those who have become wed to the ideology of "maturational development" (libidinal stages et al.) in Freud (i.e., the ego psychologists).—ED.

33. The allusion is to Lévi-Strauss's article of the same title ("L'efficacité symbolique") in *L'Anthropologie structurale.*—ED.

34. Virgil's line reads: *facilis descensus Averno.*

35. Cf. Corneille, *Le Cid* (2.2): "A vaincre sans péril, on triomphe sans gloire." (To vanquish without danger is to triumph without glory.)—ED.

36. We recall the witty couplet attributed before his fall to the most recent in date to have rallied Candide's meeting in Venice:

Il n'est plus aujourd'hui que cinq rois sur la terre,
Les quatre rois des cartes et le roi d'Angleterre.

(There are only five kings left on earth: four kings of cards and the king of England.)

37. For the antithesis of the "sacred," see Freud's "The Antithetical Sense of Primal Words." The idiom *tenir à* in this sentence means both to prize and to be a function of. The two senses—King and / as Subject—are implicit in Freud's frequent allusions to "His Majesty the Ego."—Ed.

38. From Pliny, 35.10.35: "A cobbler not beyond his sole. . . ."—Ed.

39. This proposal was openly presented by a noble Lord speaking to the Upper Chamber in which his dignity earned him a place.

40. We note the fundamental opposition Aristotle makes between the two terms recalled here in the conceptual analysis of chance he gives in his *Physics*. Many discussions would be illuminated by a knowledge of it.

41. Lacan misquotes Crébillon (as well as Poe and Baudelaire) here by writing *destin* (destiny) instead of *dessein* (scheme). As a result he is free to pursue his remarkable development on the tragic Don Juan ("multiply in objects . . . stone guest).—Ed.

42. Thus nothing shall (have) happen(ed)—the final turn in Lacan's theatre of lack. Yet within the simplicity of that empty present the most violent of (pre-)Oedipal dramas—Atreus, Thyestes—shall silently have played itself out.—Ed.

Psychoanalytic Provocateurs

1. What questions do modern psychoanalytic critics ask about a literary work? How do their areas of inquiry contrast with those of the archetypalists like Gelpi? phenomenological critics like Halliburton?

2. Certain types of criticism seem to be more useful for certain kinds of literary discourse than others. For what kind of literature does psychoanalytic criticism seem especially useful?

3. "Classic" psychoanalytic critics like Bonaparte have been accused of neglecting the specifically poetic elements of a literary text, that is, those things that make a text "literary." What reply could be made to this charge?

4. According to classical psychoanalytic critics, what unifies a poem or story?

5. Lesser writes that just as fiction's formal aspects result from the ego's defense strategies of displacement and condensation, so fiction's content derives from repressed unconscious desires. How does he demonstrate this theory in his interpretation of "The Birthmark"? Could this theory be applied to poetry? to historical essays? to criticism?

6. Often people want to reject interpretations like Holland's (Emily

Grierson is an oedipal anal retentive) or Lesser's (Aylmer fears female sexuality). How much do such negative responses tend to support psychoanalytic descriptions of the Unconscious as the site of the repressed? That is, if we object to such descriptions, do our objections tend to prove what we would deny?

7. Ego development theories of psychic harmony and ego control, such as Lesser's and Holland's, have been criticized for ignoring the anarchic, contradictory force of the Unconscious. For example, Marxist critics charge that ego development theory merely masks and so reinforces bourgeois (individualist) ideology. What charge might feminist critics levy against this theory? the New Critics?

8. Object relations theory, used here by Webster, studies the intensely personal area between internal and external reality which takes shape during early childhood experiences. In this intermediate area we first relate to the world through transitional objects, objects that are both inside and outside of ourselves; later, we perpetuate this paradoxical relationship through creative, symbolic play. What does this approach add to your appreciation of Yeats's golden bird?

9. Bloom's theory of the anxiety of influence suggests that a poet's relation to his poetic precursors—Yeats's relation to Shelley, for example—resembles the Oedipal relationship between son and father. How might this hypothesis be applied to Dickinson?

10. Bloom's theory that every reading is a misreading or "misprisioning" has been cheerfully appropriated by many semiotic, Marxist, and feminist critics. Why?

11. Lacan's reading of "The Purloined Letter" can be seen as a practice of reader-response deconstruction. Elizabeth Wright declares that from this perspective "a text will be first and foremost a discourse of desire, with the result that the emphasis will be not on an appropriation of the author's meaning but on an expropriation [of the text] by the reader" (*Modern Literary Theory: A Comparative Introduction,* ed. Ann Jefferson and David Robey [Totowa, N.J.: Barnes and Noble Books, 1982], 129). Wright goes on to suggest that by substituting "the text" for the stolen letter, we can construct a model of the reading process. Thus, at (A), the blind King's position, we might place the reader who believes that the authorial ego establishes the text's one true meaning; at (B), the Queen's first position, the competent reader who allows for pluralist yet stable readings; and at (C), the Minister-Dupin's position, relativistic deconstructionists like Lacan who take "into account the problematic relationship between author and text" (130). Discuss her suggestion.

12. Lacan is concerned with the effects of the special ambiguity of texts which, like the stolen "letter," both reveal and conceal. From this viewpoint, how is the "Seminar" both an interpretation and about interpretation?

CHAPTER 7

Reader-Response Criticism

READER-RESPONSE CRITICS ASK, What part does the reader play in the reading process? Theoretical interest in this question is fairly recent. In part it stems from structuralist and post-structuralist studies of language; in part from psychoanalytical analyses of the author's or reader's mind; and in part, from renewed interest in how composition and reading interrelate.

Reader-response theorists cover a wide spectrum. At one extreme are those who see readers as passive, their responses controlled by the text (the "inscribed" reader), or by the sociohistorical conditions (Marxist social realism), or by the author's intentions (Georges Poulet's phenomenological view of shared consciousness.) At the other extreme are critics like Stanley Fish and David Bleich who see readers as active creators of meaning. For these, "meaning" is redefined as "the experience the reader has in reading."

The middle ground between these positions is held by critics who see reading as a process of text production involving some interactive combination of language-reader-text-author. Jacques Lacan, with his psychostructural reading of "The Purloined Letter," could be included here. Other critics in this category are Yury M. Lotman, who proposes that, unlike other texts, literary texts establish a dialogic interaction which "frees" the reader; Michael Riffaterre, who suggests that meaning, a property of language, must be actualized by the reader; and Wolfgang Iser, who holds that the reader co-creates because he must fill in the gaps or implications unstated in the text. Critics in this middle ground often investigate the conventions and interpretive strategies of reading: Roland Barthes, in *S/Z*, explores how readers help determine how the text is written; Jonathan Culler explores how readers internalize communal conventions and so gain literary competence.

Focus on the reader's role has significant implications for literary studies. It problemizes the epistemological question, How is meaning produced? and simultaneously, the psychological question, How are we, as subjects, constituted? If we, as readers, play an important role in making meaning, do we do this as autonomous individuals (the humanist view), or as the products of signing systems which are "always already there" (the structuralist view)? Attention to the reader's role also calls into question any "objective" or neutral description of literature since every reading can be seen to be laden with human interests and values. And finally, this focus makes us aware that theories of reading affect the way the average reader responds to literary discourse: instead of acceding to an expert's opinion of the text's "true" meaning, readers are encouraged to heed their own responses.

Norman N. Holland and "A Rose for Emily"—Some Questions Concerning Psychoanalytic Criticism

WAYNE A. TEFS

Tefs responds to Holland's essay on "A Rose for Emily" (see Chapter 6) by charging, first, that Holland's genetic model "anaesthetizes" the story's punch, and second, that psychoanalysis must be performed not on a character's mind but on an actual human mind—the author's or the reader's. By calling attention to the crucial role of the reader, Tefs presages Holland's move to a reader-centered theory of interpretation. Holland's subsequent position, described in his 5 *Readers Reading* (1975), holds that as readers we match our individual fantasies to the text so that interpretation becomes a function of one's identity themes.

WHEN I RECEIVED Norman N. Holland's recent "Fantasy and Defense in Faulkner's 'A Rose For Emily,'"[1] I eagerly perused it to see what Professor Holland had to say about Faulkner's widely-read story. My response, not unlike that of a number of others who read the paper about the same time, was dissatisfaction with Professor Holland's rigorous and observant analysis of the story; I felt, to use Frederick Crews' happy term, that the paper had quite successfully "anaesthetized" the story.

From "Norman N. Holland and 'A Rose for Emily'—Some Questions Concerning Psychoanalytic Criticism," by Wayne A. Tefs, *The Sphinx: A Magazine of Literature and Society* 2 (1974): 50–57. Copyright 1974 by *The Sphinx: A Magazine of Literature and Society.* Reprinted by permission of *The Sphinx.*

This response was puzzling since it was unique in my reading of Holland's work, from his *Psychoanalysis and Shakespeare*, to *The Dynamics of Literary Response*, and recent essays, such as "The 'Unconscious' of Literature." I want in this essay to try and determine why "Fantasy and Defense in Faulkner's 'A Rose for Emily'" left me with the impression that there was a large gap between those things in the story which affected me and the things Holland isolated as central to a response to the story. . . .

. . .[E]ven after reading this detailed and carefully integrated study I cannot help feeling that I have been short-changed. The reason appears to be in Holland's near-neglect of the horrifying final paragraphs. For this reader at least, the final revelation has been anaesthetized by Holland's carefully-worked model. That deep sense of terror and horror (springing from primal scene anxieties which emerge from the common Faulknerian incest motif) has similarly been anaesthetized. In quoting the final paragraphs of the story I want to emphasize again the feeling that I have that Holland's analysis fails to account for the portion of the story that elicits my primary response:

> The man himself lay in the bed.
>
> For a long while we just stood there, looking down at the profound fleshless grin. The body had apparently once lain in the attitude of an embrace, but now the long sleep that outlasts love, that conquers even the grimace of love, had cuckolded him. What was left of him, rotten beneath what was left of the nightshirt, had become inextricable from the bed in which he lay; and upon him and upon the pillow beside him lay that even coating of the patient and biding dust.
>
> Then we noticed that in the second pillow was the indentation of a head. One of us lifted something from it, and leaning forward, that faint and invisible dust dry and acrid in the nostrils, we saw a long strand of iron-gray hair.

II

I want now to return to Holland's argument in order to examine some more deep-seated problems. Throughout the argument we are aware of the fact that Holland links Emily's adult personality traits (her stubbornness, for example) to their infantile origins. From the outset he hints "that the story, at an unconscious level, is dealing with an anal character"; later, in discussing control, the major issue of the story, he notes that it "plays an important part in the anal stage of development, in adults with predominantly anal characters, and in this story." When he comes to a psychological depth discussion of Emily he quotes [Erik H.] Erikson to the effect that "this stage, therefore becomes decisive for the ratio between loving good will and hateful self-insistence, . . ." indicating that Emily's stubbornness is determined by this infantile stage. Finally, he analogizes Miss Emily to the child who is being trained and quotes Dr.

Spock to support his thesis that "letting go and holding on" is the unconscious core in Miss Emily, and the story: "Towards the parent trying to regulate the feces that come from its body, Dr. Spock notes the way the child is 'apt to fight in rage and terror, as if he thought he was going to remove a very part of his body,' or at least will become 'worried to see this object, which he considers part of himself, snatched away.'" In short, then, Holland follows through his earliest suggestion that the story, at an unconscious level, is dealing with an anal character. The Miss Emily sketched by Holland is characterized (in terms of symbols, traits and potentials) by the anal stage of development.

In following this procedure (i.e., in locating adult character traits in their infantile origins) Holland is carefully emulating Freud's clinical methodology. In his work with the "Wolf Man," for example, Freud differentiated three periods in the "Wolf Man's" life—the earliest infantile period of dependency, the period at which the young child (of approximately four years) revived his earliest (in this case, primal scene) impressions, and the adult period during analysis when the "Wolf Man" was attempting to understand himself and his development. In order to understand the "Wolf Man" Freud moved directly from period three (adult) to period two (infantile memory), neglecting the entire period in between: "The patient justifiably disregards the three periods of time and puts his present ego into the situation which is so long past. And in this we follow him, since with correct self-observation and interpretation the effect must be the same as though the distance between the second and third periods of time could be neglected."[2] One notes here the ease with which Freud dismisses the twenty-year space of time between the two periods as unimportant to the development of the individual.

The road to understanding human development is clearly outlined in Freud's method as presented above: one traces back adult character traits to their genesis in infantile development. Accordingly, when Holland seeks to understand Emily, he relates the adult character traits evident in the story to generalized infantile development. Hence when Holland wants to tell us something about Emily he characteristically phrases his observations in terms that apply to infantile orientations: "regressing from the little girl's oedipal wish," "Miss Emily, like a child being trained," and "Deprived, Miss Emily, and the story as a whole, regress to the anal stage." The ease with which Holland leaps backward from adult character traits to infantile orientations is apparent; it may be susceptible to the criticism of psychoanalysis that Daniel Yankelovich and William Barrett refer to as "genetic determinism":

> Psychoanalysts rely heavily upon the "genetic" point of view (the reconstruction of the past) because a neurotic conflict always bears the stamp of its origins. Thus, psychoanalysts become acutely sensitized to patients' references to their bodies, and to the symbolism of incorporat-

ing, penetrating, and expelling from the body. But it is a mistake to equate an adult personality trait that shows signs of infantile origins with these origins itself. . . . Between ordinary adult personality traits and infantile urges there are layers upon layers of relationships, experiences, values and meanings. From infancy to adulthood is a long time, and there is a lot more going on by way of development, identifications, learning, and transformations of personality than is accounted for in the present metapsychology.[3]

III

More serious, it seems to me, is Holland's position that Emily is a suitable subject for depth analysis. In *The Dynamics of Literary Response* Holland has indicated that a literary character, such as Emily, comes alive, or seems to have life for readers because readers "recreate a dramatic character," and "give [him] a sense of reality."[4] Working from the conclusions of the Heider-Simmel experiments,* Holland goes on to explain that readers recreate characters in order to deal with tensions that exist in themselves: "The plot or incidents cause me to have certain feeling or wishes or tensions. I feel these tensions from the play as tensions in myself, but, both intellectually and emotionally, I attribute these tensions to the characters as motives: I project or bestow my feelings on the characters. . . . I take the character in because he offers me a way of dealing with the events and incidents [the writer] has created and which are creating tensions in me as I take the whole play in." The conclusion he reaches is, "The characters are real or not real only as we endow the characters with our wishes and defenses."

Yet throughout his discussion of "A Rose for Emily" Holland concentrates on Emily as a character, analyzing her character actions and posing psychoanalytic conclusions about them. Although he occasionally considers the town, Holland's central focus is on the mind of Emily. This appears especially odd in view of Holland's own statements in the essay— ". . . When one studies a literary work psychoanalytically, one does so in terms of three possible minds. Of these, only the author and the reader

*Conducted by psychologists Fritz Heider and Marianne Simmel on girls at Smith College, 1944: "To a group of undergraduates, they showed an animated cartoon detailing the aventures of a large black triangle, a small black triangle, and a circle, the three of them moving in various ways in and out of a rectangle. After the short came the main feature: the psychologists asked for comments, and the Smith girls 'with great uniformity' described the big triangle as 'aggressive,' 'pugnacious,' 'mean,' 'temperamental,' 'irritable,' 'power-loving,' 'possessive,' 'quick to take offense,' and 'taking advantage of his size' (it was, after all, the larger triangle). Eight per cent of the girls went so far as to conclude that this triangle had a lower I.Q. than the other. . . .

What the experiment shows is that realism, like beauty, is in the eye of the beholder. From the lines we are hearing, *we* recreate the characters, the words on the page controlling and shaping the characters we create." Norman N. Holland, *The Dynamics of Literary Response* (New York: Oxford University Press, 1968), 272.

can claim the fullness of life." Holland's analysis of Emily in terms of anal characteristics seems to wrench the focus of psycho-literary study toward the least important mind—that of the story's protagonist.

This raises the question whether it is possible to make meaningful psychoanalytic statements about a literary character. Since a literary character, such as Emily, is composed only of isolated bits of behaviour and selected character traits, the literary character may not provide a large enough context for a psychoanalytic explanation. It may be that Holland's careful analysis of Emily "feels" inadequte even as a psycho-analytic explanation because the explanation is not within the context of a whole character. Indeed, because we do not have an Emily who is a whole character it may be that the application of psychoanalysis to a liter-ary character is inevitably inadequate. An analogy may help clarify this point. When an analyst interprets a dream, he relates the material of the dream to a real mind (the dreamer's); he goes on to use this bit of a case history in relation to the rest of what he knows about his patient. In brief, he works the dream interpretation into the framework of a case history, which is the history of a particular mind. He does not consider the events or characters of a dream outside of their relationship to a par-ticular mind. He regards the dream within the context of the patient's whole history—and he composes a psychoanalytic narrative that in-cludes the dream, but always within its context.

If we follow this analogy we see that a psycho-literary reading loses its context if it is not related to a particular mind. The reason Holland's analysis of "A Rose for Emily" seems anaesthetic is that it does not give the feeling that a person in a historical time (Holland himself) is relating to the elements so clearly outlined. The sense of relatedness between the work and the reader has been lost in the "analysis" of Miss Emily.

NOTES

1. Norman N. Holland, "Fantasy and Defense in Faulkner's 'A Rose for Em-ily,'" *Hartford Studies in Literature* 4 (1972): 6. All further references are to this text unless otherwise noted.

2. Sigmund Freud, "From the History of an Infantile Neurosis (1918 [1914])," in *The Wolf-Man: by the Wolf-Man*, ed., with notes, an introduction, and chapters by Muriel Gardner (New York: Basic Books, 1971), 189.

3. Daniel Yankelovich and William Barrett, *Ego and Instinct: The Psychoana-lytic View of Human Nature: Revised* (New York: Random House, 1970), 313.

4. Norman N. Holland, *The Dynamics of Literary Response* (New York: Oxford University Press, 1968), 273 and 277. The following two references are also to this text.

How Readers Make Meaning

ROBERT CROSMAN

Crosman asks, How do readers make meaning? He answers that each reader responds to a text according to his or her own psychological and social constraints. The differences in the readings, as between his own and his student's, are then negotiated according to certain conventional strategies. He then asks another hard question: How can different readers' interpretations be equally valid? He grounds his answer here on deconstructionist views of the nature of the "open" text. That is, "A Rose for Emily" is ambiguous, vague, "a jumble of 'features' or 'elements.'" To read this story is to negotiate, by way of the codes of reading, a series of oppositions that the text itself has left unresolved.

FOR A NUMBER OF YEARS now I have been arguing that readers make the meanings of literary texts, and that accordingly there is no such thing as "right reading." Such a conclusion troubles most students of literature, and raises a host of questions, some of which—like "By what authority can I tell a student his interpretation is wrong?" or "How then can English be called a discipline?"—are questions of campus politics that are, theoretically at least, very easily answered. The problem for us is to answer the much more complex question of *how* readers make meaning: under what impulses or constraints, following what conventions or strategies? Beyond this lies a second thorny question: are different readers' results all equally valid? [1]

I want to try answering these general questions by looking at a specific text—William Faulkner's short story "A Rose for Emily"—and two antithetical interpretations of it. My contention is that although these interpretations contradict each other, both are valid. How this can be, it will be my task to explain. The two readers are myself and one of the students in a course called "Responses to Literature" that I taught at Trinity College in 1976. Our procedure was to read a text, and then immediately to write in our journals about our thoughts, feelings, and fantasies during and after reading. Here first is my journal entry, warts and all, exactly as I wrote it:

> This is a story I had never actually read, though I had heard of
> it, read something about it, and in particular knew its ending, which

From *College Literature* 9 (1982): 207–15. Copyright 1982 by West Chester State College. Reprinted by permission of *College Literature*.

357

kept me from feeling the pure shock that the reader must feel who knows nothing of what is coming. Even so I felt a shock, and reacted with an audible cry of mingled loathing and pleasure at the final and most shocking discovery: that Emily has slept with this cadaver for forty years. The loathing is easy enough to explain: the problem is to explain the pleasure. But before trying, let me record other parts of my "response."

I found my mind wandering as I read this story; there were paragraphs I had to reread several times. For one reason or another I was "uninvolved" with the story, perhaps a product of the circumstances under which I read it, but possibly also a response to the story itself. There are various reasons why I might tonight shun wrestling with a "serious" story, but perhaps I also shrank from the "horror" I knew was coming. Perhaps the story of a woman killing her faithless lover is not one I particularly want to hear. I've known about this story for years, yet had no urge to read it, perhaps because I knew what it contained.

She kills him. What do I care about him?—he's hardly in the story at all. But I noticed the repeated differentiation at the story's beginning between men and women, and the put-downs of women. The story seemed to be setting me up for some attitude toward women, and even though I noticed this, I did take the attitude: women are mean, ill-willed, and therefore (though not men's equals) menacing. Miss Emily is menacing. But at first she seems grotesque and stupid: her house smells bad; she's fat, with a dead look; she faces down the fathers [i.e. the aldermen] by (apparently) missing their point. Only gradually do I see the force of her will, that just because she doesn't go out or *do* anything doesn't mean that she isn't in control.

The scene with the rat-poison is crucial here: Miss Emily got her way, and the fact that her way is inscrutable, though surely menacing (arsenic), only makes it worse. The whole feeling of the story is of a mystery, something to do with male-female relationships, as well as time, perhaps, but a mystery one doesn't entirely want solved. Perhaps because I knew what was coming my mind wandered, putting even further distance between myself and the disgusting (but fascinating) revelation of the "bedroom" scene at the end. But the distancing is there in the story itself. The time-lags, the mysteriousness, the indirection, all put barriers between you and the story's subject.

So this is what I'd say at first reading, anyway. As far as response goes, mine is a considerable *fear* of the discovery I know is waiting, the sex-and-death thing, though there is a *fascination*, too. As far as the story's technique goes, I think it sets up shields of various sorts, that hide the ultimate truth, yet that have chinks that give us inklings, and the effect of secrets-not-entirely-hidden, of horrible-premonitions-defended-against, is what I'd guess is the technique that seems to arouse my feelings.

Now let me admit, right off, that this isn't an "unmediated" response to Faulkner's story. It was written not during but immediately after reading the story, by a relatively sophisticated, self-conscious reader, who also had some foreknowledge of the story's shocking climax. Most of all, it is a *written account* of a response, and so subject to all kinds of misrepresentation on my part *as I wrote it*. Also it was written by someone who has had considerable exposure to psychotherapy, and who therefore is somewhat at ease when expressing a taboo pleasure at contemplating necrophilia, an activity that is widely considered (and no doubt really is) loathsome to engage in.

Nonetheless, all this said, my response should give comfort to literary Freudians. For what I saw in "A Rose for Emily" was pretty certainly a "primal scene." Both my fear and my interest, my loathing and pleasure, derived, at least in part, from remembered childish speculation as to what went on in the parental bedroom. The structure of the story's plot is to set up a dark and impenetrable mystery—what is troubling Emily?—and to penetrate deeper and deeper into her past in hopes of getting an answer. Formally the pleasure is derived from solving the mystery, but the solution is a shocking one. My unconscious *knew* all along that nothing good went on behind a locked bedroom door, but now it has proof, and has won a victory over my conscious mind, which assured me it was none of my business. My conscious mind, meanwhile, has to content itself with solving a puzzle, with the self-evident reflection that after all Emily and Homer aren't Mom and Dad, and that, anyway, "it's only a story."

Beyond the illicit pleasure of letting a taboo thought become momentarily conscious, there was more bad news for my conscious mind in my response to "A Rose for Emily," for it turns out that my unconscious is a nasty little sexist, as I dutifully though rather reluctantly reported in my journal: "women are mean, ill-willed, men's inferiors, and menacing." I don't approve of such feelings, or consciously agree with them—some of my best friends are women—but they are *there* lying in wait for me when I read Faulkner. My shocked response to the imagined scene of Emily bedding down with Homer Barron's decomposing body, and my related interest at male/female antagonism and conflict in the story are only the beginnings of an interpretation, of course, but any class I would teach, or essay I would write on the story would feature such interests prominently.

In sharp contrast to my response was that of my student, Stacy. Since her notebook remained in her possession, I will summarize from memory her entry on "A Rose for Emily." Surprisingly, Stacy did not mention the terrible denouement of the story—the discovery of Homer Barron's remains in Emily's bed. On questioning, she said that Emily's poisoning of Homer remained shadowy and hypothetical in her mind, and she had completely missed the implication of the strand of Emily's hair found on the pillow next to the corpse. Instead, Stacy had written a rather poetic reverie about her *grandmother*, of whom she was strongly reminded by

Emily. The grandmother lived, Stacy wrote, shut away in a house full of relics and mementos of the past. Events of long ago, and people long dead, were more real to her than the world of the present, but Stacy found very positive things in her grandmother, and (by implication) in Emily as well: endurance, faith, love. She even identified the frail, pretty woman with Faulkner's picture of Emily when young: "a slender figure in white."

The contrast between our two reactions to the story was striking, and cause for discussion in class. In a more conventional course, I might have been tearing my hair over a student who so "missed the point" of the story as to ignore in her interpretation the terrifying climax of Emily's story, and who did not even notice the grizzly implications of that strand of iron-grey hair on the pillow beside Homer Barron. But what I found myself doing, instead, was to go back over the story and see how much of its meaning *I* had missed, how much there was in Faulkner's picture of Emily that *was* attractive, noble, tragic. Deprived of all normal suitors by a domineering father, she had clung to that father, even in death; deprived of her father, she had found a suitor outside the limits of respectability for a woman of her class and background; threatened with his loss as well she found a way to keep him, and then she remained true to him all the days of her life. Certainly it is hard entirely to like a Juliet who poisons her Romeo, yet remember that this is an extraordinarily evasive, indirect story, in which the reader can easily overlook unwanted implications. No poisoning actually occurs in its pages; the deed is left for the reader to infer. Stacy found it easy to ignore, and when confronted with it, accepted it as a qualification, but not a refutation of her admiration for Emily: just as I was able to modify my interpretation of the story without giving up my spontaneous horror, so Stacy could acknowledge the horror, without surrendering her view of Emily as embodying positive values.

What happened between Stacy and me is a perfectly familiar event in the lives of all of us: we communicated our differing interpretations to each other and both learned from the exchange. I wasn't right and she wrong, nor vice versa. Nor did we emerge from the exchange with identical interpretations of the story: Emily will doubtless never be as noble a character for me as she is for Stacy. Nonetheless, each of us improved his or her sense of understanding the story by sharing it with the other. Similarly, I can imagine no essay that I might read on "A Rose for Emily" that would leave my sense of the story entirely unchanged, nor any essay that would completely obliterate my old sense of the story. Meaning, as David Bleich has so eloquently argued, is constituted by individual readers as response, and is then negotiated by them into group knowledge. Readers, first individually and then collectively, make meaning.

Now what, we might want to ask, must Faulkner's text be like, if Stacy's interpretation and mine are both "right"—both defensible, that is, under the laws of logic and evidence? The obvious answer is that the text must be ambiguous. Indeed we have already seen its ambiguity with reference to Emily's own character. A figure of pathos as a young girl under her father's thumb, she develops in later years into a formidable figure herself. Victimized first by her father and then by Homer Barron, she turns the tables and becomes a victimizer; but even in this latter role she is ambiguous—the villainous-heroic resolver of an impossible situation. Even physically our imaginations must hover between the picture of Emily as a slender, girlish, angelic creature, and that of the older Emily: "She looked bloated, like a body long submerged in motionless water, and of that palid hue." To complicate matters still further, the advanced-age description occurs earlier in the story.

The ambiguities of Emily's character are echoed in those of the other people portrayed in the story. The fact is that, like Emily, all characters in this story are seen through such a veil of vagueness, of mysteriousness, of innuendo pointing in no clearly defined direction, that whatever stance a reader takes toward any of the characters is conjecture based on little real information.

Equally vague and contradictory are the subjects and themes that we find in the story. Take the issue that spoke to me most at first reading: the man/woman polarity. The narrator (although typically given no name, age, sex, or other distinguishing characteristic) begins in the first sentence to distinguish between the sexes:

> When Miss Emily Grierson died, our whole town went to her funeral: the men through a sort of respectful affection for a fallen monument, the women mostly out of curiosity to see the inside of her house. . . .

In contrast to women, men seem high-minded here, capable of a gallantry echoed in Judge Stevens' refusal to force Emily to clean her house: "'Dammit, sir,' Judge Stevens said, 'will you accuse a lady to her face of smelling bad?'" When Emily begins her "affair" with Homer Barron (the exact nature of which is, to put it mildly, unclear) it is "the ladies" who try to meddle, while "the men did not want to interfere." Struggle is certainly there between men and women, but my initial interpretation of the story as "bad woman destroys good man" suppresses a good deal of evidence that it is the men, father and lover, who are ultimately responsible for Emily's pitiful condition. If she later turns the tables on them and wins a series of victories, isn't this an instance of the underdog triumphing? Emily's "victories" are, in any case, utterly grotesque (she succeeds in buying arsenic from the reluctant druggist, she succeeds in "keeping" her faithless lover) and could as easily be called *moral defeats*. If there is a battle of the sexes in "A Rose for Emily," the reader must decide who wins.

Other polarities are equally ambiguous. The story sets up tensions—

or allows tensions to be felt—between age and youth, parent and child, black and white, individual and group, North and South, past and present, love and hate, and perhaps most of all between life and death. The picture (not actually in the story, but imperatively implied by it in my experience) of "bloated" corpselike Emily lying with her decomposing lover is as vivid an image of death-in-life as I know: Emily already dead in a sense, Homer still alive to her (despite the stink, the "fleshless grin"). Which one of them is deader? Which one would you rather be? Nowhere in literature do I remember the line between death and life so definitively rubbed out.

Indeed, I find it tempting to picture Faulkner's story as a series of widening concentric rings, with the dead/alive lovers at their center. As we move outward, we reach progressively wider polarities: the family (Emily/Father), the community (individual/group; men/women; older/younger generations), the nation (North/South: "And now Miss Emily had gone to join the representatives of those august names where they lay in the cedar-bemused cemetery among the ranked and anonymous graves of Union and Confederate soldiers who fell at the battle of Jefferson"), and the universe (past/present; life/death). "What is true at the center," the story seems to say, "is equally true at every wider circumference." But what (I ask) is true at the center? Those lovers on their bed seem to be a hieroglyph of some profound truth about life, death, time—about *everything*, in fact. But any attempt to pin it down, to state its meaning, excludes other equally possible interpretations—which doesn't mean that we shouldn't interpret, but only that we should have some humility about the status of our results.

Finally, with respect to the story's technique, we find the same sort of ambiguities. I mentioned in my original journal entry the extraordinary indirection with which the story is told. The narrator is anything but omniscient, reporting only what is common knowledge in Jefferson, and even then withholding foreknowledge of earlier events—such as the cause of the bad smell emanating from Emily's house in the months following Homer's disappearance—until the right moment comes to spring it on the reader.

The narrator is himself a "reader" of Emily's story, trying to put together from fragments a complete picture, trying to find the meaning of her life in its impact upon an audience, the citizens of Jefferson, of which he is a member. He disregards chronology, working generally backward from recent events to ever-earlier ones, as if seeking their explanation in a receding past that never throws quite enough light. Displaced chronology and the narrator's carefully limited point of view are two sources of the story's murkiness, which leaves us constantly guessing about events— What caused the smell? Why did Emily buy arsenic? What happened to Homer? Yet the narrator can be wonderfully, or cruelly, explicit too in his handling of details.

To read Faulkner's story, then, is to negotiate a series of oppositions that the text itself has left unresolved. We feel compelled to resolve its ambiguities, but however we do so, some of the evidence will have to be ignored. Small wonder if Stacy and I each constructed our interpretations out of different bits of this conflicting, shifting, and incomplete mass of evidence, each of us ignoring what didn't fit.

It is often argued, when this point is reached, that the text in question is in a special (though daily widening) category of texts whose meaning is, in effect, "everything is ambiguous." Modern critics—New Critical, Structuralist, semiotic, deconstructive—are fond of finding this message everywhere they look. I confess a fondness for it myself, yet I remember that at first "A Rose for Emily" had a definite meaning for me; that only second, more "mature" thoughts softened it into a structure of irresolvable ambiguities. I am not convinced, in other words, that ambiguity is the *meaning* of Faulkner's story. I think, rather, that it is the *nature* of this text to be ambiguous, and that meaning is what the reader makes, by choosing among its paired, antithetical elements. I hope to have demonstrated this contention with respect to "A Rose for Emily." I cannot hope to prove here, but do affirm my belief that all literary texts are by nature ambiguous, and that the reader makes their meaning.

In his extensive inquiry into the psychology of reading, *5 Readers Reading*, Norman Holland asks what is the nature of a text, and then shrugs his shoulders:

> A reader reads something, certainly, but if one cannot separate his "subjective" response from its "objective" basis, there seems no way to find out what that "something" is in any impersonal sense. It is visible only in the psychological processes the reader creates in himself by means of the literary work. (p. 40)[2]

Certainly Holland has a point: it is impossible to discover a situation in which a text can be observed without an observer (a reader) being present. Yet it is well to remember that this predicament is shared by all the sciences, even by particle physics, which nonetheless goes on finding leptons and quarks, the sub-subatomic particles of matter. Moreover, if it is impossible to describe the *text* with certainty, that same limitation applies, in spades, to describing with certainty the reader's "psychological processes"—approximation and plausibility are the most we can hope for in either enterprise.

Holland writes as if a solitary reader confronted a solitary text in a void, equipped only by the internal psychological processes described by Freud. This is for Holland a fruitful hypothesis; yet, from another, equally sound, point of view, the individual reader is a member of a society, a product of a lifetime of education whose substance is the learning of conventions shared by other members of society. The very language in which the literary text is written is the product not of his own psyche but of a human community ongoing over millennia. It seems clear that the individual reader reads, in part at least, according to conventions, strategies, and expectations that he has learned from other human beings and that he shares with them.

Remember, for example, that though Stacy and I interpreted Emily in antithetical ways, we both shared a reading strategy: call it reading-for-character. It would seem that the text could accordingly be described as embodying the "character-reading code," put there by Faulkner, who knew the code as well as anyone. This is the approach of the relatively new discipline of Semiotics, whose goal is to specify all the codes operating in a text and thus to read "scientifically." In practice, though, the name and nature of the codes are variable with the critic and the work, and the codes become so numerous and so redundant that instead of achieving with their help a specific meaning we are left, once again, contemplating the universal aesthetic message of ambiguity.

We are on firmer ground, I think, when we think of the "codes" as in the reader, not in the text, and call them "reading conventions" or "reading strategies." Stacy and I (and many others) read "A Rose for Emily" as a portrait of its heroine's character, but that's not *all* we read it as, and other readers will apply entirely different strategies: the Marxist will read for (and find) representations of a decaying class-structure and social victimization, a deconstructionist will read it as a self-consuming artifact, allegorizing readers of all sorts will read for all sorts of symbols, a Structuralist will read for structures; and in no case (except perhaps by majority-rule) can we exclude any of these strategies from validity, though some will interest us more than others.

But if the "codes" are in the reader, what is in the text? I suggest that when we look closely at texts what we find are not "codes"—consistent, coherent, smoothly concatenated—but a jumble of "features" or "elements." The maddening thing is that these elements seem to spring into being only when a reader is present—that is, when a reading strategy is being applied. The reader's freedom is limited both by the elements in the story, and by the codes he has learned from his culture, but since he *is* free to select which codes he applies, which elements he constitutes, he is in practice no more constrained by them than putting on a pair of sneakers compels me to run. What he *is* forced to do is to apply *some* strategy, look at *some* elements of the text (since that, after all, is what reading is) and in so doing he joins a community of which all other readers, and the author himself, are members—he enters, that is, a dialogue, all of whose voices speak within him, all of whose roles he plays.

It is my conclusion—a tentative conclusion, as always—that such issues are never definitively settled; that since literary texts are richly ambiguous, individual readers do resolve those ambiguities, fill in the hermeneutic gaps, with their own individual psychological makeups, their own "identity themes," to borrow Holland's phrase. But reader and text do not exist in a void. Rather, they are framed by a vast series of linguistic, literary, and cultural conventions of interpretation, some of which, at least, readers cannot help knowing and using, since that is what "reading" is. These conventions, or codes, are *so* numerous, however, and so mutually contradictory, that the individual reader still exercises considerable freedom in the way he interprets, merely by his choice and emphasis among the conventions.

Reading is *both* a solitary *and* a communal enterprise; we read *both* for self-discovery *and* to learn about the world; and we go on learning, after we have read a text, by sharing our interpretation with others, and by letting their interpretations enrich our own.

I won't pretend that disagreements, even violent disagreements, can't occur. Many of them are due to the pernicious belief in "right reading": the idea that if you and I disagree, one of us is wrong, and it better not be me! But disagreements can also result from real moral or political differences. Even here, though, negotiation and compromise may be a more useful approach than the verbal equivalent of war, however stimulating and entertaining a quarrel may be.

Still, it helps to remember that these disagreements are not epistemological but political, whether on or off the campus. I had only to *offer* my interpretation of "A Rose for Emily" for Stacy to change hers, but if she had resisted mine completely, I would still have listened to hers and learned from it, confident that sooner or later she would follow my example. Telling her that she was "wrong" would have been not only unhelpful but untrue. Her interpretation was *not* wrong; it was merely partial, incomplete, and *all* interpretations are incomplete. Literary study *is* a discipline not because it gives *certain* answers—no field of inquiry does that—but because it is eternally in the business of developing procedures for assembling evidence and answering questions about an area of human experience that human beings collectively judge to be important and worthy of inquiry. Literary theory, I submit, is nothing more nor less than the study, with regard to literary texts, of how readers make meaning.

NOTES

1. "How Readers Make Meaning" is a sequel to my earlier article, ("Do Readers Make Meaning?") printed in *The Reader in The Text: Essays on Audience and Interpretation*, ed. Susan R. Suleiman and Inge Crosman (Princeton: Princeton University Press, 1980), 149–64. "How Readers" was delivered in an earlier form to the Theories of Reading Conference sponsored by the Society for Critical Exchange and Indiana University and held in Bloomington on 28–30 September 1981.

Those acquainted with "reader-response" theories will recognize, throughout my essay, bits and pieces of the ideas and methods of Norman Holland, David Bleich, Wolfgang Iser, Jonathan Culler, and Stanley Fish, and of Structuralism ("binary opposition"), Semiotics ("codes"), and deconstruction (Derrida: "the reader writes the text"). Those for whom these names and slogans are not household words will find a useful, 23-page bibliography by Inge Crosman in Suleiman and Crosman. More on these matters will also be found in my essay "The Twilight of Critical Authority," *Annals of Scholarship* 1, no. 1 (Winter, 1980) and in the first chapter of my book *Reading Paradise Lost* (Bloomington: Indiana University Press, 1980).

    2. [Holland, 5 *Readers Reading* (New Haven: Yale University Press, 1975).]

Styles of Reading

GEORGE L. DILLON

Dillon's essay exemplifies what we might call reader-response narratology—a study of how readers read (perform) narrative. He argues that our interpretations depend on how we answer the questions we ask when we read. So Dillon analyzes how students use comprehension skills of inferring and connecting— what he calls "event chaining"—to read the narrative sequence of "A Rose for Emily." He finds that not only do student readers cluster into several groups, but critics as well fall into these same groupings. Dillon's conclusion that our "styles of reading" exist prior to and form the basis of critical approaches underscores a semiotic view of the interrelationship of discourse systems: "We understand literature and life in the same or similar ways."

ONE OF THE THINGS READERS DO with stories is to talk about them. These stories have not said it all, and readers derive evident pleasure from completing them, commenting on them, making them their own in various ways. Christine Brooke-Rose has recently called attention to the strategic incompleteness of good stories—spelling everything out treats the reader as stupid—and has suggested a classification of stories according to the tasks they leave to readers, or in which they entangle readers.[1] If we look at actual, published discussions of a story, however, we find no two of them answering the same set of questions, which suggests that we should look for questions (pre)inscribed in the reader as well as the text—the text, it is a matter of fact, has not very narrowly constrained the set of questions the readers have posed. As soon as we raise the matter of the actual performance of readers, however, we encounter

From *Poetics Today* 3, no. 2 (1982): 77–88. Copyright 1982 by The Porter Institute for Poetics and Semiotics, Tel Aviv University. Reprinted by permission of The Porter Institute for Poetics and Semiotics, Tel Aviv University.

a plethora of variables, and it has become something of a fashion in discussions of reading to enumerate them, often, it seems, to frighten scholars back to the study of narrative competence and the ways texts constrain, or should constrain interpretations. Here, for example, is the list of Gerald Prince, a theorist who, though a strong believer in narrative competence, is a sceptic about the study of narrative performance:

> Of course, a given reader may be very tired or not at all, very young or very old, in a good mood or in a bad one; he may have a very good or a very deficient memory, a very great or very limited capacity for decentration, a considerable or moderate attention span; he may be a more or less experienced reader; he may be reading the text for the first, second, or tenth time; he may find the sentences and situations presented more or less familiar; he may want to read for fun or out of a sense of duty; he may show particular interest in the language, the plot, the characters, or the symbolism; he may hold one set of beliefs or another; and so on. In other words, his physiological, psychological, and sociological conditioning, his predispositions, feelings, and needs may vary greatly and so may his reading: his knowledge, his interests, and his aims determine to a certain extent the conventions, assumptions, and presuppositions he takes to underlie the text, the kinds of connections he is particularly interested in making, the questions he chooses to ask, and the answers he brings to them.[2]

Barbara Herrnstein Smith offers a similar list of factors that may influence how and how much a reader may construct of the "chronology of events" which underlies a narrative.[3] If we are concerned with how people actually do read stories, however, these lists outline an area for research. Idiosyncratic variation may be a bogeyman; on the other hand, it may pose serious threats to communication, requiring rigorous methodological rules and the exercise of institutional authority. Perhaps there are underlying regularities which *in fact* shape readers' performances; perhaps there are none. In this article, I will examine readings of Faulkner's "A Rose for Emily," and focus initially on one area of variation—the answers readers have given to questions about the chronological sequence, or "event chain," of the story—to see how wild the variation is and what hope there may be of identifying regularities of performance.

One reason for focusing on event chains is that these have been among the most intensively studied of the many aspects of story comprehension. The term *event chain* is being used in a slightly technical way to refer to a graph connecting material in a story as events and causes of events, actions and motives of actions, enablements of events or actions, responses to events or actions and consequences of these. Readers employ two basic operations in building event chains: connection and inference. No story I know of spells out all of the terms and connections in an event chain (Miss Emily's motive for murdering Homer Barron, for example, is left for the reader to infer, as is the connection of the arsenic to the murder), and a story that did spell them all out would treat the reader as inconceivably stupid. Two distinctions are in order here: event chains are not precisely chronological, though I think they do correspond closely to what Professor Smith means by chronological sequences, that is, a certain sequentiality is implicit in the notions of motive, action, cause, response, and consequence, but not necessarily clock or calendar time, nor do pieces of the overall chain have to be strictly ordered; different sequences may overlap. This point is quite clear in regard to "A Rose for Emily": it seems possible to establish a chronology of the story that orders all of its major incidents, though it is very difficult to do so,[4] and it is not necessary to have worked out such a time scheme in order to get major portions of the event chain straight. Second, event chains are not "plots" in the sense defined by story grammars, nor in the traditional "rising-falling" interpretation.[5] That is, they are shapeless and open-ended; they do not account for any sense of beginning, climax, or conclusion. I assume that such structures can be fitted over them, or parts of the chains explained in terms of these notions—or not, as the reader desires. Hence event chains are part of the comprehension of all narratives; indeed, of all happenings, not just stories. One final proviso—we probably should not speak of "the event chain" but of "event chaining," since what a reader infers and connects, and how far he or she carries some sequence, is the reader's choice.

When we survey the published criticism of "A Rose for Emily," we find a large and bewildering array of questions about the event chain that have been answered. These include:

1. Why weren't there suitable suitors for Emily?
2. How does Emily respond to being denied suitors?
3. Why does Emily take up with Homer Barron?
4. What happened when he left? Did he abandon her? Why did he come back?
5. Why did she kill him?
6. Why did the smell disappear after only one week?
7. What did Miss Emily think of the men scattering lime around her house?
8. How did the hair come to be on the pillow? How much hair is a *strand*?
9. What was her relationship to Tobe?
10. Did she lie beside the corpse? How often, for what period of years?
11. Why did she not leave the house for the last decade of her life?
12. Did she not know Colonel Sartoris had been dead ten years when she faced down the Aldermen?

13. How crazy was she (unable to distinguish fantasy from reality)?

14. Why does she allow so much dust in her house?

There is also one question that has been asked but not answered, as far as I know: What transpired when the Baptist minister visited her? As the specialists in story comprehension have noted, once we realize that a Story Comprehender must have the power to carry out inferences in order to comprehend even the simplest story and give it that power, the problem becomes one of limiting the inferences drawn to some "relevant" subset of the possible ones. William Warren, David Nicholas, and Tom Trabasso suggest a first approximation of "relevance" as some inference that advances the main story line,[6] but it is not clear how to apply this principle to the fourteen questions and answers, since every one of those questions was answered by at least one critic who felt the answer was relevant to the interpretation of the story—relevant to determining her motives, naming her actions, and so on. Of course, some of these event-chain inferences are stimulated by the particular interpretation a critic is putting forth, but there does not seem to be any basis on which to separate those inferences that are made independent of an interpretation from those which are not; event chaining is not an autonomous activity, but rather is subject to varying degrees of top-down guidance. People do not agree on the story to then disagree on the interpretation. It is simply not true that, as Wolfgang Iser claims, "On the level of plot, then, there is a high degree of intersubjective consensus," with subjective variation arising at the level of significance.[7] In fact, when we look at the list of questions that have been answered, the constructon of event chains seems wildly unconstrained.

If we look at whole readings, however, some system and pattern does emerge. There are two surveys of the criticism of this story, and both find it fairly easy to group the readings into three classes (though the classes are somewhat differently defined).[8] We could group the readings according to what one might call "approaches," suggesting by that term some set of general questions readers taking a particular approach tend to pose of texts they read. This notion can be pushed in two, opposite directions. Taking it one way, we could argue that the variation considered so far does not directly reflect the way readers read but the way critics write about stories when they have an eye toward publication; the facts presented so far pose questions for the sociology of literature, or the history of literary criticism, not for the theory of reading. Taken the other way, these approaches could be viewed as personal styles or preferences in reading that happen to have acquired some public sanction. We generally have some style of reading before we know much about "approaches," after all, though we may learn other questions to ask when we study literature. In any case, one must have learned the approach in order to use it, so an approach is to some degree part of the cognitive equipment of a reader who employs it, however imperfectly integrated into his other modes of thinking it may be. Some light on the matter is shed, I think, by the very copious transcripts of interviews with undergraduate English majors about "A Rose for Emily" published by Norman Holland in 5 *Readers Reading.*

Holland's students also show three distinct approaches, and these approaches match up with the types of approaches in the published criticism. Though the student subjects may have gotten some leads from the criticism and they may be editing their responses to various degrees when presenting them to Professor Holland, they do seem to be giving what they feel are their own responses and to be responding in somewhat original—but consistent—ways to his questions. Also, because Holland has them talk about three stories, they could not have been greatly influenced by any one piece of published criticism, and indeed, the criticism they chose to be influenced by as much reflects their cognitive styles as it determines them. Holland's study strongly suggests that there are styles of reading stories, characteristic ways that readers interrogate texts, and that the "approaches" in the criticism are indeed rooted in the critics' own styles of reading and appeal to like-minded readers. I will illustrate this correspondence for three basic styles, which I will call the Character-Action-Moral (CAM) style, the Digger for Secrets style, and the Anthropologist style.

The CAM style differs markedly from the other two in treating the meaning (or significance) as more or less evident in the story: the reader makes the text his own, and makes the reading more apparent, by elaborating the event chain in the direction of the main character's traits, motives, thoughts, responses, and choices. To do this, CAM readers treat the world of the text as an extension or portion of the real world, the characters as real persons, so that we will recognize the experience of characters as being like our own experience; hence it can be understood or explained just as we would understand our own experience. Thus, the inferences they draw are based on commonsense notions of the way the world is, people are, etc. The other two styles appropriate the text not by immersion, but by analytic distance, probing and abstracting behind what is said; they assume that the world of the text is an edited version of our world—a *structure* rather than a glimpse or fragment. The CAM reader works by amalgamating the story into the body of his own beliefs and practical axioms about how life is or should be, the analytic styles by postulating the otherness or strangeness of the text.

The standard CAM reading contains lists of traits that account for the actions of the main character in a straightforward evaluative fashion (Brooks and Warren: "What is Miss Emily like? What are the mainsprings of her character?" p. 411).[9] The actions are assumed to be pointers toward relatively permanent and pervasive characteristics, and one often finds "it could be otherwise" speculations in CAM readings (e.g., "A Rose for Emily" could have had a happy outcome if Homer Barron had been a marrying man—West; [10] if another man had proposed to Emily after she finished with Homer, she would have declined the offer because she felt herself already married—Sam, in Holland [pp. 138–39]). That is, the notion of character seems to presuppose the freedom of individuals to choose their responses to their situations, and stories like "A Rose for Emily" are treated as collisions between characters and situations—as *tragedies*, in the traditional Butcher/Bradley sense:

> Perhaps the horrible and the .admirable aspects of Miss Emily's final deed arise from the same basic fact of her character: she insists on meeting the world on her own terms. She never cringes, she never begs for sympathy, she refuses to shrink into an amiable old maid, she never accepts the community's ordinary judgments or values. This independence of spirit and pride can, and does in her case, twist the individual into a sort of monster, but, at the same time, this refusal to accept the hero values carries with it a dignity and courage. (Brooks and Warren, 413)

(Brooks and Warren later suggest Lear and Hamlet as parallels, but their language suggests Richard III as closer to hand.) We can see here the way the common notion of tragedy directs the reading toward character analysis; it also introduces three other questions, namely, those of awareness, tragic flaw, and moral. The evoking or constructing of character seems to lead directly to inference on the character's thoughts. When done naïvely, the results are fairly obtrusive, as when Holland's Sam says Emily has an awareness that "things were moving on, that things were changing, and yet, a similar awareness that she was unable to change along with them" (p. 137). More subtle is a partial merging of reader's and character's points of view. The reader talks about the character in terms the character himself might use: "She lost her honor, and what else could she do but keep him [Homer] forever, make him hers in the only way she possibly could?" (Sam, p. 137). This is remarkably similar to statements in the published readings of Brooks and Warren and West:

> Emily's world, however, continues to be the Past (in its extreme form it is death), and when she is threatened with desertion and disgrace, she not only takes refuge in that world, but she also takes Homer with her, in the only manner possible. (West, 195)
>
> She would marry the common laborer, Homer Barron, let the community think what it would. She would not be jilted. And she would hold him as a lover. But it would all be on her own terms. (Brooks and Warren, 413–14)

> From the moment that she realizes that he will desert her, tradition
> becomes magnified out of all proportion to life and death, and she con-
> ducts herself as though Homer really had been faithful—as though this
> view represented reality. (West, 195–96)

This construction of an inner logic for the character is essential to
the drawing of the moral: once we have realized the character's viewpoint, we can see the fatal flaw, the impulses or tendencies in ourselves
that we should not give in to. If this immersion and identification with
the character (which is plainly the identification of the character with the
reader, in terms of himself) fails, then the story is, as Lionel Trilling concluded of "A Rose for Emily," without larger human import.[11] In this
story, the CAM reader must direct his attention away from the details
that suggest Miss Emily is not "like us" (above all, the questions about
sleeping next to the corpse). The published critics can simply maintain
silence on the question; Holland raised it, however, in his interviews, and
Sam simply refused to pursue it. Even lines of inference that would attribute dark or complex motives are avoided or treated as normal. In regard to question (2) (Why Homer?), West discreetly suggests the usual,
healthy, sexual urges, without considering that Homer is the utter subversion of Grierson hauteur and a most improbable candidate for a husband, that Emily flaunts her involvement, and so on. It is to Sam's credit
that he records this as a "gap" in the story (according to his characterization of her as a tragic heroine).

Sam, in fact, has difficulty establishing a basic identification in the
other two stories he read. In the case of Fitzgerald's "Winter Dreams," he
finds Dexter's idealizing of Judy Jones a bit silly, concludes that neither
that idealizing nor his actions reflect a tragic flaw, and complains that the
moral to be drawn is obvious and banal: "We're taught this lesson through
every damn novel, you know. . . . The lesson of the past, the knowledge,
the realization in every hero throughout the damn thing that it cannot be
retraced, that you try ceaselessly to recapture the past and that it forever
eludes you" (p. 309). The story lavishly traces Dexter's thoughts, and it
seems simply not to have left Sam enough of the kinds of questions he
likes to answer. Sam does engage in some "it could have been otherwise"
speculation and elaborates certain details of Judy's "fall" into housewif-
ery, but on the whole, the story is too familiar and too explicit for him to
take a great interest in it. He has even greater difficulty with Hemingway's "The Battler." Although he at first praises the story because he
thinks "it's a valuable look at Nick Adams" (p. 319), he also complains
that "we don't get much into Nick's mind" (p. 326)—which is certainly
true, and a bit of an enigma if you are looking for meaning in terms of
the impact of Nick's experience on him. Sam cannot find a plot with a
significant, life-altering decision in it, and he says, "I don't know what it's
doing if it's not doing symbolic things" (p. 319). And obviously, Sam's

style of reading doesn't have much use for symbolism, since symbolism is mainly used to get beyond, behind, or beneath the conscious awareness that characters have of the reasons and implications of their actions. His two comments on symbolic or emblematic significance of details in "A Rose for Emily" point right back to the characters and their relationships: Her house represents "her whole way of life" (p. 136) and the tableau of Emily's father standing on the porch with a horsewhip driving away suitors symbolizes "the kind of relationship they had" (p. 137). Sam's wording is pedestrian, but Brooks and Warren and West say essentially the same thing (West, 193; Brooks and Warren, 411).

In sum, then, the CAM style is not afraid to state the obvious; it does not try to be ingenious or clever, but solid and useful; it does not assume the author is fashioning puzzles for us to solve, or playing tricks on us. The story conceals nothing—it is merely, of necessity, incomplete. For Diggers for Secrets, however, the story enwraps secrets, the narrator hides them—much as Miss Emily, and the narrator, conceal the body of Homer Barron—and the reader must uncover them. The title of Edward Stone's *A Certain Morbidness* suggests how he will read "A Rose for Emily."[12] Diggers for Secrets expect narrators to screen us from the "reality,"

> But when, during her early spinsterhood, her father dies and she refuses for three days to hand his putrefying body over for burial, we are shocked by this irrational action, even though in keeping with his standpoint of noncommitment Faulkner tries to minimize it ("We remembered all the young men her father had driven away, and we knew that with nothing left, she would have to cling to that which had robbed her, as people will"). (Stone, 96)

and expect the author only to give us clues:

> For Faulkner, so far from withholding all clues to Homer Barron's whereabouts, scatters them with a precise prodigality; since his is a story primarily of character, it is to his purpose to saturate our awareness of Miss Emily's abnormality as he goes, so that the last six shocking words merely put the final touch on that purpose. (p. 65)

Sebastian, who is Holland's Digger, also comments on the evenhandedness of the narrator, whom he describes as switching sides (p. 177), and he too finds the maxim about holding on to that which robbed her a screen rather than an explanation: "Shouldn't have put that in, Bill," he says (p. 186). He even proposes to see through the author: "I wanted to see what unconscious things he would reveal about the South" (p. 186).

When Diggers for Secrets explain the psychology of characters, they employ the categories of depth and abnormal psychology (Stone even quotes Kraft-Ebbing's *Psychopathia Sexualis*) and frequently "diagnose" motives the characters would not be aware of and in terms they might well not accept. Sebastian uses the terms *sexuality, obsession,* and *necrophilia* heavily and confidently, but he still falls short, in eloquence at least, of Irving Malin and Edward Stone:

> Her passionate, almost sexual relationship with her dead father forces her to distrust the living body of Homer and to kill him so that he will resemble the dead father she can never forget.
>
> Not only does this obsessed spinster continue for some years to share a marriage bed with the body of the man she poisoned—she evidently derives either erotic gratification or spiritual sustenance (both?) from these ghastly nuptials. She becomes, in short, a necrophile or a veritable saprophytic organism; for we learn that the "slender figure in white" that was the young Miss Emily becomes, as though with the middle-aged propriety that the marriage customarily brings, fat! (Stone, 96)

Notice the assurance with which the "sleeping" questions are answered; Malin seems to ignore the dust on the bed. In a similar vein, Sebastian draws numerous inferences about the Negro servant Tobe's complicity in Emily's crime, about her "affair" with Homer, about the details of her sleeping with his corpse (how can a woman perform an act of necrophilia on a man?), and so on.

Symbolism being a ready avenue to non-obvious meanings, these readers find symbolic significances and secrets in details that the CAM readers either pass over or handle prosaically: Miss Emily's house for Stone is an isolated fortress, a forbidden, majestic stronghold; for Malin, Homer Barron represents "wild virility" (compare West's "earthiness"); for Sebastian, the title is richly ironic, "an unforgiveable irony in one sense: 'A Rose by any other name would not smell half as sweet!' There's not much sweetness about *her* rose. So I think the title refers to the decomposition of living matter, and so I take it ironically" (p. 182). Lest this seem jejune, note should be taken that William T. Going suggested this significance in *The Explicator.*[13] One expects such ironies from an author presumed to conceal.

An interesting feature of "A Rose for Emily" is that it contains not only a literal hidden secret (which Sebastian objects to as a bit too overt) but a "reader" as well (the narrator). That is, people who habitually look for the dirty reality behind appearances are open to the charge of prurience, a charge that would be easy to level at these readers, and one that the story conveniently allows us to displace onto the narrator ("the community") instead. So the taint of corruption spreads to the town, all these readers say, but, of course, not to *us.*[14] Thus in a sense, the abnormal becomes normal, and the story acquires the universality that raises it from case history to literature. The search for the abnormal and perverse finally leads back to the unacknowledged parts of our selves.

One would suppose that Diggers for Secrets would never be at a loss for things to discover in a story, but this is not the case, at least for Sebastian, who found "Winter Dreams" and "The Battler" less to his taste. In the case of "Winter Dreams," the illusion to be penetrated seems too obvious (Dexter's romanticizing of Judy Jones); in the case of "The Battler," he pursues many symbolic possibilities and explores the suggestion of homosexual undercurrents, but is dissatisfied because he can conclude nothing; the story may be rich in depths, but they do not converge as a secret to be discovered. In short, he plays detective with the text, and wants to know when he has won the game. Other Diggers are less demanding, and seem to assume that if they have dug it up, it must be a secret. Philip Young's lead to his discussion of "The Battler" promises things of darkness if not secrets:

> People who complain about the sordid nature of many of Hemingway's stories seldom if ever cite this one, perhaps because the unpleasantness is more in the undertones and in things not said than in the outer events, which, though not happy, are not entirely extraordinary in our time. But if the subtleties are drawn out and examined, "The Battler" is as unpleasant as anything its author ever wrote.[15]

One should not suppose that Diggers for Secrets are exclusively attuned to tabooed "realities"—Stone detects a reference to a Yankee general who raided Mississippi in the Civil War in the name *Grierson*—but it is reasonable to expect them to be there, and touched indirectly, in literature. The reader then plays beat-the-censor with the author.

Though the Diggers for Secrets make use of abstractive codes that explain what is going on in the story, their interest in "what's really going on" does, as we have seen, lead to inferences elaborating the event chain. The third group, the Anthropologists, have much less to say about events than either of the first two groups. Their interest, rather, is in identifying the cultural norms and values that explain what characters indisputably do and say. Like Diggers for Secrets, these readers go beneath the surface and state things that are implicit and not said, though what they bring out is not a secret, but the general principles and values which the story illustrates as an example. To some degree, early readings that talk of a conflict in "A Rose for Emily" between the North and the South, or old versus new South, outline this approach, but these readings tended to be brief and schematic, as if critics were not willing to reopen old wounds.[16] And, too, Faulkner was on record as not intending such an interpretation.[17] When a reader is especially engaged in the critique of the norms and values of American society, however, the story takes on interest as an extended exemplum. Thus the two instances of this style of reading, Holland's Shep and Judith Fetterley, are both radicals. For Shep, who is Hoiland's example of a sixties radical, the characters and events of the story exemplify forces of social struggle—class struggle, racial struggle, and above all the struggle between true and false values. Thus he says Emily's father represents the old code, the dead hand of the past; Homer Barron represents the forces of aimless technology; Emily herself was, he says, "perpetuating the same ethos in which her father lived" (p. 61); "In a way, Miss Emily is a descendant of the culture hero, except that she's a descendant of the culture hero in his waning phase" (p. 166); "They had a very rigid formal code and it was perhaps very much a dead code by the time she got her hands on it, but it represented something which the new people weren't able to offer an adequate substitute for" (p. 161). Proceeding at such a lofty plane, he is fairly indifferent to the detailed goings-on of the event chain, though he does infer Emily's response to the lime-scattering incident—namely, scorn for the men—and he is willing to speculate under Holland's urging. He offers two motives for the murder, first, simple revenge, to keep him from leaving her; but he also evolves a second, mythic explanation, which I quote at some length:

> She can reverse the social decay process by putting her lover, representative of all of them ["the newcomers"] through a physical decay process and coming to relish the sight. This would also give some sort of, quote, explanation, unquote, for her necrophilic hangups. The fact that she wanted her father's body around to . . . preserve it from decay—she was denying the end of the line thing symbolized by putting it underground and letting the earth have it. (p. 171)

Though he judges that this attempt failed:

> She feels personally that with Homer she managed to offset the decay process around her and, for that matter, within her, as she represents the tradition . . . she doesn't really do it. Becoming "Barron," she didn't prevail in the way that she thought she had. For her, maybe, she went to the grave triumphant, but for everyone else, she went to the grave dead. I think that's the judgment that has to be made, after all. Aw, hell—drive through Jefferson, Mississippi, Oxford, Mississippi, and you can see this judgment has to be made. (p. 174)

So there is a double or triple pattern of explanation here—commonsense psychology (she wanted revenge), operation of social forces, and mythic patterns; these explanations seem somewhat detached from each other and so the reading is not completely totalized.

If Shep is an example of a sixties radical, then Judith Fetterley, in her book *The Resisting Reader*[18] represents a kind of seventies version of the same basic style of reading. Fetterley focuses on stating the social norms and codes that explain the events of the story—there is very little in the way of constructive activity of motives, actions, responses, and consequences, except for a brief discussion of the lime-scattering incident. She also offers two motives for the murder: first, that Emily murdered Homer because she had to have a man (thus illustrating the brainwashing of the code), but she also offers the following symbolic/mythic account:

> Having been consumed by her father, Emily in turn feeds off Homer Barron, becoming, after his death, suspiciously fat. Or, to put it another way, it is as if, after her father's death, she has reversed his act of incorporating her by incorporating and becoming him, metamorphosed from the slender figure in white to the obese figure in black whose hair is "a vigorous iron-gray, like the hair of an active man." She has taken into herself the violence in him which thwarted her and has reenacted it upon Homer Barron. (pp. 42–43)

On first reading, this seems very much like Stone's celebration of Faulkner's "ghoulish evolution" of the gothic, but on closer examination, the passage is really suggesting a crude form of retributive justice, a pointed, if lurid, warning to the upholders of patriarchy. It is striking that the same elementary operations—*connecting* her growing fat to Homer's murder and *inferring* a causal link—result in such different explanations.

Like Shep, Fetterley makes heavy use of symbolic interpretation and the logic of example: Emily's confinement by her father represents confinement of women by patriarchy; the remission of taxes signifies continued dependence of women on men; the men's treatment of her, and her ability to buffalo them and commit murder without punishment, are explained in terms of the code of the "lady" who is assumed to be out of touch with reality, and must be kept so; Emily represents the town itself, and in discovering her nature, they discover their own. The focus of Fetterley's interest is in flushing the codes out of hiding and explaining what happens in terms of them, though it is not a totalizing reading in that she doesn't claim to have explained everything in the story in terms of the codes; this treatment represents the extreme of abstraction away from the events and surface of the story toward allegory and parable. That's what it means to be a Resisting Reader: to refuse to give yourself to the work, to accept any of its givens—and in fact, to bring precisely those axioms into question.

Clearly, then, these three styles or approaches are asking different questions of the text, and constructing what are to various degrees different stories in the course of answering them. We may think of them as concentrating their attentions on different codes in the Barthian sense: The CAM style is oriented toward the proairetic code, the Digger style toward the hermeneutic code, and the Anthropologist toward the referential code (cultural norms). I do not have any evidence for styles especially concentrated on the semic or symbolic codes, and, while these three styles surely do not exhaust the possibilities,[19] it seems unlikely that "semic" or "symbolic" styles will turn up. Semic (naming, categorizing, schematizing) and symbolic moves are scattered over the three styles we have considered and are deployed in different ways in each style. Similarly, I don't think we should expect to find a structuralist style as such: the basic moves of structural analysis (finding contrasting groups and repetitions of patterns) are used by CAM readers as well as by the more analytically inclined; the latter readers, however, are more likely to come up with non-obvious mythic or psychoanalytic patterns. In fact, these parallels perhaps should be taken as a glimmering of "objectivity" (or intersubjective consensus) about the text: Readers predisposed to a certain style of reading will, when faced with the same text, come up with some very similar stories along with some very similar explanations.

Second, and lastly, the notion that these styles are, or can become, general patterns of thinking, rather than a learned decorum of literary criticism, seems to derive support from the consideration that we also exhibit differences of styles in thinking about real people and events. We think of ourselves and others as conscious, moral agents shaping our destinies in situations benign and hostile, but also as mysteries to ourselves and others, and/or as enacting typical social roles and attitudes. There is some basis for concluding that we understand literature and life in the same or similar ways, and that some of the ways we read literature will be applied in reading others of life's texts.

NOTES

1. Brooke-Rose, "The Readerhood of Man," in *The Reader in the Text,* ed. Susan R. Suleiman and Inge Crosman (Princeton: Princeton University Press, 1980), 120–48.

2. Prince, "Notes on the Text as Reader," in *Reader in the Text,* ed. Suleiman and Crosman, 229.

3. Smith, "Narrative Versions, Narrative Theories," *Critical Inquiry* 7 (1980): 213–36.

4. At least five chronologies have appeared in print, all differing: William T. Going, "Chronology in Teaching 'A Rose for Emily,'" *Exercise Exchange* 5 (1958): 8–11; Robert W. Woodward, "The Chronology of 'A Rose for Emily,'" *Exercise Exchange* 13 (1966): 17–19; Paul D. McGlynn, "The Chronology of 'A Rose for Emily,'" *Studies in Short Fiction* 6 (1969): 461–62; Helen E. Nebeker, "Chronology Revisited," *Studies in Short Fiction* 8 (1971): 471–73; and Menakhem Perry, "Literary Dynamics: How the Order of a Text Creates Its Meaning," *Poetics Today* 1 (1979): 35–63; 311–61.

5. There is a lengthy discussion of the story structure of "A Rose for Emily" in William O. Hendriks, "'A Rose for Emily': A Syntagmatic Analysis," *PTL* 2 (1977): 257–95.

6. Warren, Nicholas, and Trebasso, "Event Chains and Inferences in Understanding Narratives," in *New Directions in Discourse Processing,* ed. Roy O. Freedle (Norwood, N.J.: Ablex Publishing, 1979).

7. Wolfgang Iser, *The Act of Reading* (Baltimore: Johns Hopkins University

Press, 1978), 123. Iser's definition of *significance* as "the reader's absorption of the meaning into his own existence" (p. 151) leaves us in need of an intermediate term between it and *plot* (event chains)—something like *explanation,* which is constructed to account for events (e.g., in terms of character traits, maxims of behavior, mythic patterns, etc.) but which is not necessarily the amalgamation of the story into the reader's subjectivity. For one thing, explanation need not be evaluative. I am using *interpretation* in a broad sense here to mean the reader's commentary minus any plot summary, though even the latter is usually tailored to fit the commentary.

8. See Norman Holland, *5 Readers Reading* (New Haven: Yale University Press, 1975), 21–24 (cited in the text as Holland, or Holland's Sam); and Perry, "Literary Dynamics," 62–63 et passim.

9. Cleanth Brooks and Robert Penn Warren, *Understanding Fiction* (New York: Crofts, 1948), 409–14. Cited in the text as Brooks and Warren.

10. Ray B. West, "Atmosphere and Theme in Faulkner's 'A Rose for Emily,'" in *William Faulkner: Four Decades of Criticism,* ed. Linda W. Wagner (East Lansing: Michigan State University Press, 1973), 192–98. Cited in the text as West.

11. Trilling, "Mr. Faulkner's World," *The Nation* 4 November 1931: 491–92.

12. Stone, *A Certain Morbidness* (Carbondale: Southern Illinois University Press, 1969). Cited in the text as Stone.

13. Going, *The Explicator* 16 (February 1958), item 27.

14. For Ruth Sullivan, however, the narrator is a prying, probing voyeur, and so are we readers. See "The Narrator in 'A Rose for Emily,'" *Journal of Narrative Technique* 1 (1971): 159–78.

15. See C. W. M. Johnson, "Faulkner's 'A Rose for Emily,'" *Explicator* 6 (1948), item 45; and other references cited in the footnote in Perry, "Literary Dynamics," 346.

16. Frederick Gwynn and Joseph L. Blotner, *Faulkner in the University* (New York: Vintage Books, 1965), 47–48.

17. There is one style which I find attested only in Holland's interviews (and in some of the papers of David Bleich's students), that we might call the Visualizer style, the style of Holland's Sandra, whose comments on all three stories are strongly weighted to descriptions of characters' expressions and feelings, decors and other physical details and commentary on the suitability of words, images and tonal effects in the narration. This is perhaps the most surface- or craft-conscious of the styles, and the reason it does not appear in the published readings is that it is more a style of appreciation than explanation, or, to put it another way, it is more concerned with explaining the details of the style and presentation ("discourse" in Seymour Chatman's terminology) than with the story. Academic criticism of fiction, it appears, has been concerned with stories, not discourse.

18. Fetterley, *The Resisting Reader* (Bloomington and London: Indiana University Press, 1978).

19. Holland of course would explain these consistencies in terms of basic, immutable personality themes (or styles), but I do not think we need to accept this grounding of cognitive styles in deeper, unconscious entities. Similarly, we can account for judgments of taste and lack of things to say in terms of matches and mismatches between cognitive styles of reading and texts; blocking and denial need not be involved. At issue really is the learnability of these approaches.

The Text and the Structure of Its Audience

YURY M. LOTMAN

Lotman schematizes the author-reader transaction by suggesting that texts create their own "ideal" readers. To illustrate this, he distinguishes between two kinds of textual discourse: one, an impersonal, generalized discourse merely dependent on the reader's knowing the language; the other, a personal discourse encoding shared author-reader memory systems. Literary texts partake of this latter discourse. The reader enters the poem as a part of a game: he or she becomes the author's intimate friend; they share a private memory. This frees the reader by enabling him "to recall what his memory did not know."

THE IDEA THAT EVERY MESSAGE is oriented toward a definite audience and is fully realized only in the consciousness of that audience is not a new one. There is a story about an episode in the life of the famous mathematician P. L. Chebyshev. At one of his lectures on the subject of the mathematical aspects of cutting clothes, there appeared an unexpected audience consisting of tailors, fashionable ladies, and so on. However, the first sentence spoken by the lecturer—"Let us suppose for simplicity's sake that the human body has the form of a sphere"—put them to flight. Only mathematicians who found nothing surprising in this opening remark remained in the hall. The text selected its own audience, creating it in its own image.

What is of much greater interest is to examine the actual mechanisms of interaction between the text and its addressee. It is obvious that when the codes of addresser and addressee do not coincide (and they coincide only as a theoretical assumption which is never realized in practical communication), then the text of the message is deformed in the process of decoding by the receiver. For the moment, however, we are here concerned with the other aspect of this process—how the message affects the addressee, transforming his appearance. This phenomenon is bound up with the fact that any text (and especially a literary one) contains in itself what we should like to term the *image of the audience* and that this image actively affects the real audience by becoming for it a kind of normatizing code. This is imposed on the consciousness of the audi-

From *New Literary History* 14 (1982): 81–87. Translated by Ann Shukman. First published as "Tekst i struktura auditorii," in *Trudy po znakovym sistemam: Papers on Sign Systems* 9 (Tartu, 1977). Copyright 1982 by New Literary History, The University of Virginia. Reprinted by permission.

ence and becomes the norm for its own image of itself, being transferred from the text into the sphere of the real behavior of the cultural collective.

In this way, between text and audience a relationship is formed which is characterized not as passive perception but rather as a dialogue. Dialogic speech is distinguished not only by the common code of two juxtaposed utterances, but also by the presence of a common memory shared by addresser and addressee.[1] The absence of this factor makes a text undecipherable. In this respect it could be suggested that any text is characterized not only by code and message, but also by orientation toward a particular type of memory (the structure of memory and the character of its content).

From this point of view, two types of speech activity can be distinguished. The one is directed toward an abstract addressee the extent of whose memory is reconstructed by the addresser as typical of anyone speaking the given language. The other is directed to an actual interlocutor whom the speaker sees or with whom the writer is personally acquainted and the extent of whose memory is perfectly well known to the addresser. This opposition of two types of speech activity should not be identified with the antithesis "written forms of speech/oral form of speech."[2] Such an identification led Josef Vachek, for instance, to the notion that the relationships "phoneme/grapheme" and "oral message/written message" were of the same type. This notion set Vachek at odds with [Ferdinand de] Saussure. He pointed out the contradiction between the proposition about the independence of linguistic facts from the material substance of their expression—"If signs and their correlations are the sole value, they must receive equal expression in any material including therefore also written, in particular alphabetic, signs"—and the specific structural distinction in the nature of written and oral communications: "As against this we must point to the fact that written utterances, at least in cultural linguistic collectives, reveal a certain independence in relation to the oral."[3] Vachek explains the nature of this autonomy as follows: "An oral utterance consists in reacting to a fact as directly as possible; the written utterance fixes a certain relation to a situation for a longer period."[4]

Yet the grapheme and the text (whether written or printed) are phenomena that are in principle different. The former belongs to the language code and in reality is indifferent to the nature of its material embodiment. The latter is a functionally specific message. It can be demonstrated that the qualities that distinguish a written message from an oral one are determined not so much by the technique of explication as by the relationship to the functional opposition "official/intimate." The quality is determined not by the materiality of the expression of the text but by its relationship to texts that have an opposing function. Such oppositions include "oral/written," "printed/not printed," "pronounced ex cathedra/confidential communication." All these oppositions can be reduced to the opposition "official/authoritative//unofficial/not authoritative." It is indicative that when comparing the oppositions "oral/written (handwritten)" and "written (handwritten)/printed," "handwritten" in the first case is equivalent to "printed" and in the second to "oral."

At this juncture we should point out that the choice of these functional groups depends on the character of the addressee constructed by the text itself. Communication with an interlocutor is possible only given some common memory. Yet in this respect there are differences of principle between the text directed to any addressee and the text which has in view a certain specific and personally known addressee. In the first case the extent of the memory of the addressee is constructed as one that is obligatory for anyone speaking that language. His memory is without individuality, abstracted, and contains in itself only an irreducible minimum. Of course the poorer the memory the more detailed and extensive must the message be and the less possibility there is for ellipses and passing things over in silence. The official text constructs an abstract interlocutor, the bearer of only a generalized memory deprived of personal and individual experience. Such a text can be addressed to all and sundry. It is distinguished by the detail of its explanations, the absence of implied meanings, abbreviations, or allusions, and by its closeness to normative correctness.

The text addressed to a personally known addressee, a person designated for us not by a pronoun but by a proper name, is constructed quite differently. The extent of his memory and the character of its content is familiar to us and intimately known. In this case there is no need to burden the text with unnecessary details which are already to be found in the memory of the addressee. An allusion is enough to actualize them. This text will develop elliptical constructions, a localized semantics, and tend to use a "domestic" and "intimate" lexis. This text will be valued not only by the degree of its comprehensibility to the given addressee, but also by the degree of its incomprehensibility to others.[5] In this way orientation toward one or the other type of addressee-memory involves recourse to either "a language for others" or "a language for oneself"—in fact to one of the two opposing structural potentialities concealed in natural language. In this way being in possession of a comparatively incomplete set of linguistic and cultural codes, we can, on the basis of the analysis of a given text, make out whether it is oriented to "our own" or to "someone else's" audience. If we reconstruct the character of the "general memory" needed to understand it, we will obtain an "image of the audience" concealed in the text. From this it follows that the text contains within itself a miniature system of all links in the communicative chain, and just as we can abstract from it the author's position, so we can reconstruct also the ideal reader. The text, even when taken in isolation (but given, of course, certain information about the structure of the culture that created it), is a most valuable source of judgments about its own pragmatic connections.

This question becomes more complex and has special importance when we turn to literary texts. In the literary text, orientation toward a certain type of collective memory, and consequently toward a structure of the audience, acquires a character that is different in principle. It ceases to be automatically implied in the text and becomes a signified (i.e., free) artistic element which can enter the text as part of a game.

We can illustrate this with examples from Russian poetry of the eighteenth and early nineteenth centuries.

In the hierarchy of poetic genres in the eighteenth century, the determinant was the notion that the more abstract the addressee to which the poem was addressed, the more valuable was the poetry. The person to whom the poem was addressed was constructed as the bearer of the most abstract, culturally and nationally generalized memory.[6] Even if it was a question of a fully real and known addressee, known personally to the poet, the prestige of the text as a poetic text demanded that he be treated in this way, just as if the author and the addressee enjoyed a generalized memory only as members of the single State collective and as bearers of one language. The actual addressee was raised up the scale of values, becoming "one of many." Maikov, for instance, begins his poem addressed to Count Z. G. Chernyshev as follows:

O thou, hero tested by fortunes,
Whom the Russian State saw as its leader
And learnt how lofty was thy soul,
When you campaigned against Frederick!
Then, when that monarch became our ally,
He himself tested thy valour and reason.[7]

The poet assumes that the facts of Chernyshev's biography were not contained in Chernyshev's memory (since they were not contained in the memory of other readers), and in the poem addressed to Chernyshev himself, the poet has to recall and explain who Chernyshev is. To omit this information, which is well known to the author and to the addressee, would be impossible because to do so would place the solemn address into the lower category of the nonliterary text addressed to an actual person. No less typical are instances of abbreviations in analogous texts. When Derzhavin wrote the lapidary inscription "Here lies Suvorov" for the tomb of Suvorov,[8] he made the assumption that all the information which might, according to custom, be engraved on the tomb was already inscribed in the general memory of history and of the State and therefore could be omitted.

The opposite pole is the structuring of the audience in Pushkin's texts. Pushkin consciously omits as well known, or refers to by a hint in the printed text, things which clearly could be known only to a very small circle of select friends. For instance, in the fragment "Women" there are the lines:

> Even I am allowed to speak
> With the words of the prophetic poet:
> Temira, Daphne and Lileta—
> Like a dream that I have long forgot.[9]

The modern reader wanting to find out who is meant by the "prophetic poet" must turn to a commentary and will establish that it is Del'vig who is being referred to and the lines from his poem "Fani":

> Temira, Daphne and Lileta
> Long since like a dream I have forgot
> And only my skilful verse preserves them
> For the poet's memory.[10]

We must not forget that Del'vig's poem was published only in 1922. In 1827, when Pushkin wrote his fragment, the poem was not published nor even known to his contemporaries, i.e., the mass of readers in the 1820s, since Del'vig was exceptionally severe toward his early verses, very choosy about which ones he printed, and did not circulate copies of the rejected ones.

Pushkin, then, was referring his readers to a text which they could not possibly have known. What was the point? The point was that among the potential readers of *Eugene Onegin* there was a small group for whom the allusion was obvious, and that was the circle of Pushkin's Lycée friends (Del'vig's poem was written at the Lycée), and possibly also the close group of friends in the post-Lycée period.[11] In this circle Del'vig's poem undoubtedly was well known.

In this way Pushkin's text firstly divided its audience into two groups: an extremely small group to whom the text was comprehensible and intimately familiar, and the main mass of the readership, who were aware of an allusion but could not decipher it. But the realization that the text required the position of intimate familiarity with the poet forced its readers to *imagine* themselves in just such a relationship with the verses. As a result the second effect of the text was that it put *each* reader into the position of intimate friend of the poet, one who shared with him a special, unique memory and who thus was capable of explaining the allusions. The reader here was included in a game, a game that is the opposite to the one whereby a baby is referred to by his official name, which is the shift of intimately familiar persons into the position "all and sundry" (see, for example, Tolstoy's *Family Happiness:* "'Ivan Sergeevich,' said my husband, touching him with his finger under his little chin. But I quickly wrapped Ivan Sergeevich up again. No one but me should look at him for long"), and a game that is analogous to the one when adults and distant acquaintances use the "baby" name of another grown-up.

In the actual speech act, however, the use of official or intimate language (or rather of the hierarchy "official/intimate") by a person is determined by his extralinguistic relationship to the speaker or hearer. The literary text makes it readership familiar with the system of positions on that hierarchy and allows it freely to move into the slots indicated by the author. It turns the reader, during the course of his reading, into a person with that degree of acquaintanceship with the author which the author chooses to indicate. In fact the author changes the extent of the reader's memory, since the reader, when he receives a text of the work by virtue of the make-up of human memory, is able *to recall what his memory did not know.*

On the one hand the author imposes on the readership its type of memory, and on the other the text preserves in itself the image of the readership.[12] The attentive researcher can extract it in his analysis of the text.

NOTES

1. O. G. Revzina, I. I. Revzin, "A Semiotic Experiment on Stage: The Violation of the Postulate of Normal Communication as a Dramatic Device," *Semiotica* 14, no. 3 (1975): 245–68. Originally published in *Trudy po znakovym sistemam* [Papers on sign systems], 5 (Tartu, 1971).

2. Josef Vachek, "Zum Problem der geschriebenen Sprache," in *A Prague School Reader in Linguistics* (Bloomington, 1964), 441–52, also published in *Travaux du Cercle Linguistique de Prague* 8 (1939): 94–104, and in Russian as "K probleme pis'mennogo yazyka," in *Prazhskii lingvisticheskii kruzhok* (Moscow, 1967); Vachek, "Written Language and Printed Language," in *A Prague School Reader,* 453–60, also published in *Recueil Linguistique de Bratislava* 1 (1948): 67–75, and in Russian as "Pis'mennyi yazyk i pechatnyi yazyk," in *Prazhskii;* Jan Baudouin de Courtenay, *Ob otnoshenii russkogo pis'ma k russkomu yazyku* (St. Petersburg, 1912).

3. Vachek, "Zum Problem," 445.

4. Vachek, "Zum Problem," 445.

5. The identification of a generally comprehensible message addressed to all and sundry with what is official and authoritative is a feature only of a certain cultural orientation. In cultures where the highest cultural values are ascribed to texts intended to communicate with God (deriving from God or addressed to Him), the notion that one of the participants in the communication has a limitless memory may turn the text into one that is quite esoteric. A third party drawn into this communicative act will value just the incomprehensibility of the message as a sign of its viability in some mysterious spheres. In this case incomprehensibility is the same as authority.

6. This said, however, it is not a question of the real memory of a national collective but of an ideal general memory of an ideal national unity reconstructed according to the theories of the eighteenth century.

7. Vasily Maikov (1728–78), *Izbrannye proizvedeniya* [Selected works] (Moscow and Leningrad, 1966), 276.

8. G. R. Derzhavin (1743–1816), *Stikhotvoreniya* [Poems] (Leningrad, 1947), 202.

9. A. S. Pushkin (1799–1837), *Polnoe sobranie sochinenii* [Complete collection of works], VI (Academy of Sciences, USSR, 1937), 647. This fragment, from the original variant of chapter 4 of *Eugene Onegin,* was published in *Moskovskii Vestnik,* no. 20 (1827): 365–67.

10. A. A. Del'vig (1798–1831), *Neizdannye stikhotvoreniya* [Unpublished poems] (Petrograd, 1922), 50.

11. Cf. Pushkin's poem of 1819, "To Shcherbinin":

I shall say to you at the gates of the grave:
"Do you remember Fanny, my dear?"
And we shall both smile quietly.

(Complete collection, 2 [1947], bk. 1, p. 88)

12. This is bound up with the difference of principle between the nature of address in the literary and nonliterary text. The nonliterary text is (normally) read by the person to whom it is addressed. Reading other people's letters or learning the contents of messages intended for someone else is ethically proscribed. The literary text as a rule is not received by the one to whom it is addressed: a love lyric becomes a printed object, the intimate diary or correspondence is made public property. One of the working features of the literary text could be seen as the difference between the formal and the real addressee. For as long as the poem containing a confession of love is known solely to the person who inspired this feeling in its author, functionally speaking the text is not a literary one. But once published in a journal it becomes a work of art. B. V. Tomashevskii made the suggestion that Pushkin gave Anna Petrovna Kern the poem when it had long since been written, and not written for her. [Reference to one of Pushkin's most famous lyrics, "I remember a wonderful moment."—Translator.] In this case there was a reverse process: the text of art was functionally narrowed down to a fact of biography. (Publication once more turned it into a fact of art. It must be emphasized that the decisive significance is not the comparatively chance fact of publication but the intention for public use.) In this regard the police agent reading other people's letters experiences emotions remotely resembling aesthetic ones. See, in Gogol's play *The Government Inspector,* the postmaster Shpekin's remarks: "It's highly interesting reading: some letters you read with pleasure. They describe all kinds of goings on . . . and such edification. . . . Better than in the *Moscow News*" (act 1, scene 2).

"Play with the addressee" is a characteristic of the literary text. But it is just such texts, addressed, as it were, not to the one who uses them, that become for the reader a school of reincarnation, teaching him the capacity to change perspective on the text and to play with different types of social memory.

Reader-Response Provocateurs

1. No firm decision has been made about whether or not "subjective" reader-response theories should be used in literature courses.

Proponents claim it reinvigorates and democratizes literary discourse. Opponents charge it breaks down cultural conventions and leads to discursive anarchy. Discuss.

2. Suppose you were asked to respond to a story you have just read. What difference would it make if you were talking with a friend or with an authority in the field? What difference if you were reading a classic story for the umpteenth time or a story in this Sunday's newspaper? What difference if you were in a good mood or a bad mood? Is any text we read ever exempt from such considerations or do we always, in some sense, construct the text we read?

3. Tefs charges that Holland "anaesthetizes" Faulkner's story. Does he? Is Tefs's argument that one can psychoanalyze the reader's or the author's mind but not the character's valid?

4. Crosman's essay raises some problematics of response theory. For example, why would his essay be more convincing if he had quoted Stacy instead of summarizing her interpretation from memory?

5. Dillon's categories would include most of the critics presented in this text, but not all. Who would be excluded? Lacan? Dillon? others?

6. Lotman asserts that a literary text, as opposed to other texts, sets up a special relationship with the reader. Is it possible that these other impersonal, generalized texts might enable us to recall what our memories "do not know" as he claims literary texts do? Compare your own experience of reading, for example, *Newsweek,* with reading "Sailing to Byzantium."

CHAPTER 8

Deconstructionist Criticism

"DECONSTRUCTION" DESIGNATES COMPLEX DISCURSIVE strategies that try to account for the paradoxical linguistic and nonlinguistic conditions that make reflective thought possible. Deconstruction—the term is philosopher Jacques Derrida's—operates from the theoretical perspective of Continental post-structuralism. As I commented in the Con-Text, post-structuralism challenges traditional literary assumptions about textual coherence and about the special status of literature. As a result, deconstruction has served as a flash-point for controversy. Deconstruction's admirers see it as a way that begins to let us question the presuppositions of the language we think in. Its detractors condemn its subtle and convoluted readings as narcissistic self-reflexivity.

You recall that post-structuralists, much more than earlier structuralists, emphasize the fluidity and contradictoriness of signification, the arbitrary and differential aspects of language. From the post-structuralist view, "rose" in Gertrude Stein's "A rose is a rose is a rose . . ." is three different signs, distinguished one from another in time and space. They reject as false the commonsense notion that words refer to stable entities, or ideas, even though they are aware that this view still rules our thinking. Indeed, post-structuralist philosophers contend that key concepts such as truth, origin, nature, reason, meaning, self, God, and so on which have ordered and dominated Western thought, have taken on a kind of originary self-sufficiency, or self-presencing. These have become signs *of* Being, signifiers transformed into "transcendental" signifieds.

However, if we would contest this centered habit of thinking—what Derrida calls "logocentrism"—we find ourselves caught in a catch-22: we have to speak the very language we would query. To question reason, we must reason; to challenge meaning, we must mean. As Derrida puts it, If we would pretend to speak Chinese to a Chinese person, we must speak Chinese.

Although we cannot get outside of our logocentric way of thinking, deconstructionist philosophers such as Maurice Merleau-Ponty, Jean-François Lyotard, and Derrida suggest that we can call it into question by foregrounding its differential signifying structures. That is to say, we can critique the presuppositions of the discourse in which these powerful concepts are inscribed.

In part this means demonstrating that these seemingly self-sufficient notions (like truth, nature, self, origin, and such) function as the dominant partners of a hierarchal binary. We see that each superior concept defines itself by negating its opposite, its inferior other: Truth = not-fiction, self = not-other, Man = not-woman. Deconstruction shows that such superiority is a function of and so dependent upon a hidden differential relationship. Deconstruction tries to show how these main concepts suppress within themselves their conceptual opposites: Truth/(fiction), Presence/(sign), Self/(other), Origin/(end), Nature/(civilization), Cause/(effect), Speech/(writing), God/(man), Man/(woman), and so on. For example, the opposite of "man" is "woman": man is not-woman. Yet as everyday phrases such as "Mankind," "The History of Man," "Peace on earth, Good will to Man," make clear, "man" maintains its primacy by containing and so suppressing "woman."

Deconstruction attempts to resist, as well as to account for, this logocentric habit of thought by a series of adroit maneuvers we might bluntly call reversal, displacement, and reinscription. By reversing the oppositional pairs and by displacing the primary term, deconstruction draws attention to the relations of difference which make meaning possible: fiction/truth, sign/presence, other/self, woman/man.

Reversal and displacement, however, are negative moves which could suggest a mere substitution of underdogs for top dogs. Deconstruction aims at something very different. It attempts to rethink the once-interior term by reinscribing, or rewriting, the term. Deconstructionists argue that, because they have deconstituted the term's former definition, the newly inscribed notion does not function the same as before. It is no longer merely the negative image of the dominant term. Derrida's *Of Grammatology*, for instance, painstakingly reverses the oppositional binary Speech/(writing), which represents writing as the negative trace of presenced Speech, and reinscribes a new sense of "writing" as writing/speech.

Deconstructive American literary critics Paul de Man, J. Hillis Miller, and Geoffrey Hartman focus less on the problematic conditions of conceptual thought and more on the rhetorical, self-reflexivity of the text. Since the late 1960s, these critics' post-structuralist theories and deconstructionist readings have countered the mainstream of Anglo-American criticism which emphasizes interpretation. In contrast, their deconstructive maneuvers probe the text's rhetorical density—its textual metaphors, metonymies, verbal ambiguities, tropes, figures, and images. They are concerned to show how these rhetorical strategies disclose *aporias,* or gaps where the text begins to undo itself, to comment on itself, and thus to become its own object.

Other deconstructive literary critics, more interested in the reader's role, take yet a different tack. They question the autonomy of the literary text by opening the reading process to the reader. They analyze the structures of nonclosure which allow us to reflect upon the text. Barbara Johnson, for example, deconstructs Derrida's reading of Lacan's reading of "The Purloined Letter" by exploring how the reader's frame of reference participates in the differential structures that make meanings possible.

Finally, a comment on the circularity inherent in any introductory explanation of deconstruction. As you will have noticed, I have used logocentric thinking throughout this logical account of deconstructive strategies, critical groups, and issues. But this is not the way a deconstructionist would think or talk. As Jacques Derrida argues in the following essay, a truly post-structuralist commentary would be decentered.

Structure, Sign, and Play in the Discourse of the Human Sciences

JACQUES DERRIDA

In this reading of Claude Lévi-Strauss's works, Jacques Derrida critiques structuralist assumptions that perpetuate a logocentric, or centered, way of thinking. Derrida shows how structuralist binary thinking allows one term of an opposition to conceal and so repress another. For although structuralists recognize the necessity of binary thinking, Derrida contends they do not rigorously question its operative conditions. As a result, structuralists are still conceptually trapped within unexamined logocentric frames. In contrast, deconstruction demonstrates that all reflexive thought is constituted within the paradoxical, differential play of language. Deconstruction highlights the presuppositions constitutive of binary thinking. It indicates how the primordial structure of repetition accounts for the self-presencing of logocentric thought. Finally, since language contains within itself its

From *Writing and Difference,* trans. Alan Bass (Chicago: University of Chicago Press, 1978). © 1978 by The University of Chicago. Reprinted by permission.

own conditions of deconstruction, Derrida will show how structuralist texts like Lévi-Strauss's can be made to embarrass their own logic.

Derrida prefaces his critique of logocentrism with a brief history of structure, which, he notes, parallels the history of reflective thinking. In the past, logocentric thought ascribed a center, or organizing principle, to structural systems. Likewise, the same self-centering or privileging ordered our scientific and philosophical thinking, our traditional episteme. Then came the breakthrough enabling us to think "the structurality of structure" (to think the language which makes thought possible). The insights of Nietzsche, Freud, Heidegger, Saussure, and others had ruptured logocentric thought. We began to see that thought occurs within the differential play of language. We realized that questions of structure can only be asked from a point of view that is not privileged. These insights decentered the notion of structure. Now the structurality of structure could be understood as a function analogous to the differential play of the signifier.

But, as Derrida shows, this post-structuralist position is difficult to maintain. We are still caught in the double-bind of drawing on the very discourse we would question. What language can we use to pose the problem of the conditions of language that we use? We cannot seem to escape the logocentric habit (what he calls here "the metaphysical reduction") of taking the sign to be a sign *of* a self-presenced idea. Lévi-Strauss tried to transcend the intelligible/sensible opposition by using signs. But he failed to grasp that the paradoxical concept of sign functions on this very opposition.

According to Derrida, the history of the human sciences parallels the history of structure and of philosophy. Indeed, Lévi-Strauss's anthropological studies to determine the syntax of South American mythological systems could only have taken place after European culture stopped considering itself as the signified norm, "the culture of reference." Yet Lévi-Strauss, disciple of Saussurean structuralism, is himself caught in the double-bind of logocentric reduction. The binary opposition, nature/culture, so fundamental to Western discourse, weaves throughout all his works. Lévi-Strauss did not accept the truth of these notions, yet he could not do without them.

Because Lévi-Strauss recognized that the logic of such conceptual oppositions as nature/culture, even though no longer valid historically, needed to be investigated, he devised a strategy he called "bricolage." This means using logocentric tools (concepts) but discounting their truth value. Derrida commends these bricolage tactics when, as with the Bororos myths, they are used to question the status of mythological discourse, to let myth reflect upon itself. Then bricolage decenters mythological discourse and opens it up to the discursive play of difference. In these instances, Lévi-Strauss's "myth of mythology" signals a new mythomorphic episteme, one which takes the form of what it speaks.

Overall, though, Derrida faults Lévi-Strauss's strategy of bricolage for failing to pose the basic problem of metaphysical reduction (logocentrism). Derrida contends that the ethnologist's use of traditional concepts, even though they are not accorded a truth value, does not let him distinguish among levels of discourse. As a result, Lévi-Strauss does not ask the fundamental question, Are all discourses myths? Or, in other words, What is the relation between centered empirical thought (in which signs are signs *of* stable ideas) and decentered mythopoetic thought (in which signs follow the differential play of the signifier)? Bricolage cannot pose the question of the status of a discourse which is trying to deconstruct itself.

Thus although structuralism claims to critique the assumptions of empiricism, Derrida argues that Lévi-Strauss is still confined within that traditional episteme. The latter's contradictory reasons for not "totalizing" his account of myths (It is *impossible* to gather all myths; and; It is *useless* to gather all myths) give him away. Derrida contends the real reason Lévi-Strauss cannot gather all myths has to do with the field of language as an infinite play of signifiers. Language excludes totalization because signification always involves absence, something is always missing.

Derrida calls this something that is always missing the "movement of supplementarity." (This term is related to other complicated Derridean notions such as "différance," "arche-trace," and "writing.") The sign, which takes the place of the always absent center, is added as surplus. The play of signification, then, supplements a lack on the part of the signified. Thus we can see that the relationship of complementarity between signifier and signified is the very condition of the use of symbolic thought— thought which operates in spite of the contradiction proper to it. Lévi-Strauss's description of "mana," a sign of zero symbolic value which can mean anything and nothing, comes close to suggesting this lack, this play of supplementarity.

Thus we can see why, Derrida says, Lévi-Strauss's writings so often mention play. (For Derrida, "play" suggests both play as game and play as free movement within a bounded space, as in a car's "play of the wheel.") Derrida suggests that we should deconstruct the logocentric concepts of history and of presence which have traditionally been opposed to play: History/(play) and Presence/(play). By reversing, displacing, and reinscribing them as play/history and play/presence, Derrida suggests we can begin to do something structuralists like Lévi-Strauss were unable to do. We can begin to step outside, to decenter, traditional logocentric thought.

> We need to interpret interpretations more than to interpret things.
>
> —Montaigne

PERHAPS SOMETHING HAS OCCURRED in the history of the concept of structure that could be called an "event," if this loaded word did not entail a meaning which it is precisely the function of structural—or structuralist—thought to reduce or to suspect. Let us speak of an "event," nevertheless, and let us use quotation marks to serve as a precaution. What would this event be then? Its exterior form would be that of a *rupture* and a redoubling.

It would be easy enough to show that the concept of structure and even the word "structure" itself are as old as the *epistēmē*—that is to say, as old as Western science and Western philosophy—and that their roots thrust deep into the soil of ordinary language, into whose deepest recesses the *epistēmē* plunges in order to gather them up and to make them part of itself in a metaphorical displacement. Nevertheless, up to the event which I wish to mark out and define, structure—or rather the structurality of structure—although it has always been at work, has always been neutralized or reduced, and this by a process of giving it a center or of referring it to a point of presence, a fixed origin. The function of this center was not only to orient, balance, and organize the structure—one cannot in fact conceive of an unorganized structure—but above all to make sure that the organizing principle of the structure would limit what we might call the *play* of the structure. By orienting and organizing the coherence of the system, the center of a structure permits the play of its elements inside the total form. And even today the notion of a structure lacking any center represents the unthinkable itself.

Nevertheless, the center also closes off the play which it opens up and makes possible. As center, it is the point at which the substitution of contents, elements, or terms is no longer possible. At the center, the permutation or the transformation of elements (which may of course be structures enclosed within a structure) is forbidden. At least this permutation has always remained *interdicted* (and I am using this word deliberately). Thus it has always been thought that the center, which is by definition unique, constituted that very thing within a structure which while governing the structure, escapes structurality. This is why classical thought concerning structure could say that the center is, paradoxically, *within* the structure and *outside it*. The center is at the center of the totality, and yet, since the center does not belong to the totality (is not part of the totality), the totality *has its center elsewhere*. The center is not the center. The concept of centered structure—although it represents coherence itself, the condition of the *epistēmē* as philosophy or science—is contradictorily coherent. And as always, coherence in contradiction expresses the force of a desire.[1] The concept of centered structure is in fact the concept of a play based on a fundamental ground, a play constituted on the basis of a fundamental immobility and a reassuring certitude, which itself is beyond the reach of play. And on the basis of this certitude anxiety can be mastered, for anxiety is invariably the result of a certain mode of being implicated in the game, of being caught by the game, of being as it were at stake in the game from the outset. And again on the basis of what we call the center (and which, because it can be either inside or outside, can also indifferently be called the origin or end, *archē* or *telos*), repetitions, substitutions, transformations, and permutations are always *taken* from a history of meaning [*sens*]—that is, in a word, a history—whose origin may always be reawakened or whose end may always be anticipated in the form of presence. This is why one perhaps could say that the movement of any archaeology, like that of any eschatology, is an accomplice of this reduction of the structurality of structure and always attempts to conceive of structure on the basis of a full presence which is beyond play.

If this is so, the entire history of the concept of structure, before the rupture of which we are speaking, must be thought of as a series of substitutions of center for center, as a linked chain of determinations of the center. Successively, and in a regulated fashion, the center receives different forms or names. The history of metaphysics, like the history of the West, is the history of these metaphors and metonymies. Its matrix—if you will pardon me for demonstrating so little and for being so elliptical in order to come more quickly to my principal theme—is the determination of Being as *presence* in all senses of this word. It could be shown that all the names related to fundamentals, to principles, or to the center have always designated an invariable presence—*eidos, archē, telos, energeia, ousia* (essence, existence, substance, subject) *alētheia*, transcendentality, consciousness, God, man, and so forth.

The event I called a rupture, the disruption I alluded to at the beginning of this essay, presumably would have come about when the structurality of structure had to begin to be thought, that is to say, repeated, and this is why I said that this disruption was repetition in every sense of the word. Henceforth, it became necessary to think both the law which somehow governed the desire for a center in the constitution of structure, and the process of signification which orders the displacements and substitutions for this law of central presence—but a central presence which has never been itself, has always already been exiled from itself into its own substitute. The substitute does not substitute itself for anything which has somehow existed before it. Henceforth, it was necessary to begin thinking that there was no center, that the center could not be thought in the form of a present-being, that the center had no natural site, that it was not a fixed locus but a function, a sort of nonlocus in which an infinite number of sign-substitutions came into play. This was the moment when language invaded the universal problematic, the moment when, in the absence of a center or origin, everything became discourse—provided we can agree on this word—that is to say, a system in which the central signified, the original or transcendental signified, is never absolutely present outside a system of differences. The absence of the transcendental signified extends the domain and the play of signification infinitely.

Where and how does this decentering, this thinking the structurality of structure, occur? It would be somewhat naïve to refer to an event, a doctrine, or an author in order to designate this occurrence. It is no doubt part of the totality of an era, our own, but still it has always already begun to proclaim itself and begun to *work*. Nevertheless, if we wished to choose several "names," as indications only, and to recall those authors in whose discourse this occurrence has kept most closely to its most radical formulation, we doubtless would have to cite the Nietzschean critique of metaphysics, the critique of the concepts of Being and truth, for which were substituted the concepts of play, interpretation, and sign (sign without present truth); the Freudian critique of self-presence, that is, the critique of consciousness, of the subject, of self-identity and of self-proximity or self-possession; and, more radically, the Heideggerean destruction of metaphysics, of onto-theology, of the determination of Being as presence. But all these destructive discourses and all their analogues are trapped in a kind of circle. This circle is unique. It describes the form of the relation between the history of metaphysics and the destruction of the history of metaphysics. There is no sense in doing without the concepts of metaphysics in order to shake metaphysics. We have no language—no syntax and no lexicon—which is foreign to this history; we can pronounce not a single destructive proposition which has not already had to slip into the form, the logic, and the implicit postulations of precisely what it seeks to contest. To take one example from many: the metaphysics of presence is shaken with the help of the concept of *sign*. But, as I suggested a moment ago, as soon as one seeks to demonstrate in this way that there is no transcendental or privileged signified and that the domain or play of signification henceforth has no limit, one must reject even the concept and word "sign" itself—which is precisely what cannot be done. For the signification "sign" has always been understood and determined, in its meaning, as sign-of, a signifier referring to a signified, a signifier different from its signified. If one erases the radical difference between signifier and signified, it is the word "signifier" itself which must be abandoned as a metaphysical concept. When Lévi-Strauss says in the preface to *The Raw and the Cooked* that he has "sought to transcend the opposition between the sensible and the intelligible by operating from the outset at the level of signs,"[2] the necessity, force, and legitimacy of his act cannot make us forget that the concept of the sign cannot in itself surpass this opposition between the sensible and the intelligible. The concept of the sign, in each of its aspects, has been determined by this opposition throughout the totality of its history. It has lived only on this opposition and its system. But we cannot do without the concept of the sign, for we cannot give up this metaphysical complicity without also giving up the critique we are directing against this complicity, or without the risk of erasing difference in the self-identity of a signified reducing its signifier into itself or, amounting to the same thing, simply expelling its signifier outside itself. For there are two heterogenous ways of erasing the difference between the signifier and the signified: one, the classic way, consists in reducing or deriving the signifier, that is to say, ultimately in *submitting* the sign to thought; the other, the one we are using here against the first one, consists in putting into question the system in which the preceding reduction functioned; first and foremost, the opposition between the sensible and the intelligible. For the *paradox* is that the metaphysical reduction of the sign needed the opposition it was reducing. The opposition is systematic with the reduction. And what we are saying here about the sign can be extended to all the concepts and all the sentences of metaphysics, in particular to the discourse on "structure." But there are several ways of being caught in this circle. They are all more or less naïve, more or less empirical, more or less systematic, more or less close to the formulation—that is, to the formalization—of this circle. It is these differences which explain the multiplicity of destructive discourses and the disagreement between those who elaborate them. Nietzsche, Freud, and Heidegger, for example, worked within the inherited concepts of metaphysics. Since these concepts are not elements or atoms, and since they are taken from a syntax and a system, every particular borrowing brings along with it the whole of metaphysics. This is what allows these destroyers to destroy each other reciprocally—for example, Heidegger regarding Nietzsche, with as much lucidity and rigor as bad faith and misconstruction, as the last metaphysician, the last "Platonist." One could do the same for Heidegger himself, for Freud, or for a number of others. And today no exercise is more widespread.

WHAT IS THE RELEVANCE OF this formal schema when we turn to what are called the "human sciences"? One of them perhaps occupies a privileged place—ethnology. In fact one can assume that ethnology could have been born as a science only at the moment when a decentering had come about: at the moment when European culture—and, in consequence, the history of metaphysics and of its concepts—had been *dislo-*

cated, driven from its locus, and forced to stop considering itself as the culture of reference. This moment is not first and foremost a moment of philosophical or scientific discourse. It is also a moment which is political, economic, technical, and so forth. One can say with total security that there is nothing fortuitous about the fact that the critique of ethnocentrism—the very condition for ethnology—should be systematically and historically contemporaneous with the destruction of the history of metaphysics. Both belong to one and the same era. Now, ethnology—like any science—comes about within the element of discourse. And it is primarily a European science employing traditional concepts, however much it may struggle against them. Consequently, whether he wants to or not—and this does not depend on a decision on his part—the ethnologist accepts into his discourse the premises of ethnocentrism at the very moment when he denounces them. This necessity is irreducible; it is not a historical contingency. We ought to consider all its implications very carefully. But if no one can escape this necessity, and if no one is therefore responsible for giving in to it, however little he may do so, this does not mean that all the ways of giving in to it are of equal pertinence. The quality and fecundity of a discourse are perhaps measured by the critical rigor with which this relation to the history of metaphysics and to inherited concepts is thought. Here it is a question both of a critical relation to the language of the social sciences and a critical responsibility of the discourse itself. It is a question of explicitly and systematically posing the problem of the status of a discourse which borrows from a heritage the resources necessary for the deconstruction of that heritage itself. A problem of *economy* and *strategy.*

If we consider, as an example, the texts of Claude Lévi-Strauss, it is not only because of the privilege accorded to ethnology among the social sciences, nor even because the thought of Lévi-Strauss weighs heavily on the contemporary theoretical situation. It is above all because a certain choice has been declared in the work of Lévi-Strauss and because a certain doctrine has been elaborated there, and precisely, in a *more or less explicit manner,* as concerns both this critique of language and this critical language in the social sciences.

In order to follow this movement in the text of Lévi-Strauss, let us choose as one guiding thread among others the opposition between nature and culture. Despite all its rejuvenations and disguises, this opposition is congenital to philosophy. It is even older than Plato. It is at least as old as the Sophists. Since the statement of the opposition *physis/nomos, physis/technē,* it has been relayed to us by means of a whole historical chain which opposes "nature" to law, to education, to art, to technics— but also to liberty, to the arbitrary, to history, to society, to the mind, and so on. Now, from the outset of his researches, and from his first book (*The Elementary Structures of Kinship*) on, Lévi-Strauss simultaneously has experienced the necessity of utilizing this opposition and the impossibility of accepting it. In the *Elementary Structures*, he begins from this axiom or definition: that which is *universal* and spontaneous, and not dependent on any particular culture or on any determinate norm, belongs to nature. Inversely, that which depends upon a system of *norms* regulating society and therefore is capable of *varying* from one social structure to another, belongs to culture. These two definitions are of the traditional type. But in the very first pages of the *Elementary Structures* Lévi-Strauss, who has begun by giving credence to these concepts, encounters what he calls a *scandal*, that is to say, something which no longer tolerates the nature/culture opposition he has accepted, something which *simultaneously* seems to require the predicates of nature and of culture. This scandal is the *incest prohibition*. The incest prohibition is universal; in this sense one could call it natural. But it is also a prohibition, a system of norms and interdicts; in this sense one could call it cultural:

> Let us suppose then that everything universal in man relates to the natural order, and is characterized by spontaneity, and that everything subject to a norm is cultural and is both relative and particular. We are then confronted with a fact, or rather, a group of facts, which, in the light of previous definitions, are not far removed from a scandal: we refer to that complex group of beliefs, customs, conditions and institutions described succinctly as the prohibition of incest, which presents, without the slightest ambiguity, and inseparably combines, the two characteristics in which we recognize the conflicting features of two mutually exclusive orders. It constitutes a rule, but a rule which, alone among all the social rules, possesses at the same time a universal character.[3]

Obviously there is no scandal except within a system of concepts which accredits the difference between nature and culture. By commencing his work with the *factum* of the incest prohibition, Lévi-Strauss thus places himself at the point at which this difference, which has always been assumed to be self-evident, finds itself erased or questioned. For from the moment when the incest prohibition can no longer be conceived within the nature/culture opposition, it can no longer be said to be a scandalous fact, a nucleus of opacity within a network of transparent significations. The incest prohibition is no longer a scandal one meets with or comes up against in the domain of traditional concepts; it is something which escapes these concepts and certainly precedes them—probably as the condition of their possibility. It could perhaps be said that the whole of philosophical conceptualization, which is systematic with the nature/culture opposition, is designed to leave in the domain of the unthinkable the very thing that makes this conceptualization possible: the origin of the prohibition of incest.

This example, too cursorily examined, is only one among many others, but nevertheless it already shows that language bears within itself the necessity of its own critique. Now this critique may be undertaken along two paths, in two "manners." Once the limit of the nature/culture opposition makes itself felt, one might want to question systematically and rigorously the history of these concepts. This is a first action. Such a systematic and historic questioning would be neither a philological nor a philosophical action in the classic sense of these words. To concern oneself with the founding concepts of the entire history of philosophy, to deconstitute them, is not to undertake the work of the philologist or of the classic historian of philosophy. Despite appearances, it is probably the most daring way of making the beginnings of a step outside of philosophy. The step "outside philosophy" is much more difficult to conceive than is generally imagined by those who think they made it long ago with cavalier ease, and who in general are swallowed up in metaphysics in the entire body of discourse which they claim to have disengaged from it.

The other choice (which I believe corresponds more closely to Lévi-Strauss's manner), in order to avoid the possibly sterilizing effects of the first one, consists in conserving all these old concepts within the domain of empirical discovery while here and there denouncing their limits, treating them as tools which can still be used. No longer is any truth value attributed to them; there is a readiness to abandon them, if necessary, should other instruments appear more useful. In the meantime, their relative efficacy is exploited, and they are employed to destroy the old machinery to which they belong and of which they themselves are pieces. This is how the language of the social sciences criticizes *itself*. Lévi-Strauss thinks that in this way he can separate *method* from *truth*, the instruments of the method and the objective significations envisaged by it. One could almost say that this is the primary affirmation of Lévi-Strauss; in any event, the first words of the *Elementary Structures* are: "Above all, it is beginning to emerge that this distinction between nature and society ('nature' and 'culture' seem preferable to us today), while of no acceptable historical significance, does contain a logic, fully justifying its use by modern sociology as a methodological tool."[4]

Lévi-Strauss will always remain faithful to this double intention: to preserve as an instrument something whose truth value he criticizes.

On the one hand, he will continue, in effect, to contest the value of the nature/culture opposition. More than thirteen years after the *Elementary Structures, The Savage Mind* faithfully echoes the text I have just quoted: "The opposition between nature and culture to which I attached much importance at one time . . . now seems to be of primarily methodological importance." And this methodological value is not affected by its "ontological" nonvalue (as might be said, if this notion were not suspect here): "However, it would not be enough to reabsorb particular humanities into a general one. This first enterprise opens the way for others which . . . are incumbent on the exact natural sciences: the reintegration of culture in nature and finally of life within the whole of its physico-chemical conditions."[5]

On the other hand, still in *The Savage Mind*, he presents as what he calls *bricolage* what might be called the discourse of this method. The *bricoleur*, says Lévi-Strauss, is someone who uses "the means at hand," that is, the instruments he finds at his disposition around him, those which are already there, which had not been especially conceived with an eye to the operation for which they are to be used and to which one tries by trial and error to adapt them, not hesitating to change them whenever it appears necessary, or to try several of them at once, even if their form and their origin are heterogenous—and so forth. There is therefore a critique of language in the form of *bricolage*, and it has even been said that *bricolage* is critical language itself. I am thinking in particular of the article of G. Genette, "Structuralisme et critique littéraire," published in homage to Lévi-Strauss in a special issue of *L'Arc* (no. 26, 1965), where it is stated that the analysis of *bricolage* could "be applied almost word for word" to criticism, and especially to "literary criticism."

If one calls *bricolage* the necessity of borrowing one's concepts from the text of a heritage which is more or less coherent or ruined, it must be said that every discourse is *bricoleur*. The engineer, whom Lévi-Strauss opposes to the *bricoleur*, should be the one to construct the totality of his language, syntax, and lexicon. In this sense the engineer is a myth. A subject who supposedly would be the absolute origin of his own discourse and supposedly would construct it "out of nothing," "out of whole cloth," would be the creator of the verb, the verb itself. The notion of the engineer who supposedly breaks with all forms of *bricolage* is therefore a theological idea; and since Lévi-Strauss tells us elsewhere that *bricolage* is mythopoetic, the odds are that the engineer is a myth produced by the *bricoleur*. As soon as we cease to believe in such an engineer and in a discourse which breaks with the received historical discourse, and as soon as we admit that every finite discourse is bound by a certain *bricolage* and that the engineer and the scientist are also species of *bricoleurs*, then the very idea of *bricolage* is menaced and the difference in which it took on its meaning breaks down.

This brings us to the second thread which might guide us in what is being contrived here.

Lévi-Strauss describes *bricolage* not only as an intellectual activity but also as a mythopoetical activity. One reads in *The Savage Mind*, "Like *bricolage* on the technical plane, mythical reflection can reach brilliant unforeseen results on the intellectual plane. Conversely, attention has often been drawn to the mythopoetical nature of *bricolage*."[6]

But Lévi-Strauss's remarkable endeavor does not simply consist in proposing, notably in his most recent investigations, a structural science of myths and of mythological activity. His endeavor also appears—I would say almost from the outset—to have the status which he accords to his own discourse on myths, to what he calls his "mythologicals." It is here that his discourse on the myth reflects on itself and criticizes itself. And this moment, this critical period, is evidently of concern to all the languages which share the field of the human sciences. What does Lévi-Strauss say of his "mythologicals"? It is here that we rediscover the mythopoetical virtue of *bricolage*. In effect, what appears most fascinating in this critical search for a new status of discourse is the stated abandonment of all reference to a *center*, to a *subject*, to a privileged *reference*, to an origin, or to an absolute *archia*. The theme of this decentering could be followed throughout the "Overture" to his last book, *The Raw and the Cooked*. I shall simply remark on a few key points.

1. From the very start, Lévi-Strauss recognizes that the Bororo myth which he employs in the book as the "reference myth" does not merit this name and this treatment. The name is specious and the use of the myth improper. This myth deserves no more than any other its referential privilege: "In fact, the Bororo myth, which I shall refer to from now on as the key myth, is, as I shall try to show, simply a transformation, to a greater or lesser extent, of other myths originating either in the same society or in neighboring or remote societies. I could, therefore, have legitimately taken as my starting point any one representative myth of the group. From this point of view, the key myth is interesting not because it is typical, but rather because of its irregular position within the group."[7]

2. There is no unity or absolute source of the myth. The focus or the source of the myth are always shadows and virtualities which are elusive, unactualizable, and nonexistent in the first place. Everything begins with structure, configuration, or relationship. The discourse on the acentric structure that myth itself is, cannot itself have an absolute subject or an absolute center. It must avoid the violence that consists in centering a language which describes an acentric structure if it is not to shortchange the form and movement of myth. Therefore it is necessary to forego scientific or philosophical discourse, to renounce the *epistémé* which absolutely requires, which is the absolute requirement that we go back to the source, to the center, to the founding basis, to the principle, and so on. In opposition to *epistemic* discourse, structural discourse on myths—*mythological* discourse—must itself be *mythomorphic*. It must have the form of that of which it speaks. This is what Lévi-Strauss says in *The Raw and the Cooked*, from which I would now like to quote a long and remarkable passage:

> The study of myths raises a methodological problem, in that it cannot be carried out according to the Cartesian principle of breaking down the difficulty into as many parts as may be necessary for finding the solution. There is no real end to methodological analysis, no hidden unity to be grasped once the breaking-down process has been completed.

Themes can be split up *ad infinitum*. Just when you think you have dis-
entangled and separated them, you realize that they are knitting together again in response to the operation of unexpected affinities.
Consequently the unity of the myth is never more than tendential and
projective and cannot reflect a state or a particular moment of the myth.
It is a phenomenon of the imagination, resulting from the attempt at
interpretation; and its function is to endow the myth with synthetic form
and to prevent its disintegration into a confusion of opposites. The science of myths might therefore be termed "anaclastic," if we take this old
term in the broader etymological sense which includes the study of both
reflected rays and broken rays. But unlike philosophical reflection, which
aims to go back to its own source, the reflections we are dealing with
here concern rays whose only source is hypothetical. . . . And in seeking
to imitate the spontaneous movement of mythological thought, this essay, which is also both too brief and too long, has had to conform to the
requirements of that thought and to respect its rhythm. It follows that
this book on myths is itself a kind of myth.[8]

This statement is repeated a little farther on: "As the myths themselves
are based on secondary codes (the primary codes being those that provide the substance of language), the present work is put forward as a tentative draft of a tertiary code, which is intended to ensure the reciprocal
translatability of several myths. This is why it would not be wrong to consider this book itself as a myth: it is, as it were, the myth of mythology."[9]
The absence of a center is here the absence of a subject and the absence
of an author: "Thus the myth and the musical work are like conductors
of an orchestra, whose audience becomes the silent performers. If it is
now asked where the real center of the work is to be found, the answer is
that this is impossible to determine. Music and mythology bring man
face to face with potential objects of which only the shadows are actualized. . . . Myths are anonymous."[10] The musical model chosen by Lévi-
Strauss for the composition of his book is apparently justified by this
absence of any real and fixed center of the mythical or mythological
discourse.

Thus it is at this point that ethnographic *bricolage* deliberately assumes its mythopoetic function. But by the same token, this function
makes the philosophical or epistemological requirement of a center appear as mythological, that is to say, as a historical illusion.

Nevertheless, even if one yields to the necessity of what Lévi-Strauss
has done, one cannot ignore its risks. If the mythological is mythomorphic, are all discourses on myths equivalent? Shall we have to abandon any epistemological requirement which permits us to distinguish
between several qualities of discourse on the myth? A classic, but inevitable question. It cannot be answered—and I believe that Lévi-Strauss
does not answer it—for as long as the problem of the relations between
the philosopheme or the theorem, on the one hand, and the mytheme or

the mythopoem, on the other, has not been posed explicitly, which is no small problem. For lack of explicitly posing this problem, we condemn ourselves to transforming the alleged transgression of philosophy into an unnoticed fault within the philosophical realm. Empiricism would be the genus of which these faults would always be the species. Transphilosophical concepts would be transformed into philosophical naïvetés. Many examples could be given to demonstrate this risk: the concepts of sign, history, truth, and so forth. What I want to emphasize is simply that the passage beyond philosophy does not consist in turning the page of philosophy (which usually amounts to philosophizing badly), but in continuing to read philosophers *in a certain way*. The risk I am speaking of is always assumed by Lévi-Strauss, and it is the very price of this endeavor. I have said that empiricism is the matrix of all faults menacing a discourse which continues, as with Lévi-Strauss in particular, to consider itself scientific. If we wanted to pose the problem of empiricism and *bricolage* in depth, we would probably end up very quickly with a number of absolutely contradictory propositions concerning the status of discourse in structural ethnology. On the one hand, structuralism justifiably claims to be the critique of empiricism. but at the same time there is not a single book or study by Lévi-Strauss which is not proposed as an empirical essay which can always be completed or invalidated by new information. The structural schemata are always proposed as hypotheses resulting from a finite quantity of information and which are subjected to the proof of experience. Numerous texts could be used to demonstrate this double postulation. Let us turn once again to the "Overture" of *The Raw and the Cooked,* where it seems clear that if this postulation is double, it is because it is a question here of a language on language:

> If critics reproach me with not having carried out an exhaustive inventory of South American myths before analyzing them, they are making a grave mistake about the nature and function of these documents. The total body of myth belonging to a given community is comparable to its speech. Unless the population dies out physically or morally, this totality is never complete. You might as well criticize a linguist for compiling the grammar of a language without having complete records of the words pronounced since the language came into being, and without knowing what will be said in it during the future part of its existence. Experience proves that a linguist can work out the grammar of a given language from a remarkably small number of sentences. . . . And even a partial grammar or an outline grammar is a precious acquisition when we are dealing with unknown languages. Syntax does not become evident only after a (theoretically limitless) series of events has been recorded and examined, because it is itself the body of rules governing their production. What I have tried to give is an outline of the syntax of South American mythology. Should fresh data come to hand, they will be used to check or modify the formulation of certain grammatical laws,

so that some are abandoned and replaced by new ones. But in no instance would I feel constrained to accept the arbitrary demand for a total mythological pattern, since, as has been shown, such a requirement has no meaning.[11]

Totalization, therefore, is sometimes defined as *useless,* and sometimes as *impossible.* This is no doubt due to the fact that there are two ways of conceiving the limit of totalization. And I assert once more that these two determinations coexist implicitly in Lévi-Strauss's discourse. Totalization can be judged impossible in the classical style: one then refers to the empirical endeavor of either a subject or a finite richness which it can never master. There is too much, more than one can say. But nontotalization can also be determined in another way: no longer from the standpoint of a concept of finitude as relegation to the empirical, but from the standpoint of the concept of *play.* If totalization no longer has any meaning, it is not because the infiniteness of a field cannot be covered by a finite glance or a finite discourse, but because the nature of the field—that is, language and a finite language—excludes totalization. This field is in effect that of *play,* that is to say, a field of infinite substitutions only because it is finite, that is to say, because instead of being an inexhaustible field, as in the classical hypothesis, instead of being too large, there is something missing from it: a center which arrests and grounds the play of substitutions. One could say—rigorously using that word whose scandalous signification is always obliterated in French—that this movement of play, permitted by the lack or absence of a center or origin, is the movement of *supplementarity.* One cannot determine the center and exhaust totalization because the sign which replaces the center, which supplements it, taking the center's place in its absence—this sign is added, occurs as a surplus, as a *supplement.*[12] The movement of signification adds something, which results in the fact that there is always more, but this addition is a floating one because it comes to perform a vicarious function, to supplement a lack on the part of the signified. Although Lévi-Strauss in his use of the word "supplementary" never emphasizes, as I do here, the two directions of meaning which are so strangely compounded within it, it is not by chance that he uses this word twice in his "Introduction to the Work of Marcel Mauss," at one point where he is speaking of the "overabundance of signifier, in relation to the signifieds to which this overabundance can refer":

> In his endeavor to understand the world, man therefore always has at his disposal a surplus of signification (which he shares out amongst things according to the laws of symbolic thought—which is the task of ethnologists and linguists to study). This distribution of a *supplementary* allowance [*ration supplémentaire*]—if it is permissible to put it that way— is absolutely necessary in order that on the whole the available signifier

and the signified it aims at may remain in the relationship of complementarity which is the very condition of the use of symbolic thought.[13]

(It could no doubt be demonstrated that this *ration supplémentaire* of signification is the origin of the *ratio* itself.) The word reappears a little further on, after Lévi-Strauss has mentioned "this floating signifier, which is the servitude of all finite thought":

> In other words—and taking as our guide Mauss's precept that all social phenomena can be assimilated to language—we see in *mana, Wakau, oranda* and other notions of the same type, the conscious expression of a semantic function, whose role it is to permit symbolic thought to operate in spite of the contradiction which is proper to it. In this way are explained the apparently insoluble antinomies attached to this notion. . . . At one and the same time force and action, quality and state, noun and verb; abstract and concrete, omnipresent and localized— *mana* is in effect all these things. But is it not precisely because it is none of these things that *mana* is a simple form, or more exactly, a symbol in the pure state, and therefore capable of becoming charged with any sort of symbolic content whatever? In the system of symbols constituted by all cosmologies, *mana* would simply be a zero symbolic value, that is to say, a sign marking the necessity of a symbolic content *supplementary* [italics added] to that with which the signified is already loaded, but which can take on any value required, provided only that this value still remains part of the available reserve and is not, as phonologists put it, a group-term.

Lévi-Strauss adds the note:

> Linguists have already been led to formulate hypotheses of this type. For example: "A zero phoneme is opposed to all the other phonemes in French in that it entails no differential characters and no constant phonetic value. On the contrary, the proper function of the zero phoneme is to be opposed to phoneme absence" (R. Jakobson and J. Lutz, "Notes on the French Phonemic Pattern," *Word* 5, no. 2 [August 1949]: 155). Similarly, if we schematize the conception I am proposing here, it could almost be said that the function of notions like *mana* is to be opposed to the absence of signification, without entailing by itself any particular signification.[14]

The *overabundance* of the signifier, its *supplementary* character, is thus the result of a finitude, that is to say, the result of a lack which must be *supplemented*.

It can now be understood why the concept of play is important in Lévi-Strauss. His references to all sorts of games, notably to roulette, are very frequent, especially in his *Conversations*,[15] in *Race and History*,[16] and in *The Savage Mind.* Further, the reference to play is always caught up in tension.

Tension with history, first of all. This is a classical problem, objections to which are now well worn. I shall simply indicate what seems to me the formality of the problem: by reducing history, Lévi-Strauss has treated as it deserves a concept which has always been in complicity with a teleological and eschatological metaphysics, in other words, paradoxically, in complicity with that philosophy of presence to which it was believed history could be opposed. The thematic of historicity, although it seems to be a somewhat late arrival in philosophy, has always been required by the determination of Being as presence. With or without etymology, and despite the classic antagonism which opposes these significations throughout all of classical thought, it could be shown that the concept of *epistēmē* has always called forth that of *historia*, if history is always the unity of a becoming, as the tradition of truth or the development of science or knowledge oriented toward the appropriation of truth in presence and self-presence, toward knowledge in consciousness-of-self. History has always been conceived as the movement of a resumption of history, as a detour between two presences. But if it is legitimate to suspect this concept of history, there is a risk, if it is reduced without an explicit statement of the problem I am indicating here, of falling back into an ahistoricism of a classical type, that is to say, into a determined moment of the history of metaphysics. Such is the algebraic formality of the problem as I see it. More concretely, in the work of Lévi-Strauss it must be recognized that the respect for structurality, for the internal originality of the structure, compels a neutralization of time and history. For example, the appearance of a new structure, of an original system, always comes about—and this is the very condition of its structural specificity—by a rupture with its past, its origin, and its cause. Therefore one can describe what is peculiar to the structural organization only by not taking into account, in the very moment of this description, its past conditions: by omitting to posit the problem of the transition from one structure to another, by putting history between brackets. In this "structuralist" moment, the concepts of chance and discontinuity are indispensable. And Lévi-Strauss does in fact often appeal to them, for example, as concerns that structure of structures, language, of which he says in the "Introduction to the Work of Marcel Mauss" that it "could only have been born in one fell swoop":

> Whatever may have been the moment and the circumstances of its appearance on the scale of animal life, language could only have been born in one fell swoop. Things could not have set about acquiring signification progressively. Following a transformation the study of which is not the concern of the social sciences, but rather of biology and psy-

chology, a transition came about from a stage where nothing had a meaning to another where everything possessed it.[17]

This standpoint does not prevent Lévi-Strauss from recognizing the slowness, the process of maturing, the continuous toil of factual transformations, history (for example, *Race and History*). But, in accordance with a gesture which was also Rousseau's and Husserl's, he must "set aside all the facts" at the moment when he wishes to recapture the specificity of a structure. Like Rousseau, he must always conceive of the origin of a new structure on the model of catastrophe—an overturning of nature in nature, a natural interruption of the natural sequence, a setting aside *of* nature.

Besides the tension between play and history, there is also the tension between play and presence. Play is the disruption of presence. The presence of an element is always a signifying and substitutive reference inscribed in a system of differences and the movement of a chain. Play is always play of absence and presence, but if it is to be thought radically, play must be conceived of before the alternative of presence and absence. Being must be conceived as presence or absence on the basis of the possibility of play and not the other way around. If Lévi-Strauss, better than any other, has brought to light the play of repetition and the repetition of play, one no less perceives in his work a sort of ethic of presence, an ethic of nostalgia for origins, an ethic of archaic and natural innocence, of a purity of presence and self-presence in speech—an ethic, nostalgia, and even remorse, which he often presents as the motivation of the ethnological project when he moves toward the archaic societies which are exemplary societies in his eyes. These texts are well known.[18]

Turned towards the lost or impossible presence of the absent origin, this structuralist thematic of broken immediacy is therefore the saddened, *negative,* nostalgic, guilty, Rousseauistic side of the thinking of play whose other side would be the Nietzschean *affirmation,* that is the joyous affirmation of the play of the world and of the innocence of becoming, the affirmation of a world of signs without fault, without truth, and without origin which is offered to an active interpretation. *This affirmation then determines the noncenter otherwise than as loss of the center.* And it plays without security. For there is a *sure* play: that which is limited to the *substitution* of *given* and *existing, present,* pieces. In absolute chance, affirmation also surrenders itself to *genetic* indetermination, to the *seminal* adventure of the trace.

There are thus two interpretations of interpretation, of structure, of sign, of play. The one seeks to decipher, dreams of deciphering a truth or an origin which escapes play and the order of the sign, and which lives the necessity of interpretation as an exile. The other, which is no longer turned toward the origin, affirms play and tries to pass beyond man and humanism, the name of man being the name of that being who, throughout the history of metaphysics or of ontotheology—in other words, throughout his entire history—has dreamed of full presence, the reassuring foundation, the origin and the end of play. The second interpretation of interpretation, to which Nietzsche pointed the way, does not seek in ethnography, as Lévi-Strauss does, the "inspiration of a new humanism" (again citing the "Introduction to the Work of Marcel Mauss").

There are more than enough indications today to suggest we might perceive that these two interpretations of interpretation—which are absolutely irreconcilable even if we live them simultaneously and reconcile them in an obscure economy—together share the field which we call, in such a problematic fashion, the social sciences.

For my part, although these two interpretations must acknowledge and accentuate their difference and define their irreducibility, I do not believe that today there is any question of *choosing*—in the first place because here we are in a region (let us say, provisionally, a region of historicity) where the category of choice seems particularly trivial; and in the second, because we must first try to conceive of the common ground, and the *différance* of this irreducible difference. Here there is a kind of question, let us still call it historical, whose *conception, formation, gestation*, and *labor* we are only catching a glimpse of today. I employ these words, I admit, with a glance toward the operations of childbearing—but also with a glance toward those who, in a society from which I do not exclude myself, turn their eyes away when faced by the as yet unnamable which is proclaiming itself and which can do so, as is necessary whenever a birth is in the offing, only under the species of the nonspecies, in the formless, mute, infant, and terrifying form of monstrosity.

NOTES *

1. The reference, in a restricted sense, is to the Freudian theory of neurotic symptoms and of dream interpretation in which a given symbol is understood contradictorily as both the desire to fulfill an impulse and the desire to suppress the impulse. In a general sense the reference is to Derrida's thesis that logic and coherence themselves can only be understood contradictorily, since they presuppose the suppression of *différance*, "writing" in the sense of the general economy. Cf. "La pharmacie de Platon," in *La dissemination*, 125–26, where Derrida uses the Freudian model of dream interpretation in order to clarify the contractions embedded in philosophical coherence.

2. Lévi-Strauss, *The Raw and the Cooked*, trans. John and Doreen Wightman (New York: Harper and Row, 1969), 14. (Translation somewhat modified.)

3. Lévi-Strauss, *The Elementary Structures of Kinship*, trans. James Bell, John von Sturmer, and Rodney Needham (Boston: Beacon Press, 1969), 8.

4. Ibid., 3.

*Notes by the translator, Alan Bass.—ED.

5. Lévi-Strauss, *The Savage Mind* (London: George Weidenfeld and Nicolson; Chicago: University of Chicago Press, 1966), 247.

6. Ibid., 17.

7. Lévi-Strauss, *The Raw and the Cooked*, 2.

8. Ibid., 5–6.

9. Ibid., 12.

10. Ibid., 17–18.

11. Ibid., 7–8.

12. TN. This double sense of supplement—to supply something which is missing, or to supply something additional—is at the center of Derrida's deconstruction of traditional linguistics in *De la grammatologie*. In a chapter entitled "The Violence of the Letter: From Lévi-Strauss to Rousseau" (149ff.), Derrida expands the analysis of Lévi-Strauss begun in this essay in order further to clarify the ways in which the contradictions of traditional logic "program" the most modern conceptual apparatuses of linguistics and the social sciences.

13. "Introduction à l'oeuvre de Marcel Mauss," in Marcel Mauss, *Sociologie et anthropologie* (Paris: P.U.F., 1950), xlix.

14. Ibid., xlix–l.

15. George Charbonnier, *Entretiens avec Claude Lévi-Strauss* (Paris: Plon, 1961).

16. Lévi-Strauss, *Race and History* (Paris: Unesco Publications, 1958).

17. Lévi-Strauss, "Introduction à l'oeuvre de Marcel Mauss," xlvi.

18. TN. The reference is to *Tristes tropiques*, trans. John Russell (London: Hutchinson, 1961).

The Frame of Reference: Poe, Lacan, Derrida

BARBARA JOHNSON

Johnson emphasizes the crucial role of the reader in her deconstruction of Derrida's essay "The Purveyor of the Truth" which, in turn, deconstructs Lacan's essay "Seminar on 'The Purloined Letter'" (reprinted, above, in Chapter 6). Earlier versions of both essays appeared in *Yale French Studies:* Derrida's in no. 52 (1975) and Johnson's in nos. 55–56 (1977). Subsequently, Johnson revised her response (the revised essay is reprinted below) as did Derrida, whose newly translated version is retitled *The Post Card* (Chicago: University of Chicago Press, 1987). These articles, one commenting on another, have begun a dialogue which

From *Psychoanalysis and the Question of the Text*, ed. Geoffrey Hartman (Baltimore: Johns Hopkins University Press, 1978), 149–71. Copyright 1978 The Johns Hopkins University Press.

still reverberates today. The original essays along with the revised versions are well worth consulting as examples of the open reflexivity of deconstructive reader-response criticism.

A brief comment on Derrida's "Purveyor of the Truth" which Johnson discusses in relation to Lacan might be helpful at this point. While Derrida agrees with Lacan that the symbolic order (language) constitutes the subject (ourselves), he faults the way Lacan's "Seminar" demonstrates this. Derrida complains that Lacan's method is logocentric: It strips away and discards the "scene of writing" of "The Purloined Letter," that is, the literary and fictional dimension of Poe's story which resists being completely transformed into content. As a result, Lacan's analysis of two scenes from the story ignores the movement of supplementarity and falls prey to metaphysical reduction. It reduces the signifier to the letter, the letter to castration, and castration to (maternal) phallus. Derrida concludes that instead of showing how language works to decenter the self, Lacan falls into the trap he set out to avoid—logocentrism.

In her turn, Johnson accuses Derrida of slipping into the logocentric habits he faults Lacan for. She contends that Derrida "frames" Lacan for "interpretive malpractice" which Derrida himself commits. This insight leads Johnson to her central question, "What can this frame teach us about the nature of the act of reading?" Her answer is that each reader interprets within a paradoxical frame of reference which allows him insight at the same time as it blinds him.

A LITERARY TEXT THAT BOTH ANALYZES itself and shows that it actually has neither a self nor any neutral metalanguage with which to do the analyzing calls out irresistibly for analysis. And when that call is answered by two eminent thinkers whose readings emit an equally paradoxical call to analysis of their own, the resulting triptych, in the context of the question of the act of reading (literature), places *its* would-be reader in a vertiginously insecure position.

The three texts in question are Edgar Allan Poe's short story "The Purloined Letter,"[1] Jacques Lacan's "Seminar on 'The Purloined Letter,'"[2] and Jacques Derrida's reading of Lacan's reading of Poe, "The Purveyor of Truth" (Le Facteur de la Vérité).[3] In all three texts, it is the *act of analysis* that seems to occupy the center of the discursive stage and the *act of analysis of the act of analysis* that in some way disrupts that centrality, subverting the very possibility of a position of analytical mastery. In the resulting asymmetrical, abysmal structure, no analysis—including this one—can intervene without transforming and repeating other elements in the sequence, which is thus not a stable sequence, but which nevertheless produces certain regular effects. It is the functioning of this regularity, and the structure of these effects, that will provide the basis for the present study.

Any attempt to do "justice" to three such complex texts is obviously out of the question. But it is precisely the *nature* of such "justice" that *is* the question in each of these readings of the act of analysis. The fact that the debate proliferates around a crime story—a robbery and its undoing—can hardly be an accident. Somewhere in each of these texts, the economy of justice cannot be avoided. For in spite of the absence of mastery, there is no lack of *effects of power*.

I shall begin by quoting at some length from Lacan's discussion of "The Purloined Letter" in order to present both the plot of Poe's story and the thrust of Lacan's analysis. Lacan summarizes the story as follows. . . .

[Johnson here quotes Lacan's summary. See pp. 327–30, this volume.]

Thus, it is neither the character of the individual subjects, nor the contents of the letter, but the *position* of the letter within the group that decides what each person will do next. It is the fact that the letter does *not* function as a unit of meaning (a signified) but as that which produces certain effects (a signifier) that leads Lacan to read the story as an illustration of "the truth which may be drawn from that moment in Freud's thought under study—namely, that it is the symbolic order which is constitutive for the subject—by demonstrating . . . the decisive orientation which the subject receives from the itinerary of a signifier" (*SPL*, 40 [p. 325, this volume]). The letter acts like a signifier precisely to the extent that its function in the story does not require that its meaning be revealed: "the letter was able to produce its effects *within* the story: on the actors in the tale, including the narrator, as well as *outside* the story: on us, the readers, and also on its author, without anyone's ever bothering to worry about what it *meant*."[4] "The Purloined Letter" thus becomes for Lacan a kind of *allegory of the signifier*.

Derrida's critique of Lacan's reading does not dispute the validity of the allegorical interpretation on its own terms, but questions rather its implicit presuppositions and its modus operandi. Derrida aims his objections at two kinds of targets: (1) what Lacan *puts into* the *letter*, and (2) what Lacan *leaves out of* the *text*.

1. *What Lacan puts into the letter.* While asserting that the letter's meaning is lacking, Lacan, according to Derrida, makes this lack into *the* meaning of the letter. But Derrida does not stop there: he goes on to assert that what Lacan means by that lack is the truth of lack-as-castration-as-truth: "The truth of the purloined letter is the truth itself. . . . What is veiled/unveiled in this case is a hole, a nonbeing (*non-étant*); the truth of being (*l'être*), as nonbeing. Truth is "woman" as veiled/unveiled castration" (*PT*, 60–61). Lacan himself, however, never uses the word "castration" in the

text of the original seminar. That it is suggested is indisputable, but Derrida, by filling in what *Lacan* left blank, is repeating precisely the gesture of blank-filling for which he is criticizing Lacan.

2. *What Lacan leaves out of the text.* This objection is itself double: on the one hand, Derrida criticizes Lacan for neglecting to consider "The Purloined Letter" in connection with the other two stories in what Derrida calls Poe's "Dupin Trilogy." And on the other hand, according to Derrida, at the very moment Lacan is reading the story as an allegory of the signifier, he is being blind to the disseminating power of the signifier in the *text* of the allegory, in what Derrida calls the "scene of writing." To cut out part of a text's frame of reference as though it did not exist and to reduce a complex textual functioning to a single meaning are serious blots indeed in the annals of literary criticism. Therefore it is all the more noticeable that Derrida's own reading of Lacan's text repeats precisely the crimes of which he accuses it: on the one hand, Derrida makes no mention of Lacan's long development on the relation between symbolic determination and random series. And on the other hand, Derrida dismisses Lacan's "style" as a mere ornament, veiling, for a time, an unequivocal message: "Lacan's 'style,' moreover, was such that for a long time it would hinder and delay all access to a *unique* content or a single unequivocal meaning determinable beyond the writing itself" (*PT,* 40). The fact that Derrida repeats the very gestures he is criticizing does not in itself invalidate his criticism of their *effects,* but it does render problematic his statement condemning their *existence.* And it also illustrates the transfer of the repetition compulsion from the original *text* to the scene of its *reading.*

In an attempt to read this paradoxical encounter more closely, let us examine the way in which Derrida deduces from Lacan's text the fact that, for Lacan, the "letter" is a symbol of the (mother's) phallus. Since Lacan never uses the word "phallus" in the seminar, this is already an *interpretation* on Derrida's part, and quite an astute one at that. Lacan, as a later reader of his own seminar, implicitly agrees with it by placing the word "castrated"—which had not been used in the original text—in his "Points" presentation. The disagreement between Derrida and Lacan thus arises not over the *validity* of the equation "letter = phallus," but over its *meaning.*

How, then, does Derrida derive this equation from Lacan's text? The deduction follows four basic lines of reasoning:

1. The letter "belongs" to the Queen as a substitute for the phallus she does not have. It feminizes (castrates) each of its successive holders and is eventually returned to her as its rightful owner.

2. Poe's description of the position of the letter in the Minister's apartment, expanded upon by the figurative dimensions of Lacan's text, suggests an analogy between the shape of the fireplace, from the center

of whose mantelpiece the letter is found hanging, and that point on a woman's anatomy from which the phallus is missing.

3. The letter, says Lacan, cannot be divided: "But if it is first of all on the materiality of the signifier that we have insisted, that materiality is *odd* [singulière] in many ways, the first of which is not to admit partition" (*SPL,* 53 [p. 333, this volume]). This indivisibility, says Derrida, is odd indeed, but becomes comprehensible if it is seen as an *idealization* of the phallus, whose integrity is necessary for the edification of the entire psychoanalytical system. With the phallus safely idealized the so-called "signifier" acquires the "unique, living, non-mutilable integrity" of the self-present spoken word, unequivocally pinned down to and by the *signified.* "Had the phallus been per(mal)chance divisible or reduced to the status of a partial object, the whole edification would have crumbled down, and this is what has to be avoided at all cost" (*PT,* 96–97).

4. Finally, if Poe's story "illustrates" the "truth," as Lacan puts it, the last words of the seminar proper seem to reaffirm that truth in no uncertain terms: "Thus it is that what the 'purloined letter' . . . means is that *a letter always arrives at its destination*" (*SPL,* 72 [p. 346, this volume]; emphasis mine). Now, since it is unlikely that Lacan is talking about the efficiency of the postal service, he must, according to Derrida, be affirming the possibility of unequivocal meaning, the eventual reappropriation of the message, its total equivalence with itself. And since the "truth" Poe's story illustrates is, in Derrida's eyes, the truth of veiled/unveiled castration and of the transcendental identity of the phallus as the lack that makes the system work, this final sentence in Lacan's seminar seems to affirm both the absolute truth of psychoanalytical theories and the absolute decipherability of the literary text. Poe's message will have been totally, unequivocally understood and explained by the psychoanalytical myth. "The hermeneutic discovery of meaning (truth), the deciphering (that of Dupin and that of the seminar), arrives itself at its destination" (*PT,* 66).

Thus, the law of the phallus seems to imply a reappropriating return to the place of true ownership, an indivisible identity functioning beyond the possibility of disintegration or unrecoverable loss, and a totally self-present, unequivocal meaning or truth. The problem with this type of system, counters Derrida, is that it cannot account for the possibility of sheer accident, irreversible loss, unreappropriable residues, and infinite divisibility, which are in fact necessary and inevitable in the system's very elaboration. In order for the circuit of the letter to end up confirming the law of the phallus, it must begin by transgressing it: the letter is a sign of high treason. Phallogocentrism mercilessly represses the uncontrollable multiplicity of ambiguities, the disseminating play of *writing,* which irreducibly transgresses any unequivocal meaning. "Not that the letter never arrives at its destination, but part of its structure is that it is always capable of not arriving there. . . . Here dissemination threatens the law of the signifier and of castration as a contract of truth. Dissemination mutilates the unity of the signifier, that is, of the phallus" (*PT*, 66). In contrast to Lacan's *Seminar*, then, Derrida's text would seem to be setting itself up as a *Disseminar*.

From the foregoing remarks, it can easily be seen that the disseminal criticism of Lacan's apparent reduction of the literary text to an unequivocal message depends for its force upon the presupposition of unambiguousness in *Lacan's* text. And indeed, the statement that a letter always reaches its destination seems straightforward enough. But when that statement is reinserted into its context, things become palpably less certain:

> Is that all, and shall we believe we have deciphered Dupin's real strategy above and beyond the imaginary tricks with which he was obliged to deceive us? No doubt, yes, for if "any point requiring reflection," as Dupin states at the start, is "examined to best purpose in the dark," we may now easily read its solution in broad daylight. It was already implicit and easy to derive from the title of our tale, according to the very formula we have long submitted to your discretion: in which the sender, we tell you, receives from the receiver his own message in reverse form. Thus it is that what the "purloined letter," nay, the "letter in sufferance" means is that a letter always arrives at its destination. (*SPL*, 72 [pp. 345–46, this volume])

The meaning of this last sentence is problematized not so much by its own ambiguity as by a series of reversals in the preceding sentences. If the best examination takes place in darkness, what does "reading in broad daylight" imply? Could it not be taken as an affirmation not of actual lucidity but of *delusions* of lucidity? Could it not then move the "yes, no doubt" as an answer not to the question "have we deciphered?" but to the question "shall we *believe* we have deciphered?" And if this is possible, does it not empty the final affirmation of all unequivocality, leaving it to stand with the *force* of an assertion, without any definite content? And if the sender receives from the receiver his own message backwards, who is the sender here, who is the receiver, and what is the message? I will take another look at this passage later, but for the moment its ambiguities seem sufficient to problematize, if not subvert, the presupposition of univocality that is the very foundation on which Derrida has edified his interpretation.

Surely such an oversimplification on Derrida's part does not result from mere blindness, oversight, or error. As Paul de Man says of Derrida's similar treatment of Rousseau, "the pattern is too interesting not to be deliberate."[5] Derrida's consistent forcing of Lacan's statements into systems and patterns from which they are actually trying to escape must correspond to some strategic necessity different from the attentiveness to the letter of the text that characterizes Derrida's way of reading Poe. And in fact, the more one works with Derrida's analysis, the more convinced one becomes that although the critique of what Derrida *calls* psychoanalysis is entirely justified, it does not quite apply to what Lacan's text is actually saying. What Derrida is in fact arguing against is therefore not Lacan's text but Lacan's power, or rather, "Lacan" as the apparent cause of certain *effects of power* in French discourse today. Whatever Lacan's text may say, it *functions*, according to Derrida, as if it said what *he* says it says. The statement that a letter always reaches its destination may be totally undecipherable, but its assertive force is taken all the more seriously as a sign that Lacan himself has everything all figured out. Such an assertion, in fact, gives him an appearance of mastery like that of the Minister in the eyes of the letterless Queen. "The ascendancy which the Minister derives from the situation," explains Lacan, "is attached not to the letter but to the character it makes him into."

Thus Derrida's seemingly "blind" reading, whose vagaries we are following here, is not a mistake, but the positioning of what can be called the "average reading" of Lacan's text, which is the *true* object of Derrida's deconstruction. Since Lacan's text is *read* as if it said what Derrida says it says, its actual textual functioning is irrelevant to the agonistic arena in which Derrida's analysis takes place. If Derrida's reading of Lacan's reading of Poe is thus actually the deconstruction of a reading whose status is difficult to determine, does this mean that Lacan's text is completely innocent of the misdemeanors of which it is accused? If Lacan can be shown to be opposed to the same kind of logocentric error that Derrida is opposed to, does that mean that they are both really saying the same thing? These are questions that must be left, at least for the moment, hanging.

But the structure of Derrida's *transference of guilt* from a certain *reading* of Lacan onto Lacan's *text* is not indifferent in itself, in the context of what, after all, started out as a relatively simple crime story. For what it amounts to is nothing less than—a *frame*. And if Derrida is thus framing Lacan for an interpretative malpractice of which he himself is, at least in part, the author, what can this frame teach us about the nature of the act of reading, in the context of the question of literature and psychoanalysis?

Interestingly enough, one of the major crimes for which Lacan is being framed by Derrida is precisely the psychoanalytical reading's elimination of what Derrida calls the literary text's *frame*. That frame here consists not only of the two stories that precede "The Purloined Letter," but of the stratum of narration through which the stories are told, and, "beyond" it, of the text's entire functioning as *écriture*.

It would seem that Lacan is guilty of several sins of omission: the omission of the narrator, of the nondialogue parts of the story, and of the other stories in the trilogy. But does this criticism amount to a mere plea for the inclusion of what has been excluded? No, the problem is not simply quantitative. What has been excluded is not homogeneous to what has been included. Lacan, says Derrida, misses the specifically literary dimension of Poe's text by treating it as a "real drama," a story like the stories a psychoanalyst hears every day from his patients. What has been left out is precisely *literature* itself.

Does this mean that the "frame" is what makes a text literary? In a recent issue of *New Literary History* devoted to the question "What is Literature?" and totally unrelated to the debate concerning the purloined letter, this is precisely the conclusion to which one of the contributors comes: "Literature is language, . . . but it is language around which we have drawn a *frame*, a frame that indicates a decision to regard with a particular self-consciousness the resources language has always possessed."[6]

Such a view of literature, however, implies that a text is literary *because* it remains inside certain definite borders: it is a many-faceted object, perhaps, but still, it is an object. That this is not quite what Derrida has in mind becomes clear from the following remarks:

> By overlooking the narrator's position, the narrator's involvement in the content of what he seems to be recounting, one omits from the scene of writing anything going beyond the two triangular scenes.
>
> And first of all one omits that what is in question—with no possible access route or border—is a scene of writing whose boundaries crumble off into an abyss. From the simulacrum of an overture, of a "first word," the narrator, in narrating himself, advances a few propositions that carry the unity of the "tale" into an endless drifting off course: a textual drifting not at all taken into account in the seminar. (*PT*, 100–101; translation modified)

> These reminders, of which countless other examples could be given, alert us to the effects of the frame, and of the paradoxes in the parergonal logic. Our purpose is not to prove that "The Purloined Letter" functions within a frame (omitted by the seminar, which can thus be assured of its triangular interior by an active, surreptitious limitation starting from a metalinguistic overview), but to prove that the structure of the framing effects is such that no totalization of the border is even possible. Frames are always framed: thus, by part of their content. Pieces without a whole, "divisions" without a totality—this is what thwarts the dream of a letter without division, allergic to division. (*PT*, 99; translation modified)

Here the argument seems to reverse the previous objection: Lacan has eliminated not the frame but the unframability of the literary text. But what Derrida calls "parergonal logic" is paradoxical precisely because *both* of these incompatible (but not totally contradictory) arguments are equally valid. The total inclusion of the "frame" is both mandatory and impossible. The "frame" thus becomes not the borderline between the inside and the outside, but precisely what subverts the applicability of the inside/outside polarity to the act of interpretation.

What enables Derrida to problematize the literary text's frame is, as we have seen, what he calls "the scene of writing." By this he means two things:

1. The textual signifier's resistance to being totally transformed into a signified. In spite of Lacan's attentiveness to the path of the letter in Poe's story as an illustration of the functioning of a signifier, says Derrida, the psychoanalytical reading is still blind to the functioning of the signifier *in the narration itself*. In reading "The Purloined Letter" as an *allegory* of the signifier, Lacan, according to Derrida, has made the "signifier" into the story's truth: "The displacement of the signifier is analyzed as a signified, as the recounted object in a short story" (*PT,* 48). Whereas, counters Derrida, it is precisely the *textual* signifier that resists being thus totalized into meaning, leaving an irreducible residue: "The rest, the remnant, would be 'The Purloined Letter,' the text that bears this title, and whose place, like the once more invisible large letters on the map, is not where one was expecting to find it, in the enclosed content of the 'real drama' or in the hidden and sealed interior of Poe's story, but in and as the open letter, the very open letter which fiction is" (*PT,* 64).

2. The actual writings—the books, libraries, quotations, and previous tales—that surround "The Purloined Letter" with a *frame* of (literary) *references*. The story begins in "a little back library, or book-closet" (*Poe,* 199) where the narrator is mulling over a previous conversation on the subject of the two previous instances of Dupin's detective work as told in Poe's two previous tales (the first of which recounted the original meeting between Dupin and the narrator—in a *library*, of course, where both were in search of the same rare book). The story's beginning is thus an infinitely regressing reference to previous writings. And therefore, says Derrida, "nothing begins. Simply a drifting or a disorientation from which one never moves away" (*PT,* 101). Dupin himself is in fact a walking library: books are his "sole luxuries," and the narrator is "astonished" at "the vast extent of his reading" (*Poe,* 106). Even Dupin's last, most seemingly personal words—the venomous lines he leaves in his substitute letter to the Minister—are a quotation; a quotation whose transcription and proper authorship are the last things the story tells us. "But," concludes Derrida, "beyond the quotation marks that surround the entire story, Dupin is obliged to quote this last word in quotation marks, to recount his signature: that is what I wrote to him and how I signed it. What is a signature within quotation marks? Then, within these quotation marks, the seal itself is a quotation within quotation marks. This remnant is still literature" (*PT,* 112–13).

It is by means of these two extra dimensions that Derrida intends to show the crumbling, abysmal, nontotalizable edges of the story's frame. Both of these objections, however, are in themselves more problematic and double-edged than they appear. I shall begin with the second.

"Literature," in Derrida's demonstration, is indeed clearly the beginning, middle, and end—and even the interior—of the purloined letter. But how was this conclusion reached? To a large extent, by listing the books, libraries, and other writings *recounted* in the story. That is, by following the *theme*, not the functioning, of "writing" within "the content of a representation." But if the fact that Dupin signs with a quotation, for example, is for Derrida a sign that "this remnant is still literature," does this not indicate that "literature" has become not the signifier but the *signified* in the story? If the play of the signifier is really to be followed, doesn't it play beyond the range of the *seme* "writing?" And if Derrida criticizes Lacan for making the "signifier" into the story's "signified," is Derrida not here transforming "writing" into "the written" in much the same way? What Derrida calls "the reconstruction of the scene of the signifier as a signified" seems indeed to be "an inevitable process" in the logic of reading the purloined letter.

Derrida, of course, implicitly counters this objection by protesting—twice—that the textual drifting for which Lacan does not account should not be considered "the *real subject* of the tale," but rather the "remarkable ellipsis" of any subject. But the question of the seemingly inevitable slipping from the signifier to the signified still remains. And it remains not as an *objection* to the logic of the frame, but as its fundamental *question*. For if the "paradoxes of parergonal logic" are such that the frame is always being framed by part of its contents, it is precisely this slippage between signifier and signified (which is *acted out* by both Derrida and Lacan against their intentions) that best illustrates those paradoxes. If the question of the frame thus problematizes the object of any interpretation by setting it at an angle or fold with itself, then Derrida's analysis errs not in opposing this paradoxical functioning to Lacan's allegorical reading, but in not following the consequences of its own insight far enough.

Another major point in Derrida's critique is that psychoanalysis, wherever it looks, is capable of finding only itself. The first sentence of *The Purveyor of Truth* is: "Psychoanalysis, supposing, finds itself" (La psychanalyse, à supposer, se trouve). In whatever it turns its attention to, psychoanalysis seems to recognize nothing but its own (Oedipal) schemes. Dupin finds the letter because "he knows that the letter finally *finds itself* where it must *be found* in order to return circularly and adequately to its proper place. This proper place, known to Dupin and to the psychoanalyst who intermittently takes his place, is the place of castration" (*PT*, 60; translation modified). The psychoanalyst's act, then, is one of mere *recognition* of the expected, a recognition that Derrida finds explicitly stated as such by Lacan in the words he quotes from the seminar: "Just so does the purloined letter, like an immense female body, stretch out across the Minister's office when Dupin enters. But just so does he already *expect to find it* (emphasis mine—Derrida) and has only, with his eyes veiled by green lenses, to undress that huge body" (*PT*, 61–62; original emphasis and brackets restored).

But if recognition is a form of blindness, a form of violence to the otherness of the object, it would seem that, by lying in wait between the brackets of the fireplace to catch the psychoanalyst at his own game, Derrida, too, is "recognizing" rather than reading. All the more so, since he must *correct* Lacan's text at another point in order to make it consistent with his critique. For when Lacan notes that the "question of deciding whether Dupin seizes the letter above the mantelpiece as Baudelaire translates, or beneath it, as in the original text, may be abandoned without harm to the inferences of those whose profession is grilling" (*SPL*, 66–67 [p. 342, this volume]), Derrida protests: "Without harm? On the contrary, the harm would be decisive, within the Seminar itself: *on* the mantelpiece, the letter could not have been . . . 'between the legs of the fireplace'" (*PT*, 69). Derrida must thus rectify Lacan's text, eliminate its apparent contradiction, in order to criticize Lacan's enterprise as one of rectification and circular return. What Derrida is doing here, as he himself says, is recognizing a certain classical conception of psychoanalysis: "From the beginning," writes Derrida early in his study, "*we recognize* the classical landscape of applied psychoanalysis" (*PT*, 45; emphasis mine). It would seem that the theoretical frame of reference that governs recognition is a constitutive element in the blindness of any interpretative insight. And it is precisely that frame of reference that allows the analyst to frame the author of the text he is reading for practices whose locus is simultaneously beyond the letter of the text and behind the vision of its reader. The reader is framed by his own frame, but he is not even in possession of his own guilt, since it is that guilt that prevents his vision from coinciding with itself. Just as the author of a criminal frame transfers guilt from himself to another by leaving signs that he hopes will be read as insufficiently erased traces or referents left by the other, the author of any critique is himself framed by his own frame of the other, no matter how guilty or innocent the other may be.

What is at stake here is thus the question of the relation between referentiality and interpretation. And here we find an interesting twist: while criticizing Lacan's notion of the phallus as being *too* referential, Derrida goes on to *use* referential logic against it. This comes up in connection with the letter's famous "materiality" that Derrida finds so odd. "It would be hard to exaggerate here the scope of this proposition on the indivisibility of the letter, or rather on its identity to itself inaccessible to dismemberment, . . . as well as on the so-called materiality of the signifier (the letter) intolerant to partition. But where does this idea come from? A torn-up letter may be purely and simply destroyed, it happens" (*PT*, 86–87; translation modified). The so-called materiality of the signifier, says Derrida, is nothing but an idealization.

But what if the signifier were precisely what puts the polarity "materiality/ideality" in question? Has it not become obvious that neither Lacan's description ("Tear a letter into little pieces, it remains the letter that it is") nor Derrida's description ("A torn-up letter may be purely and simply destroyed, it happens") can be read *literally?* Somehow, a rhetorical fold (*pli*) in the text is there to trip us up whichever way we turn. Especially since the expression "it happens" (*ça arrive*) uses the very word on which the controversy over the letter's *arrival* at its destination turns.

This study of the readings of "The Purloined Letter" has thus arrived at the point where the *word* "letter" no longer has any literality. But what is a letter that has no literality?

It seems that the letter can only be described as that which poses the question of its own rhetorical status. It moves *rhetorically* through the two long, minute studies in which it is presumed to be the literal object of analysis, *without* having any literality. Instead of simply being explained by those analyses, the rhetoric of the letter problematizes the very rhetorical mode of analytical discourse itself.

The letter in the story—and in its readings—acts as a signifier not because its contents are lacking, but because its rhetorical function is not dependent on the identity of those contents. What Lacan means by saying that the letter cannot be divided is thus not that the phallus must remain intact, but that the phallus, the letter, and the signifier *are not substances.* The letter cannot be divided because it only functions *as* a division. It is not something with "an *identity* to itself inaccessible to dismemberment" as Derrida interprets it; it is a *difference.* It is known only in its effects. The signifier is an articulation in a chain, not an identifiable unit. It cannot be known in itself because it is capable of "sustaining itself *only* in a displacement" (*SPL,* 59 [p. 337, this volume]; emphasis mine). It is localized, but only as the nongeneralizable locus of a differential relationship. Derrida, in fact, enacts this law of the signifier in the very act of opposing it:

> Perhaps only one letter need be changed, maybe even less than a letter in the expression: "missing from its place" ["manque à sa place"]. Perhaps we need only introduce a written "a," i.e. without accent, in order to bring out that if the lack *has* its place ["le manque a sa place"] in this atomistic topology of the signifier, that is, if it occupies therein a specific place of definite contours, the order would remain undisturbed. (*PT,* 45)

While thus criticizing the hypostasis of a lack—the letter as the *substance* of an absence—(which is not what Lacan is saying), Derrida is *illustrating* what Lacan *is* saying about both the materiality and the localizability of the signifier *as the mark of difference* by operating on the letter as a material locus of differentiation: by removing the little signifier " ` ," an accent mark that has no meaning in itself.[7]

The letter as a signifier is thus not a thing or the absence of a thing, nor a word or the absence of a word, nor an organ or the absence of an organ, but a *knot* in a structure where words, things, and organs can neither be definably separated nor compatibly combined. This is why the exact representational position of the letter in the Minister's apartment both matters and does not matter. It matters to the extent that sexual anatomical difference creates an irreducible dissymmetry to be accounted for in every human subject. But it does not matter to the extent that the letter is not hidden *in* geometrical space, where the police are looking for it, or in anatomical space, where a literal understanding of psychoanalysis might look for it. It is located "in" a *symbolic* structure, a structure that can only be perceived in its effects and whose effects are perceived as repetition. Dupin finds the letter "in" the symbolic order not because he knows where to look, but because he knows *what to repeat*. Dupin's "analysis" is the *repetition* of the scene that led to the necessity of analysis. It is not an interpretation or an insight, but an act. An act of untying the knot in the structure by means of the repetition of the act of tying it. The word "analyze," in fact, etymologically means "untie," a meaning on which Poe plays in his prefatory remarks on the nature of analysis as "that moral activity which disentangles" (*Poe*, 102). The analyst does not intervene by giving meaning, but by effecting a *dénouement*.

But if the act of (psycho)analysis has no identity apart from its status as a repetition of the structure it seeks to analyze (to untie), then Derrida's remarks against psychoanalysis as being always already *mise en abyme* in the text it studies and as being only capable of finding *itself*, are not objections to psychoanalysis but in fact a profound insight into its very essence. Psychoanalysis is in fact itself the primal scene it is seeking: it is the *first* occurrence of what has been repeating itself in the patient without ever having occurred. Psychoanalysis is not itself the *interpretation* of repetition; it is the repetition of a *trauma of interpretation*—called "castration" or "parental coitus" or "the Oedipus complex" or even "sexuality." It is the traumatic deferred interpretation not *of* an event, but *as* an event that never took place as such. The "primal scene" is not a scene but an *interpretative infelicity* whose result was to situate the interpreter in an intolerable position. And psychoanalysis is the reconstruction of that interpretative infelicity not as *its* interpretation, but as its first and last act. Psychoanalysis has content only insofar as it repeats the dis-content of what never took place.

In a way, I have come back to the question of the letter's destination and of the meaning of the enigmatic "last words" of Lacan's seminar. "The sender," writes Lacan, "receives from the receiver his own message in reverse form. Thus it is that what the 'purloined letter,' nay, the 'letter in sufferance' means is that a letter always arrives at its destination" (*SPL*, 72). What the reversibility of the direction of the letter's movement between sender and received has now come to stand for is precisely the fact, underlined by Derrida as if it were an objection to Lacan, that *there is no position from which the letter's message can be read as an object:* "no neutralization is possible, no general point of view" (*PT,* 106). This is also precisely the "discovery" of psychoanalysis—that the analyst is *involved* (through transference) in the very "object" of his analysis.

Everyone who has held the letter—or even beheld it—including the narrator, has ended up having the letter addressed to him as its destination. The reader is comprehended by the letter: there is no place from which he can stand back and observe *it.* Not that the letter's meaning is subjective rather than objective, but that the letter is precisely that which subverts the polarity subjective/objective, that which makes subjectivity into something whose position in a structure is situated by the passage through it of an object. The letter's destination is thus *wherever it is read,* the place it assigns to its reader as his own partiality. Its destination is not a place, decided a priori by the sender, because the receiver *is* the sender, and the receiver is whoever receives the letter, including nobody. When Derrida says that a letter *can* miss its destination and be disseminated, he reads "destination" as a place that preexists the letter's movement. But if, as Lacan shows, the letter's destination is not its literal addressee, nor even whoever possesses it, but whoever is possessed *by* it, then the very *disagreement* over the meaning of "reaching the destination" is an *illustration* of the nonobjective nature of that "destination." The rhetoric of Derrida's differentiation of his own point of view from Lacan's *enacts* that law:

> Thanks to castration, the phallus always stays in its place in the transcendental topology we spoke of earlier. It is indivisible and indestructible there, like the letter that takes its place. And that is why the *interested* presupposition, never proved, of the letter's materiality as indivisibility was indispensable to this restricted economy, this circulation of propriety.
>
> The difference I am *interested* in here is that, a formula to be read however one wishes, the lack has no place of its own in dissemination. (*PT,* 63; translation modified, emphasis mine)

The play of *interest* in this expression of difference is quite too interesting not to be deliberate. The opposition between the "phallus" and "dissemination" is not between two theoretical objects but between two interested positions. And if sender and receiver are merely the two poles of a reversible message, then Lacan's *substitution* of "destin" for "dessein" in the Crébillon quotation—a misquotation that Derrida finds revealing enough to end his analysis upon—*is* in fact the quotation's message. The sender (*dessein*) and the receiver (*destin*) of the violence that passes between Atreus and Thyestes are *equally* subject to the violence the letter *is.*

The *sentence* "a letter always arrives at its destination" can thus either be simply pleonastic or variously paradoxical: it can mean "the only message I can read is the one I send," "wherever the letter is, is its destination," "when a letter is read, it reads the reader," "the repressed always returns," "I exist only as a reader of the other," "the letter has no destination," and "we all die." It is not any one of these readings, but all of them and others in their very incompatibility, that repeat the letter in its way of reading the act of reading. Far from giving us the seminar's final truth, these last words, and Derrida's readings of them, can only *enact* the impossibility of any ultimate analytical metalanguage, the eternal oscillation between unequivocal undecidability and ambiguous certainty.

NOTES

An extended version of this essay can be found in *Yale French Studies*, nos. 55–56 (1977) (special issue entitled "Literature and Psychoanalysis"), 457–505.

1. In Edgar Allan Poe, *Great Tales and Poems of Edgar Allan Poe* (New York: Pocket Books, 1951), 199–219, hereafter designated as *Poe*.

2. In Jacques Lacan, *Ecrits* (Paris: le Seuil, 1966). Quotations in English are taken, unless otherwise indicated, from the partial translation in *Yale French Studies*, no. 48 (1972) (special issue entitled *French Freud*), 38–72, hereafter designated as *SPL*. [Reprinted, above, in Chapter 6.]

3. This article was published in French in *Poétique* 21 (1975): 96–147, and, somewhat reduced, in English in *Yale French Studies*, no. 52 (1975) (special issue entitled *Graphesis*), 31–113. Unless otherwise indicted, references are to the English version, hereafter designated as *PT*.

4. Lacan, *Ecrits*, 57; translation and emphasis mine. Not translated in *SPL*.

5. Paul de Man, *Blindness and Insight* (New York: Oxford University Press, 1971), 140.

6. Stanley E. Fish, "How Ordinary is Ordinary Language?," *New Literary History* 5 (Autumn, 1973): 52 (emphasis mine).

7. It is perhaps not by chance that the question arises here of whether or not to put the accent on the letter "a." The letter "a" is perhaps the purloined letter par excellence in the writings of all three authors: Lacan's "objet *a*," Derrida's "différance," and Edgar Poe's middle initial, A, taken from his foster father, John Allan.

Deconstructionist Provocateurs

1. The English translation of Derrida's "Structure, Sign, and Play" is more logocentric and less decentered than the original French. Derrida attempts to write in the form of what he speaks: decentered discourse. As a result, Derrida's original French exploits verbal ambiguities and nuances, creates neologisms, makes etymological puns, and employs a dense and elliptical style. Most of this is untranslatable. Alan Bass, the

translator of *Writing and Difference* from which this essay is taken, comments that as a translator he was constantly aware of what he was sacrificing. He reveals that he was "often tempted to use a language that is a compromise between English as we know it and English as he would like it to be in order to capture as much of the original text as possible" (xiv). Bass concludes this cannot be done because such a translation would make sense only if read along with the original French. Discuss how the general problems of translation, as well as the particular problem of Derrida's writings, reflect deconstructionists' interest in the relation between centered and decentered discourse.

2. How closely does Johnson's paradoxical "frame of reference" correspond to Derrida's "movement of supplementarity?"

3. What frame of reference does Johnson's essay use to critique Derrida and Lacan?

4. What is your frame of reference for reading these deconstructionist essays? Can post-structuralist perspectives help us see around the corners of our traditional ways of thinking?

CHAPTER **9**

Humanist Criticism

HUMANISM PLACES THE INDIVIDUAL HUMAN BEING (or, more accurately, the Western concept of "man") at the center of things. The individual, as a free, unified, and autonomous self, expresses his thoughts and feelings through language. Literature and art interact directly. Since humanists view human nature, or the self, as essentially unchanging, they see literature as a fairly stable body of human achievement, a cluster of great works by great authors. While they allow for changes and additions in this literary canon, they hold that the canon, as indeed the individual human being, retains an essential identity over time and space.

Humanist critics evaluate as well as interpret literature. They hold that literature and culture have value insofar as they enhance our experience of life and develop our potential as human beings. They fault much contemporary criticism for being too theoretical and thus divorced from our immediate concerns. They feel such academic criticism is neither useful to students confronting imaginative literature, nor relevant to culture in general.

Instead, humanist critics would emphasize general ideas that they feel give meaning and value to literary study; they would make criticism part of a broader cultural perspective. Their commonsense stance on the relation of literature and life overlaps with certain types of phenomenological and sociological criticism. Indeed, their methodology integrates New Critical close reading with awareness of the intention of the author and awareness of the cultural and philosophical contexts of the work. Words, like disposable cellophane wrappers, say what authors mean. As Lipking writes, humanists want to talk about poems "as if they were things made in a person's head."

The Practice of Theory

LAWRENCE I. LIPKING

Lipking's sly spoof of a deconstructionist reading of Yeats's poem, delivered at the 1983 Association of Departments of English Summer Seminar at Southwest Texas State University, is really a defense of humanism against post-structuralist language theories challenging the authority of the author, the unity of the text, and the centrality of meaning. Lipking does not attack the deconstructionists frontally but instead undercuts their method by poking fun at the confusion and fear we all feel when confronted with an endless multiplicity of possible meanings. His summary of those fears neatly encapsulates post-structuralist aims which humanists oppose: "[Deconstruction] would force us all to reexamine our language, to build curricula in which theory or the contest of ideas played a major part, to question texts instead of passing them on, and to admit to our students that we do not know whether what we are doing has any value."

I HAVE BEEN ASKED to talk about poststructuralism in the classroom—the uses of contemporary literary theory in teaching undergraduates, as well as some of its consequences—and that is what I intend to try to do. But I had better admit at once that in some respects this invitation strikes me as comic. To begin with, you have asked the wrong person. Deconstruction is not my game. It is a bit as if a sheep had been commissioned to say something sympathetic about wolves, from a wolf's point of view. Even with the best intentions, he could not help feeling sheepish—especially when the thought of those teeth crossed his mind. Yet there are worse things for a sheep to try to do, of course, than to think like a wolf. It may give him a fresh perspective on life and even, in some situations, make it possible for him to survive. . . .

A more serious objection to my project, however, might be offered by many theorists themselves: Does theory belong in the classroom? One currently fashionable line of argument would insist that it does not. The truth of a difficult idea, such critics maintain, does not depend on its accessibility to undergraduates or its ability to generate plausible "readings." Theory must be judged by its own standards, not by its immediate practical uses, and not everyone is equally qualified to pursue it. Indeed, the pragmatic American tendency to rush every new idea into the classroom, reducing an adventure of thought to a pedagogical exercise, accounts for the weakness of our theory in relation to the Continental model. Truth stands on a high hill, and salespersons like to take short-cuts. Better to keep our students and theory apart.

This view is of course elitist. That makes it un-American but not nec-essarily wrong. And young theorists seem to me entitled to this line of defense, at least up to a point. The excitement of much current intellec-tual debate about literature has been stirred by the number of questions that remain to be answered. It seems that everything that literary critics once thought they knew about—the author, the reader, the meaning, the structure, the world—is called into question. Nor should one under-estimate the sense of possibility that has resulted. At least a dozen times, during the past few years, some bright young person has told me how fortunate she feels to be alive at a moment when literary theory has come to the forefront, when our own field has replaced philosophy, linguistics, history, psychology at the frontier of knowledge. So much is still to be done! Each time I have replied the same way: how lucky for you that you think that! And however ironic, my comment is also sincere. Young theo-rists must be granted a piece of the future, a chance to work out their ideas without being called instantly to account. They need some time to be muddled, or even to find the truth. And the classroom may not be the best place for that search. Our students do not refute our ideas by failing to understand them—fortunately for us!

But can theory be *kept* from the classroom? Another group of theo-rists strongly denies it. Even the most naive discussion of a literary work, they would argue, is based on assumptions and presuppositions that de-termine what can be seen and what can be talked about. Theory sur-rounds us like the air we breathe. In a recent survey in *New Literary History* (Winter, 1983), which asked a wide sample of scholars how the-ory had affected their teaching, about half the respondents replied that everything they do partakes of theory. "Any study of literature is im-plicitly or explicitly a theoretical study, even if, and in a sense all the more tellingly when, it denies itself as such" (427). Thus literary histo-rians and critics who consider their work unrelated to theory, on this analysis, are self-deluded; they obey principles all the more dogmatic for never being brought out in the open. And the practice of every class-room reflects the assumptions that teachers and students bring with them. There is no way out of this circle. Consider the depth of the epis-temological and psychological problems raised by a reader who says, "I know what I like." Knowing and liking can hardly be taken for granted. From this point of view the classroom necessarily functions as a labora-tory where the usefulness of theories is tested or as an arena where they fight for supremacy. In literary studies there may be good theories and bad theories; but no sanctuary exists in which there are no theories.

To some extent this disagreement about whether theory belongs in the classroom is more apparent than real. It results from different definitions of theory. The first group tends to regard literary theory as a rigorous and strenuous field of knowledge, related to philosophy and often to science, whose object is to formulate axioms and laws of inquiry that may or may not bear any relation to concrete works of literature or common sense. Adherents of this view often justify it by its future. Literary theory, they may say, does not yet exist; and to ask it to demonstrate its usefulness when its very possibility has yet to be established is clearly a hostile demand. But the second group regards theory more descriptively, as the principles or rules of procedure that motivate what we actually do with texts. Seen this way, theory is not only possible but necessary and inevitable. It is the breath and finer spirit of all practice, practice itself in a self-reflective mood. Hence all teaching departs from and turns back into theory, insofar as the purpose of teaching is to make students conscious of what they are doing. Where instinctive reading was, there theory shall be.

These two positions, distinct as they are in logic, may easily coexist in the same mind. In fact they usually do. However reluctant to prostitute his ideas for the sake of undergraduates, the philosopher who is also a teacher can seldom resist the temptation to tell them the truth. And more than one literary theorist conceives her work as bringing reports from the frontline of the classroom to the command post of *Boundary 2*. Theory and practice mingle in unholy alliance like writing papers and grading them or having a taste for reading and getting a job. We make our livings by juggling the two together. It is only natural, then, for professors to feel that their own most stringent ideas are just what the public needs. Nothing is more common, in contemporary American criticism, than a strange combination of elitism and evangelism. On the one hand the critic insists on the right to follow his ideas to their ultimate, most uncanny consequences, free from the constraints of ordinary language, common readers, authorial intentions, historical conventions, or even "the work." On the other hand he often claims that his own work provides an example from which other readers might profit, a hermeneutic model that might redeem the rest of humanity from its shortsightedness. A particularly heady atmosphere of such elitism and evangelism accounts for much of the Early Christian air around New Haven. I do not want to claim that I am about it. Like most other literary critics, I too both take pride in the uniqueness of my insights and think that everyone else ought to share them. But most of the public refuses to rise to our heights, and before we can convert them we must find some common ground. For professors that ground is usually the classroom.

There is another reason why some of the most refined contemporary literary theory seems adaptable to undergraduate teaching. To a high degree the form of that theory *is* practice. However esoteric, most theorists begin with a text, and they arrive at their generalizations not through direct statement but through teasing them out of that text.

Sometimes the text is a philosophical treatise, sometimes a poem, and often, of late, a chance remark, a piece of marginalia, or a fragment in a notebook ("I have forgotten my umbrella"). But whatever the provenance of the text or the use to which the text is put, the method of theory still tends toward close reading. One way of describing recent developments in criticism would be as an intensification of close reading, New Criticism with a vengeance, in which the reading eventually becomes so close—like a page held a few inches from the eye—that the sentences break into fragments and the words dissolve into syllables. ("Atone" turns into "at one" and "therapist" parts to reveal "the rapist.") Most deconstructionists, to be sure, reject this association with close reading. They prefer to regard their enterprise not as a method but as the subversion of any method, not as close reading but as the detonation, primed from within, of any stable reading. So be it. Yet whatever the intention behind the deconstruction of texts, its surface manifestations often bear a remarkable resemblance to old-fashioned explication. Indeed, in standard professional terms (such as the comments of readers for *PMLA*) the main effect of recent theory has been to lend a new impetus and sense of importance to finer and finer close readings. Most of the practical criticism that reaches the *PMLA* editorial board these days begins and ends with theoretical statements, sometimes quite esoteric. But in between lies the reading. Theory itself requires it. And any teacher who is willing to spend a few days mastering the vocabulary of such explications will find much that can be passed on to his or her own students.

How might this work in practice? Poststructuralists have tended to be quite reticent about the use of their ideas in literature courses (aside from courses in literary theory). But let me provide an example. I take, as my exhibit, a poem that gets taught to a great many undergraduates, "Sailing to Byzantium." The choice of this text seems appropriate for several reasons. First, it is canonical. Many teachers know it by heart and probably feel fairly certain that they understand it. Second, it has served more than one generation of critics as a test case for their methods. For several of the New Critics it seemed a perfect verbal icon or type of the concrete universal, a timeless artifact whose form and theme alike expressed the fusion of structure and content, or nature and art, that every great poem embodies. Yet other sorts of critics had no trouble adapting it to their own methods of analysis, as when Northrop Frye observed it in all the archetypes of the comic vision: "the city, the tree, the bird, the community of sages, the geometrical gyre and the detachment from the cyclic world." If any theory of poetry works, it ought to be able to account for "Sailing to Byzantium." Yet a third reason for choosing this poem is that for me, and I suspect for some other readers, it has gone a bit dead. We know what to say about it and may be quite skilled at getting our students to say the same things, but its formal perfection often leaves us cold; and students are wonderfully quick at picking up such attitudes,

about the texts of the poem, its historical and biographical background, or even the minimal information that some teachers will think necessary to allow students to make basic sense of the poem (where is that country? what is Byzantium? how old was W. B. Yeats?). The Norton Anthology is good enough for me. In fact it is far too good, since it insists on providing interpretations—"The theme of this poem, though not the treatment, is similar to that of Keat's *Ode on a Grecian Urn*"—whereas all I want is a glossary or word-hoard that will supply all the possible meanings of "perne" and "gyre" as well as their etymologies. The rest does not matter, because in this class "Sailing to Byzantium" will not be an illustration of the doctrine in *A Vision,* an autobiographical testament, an example of a poetic genre, a symbol of art, a verbal icon, or anything else except a piece of language. Students who have done homework on the "sources" or "meaning" of the poem will be told to shut up or, more subtly, questioned until it becomes obvious that they do not know what they are talking about. I will give no quizzes here. The language is all that counts.

But does "Sailing to Byzantium" make any sense when regarded strictly as a piece of language? That question is exactly what provides the energy for class discussion. *"Does this make sense?"* I ask again and again; and, unlike older critics and teachers, I do not coerce my students by implying that the perfect coherence and correctness of the sense will become manifest if they work hard enough to decipher it. One of my own teachers used to say, "It is not the poem that is on trial here but you"; in this class, though, the poem is on trial. We notice, for instance, its tendency to contradict itself. When the class is asked why soul should "louder sing / For every tatter in its mortal dress," one student answers that the soul is desperately singing to try to drown out the sound of ripping, and another student thinks that the soul is singing in celebration of those tatters, which bring it closer to freedom; and, after other students have had their say, we do not try to resolve this contradiction or find the proper meaning as it appeared to Yeats. Instead we observe the duplicity of that word "for," which can signify either "in spite of" or "on behalf of" as well as many other things. Thus the line does not make sense, if by sense we understand a single unequivocal meaning or even the Aristotelian logic that asserts that nothing can be both itself and not itself at the same time. Language goes its own way; it does not obey Aristotle or Yeats or Humpty-Dumpty.

Read in this light, a surprising amount of "Sailing to Byzantium" turns out not to make any sense or to make so many senses that no interpretation can make sense of them. I will not rehearse the difficulty of generations of schoolchildren with the syntax of "Nor is there singing school but studying" (probably that was what they asked the old man about when he walked through the long schoolroom questioning). Does it imply that there is, or is not, a singing school? My students will not be forced to choose. Is the artifice of eternity something permanent (an eternal artifice) or something evanescent (an illusion without any substance)? My students will not have to make up their minds. What is the syntax of the opening "That" (which Yeats himself once said was the worst syntax he ever wrote)? In this classroom all answers will be entertained.

Perhaps this sounds like total permissiveness, an extreme version of the situation encouraged by some reader-response theorists in which each student is invited to use the text in order to make up some poem of his or her own, through free association or a homemade personal identity kit. But that is not my scheme. I do not ask my class, "Does this make sense *for you?*" Instead, the more austere form of the question—"Does this make sense?"—directs attention away from personal responses and toward the condition of language that makes variant responses possible or even inevitable. The cacophony of voices in my classroom does not result from rampant individualism. Rather, it reflects the cacophony within the language of the poem—its multiple, uncontrollable meanings. Anything goes, not because I have permitted it, but because language itself, as an arbitrary and unstable system of differences, must be capable of saying anything.

Nor does this cacophony stop at the level of the phrase and the sentence. It applies as well to the whole structure of the poem, to the story or allegory of meaning it tries to construct. In my classroom we spend most of our time looking squarely at a "fact" that most other classrooms spend all their time trying to avoid. To put it simply: in strict logical terms most of "Sailing to Byzantium" does not work. The elementary polarities that seem to provide its frame—the dialectic of "that country" and Byzantium, of young and old, of time and timelessness, of body and soul, above all of nature and art—do not hold up under a careful reading. Thus the schematic contrast of "Whatever is begotten, born, and dies" with "what is past, or passing, or to come" does not satisfy my students. They notice that some of the parallelism is false; that "lives," for instance, would match "passing" much better than "born" does and that the relation of "begotten" to "past" is far from obvious. Even the neat contrast between "dies" and "to come," the time-bound state of the living and the eternity of the artifice, does not quite work, since the fact that birds die does not keep their songs too from being repeated eternally by later generations. The poem has deliberately fudged such issues. My students begin to realize that their own confusions respond to something confused or ungraspable in "Sailing to Byzantium" itself.

A similar analysis might be applied to every element of the poem. I will spare you the details. But one point of internal contradiction is so important and obvious that it is noticed by a great many students, and even some critics. When the speaker claims that "Once out of nature I shall never take / My bodily form from any natural thing," he seems to ignore the blatant fact that every bodily form must be taken from nature, whether the form of a bird or simply the golden form embodied by an artist. In a famous letter, Sturge Moore told Yeats that "Sailing to Byzantium" had let him down in the fourth stanza, "as such a goldsmith's bird is as much nature as a man's body, especially if it only sings like Homer and Shakespeare of what is past or passing or to come to Lords and Ladies"; and Yeats was impressed enough by the point to write "Byzantium," since Moore had showed him "that the idea needed exposition." But neither Moore nor Yeats saw how deep the criticism went. The false opposition between nature and art begins not in the fourth stanza but in the first, where the description of "nature" is thoroughly conditioned by "art." The lushness and prettiness of "that country," where the young are always in one another's arms and the salmon are always running, has a basic artificiality that only a poet could overlook. No student overlooks it. The poem composes a colorful postcard that resembles Ireland no more than a travel brochure. Indeed, the language itself confesses its interest in "sensual music"—not the unmediated country of the senses but the senses patterned by art. Insofar as any form can be "out of nature," the form of the first stanza already achieves that state. Hence the speaker's departure from nature, attained with such seeming difficulty, is actually always already present, contained in the framework or dialectic that allows the poem to begin. It is easy to leave nature if you have never been there in the first place—or impossible if you have been.

Seen in this way, the opposition of nature and art in "Sailing to Byzantium" may be understood for what it is: not a reference to anything existing in "the world" but a system of differences in which each term gives meaning to the other. That country and Byzantium are equally unreal; they acquire significance only by being contrasted with each other. Hence a student who has never learned to equate that country with Ireland or Byzantium with what Yeats said about it may well have an advantage in analyzing the poem; no irrelevant images or "facts" will interfere with the self-contained system of language that is all we can know or need to know.

At this point of the discussion my students, if they have been paying attention, have been born into structuralism. But we have not yet accounted for the full extent to which "Sailing to Byzantium" does not work—the unease with which we perceived not only the artificiality of its system of differences but the slippage or instability in the system. It is time to enter the poststructuralist age. Let us read even closer.

We come back to "That." By this time even that somewhat jaundiced engineer in the back row is ready to wave his hand and explain the point of "That": it contrasts with "this," the holy city to which the speaker has sailed, about which we know the one important thing: it is the opposite of "That." But teacher is not so easy to please. Once again I ask my magic question: Does this make sense? How can a "that" be specified so soon, before the system of the poem or of language has established a place for it? Doesn't it seem to propose that "That" might exist prior to a system or syntax, as if a "that" could be there without a "this"? After a long pause, one of the brighter students suggests that the speaker seems to be point-ing—pointing toward something outside of language, something we cannot see. The footnote tells us "Ireland." But "Ireland" is also a mere form of language, a word that substitutes for whatever the speaker is pointing at, a word that does not satisfy our search for what the speaker sees. Perhaps later we will know.

But later never comes. The absent referent of "That" will never ma-terialize on the page. Nor is there any evidence that the speaker himself ever knew exactly what he was talking about. By pointing outside the sys-tem of language, the poem creates the illusion of a presence somewhere else. But that presence is communicated only through absences and de-ferrals, the endless strategies through which language tempts us to be-lieve that we will arrive at a meaning. There is never an end to this process. It is not only the poem that does not work but the whole system of language to which it belongs. No matter how long the class stays on after the bell, it will never explain away *that*. No, it does not make sense.

Perhaps I can clarify this point by reading the allegory of "Sailing to Byzantium" once more, as a struggle between the medium of language in which the poet lives and the pure significance he hopes some day to find. At the moment his sense is still entrapped in words. Consider the resonance of a phrase like "Fish, flesh, or fowl." It asks for an analysis that has nothing to do with meaning and everything to do with sounds. The consonants of the first noun are modulated by the "l" introduced in the second, and that "l" then resolves the phrase as a whole. At the same time the vowels gradually open until the initial pinched "i" has length-ened into the diphthong "ow." Reverse the sequence—"fowl, flesh, or fish"—and the phrase would become harsh and constricted; substitute "meat" for "flesh" and it becomes grotesque. What shall we conclude? Clearly the effect depends not on meaning, let alone "unageing intel-lect"; it would not survive translation to another language, like Byzantine Greek. Rather, it depends on "sensual music," the pleasant way that cer-tain cadences strike the ear. Linguistically, one might say that the empha-sis has fallen on the signifier, not the signified, on the words, not their significance.

But such music does not seem good enough for the speaker. He wants another artistic world in which the signifier and the signified are one and the music explains itself. Byzantium, as he conceives it, is such a world. There the sages are at once the medium and the message, the ar-tifact and its interpreters. They speak directly to the soul and teach it how to sing without the need for any mediation, in a universal language (there is no indication that Yeats thought his soul would need to learn Greek in order to talk to its masters). In Byzantium the arbitrariness of the sign disappears, and the song itself makes the world of which it sings.

Yet the poem itself does not, of course, arrive there. It is only "sailing" to Byzantium. At best it projects that state of a seamless union between word and meaning, subject and object, signifier and signified, into the future. It does not, it cannot, reach that state. Language does not allow such perfection or such closure. As we have already seen, the poem contains the evidence of its own betrayal, a deconstruction of its own distinctions between nature and art or time and the timeless. "The idea," Yeats thought, "needed exposition"; but that exposition could only be another poem, which leads in turn to another poem in an infinite regress of explanations and resolutions that never quite work. We do not command our own language, and we cannot escape it. Hence the true "meaning" of "Sailing to Byzantium," as revealed by rigorous close reading, is the impossibility of ever arriving at a true meaning. The closer we come to Byzantium, the more we discover that we have never left home. The soul will never stand outside itself and "know what it is." At home and abroad we swim in a sea of language.

At this point the class is still, and I realize that for the past few minutes I have done all the talking. Nothing to say, at such moments, but "Class dismissed." But fellow teachers may want to ask a few more questions. What use has this exercise been? Does it furnish a model of teaching literature that ought to be exported to other classrooms? What are its implications for undergraduate education or for the future of our profession? These are hard questions, and I will not pretend that I have all the answers. But a theory so dedicated to exploring the self-consciousness and inner contradictions of literature can hardly avoid the demand to be self-conscious about its own practice. If poststructuralism turns out not to have been a mere fashion or elite amusement, then its consequences will eventually affect us all. Let us try some tentative comments on where this analysis leads.

To begin with, I will admit something that most of you have already suspected: my account of that classroom session was rather too neat. Perhaps it was even phony. For it left out one crucial element that every teacher knows about, the resistance of students. I do not mean only dumb resistance, the silence or apathy of those who have not done the reading or who will never be persuaded, by any means, to pay attention to something as hard and beautiful and unlike a videogame as a poem by Yeats. I mean also the resistance of the good students, those who genuinely take pleasure in some poetry and want to understand it. Those students are also uneasy. Many of them were intrigued by "Sailing to Byzantium" when they read it—some of them even loved it—and came to class prepared to share their pleasure, to learn more about Yeats and his kind of poetry, to grasp the theme and story better, and to find out how the poem works. They may also have looked forward to praising it or to hearing why Yeats was "great." But some of them now perceive the class as having been a subtle—or not so subtle—attack on "Sailing to Byzantium," an analysis of how the poem does not make sense and does not work. Nor are they consoled to hear, now and in later classes, that all the other poems they like do not work in just the same way. They resisted the teacher while he was asking questions, and now that he has finished they continue to resist him. On the final examination they will ignore the classroom discussion and put down some chestnuts gathered from the Norton Anthology. ("In his old age, the poet repudiates the world of biological change, . . . putting behind him images of breeding and sensuality to turn to 'monuments of unageing intellect,' in a world of art and artifice outside of time.") They will get a B−.

How much notice does a theorist need to take of such resistance? The answer will vary from teacher to teacher. If self-satisfied, he may not notice it at all; if skillful, she may overcome it; if discouraged, he may resolve to give up teaching entirely or to stop mixing theory with practice. But a young teacher might become more self-conscious about her theory. One respondent to the *NLH* survey, a graduate student who had just taught his first course in theory, was honest enough to confess that it did not live up to his expectations: the students "had serious difficulties in the 'application' of theory to literary texts" because of "a marked resistance to the positing of representation as a theoretical problem" (434). I like that graduate student and have hopes for his future. But the problems he faces with undergraduates will not go away.

Let me state them more fully. The power of the poststructuralist reading, even in the sheepish version I have given of it, lies in its relentless questioning of texts. In one respect it can afford to pursue its analysis much further than conventional critical methods can, since it does not consider itself obliged to offer a defense of the value or coherence of the works it questions. The New Critical program included a vision of the uniqueness of literature and, at one extreme, even a kind of political and religious salvation through poetry; I. A. Richards, its distant father, thought that learning how to read better might help people to understand each other better and perhaps save the world. Most poststructuralists consider such ideas crackpot. Since "language speaks, not man" (in Heidegger's celebrated wordplay), our efforts to master ourselves by mastering language are bound to fail. Moreover, the effort to confer a special privilege on literary language by insisting on its ineffable, incarnational superiority to all other writing or on its more immediate contact with "the world's body" seems a basic misunderstanding of the principles of writing, which is not related to any hierarchy of values or to any world except the world of writing. Poststructuralists know better. They know that literary works cannot be traced to any point of origin (no author; no reality) and that literature is just like all other kinds of writing, only more so (the more so is what makes it interesting to study). The methods by which poetry tries to convince us that we are in the presence of someone, some emotion, some immediate experience are interesting precisely because of the manifold ways in which they fail. The answer ends, the questioning goes on.

This line of thought does have power. Anyone who has ever written a poem can testify, if honest, to how much of it escapes control, to how many internal contradictions must be papered over. Language runs away with us. The same thing is true of freshman papers, and the poems of Yeats. And by refusing to deny the fissures and instabilities of writing, even when that writing is endorsed by a brand name like Shakespeare or Yeats, the teacher and student alike can become conscious of the problems they share with every creature who writes. For many young theorists that consciousness has been liberating. It seems to offer a way not merely of seeing literature but of seeing through it. And it also corresponds to the skepticism about authority, the doubt that the elders knew what they were talking about, that now seems so much a part of American life. If some of the idealistic students in my classroom are disappointed at watching Yeats torn down, a few of the others are delighted that the poem is at last getting what it deserves: a long, hard look that spares nothing. The poet himself, after all, advised us to cast a cold eye.

To what extent such skepticism represents a reasoned position, and to what extent it reflects an impatience with learning, a hostility toward the past, or even a general resentment on the part of the young and unemployed toward those whose jobs have given them an interest in preserving civilization is a problem far too difficult for me to solve. But in the more limited arena of literary criticism, the politics of interpretation undoubtedly plays a significant role. For anyone who reads much criticism today, one striking phenomenon is how many essays end with a celebration of indeterminacy and a denunciation of all interpreters who think they can find the key to a piece of writing. My own reading of "Sailing to Byzantium" could easily be adapted to this vein by heaping scorn on earlier critics who thought they had discovered its meaning. These conclusions often puzzle me for two related reasons. First, I am never quite sure who *are* those benighted dogmatists who stir such rage. Most of the conservative literary historians and critics I know are modest people who would never dream of saying that their work had put an end to interpretation once and for all. Second, the denunciation of dogmatism often concluded an example of close reading that seems very sure of itself, very closed to alternative possibilities. Many of you will have noticed that my allegorizing of "Sailing to Byzantium" as a text about the very gap between signifier and signified that it pretends to resolve was advanced with no ifs, ands, or buts. It is always someone else's dogma that seems at issue.

I do not accuse such critics of bad faith. The more sophisticated among them would readily admit their own blind spots, on the grounds that writing itself depends on presuppositions and biases, built right into the frame that is the condition of its possibility. But this admission seldom results in much fellow feeling or charity toward the blind spots of others. Many of our best young critics seem to feel oppressed. Traditional methods of reading, and sometimes the prestige of the literary canon itself, hang like a weight on the spirit. I always respect such feelings. While the oppressed may be guilty of injustice to others, they are seldom wrong about their own oppression. But whatever the cause, much of the current practice of poststructuralism bears an overt political message: authority is not to be trusted. In strict political terms, as many have noted, this message can hardly be considered threatening, since it almost never is accompanied by a program or by any agreement about what should be done to change the situation. A refusal to accept Yeats's intention as relevant to "Sailing to Byzantium" does not get us much closer to manning the barricades. Yet a teaching founded on such principles would eventually change our profession. It would force us all to reexamine our language, to build curricula in which theory or the contest of ideas played a major part, to question texts instead of passing them on, and to admit to our students that we do not know whether what we are doing has any value.

I do not think it will happen. One reason, of course, is simply the power and torpor of institutions. There is something comical about the idea that most professors or literary historians might suddenly stop what they were doing, convert from Saul to Paul or Jack to Jacques, begin reading theory, and start to speak in tongues of *paragones* or *écriture*. Moreover, the political moment seems wrong. Not long ago I heard an eloquent young deconstructionist, trained in the sixties, argue that the old literary faiths seem obsolete to people of his generation, only to be interrupted by a recent Ph.D. who protested that to people of her generation his jargon sounded like nonsense. The times, they are changing—backwards.

But there seem to me two better reasons why poststructuralism, at least in its purest and most rigorous forms, does not have a particularly bright future in American classrooms; and on this sheeplike note I shall end. The first is that, in my own admittedly fallible and tentative opinion, the theoretical arguments of deconstruction do not support the ardent claims on its behalf. Even if we grant its premises, not much seems to follow from them. I urge you not to take my word for this. In the past few months some introductory primers to deconstruction have been pouring out of the presses. They are accessible and, for the most part, clearly written, and they can be read in an evening. Anyone who grumbles about deconstruction without quite knowing what it is should certainly read one. Then, if you like, you too can teach your students how to make sense of a poem—or how not to make it.

But you will not find all the answers in those books; and I do not think you will find them in [Jacques] Derrida either. Specifically, what deconstruction (and its adaptations to literary theory) has not yet achieved is a way of addressing the concerns of those bright, resistant undergraduates whom I spoke of before. Let me put some words in their mouths. Why are we supposed to talk about poems as if they were only pieces of language? Can't we talk about them instead in other ways, as if they were things made in a person's head, or pictures, or feelings, or one person talking to another? Are there some reasons why all these other ways are wrong, something that you're not telling us (you seem very pleased with yourself)? Or is it just that you're afraid that if we talk about those things you won't be able to control the discussion?

Next: Why aren't we allowed to talk about "Sailing to Byzantium," or even about a novel, as if it had something to do with life? You explained to us that novels can give us only a screen of words, not life firsthand, and we see that; but why can't we talk about both, about life and the words? Anyway, would the words mean anything at all if we didn't sense life behind them? You bore us with all your words. We want to know how to live, and that's why we learned how to read in the first place.

Finally: Did you really mean it when you said that writing is never finished and never makes sense, just like our papers? Aren't our papers different from "Sailing to Byzantium"? Don't you honestly think that "Sailing to Byzantium" is a great poem, better than the article that you wrote about it in *Diacritics*? Then why won't you tell us why? Why did you become a teacher in the first place? We think that we'll switch to economics.

Kids can be so cruel.

I do not think that all these questions are completely fair; and some of them you will find answered, more or less ingeniously, in the books I have mentioned. But the present state of deconstruction does not seem comfortable with such questions and tends to answer them quite indifferently. The issues of pluralism, representation, and evaluation have been put in abeyance, at least until someone in Paris rediscovers them. Thus theory decrees that readers must fend for themselves. If a conflict arises between current speculations and the questions raised by students, many poststructuralists would prefer to replace the students rather than the theory. I honor their choice. But it also means that their theories must stop at the doors of the classroom. To a large extent that has happened. Despite the buzz and swarm of theorists in motion and the alarm they set off in many circles, most of the practice of teaching literature to undergraduates still goes on in the same old way. Deconstructionists and their enemies tend to agree that theory is too high a thing to be grounded in adolescents.

Yet a healthier reason for the uncertain state of deconstruction in the classroom may also be put forward: it has too many rivals. Up to this point I have been talking about contemporary literature theory as if it were identical with the term "poststructuralism" and about poststructuralism as if it meant the same thing as deconstruction. That was convenient for my argument and made it possible for me to give this talk. But it does not correspond to reality (even that weak form of reality connected with theory). The most prominent feature of the American theoretical scene, as most of us know, is its diversity: semioticians, reader responders, Marxists, psychoanalysts, feminists, phenomenologists, hermeneuts, mythographers, not to mention some unreconstructed New Critics and neo-Aristotelians. There is even one growing school of theorists devoted to the proposition that theory is useless and ought to be discontinued. The number and wealth of these schools may be considered a source of dismay or of pride. A European might conclude that every American concern eventually turns into a supermarket. But to me our republic of theory signifies health.

Indeed, what gives me most hope about our younger theorists, the generation just now emerging, is that so many are frankly eclectic. In strict logical terms, deconstruction may or may not be compatible with feminism, archetypal criticism, Saint Thomas Aquinas, word processing, and what goes on in the classroom; but flexible minds join points even further apart. The practice of theory will be the result of such joining. In the most recent MLA *Job Lists,* a considerable number of entries end with the words "and theory": medieval literature and theory, Victorian poetry and theory, contemporary film and theory, and so on. Those listings may be illogical, but to me they seem just right. For the future of theory in our profession depends on those "and"s: the way that our bright young people test their ideas, not in the purity of a vacuum chamber, but in the cunning corridors of history and the murk of undergraduate minds. I think they will do it well.

Humanist Provocateurs

1. Like all parodies, Lipking's imitation of deconstructive criticism somewhat distorts what it imitates. What are these distortions?

2. Lipking asserts that deconstruction "would force us all to reexamine our language, to build curricula in which theory or the contest of ideas played a major part, to question texts instead of passing them on, and to admit to our students that we do not know whether what we are doing has any value." Take up his list point-by-point: Which of these would you as a critic not be willing to do?

SELECTED BIBLIOGRAPHY

Handbooks on Critical Theory

*Belsey, Catherine. *Critical Practice*. London: Methuen, 1980.

Culler, Jonathan. *Structuralist Poetics: Structuralism, Linguistics, and the Study of Literature*. Ithaca: Cornell University Press, 1975.

*Eagleton, Terry. *Literary Theory: An Introduction*. Minneapolis: University of Minnesota Press, 1983.

Ellis, John M. *The Theory of Literary Criticism: A Logical Analysis*. Berkeley: University of California Press, 1974.

Felperin, Howard. *Beyond Deconstruction: The Uses and Abuses of Literary Theory*. Oxford: Clarendon, 1985.

Hawkes, Terence. *Structuralism and Semiotics*. Berkeley: University of California Press, 1977.

*Jefferson, Ann, and David Robey, eds. *Modern Literary Theory: A Comparative Introduction*. New York: Barnes and Noble, 1982.

Lentricchia, Frank. *After the New Criticism*. Chicago: University of Chicago Press, 1980.

New Criticism

*Booth, Wayne C. *The Rhetoric of Fiction*. Chicago: University of Chicago Press, 1961.

*Brooks, Cleanth. *The Well-Wrought Urn: Studies in the Structure of Poetry*. 1947. New York: Harcourt Brace, 1956.

*Brooks, Cleanth, and Robert Penn Warren, eds. *Understanding Poetry*. New York: Henry Holt, 1938.

Eliot, T. S. *Selected Essays*. New York: Harcourt Brace, 1963.

Empson, William. *Seven Types of Ambiguity*. New York: New Directions, 1947.

*Indicates a useful text with which to start one's study.

Heilman, Robert B. *This Great Stage*. Baton Rouge: Louisiana State University Press, 1948.

*Kermode, Frank. *Romantic Image*. London: Routledge & Kegan Paul, 1957.

Krieger, Murray. *The New Apologists for Poetry*. Minneapolis: University of Minnesota Press, 1956.

Ransom, John Crowe. *The New Criticism*. New York: New Directions, 1941.

*Richards, I. A. *Principles of Literary Criticism*. 1925. London: Routledge & Kegan Paul, 1959.

Tate, Allen. *Collected Essays*. Denver: Alan Swallow, 1959.

*Wimsatt, W. K., Jr. *The Verbal Icon*. 1958. Lexington: University of Kentucky Press, 1967. Includes "The Affective Fallacy" and "The Intentional Fallacy" co-authored with Monroe C. Beardsley.

Phenomenological Criticism

Blanchot, Maurice. *The Siren's Song: Selected Essays by Maurice Blanchot*. Ed. Gabriel Josipovici. Trans. Sacha Rabinovitch. Bloomington: Indiana University Press, 1982.

Heidegger, Martin. *Poetry, Language, Thought*. Trans. Albert Hofstadter. New York: Harper & Row, 1971.

*Hirsch, E. D., Jr. *Validity in Interpretation*. New Haven: Yale University Press, 1967.

Ingarden, Roman. *The Literary Work of Art: An Investigation on the Borderlines of Ontology, Logic, and Theory of Literature*. Trans. George G. Grabowicz. Evanston, Ill.: Northwestern University Press, 1973.

Lawell, Sarah N. *Critics of Consciousness: The Existential Structures of Literature*. Cambridge, Mass.: Harvard University Press, 1968.

Magliola, Robert R. *Phenomenology and Literature: An Introduction*. West Lafayette, Ind.: Purdue University Press, 1977.

Merleau-Ponty, Maurice. *The Visible and the Invisible*. Evanston, Ill.: Northwestern University Press, 1968.

*Miller, J. Hillis. *Charles Dickens: The World of his Novels*. Cambridge, Mass.: Harvard University Press, 1958.

———. *The Disappearance of God*. Cambridge, Mass.: Harvard University Press, 1963.

Poulet, Georges. *Studies in Human Time*. Trans. Elliott Coleman. Baltimore: Johns Hopkins University Press, 1977.

Ricoeur, Paul. *The Conflict of Interpretations: Essays on Hermeneutics*. Evanston, Ill.: Northwestern University Press, 1974.

Valdés, Mario J. *Shadows in the Cave: A Phenomenological Approach to Literary Criticism Based on Hispanic Texts*. Toronto: University of Toronto Press, 1982.

Archetypal Theory

*Bodkin, Maude. *Archetypal Patterns in Poetry: Psychological Studies of Imagination*. London: Oxford University Press, 1934.

Campbell, Joseph. *The Hero with a Thousand Faces*. 1959. Princeton: Princeton University Press, 1968.

Cornford, F. M. *The Origin of Attic Comedy.* Ed. Theodor H. Gaster. 1949. Garden City, N.Y.: Anchor, 1961.

Eliade, Mircea. *The Myth of the Eternal Return or, Cosmos and History.* Trans. Willard R. Trask. Princeton: Princeton University Press, 1954.

Fiedler, Leslie. *Love and Death in the American Novel.* 1960. Rev. ed. New York: Stein and Day, 1966.

Frye, Northrop. *Fables of Identity: Studies in Poetic Mythology.* New York: Harcourt, Brace & World, 1963.

———. *A Natural Perspective: The Development of Shakespearean Comedy and Romance.* New York: Harcourt, Brace & World, 1965.

Girard, René. *Violence and the Sacred.* Trans. Gregory Patrick. Baltimore: Johns Hopkins University Press, 1977.

Graves, Robert. *The White Goddess: A Historical Grammar of Poetic Myth.* 1948. New York: Octagon, 1972.

Harrison, Jane. *Themis.* 1912. Boston: Carrier Pigeon, 1963.

*Jung, C. J. *The Archetypes and the Collective Unconscious.* Trans. R. F. C. Hull. 2d ed. Princeton: Princeton University Press, 1968.

Murray, Gilbert. *Euripides and his Age.* 2d ed. London: Oxford University Press, 1946.

Pratt, Annis. *Archetypal Patterns in Women's Fiction.* Bloomington: Indiana University Press, 1982.

Sebeok, Thomas A., ed. *Myth: A Symposium.* Bloomington: Indiana University Press, 1955.

Smith, Henry Nash. *Virgin Land: American West as Symbol and Myth.* 1950. Cambridge, Mass.: Harvard University Press, 1970.

Strelka, Joseph P., ed. *Literary Criticism and Myth.* [University Park]: Pennsylvania State University Press, 1980.

Turner, Victor. *Dramas, Fields, and Metaphors: Symbolic Action in Human Society.* Ithaca: Cornell University Press, 1974.

———. *From Ritual to Theatre: The Human Seriousness of Play.* Performing Arts, 1982.

*Vickery, John, ed. *Myth and Literature: Contemporary Theory and Practice.* Lincoln: University of Nebraska Press, 1969.

Genre Criticism

Bruss, Elizabeth W. *Autobiographical Acts: The Changing Situation of a Literary Genre.* Baltimore: Johns Hopkins University Press, 1977.

Colie, Rosalie L. *The Resources of Kind: Genre Theory in the Renaissance.* Ed. Barbara K. Lewalski. Berkeley: University of California Press, 1973.

Crane, R. S. "The Concept of Plot and the Plot of *Tom Jones.*" In *Critics and Criticism,* ed. R. S. Crane. Chicago: University of Chicago Press, 1952.

*Debrow, Heather. *Genre.* London: Methuen, 1982.

Eichenbaum, Boris. "The Theory of the Formal Method." In *Russian Formalist Criticism,* ed. Lee T. Lemon and Marion J. Reis. Lincoln: University of Nebraska Press, 1965.

Empson, William. *Some Versions of Pastoral.* New York: New Directions, 1974.

*Fowler, Alastair. *Kinds of Literature: An Introduction to the Theory of Genres and Modes.* Cambridge, Mass.: Harvard University Press, 1982.

443

*Frye, Northrop. *Anatomy of Criticism: Four Essays*. Princeton: Princeton University Press, 1957.

Hernandi, Paul. *Beyond Genre: New Directions in Literary Classification*. Ithaca: Cornell University Press, 1972.

Hirsch, E. D. Chap. 3, "The Concept of Genre." In *Validity in Interpretation*. New Haven: Yale University Press, 1967.

Rosmarin, Adena. *The Power of Genre*. Minneapolis: University of Minnesota Press, 1985.

Smith, Barbara Herrnstein. *Poetic Closure: A Study of How Poems End*. Chicago: University of Chicago Press, 1968.

Todorov, Tzvetan. *The Fantastic: A Structural Approach to a Literary Genre*. Trans. Richard Howard. Ithaca: Cornell University Press, 1975.

*———. "The Origin of Genres." *New Literary History* 8 (1976): 159–70.

Tomashevsky, Boris. "Literary Genres." Trans. L. M. O'Toole. *Formalism: History, Comparison, Genre*. Russian Poetics in Translation, no. 5. Colchester, Essex: University of Essex Press, 1978.

STRUCTURALIST-SEMIOTIC CRITICISM

A Barthes Reader. Ed. Susan Sontag. New York: Hill and Wang, 1982.

Barthes, Roland. *Image, Music, Text*. Trans. Stephen Heath. New York: Hill and Wang, 1977.

———. "An Introduction to the Structural Analysis of Narrative." *New Literary History* 6 (1974): 137–72.

*———. *Mythologies*. Trans. Annette Lavers. 1957. New York: Hill and Wang, 1972.

———. *S/Z*. Trans. Richard Miller. New York: Hill and Wang, 1974.

Benveniste, Emile. *Problems in General Linguistics*. Coral Gables: University of Miami Press, 1973.

Blonsky, Marshall, ed. *On Signs*. Baltimore: Johns Hopkins University Press, 1985.

Chatman, Seymour. *Story and Discourse*. Ithaca: Cornell University Press, 1978.

Coward, Rosalind, and John Ellis. *Language and Materialism: Developments in Semiology and the Theory of the Subject*. London: Routledge & Kegan Paul, 1977.

*Culler, Jonathan. *Structuralist Poetics: Structuralism, Linguistics, and the Study of Literature*. Ithaca: Cornell University Press, 1975.

———. *The Pursuit of Signs: Semiotics, Literature, Deconstruction*. Ithaca: Cornell University Press, 1981.

Deely, John. *Introducing Semiotics: Its History and Doctrine*. Bloomington: Indiana University Press, 1982.

Eco, Umberto. *A Theory of Semiotics*. Bloomington: Indiana University Press, 1976.

Ehrmann, Jacques, ed. *Structuralism*. Special Issue. *Yale French Studies* 36–37 (1966): Published as *Structuralism*. Ed. Jacques Ehrmann. Garden City, N.Y.: Doubleday-Anchor, 1970.

Elam, Keir. *The Semiotics of Theatre and Drama*. London: Methuen, 1980.

Fiske, John, and John Hartley: *Reading Television*. London: Methuen, 1978.

Genette, Gerard. *Narrative Discourse: An Essay in Method*. Trans. Jane E. Lewin. 1972. Ithaca: Cornell University Press, 1980.

Greimas, A. J., et al., eds. *Sign, Language, Culture*. The Hague: Mouton, 1970.

*Hawkes, Terence. *Structuralism and Semiotics.* Berkeley and Los Angeles: University of California Press, 1977.

Heath, Stephen. *Questions of Cinema.* Bloomington: Indiana University Press, 1981.

Jacobson, Roman. "Linguistics and Poetics." In *Style in Language,* ed. Thomas A. Sebeok. Cambridge, Mass.: MIT Press, 1960. Also in *Essays on the Language of Literature,* ed. Seymour Chatman and Samuel R. Levin. Boston: Houghton Mifflin, 1967.

———. *Verbal Art, Verbal Sign, Verbal Time.* Minneapolis: University of Minnesota Press, 1984.

Jameson, Fredric. *The Prison House of Language: A Critical Account of Structuralism and Russian Formalism.* Princeton: Princeton University Press, 1972.

Kristeva, Julie. *Desire in Language: A Semiotic Approach to Literature and Art.* Trans. Thomas Gora et al. New York: Columbia University Press, 1980.

Kurzweil, Edith. *The Age of Structuralism: Levi-Strauss to Foucault.* New York: Columbia University Press, 1980.

Lane, Michael, ed. *Introduction to Structuralism.* New York: Basic Books, 1979.

Lévi-Strauss, Claude. *The Savage Mind.* Chicago: University of Chicago Press, 1966.

*Lodge, David. *Working with Structuralism: Essays and Reviews on Nineteenth and Twentieth-Century Literature.* London: Routledge & Kegan Paul, 1981.

MacCabe, Colin. *Tracking the Signifier: Theoretical Essays: Film, Linguistics, Literature.* Minneapolis: University of Minnesota Press, 1985.

*Macksey, Richard, and Eugenio Donato, eds. *The Structuralist Controversy: The Languages of Criticism and the Sciences of Man.* Baltimore: Johns Hopkins University Press, 1972.

On Narrative. Critical Inquiry 7 (1980).

Peirce, Charles S. *Semiotics and Significs.* Ed. C. S. Hardwick. Bloomington: Indiana University Press, 1977.

Piaget, Jean. *Structuralism.* Ed. and trans. Chaninah Maschler. New York: Basic, 1970.

Propp, Vladimir. *The Morphology of the Folk Tale.* 2d ed. Ed. Louis A. Wagner. Austin: University of Texas Press, 1968.

Riffaterre, Michael. *Semiotics of Poetry.* Bloomington: Indiana University Press, 1978.

———. *Text Production.* Trans. Terese Lyons. New York: Columbia University Press, 1983.

Rimmon-Kenan, Shlomith. *Narrative Fiction: Contemporary Poetics.* London: Methuen, 1983.

*Robey, David, ed. *Structuralism: An Introduction.* Oxford: Clarendon, 1973.

Saussure, Ferdinand de. *Course in General Linguistics.* Trans. Wade Baskin. New York: McGraw-Hill, 1966.

*Scholes, Robert. *Semiotics and Interpretation.* New Haven: Yale University Press, 1982.

———. *Structuralism in Literature: An Introduction.* New Haven: Yale University Press, 1974.

Sturrock, John, ed. *Structuralism and Since.* New York: Oxford University Press, 1979.

Todorov, Tzvetan. *Introduction to Poetics*. Trans. Richard Howard. Minneapolis: University of Minnesota Press, 1981.

———. *The Poetics of Prose*. Trans. Richard Howard. Ithaca: Cornell University Press, 1977.

Valdés, M., and O. Miller, eds. *Interpretation of Narrative*. Toronto: University of Toronto Press, 1970.

Williamson, Judith. *Decoding Advertisements: Ideology and Meaning in Advertising*. London: M. Boyers, 1980.

Sociological Criticism: *Historical*

Auerbach, Erich. *Mimesis: The Representation of Reality in Western Literature*. Trans. Willard R. Trask. Princeton: Princeton University Press, 1953.

Burke, Kenneth. *Attitudes Toward History*. 3d ed. 1937. Berkeley: University of California Press, 1984.

Foucault, Michel. *The History of Sexuality*. Volume 1, *An Introduction*. Trans. Robert Hurley. New York: Random House, 1980.

———. *Language, Counter-Memory, Practice: Selected Essays and Interviews*. Trans. Donald F. Bouchard and Sherry Simon. Ithaca: Cornell University Press, 1977.

LaCapra, Dominick. *History and Criticism*. Ithaca: Cornell University Press, 1985.

LaCapra, Dominick, and Steven L. Kaplan, eds. *Modern European Intellectual History: Reappraisals and New Perspectives*. Ithaca: Cornell University Press, 1982.

Lovejoy, Arthur O. *Essays in the History of Ideas*. Baltimore: Johns Hopkins University Press, 1948.

McGann, Jerome J. *The Beauty of Inflections: Literary Investigations on Historical Method and Theory*. Oxford: Clarendon, 1985.

*———, ed. *Historical Studies and Literature and Society*. Madison: University of Wisconsin Press, 1985.

Said, Edward W., ed. *Literature and Society*. Baltimore: Johns Hopkins University Press, 1986.

———. *The World, the Text, and the Critic*. Cambridge, Mass.: Harvard University Press, 1983.

Spitzer, Leo. *Linguistics and Literary History: Essays in Stylistics*. Princeton: Princeton University Press, 1948.

Steiner, George. *After Babel: Aspects of Language and Translation*. New York: Oxford University Press, 1975.

Tindall, William York. *Forces in Modern British Literature, 1885–1946*. New York: Knopf, 1947.

Trilling, Lionel. *Beyond Culture: Essays on Literature and Learning*. New York: Viking, 1968.

Weimann, Robert. *Structure and Society in Literary History: Studies in the History and Theory of Historical Criticism*. Baltimore: Johns Hopkins University Press, 1984.

*Wellek, Rene. *Concepts of Criticism*. Ed. Stephen G. Nichols, Jr. New Haven: Yale University Press, 1963.

Wellek, Rene, and Austin Warren. *Theory of Literature*. New York: Harcourt, Brace, 1949.

White, Hayden. *Metahistory: The Historical Imagination in Nineteenth-Century Europe*. Baltimore: Johns Hopkins University Press, 1974.

———. *Tropics of Discourse: Essays in Cultural Criticism.* Baltimore: Johns Hopkins University Press, 1985.

Sociological Criticism: *Marxist*

Althusser, Louis. *Lenin and Philosophy and Other Essays.* Trans. Ben Brewster. New York: Monthly Review, 1971.

Bakhtin, Mikhail. *The Dialogic Imagination: Four Essays.* Trans. Caryl Emerson and Michael Holquist. Austin: University of Texas Press, 1981.

*Baxandall, Lee, ed. *Radical Perspectives in the Arts.* Baltimore: Penguin, 1972.

*Baxandall, Lee, and Stefan Morawski, eds. *Marx and Engels on Literature and Art.* St. Louis: Telos, 1973.

Benjamin, Walter. *Illuminations.* Ed. Hannah Arendt. Trans. H. Zohn. New York: Harcourt Brace, 1968.

Bennett, Tony. *Formalism and Marxism.* London: Methuen, 1979.

Brecht, Bertold. *Brecht on Theatre.* Trans. John Willett. New York: Hill and Wang, 1964.

Burke, Kenneth. *A Rhetoric of Motives.* Berkeley: University of California Press, 1969.

*Caudwell, Christopher. [Christopher St. John Sprigg.] *Illusion and Reality: A Study of the Sources of Poetry.* New ed. New York: International, 1963.

Craig, David, ed. *Marxists on Literature: An Anthology.* Harmondsworth: Penguin, 1975.

Demetz, Peter. *Marx, Engels and the Poets: Origins of Marxist Literary Criticism.* Trans. Jeffrey L. Sammons. Chicago: University of Chicago Press, 1967.

*Eagleton, Terry. *Criticism and Ideology: A Study in Marxist Literary Theory.* New York: Schocken, 1978.

*———. *Marxism and Literary Criticism.* Berkeley: University of California Press, 1976.

"Forum on Mikhail Bakhtin." Ed. Gary Saul Morson. *Critical Inquiry* 10 (1983): 225–319.

Goldmann, Lucien. *The Hidden God.* Trans. Phillip Thody. 1955. Atlantic Highlands, N.J.: Humanities, 1976.

Jameson, Fredric. *Marxism and Form: Twentieth-Century Dialectical Theories of Literature.* Princeton: Princeton University Press, 1971.

———. *The Political Unconscious: Narrative as a Socially Symbolic Act.* Ithaca: Cornell University Press, 1981.

Lang, Berel, and Forrest Williams, eds. *Marxism and Art: Writings in Aesthetics and Criticism.* New York: McKay, 1972.

Lenin, V. I. *On Literature and Art.* Moscow: Progress Publishers, 1967.

LeRoy, Gaylord, and Ursula Beitz, eds. *Preserve and Create: Essays in Marxist Literary Criticism.* New York: Humanities, 1973.

Lukács, George. *The Historical Novel.* Trans. Hannah Mitchell and Stanley Mitchell. 1962. Lincoln: University of Nebraska Press, 1983.

———. *Studies in European Realism.* Trans. Edith Bone. New York: Grosset and Dunlap, 1964.

Macherey, Pierre. *A Theory of Literary Production.* Trans. Geoffrey Wall. London: Routledge & Kegan Paul, 1978.

Marcuse, Herbert. *The Aesthetic Dimension: Toward a Critique of Marxist Aesthetics.* Boston: Beacon, 1978.

Ryan, Michael. *Marxism and Deconstruction: A Critical Articulation.* Baltimore: Johns Hopkins University Press, 1984.

Sartre, Jean-Paul. *What Is Literature?* London: Peter Smith, 1978.

*Solomon, Maynard, ed. *Marxism and Art: Essays Classic and Contemporary.* 1973. Detroit: Wayne State University Press, 1979.

Williams, Raymond. *Marxism and Literature.* Oxford: Oxford University Press, 1977.

SOCIOLOGICAL CRITICISM: *FEMINIST*

Abel, Elizabeth, ed. *The Signs Reader.* Chicago: University of Chicago Press, 1982.

———. *Writing and Sexual Difference.* Special Issue, *Critical Inquiry* 8, no. 2 (1981): 173–403. Also published as *Writing and Sexual Difference.* Chicago: University of Chicago Press, 1982.

*Donovan, Josephine, ed. *Feminist Literary Criticism: Explorations in Theory.* Lexington: University Press of Kentucky, 1975.

Eisenstein, Hester, and Alice Jardine, eds. *The Future of Difference.* Boston: G. K. Hall, 1980.

*Ellman, Mary. *Thinking About Women.* New York: Harcourt Brace Jovanovich, 1968.

Evans, Mari, ed. *Black Women Writers (1950–1980): A Critical Evaluation.* Garden City, N.Y.: Doubleday Anchor, 1984.

*Fetterley, Judith. *The Resisting Reader: A Feminist Approach to American Fiction.* Bloomington: University of Indiana Press, 1977.

Gelpi, Barbara Charlesworth, ed. *Feminist Theory.* Special Issue, *Signs* 7 (1982): 513–738.

Gilbert, Sandra, and Susan Gubar. *The Madwoman in the Attic: The Woman Writer and the Nineteenth-Century Literary Imagination.* New Haven: Yale University Press, 1979.

Greene, Gayle, and Coppelia Kahn. *Making a Difference: Feminist Literary Criticism.* New York: Methuen, 1985.

Heilbrun, Carolyn. *Toward a Recognition of Androgyny.* 1973. New York: Harper & Row, 1974.

*Kolodny, Annette. "Dancing Through the Minefields." *Feminist Studies* 6 (1980): 1–25.

———. "A Map for Rereading: Or, Gender and the Interpretation of Literary Texts." *New Literary History* 11 (1980): 451–57.

Lauretis, Teresa de., ed. *Feminist Studies/Critical Studies.* Bloomington: Indiana University Press, 1986.

Marks, Elaine, and Isabelle de Cortivron, eds. *New French Feminisms: An Anthology.* Amherst: University of Massachusetts Press, 1980.

Millett, Kate. *Sexual Politics.* 1970. Garden City, N.Y.: Doubleday, 1971.

Moers, Ellen. *Literary Women.* Garden City, N.Y.: Doubleday, 1972.

Moi, Toril. *Sexual/Textual Politics.* New York: Methuen, 1985.

Rich, Adrienne. *On Lies, Secrets, and Silence: Selected Prose 1966–1978.* New York: Norton, 1979.

Rogers, Katherine M. *The Troublesome Helpmate: A History of Misogyny in Literature.* Seattle: University of Washington Press, 1966.

*Showalter, Elaine. *A Literature of Their Own: British Women Novelists From Bronte to Lessing.* Princeton: Princeton University Press, 1977.

*———, ed. *The New Feminist Criticism: Essays on Women, Literature, and Theory.* New York: Pantheon, 1985.

Spacks, Patricia Meyer. *The Female Imagination.* New York: Knopf, 1975.

Spender, Dale. *Man Made Language.* London: Routledge & Kegan Paul, 1980.

Treichler, Paula A. et al. *For Alma Mater: Theory and Practice in Feminist Scholarship.* Urbana: University of Illinois Press, 1985.

Walker, Alice. *In Search of Our Mother's Gardens: Womanist Prose.* San Diego: Harcourt Brace Jovanovich, 1983.

*Woolf, Virginia. *A Room of One's Own.* 1929. New York: Harcourt Brace Jovanovich, 1981.

———. *Three Guineas.* 1938. New York: Harcourt Brace Jovanovich, 1966.

PSYCHOANALYTIC CRITICISM

Bloom, Harold. *The Anxiety of Influence: A Theory of Poetry.* New York: Oxford University Press, 1973.

———. *A Map of Misreading.* New York: Oxford University Press, 1975.

Crews, Frederick C. *The Sins of the Fathers: Hawthorne's Psychological Themes.* New York: Oxford University Press, 1966.

Davis, Robert Con, ed. *Lacan and Narration: The Psychoanalytic Difference.* Baltimore: Johns Hopkins University Press, 1984.

Felman, Shoshana, ed. *Literature and Psychoanalysis: The Question of Reading: Otherwise.* Baltimore: Johns Hopkins University Press, 1982. Originally appeared as *Yale French Studies* 55/56 (1977).

Freud, Anna. *The Ego and the Mechanisms of Defense. The Writings of Anna Freud* 2. New York: International University Press, 1967.

*Freud, Sigmund. *Jokes and Their Relation to the Unconscious. The Standard Edition of the Complete Psychological Works of Sigmund Freud* 8. London: Hogarth, 1953.

*———. *The Interpretation of Dreams. S. E.* 4 and 5. London: Hogarth, 1953.

———. *New Introductory Lectures. S. E.* 22. London: Hogarth, 1964.

Gallop, Jane. *The Daughter's Seduction: Feminism and Psychoanalysis.* Ithaca: Cornell University Press, 1982.

Gilligan, Carol. *In a Different Voice: Psychological Theory and Women's Development.* Cambridge, Mass.: Harvard University Press, 1982.

Hartman, Geoffrey H., ed. *Psychoanalysis and the Question of the Text.* Baltimore: Johns Hopkins University Press, 1978.

Hartman, Heintz. *Essays on Ego Psychology: Selected Problems in Psychoanalytic Theory.* New York: International University Press, 1965.

Holland, Norman. *The Dynamics of Literary Response.* New York: Norton, 1975.

———. *Poems in Persons: An Introduction to the Psychoanalysis of Literature.* 1973. New York: Norton, 1975.

Jones, Ernst. *Hamlet and Oedipus.* New York: Norton, 1976.

Klein, Melanie, and Joan Rivere, eds. *Love, Hate and Reparation.* New York: Norton, 1964.

Kris, Ernst. *Psychoanalytic Explorations in Art.* 1952. New York: Schocken, 1964.

*Kurzweil, Edith, and William Phillips, eds. *Literature and Psychoanalysis.* New York: Columbia University Pres., 1983.

Lacan, Jacques. *Écrits.* Trans. Alan Sheridan. London: Tavistock, 1977.

Lemaire, Anika. *Jacques Lacan.* Trans. David Macey. 1970. London: Routledge & Kegan Paul, 1977.

Lesser, Simon O. *Fiction and the Unconscious.* 1957. Chicago: University of Chicago Press, 1975.

*Meisel, Perry, ed. *Freud: A Collection of Critical Essays.* Twentieth-Century Views. Englewood Cliffs, N.J.: Prentice Hall, 1981.

Mitchell, Janet. *Psychoanalysis and Feminism.* New York: Vintage/Random House, 1974.

Psychology and Literature: Some Contemporary Directions. New Literary History 12, no. 1 (1980).

Ricoeur, Paul. *Freud and Philosophy.* New Haven: Yale University Press, 1970.

Skura, Meredith Ann. *The Literary Use of the Psychoanalytic Process.* New Haven: Yale University Press, 1981.

Smith, Joseph H., ed. *The Literary Freud: Mechanisms of Defense and the Poetic Will.* New Haven: Yale University Press, 1980.

Winnicott, D. W. *Playing and Reality.* London: Tavistock, 1971.

*Wright, Elizabeth. *Psychoanalytic Criticism: Theory in Practice.* London: Methuen, 1984.

READER-RESPONSE CRITICISM

*Bleich, David. *Reading and Feelings: An Introduction to Subjective Criticism.* Urbana, Ill.: National Council of Teachers of English, 1975.

———. *Subjective Criticism.* Baltimore: Johns Hopkins University Press, 1978.

Crosman, Robert. *Reading Paradise Lost.* Bloomington: Indiana University Press, 1980.

Dillon, George. *Language Processing and the Reading of Literature: Towards a Model of Comprehension.* Bloomington: Indiana University Press, 1978.

Eco, Umberto. *The Role of the Reader: Explorations in the Semiotics of Texts.* Bloomington: Indiana University Press, 1979.

*Fish, Stanley E. *Is There a Text in This Class? The Authority of Interpretive Communities.* Cambridge, Mass.: Harvard University Press, 1980.

Freund, Elizabeth. *Return of the Reader.* New York: Methuen, 1986.

*Holland, Norman. *Poems in Persons: An Introduction to the Psychoanalysis of Literature.* 1973. New York: Norton, 1975.

———. *5 Readers Reading.* New Haven: Yale University Press, 1975.

———. "Unity Identity Text Self." *PMLA* 90 (1975): 813–22.

Holub, Robert C. *Reception Theory: A Critical Introduction.* London: Methuen, 1984.

Iser, Wolfgang. *The Act of Reading: A Theory of Aesthetic Response.* Baltimore: Johns Hopkins University Press, 1978.

Jauss, Hans Robert. *Towards an Aesthetic of Reception.* Trans. Timothy Bahti. Minneapolis: University of Minnesota Press, 1982.

Johnson, Barbara. *The Critical Difference: Essays in the Contemporary Rhetoric of Reading.* Baltimore: Johns Hopkins University Press, 1980.

Lotman, Yury. *The Structure of the Artistic Text.* Trans. Ronald Vroon. Ann Arbor: Michigan Slavic Publications, 1977.

Mailloux, Steven J. *Interpretive Conventions: The Reader in the Study of American Fiction.* Ithaca: Cornell University Press, 1982.

Richards, I. A. *Practical Criticism: A Study of Literary Judgement.* 1929. New York: Harcourt, Brace, 1935.

Riffaterre, Michael. *Semiotics of Poetry.* Bloomington: Indiana University Press, 1978.

Rosenblatt, Louise. *Literature as Exploration.* 1937. New York: Noble and Noble, 1968.

———. *The Reader, The Text, The Poem: The Transactional Theory of the Literary Work.* Carbondale, Ill.: Southern Illinois University Press, 1978.

Spanos, William V. et al. *The Question of Textuality: Strategies of Reading in Contemporary American Criticism.* Bloomington: Indiana University Press, 1982.

*Suleiman, Susan, and Inge Crosman, eds. *The Reader in the Text: Essays on Audience and Interpretation.* Princeton: Princeton University Press, 1980.

*Tompkins, Jane P. *Reader-Response Criticism: From Formalism to Post-Structuralism.* Baltimore: Johns Hopkins University Press, 1980.

Deconstructionist Criticism

Arac, Jonathan, et al., eds. *The Yale Critics: Deconstruction in America.* Minneapolis: University of Minnesota Press, 1983.

Bloom, Harold, Paul de Man, Jacques Derrida, Geoffrey H. Hartman, J. Hillis Miller. *Deconstruction and Criticism.* New York: Continuum, 1979.

*Culler, Jonathan. *On Deconstruction: Theory and Criticism after Structuralism.* Ithaca: Cornell University Press, 1982.

DeMan, Paul. *Allegories of Reading: Figural Language in Rousseau, Nietzche, Rilke, and Proust.* New Haven: Yale University Press, 1979.

*———. *Blindness and Insight: Essays in the Rhetoric of Contemporary Criticism.* New ed. Minneapolis: University of Minnesota Press, 1983.

Derrida, Jacques. *Of Grammatology.* Trans. Gayatri Spivak. Baltimore: Johns Hopkins University Press, 1977.

———. *Writing and Difference.* Trans. Alan Bass. Chicago: University of Chicago Press, 1978.

Gasché, Rodolphe. "Deconstruction as Criticism." *Glyph* 6 (1979): 177–215.

Harari, Josue V., ed. *Textual Strategies: Perspectives in Post-Structuralist Criticism.* Ithaca: Cornell University Press, 1979.

Hartman, Geoffrey H. *Criticism in the Wilderness: The Study of Literature Today.* New Haven: Yale University Press, 1980.

———. *Saving the Text: Literature / Derrida / Philosophy.* Baltimore: Johns Hopkins University Press, 1981.

Leitch, Vincent B. *Deconstructive Criticism: An Advanced Introduction and Survey.* New York: Columbia University Press, 1982.

Lyotard, Jean-François. *The Postmodern Condition: A Report on Knowledge.* Trans. Geoff Bennington and Brian Massumi. Minneapolis: University of Minnesota Press, 1984.

Miller, J. Hillis. *Fiction and Repetition: Seven English Novels.* Cambridge, Mass.: Harvard University Press, 1982.

Norris, Christopher. *Deconstruction, Theory and Practice*. London: Methuen, 1982.

Ulmer, Gregory L. *Applied Grammatology: Post(e)-Pedagogy from Jacques Derrida to Joseph Beuys*. Baltimore: Johns Hopkins University Press, 1985.

Young, Robert, ed. *Untying the Text: A Post-Structuralist Reader*. Boston: Routledge & Kegan Paul, 1981.

HUMANIST CRITICISM

Altieri, Charles. *Act and Quality: A Theory of Literary Meaning and Humanistic Understanding*. Amherst: University of Massachusetts Press, 1981.

Auerbach, Erich. *Scenes from the Drama of European Literature*. Minneapolis: University of Minnesota Press, 1984.

Booth, Wayne C. *Critical Understanding: The Powers and Limits of Pluralism*. Chicago: University of Chicago Press, 1979.

Crane, R. S. *The Idea of the Humanities, and Other Essays Critical and Historical*. Chicago: University of Chicago Press, 1967.

Graff, Gerald. *Literature Against Itself: Literary Ideas in Modern Society*. Chicago: University of Chicago Press, 1979.

Hirsch, E. D. *The Aims of Interpretation*. Chicago: University of Chicago Press, 1976.

Krieger, Murray, and Larry Dembo, eds. *Directions for Criticism: Structuralism and Its Alternatives*. Madison: University of Wisconsin Press, 1977.

Lanham, Richard A. *Literacy and the Survival of Humanism*. New Haven: Yale University Press, 1983.

Leavis, F. R. *The Common Pursuit*. 1952. London: Hogarth, 1985.

———. *Revaluation: Tradition and Development in English Poetry*. 1947. New York: Norton, 1963.

Steiner, George. *Language and Silence*. New York: Atheneum, 1982.

CONTRIBUTORS

CHARLES R. ANDERSON has taught at Johns Hopkins University, where he served as chairman of the English Department; at Heidelberg University; at the University of Rome; at Nagano Seminar in Japan; and at the University of Torino in Italy. His publications include *Emily Dickinson's Poetry: Stairway of Surprise* (winner of the Christian Gauss Award in 1961), *The Magic Circle of Walden* (1968) and, *Person, Place and Theme in Henry James* (1977). He is the editor of *The Centennial Edition of Sidney Lanier* (1946), *American Literary Masters* (1965), and *Thoreau's Vision: The Major Essays* (1973).

LIAHNA BABENER is president of the Popular Culture Association, a group that has nurtured her sustained interest in the literature of detection. She has been head of the Department of English at Montana State University and chair of American Studies at Grinnell College. Professor Babener has published articles on detective fiction and she is completing a book, *Growing Up in the Heartland: Autobiographies by Midwesterners*.

ROLAND BARTHES, professor at the College de France at his death in 1980, is a leading critic. His writings herald major shifts in modern thinking about writing and language: *Writing Degree Zero* (1953; English translation 1968), *Mythologies* (1957; English translation 1972), *Criticism and Truth* (1966), *Elements of Semiology* (1968), *System of Fashion* (1967), and *S/Z* (1970). His later works include *The Pleasure of the Text* (1975) and *The Empire of Signs* (1970).

HAROLD BLOOM, the DeVane Professor of the Humanities at Yale University, has vigorously defended and reinterpreted the Romantic tradition in his writings. Some of his books include *Yeats* (1970), *The Ringers in the Tower* (1971), *The Anxiety of Influence: A Theory of Poetry* (1973), *Kabbalah and Criticism* (1975), *Poetry and Repression: Revisionism from Blake to Stevens*

(1976), *Wallace Stevens: The Poems of Our Climate* (1977). Professor Bloom is the general editor of *The Art of the Critic* series, *The Critical Perspective* series, and the *Major Authors Edition of the New Moulton's Library of Literary Criticism.*

MARIE BONAPARTE was a French psychoanalyst who studied with Freud. Along with *The Life and Works of Edgar Allan Poe: A Psycho-Analytic Interpretation,* she is chiefly known in English-speaking countries for her *Female Sexuality* (1953) and *Myths of War* (1947).

BERTOLT BRECHT was a German dramatist, poet, and theatrical director who espoused communist views. His better-known plays are *The Three-Penny Opera* (1928; English translation 1955), *The Life of Galileo* (1938–39; English translation 1947), *Mother Courage and Her Children* (1939; English translation 1941), and *The Caucasian Chalk Circle* (1944–45; English translation 1948).

CLEANTH BROOKS's major critical writings include *Modern Poetry and the Tradition* (1939), *The Well Wrought Urn: Studies in the Structure of Poetry* (1947), and *Literary Criticism: A Short History,* with W. K. Wimsatt, Jr. (1957). He was co-author, with Robert Penn Warren, of the influential college text *Understanding Poetry: An Anthology for College Students* (1938; 1960). He has served as Gray Professor of Rhetoric at Yale University.

SEYMOUR CHATMAN is professor of rhetoric at the University of California, Berkeley. His recent writings deal with narratology: *Story and Discourse: Narrative Structure in Fiction and Film* (1978) and *Antonioni, or the Surface of the World* (1985). He is currently at work on another book on narrative structure.

ROBERT CROSMAN, professor at Tufts University, has taught literature, reader-oriented criticism, and creative writing at Williams College, Trinity College, the University of Constance, and Boston University. Some of his recent publications include "Do Readers Make Meaning?" in *The Reader in the Text* (ed. Suleiman and Crosman [1980]), *Reading Paradise Lost* (1980), and "Is There Such a Thing As Misreading?" in *Criticism and Critical Theory* (ed. Hawthorn [1984]).

JACQUES DERRIDA, French philosopher and essayist, teaches the history of philosophy at the Ecole normale supérieure in Paris. His essays have been collected in *Writing and Difference* (1967; English translation 1978), *On Grammatology* (1967; English translation 1976), *Disseminations* (1972; English translation 1981), *Margins of Philosophy* (1972; English translation 1982), and *Spurs: Nietzsche's Styles / Eperons: Les styles de Nietzsche* (1976; English translation 1979).

GEORGE L. DILLON is professor of English and director of composition at the University of Washington. He has published articles on semantics, the processing of written texts, and the intersection of discourse theory and rhetoric. His books include *Introduction to Contemporary Linguistic Semantics* (1977) and *Constructing Texts: Elements of a Theory of Composition and Style* (1981).

TERRY EAGLETON, tutorial fellow at Wadham College, Oxford University, has published *Criticism and Ideology* (1975), *Marxism and Literary Criticism* (1976), *The Rape of Clarissa: Writing, Sexuality, and Class-Struggle in Richardson* (1982), *Literary Theory: An Introduction* (1983), *The Function of Criticism* (1984), and *Shakespeare* (1986).

JUDITH FETTERLEY teaches English and women's studies at the State University of New York at Albany. She has been active in the National Women's Studies Association since its inception in 1977 and is presently a general editor of the Rutgers University Press series on American Women Writers. Her books include *The Resisting Reader: A Feminist Approach to American Fiction* (1978) and *Provisions: A Reader from 19th Century American Women* (1985).

NORTHROP FRYE is university professor at the University of Toronto. Some of his extensive publications include *Fearful Symmetry: A Study of William Blake* (1947), *Anatomy of Criticism* (1957), *Fables of Identity: Studies in Poetic Mythology* (1963), *The Well-Tempered Critic* (1966), *A Natural Perspective: The Development of Shakespearean Comedy and Romance* (1965), *The Secular Scripture: A Study of the Structure of Romance* (1976), and *The Great Code: The Bible and Literature* (1982).

SANDRA M. GILBERT teaches English and American literature at the University of California, Davis. She has published articles, two books of poetry, and *Acts of Attention: The Poems of D. H. Lawrence* (1972). Along with Susan Gubar, she coauthored *The Madwoman in the Attic: The Woman Writer and the Nineteenth-Century Literary Imagination* (1979) and coedited *Shakespeare's Sisters: Feminist Essays on Women Poets* (1979) as well as *The Norton Anthology of Literature by Women* (1985).

ALBERT GELPI is the Coe Professor of American Literature at Stanford University. His books are *Emily Dickinson: The Mind of the Poet* (1971), *The Tenth Muse: The Psyche of the American Poet* (1975), and the forthcoming *A Coherent Splendor: The American Poetic Renaissance 1910–1950*. He edited *The Poet in America 1650 to the Present* and *Wallace Stevens: The Poetics of Modernism* (1985), and coedited *Adrienne Rich's Poetry* (1975).

DAVID HALLIBURTON is professor of English, comparative literature, and modern thought and literature at Stanford University. His writings include *Edgar Allan Poe: A Phenomenological View* (1973), and, more recently, *Poetic Thinking: An Approach to Heidegger* (1981). He is currently at work on a book entitled *The Fateful Discourse of Worldly Things*.

NIKOLAUS HAPPEL, German scholar and critic, has written about English, Welsh, and American authors for the West German publication *Die Neueren Sprachen.*

JOHN HEATH-STUBBS, English poet and critic, was appointed Gregory Fellow in Poetry at the University of Leeds in 1952. He has published eight books of poetry as well as the critical work on English poets, *The Darkling Plain* (1950).

DICK HEBDIGE is associated with the faculty of art and design at the Polytechnic of Wolverhampton and with the Centre for Contemporary Cultural Studies at the University of Binghamton. Some of his publications include *Reggae Rastas and Rudies: Style and the Subversion of Form* (1974), *Subcultural Conflict and Criminal Performance in Fulham* (1976), and *Subculture: The Meaning of Style* (1979).

ROBERT B. HEILMAN is professor emeritus of English at the University of Washington. His many publications include an historical study, *America in English Fiction 1760–1800* (1937; 1968); an anthology, *Modern·Short Stories* (1950; 1971), and editions of eighteenth- and nineteenth-century British novelists. His studies in drama are *Magic in the Web: Action and Language in Othello* (winner of the Explicator Prize in 1956) and *The Ways of the World: Comedy and Society* (winner of the Christian Gauss Prize in 1978).

NORMAN N. HOLLAND, James H. McNulty Professor of English at the State University of New York at Buffalo, is founder and director of the SUNY Center for the Psychological Study of the Arts. His publications include *The Dynamics of Literary Response* (1968), *Poems in Persons* (1973), and *5 Readers Reading* (1975).

ANTHONY L. JOHNSON, professor of English language and literature at Florence University, is a poet and critic. In addition to many articles and two volumes of poetry, he is the author of *Sign and Structure in the Poetry of T. S. Eliot, Readings of "Anthony and Cleopatra" and "King Lear,"* and *Fonetica e grafia inglesi.* Professor Johnson serves as review editor of *Poetics Today.*

BARBARA JOHNSON, professor of romance languages and literature at Harvard University, is the author of *Defigurations du language poetique* (1979), *The Critical Difference* (1980), and *Critical Transitions: Deconstruction, Feminism, and Other Inflections of Difference* (1986). She has translated Jacques Derrida's *La Dissémination* and serves as editor for the *Yale French Series.*

French psychoanalyst JACQUES LACAN directs the Ecole Freudienne de Paris and teaches at the Ecole normale supérieure. Dr. Lacan's translated volumes include *The Language of the Self: The Function of Language in Psychoanalysis* (1968), *Ecrits: A Selection* (1977), and *Speech and Language in Psychoanalysis* (1981).

SIMON O. LESSER had training in literature at the University of Chicago, Kenyon College, and Columbia University, and in psychology at the Chicago and the New York Psychiatric Institutes as well as the Washington School of Psychiatry. His writings have appeared in *Daedalus, Modern Fiction Studies,* and *Partisan Review,* and in more than a dozen anthologies. His major essays have been collected in *The Whispered Meanings: Selected Essays of Simon O. Lesser* (ed. Sprich and Noland [1977]). Before his death in 1979, Mr. Lesser taught at the University of Massachusetts.

LAWRENCE I. LIPKING is Chester D. Tripp Professor of Humanities at Northwestern University, where he founded the Program in Comparative Literature and Theory in 1982. His books include *The Ordering of the Arts in Eighteenth-Century England* (1970), *Modern Literary Criticism 1900–1970* (coedited with A. Walton Litz, 1971), *The Life of the Poet* (winner of the Christian Gauss Award in 1981), and the forthcoming *Abandoned Women and Poetic Traditions.*

YURY M. LOTMAN, professor of Russian literature at Tartu University, is a Soviet scholar and structuralist. He has published more than 300 articles and works on eighteenth- and early nineteenth-century Russian literature. Some of his translated books are *The Analysis of the Poetic Text* (1972), *The Semiotics of the Cinema* (1976), and *The Structure of the Artistic Text* (1977).

JEROME J. MCGANN, the Doris and Henry Dreyfuss Professor in the Humanities at the California Institute of Technology, has written extensively on literary history. His more recent books include *The Romantic Ideology: A Critical Investigation* (1983), *A Critique of Modern Textual Criticism* (1983), and *The Beauty of Inflections: Literary Investigations in Historical Method and Theory* (1985). He edited the first volume of *Lord Byron: The Complete Poetical Works, Historical Studies and Literary Criticism* (1985), and *Textual Criticism and Literary Interpretation* (1985).

DOROTHY MCFARLAND, who lives in Leverett, Massachusetts, is an independent scholar. Her published books are *A Handbook of Faulkner* (1964), *Willa Cather* (1982), *Flannery O'Connor* (1976), and *Simone Weil* (1983). In addition, she is co-translator of an anthology of Simone Weil's works entitled *Formative Writings, 1929–1941* (1986).

JOHN R. MAY, chairman and professor of English at Louisiana State University, is the author of *Toward a New Earth: Apocalypse in the American Novel* (1972) and *The Pruning Word: The Parables of Flannery O'Connor* (1976). He has coauthored two books on film, *Film Odyssey: The Art of Film as Search for Meaning* (1976) and *The Parables of Lina Wertmuller* (1977); edited a collection of original essays on religion and culture, *The Bent World* (1981); and coedited *Religion in Film* (1982).

BENITA A. MOORE teaches English and religious studies at Marycrest College in Davenport, Iowa. Her research has focused on language as sacrament in Walker Percy and, more recently, on the angle of convergence between deconstruction and feminist critical theory.

457

ERIC MOTTRAM writes on cultural studies, on nineteenth- and twentieth-century American and British writers, and on modern Hungarian poetry. Some of his recent publications include "Ross Macdonald and the Past of a Formula" in *Art in Crime Writing: Essays on Detective Fiction* (ed. Benstock [1983]), "Fears of Invasion in American Culture" in *The Origins and Originality of American Culture* (ed. Tibor [1984]), and "'Man under Fortune': Bases for Ezra Pound's Poetry" in *Modern American Poetry* (ed. Butterfield [1984]).

GILBERT H. MULLER, professor of American and comparative literature at LaGuardia Community College of the City University of New York, has published in *The Georgia Review, The Nation, The New Republic, The New York Times* and *Studies in Short Fiction*. His books include *Nightmares and Visions: Flannery O'Connor* (1972), *John A. Williams* (1984), *The American College Handbook of Contemporary English* (1985), and, as co-editor, *The McGraw-Hill Short Prose Reader* (1979).

MARJORIE PERLOFF, professor of English and comparative literature at Stanford University, has written widely on poetics. Some of her more recent books are *The Poetics of Indeterminacy: Rimbaud to Cage* (1981), *The Dance of the Intellect: Studies in the Poetry of the Pound Tradition* (1985), and *The Futurist Moment: Avant-Garde, Avant-Guerre and the Language of Rupture* (1986). Dr. Perloff writes a column for *American Poetry Review* and is the poetry correspondent for *Sulfur*.

ADRIENNE RICH is one of today's leading feminist poets and theorists. To date she has published a dozen books of poetry, including *Diving into the Wreck* (co-winner of the 1974 National Book Award), *The Dream of a Common Language: Poems 1974–1977* (1978), and *A Wild Patience Has Taken Me This Far: Poems 1978–1981* (1981). Her critical books include *Of Woman Born: Motherhood as Experience and Institution* (1976) and *On Lies, Secrets, and Silence: Selected Prose 1966–1978* (1979). She is coeditor of the lesbian-feminist journal *Sinister Wisdom*.

ROBERT SCHOLES is chairman and Alumni/Alumnae University Professor of English and Comparative Literature at Brown University. He is the author of many critical studies on fiction, including *The Nature of Narrative* (with Robert Kellogg, 1968), *Structuralism in Literature* (1974), *Science Fiction: History, Science, Vision* (with Eric Rabkin, 1977), *Fabulation and Metafiction* (1979), *Semiotics and Interpretation* (1982), and *Textual Power* (1985).

ELLA SHOHAT has published articles on film in *Screen, Film Quarterly, Critical Arts,* and *Proza* (Tel Aviv). Her essay on Israeli cinema will be part of the forthcoming *World Cinema Since 1945*. She is currently completing her doctoral dissertation on Israeli cinema at New York University.

ROBERT STAM teaches in the cinema studies department at New York University. He is the coauthor of *Brazilian Cinema* (1982) and the author of

Reflexivity in Film and Literature: From Don Quixote to Jean-Luc Godard (1985). He is currently the recipient of a Guggenheim Fellowship.

WAYNE A. TEFS, a Woodrow Wilson Fellow, has taught and lectured at several universities and currently serves as head of the English department at St. John's Ravenscourt School, Winnipeg, Canada. He has published two novels and is a regular contributor to literary journals.

WILLIAM YORK TINDALL, critic and literary historian, is professor emeritus of the Graduate School at Columbia University where he lectured on contemporary literature. He has authored some dozen books, including the well-known *Forces in Modern British Literature* (1947), *James Joyce: His Way of Interpreting the Modern World* (1950), *The Literary Symbol* (1955), *The Joyce Country* 1960, *Wallace Stevens* (1961), *Samuel Beckett* (1964), *W. B. Yeats* (1966), and *A Reader's Guide to Finnegan's Wake* (1968).

ROBERT PENN WARREN, professor emeritus of Yale University, is the author of eleven volumes of poetry, two plays, ten novels, two books of short stories, several books on the Southern legacy, and three volumes of criticism: *Selected Essays* (1958; 1964), *A Plea in Mitigation: Modern Poetry and the End of an Era* (1966), and *Democracy and Poetry* (1975). He is coauthor, along with Cleanth Brooks, of *Understanding Poetry: An Anthology for College Students* (1938; 1960) and *Understanding Fiction* (1943; 1959), as well as editor of several American literature texts.

BRENDA S. WEBSTER is an independent scholar, fiction writer, and translator. Her critical books are *Yeats: A Psychoanalytic Study* (1973) and *Blake's Prophetic Psychology* (1983). She has translated poetry from the Italian for *The Other Voice* (1976), *The Penguin Book of Women Poets* (1979), and *Women Poets of the World* (1983).

INDEX